THE AMERICAN OCCU-
PATION OF GERMANY

Edward N. Peterson is professor of history and chairman of the Department of History at the University of Wisconsin, River Falls. He received the B.A., M.A., and Ph.D. (1953) degrees from the University of Wisconsin.

Professor Peterson has published articles in both American and German scholarly journals; he is the author of two previous books: *Hjalmar Schacht: For and Against Hitler* (1954) and *The Limits of Hitler's Power* (1969).

THE AMERICAN OCCU-
PATION OF GERMANY
RETREAT TO VICTORY

EDWARD N. PETERSON

University of Wisconsin-River Falls

Wayne State University Press

Detroit, 1977

Library of Congress Cataloging in Publication Data

Peterson, Edward Norman.
The American Occupation of Germany.

Bibliography: p.
Includes index.
1. Germany (Territory under Allied occupation, 1945–
1955. U.S. Zone)   2.   Berlin question (1945–   )
I.   Title.
DD257.4.P43   940.53′144′0943   77-28965
ISBN 0-8143-1588-7

The research for this volume and costs associated with its publication were supported through
grants from the National Endowment for the Humanities, an independent federal agency.

Contents

Preface

Although a background study of the occupation of Germany began unintentionally with my service as an infantry private and military intelligence sergeant in Germany from 1945 to 1947, a more formal study began with the research for my book on policy implementation in Nazi Germany, *The Limits of Hitler's Power.* That research involved interviews and documents concerning the Berlin government, the Bavarian government, and the city governments in four Bavarian communities in order to analyze policy implementation from top to bottom in the chain of command. That research, and particularly the interviews, led to a renewed interest in the occupation and a curiosity about how the deplorable conditions of hunger and apathy that I had seen more than twenty years before could be explained. Judging by my findings about the authoritarian chain of command before 1945, it seemed likely that the apparent problems of American military government, so at variance with the policy expressed by the American civilian government, could be better understood if one studied the process of military government from top to bottom. One could presumably understand why the supposed American superpower, despite its victory in 1945, seemed so weak in the occupation. As ran the complaint of the times: America can win a war but it always loses the peace. It would perhaps explain why the American dream became for many people a German nightmare.

My suspicion of internal problems at the top was more than confirmed by the large numbers of contemporary reports by participants in military government and by the journalists observing them. Most of these bitterly criticized a supposedly harmful policy which was created by incompetence and conflict within the Washington bureaucracy and the Berlin military bureaucracy. To probe beneath these very critical contemporary reports, I needed to look at archival materials in the United States, private papers, and official papers, some of which were still classified. The many boxes of Office of Military Government of the United States (OMGUS) documents at the Washington National Record Center, and the cables sent by General Lucius

7

D. Clay to Washington, stored at the National Archives, evidenced the conflicts at the top but gave disturbingly few insights into local policy implementation. The fragmentary reports of local units were composed of bland (usually statistical) reports of progress made, occasionally bitter accounts of German resistance to the occupation, and even more occasionally a candid inspection report stating that the local units were not implementing policy for reasons of sloth or confusion. The impression of failure persists in the official histories commissioned by OMGUS and its successor, the High Commission for Germany (HICOG), located at the Library of Congress and at U.S. Army Headquarters in Heidelberg. Private papers, located at various archives, were usually angry about the tragic errors perceived as endemic in the Washington establishment or in the Berlin OMGUS establishment.

My effort to find and interview officers who had served in the four local communities was relatively unsuccessful. Many could not be found. Those I could locate and interview were very critical of their commanders and local policy implementation. Some regarded the policies as ridiculous and themselves as incompetent to their tasks. Those with whom I corresponded were usually vague and general, increasing my suspicion that the local reality had been vague and general.

But it was a greater shock to discover that the German memory was much less filled with details about military government than it had been about Hitler's less recent government. The closer to the people that I came, the less evidence of an American military government I found. There were individual memories, sometimes very fond, of individual Americans, but those Germans I interviewed at great length remembered very little of substance that military government had done: a bicycle burned for trespassing on an off limits street, a house requisitioned, coffee or cigarettes acquired. (Nightmares of the Nazi period are much more sharply etched, which suggests that fear is an aid to memory and that the occupation was not feared.) A few mayors or interpreters remembered a few military governors. The hunger of those years of the black market is remembered, as is, in a vaguely grateful way, the Marshall Plan. Clay's resistance to the Russians, formally begun with the 1948 Berlin blockade, was more clearly recalled, but very little else.

The ghostlike memories were only partially fleshed out by my searching through the German documents. They were relatively scarce and the standard explanation was that "when the Americans came they fired the record keepers, so our records for that period are poor." Although I investigated every possible source of documentation, and often found German officials so generous that I could pile boxes of documents in the back of my station wagon and sift through them seven days a week, there was little of substance except correspondence detailing complaints and criticism. Yet it was not so much that the occupation was evident in the spirit of official praise or in the spirit of bitter American critics, it was barely there at all. Even the German news-papers, helpfully preserved in a Bavarian state newspaper archive, gave rare glimpses of military government activity. Weeks, then months, of newspapers carried no MG news, and then perhaps would publish the picture of an officer coming or going, saying that he wanted to help, when he came, or that he hoped that he had helped as he left. My feeling was comparable to the sensation of seeing the modern West Germany and remembering the ruins of 1945. The military government reality has simply been replaced with other realities. One knew that once something had existed, but was now all in the mind.

The materials for the analysis of U.S. policy formation and implementa-tion at the higher levels of the civilian and military government are relatively abundant, even if we will never know what President Roosevelt would have done with an occupation. The documentation of the local communities is largely of trivial matters, as, for example, of whether the commander will get the flowers he requested from the city gardener. An exception is the material related to the mass firings of officials in the summer and fall of 1945, and the complaints thereafter that they were being rehired. Surely things happened locally which did not enter the documents—oral instructions are less danger-ous than those in writing—and surely some events have escaped the memories of participants on both sides of the Atlantic. Presumably some bits of scandal were tactfully not told me, and I have tactfully omitted those that were if they concerned specific participants still living. Yet those happenings not recorded nor remembered were probably expressions of personal, not official, policy desires, and were probably even more trivial than the concerns recorded.

The humbling conclusion gradually formed that the occupation's "ac-tion" occurred largely in Clay's headquarters and consisted primarily of Americans arguing with Americans about what could or should be done. It rarely involved interaction with Germans. Americans at the top level had also to interact with the British, which they did relatively successfully, and with the French and Russians, relatively unsuccessfully, to accomplish their goals of keeping their zone alive. Because of the wartime Allies, OMGUS was much restrained in accomplishing its goals even at the top level. The result was that OMGUS affected the timing of the recreation of a West German government more than its substance. It slightly delayed and briefly annoyed the Bavarian government. It very quickly upset and briefly annoyed city governments. It passed by village governments barely noticed.

Much of this effect or noneffect was indeed related to the lack of power that I had originally assumed. The capacity of a broadly based domestic party to control a bureaucracy and a people, though limited, is vastly greater than that of an alien army. Indeed, the American military government could have achieved very little with bayonets or bombs, but that it compelled the Germans so little was also the result of American virtues. The attitudes of these conquerors included ideals of freedom and democracy, though these ideals were occasionally obscured by hatred and pride. No subservient cadre was brought along as the American army's camp follower. MG's noninterference further reflects the pragmatism which Americans also espouse and which was shown early by Clay in most matters. He recognized that the theories from Washington would not mesh with the more compelling realities in Germany. First and foremost, Clay realized that Americans could not govern Germans. The wisdom of the occupation, sometimes belated, was derived in large part from the growing awareness that there were problems which America, in spite of its supposed power, could not solve. It was a wisdom created by necessity. A reading of the research results might even remind one of the classic advice given America in the 1960s about another effort to dominate an alien people: "Call it victory and get out."

The American victory in the occupation seems in essence a retreat from policies based on interference which would not work to other policies based on noninterference. Those more workable policies meant the rapid return of authority to the Germans. The occupation worked when and where it allowed the Germans to govern themselves. Under Clay's generally perceptive policy, OMGUS returned ever more freedom to the Germans and then fought to get the British and the French to do the same, and then fought unsuccessfully to get the Russians to restore the freedoms that most Germans wanted. The victor quickly became the ally, which in some ways it had to be already in 1945.

This evolution of occupation policy thus became enmeshed with the evolution of American foreign policy with the former Allies. In the pages that follow, I briefly examine how that foreign policy affected occupation policy, and how Clay's occupation policy affected foreign policy. In the past ten years, the so-called revisionists have argued that Clay was a major instigator, for ideological reasons, of the Cold War. My narrative briefly touches on the Cold War as it involved Germany, but gives only marginal support to the revisionist argument. Clay was primarily compelled by his need to find ways of keeping some forty million Germans alive as something more than recipients of welfare from the American taxpayer.

My analysis starts at the top of the chain of command and examines the hectic activity in Washington and Berlin, then moves to the arguments between Americans and Germans at the intermediate level in Munich, and at last reaches the inaction at the bottom in four Bavarian communities. It seems to me that what I have found is a withdrawal which led to success, a retreat from policies which were dictatorial and un-American in their claim to the right to rule other peoples to new policies which were democratic and American in their acceptance of the equality of all men, even Germans, in their capacity to govern themselves. The evidence could be considered a reaffirmation of the Jeffersonian principle that the government which governs least governs best. In this sense the American military government represents a retreat to victory.

In addition to the support from many archives and libraries, which I have noted in my bibliography, I must express special gratitude to the Social Science Research Council and the National Endowment for the Humanities. Their support made possible the travel in the United States and Germany requisite to the study of scattered sources.

A further word of thanks is due to Sherwyn Carr and her skill and patience in improving the literary quality of the manuscript.

Abbreviations

Washington Organizations

AGWAR	Adjutant General, War Department
CAD	Civil Affairs Division: office for military government in War Department, 1942–49
CCS	Combined Chiefs of Staff: coordinating committee for British-American general staffs, 1942–45
DOD	Department of Defense: organization to coordinate War Department and Navy Department, created 1947
EAC	European Advisory Commission: British-American-Russian committee to coordinate postwar planning, 1943–45
ECA	Economic Cooperation Administration: agency for the Marshall Plan, 1947–
ERP	European Recovery Program: Marshall Plan
FEA	Foreign Economic Administration: wartime agency to coordinate economic policy overseas
IPCOG	Informal Policy Committee on Germany: interdepartmental committee, early 1945
JCS	Joint Chiefs of Staff: chiefs of Army, Navy and Air Force
NSC	National Security Council: postwar supreme defense committee
OSS	Office of Strategic Services: wartime predecessor of Central Intelligence Agency
SD	State Department
SWNCC	State-War-Navy Coordinating Committee: 1944–45
WARCAD	War Department, Civil Affairs Division

WARSEC   Secretary of War

WD   War Department

WSC   Working Security Committee: interdepartmental committee,
           1944

American/Allied Organizations in Germany

ACC   Allied Control Council: central organ for Germany, 1945–48

BICO   Bipartite Control Office: British-American office for Bizonia,
           1946–49

CIC   Counter Intelligence Corps

COSSAC   Chief of Staff, Supreme Allied Command

ETOUSA   European Theater of Operations, United States Army

GYA   German Youth Activities: 1945–49

G-2   Intelligence section of a general staff

G-5   Civil affairs section of a general staff

HICOG   High Commission for Germany: replacement for military
           government in 1949

IARA   Inter-allied Reparations Agency

ICD   Information Control Division: OMGUS office to regulate pub-
           lishing and broadcasting

IRO   International Relief Organization

JEIA   Joint Export-Import Agency: British-American trade control
           agency

MG   Military Government: 1945–49

OMGB   Office of Military Government, Bavaria: 1945–49

OMGUS   Office of Military Government, United States: 1945–49

PWD   Psychological Warfare Division: wartime propaganda office;
           predecessor to the ICD in occupation

RGCO   Regional Government Coordinating Office: OMGUS liaison to
           the zonal Landerrat

SHAEF   Supreme Headquarters, Allied Expeditionary Forces: Eisen-
           hower's wartime headquarters

SMA   Soviet Military Administration

UNRRA	United Nations Relief and Rehabilitation Administration
USFET	United States Forces, European Theater: successor to SHAEF, 1945
USGCC	United States Group Control Council: military government as part of ACC, 1945

German Organizations

BP	Bavarian Party: 1946–
BVP	Bavarian Peoples' Party: Catholic party, 1919–33
CDU	Christian Democratic Union: conservative party, 1945–
CSU	Christian Social Union: Bavarian conservative party, 1945–
FDP	Free Democratic Party: liberal party, 1945–
KPD	Communist Party of Germany
NS/NSDAP	National Socialist German Workers' Party (Nazi)
SA	Sturm Abteilung: Nazi paramilitary organization
SS	Schutzstaffel: Nazi organization involved with police and concentration camps; in war as special army units
SPD	Social Democratic Party of Germany

THE AMERICAN OCCU-
PATION OF GERMANY

1 Policy Confusion in Washington

In the days of American innocence, which some say ended during World War II and others say persisted until Watergate, it was commonly assumed that the American people elected a president who executed laws and policies created by Congress in a simple and straightforward fashion. The people spoke; Congress listened; the president acted. This was the process by which America went to war, won the war, and set about guaranteeing the peace. The initiated, however, have all along known differently. If one looks below the surface of Washington's attempts to formulate policies to guide America's postwar occupation of Germany, it becomes evident that this pleasing image of a reasonable government creating and executing policy is a vast oversimplification. One should expect human institutions to be subject to human frailty, but the story of German policy formation, now well known to the experts, is an amazing tale of clashing personalities and bureaucratic structures, which together delayed and obscured policy goals to an extraordinary degree.

In order to understand the story, one has to begin at the top, with Presidents Roosevelt and Truman, and work his way down through the governmental maze. Out of the darkness of obscure but knowledgeable civil servants should have come the sober expert judgments to which the presidents should have added their broader wisdom and made broad policy decisions. These informed decisions should then have been implemented by skilled executives. It would appear, in fact, that this intelligent interchange seldom occurred, and as a result, few clear policies were formulated, at least until the occupation had begun.

The following chapter explores Washington's struggle to achieve a German policy. It suggests the positive, negative, or, more often, merely passive contributions of the presidents, the slight influence of cabinet ministers, and the frantic efforts of their underlings to produce vague but meaningful statements acceptable to their superiors. One might conclude that most of these activities were mere sound and fury, which came in time to signify very little. Of those persons who attained a policy-making level, most achieved high office for reasons completely unrelated to German policy. People were chosen because of personal likes and dislikes, or for reasons of domestic policy; others were selected because someone felt comfortable with them or because they could be pushed around or ignored. They held power without a policy base, a situation that was particularly characteristic of the Roosevelt administration. Roosevelt himself attained his power in 1940 for reasons only faintly related to a German policy, and he retained it in 1944, when the public knew only that he intended to defeat the German armies.

Roosevelt, Truman, and German Policy

The problem of defining occupation policy originated in Washington. Its personalities and institutions were ill adapted to deciding on a German policy, and even less adapted to implementing whatever policy was somehow adopted. Franklin Delano Roosevelt was praised as the master politician who saved the country from depression and revolution, and then praised more as the statesman who saved the world from Hitler and Tojo. He was later cursed by Cold War warriors, who claimed that his naiveté toward Stalin lost the peace. More recently, revisionists have seen again the states-man, whose tragic death interrupted the policy of conciliation which would have prevented the Cold War. In fact, his effect on occupation policy was to delay and obscure.

Critics of occupation policy have castigated his inability to compel the bulky bureaucracies which multiplied in his New Deal.[1] A minority view is that FDR had learned well how to administer in the Navy Department in World War I and as governor of New York, but most experts agree with James MacGregor Burns: "Again and again Roosevelt flouted the central rule of administration that the boss must coordinate the men and agencies under him."[2] They also agree that FDR was too secretive for anyone to be sure of his intentions and that his thought process was hard to follow. Henry Stimson, trying to set army policy, was upset: "Conferences with the President are difficult matters. His mind does not follow easily a consecutive chain of thought, but he is full of stories and incidents and hops about in his discussion from suggestion to suggestion and it is very much like chasing a vagrant beam of sunshine around a vacant room." Most of Stimson's troubles came from "the topsy-turvy, upside-down system of poor administration with which Mr. Roosevelt runs the Government."[3] Dean Acheson corroborated the confusion but would not dismiss it as organizational confusion which permitted him to keep power in his own hands by playing off his colleagues one against the other. "This, I think, is nonsense. Such is a policy of weakness and Roosevelt was not a weak man. Furthermore, it did not keep power in his own hands: it merely hindered the creation of effective power by anyone." Administration was chaotic because "he did not know any better." Particularly in foreign policy, Acheson thought, he lacked a command of the very complex facts.[4]

Yet FDR, who frustrated bureaucrats, was himself frustrated by bureaucratic resistance, particularly the State Department's. As he complained: "You should go through the experience of trying to get any changes in the thinking, policy, and action of the career diplomats and then you'd know what a real problem was."[5] An aide noted: "Half of a President's suggestion . . . can be safely forgotten by a Cabinet member. And if the President asks about a suggestion a second time, he can be told that it is being investigated. If he asks a third time, a wise cabinet officer will give him at least part of what he suggests. But only occasionally, except about the most important matters, do Presidents ever get around to asking three times."[6]

Policy creation and implementation depend in large part on those men closest to the president, who have power because they have the president's attention.[7] During Roosevelt's presidency the most influential man was Harry Hopkins, who had started as a social worker, risen to direction of the national antidepression program, and finally became FDR's alter ego.[8] In terms of German policy, he used his influence to maintain good relations with both Churchill and Stalin, at German expense if necessary. His major contribution to policy was probably to moderate FDR's fanciful ideas.

It is difficult to trace any consistent German policy during FDR's administration because he operated in such a private world. The constitutional system encouraged secretiveness and poor administration because, unlike Churchill, FDR did not need to clear decisions with his cabinet or with anyone else.[9] Roosevelt's view of Germany and how it should be handled is, however, clear up to a point: it must be weakened and punished.[10] State Department experts had an unending fight with his antipathy to Germany, which was based in part on his experiences in the Germany of Kaiser Wilhelm, such as being arrested four times in one day. Cordell Hull thought him too intelligent not to recognize at times that his views were highly subjective, yet his conviction was strong enough that he rejected the idea of assisting the German resistance movement.[11] When the Joint Chiefs of Staff asked him to relent on his unconditional surrender doctrine, he replied: "Please note that I am not willing at this time to say that we do not intend to destroy the German nation."[12]

Resting somewhere near this whimsical antipathy toward the Germany of his childhood was his sometime grand design for peace, in which Germany and most of Europe would be included in the Russian sphere of influence. Francis Cardinal Spellman's notes of an interview 3 September 1944 show a Roosevelt of very hard power politics.

> "It is planned to make an agreement among the Big Four. Accordingly the world will be divided into spheres of influence. China gets the Far East; the U.S., the Pacific; Britain and Russia, Europe and Africa. But as Britain has predominately colonial interests, it might be assumed that Russia will predominate in Europe. Although Chiang will be called in on the great decisions concerning Europe, it is understood that he will have no influence on them. The same thing might become true—although to a lesser degree—for the U.S.....
> [Stalin] would certainly receive Finland and the Baltics, the eastern half of Poland, Bessarabia. There is no point to oppose these desires of Stalin, because he has the power to get them anyway. So better give them gracefully. Still it is absolutely not sure whether Stalin will be satisfied with these boundaries....Be that as it may," he added, "the U.S. and British cannot fight the Russians."[13]

FDR had apparently decided his power was too limited to counter the Russians in Germany.[14] Whether his policy was one of grand design or petty whimsy, FDR accomplished little politically in regard to postwar Germany. What he chiefly did was to get in the way of his professionals.[15] He hardened and obscured policy, keeping his administrators from making decisions on Germany until after he died on 12 April 1945.

His successor, Harry S Truman, has lately been much admired for his directness, contrasted with the deviousness of Roosevelt, and for the decisiveness exemplified in "the buck stops here." Contemporaries were frequently much more critical, and he was given low ratings by the opinion polls during the Korean War. Among historians his reputation has also varied. Historians of the Cold War period have tended to regard him as the strong president who saved the world, including West Germany, from communism by his courageous, quick response to Stalin's challenge with the Berlin airlift. A large number of revisionist historians, those who have reexamined the origins of the Cold War, have come to the conclusion that he was a mediocrity, who tried and failed to bully the Russians into surrendering what they had won by war's great sacrifice, an uninformed president-by-chance, who departed from Roosevelt's grand design.[16] Both views of Truman have flaws.

The uninspiring process by which he was made vice-president has made him look like an accidental, unqualified president. Yet many who served under Truman rated him higher than Roosevelt as a decision-maker and administrator. What he lacked in charm he made up in common sense and hard work. Associates have praised how fast he learned.[17] Truman described himself as one who had read everything in the Independence, Missouri, library, so that he possessed the historical background necessary for the presidency. Such skill and knowledge would be difficult to demonstrate in his

German policy, however, because his contribution to forming occupation policy seems neither extensive nor profound. He was rarely involved, and then only in terms of a general principle that was more anti-Russian than pro-German or anti-German. Between Potsdam in 1945 and Berlin in 1948, Truman acted less than Roosevelt did before—he was not even vetoing policy. He more clearly left matters to subordinates, and his selection of subordinates shows little relevance to any foreign policy, let alone a German one. And Truman found his power over these subordinates limited. In 1952 he told Richard Neustadt of Eisenhower's coming frustrations. "He'll sit here and he'll say, 'Do this! Do That!' *And nothing will happen.*" Truman saw that his authority was limited by what he could persuade people to do, and "to persuade is to bargain."[18]

What is most relevant to assessing Truman's German policy is that his administration had a split personality on the issue. It developed a program of liberal reform at home and conservative containment abroad, led by a fairly closely knit band of bankers and lawyers, soldiers and diplomats.[19] Reinforcing the conservative tendency in foreign policy was Truman's conviction that the only way to get along with the Russians was to get tough, which in time meant a softer policy toward Germany. Another source of pressure against Russia came from the State Department, from Foreign Service officers long suspicious of the Soviet Union but previously unable to influence policy. George Kennan became their spokesman. The military too shifted steadily from its support of Roosevelt's policy of conciliation.[20] No other major country gave its top military leaders such power during this period.

Truman had no Hopkins as such. He believed in using departments, not White House operatives, to run the government. His closest associate was Clark Clifford, who acted not as an executive but as an adviser, using his intellectual influence to affect policy formation.[21] His advice on foreign affairs was premised on a tough pragmatism. His most singular statement was the memorandum of 24 September 1946 which proposed a military containment of Russia to add to the political containment envisaged by Kennan. Yet neither president nor staff was particularly interested in the occupation.[22] Government and nation were largely indifferent to the problems. Truman, at rare crises like Berlin, tipped the balance between firmness and retreat, but real interest and power were to be found on the level where the action was: with the bureaucrats and with General Lucius D. Clay.

The Role of the State Department

The State Department may have been the best qualified in Washington to make decisions on German policy, but it rarely had the loudest voice. Lacking both a constituency to pressure the Congress and impressive hardware to prove they were defending the country, diplomats were largely ignored. Besides low prestige, the department suffered from weak organization and weak secretaries of state, none of whom had any particular aptitude for formulating occupation policy until the evolution of policy was nearly finished.

Cordell Hull, sixty-one years old when he was appointed secretary of state in 1933, had been a congressman from the Cumberland mountains from 1906 to 1930. "He was totally lacking in diplomatic experience. . . . his selection involved considerations founded in the expediencies of domestic political maneuver."[23] He stayed in office partly because of the nation's intense concentration on domestic affairs; he was left to his own devices until Roosevelt became interested in foreign policy. He had a modest success with reciprocal trade and the Good Neighbor policy for Latin America during the thirties, but his position eroded quickly once the war started. He did not even sit with the War Council. Since Hull was one of the least influential members at the White House, "it was more or less an accident whether or not the views of senior officials [in the State Department] got serious hearings."[24] He had little effect on German policy because he was an ineffective spokesman for his experts and exercised only a feeble restraint on FDR's personal diplomacy.

Hull was also unable to control his department, partly because the FDR system led to the long feud with his nominal assistant, Sumner Welles, whom FDR respected more than State's professionals. Acheson described Hull's department as nineteenth-century; power lay with division chiefs, unequipped for appraisals of capability based on quantitative and technical judgments. Days were filled with meetings, necessary mostly because jurisdictions were so confused.[25] The department was a vessel adrift, pushed about by collisions with the more purposeful craft of more vigorous men in the cabinet. That its ability and knowledge often went to waste is amply evident in the evolution of German policy.

Hull's waning health meant that there was even less professional influence in the crucial year of 1944, and matters got little better with the appointment of Edward R. Stettinius, Jr. He was secretary for only a few months, but these came at the end of the war when long-postponed decisions had to be made. His appointment was also irrelevant to policy. Handsome and vigorous, only forty-four, in front of a newsreel camera he seemed an ideal choice for secretary, and to revisionists he has seemed an ideal representative of big business. Born the son of a partner of J. P. Morgan, he had gone from General Motors to U.S. Steel, becoming chairman of the board at thirty-eight. Yet he was not a stereotypical big businessman and administrator. He attracted the attention of FDR because he was atypical; he had not wanted to reduce wages as prices went down.

In August 1939, Stettinius was made chairman of the War Resources Board, as a member of the business community whom FDR could use politically. Although the board rapidly failed, he was trusted by Hopkins; after being appointed head of the Lend-Lease program in September 1941, he was chosen, on Hopkins's suggestion, to replace Welles in late 1943.[26] FDR assumed Stettinius would clean up the administrative mess, telling Mrs. Stettinius: "Ed is going to raise Hell in the State Department . . . and he will do it with my blessing." His reforms of the organization emphasized better public relations. He brought in an able top level staff: Joseph Grew, William Clayton, Nelson Rockefeller, and Dean Acheson.[27] When Hull retired in early October, Stettinius was chosen to replace him so that FDR could be even more his own secretary of state.[28] Like his successors, Stettinius was usually on the road. Whatever his merits as administrator and traveling man, mostly for the United Nations, he left scant imprint on policy. Any impact he had on German policy could only have been the negative one of not getting approval for his professionals' policy, but instead bending affably to Roosevelt's amateurs.

Policy implementation was further weakened by yet another politician appointed for reasons irrelevant to policy, although James Byrnes had made a remarkable record. After successful service as a senator, he was appointed to the Supreme Court in June 1941. With the chaos in the war economy, Byrnes was made head, in October 1942, of the Office of Economic Stabilization. As such he became "the assistant president," with Roosevelt turning over to him much of the management of domestic affairs. Despite this internship, Byrnes was passed over for vice-president. Embittered, he asked for the State Department. He was turned down, but as consolation the president unexpectedly asked him to come along to Yalta. This experience constituted his background in foreign affairs.

After FDR's funeral, Truman asked Byrnes whether he would be interested in the State Department, and later commented: "He almost jumped down my throat in taking me up on it."[29] Apparently most of Truman's reasons for selecting Byrnes were irrelevant to foreign policy: he was apprehensive about the commitments made at Yalta; Byrnes should be able to tell him about them. He had always stood in awe of the quick-witted, sharp-tongued South Carolinian. Truman also sensed Byrnes's resentment, and "as allergic as any man alive to an accusation of disloyalty, felt a compulsion to propitiate Byrnes's hurt feelings as well as his own unreasoningly troubled conscience."[30] As the president became more sure of himself and of his ideas for foreign policy, "an estrangement inevitably grew between them." Byrnes submitted his resignation in April 1946, "on advice of doctor."[31] State's professionals did not regret his going, for he had had little contact with them. He was usually on the road or with his trusted clique. As Ernest Penrose said: "The Department was not run, it just jerked along."[32] His lack of leadership was another reason why Washington had little control over Germany during the key years of the occupation. During Byrnes's first nine months, his contribution to policy was to compromise with Russia, at German expense if necessary. His later contribution was to compromise with Clay's pressure from Berlin.

George C. Marshall's appointment was, like Byrnes's, more for reasons of personality than policy. His skill was in coping with a bureaucracy, most of his life having been spent in the military bureaucracy.[33] By 1 September 1939 he was army chief of staff, after Hopkins had called him to FDR's attention. Chief of staff throughout the war, he was called "the organizer of victory." Truman had long been one of his staunchest admirers, dating from his appearances before congressional committees, and had complete faith in him, though he "was awed by and never seemed relaxed with him."[34] It was also good politics to have the enormously respected general to gain Republican support.

Marshall's strength came from his careful planning and self-control. "Even those who had worked closely with him knew little of Marshall the man. They described him as cool, courteous, and impersonal, a man with an orderly mind, a clear sense of authority, and a great capacity for work."[35] His major effort was to bring some order into the bureaucracy by straightening out the lines of authority under Acheson (later under Robert Lovett), who acted as chief of staff. Marshall kept himself remote from subordinates. The orders came from Acheson. Marshall did not want to listen to long expert discussions: "Gentlemen, don't fight the problem; decide it." The machine operated more efficiently, but not so much from the top down as from the bottom up. German policy was much governed by tactical information from the front, that is, by pressures from Germany, rather than by any preferences of Marshall or Truman. He generally tried to do what Clay wanted, insofar as the Allies permitted, as he did so with as little personal ideological conflict as he had felt in allying with the Soviet Union during the war.

Acheson held the secretaryship 1949–52, having gained it by serving first as assistant secretary. He was the first in this period to have an articulate concept of international relations, which he saw as power politics. Within the administration he did everything right to keep his power. He had daily conferences with Truman, who rarely ignored his advice. "Truman's primary loyalty was to Acheson; where Acheson led, he followed."[36] He kept excellent staff men and rarely left Washington. Acheson even had a specific German policy, although it was largely set by Clay. He wanted to permit internationally minded Germans to gain control of their country so that the Bonn government would become a source of stability in European politics. Nevertheless, his leadership was weakened by the irrelevant and irrational arguments of the time. For all of his command of his field, he could not satisfy the

Republicans, stimulated by Senator Joseph McCarthy, who said he was "soft on communism."[37] As Marshall's and Truman's chief adviser, his contribution to the formation of German occupation policy was largely to translate reports from the field into a relatively consistent policy of anticommunism.

The Role of the War Department

The study of German policy would be relatively simple had it remained in the State Department's domain. The diplomats, however, were usually advisers to soldiers and often existed as little more than bystanders, partly because they realized they did not have the competence to provide a government of occupation. German policy was normally made at some level of the War Department, although the personnel of that department resisted the responsibilities for being in charge of millions of Germans almost as strenuously as did the State Department. The army had always ended up being responsible for the territories won in wars, but preferred not to be given the enormous burden.

The senior statesman willing and eager to assume the burden of the War Department was Henry L. Stimson, who was old enough to have been secretary of war for President Taft. He was brought back in despite his advanced age and the physical infirmities which meant that he often could not spend more than two or three hours a day at his desk. His contacts from Yale and in the law firm of the statesman Elihu Root had opened doors to wealth and a political career. Though he came from the federal bench, he was scarcely of the judicial temperament. "Around his waist he wore, as a perpetual reminder, the belt of a German soldier he had killed in the First World War. He loved a job to do and he flourished in the feeling of combat." He had learned from his father "to mistrust the Prussian and admire the French."[38] His belligerence and the fact that he was a Republican whose appointment might confound the Republican party in the year of the election got him the job when FDR finally brought himself to fire Harry Woodring, who had opposed warlike activity.[39]

There was also an element of chance in Stimson's appointment. It was arranged by Grenville Clark, a man of influence because he came from the Yale/Harvard breeding ground for government lawyers.[40] Knowing them and knowing Stimson was bored, he took his idea to Justice Felix Frankfurter, one of the power brokers. They made up a package, including the younger Robert Patterson, a former partner in Clark's law firm. Frankfurter took it to FDR, who knew that Patterson had tried to enlist as a private, so keen was he for fighting. The package was odd though, in that Patterson, unlike so many others in FDR's administration, was willing to cooperate with his cabinet boss. Stimson's contributions to policy were usually more moderate than those of his peers. When his voice was heard, and his was not the only voice heard from the War Department, it counseled fair treatment to the Germans.

Patterson succeeded him as secretary of war in the fall of 1945, the obvious choice by virtue of his dependability and industry. He was not a philosopher but a man of action, hard-working, self-confident, and most importantly, "fearless." He was also high-minded, forceful, zealous, and heartily profane. In the hands of the Washington brass, he was a blunt instrument to be used against the civilians, with his simplistic answer to issues: "We've got to win the war."[41] The Patterson-Clay correspondence after the war shows a Patterson very loyal to Clay, encouraging him in every possible way and limiting him scarcely at all.[42]

In 1940 Stimson found the War Department in no shape to conduct its business because of top level feuding and years of neglect. The situation seemed to him "perfectly horrible." To gain some control he brought in a first-class staff, including John J. McCloy, Robert Lovett, and Harvey Bundy, all able to stand up to his rage and "overweening presence." But Stimson had dubious success in dealing with a war bureaucracy so vastly expanded. As he reflected, he could never lay his hands on its slowly moving parts; he never had the feeling, as he did in 1911, that he knew all that was going on and that he was "running the whole show."[43] His method of control was to see as many officials in the course of a day as time and his health permitted and to ask as many questions as he could think of. Unfortunately for him, some subordinates allied with Henry Morgenthau against him, and turned "important segments of the planning into wrong channels."[44]

Stimson's assistant secretary, John J. McCloy, was of particular significance in German policy. His role, like Stimson's, was more often buffer than initiator. "While he did not press vigorously for the adoption of moderate concepts, he occasionally vetoed radical ones."[45] His vitality and acute sense for the location of real influence, brought him ever more important assignments from Stimson: Lend-Lease, Japanese relocation, military government in conquered areas, and eventually planning for Germany. In 1945 he was assumed by most to be the logical military governor of Germany, but he only gained the post of high commissioner for Germany in 1949. By that time it was important that his wife was related to Konrad Adenauer and that both McCloys exhibited keen admiration for German culture. The luxury of such admiration was denied him as assistant secretary 1940–45, when he was well aware of the anti-German tides that were running. His survival ability was more evident than any particular German policy line; he would strike this way and that in the close infighting that took place among the departments. He could claim afterwards that he restrained Morgenthau's irrationality, and sometimes he had.

When the Department of War was merged with the Navy Department into the Department of Defense in 1947, James Forrestal assumed that unified command. His career ended in a mental breakdown while he was in office, and he committed suicide soon after his loss of power. He has since become the center of historical controversy, for revisionists regard him as the leader—at some stage mentally ill—of the right-wing push which brought on the Cold War and altered occupation policy.[46] This view oversimplifies Forrestal's ideology, personality, and influence on German-Russian policy. In fact, his main sponsor at the White House was William Douglas, the symbol of liberalism, and he had moved from Wall Street to Washington not as a result of policy change, but as part of FDR's complex relationship with Irish Democrats and Catholics.[47] His power was a matter of accident and personality, not policy. A boy wonder on Wall Street in the twenties, he was involved in a manipulation verging on income tax evasion, and subjected to a congressional investigation. Perhaps because of this experience, he later supported the New Deal with its Security and Exchange Act, which support gained the favorable attention of Hopkins. When FDR was looking for someone with a background in finance and banking, Forrestal appeared to be a natural choice because he was not a typical banker.

In June 1940 Forrestal was made one of six special assistants to FDR, but he stayed only two months, since it seemed he was only an errand boy. By coincidence Congress had just created the post of undersecretary of the navy. Forrestal told several Roosevelt advisers he would like the job, and he got it. His assignment was "nonpolitical"—he was to take charge of procurement and contract negotiations, taxes, and other legal matters—but it involved liaison with many other agencies. He built it into a powerful position, gathering a group of men willing to work and be loyal to him. He took a comprehensive view of his duties, and few in government, certainly not Secretary of the Navy Frank Knox, could match his drive. When Knox died in 1944, Forrestal's appointment as his successor was a foregone conclusion.

Forrestal's influence on German policy, however, was limited by his own personality and opinions on other issues. An early advocate of military preparedness against Russia, he had since August 1943 been investigating those who might "wrongly" influence opinion. His office became a clearing house of information on communist influence. Forrestal had been much impressed by Averell Harriman's warnings in early 1945 and by Stalin's belligerent 9 February 1946 speech. This view of Russia happened to fit in with Truman's thinking, but Forrestal's opposition to Truman's pro-Zionist policy irritated the president.[48] He was one of the least conciliatory of men, and least inclined to retreat when it was strategic to do so, or to mind his own business. His relations with his cabinet colleagues and Truman were often strained. Truman distrusted his domestic and foreign views. He did not fit in socially, although his effort to do so included losing at poker. Other than adding push to an anticommunist policy, which could be seen as pro-German, even the vigorous Forrestal seems not to have been able to alter Clay's policy.

The Role of the Joint Chiefs of Staff

The Joint Chiefs of Staff (JCS) was basically a wartime body. Peacetime power in the military had rested with autonomous bureau chiefs. Marshall, by allying with Stimson and FDR, gained a measure of JCS control over these bureaus.[49] JCS power derived partly from their personal relations with FDR, who liked to consort with military leaders, assuming himself able to speak on equal terms. With that support the JCS moved into a vacuum of power; the willingness of Congress to give the military whatever it asked meant that Congress lost its control over U.S. global strategy.[50] Yet while the JCS could possibly have implemented a consistent and rational policy, in getting power its members lost their independence of view, or so Samuel Huntington concluded. They gave up a professional military point of view and accepted that of the amateur civilians whose power theirs had displaced.

The JCS had been thinking in terms of a permanent power struggle, while civilians were hoping for permanent peace. Their attitude meant that by 1945 JCS insisted on a tough German policy, contrary to their earlier analysis of an unsentimental power balance. In 1939 and 1940 the military had urged avoiding action which would give the Axis an excuse for war. Hopkins, Stimson, Knox, Harold Ickes, and Morgenthau favored more dangerous measures; while FDR and Hull wavered, FDR was more inclined to the belligerence of the civilians. The final American decisions which were made in the last part of November 1941 and "which precipitated the conflict, were reached virtually without military participation and decidedly without military approval."[51] The key decisions, prior to and early in the war, were civilian decisions: to concentrate on military defeat of the Axis to the exclusion of other considerations, to postpone political decisions, to demand unconditional surrender, and to defeat Germany before Japan. The top level military came to adopt these objectives.[52]

Foreign policy was conducted under military secrecy and with surface harmony, in contrast to the vicious fighting over economic mobilization which became an open scandal. Yet the result of public debate was preferable, for U.S. economic mobilization was rapid as compared to that of Germany and Japan, whereas the undebated foreign policy remained undeveloped. The JSC emerged from its long top secret deliberations with a foolish policy on Germany, one dictated from haste and fear of a belligerent civilian, Morgenthau.

The Role of the Civil Affairs Division

In the Pentagon's occupation policy structure, the Civil Affairs Division (CAD) supposedly made most of the implementation-of-policy decisions on Germany when it was assigned the task of coordinating policy for liberated and conquered territories. Its antecedent was a small military government division created in July 1942 in the provost marshall general's office. Its charter had authorized it to plan broadly, but it could do no more than plan a bit of training.[53] The only notable action it took, creating a school of military government at the University of Virginia, got it into trouble. The school nearly died in October, when at a cabinet meeting FDR made it clear that the occupation was to be a State Department matter. Earl Ziemke assumed that the president either did not know or did not accept the army doctrine that the theater commander had to be the military governor at least until the hostilities ended. Stimson avoided the issue, fearing that he could precipitate a decision that could in one stroke force the army out of military government. Attacks within the army stressed the allegedly second-rate quality of the faculty and the reactionary content of the courses. Ziemke concedes that there was some basis for believing that the officers sent to the school were of low quality, because the priority of its claim on talent was low. General Cornelius Wickersham complained that of 250 officers, only 38 would make suitable students, and these were "nothing to brag about."[54]

On 18 November 1942 FDR gave Hull "full authority for economic, political, and fiscal questions in liberated territories." The State Department set up the Office of Foreign Territories, which accomplished little and was soon dissolved. Civilians had no power to solve the problem of getting supplies to North Africa, being helpless without military support. Finally it became clear that the president's policy of establishing civilian-coordinated leadership had failed, and he was forced to request that the War Department assume responsibility for supply. Civilians were given one more chance at power when the Foreign Economic Administration was created in September 1943, with the supposed advantage of being located in the Office for Emergency Management of the Executive Office of the President. It was constantly in conflict with other agencies, so that for a while utter confusion reigned, until on 10 November 1943 the president recognized that the army would have to take the primary role.[55]

CAD had been created 1 March 1943 as a consequence of the North African problems. It was commanded from April 1943 to April 1946 by Major General John Hilldring. Subordinate to both Stimson and JCS, CAD power was limited by the delays in decision-making in both Marshall's Operations Division and JCS. As a staff rather than a command division, it confined its activities to planning, supervising, and locating information and personnel. Its creation led to a civil affairs, or G-5, section for each command staff.

CAD was immediately made responsible for ameliorating the misery caused by the war, an effort doomed in advance to failure, and to the training of military government officers. Several hundred men were recruited from surplus officers in various army units and sent to Fort Custer, Michigan, for a month's training, and then distributed among civil affairs training schools on various campuses. The supply from these schools was insufficient, so the division was staffed with direct commission officers, many of them lawyers straight from civilian life with the barest of orientation and training. The program, at its height in the latter part of 1943, trained 700 officers at Fort Custer in a single month. By the early spring of 1944 most had arrived in England for more training, which many officers, especially those who had been in North Africa and Italy, felt served no useful purpose.[56] Because the planning at supreme headquarters (SHAEF) had not progressed to specifics, the courses contained little that the students had not heard at least once before, although increased time was devoted to language and military training, calisthenics, and marching.[57] A pinpoint location had been set for each detachment, but for security reasons they could not be told what it was. They were all changed later anyway.

CAD was also supposed to accumulate materials, largely from the Office of Strategic Services (OSS), to be incorporated into a handbook on Germany and for civil affairs guides. Little was available when it was needed, and the publications did not reach Europe until late 1945, after the need for them had passed.[58] "Intelligence" was basically general information, which so-called experts on Germany could lecture on. British intelligence was found to be superior to the OSS reports, which were mostly summaries of opinions of various experts consulted by the organization. CAD emphasized the combat functions of military government and how to help the advancing armies; "relatively little attention was paid to the job of military government after hostilities had ceased." This emphasis partly explains why commanders "never fully realized the importance of activating political parties, labor unions and various cultural groups, reconstructing the German governmental system, re-educating the Germans, and other long range problems."[59] Military government did not get superior officers; the ablest usually went to combat duties or staff jobs.

CAD commander John Hilldring had been an infantry general but had suffered a heart attack while commanding a division.[60] Marshall found him a Pentagon job. When Hilldring took charge of CAD, Stimson explained he did not want the army to have anything to do with making policy. Marshall asked him: "Do you know what your duties are?" When Hilldring said yes, Marshall answered: "Well, I don't think you really do. Your mission is to start planning from the day you go into business, how you're going to get out of it as fast as possible. . . . The reason is that we have never regarded it as part of the proper duty of the military to govern."[61] Hilldring took seriously Marshall's advice to retreat, and he remained skeptical of subordinates' plans for reform and reeducation. CAD therefore was basically conservative; its instructions were to keep the "laws, customs and institutions of government."[62]

Hilldring's assistant, Ernest Gross, later said that Hilldring contributed little to policy formation, and that area commanders were allowed wide discretion in implementing it. CAD was mostly a buffer for theater commanders.[63] Although Hilldring's office supposedly issued policy directives, how feeble its command function actually was is evident in Hilldring's cable to W. Bedell Smith, Eisenhower's chief of staff. Referring to a letter asking when certain plans might be available for examination, Hilldring humbly accepted Smith's criticism that his request was highly improper, saying, "only your generous and charitable nature could have been responsible for your not blowing me out of the water because of it. Thanks. . . . My only alibi is that I don't know much about this civil affairs business. . . . Heaven knows, nothing is farther from my mind than to cause you trouble or irritation, no matter how slight." He later wrote how tenuous he felt his position to be, with generals looking for a job and likely to be assigned to CAD despite their lack of qualifications.[64]

In the days before military government became a reality in Germany, CAD frequently had a crippling effect on German policy inside the bureaucracy, partly because it had "little appreciation for Germany." Its key staff officers were influential liberal civilians, like John Boettinger, the president's son-in-law. The most energetic of the staff was the chief of Planning Branch, Colonel David Marcus, later a hero in Israel.[65] The staff's unsympathetic policy put CAD into general conflict with the State Department, delaying planning. CAD often refused to take part in the discussions with civilians, insisting that the occupation was purely a military matter; there was no need for interdepartmental committees; when the time came the JCS would issue any necessary orders. The CAD staff, largely civilian lawyers, said Philip Mosely, "seemed to regard the jurisdiction and prestige of the military service as they might the interests of a client, to be defended by every device of argument, delay, obstruction, and veto against an 'adversary,' " the adversary in this case being the State Department.[66] The process reminded him of "the procedures of Soviet negotiators in their more intransigent moods."[67]

Hilldring, in defense of CAD's obstructive behavior, blamed it on confusion among higher authorities. "First there was no organization in Washington capable of hammering out these military government policies and decisions except the War Department. There wasn't even a clear and lasting decision as to what civilian departments and agencies of the government should participate in the making of policy. . . .This very bitter and troublesome controversy was never resolved."[68] The State Department also had no coordinating agency until Hilldring moved there in 1946. Departmental coordination was attempted by the State–War–Navy Coordinating Committee, which lived only from December 1944 to August 1945.[69] CAD was dissolved in 1949, as was Hilldring's Office for Occupied Areas.

Before the occupation began CAD had little to communicate because Washington produced only arguments about theories. After the war facts began to pour in, along with more realistic recommendations from the command in Germany. CAD facilitated the U.S. Office of Military Government (OMGUS) decision-making by clearing it in Washington. It seems not to have been a control office, but rather a relay station for messages. Its earlier impact on Washington planning was to toughen it, or to delay it.

The Minor Role of Congress and Public Opinion

Before leaving the institutions and personalities of Washington, one should remember Congress, supposedly advising and consenting. It played only an infrequent role in occupation policy. During the war it was ignored because such matters were for the military to decide. After the war two committees had a minor and negative impact. The Kilgore Committee, during 1945, was alert to stories that the military was coddling Nazis; Kilgore called Clay "nothing but a fascist."[70] Yet with the Republican victory in 1946, some suspected Clay of being pro-Russian. The Taber Committee intervened in 1948 and called a halt to the denazification that Kilgore had pushed.

Acheson described the congressional role by quoting Woodrow Wilson: "Congress stands almost helplessly outside of the departments. Even the special irksome, ungracious investigations . . . do not afford it more than a glimpse of the inside of a small province of federal administration. . . . it cannot often fathom the waters of the sea in which the bigger fish of the civil service swim and feed."[71] Yet the civil servant could blame unreasonable politicians. Acheson also said: "I was a frustrated schoolteacher persisting against overwhelming evidence to the contrary that the human mind could be moved by facts and reason." Kennan thought similarly: "Washington's reactions were deeply subjective, influenced more by domestic-political moods and institutional interests than by any theoretical considerations of our international position."[72]

In this hodgepodge of leaders and institutions, each frustrating the other, there is little evidence of insight or decisiveness about German or European realities. Politicians were more oriented to gaining power in Washington than to the intelligent use of power in Europe, although they did have a veto power in the evolution of occupation policy. They sometimes got in the way of policy decided by subordinates, but they were too diverted to do more. The government and the people were too deeply involved in the economic problems of moving from a wartime to a peacetime economy to think carefully about a defeated Germany, and attitudes about Germany in 1945 were hardened for a generation by the discovery that the propaganda about German atrocities was even exceeded by the realities of Auschwitz.

Washington, the Allies, and Occupation Policy

Before moving to the level of military government in Germany, its creation and implementation of policy, it is necessary to trace quickly the conflict which persisted at the top level among the various governments allied against Germany. Washington's power to implement a policy was affected not only by its internal conflicts but also by the conflicting interests of its former enemy and its wartime Allies. The United States did not have the power to win the war alone, and would not be able to win the peace in Germany alone. What the Allies wanted would seriously complicate the task of OMGUS in governing its zone. Further, what the Germans of the U.S. zone wanted would seriously complicate the task of the United States in dealing satisfactorily with its Allies.

The ability to coerce or persuade the Germans or the Allies was limited most seriously by FDR's decision, made before Pearl Harbor, to fight the Japanese at the same time as the Germans, ignoring the advice of his professional soldiers that the United States was not ready to do either. The scattering of U.S. resources increased "the gap between promise and reality," which James Burns thought destroyed the victorious alliance. He assumed that the failure to aid Russia seriously before 1944 occurred despite FDR's honest intentions. Stalin assumed it was duplicity.[73] In May 1942, FDR promised Molotov a second front that year, but Churchill refused and the United States was powerless to invade the continent alone. A substitute for the second front, the doctrine of "unconditional surrender," enunciated at Casablanca January 1943, was supposed to please Stalin, but he reasonably argued that it served only to unite the Germans. FDR rejected both British and Russian urgings to alter it. William McNeill has a persuasive explanation: "the President did not want to have dealings with any group such as the German officer corps. He was not willing to accept the only alternative wielders of power."[74] Not the slogan but the attitude prolonged the war. In maintaining it, FDR closed a power option. His refusal to negotiate was based on the false image of a degenerate German race, sold by war propaganda and bought by American leaders. Kennan, who had had closer contact with them, rejected the image of "the German people as a mass of inhuman monsters, solidly behind Hitler and consumed with a demonic enthusiasm for the ruin and enslavement of Europe."[75] The tension which existed from the beginning of occupation policy between those like George Shuster, who wanted to work with the Germans, and those like Henry Morgenthau, who wanted to punish them, was finally resolved only after Clay, and through him Washington, learned the facts of German life.

Allied agreements, so general as to be amenable to widely divergent interpretations, began to take shape at the Teheran Conference in November 1943. There the Big Three apparently agreed to crush Germany by partition.[76] Roosevelt suggested seven parts, with the Ruhr and Saar under international control. Stalin demanded large quantities of German machinery and "at least four million Germans" for reconstruction. Although FDR thought his conciliation at the expense of Germans had broken through Stalin's suspicion, Milovan Djilas heard Stalin's reaction. "Churchill is the kind who, if you don't watch him, will slip a kopeck out of your pocket!... Roosevelt is not like that. He dips in his hand only for bigger coins." Actually Americans were too confused to pick pockets; right hands never knew where left hands were.[77] For example, Eisenhower could assume in the following months that he had an occupation mission, but "its nature and purposes were almost totally unknown."[78]

The Teheran meeting delegated the task of working out Allied policy on occupied territories to the European Advisory Commission (EAC).[79] The committee met first in January 1944, with Russian ambassador F. T. Gusev, British diplomat William Strang, and U.S. ambassador John Winant, a friend of FDR's and a teacher and former governor.[80] A State Department committee recommended in the spring of 1944 against partitioning and harsh peace, but State did not decide policy.[81] Its EAC delegates were held on such a short leash they could not join in Strang's effort to make meaningful decisions. "The American representative could come up with no thoughts and make no suggestion to his colleagues which had not already come to him as instructions from Washington[which] appeared to have a total absence of thoughts, and only the tardiest and most grudging of suggestions."[82]

The issue of occupation zones provides a good example of Washington confusion and CAD obstruction. Returning from Teheran, the president had discussed zones with military aides, using a map prepared by JCS which set forth a Soviet zone with only 22 percent of 1937 Germany.[83] Although CAD had been talking about a Russian zone with about 80 percent, it gave Winant this 22 percent plan. He recognized that the Russians would react violently, and requested clarification, but CAD refused to elaborate and a deadlock lasted for many weeks. When Kennan was able to get audience with FDR 2 April 1944, the president showed surprise: "Why, that's just something I once drew on the back of an envelope."[84] FDR reversed himself, permitting EAC to accept the British suggestion already approved by Moscow.

Policy guides sent to Winant were late, unreasonable, and mostly irrelevant.[85] The War Department did not so much have a policy as a desire to keep its options open. When the State Department tried to use the interdepartmental Working Security Committee (WSC) there were interminable clearance problems.[86] In desperation Winant sent a long prophetic cable to FDR in mid-August 1944, suggesting material aid to help restore Russia and end her suspicions; it must be done before the war ended, otherwise rivalry over Germany and reparations would follow it. He received no reply, for just at this time Morgenthau was diverting FDR's attention, first into his famous policy aberration, the Morgenthau Plan, and then, as a reaction to the storm it created, deeper into the "policy of no policy," or "decision by postponement." Treasury Department intervention had come precisely when the War Department, having long prevented decisions, had suddenly concluded that policy decisions were urgently needed, and immediately after the State Department, in the Pasvolsky-Acheson document, had decided openly to oppose dismemberment and to favor raising the standard of living to reconcile the German people under democratic leaders to the peace settlement.[87] The policy of 1947 was thus ready by August 1944, but folly intervened.

The Morgenthau Plan and JCS Document 1067

Few things better demonstrate the human capacity for error, even in a democracy where power is supposedly balanced, than the fact that Morgenthau had a perfectly outrageous idea—to deindustrialize Germany—and it seemed to become policy. That it did reflected FDR's prejudice and that he had no professional adviser on Germany. The Morgenthau Plan is the most commented-upon aspect of policy progression, not the least reason for which is that Morgenthau's chief adviser, Harry Dexter White, was described during the McCarthy era as a Communist. This assertion proved to some more simple-minded observers that the Morgenthau Plan, as well as the early occupation policy, was part of "the Communist conspiracy."[88] It would be much more accurate to see the plan as the result of normal factors: confusion, ignorance, hatred, and even historical accident.

When White and Morgenthau were on a flight to Europe 5 August 1944, White showed him the Pasvolsky-Acheson document accepted the day before.[89] Its moderation incensed him. That began the detour in which the secretary of treasury used his emotional closeness to his neighbor the president to divert policy. Morgenthau lunched with Eisenhower to try to change army plans;[90] he also told Eden about the State Department plan. Eden was surprised that State, after Teheran, was considering a united rather than a dismembered Germany. Hull was more surprised that at Teheran FDR had decided on dismemberment, saying: "I have never been permitted to see the minutes of the Teheran Conference."[91] Roosevelt, though embarrassed that Hull had been told what had been decided at Teheran, agreed with Morgenthau: "We have to be tough with Germany and I mean the German people not just the Nazis. We either have to castrate the German people or you have got to treat them in such a manner so they can't just go reproducing people who want to continue the way they have in the past."[92] When Morgenthau returned to the president on 25 August, with an example of what he regarded as softness in the army's *Handbook for Military Government in Germany,* Roosevelt then told Forrestal and Stimson that the Germans should be allowed "simply a subsistence level of food."[93]

Morgenthau was in a good position to approach his neighbor Franklin over the Labor Day weekend. He brought FDR the plan his staff had created in a week's crash program, wherein Morgenthau ordered that the Ruhr and Saar industry should be put out of business. FDR read the plan "slowly and carefully." He liked it, but thought it might be necessary to transfer all Germans between twenty and forty out of Germany to Central Africa. He reflected that such an action would leave a problem of what to do with the children. When returning the plan to White, Morgenthau told him FDR "is willing to go as far as I am, or he is willing to go farther than I am."[94]

Stimson regarded the plan as "just fighting brutality with brutality." On 6 September the secretaries battled bitterly in front of FDR, Hopkins supporting Morgenthau and Hull shifting to Stimson.[95] Morgenthau got another chance 9 September, when he took advantage of his knowledge of FDR's personality, arguing that his plan was the best way to help Britain, in that the destruction of the Ruhr would enable Britain to take over German markets.[96]

At the Quebec Conference 13 September, when Morgenthau and White presented their revised plan at dinner, Churchill's immediate response was negative, but Roosevelt let him talk himself out and then soothed him.[97] The next morning Churchill reversed himself and initialed a moderated version of the plan in which industry was closed down but not destroyed.[98] Stimson reflected it was "a terrible thing to think that the total power of the U.S. and the U.K. in such a critical matter as this is in the hands of two men, both of whom are similar in their impulsiveness and their lack of systematic study." He wrote FDR that the plan would be "a crime against civilization itself."[99] But the president paid more heed to public reaction. The story was leaked, through Morgenthau sympathizers apparently, and published 21 September. Presidential candidate Thomas Dewey denounced it as a policy that would increase German resistance. The majority of newspapers opposed it. Roosevelt retreated.[100]

Having impulsively followed a friend, and his own prejudice, into a briar patch, FDR reverted even more deeply into a policy of postponement. On 20 October he expressed his dislike for "making detailed plans for a country which we do not yet occupy." Yet plans had to be made and the fall of 1944 was filled with planning and pushing, with Morgenthau having the advantage that publicly FDR had supported him. How much of Morgenthau's negativism became policy is subject to controversy; some analyses regard it as more mirage than reality. It is evident, however, that the State Department plan of early August was pulled down into a whirling debate that raged until the spring of 1945. The center for the struggle was the creation and revision of the famous Joint Chiefs of Staff Document 1067, more usually referred to as JCS 1067. Morgenthau's ideas perhaps helped form the public image of JCS 1067 more than its reality. It was agreed on only as the war ended, and remained secret until the fall of 1945. It would seem to have ordered the army to tear down rather than to rebuild, and to help Germans only when help was clearly necessary to avoid disease or disorder.

The JCS had been given the task of drafting a directive for troops in Germany, and on 22 September, between the Quebec Conference and FDR's private reversal, they rapidly recommended an interim directive to the Combined Chiefs of Staff (CCS). In the transmittal from JCS to CCS, the directive was given its eternal number, JCS 1067.[101] Stimson, tired and concerned with the Pacific war, left the fight against Morgenthau to McCloy, who proved either more tactful or less moderate.[102] When Stimson, and sometimes McCloy, pushed for moderation, their subordinate CAD was pushing in the opposite direction. Hilldring, whose leading officers were allied with Morgenthau, objected to the U.S. propaganda line that with the end of the war German economic, social, and cultural reconstruction could begin. David Marcus apparently dictated the final version of the basic directive, which was very close to Morgenthau's position.[103]

The problem persisted of informing EAC and the army what the policy meant; McCloy, and even Marshall, tried to get directives cleared, but JCS avoided approving further policy statements.[104] Guidance for policy-makers came through rumors of FDR's attitudes or from gleanings from his speeches. State issued an ingenious statement on 10 November refuting the argument that the plan would help England; it said the British wanted control, not destruction, and also that the Russians would oppose destruction. FDR told Stettinius on 15 November that he liked the statement,[105] but when Morgenthau lunched with FDR a few days later he changed his mind again. A week later Stettinius asked about the statement. No reply. Another week went by, and another reminder. Then came FDR's confidential note of 4 December: "(1) we should let Germany come back industrially to meet her own needs, but not to export for some time and we know better how things are going to work out; (2) we are against reparations; (3) we do want restitution of looted property of all kinds."[106] Yet he refused to provide policy instructions, insisting that important decisions be postponed until the war had ended.

To surmount the barrier of the JCS and Morgenthau, Stettinius tried a State-War-Navy Coordinating Committee (SWNCC) on 1 December at the assistant secretary level. McCloy and Hilldring had been determined to keep the army out of policy making, but the army and the Treasury Department had gained a common goal. The army would not be responsible for keeping the German economy going. After the bad publicity from Aachen, the first city occupied, they also shared strong denazification urges. This alliance brought the first revision of JCS 1067 on 6 January, which weakened Control Council authority and made a more moderate economic statement that allowed the army to take some action; yet it also spelled out severe deindustrialization provisions.[107] SWNCC did give State some added leverage, however, and closer liaison with the president. At its 16 January meeting Forrestal denounced the mass murder, enslavement, and devastation of Germany. Stimson concurred.[108]

In addition to this struggle to decide on U.S. occupation policy before meeting with the British and Russians at Yalta, there was an argument over whether the United States should support the Russian demand for reparations from Germany. An alternative to reparations was for the United States to give the Russians a direct loan to assist their postwar reconstruction. Morgenthau was pushing for a loan of ten billion dollars to be repaid over thirty-five years. Harriman agreed that Russia should receive aid, but only if she behaved.[109] FDR decided in January not to discuss the loan at Yalta, saying: "I think it's very important that we hold this back and don't give them any promises until we get what we want."[110]

FDR's decision not to be generous to the Russians with either German or American goods contradicts one of the early criticisms of the Yalta Conference of February 1945, that an ailing or naive FDR sold out to Stalin. A subsequent interpretation of the conference emphasized instead that FDR had given little if anything to Stalin, who merely kept what his army had conquered. The revisionist school of criticism includes the interpretation that FDR, as evidenced by his opposition to reparations or a loan, had taken a Cold War position toward Stalin.

To leave the larger debate and note only what affected occupation policy, it should be pointed out that the partition of Germany, presumably decided at Teheran, was reversed.[111] It seemed to agree on a central government in an Allied Control Council, although the reality came to approximate a temporary four-way partition into the occupation zones. The zones had been agreed upon by the EAC; the Big Three had little to fuss over, except for Churchill's request that France be given a zone and a seat on the council.[112] The Russians proposed moving Poland westward, with Russia regaining eastern Poland, and the Poles gaining German lands to the Oder-Neisse rivers.[113] In reply to Roosevelt's concern over the great difficulties of transferring millions of Germans across the border, Stalin falsely reported that very few Germans remained in the area. No decision was made. The western policy of postponement had won again, or so it seemed, but in fact, the Russians, being on the spot with the power, gave the land to the Poles, who began forcing Germans out as the war ended.

The most serious division of opinion pertained to reparations. Stalin demanded that Germany be billed for twenty billion dollars, of which Russia was to be given ten billion. He wanted it not in the form of money, but rather in the form of industries to be shipped to Russia within two years. He also wanted two or three million Germans for reconstruction work over a period of ten years; they were to be selected from war criminals, active Nazis, and the unemployed.[114] The English and the Americans could not agree to this, fearing that whatever wealth Russia took out at one side of Germany would have to be replaced by the West as food and materials from the other.[115] The reparations decision, which was merely a half-hearted promise to consider the Russian suggestions later, constituted a defeat for the Russians. By agreeing to Stalin's figure as "a basis for discussion," the United States sidetracked the Soviet request for aid. By taking reparations in areas his troops had occupied, however, Stalin implemented his policy even before Potsdam. To some visitors, FDR seemed hopeful. "I got along absolutely splendidly with Stalin at Yalta." Yet to others he expressed serious concern about Russian actions in Romania in March.[116]

The defeat of Germany began the conflict which worsened Roosevelt's last days. It emerged from negotiations in Berne, Switzerland, begun 8 March between SS General Wolff and Allen Dulles of the OSS for the surrender of the German army in Italy. Stalin wrote 3 April: "The German commander on the Western Front . . . has agreed to open the front and permit the Anglo-

American troops to advance to the east, and the Anglo-Americans have promised in return to ease for the Germans the peace terms."[117] That the Germans were fighting much harder on the eastern front suggested they were hoping for a separate peace with the West. Stalin's conclusion ignored the fact that the Germans were much more afraid of a Russian than a British-American occupation, and with good reason.[118] Desperate Germans hoped to be saved by the West from Russian wrath. This hope did not mean, however, that the West considered cooperating with the Germans. Eisenhower had told Stalin he would stop at the Elbe and he did. He turned over hundreds of thousands of prisoners. Stalin's intense suspicion, at least in April 1945, was unreasonable.

Yalta had an effect on the home front battle over JCS 1067. On 28 February 1945, the day of Roosevelt's return, he asked State to carry through the Yalta understandings, apparently turning his back on Morgenthau and his plan. State jumped at the opportunity to abandon JCS 1067, and 10 March produced a moderate directive which FDR initialed 15 March.[119] The president even appointed the committee to implement the memo. For a few days this memo was policy. Stimson objected to its restrictions on zonal commanders, however, and McCloy alerted Morgenthau. On 20 March Morgenthau and White met with McCloy and Hilldring, following which Morgenthau saw FDR at another lunch and got another reversal; Roosevelt said he did not remember even having seen the 10 March directive.[120]

When the three departments' Informal Policy Committee on Germany (IPCOG) met 21 March, the discussion centered on the army's insistence on flexibility in military government. On practically every point State gave way.[121] On 22 March, the president called the three secretaries in to say he did not like the 10 March directive; he did not want to destroy German industry, but he wanted to decentralize authority. This was close to War's position; its version got another FDR "OK" and all departments signed it 23 March. It placed the dispute at his death in a "tenuous balance."[122]

By 18 April IPCOG had drafted another revision, which contained a compromise on the points of conflict.[123] On 10 May Joseph Grew explained the revised JCS 1067 briefly to Truman, who asked whether light industry would be destroyed; Grew said only in exceptional cases. Truman said he disagreed with Morgenthau, yet signed JCS 1067 as Roosevelt's policy, and sent it to Eisenhower 14 May.[124] This eighth version, JCS 1067/8, policy until July 1947, was a tortuous compromise, "an agreement glued together with careful phraseology, by avoiding issues or delegating their determination in the absence of agreement." Each side could read into it much of what it had fought for, which gave Clay the same opportunity.[125]

FDR's death came when the war was won and the peace not yet lost. Truman's decisions on Germany were soon deeply involved with his policy toward Russia. The question is when conciliation with Russia at the expense of Germany was replaced with a confrontation with Russia over Germany.[126]

The events in Germany before the Potsdam meeting July–August 1945 evidence that Truman was then more inclined to continue the policy of conciliation. He ordered the army to surrender the territory between the present eastern boundary of West Germany and roughly the Elbe River, about one-half of the German Democratic Republic, to Russia. He had not pushed taking more of Germany before the war ended,[127] although this withdrawal was contrary to the repeated advice of Churchill:

> This would be an event which . . . would be one of the most melancholy in history. . . . the Allies ought not to retreat from their present positions to the occupational line until we are satisfied about Poland and also about the temporary character of the Russian occupation of Germany, and the conditions to be established in the Russianized or Russian-controlled countries. . . . If they are not settled before the U.S. armies withdraw from Europe and the Western world folds up its war machines, there are no prospects of a satisfactory solution and very little of preventing a third world war.[128]

Instead Truman's decision was for the Hopkins mission to Moscow, which dramatized his desire to avoid Churchillian resistance and to continue Rooseveltian cooperation.

On 26–27 May Hopkins, to appease Stalin, explained that Russian dominance of the Polish government lay behind her difficulties with the United States. When Stalin answered that Russia must have a friendly Poland because it had been the entry for German armies, Hopkins said the United States would be happy to have only friendly neighbors next to Russia. Stalin said that if Russia were approached in a friendly fashion much could be achieved, but "reprisals in any form would have the opposite effect." Hopkins was convinced and reported 30 May that he had arranged the summit meeting and satisfactory compromises.[129] Churchill's fears seemed paranoid.

With Hopkins's reassurance came the significant Truman decision to evacuate American troops from eastern Germany. Although General Clay would later be associated with resistance to Russia in Germany, and in 1948 with the decision not to withdraw from Berlin, in 1945 his reports gave support to the hope that withdrawal could lead to cooperation. He reported a pleasant meeting with Marshall G. M. Zhukov, who had reasonably observed that "any steps to set up control machinery must await withdrawal into the agreed zones." Clay added that he had been treated cordially and that the question of withdrawal would have to be resolved before any further discussion with Zhukov could serve any useful purpose. "As a result of my discussion with Zhukov I am optimistic that the Russians will join in some form of control machinery when withdrawal is accomplished."[130]

The French caused more immediate frustrations. When they refused to leave Stuttgart, Truman rapidly became as incensed with de Gaulle as Roosevelt had been.[131] Yet at Potsdam, Churchill and Truman permitted

France a disastrous veto power over the three victors in Germany. By then Germany and the generals were center stage. After Potsdam, Truman symbolically left Berlin and the problem of the occupation for Clay to solve. Clay became the unforeseen star of the drama, but the script, JCS 1067, was quickly made obsolete by improvisation.

Notes

1. Roosevelt told Truman he was no administrator, but a "man of vision" (Harry S Truman, *Memoirs: Year of Decision,* I [Garden City, 1955], 12).
2. The minority view is supported by Potter, who praised FDR's powers of assimilating details assembled by close questioning of many people (David Potter in William Leuchtenberg, ed., *Franklin D. Roosevelt* [New York, 1967], 20); see also Clinton Rossiter, *The American Presidency* (New York, 1969), 117–18; A. J. Wann, *The President as Chief Administrator* (Washington, 1968). The majority, while agreeing with James MacGregor Burns, found different reasons for FDR's actions. Burns assumed the confusion was a strategy for power (*The Lion and the Fox* [New York, 1956], 371, 373). Richard Neustadt and Arthur Schlesinger, Jr., saw it as FDR's successful search for information (Neustadt, *Presidential Power* [New York, 1960], 156–57; Schlesinger, *The Age of Roosevelt,* II [Boston, 1959], 258); see also Elting E. Morison, *Turmoil and Tradition* (Boston, 1960), 488. Gabriel Kolko thought him neither intellectual nor a technician (*The Roots of American Foreign Policy* [Boston, 1969], 349–50); see also Donald Drummond, "Cordell Hull," in Norman Graebner, ed., *An Uncertain Tradition* (New York, 1961), 194; John Snell, *Wartime Origins of the East-West Dilemma over Germany* (New Orleans, 1959), 29.
3. "Roosevelt always saw to it that the authority he had perforce to delegate became in the distribution so fragmented, so offset by counterweights that no single view, no single man could achieve undue significance or influence" (Morison, 510–12); see also Eliot Janeway, *The Struggle for Survival* (New Haven, 1953). His defenders argue that this competition well served FDR's intention of keeping himself informed and in control.
4. Dean Acheson, *Present at the Creation* (New York, 1969), 16, 47; see also Anthony Eden, *The Memoirs of Anthony Eden: The Reckoning* (Boston, 1965), 433; Dwight D. Eisenhower, *Crusade in Europe* (Garden City, 1948), 218.
5. Drummond, in Graebner, 194.
6. Jonathan Daniels, *Frontier on the Potomac* (New York, 1946), 31–32.
7. The Morgenthau Plan exemplifies this reliance on amateur friends. For a critique of Morgenthau's position, see Eliot Janeway, *Economics of Crisis: War, Politics, and the Dollar* (New York, 1968), 180.
8. He knew how to keep rivals away. Janeway thought Hopkins deliberately chose incompetent men to avoid endangering his own position (*Survival,* 41–57).
9. William Langer and S. Everett Gleason, *Challenge to Isolation* (New York, 1952), 3; Richard Hofstadter, *The American Political Tradition and the Men Who Made It* (New York, 1948), 351.
10. Snell quotes two high officials: "anyone who tried to adopt a fairly tolerant attitude toward Germany was suspect" (13), and "the first problem with which we had to try to cope was, to put it brutally, an ignorant animus against Germany" (30).
11. He was arrested: "Once for running over a goose, once for carrying a bicycle into a railroad

station, once for picking cherries by the roadside and once for riding his bicycle into a forbidden area after sundown.'' At the age of nine he attended a public school in Germany and at fourteen took a bicycle tour through southwestern Germany with a tutor (William Hassett, *Off the Record with FDR* [New Brunswick, 1958], 200). Hull reported that after FDR had spoken of his early experiences, "the President suddenly brought it back to Germany by saying that, after all, it was many years ago that he had become acquainted with Germany and perhaps he didn't know so much about her as he thought'' (Snell, 31–33).

12. William McNeill, *America, Britain, and Russia: Their Cooperation and Conflict, 1941–46* (London, 1953), 488. John L. Gaddis described an FDR visit in 1919 to the Rhineland occupation, where he became angry at American reluctance to fly the American flag (*The United States and the Origins of the Cold War, 1941–47* [New York, 1972], 100).

13. Robert Gannon, *The Cardinal Spellman Story* (New York, 1962), 222–24; see also Hans-Peter Schwarz, *Vom Reich zur Bundesrepublik* (Neuwied, 1966), 47–48. Adm. William Leahy said 16 May 1944 there would be three powers after the war, with Russia much stronger than Britain (U.S. Dept. of State, *Foreign Relations of the U.S.: The Conference at Yalta* [Washington, 1955], 269 [hereafter *FRUS*]). Alan Brooke recorded 27 June 1944 Anthony Eden's similar conclusion. See Arthur Bryant, *Triumph in the West* (London, 1965); see also Robert Murphy, *Diplomat among Warriors* (Garden City, 1964), 227; Edgar Snow, *Journey to the Beginning* (New York, 1958), 344. FDR's position in March 1943 could have been to try to keep communism out of central Europe (Robert Sherwood, *Roosevelt and Hopkins* [New York, 1948], 714). Kolko thought this concern determined the Quebec decision in August 1943 to occupy as much of Germany as possible (*Roots,* 29).

14. Schwarz thought he had to conciliate (53). Revisionist logic has been that Russia should dominate her neighbors because she has the right to protect herself. See Gar Alperovitz, *Atomic Diplomacy* (New York, 1964); Barton Bernstein, ed., *Politics and Policies of the Truman Administration* (New York, 1966); Lloyd C. Gardner, *Architects of Illusion* (New York, 1967); William A. Williams, *The Tragedy of American Diplomacy* (New York, 1962). They leave unanswered whether Russia was in danger after 1945 and whether small powers have the same right.

15. "Roosevelt did not lead or define American foreign policy. . . . his advisers . . . hammered out that policy for the nation'' (Kolko, *Roots,* 349).

16. Either view can begin with Senator Truman's statement after the German attack: "If we see that Germany is winning the war, we ought to help Russia, and if Russia is winning we ought to help Germany and in that way kill as many as possible.'' Truman first used the atomic bomb, but soon recognized that it had in fact a limited political power (Berstein, *Politics,* 23; Cabell Phillips, *The Truman Presidency* [New York, 1966], 40–42, 63).

17. Dean Acheson, in Joseph Jones, *The Fifteen Weeks* (New York, 1955), 111–13.

18. Neustadt, 9–10. Although Truman is best remembered for his desk sign, The Buck Stops Here, Samuel Lubell described him as "a man fighting stubbornly, and yes courageously, to avoid decision.'' Critics described a policy stalemate (Samuel Lubell, *The Future of American Politics* [New York, 1951], 24).

19. "The inner heart of this foreign affairs government was the foursome of Forrestal, Marshall, Lovett, and Acheson'' (Samuel Huntington, *The Soldier and the State* [Cambridge, Mass., 1964], 257–60, 354, 364, 377).

20. Ibid., 380–81.

21. Clifford said: "He was comfortable with me.'' Clifford, a fellow Missourian, got to the White House when a friend was made Truman's naval aide. In January 1946 Clifford became naval aide, but he rewrote a tough speech on labor policy so skillfully that Truman made him his special counsel (Gaddis, 322; Patrick Anderson, *The Presidents' Men* [New York, 1968], 87–122).

22. "It was virtually impossible to get the White House to give attention to policy matters relating to Germany" (Harold Zink, *The United States in Germany, 1944-45* [New York, 1956], 88–89).

23. He had brought FDR needed southern support (Drummond, in Graebner, 184–86, 191–94); "Hull, like most other Americans of the epoch, had an essentially naive view of how power functions in world politics" (ibid., 196).

24. "[The State Dept.] devoted itself to relations with neutrals and minor allies and . . . plans for the U.N." (ibid., 199: Acheson, 11; McNeill, 58).

25. "The heads of all these divisions, like barons in a feudal system weakened at the top by mutual suspicions and jealousy between king and prince, were constantly at odds" (Acheson, 15, 38). Welles was the only one in the State Dept. in favor of a harsh peace.

26. The State Dept.'s German expert said Stettinius "didn't know anything" (Interview James Riddleberger; Walter Johnson, "Edward R. Stettinius, Jr., 1944–45," in Graebner, 210). Welles was finally forced out by FDR's unwillingness to dismisss Hull. Janeway argued that FDR and Hopkins appointed Stettinius for his incompetence (*Survival,* 41–57).

27. Acheson dismissed this reorganization as only setting people into neater boxes (Acheson, 48).

28. FDR turned down James Byrnes because he might question who was boss (Sherwood, 835). Stettinius avoided conflict, yet presented department positions more "forcefully" by sending neat summaries of alternatives for FDR's approval or disapproval (Richard Walker, *Edward R. Stettinius, Jr.* [New York, 1956], 26).

29. Jonathan Daniels, *Man of Independence* (London, 1951), 265.

30. Phillips, 81–83. Truman's other reasons were Byrnes's friendliness, even temperament, informality, and parliamentary skills (Richard D. Burns, "James F. Byrnes, 1945–47," in Graebner, 224). Some revisionists have another explanation: "the President put his confidence in a man who took an extremely tough-minded view of the A-Bomb's role in diplomacy" (Alperovitz, 63). Yet Truman made the job offer before either he or Byrnes was aware of the Russian problem or the bomb as a solution. By December he was incensed at Byrnes's "lack of toughness" with Russia; Byrnes's first policy statement indicated he could deal with Russians as he had with Republicans (Burns, in Graebner, 227).

31. The understanding was that he would finish the negotiations for the minor treaties, which lasted the rest of the year (Jones, 105).

32. Phillips, 148; see also Ernest F. Penrose, *Economic Planning for the Peace* (Princeton, 1953), 345; Jones, 106.

33. Robert Ferrell, *The American Secretaries of State and Their Diplomacy,* XV (New York, 1966), 6–9. He had attracted the attention of General Pershing by standing his ground after the general had scolded his outfit.

34. While FDR was still alive Truman told the *Kansas City Star* that Marshall was "the greatest living American" (Alexander de Conde, "George Marshall," in Graebner, 245, 264).

35. Acheson, 143; Burns, 85; de Conde, in Graebner, 249–50; Harry S Truman, *Memoirs: Years of Trial and Hope,* II (Garden City, 1956), 112; George Kennan, *Memoirs, 1925-50* (Boston, 1967), 363. "Power is the key word in the Marshall vocabulary" (Schwarz, 77).

36. Norman Graebner, "Dean Acheson," in Graebner, 268–69; Gardner, 202, 207; Janeway, *Survival,* 219; Jones, 110–11.

37. Recent scholars instead see in Acheson an overreaction to communism, a rigidity and overreliance on force (Graebner, in Graebner, 272).

38. Snell, 24–27. He had spent three weeks at the front, the happiest days of his life. Stimson resembled Theodore Roosevelt, with his health problems and a compensating interest in climbing mountains and killing bears (Richard Current, "Henry Stimson," in Graebner, 169).

39. FDR said: "Woodring is a nice fellow but . . . I am so weak in getting rid of people"

(Morison, 477). Instead he worked with Deputy Louis Johnson who opposed Woodring; their feud became a scandal.

40. Henry Stimson and McGeorge Bundy, *On Active Service in Peace and War* (New York, 1948), 566–70; Janeway, *Survival*, 52.

41. Janeway, *Survival*, 145.

42. Interview Ferdinand Eberstadt, Patterson Project, 14, Columbia University Oral History; Jones, 119; Acheson, 49.

43. "By 1940 the military establishment had grown into a loose federation of agencies. . . . the system disintegrated in 1917 as it did again in 1941" (Morison, 488, 494–96, 507). Stilwell compared it to the alimentary canal: "You feed it at one end, and nothing comes out at the other but crap." Marshall admitted two days after Pearl Harbor that the department was "a poor command post" (ibid., 504–5, 541).

44. "Any historian who assumed that as Stimson preached, so all the administrative officials of the War Department practiced, would miss an essential part of the history of American policy toward Germany. More things go on inside the Pentagon than are ever dreamed of by Secretaries of War or Defense" (Penrose, 271).

45. Snell, 24; Morison, 492–93.

46. He had Kennan installed at the War College and the policy of containment prominently published (Gardner, 271; Schwarz, 63).

47. Liberal Harold Ickes described Forrestal as no "Wall Streeter" (Arnold Rogow, *James Forrestal* [New York, 1963], 41). Annoyed by the ambitions of James Farley and Joseph Kennedy, FDR decided to create still another Irish possibility (Janeway, *Survival*, 207). When he retired he went into a rigid, depressed state, convinced that communists, Jews, and persons in the White House had formed a conspiracy to get him. He made repeated efforts at suicide (Rogow, 5, 28).

48. Forrestal had ambivalent feelings toward Jews. He was critical of Jewish DPs and the Morgenthau group, "who are only interested in vengeance. . . . No one wanted the Jews," so the U.S. "might get stuck with them" (Walter Millis, *The Forrestal Diaries* [New York, 1951], 58, 134).

49. This policy-making institution had no legal basis until 1947, except that implied by an exchange of letters between Marshall and Adm. Ernest King. Harold Arnold represented the Air Corps; Adm. William Leahy presided and provided liaison with FDR.

50. The JCS were almost never overruled by FDR. "Ironic as it was, Roosevelt allowed one set of advisers to preempt the field with respect to his most important decisions. . . . this was caused directly by an American insistence that their professional military servants assume power and responsibility beyond their competence" (Huntington, 319); see also John Ries, *The Management of Defense* (Baltimore, 1964), 17.

51. The services agreed in a Joint Board estimate of mid-1941 on the goal of establishing a balance of power in Europe and Asia rather than of defeating Germany and Japan (Huntington, 331).

52. By August 1943 the JCS were accepting FDR's attitude toward Russia and making every effort to obtain her friendship (ibid., 332). When a study in the G-2 Division warned of the dangers of Russian dominance, the authors' superior told them sharply: "The Russians have no political objectives in the Balkans; they are there for military reasons only."

53. Harry Coles and Albert Weinberg, *Civil Affairs, Soldiers Become Governors*, Office of the Chief of Military History, Dept. of the Army (Washington, 1964), 63 (hereafter OCMH). The army was traditionally reluctant to enter civil affairs, "although it had eventually been assigned that responsibility in every war" (Edwin Hayward, "Coordination of Military and Civilian Civil Affairs Planning," *Annals of the American Academy,* Jan. 1950, 19, 22).

54. Earl Ziemke, *The U.S. Army in the Organization of Germany* (Washington, 1975), 14.

55. Hajo Holborn, *Germany and Europe* (New York, 1970), 266.

56. Franklin Davis, *Come as Conqueror* (New York, 1967), 73; Harold Zink, *American Military Government in Germany* (New York, 1947), 7, 12. Major Zink served with the Political Division of OMGUS.

57. Ziemke, 65.

58. CAD had difficulty finding someone to do its studies; by the end of 1944 it was only at the discussion stage with two Harvard professors (ibid., 17–18; Paul Hammond, "Directives for the Occupation of Germany," in Harold Stein, *American Civil-Military Decisions* [Birmingham, Ala., 1963] 321).

59. "They frequently lacked details, contented themselves with glittering generalities, did not make use of the most up-to-date sources available, and at times even included more errors than could have been reasonably expected" (Zink, *American,* 18, 21–24).

60. A small, semibald man with a big voice, Hilldring had joined the army in 1917. He reportedly worked fifteen hours a day, seven days a week (*Baltimore Sun,* 6 Mar. 1946; Holborn, 266–67). A German report said he had served as commander of a Rhineland city.

61. CAD's job turned out to be largely civilian supply (Interview Ernest Gross, Patterson Project, 339).

62. Hammond, 320; Coles, 23–24, 146–48.

63. Interview Ernest Gross, by author, 28 Nov. 1969.

64. Hilldring to Smith, 18 Jan. 1945, CAD File, National Archives (hereafter NA). "I am hanging on to my job by my finger tips" (Hilldring to Clay, 18 June 1945). When Hilldring moved to the State Dept. in mid-March 1946, a Clay assistant, Oliver Echols, took his place.

65. Marcus, son of a Rumanian immigrant grocer, had climbed from New York's east side to become the friend of both Governor Dewey and Mayor LaGuardia (Snell, 26).

66. "If the CAD had made studies of future policy toward Germany . . . this fact did not become evident" (Philip Mosely, "The Occupation of Germany," *Foreign Affairs,* July 1950, 584–85). Mosely was an adviser to EAC.

67. Winant urgently asked why he had received no replies to his requests for instructions; "CAD representatives even vetoed the draft message informing him that he should not expect an early reply." Mosely blamed CAD for killing his idea of a corridor linking Berlin to the western zones, because this would be decided "at the proper time and at the military level" (ibid., 586–87).

68. Hilldring to Greenfield, MCMH, Civil Affairs, File 70, Drawer 3, quoted in Philip Mettger, "Contract Research on OMGUS," Washington, 1954, Pollock Papers, Michigan State Historical Society, Ann Arbor, Mich. Gen. Morris Edwards has Hilldring's suggestions for planning ("A Case Study of Military Government in Germany during and after World War II" [Ph.D. diss., Georgetown University, 1957], 47–50).

69. In 1951 the secretary of the army's special study of CAD concluded that CAD's closeness to the secretary of war and chief of staff had made it effective in keeping the secretaries informed "with a notable absence of Secretarian intervention. There was a much less effective flow of information to the theaters." Commanders swamped CAD with undigested information; CAD swamped them with innumerable reports to write (Daniel Cox, Jr., "Findings, Conclusions, Recommendations and Analysis, concerning U.S. Civil Affairs/MG Organization," Feb. 1951, Pollock Papers).

70. John M. Blum, *From the Morgenthau Diaries* (Boston, 1967), 464.

71. Acheson, 100, 302.

72. Kennan thought he had been naive to assume that a sound analysis would have an "effect on the fast, turgid, self-centered, and highly emotional process by which the views and reactions of official Washington were finally evolved" (426).

73. Burns, 375; McNeill, 34. William Bullitt urged FDR to get definite commitments before

providing the second front (Bullitt to FDR, 12 May 1943, Roosevelt MSS). Gardner thought FDR used "Second Front Diplomacy" to influence Stalin. Second front and guarantees against Germany were his "powers." A guarantee was not necessary nor accepted when offered; the attempted use of economic power also failed (35); see also Kolko, *Roots*, 29, 39.

74. Even Eisenhower asked for a change. German generals agreed that the policy extended the war (Anne Armstrong, *Unconditional Surrender* [New Brunswick, 1961], 89, 141, 158–59; Penrose, 329; Coles and Weinberg, 217). Burns noted one more fateful result: failure to help European Jews. "The only way to persuade Hitler to relinquish his grip on his victims was by bribing him or by negotiating with him; FDR flatly opposed this as violating the policy" (397, 409); see also McNeill, 271.

75. Kennan deplored the Washington attitude that resistance leaders, aristocrats, and generals were as bad as the Nazis; he regarded Helmut von Moltke as "the greatest person, morally, that I met on either side of the battle lines in the Second World War" (126–28, 113–14, 117). Stalin and FDR joked about killing 50,000 officers (Herbert Feis, *Churchill, Roosevelt, Stalin* [Princeton, 1960], 273; *FRUS: Teheran*, 553).

76. Stalin seems to have planted the idea of dismemberment in 1941 (Ernst Deuerlein, *Die Einheit Deutschlands, 1941–49* [Frankfurt, 1957], 38, 44). In March 1943 FDR and Eden agreed on dismemberment (Hammond, in Stein, 314–15; see *FRUS: Teheran*, 183; McNeill, 324; Elmar Krautkrämer, *Deutsche Geschichte nach dem II Weltkrieg 1945–49* [Hildesheim, 1962], 10).

77. Army officials on the WSC in January 1944 said they expected the Red Army to occupy all of Germany east of the Rhine, yet at the same time the Russians were excluded from Italy (U.S. Dept. of State, *Postwar Foreign Policy Preparations*, 211–25; Bernstein, *Truman*, 19). "No other arrangement, of course, conformed to the real distribution of military power" (McNeill, 310).

78. Ziemke, 58. When Smith, his chief of staff, asked in February 1944 for guidelines, there was no agency that could give him directives, nor would there by any throughout SHAEF's existence.

79. Bruce Kuklick, "The Genesis of the European Advisory Commission," *Journal of Contemporary History*, Oct. 1969, 189–200. Its limited accomplishments Kuklick traced to its unwanted conception in a British War Cabinet blunder of July 1943; see *FRUS: Teheran*, 417–18; *FRUS: Yalta*, 155. The WSC was created December 1943 from the War, Navy, and State departments to prepare instructions for the EAC. Any of the three could veto (Gaddis, 107; William Strang, *Home and Abroad* [London, 1956], 207).

80. Winant's professionals included Kennan, Philip Mosely, and Ernest Penrose, all of whom have written bitter criticisms.

81. Blum, 329–31. This softening of policy reflected Welles's resignation.

82. Kennan, 174–75, 184. In February 1945 Winant was still trying to persuade FDR to a reasonable policy; "the difficulty he found was not so much that of overcoming an antagonistic attitude as that of inducing the President to bring his mind wholly to bear on the question" (Penrose, 204–5, 233). Ziemke notes that EAC planning showed that a fully unconditional surrender was never really contemplated. Only five fully cleared policy papers were sent, January to October 1944 (112–14, 130).

83. Franklin traced the three zones to Eden's suggestion 25 May 1943. A British commission by the end of the summer added the joint occupation of Berlin. FDR knew of it by October, but State discovered it only when EAC began to meet ("Zonal Boundaries and Access to Berlin," *World Politics*, Oct. 1963; Snell, 56; Gaddis, 111).

84. Kennan, 178–80; see *FRUS: 1944*, I, 196, for a copy of the map.

85. Kennan, 332–37; Penrose, 236.

86. Penrose, 233; Gaddis, 107–8; Mosely, 595.

87. Hammond, in Stein, 345; Ziemke also blames Russian intransigence on the prisoner of war issue (114).

88. Those who worked with White found much to criticize but little to show he was carrying out communist policy (Acheson, 82; Hammond, in Stein, 319; Janeway, 200). Morgenthau pushed toward more extreme formulation and White held back. The plan probably ran counter to the Russian need for reparations from production. Kolko described both men as anti-Russian; both were trying to integrate the USSR into the capitalist world by the use of a loan (*Roots*, 324, 338).

89. The Executive Committee on Economic Foreign Policy, created in April by State to outflank the JCS, had approved two papers 4 August for constructive policies. White was on the committee. Col. Bernard Bernstein showed Morgenthau SHAEF's handbook for MG (Gaddis, 115–17).

90. Eisenhower hedged; he had been too busy to be "specifically concerned with the future economy of Germany," but he had "an able staff section working on the problem. . . . He was very positive that he was going to treat them rough. 'I want to say that I am not interested in the German economy, and personally would not like to bolster it, if that will make it easier for the Germans' " (Blum, 335).

91. When asked what he was going to do, Hull said: "I don't have any chance to do anything. I am not told what is going on" (ibid., 338).

92. Morgenthau's solution to hereditary evil: "Completely remove these children from their parents and make them wards of the state, and have ex-US army officers, English army officers and Russian army officers run these schools and have these children learn the true spirit of democracy" (ibid., 342).

93. Morison, 607. FDR sent a stinging memo to Stimson and Hull: "This so-called Handbook is pretty bad . . . all copies should be withdrawn," if it had not already been distributed as approved policy. The OSS predicted: "Germany would resist occupation with a clandestine army and that Russia would oppose dismemberment and would not push socialization or dictatorship for fear of offending the west" (Hammond, 355). Hilldring wrote Eisenhower he and McCloy agreed with FDR (Donovan to McCloy, Assistant Secretary of War [hereafter ASW], 370.8 Ger, quoted in Mettger, chapter five).

94. Morgenthau told White: "The only thing you can sell me, or I will have any part of, is the complete shutdown of the Ruhr. . . . Just strip it. I don't care what happens to the population. . . . I would take every mine, every mill and factory and wreck it" (Blum, 351). White tried to get some coal production to aid Britain, but Morgenthau refused.

95. FDR reminisced about his Duchess County and how it was in 1810. "There is no reason why Germany couldn't go back to 1810, where they would be perfectly comfortable but wouldn't have any luxury. . . . He expounded on that at great length." Yet he annoyed Morgenthau by assuming he would not touch the steel mills right away; they might help Britain (ibid., 363).

96. Europe did not need an industrialized Germany. FDR exclaimed: "All the economists disagree, but I agree with that" (Snell, 85).

97. Morgenthau wrote in his diary: "I have never seen [Churchill] more irascible and vitriolic than he was that night. . . . He looked on the Treasury Plan, he said, as he would on chaining himself to a dead German" (Blum, 369).

98. Bankrupt Britain desperately needed the loan which Morgenthau could give them (Snell, 87). "With few exceptions neither British ministers nor American Secretaries of departments had made the study and gained the experience necessary to form a competent judgement . . . on the economic future of Germany" (Penrose, 258). Even Eden seemed shocked: "You can't do this." Churchill said that Britain would get export trade, to which Eden replied: "How do you know it is or where it is?" Churchill answered him quite testily: "Well, we will get it wherever it is" (Blum, 371).

99. Morison, 608; Mettger, chapter four; *FRUS: Yalta,* 155.
100. Morgenthau tried to see FDR 29 September, but FDR had seen the newspaper clippings (Blum, 379). FDR had to see the anger of Stimson on 3 October, whom he told lightly: "Henry pulled a boner." FDR was "frankly staggered," and had "no idea how he could have initialled this" (Morison, 609). "He had yielded to the importunities of an old and loyal friend" (Sherwood, 819). John Backer doubts Morgenthau's impact (*Priming the German Economy* [Durham, N.C., 1971], 17).
101. The CCS under British influence much preferred its more moderate statement of the spring, titled CCS 551 (Hammond, in Stein, 376). See *FRUS: Yalta,* 143–54 for the text of JCS 1067.
102. "Though [McCloy] objected to the industrial provisions in the Plan, though he had also some reservations about its political content, he was as resolved as was Morgenthau to crush Nazism" (Blum, 384). McCloy wanted any kind of directive quickly (Gaddis, 123).
103. Hammond, in Stein, 371, 391. Treasury was strengthened by the army's need for finance officers (Snell, 91–92). Ziemke noted that CAD had written an almost identical statement of economic policy two weeks before JCS 1067 was drafted (105).
104. When the British asked that CCS 551 be used, McCloy rejected their strenuous objections to JCS 1067's "excessive" arrests, the closing of schools and newspapers, and the leaving of Germany and Europe in chaos. McCloy thought the arrests were not excessive; German concentration camps could hold up to two million (McCloy to Chanler, 12 Oct. 1944, ASW 370.8 Ger; McCloy to Macready, CAD 014; 27 Oct. 1944 and 8 Nov. 1944, ASW 370.8 Ger, in Mettger, chapter five).
105. FDR wanted civilian control, fearing the army would be soft for administrative convenience (Hammond, in Stein, 398–99).
106. *FRUS: Yalta,* 174; Snell, 105; Hammond, 399; Michael Balfour, *Survey of International Affairs, 1939-46, Germany* (London, 1964), 24.
107. Hammond, in Stein, 401. State objected, but McCloy and Hilldring found nothing against it. See *FRUS: 1945,* III, 378–88, for the document.
108. Presumably these sentiments were conveyed to FDR by Stettinius and by Charles Bohlen (Snell, 117–19). State's briefing book cautioned against partition and a disruption of the German economy (12 Jan. 1945, *FRUS: Yalta,* 178–97).
109. The advantages were in getting strategic raw materials and gold, increasing tourism, and stimulating sixty million jobs (Harry D. White Papers, Princeton Library, 23; *FRUS: Yalta,* 310–15; Harriman to Stettinius, 4 Jan. 1945, 6 Jan. 1945, *FRUS: Yalta.*
110. Morgenthau told FDR that the fear of Bolshevism was irrational; "if they wanted to get the Russians to do something they should . . . do it nice" (quoted in Bernstein, *Truman,* 30–31). See *FRUS: 1945,* III, for the Morgenthau memo, 1 Jan. 1945 (376) and the 17 Jan. meeting (389–92). Williams, a revisionist, emphasized the loan's defeat by Harriman, who proposed to use the Russian economic problem to get cooperation (98, 221). Yet other revisionists see in the proposed loan an American effort to dominate Russia by committing her to heavy trade with the U.S. In 1945 writers feared that reparations out of production would lead to a Russian dependence on Germany. Eden thought Russia opposed destruction of German industry because this would increase German dependence on the U.S. (Bruce Kuklick, "American Foreign Economic Policy and Germany" [Ph.D. diss., University of Pennsylvania, 1968], 284–99, 115, 121).
111. Feis, *Churchill,* 538; *FRUS: Yalta,* 611, 624–25. When Stalin pressed, Roosevelt said he still favored the division into five or seven parts, but the three secretaries should be asked to bring in a plan within twenty-four hours. "You mean a plan for the study of the question," Churchill suggested. "Yes, replied Roosevelt, "for the study of dismemberment" (see Snell, 142). The EAC, despite or because of its poor record, was given the job. Russian policy wavered on 26 March, and on 10 April, Winant was told by FDR to postpone any decision. By

21 April, Stalin in a speech said Russia would not dismember Germany (Deuerlein, 77–80).

112. Stalin had less objection to a French zone out of someone else's territory, but predicted accurately that giving them a veto would cause real problems (Feis, *Churchill*, 532).

113. Snell, 156; Diaries, William D. Leahy Papers, Library of Congress, 8 Feb. 1945.

114. The Russians estimated their damage at 128 billion dollars (McNeill, 533). The Mathews's minutes record this as "the only time during the conference that Stalin showed some emotion" (see Snell, 152; *FRUS: Yalta*, 176, 620–23, 982–83; Feis, *Churchill*, 535–37).

115. Germany would need billions to survive. This left the loan to Russia as the easier alternative, one which might have continued the alliance. Yet it took over two years before the U.S. was psychologically ready to send Marshall Plan aid to friends (Snell, 156, 166, 172; Leahy Papers, 11 Feb. 1945; see also Kennan, 224–25).

116. Snow, 343; Byrnes, *Frankly*, 52; Louis Halle, *Cold War as History* (New York, 1967), 39. Revisionists argue that the Russians gave sufficient evidence of sincerity and that free governments would probably be anti-Soviet and Russian fears made that intolerable. The fear was irrational because no neighbor, not even Germans, could threaten Russia after 1944.

117. McNeill, 570. The charge of American-German cooperation was not true, but some revisionists are suspicious (Gardner, in Bernstein, 118–19).

118. When Djilas mentioned to Stalin that Soviet soldiers regularly killed all German civilian refugees, Stalin's answer had been: "Let them have some initiative!" (Djilas, 111; Allen Dulles, *The Secret Surrender* [New York, 1969], 147, 161–65; Seweryn Bialer, *Stalin and His Generals* [New York, 1969], 516–17).

119. Stettinius to Roosevelt, *FRUS: 1945*, III, 434–38; see also minutes of conferences 13–14 Mar. 1945, 438–43, 450–57. When Stimson saw FDR, he "spoke of the old Germany with such affection that . . . it reassured me to think at bottom, he did not differ from McCloy and myself in respect to the basic reorganization to be aimed at in Germany" (Hammond, in Stein, 415–18). See State Memo, 16 Mar. 1945, *FRUS: 1945*, III, 457–58, which provided for the integrated treatment of Germany by a control council which could override zonal commanders, and "a minimum standard of living for the German people" (Walter Dorn, "The Debate Over American Occupation Policy in Germany 1944–45," *Political Science Quarterly*, Dec. 1957, 500).

120. Blum, 407; see Morgenthau's objections to State and FDR (*FRUS: 1945*, III, 460–65). Stettinius told Stimson he had not read it nor could he remember it (Hammond, in Stein, 418). Morgenthau regarded McCloy as an ally. Clay tried merely to refine the 10 March directive, but McCloy wanted it replaced (Blum, 409).

121. The army feared any further delay caused by Treasury; plans based on zonal autonomy had long since been made (Dorn, 498).

122. Hammond, in Stein, 421; see *FRUS: 1945*, III, 469–73 for State's reaction.

123. For the debate see *FRUS: 1945*, III, 484–503.

124. Stimson and Truman agreed that revenge had ruined peace treaties; their pious reservations had little effect (Herbert Feis, *Between War and Peace* [Princeton, 1960], 56n, 57).

125. Hammond, in Stein, 428; the text is in Beate von Oppen, *Documents of Germany under Occupation, 1945–54* (London, 1955). McCloy told Backer getting loopholes in 1067 was the best he could do against Morgenthau (Backer, 59). Zink thought this hodgepodge inevitable; the very complexity of American society made even clear-cut domestic policies extremely difficult; "we probably have less political consciousness than the people of any other great nation" (Zink, *American*, 120, 207).

126. Some revisionists blame Truman for immediately ending conciliation, using the atomic bomb as a diplomatic weapon and practically declaring the Cold War in his 23 April interview with Molotov, but that interview came two days before Stimson fully explained the bomb to him. (William Leahy, *I Was There* [London, 1950], 315–16; Leahy Papers, 23 Apr. 1945).

Revisionists have argued that when this toughness failed, Harriman and Grew convinced Truman to use the immediate cutback of Lend-Lease. The decision may have been forced by administration promises necessary to get the Lend-Lease Act renewed in April 1945 (Truman, I, 227; Alperovitz, 36, Bernstein, *Truman,* 27; Feis, *War,* 27: McNeill, 513). Gaddis concluded the immediate change was more in personalities than policies (196–98).

127. If he were committed to a Cold War, he would surely not have exchanged this for an indefensible piece of Berlin (Phillips, 71; Feis, *Churchill,* 603).

128. Churchill to Truman, 11 May 1945, *FRUS: Potsdam,* I, 7–9. See also cables of 18 Apr., 24 Apr. 1945, *FRUS: 1945,* III, 231, 240. A telegram 12 May 1945 spoke of an iron curtain: "Meanwhile the attention of our peoples will be occupied in inflicting severities upon Germany, which is ruined and prostrate, and it would be open to the Russians in a very short time to advance, if they chose, to the waters of the North Sea and of the Atlantic."

129. Bohlen memos on Hopkins's meeting with Stalin, 26–27 May 1945, in *FRUS: Potsdam,* I, 24–31. He stopped in Frankfurt bubbling with enthusiasm. "The most important result of the Hopkins mission to Moscow was that he and all the Americans with him thought it was a spectacular success. With obvious sincerity Hopkins said to us in Frankfurt, "We can do business with Stalin. He will cooperate!" (Murphy, 260; Hopkins to Truman, 8 June 1945, *FRUS: 1945,* III).

130. Clay to AGWAR, 6 June 1945, Clay Cables, NA; Eisenhower to JCS, 6 June 1945 in *FRUS: 1945,* III, 328–29. Clay saw virtue in Zhukov's point that he could not talk about administrative problems until he had his zone to administer. If the control council became simply a negotiating agency, "we must either establish tripartite control of West Germany or else be prepared to govern our Zone on practically an independent basis." Murphy agreed (*FRUS: 1945,* III, 331). He later wrote: "As we came to realize in time, the Russians obtained everything they wanted at the first Eisenhower-Zhukov meeting" (Murphy, 273); Truman, I, 298.

131. The French refused to evacuate Stuttgart, "so on May 4 I ordered an end to supplies to French troops." Churchill cabled the hope that the order would topple de Gaulle (Truman, I, 238, 242).

$\mathcal{2}$ Berlin Policy Formation

The implementer of Washington's central German postwar policy was the military governor in Germany. For the significant period 1945–49, he was General Lucius D. Clay, who followed a short prologue from May to November 1945 involving General Dwight D. Eisenhower and preceded a long epilogue of retreat involving John J. McCloy, 1949–52. In order to understand the paradoxical nature of U.S. occupation policy, it is necessary to follow Clay's winding path during the years of his governorship. Clay's character and circumstances influenced policy implementation, but his policy was also altered by what he learned from the Germans, and he finally came to fight against the policy ideas of Washington and of the wartime Allies, usually on behalf of the Germans. In his efforts the occupation organization frequently was of little assistance.

The dominant thread in the complex web of the story is that German needs became a major factor in policy creation and implementation, for as Clay came to perceive these needs he reshaped U.S. policy. This revised policy, transmitted to the Germans through Clay, was implemented only when the Germans could and would. Without the assistance of his alien subjects, assistance which was given if his policy accorded with their felt needs, little would have been accomplished. Moreover, in the process of creating a policy acceptable to Germans and Americans, Clay was forced to counter the policy, as he perceived it, of the Allies. As policy implementer he was forced to become a diplomat to deal with France and Britain, and eventually he had to act as a commander against Russia in the Cold War.

Eisenhower, McNarney, and Clay

After the Siegfried Line was cracked wide open in March 1945, U.S. troops poured into southern and central Germany as far as the Alps and the Elbe River. Combat was gradually replaced by military government, and the U.S. zone took form when the U.S. troops moved out of the southern section of the British zone and the western section of the Russian zone. (The French stayed in the western fringe of Germany, in South Württemberg-Baden, the Rhineland, and the Saar.) By the end of June 1945, U.S. troops and the bureaucracy of military government were located in three southern states: Hesse, North Württemberg-Baden, and Bavaria.

As Germany was divided into occupation zones, the Supreme Headquarters, Allied Expeditionary Forces (SHAEF) was replaced by U.S. Forces, European Theater (USFET), which moved from Paris to Frankfurt. U.S. Group, Control Council (ACC) was supposed to provide central coordination. (It rarely did.) A welter of army groups and their armies were at first under USFET's command. Two armies, the Third in Bavaria and the Seventh in Württemberg and Hesse, survived the demobilization of 1945. Each received directives from Frankfurt and usually passed them on to divisions, which passed them on to regiments, and so down to companies. Each unit had a fifth staff position (G-5) for civil affairs, in addition to personnel, intelligence, operations, and supply. The newly established military government (MG) had at first to use this army command structure to get its directives to the German states (*Länder*), to the counties (*Kreise*), and to the cities and villages.

The first MG commander was the hero of World War II and symbol of victory, Dwight D. Eisenhower. He showed little interest in his political job as military governor, although he had shown marked political skills during the war. Yet circumstances gave him a key position at war's end, had he cared to use it, for the president and the State Department deferred, even in matters of civilian concern, to the military for decision. Eisenhower admitted not having given the occupation much thought, saying that planning it was not his responsibility. He expected civilian control and had assumed the army would provide a garrison, not a government, except for a few weeks.[1] In fact, Eisenhower's major contribution to policy was a vengeful attitude toward the defeated, and visits to the concentration camps intensified his desire to have Germans punished. He felt that one method was by friendship with the Russians, a belief supported by Moscow's warm welcome in the summer, which made a very favorable impression on him. He rejected friendship with any Germans, even refusing the hand of a surrendering general, saying, "I won't shake hands with a Nazi."[2]

The war was scarcely over when Eisenhower took a month's vacation for victory tours and golf. In this crucial early month his deputy Clay laid MG's foundations. Ike's involvement was crisis involvement, and the few occasions when he came down from the summit of power did not enhance his wise, fatherly image. Usually he delegated decisions, so much so that observers were amazed by his lack of command. He had the authority, but he failed to exercise it. While the political general kept his peers happy by giving them wide freedom, the result was that they could frustrate Clay's efforts at implementation. If the summer of 1945 showed an Eisenhower policy, it was collapsing as he left.[3]

However small the impact of Eisenhower, that of his successor from 26 November 1945, General Joseph McNarney, was even smaller. A competent staff officer given a significant command for services rendered, he devoted his attention to the troops and let Clay run MG practically without interference. Yet severe strains developed between McNarney, the commander responsible for troop behavior, and Clay, his deputy commander, responsible for the occupation and zonal government. Quite reasonably Clay saw his control over both as necessary to proper coordination. He had the real responsibility but limited authority. Clay finally wrote McNarney in June 1946 that he intended to retire from the army. State Department adviser Robert Murphy warned Byrnes, who reassured Clay. McNarney was promoted to Washington.[4] His going left scarcely a ripple. In March 1947, Clay gained control over the occupation army.

Clay's success as a political general was derived in part from a solid political background. His great-granduncle was Henry Clay, "the great compromiser," and his father was a three-term senator from Georgia. Young Lucius served as a page in the Senate. When he attended West Point he graduated first in English and history, but at the bottom in conduct and discipline, as he had already gained a reputation as a military iconoclast. His efficiency reports were for years peppered with below average ratings, especially in tact, judgment, and common sense. Yet he was highly regarded as an engineer, beginning with his teaching of the subject upon his graduation in 1918. Progressing slowly in the Corps of Engineers, from 1933 he made excellent contacts as its spokesman with Congress. He worked closely with Hopkins to create the Works Progress Administration, and with House Speaker Sam Rayburn. In March 1942, a brigadier general at forty-four, he headed military procurement in close contact with Hopkins, Congress, and industry. In the fall of 1944 Eisenhower asked him to replace SHAEF's supply chief, and sent him first to Cherbourg to solve a harbor snarl. With that quickly accomplished, Eisenhower sent him back to Washington to plead for more ammunition. James Byrnes insisted that Clay stay to serve as his deputy director of war mobilization and reconversion—in other words, as assistant to the assistant president. With Roosevelt and Byrnes both at Yalta, "Clay was left in charge."[5]

It was James Byrnes who talked Roosevelt into appointing Clay as Eisenhower's deputy for MG, describing him as "the most competent man I had found in the executive departments . . . .Give him six months and he could run General Motors or U.S. Steel."[6] Called to FDR's office, Clay had no chance to talk. Rather than discussing policy, Roosevelt spoke of Clay's earlier experience as an engineer and of the possibility of a great waterpower development in central Europe. Clay was rushed off to Europe, expecting to stay but a few months. He said later:

> As I look back I find it amazing that I did not visit the State Department or talk with any of its officials. Nor was it suggested that I do so. No one at that time advised me of the role of the State Department in occupation matters or of its relationship to military government, and I am inclined to believe that no one had thought it out. . . . When I left Washington I knew nothing of JCS 1067. . . . Nor did I know anything of the policies and agreements which had been established in international conferences.

Murphy was first dismayed that Clay "knew virtually nothing about Germany," but discovered he had high technical skills, and more important, the political skills to deal with Washington. He could learn about Germany, "but the ability to interpret ambiguous regulations, to avoid roadblocks, to persuade obstinate officials—these universally useful political talents were bred in Clay's bones and nurtured in childhood."[7]

A slender man of medium height, with a long nose and enormous dark brown eyes, Clay combined a southern charm with a northern efficiency. "His smile was entrancing and his frown a cause for quaking."[8] Observers agreed on his intelligence, his hard work, and his ability to make judgments quickly without asking for instructions or advice. "Though he had had almost no experience coping with most of the political problems confronting the U.S. in Germany, Clay was rarely at a loss, and rather than delay action until he could consult with his experts, he often made an immediate decision."[9] B. U. Ratchford, reparations adviser, wrote in 1948 that Clay rarely dodged an issue in discussion and nearly always had an opinion. He preferred to do his own staff work and after mastering the evidence, "he reaches his decisions quickly, irreversibly and alone. Once his mind is made up and he makes it up by himself, with a mystical belief in its rightness as America Thinking—there is hardly any changing it."[10]

Yet some indecisiveness was evident in his personnel problems. He had not had experience working with large staffs and failed to get anything like full work from his thousands of officers. He was unwilling to fire anyone because an army commander was judged, back in the Pentagon, by the absence of trouble in his command. He also tried to do too much himself, not trusting many of the people about him. In return, most of his staff were frightened of him. "Few on his staff dared take any serious administrative action without his specific approval, even if his approval of the policy behind the action was well known."[11] Clay, with a background in dealing with civilians, lacked the army pomposity. Yet along with his strong personality and charm, he was a reticent man; "Clay made it difficult for even his top advisers to know at times what he really thought about a situation."

All in all, Clay's attitudes and abilities were a curious mixture of seemingly contradictory qualities. Some considered him Jeffersonian, as for example in his behavior with the press. He simply walked into a press conference, smiled an all-inclusive smile, and announced: "Gentlemen, I have nothing particular to tell you. I am at your disposal." This was part of what he called the "fish bowl," with everything there for anyone to see. On the other hand, if any subordinate wished to criticize Clay's policy, he should leave.[12] His attitudes toward business were not those of an ally; rather he then regarded business as somehow grubby. He had been regarded by some businessmen with whom he quarreled about priorities in Washington as a tough enemy. One might also regard as Jeffersonian his belief that central authority had little value if it did not rest on a firm foundation of local approval.[13] Politically his instinct, which proved correct, was to give the Germans a chance to prove themselves. He may have had tyrannical impulses, but he also had a belief in the rule of law. His belief in the need to command was countered by his belief in freedom.

Clay came as a conqueror, but when he left four years later, he had become the new hero, the savior of Berlin. During later crises he was sent back as the symbol of high regard for Germany, though through it all he remained aloof. Although to some Germans Clay behaved as *der Sieger* until 1948, German leaders who worked with him can be complimentary. Reinhold Maier remembered their first meeting, when Clay's "words fell like the blows of a hammer." Maier came to believe Clay was like the best German general staff type: cultivated, straight, taciturn, polished, clear, an intellectual type with brown, melancholy eyes. Yet Friedrich Glum thought him less "human" than Hoover. "Clay always looked so ominous when he talked to the minister-presidents and always had something to criticize." Hubertus von Loewenstein, a German historian, thought the secret of Clay's success in Germany was that he pushed his bureaucrats aside and let the natives get the job done.[14]

His attitude when he arrived was clear. He told his staff their job was to keep the allies together, in order "to punish Germany and hold it down the way it should be." He said to the press: "Our first objective is to smash whatever remaining power Germany may have with which to develop a future of power. . . . When that has been accomplished, we will begin to worry about long-range policies and long-range treatment of Germany."[15] Yet he soon wrote McCloy:

> The Germans are an industrious people. They are already at work from early in the morning until late at night trying with almost no transportation and

very limited facilities, to till the soil and clean up the debris in the cities. I do not say this out of sympathy with the Germans, but really because . . . we should face a difficult short-range problem in finding sufficient food for even a limited subsistence considerably below that of the liberated countries. I feel that the Germans should suffer from hunger and cold as I believe such suffering is necessary to make them realize the consequences of a war which they caused. Nevertheless, this type of suffering should not extend to the point where it results in mass starvation and sickness.[16]

Berlin was the place where reality would modify his belief that Germans should suffer; there he was forced to deal directly with both Germans and Russians. As was the case with most Americans, his sympathy toward Russians turned to suspicion; hatred toward Germans turned to something approximating respect or pity. "They seemed weak, cowed, and furtive and not yet recovered from the shock of the Battle of Berlin. It was like a city of the dead. I had seen nothing quite comparable in western Germany, and I must confess that my exultation in victory was diminished as I witnessed this degradation of man. I decided then and there never to forget that we were responsible for the government of human beings." Yet Clay spoke no German and showed little evidence in his early reports of "making any distinction among Germans save as they accepted or rejected what MG wanted them to do." Clay said he visited many communities and saw much suffering, but deliberately avoided contacts for fear that Germans he approached would be considered collaborators. He remained aloof "for their own good." He had to be tough with the Germans to make America unhappy with that tough policy, but he used every trip to Washington to get them more food.[17]

Clay, Washington Policy, and the Modification of JCS 1067

In theory at least, Washington had established a central policy directive in JCS 1067, but the common belief is that in practice Clay acted very much on his own. There are strong supporting arguments for that belief. Tradition gave commanders wide latitude, on the assumption that they best understood the tactical situation. Yet Clay, choosing his course among conflicting policies, increased his autonomy until he became "very nearly an independent sovereign." He had a close relationship with Secretary of War Patterson, and the fact that all orders passed through the War Department "gave Clay an opportunity to follow his own discretion to an extent which could hardly be imagined in the case of a non-military administration."[18] His special relationship with Byrnes added to Clay's power, as did the State Department's inability to assume authority. State needed War approval and

War asked Clay. A State Department official complained: "Every time we go into an international meeting, we first must make a treaty with our general."[19]

Despite such reasons for autonomy, Clay has since insisted that he complied with policy. He could have blamed JCS 1067 for his problems, and many have assumed that he was crippled by that policy document. Its position was that Clay could take no steps toward the economic rehabilitation of Germany or that were designed to maintain or strengthen the German economy. John Gimbel has stressed the error in interpretation which sees Clay implementing a JCS 1067 that he found deficient, arguing that even before Potsdam Clay found JCS 1067 flexible enough on the critical economic provisions. The Potsdam Conference in August would provide even more flexibility by promising economic unity, denying reparations from production, and promising consideration of the physical destruction and loss of territories.[20] Gimbel's argument raises the interesting question: if official policy was not the cause of the problems, what was? The policy Clay formulated himself? The failure of his subordinates to carry out his policy? The very insolubility of the original problem, namely the devastated and divided condition of postwar Germany?

That JCS 1067 was resisted by administrators from the beginning is shown by Hilldring's pressure on SHAEF: "I have sensed a lack of willingness among certain of our people in London to accept and follow the clearly laid down policies established in Washington on the highest levels. . . .It is particularly important that your officers should be advocates of 1067 and under no circumstances critical of its policies." Smith said SHAEF approved and complied.[21] Contrary to Smith's assurances, however, Clay wrote in 1950 that the replacement of the earlier manual with 1067 had had a devastating effect on morale.[22] He and economic adviser Lewis Douglas, McCloy's brother-in-law, were shown a draft of JCS 1067 in late April. "We were shocked—not at its punitive provisions but at its failure to grasp the realities of the financial and economic conditions which confronted us." Robert Murphy quotes Douglas as having exclaimed: "This thing was assembled by economic idiots! It makes no sense to forbid the most skilled workers in Europe from producing as much as they can for a continent which is desperately short of everything."[23]

Clay's first effort as military governor was to get 1067 changed: "Washington must revise its thinking relative to destruction of Germany's war potential. . . . the war has accomplished that end. . . . the industry which remains, with few exceptions, even when restored will suffice barely for a very low minimum living standard in Germany. . . .We must have freedom here to bring industries back into production." Hilldring responded that no directive could be written then that would give Clay the extra latitude he desired; long-range policy would have "to bubble up out of the facts you uncover in Germany. . . . Over the long pull I am sure it will redound to your advantage to administer Germany in the post-defeat period along lines laid down by the government. It would, in our opinion, be contrary to the interest of the army and certainly to your own interests, to be personally responsible for formulating the U.S. policy you follow in Germany.'' By 16 June 1945 Clay had taken his advice: "Like all general directives JCS 1067 can be interpreted in many ways.'' This acceptance was reflected in his 9 June order that 1067 was "the Bible,'' and must be implemented as rapidly as possible; all directors should submit plans to him showing its implementation.[24]

In fact it was Truman, the one who had made 1067 official, who chose to violate it. In June he ordered German coal production increased by twenty-five million tons in ten months to help Europe revive. It was a meaningless order because, as Stimson told him, it would have required incentives to the miners in terms of food, clothing, and housing, and incentives to the rest of the economy in terms of consumer goods—not one of which was available.[25]

With President Truman coming to Berlin to decide policy, including German policy, with Churchill and Stalin, Clay hoped for greater flexibility in or assistance with his economic problems. He probably was not yet fully aware of the difficulties that lay ahead with the wartime Allies. Truman, on the other hand, did not yet seem fully aware of the German economic troubles, but he had begun to perceive the looming shadow of Comrade Stalin.

On his way to Potsdam Truman lamented: "Wish I didn't have to go, but I do and it can't be stopped now. . . . I hate it but it has to be done.'' The voyage gave him a chance to master the complex materials accumulated for his information. He studied them, but like "a person who habitually sought simple versions from which he could arrive at quick decisions.'' He spent much time in informal talk with friends and newspapermen, in dinner concerts, movies, and card games.[26] He was under pressure to get further Soviet cooperation against Japan, but his major motive was probably to permit an early withdrawal from Europe, so that American soldiers and money could come home.[27]

Elected chairman of the conference at the first session 17 July 1945, Truman took the offensive, presenting at once his proposals for the agenda, on which Germany was only one item. Stalin presented his list; the first two items concerned reparations. On the second day, Churchill raised the most pertinent question: "What is Germany?" He and Truman would be satisfied if the answer were the 1937 boundaries. Stalin's answer was "what is left of Germany." Poland's frontiers, that is, should be decided on before the conference defined any area as German. Churchill remarked that the Soviets had already turned over these provinces to Poland "for administration," and expressed his concern about the problem of millions of refugees. Truman emphasized that "the territory in question must remain a part of Germany for reparations and settlement of the whole German problem, as agreed at Yalta, until changed by the peace settlement.'' Already moving to the position of defending Germans, Truman could not approve of Polish occupation of any part of Germany before the peace treaty and without Allied approval.[28]

When Stalin asked for the ten billion dollars "promised" at Yalta, the Allies refused to pay reparations indirectly by keeping Germany going with Allied resources. The German realities noted by the occupation government had had an effect. Reparations had been studied during the spring of 1945, until the issue had become, as Keynes said, "a hopeless muddle.'' A Truman friend, oil man Edwin Pauley, had been suddenly appointed to handle the negotiations.[29] Pauley had no experience with Russia, and like Byrnes, thought that negotiation could be accomplished in three weeks by honest compromise.[30] He learned quickly of Soviet realities.

When on 23 July Molotov showed a willingness to come down from the ten billion figure to eight billion, Byrnes suggested that each take from his own zone, which he argued illogically would give Russia the 50 percent it claimed.[31] Both reactions could be traced to the booty-gathering which was going on full speed in the Russian zone. Pauley had been deeply shocked at seeing in Berlin the mass removals, for the most part of nonwar industry.[32] He figured the maximum reparations available from a Germany of the 1937 boundaries would be five to six billion dollars, so low a figure that to mention it to the Russians would anger them. It was better to speak only in percentages. Byrnes concluded that since so many plants had been stripped, one could not know what reparations were possible. This conclusion became an important American consideration, and as did, increasingly, the conviction that only a surplus above German needs should be available for reparations. McCloy wrote Byrnes, after conferring with Clay, that reparations should only be from the surplus "*not needed for the maintenance of a reasonable measure of a self-supporting economy in Germany.*"[33]

Byrnes's "package deal" offered a tacit recognition of the western frontier of Poland, first to the eastern Neisse, then to the western Neisse, if the Soviets would come to terms on German reparations. The Russians could take what reparations they wanted from their zone and a percentage of reparations from the other zones: 15 percent in exchange for Russian goods, 10 percent as reparations. Reparations were to come out of the surplus which Germany would not need to maintain a standard of living at the central European average.[34] This reduction of the German economy was ostensibly to prevent a new danger, but Truman was no longer worried about German revival. As he told de Gaulle after Potsdam, "the German menace should not be exaggerated, for the U.S. possessed a new weapon, the atomic bomb, which could defeat any aggressor.''[35]

A charitable judgment of Potsdam and the occupation is that it permitted more flexibility than did JCS 1067; using both, Clay could choose most of his policy at his OMGUS level.[36] On the level of world politics, withholding its blessing to Russian domination was all the United States could have done with the power at hand, unless it had used the atomic bomb. That club was not in hand until August, and by early September any effort had been abandoned to use it even as a threat.[37] The United States was therefore left with economic power in the giving or withholding of its money, but this generosity ran counter to the public and congressional mood. Without a cause sufficiently disturbing to justify raising the tax demands on the public, the government, even if it had had a policy, was relatively powerless to use money as its weapon. The powerful cause materialized by 1947; it was anticommunism.

Potsdam seemed to open the way to important modification of 1067 economic policy, as was evidenced in Clay's overly optimistic 1 August report to his USGCC staff. Germany would be governed as a whole; finances, communications, external trade, and transportation would be central responsibilities. In August William Draper's Industry Division interpreted the Potsdam agreement to mean that sufficient capacity must remain in each industry to supply German needs under the agreed standard of living, with additional productive plant to provide sufficient exports to pay for required imports. The Potsdam standard of living figure was to be a minimum rather than a maximum.[38] These hopes were shaken by French protest against the agreement on 7 August and their vetoes in September. France immediately made the work of the ACC impossible and prevented the formation of central agencies, which led the Russians to believe (wrongly) that the United States was using France to sabotage the Potsdam agreement.

But there were also conflicting pressures emerging from Washington. While on the one side Morgenthau and the Kilgore Committee were ready to pounce on any sign of a soft peace, on the other experts clearly saw the harmful consequences for Europe and the United States of a thoroughly crushed German economy. Calvin Hoover in early October calculated that Potsdam would put Germany back to the worst point of the depression, with, in addition, an export deficit of 818 million marks; territory losses and occupation costs made the problem insoluble if the proposed industrial disarmament went through.[39]

In November Byron Price, after an inspection trip commissioned by Truman, reported that the primary problem was to develop exports to enable Germany to pay for necessary imports. The United States had to make some basic decisions: whether to do a competent job or to withdraw, whether to permit starvation or to ship food, and whether to permit France to defeat U.S. policy. He recommended that JCS 1067 be revised and that some competent civilian administrative personnel and advice be sent from Washington. On 20 November Truman requested the secretaries of the State, War, and Navy departments to give careful consideration to the report, "with a view to taking whatever joint action may be indicated." McCloy told Patterson, who wrote Truman, that they all basically agreed with Price and with more help for German economic recovery.[40] Despite this assurance to Truman of "basic agreement," Price's recommendations were largely ignored.

When Clay visited Washington in early November, his primary concern seems to have been not the revision of JCS 1067, the level of industry, or reparations, but French obstructionism. McCloy in late November advised against revision:

> There has been an almost continuous interchange of cables dealing with specific policy questions and these, too, have in effect modified or elaborated the basic Directive. The task of tying together in one streamlined Directive all the relevant policies... to my mind really poses a very complex problem of codification, editing and renegotiation. With recollections of the difficulties we encountered in getting Governmental agreement on JCS 1067, none of us has any illusion about the magnitude of the job getting a new comprehensive Directive. Efforts along this line might well prove to be a field day for those who have ardently criticized existing policies from divergent and extreme points of view.[41]

Therefore when the War Department, for the benefit of Congress, asked Clay what revisions of 1067 he would recommend, he replied that he did not understand the Price criticism, for MG could not have been set up effectively without JCS 1067; as modified by Potsdam, it had proved workable. Clay's efforts at policy clarification brought the liberalizing cable he desired: the United States did not propose to keep the German economy down permanently; it interpreted the Potsdam agreement to mean that the stated standard of living was a minimum, not a maximum; Germany must become self-sufficient, and self-sufficiency would include resources for rebuilding and taking care of millions of refugees.[42] Clay's so-called rejection of a change was elaborated 13 December: JCS 1067 was workable with "minor exceptions." The distance that Clay had moved toward the German view of reality is shown in his December suggestions that reparations should leave enough resources to enable Germans to subsist without external assistance; proceeds from exports should go first to pay for necessary imports. He felt it was preferable not to incorporate the many interpretations of details made in exchanges of cables, because defining would tend to destroy the directive's flexibility.[43]

Significantly, the War Department cabled Clay 3 January that if JCS 1967 did not limit his freedom of action, it was highly advisable not to make any change. Changes would involve extensive conferences at highest governmental levels, with dubious results, and would probably cause unfavorable comment in print about abandoning or tempering the previous firm stand.[44]

Clay had the right to interpret rather than to arouse the sleeping dogs of the Capitol. Since he had the right to interpret policy, he had little reason to disobey. Washington became increasingly irrelevant.

Washington showed no serious concern with Clay's policy until August 1946, when the State Department was forced to get involved because Clay was about to make public his policy summary of 19 July 1946. "Since this statement is certain to receive some publicity, I hesitate to publish it without the full concurrence of the War and State Departments." State should look it over and send any modifications quickly, "as I do feel that the need for the release of a document of this type is urgent."[45] In detail Clay's summary sounded much like what was decided at Potsdam, with the strongest emphasis on a unified economy, but the tone was less negative and revealed more of Clay's positivism.

Clay thus moved into the vacuum created by the absence of formal policy. By threatening to publish policy, he forced Washington to a decision—to stop him from publishing. Clay cabled angrily:

> Since we are and have been operating under my summary of policy, we must indeed be drifting if it does not in fact summarize our policy. It contains nothing, except perhaps our stand in Ruhr and Rhineland, which has not been published before. I did not send it back to obtain a revised policy, but as statement of policy under which we are operating now. We are really in a mess if we are unable without days of delay to give a summarized statement of policy to our own people or if we are operating at variance with U.S. policy. Unless instructed otherwise I propose to issue it to military government personnel in one week as they have been promised such a summary. Otherwise, I can only tell them we don't know what our policy is. End.[46]

With a week's deadline Washington sent its answer, which begins with lavish praise for Clay's "clarity." Several aspects of his summary (the most important) were still "under study."[47] A State Department committee was coming to Berlin to discuss his summary with him, so publication before their visit would be premature. "We do not think for a moment that you have been operating at variance with U.S. policy, but your proposed statement would give publicity to certain elements of that policy which for various reasons have not been finally determined or which are at present under review in Washington."

Clay's answer was typical of him. It was a rejection which appeared to be an acceptance of a Washington order.

> Your cable will of course be followed, but I must say that it leaves MG at sea since it is obvious from its context that we have no firm policy.... I do not understand this procedure. If the War Department desires a recommendation with respect to policy from MG, we shall be very glad to present it in writing. We are not prepared to discuss recommendations with respect to policy piecemeal with a committee sent to Berlin for this purpose. Such discussions

can only lead to misunderstandings and to misinterpretations of our views here. If our recommendations are desired, please let us know so that a comprehensive rather than a summarized statement may be prepared and submitted to Washington. . . .If . . . a recommended policy is not desired from MG, then the visit of the committee would also appear to be unnecessary.[48]

He threw his summary into the wastepaper basket, but it could not have been buried very deeply, because it was reincarnated in the famous Byrnes speech at Stuttgart 6 September.[49] The speech gave an official stamp to Clay's 1946 policies. Clay was left with Byrnes's speech as policy revision until July 1947, when Washington made Clay's 1946 practices public official policy. By then, however, the new policy was already becoming obsolete as Clay's policies were changing further. Edward Litchfield observed: ''Actually it was primarily a consolidation statement of the various policy concurrences which Washington had sent to Berlin during the intervening years in response to theater initiation. It was helpful, but it was too late to have serious effect upon the emerging political scene.'' By the time even Clay's policy was formulated, ''it was too late to accomplish many of the objectives which might otherwise have been possible.''[50] Clay lagged behind events; Washington was far to the rear.

Clay, the Allies, and the Problem of Reparations

Though Clay was occasionally dismayed with his superiors, they did not seriously prevent him from following his own policy. His victor-peers on the ACC did limit him, and perhaps forced him into the Cold War. The ACC had been created as the medium through which the four Allies could settle the questions of German economic and political development. The attempt at cooperation did not work. After over two years of Clay's patient efforts to keep the ACC alive, it died, and he was the defender of Berlin, face-to-face with an increasingly intransigent Russia.

Clay came to his duties determined to punish Germans, and therefore determined to get along with Russians, his top priority when he began.[51] He did nothing to line up the three western powers against the Russians. On some issues he sided with the Russians and British against the French, on others with the Russians and the French against the British. He said in late 1945: ''I have voted with the Russians more often than with any other delegation.'' He was the mediator in the first year—the limited success of the council probably owed more to his skill than to any other single factor.[52]

But Clay was not always trusting. As early as 2 June 1945 he ''emphatically stated that he would advise the Supreme Commander not to sign the agreement [on Berlin] unless the Russians agreed without equivocation to our having unrestricted use of roads, railroads and lines of communication." In late June he wrote McCloy of his uncertainty: "It is difficult to predict the attitude of the Russians. In our two meetings with Zhukov and Vishinski, they have been most cordial." Yet he expected "the operation of zone governments on almost an independent basis for many months, although gradually through long drawn out negotiations, we will be able to establish over-all German administrative machinery for those functions of government which require central control."[53]

French resistance to Potsdam's central administration was already a problem by 11 August; their reason was that a united Germany would be Russian-dominated. Clay cabled Washington that the French were blocking the central organs which were vital to solving the economic problem; "it would then appear essential to suggest to the Soviets and British that they join us in establishing such machinery for the US/UK/USSR zones." He requested authorization to do so.[54] A draft cable conveys Clay's dismay: "Unless there is a definite improvement in our ability to obtain results in the next two or three meetings of the Coordinating Committee and the ACC, it will be manifest to the press and to the public that Quadripartite government in Germany has failed." The French were not the only opponents: "The Soviet delegation, which has hitherto been cooperative with reference to uniform policies and to early establishment of central administrative machinery, also seems to be laboring under instructions to be obstructive."[55] On 13 October Clay proposed to the British general Brian Robertson interzonal collaboration with the Russians under the zone commanders' authority.[56]

In his visit to Washington in early November, Clay stressed that the United States must break French resistance; the Russians believed the United States and Britain supported French obstinacy and would not agree to central agencies unless the United States took a position on the French demands for the Ruhr and Rhineland.[57] Manuel Gottlieb, for three years on Clay's economic staff, agreed with the Russians: "France was receiving too much financial assistance from the U.S. to maintain such strong opposition unless it met with our acquiescence."[58] It is easier to conclude that the United States wanted economic unity because Clay needed it, but lacked the power to compel de Gaulle.

While the State Department was unsuccessfully putting pressure on France through the winter, MG expressed increasing concern about the Soviets, in particular about political gains they were making as spokesmen for German unity. On Clay's request, Hilldring prepared a letter for Patterson to use to shake up Byrnes. "The rallying cry is one of tremendous appeal to all Germans, regardless of class, religion or political affiliations, and it places the communist Party in a most favorable light as compared with other political parties in Germany."[59] In the spring of 1946 the United States, having failed to exert enough political pressure, decided to bribe the French into cooperation by conceding their permanent occupation of the Saar, provided France would agree to the early establishment of central German agencies. The bribe was also fattened with grain and coal.

Clay's desire for a central administration was bound up with the struggle for reparations. The four governing powers were first to decide on the level of production at which the Germans' standard of living would not exceed the central European average.[60] Reparations, so decided the Potsdam Conference, could be taken from any surplus decreed not essential to this level of industry. Agreement on the level was reached by 28 March 1946. In the negotiations the Russians and the French were the most severe on the Germans; the British were the least severe; Clay compromised at a low level, hoping to win an agreement for central agencies. The level of industry agreement pushed through by Clay also showed U.S. acceptance of the principle of reparations to Russia. By 31 March the first transport to Russia left from Bremen. Clay's sensational stopping of reparations on 3 May, seen by some revisionists as beginning the Cold War, could scarcely reflect his personal opposition to reparations or antagonism to Russia, because otherwise he would not have pushed the 28 March plan, which was close to the Russian desires, nor later have pushed for reparations long after his ban was lifted and Congress was trying to stop him. His motivation was rather to force Russian and French acceptance of German economic unity.[61]

Evidence of Clay's motivation was shown at the strange 26 April ACC debate, when France's General Pierre Koenig surprisingly said he could not accept a solution which did not treat Germany as an economic unit because the French zone was so poor. Soviet General Mikhail Dratvin asked whether the French position with regard to central agencies had changed, but Koenig still saw no need for such agencies. Clay asked whether the Soviet nonagreement on exports and imports resulted from the lack of central agencies. Dratvin hedged, saying he was only getting a French clarification. Clay then observed, as he had repeatedly, that reparations, exports-imports, and central machinery were interdependent and all should be referred back to each government. When Dratvin denied the relationship between reparations and exports-imports, Clay announced that because none of the main economic provisions of Potsdam had been executed, the United States would stop dismantling German industry.[62]

John Gimbel's interpretation of Clay's intentions was that this ban on reparations, contrary to Cold War theory, was directed not against Russia but against France. Since the French zone was the poorest and since reparations to Russia from western zones would be limited to 25 percent of deliveries, the threat to the Soviets would have been a weak one.[63] Yet the threat was also a weak one to France, which would get only 22.8 percent of such reparations; France did not need reparations as much and could more easily exploit its zone; France could also be bribed with territory, the Saar, which Russia no longer could. What made the United States so impatient with the French was that they could not test whether the Russians would actually permit unification until the French stopped obstructing it.

Washington-Berlin correspondence refers mostly to Russian obstruction. Acheson reacted to the ban by suggesting lifting it for sixty to ninety days if the Soviets agreed to join in common economic policies. He did not refer to the French refusal, but to the Soviet. He wanted ''above all, to put Soviet protestations of loyalty to Potsdam to the final test in order to gauge their willingness to live up to the substance as well as letter and fix blame for breach of Potsdam on Soviets, in case they fail to meet this test.'' Clay expressed his assumption of Soviet responsibility; they were ''violators'' of the demilitarization agreement by continuing war production in their zone.[64] Gottlieb, involved in the negotiations, assumed the ban was an anti-Soviet measure and unjustified. The West was asking for food and coal, supposedly surplus in the Soviet zone; when the Soviets did not yield, sanctions were applied. ''The Soviets plainly told the West that their zone would not be committed to fusion before they had in their hands a specific and irrevocable list of reparations deliveries.'' Neither side was willing to sign the blank check. Gottlieb regarded the western position as making Russia the scapegoat for the failure of their own policies to revive the German economy. To the Russians it was taking from their poor zone to give to the wealthy nations; they had no food surplus in eastern Germany available to help feed western Germany. ''For Soviet relinquishment of their zone and rights to extract reparations from it, they would receive in return a curtailed dismantling quota. The Soviets were too poor to be generous.''[65] He might have added, ''too proud to be honest.'' More basic was the U.S. refusal to assist the Russians, either directly by making the requested loan or indirectly by providing the raw materials to the Germans to pay reparations as processed goods.

Clay's explanation to Washington for his ban was that he must have economic unity with central agencies, instead of four airtight zones, a common financial policy to stop inflation, and cooperation for transportation and communication.

> In the absence of agreements essential to economic unity, we have discontinued the dismantling of reparation plants except those approved for advance deliveries, as further dismantling would result in disaster if we are unable to obtain economic unity. . . . If economic unity is obtained, there is no reason why the reparations plan should not be implemented. . . . However, if agreement cannot be obtained along these broad lines in the immediate future, we face a deteriorating German economy, which will create political unrest favorable to the development of communism in Germany and a deterrent to its

democratization. The coming winter would be critical; without unity, it would be almost unbearable.[66]

He felt that the United States should at least merge its zone with that of the British.

The summer's Paris Foreign Ministers' Conference heard Molotov appeal to German nationalism by denouncing the Morgenthau Plan and urging a German central government. Byrnes answered 11 July: "The American Government has never sought to impose a peace of vengeance upon Germany. The American Government regards the economic revival of Germany as essential to the economic revival of Europe."[67] He was not yet prepared to follow Clay's 26 May plan, but he took a cautious step. Clay protested an agreement which the State Department had worked out with France as insufficiently protective of German needs; this agreement was never ratified. "It does not provide for central German administrative agencies to operate uniformly throughout Germany through German field organizations set up for the purpose as contemplated at Potsdam." The Soviets rejected it because it involved the loss of the Saar.[68]

The Question of German Government and German Economic Recovery

Official U.S. German policy was stalemated until early 1947, with movement toward central government and economic integration stalled by the Russian and French reluctance to move. The American insistence on breaking the stalemate was accentuated by the further economic decline of Germany, and not coincidentally of all of Europe, and by the weakening, again not coincidentally, of the British political position on the continent. When the British announced their intention to withdraw their military support from the Greek government in its resistance to a left-wing rebellion, the United States was forced into some European policy decisions. American policy, which had remained ill-defined since the Potsdam Conference, moved dramatically forward with the Truman Doctrine of mid-March and the Marshall Plan, proposed 5 June. In between, and relevant to both, was the Moscow Conference on Germany. The Truman Doctrine may well have led to the failure of the Moscow Conference and that failure surely led to the Marshall Plan decision.[69]

The announcement of the Truman Doctrine, just after the Moscow Conference on Germany had begun, supposedly sabotaged its chance for success, and this conference was probably the last serious chance for Allied cooperation and German unity. The conference began with the Molotov proposal for a provisional German government with a central administration for food, industry, transportation, and post, a democratic constitution, and later elections. Marshall and Georges Bidault preferred a weaker central government, rather like a consultative council, but on 3 April the participants agreed on both a central administration and such a council. On 5 April all agreed on the Bevin Plan for the step-by-step building of a provisional government, beginning with the central administration, three years later adding the council, and nine months after that, the provisional government. The conference's rapid progress was surprising, but it remained mostly on principles and not on details, where it came to an unbridgeable contradiction between the USSR and France. Bidault insisted that the central administration be built as a committee from representatives of each of the state governments, with the right of the zonal commander to interfere. Molotov denounced the French plan and accused the United States and Britain of violating the Potsdam agreement. As the United States saw it, Molotov insisted upon an all-powerful central government at Berlin.[70]

The argument sharpened as the discussion turned again to reparations. Marshall opposed continuing the abject German poverty; in reply Molotov quoted from the agreements at Yalta and Potsdam. Marshall noted the large amount of resources taken out of East Germany, and raised the question of the Oder-Neisse. Molotov said the Polish boundary was settled; Marshall wanted a boundary commission to investigate; Bevin agreed, but Bidault, hoping Russia would support French claims to the Rhineland, had no objection to the new Polish boundary. What then became evident was France's shift away from the hope that Russia would support her bid for the Rhineland.[71]

The reparations issue continued to be the most serious hindrance to agreement on the form of German government. The Soviets wanted consumer goods from German production as "the absolute condition" for German economic unity. Having failed to profit enough from looting, they were so desirous of getting goods out of a revived Germany that they were willing to risk a revived and centralized Germany.[72] France and the United States were not. Dulles wrote Washington that Clay "over-estimated" the U.S. ability to prevent Soviet control of any unified government. Again Washington declined to trust Germans as allies against Russians, though Clay, knowing the Germans better, was inclined to do so. While Dulles was concerned for the French, whom he regarded as crucial to saving Europe, Clay was pushing German interests for the same reason. The Marshall group had stopped in Berlin on the way to Moscow 7 March and had been made thoroughly acquainted with Clay's view. Marshall returned from Moscow determined to act instead of talk, although Stalin had told him that compromises concerning

Germany could be found, that one must have patience. Marshall concluded, "the patient is sinking while the doctors deliberate." In America the emphasis was shifting from a fear of German revival to a fear of European collapse.[73]

The absurdity of forbidding Germany to export to pay its bills, thus forcing the United States to pay them, was a powerful argument to taxpayers. Journalists and congressmen, in cooperation with Clay's people, repeatedly said: "Let the Germans be put to work." Yet the German situation had not improved when, in the early months of 1947, "economic recovery throughout western Europe suddenly stalled and went into a tailspin, coinciding with the necessity for facing up to the problems of Germany at the Moscow Conference."[74] The solution was the Marshall Plan, which offered U.S. financing to a Europe cooperating for recovery. There were many fathers to its victory.[75] Gimbel argued that the real push came from Clay who had convinced Marshall and British Foreign Secretary Ernest Bevin that Marshall had to get acceptance of German recovery without raising fears of German power.[76] Truman was moved by Harriman's analysis, which also emphasized Germany: "The German economy has been living on its reserves, both human and material, and it is still on the decline. . . . We shall face one crisis after another unless steps are taken promptly to turn the downward trend upward." On 29 April Marshall called Kennan to his office; he must set up a policy planning staff without delay. Europe was in a mess, and something would have to be done; he had about ten days.[77] The concept of the later Marshall Plan was announced in June. By July the concept of containment was enunciated by Kennan in the "X" article in *Foreign Affairs*.

This positive feature of economic aid, added to the more negative feature of anticommunism with military aid, and completed by the idea of west European integration, formed the American policy which remained in principle for at least a generation to come.[78] Under the umbrella of containment Clay could push more openly for Germany, as he did in late 1947 at the London Conference where the United States and Britain came close to agreement on their ideas of a German government.

> No man in any delegation was as resolute, as informed, as clear in his conception, or as creative in his design as Lucius Clay. It was Clay who pressed for a statement of the American position on governmental problems in Moscow and initiated the conferences with the British in London. It was he who urged immediate action following the failure of the London Conference. . . . it was Clay who pressed for German government, when the British and French would have let it go by default.[79]

The Germans could scarcely have selected anyone more able to win their case with the western victors. Clay consistently helped them regain their autonomy; he was less consistently helpful in respect to reparations policy.

Clay's most urgent struggle was to keep the Germans alive. Their immediate survival required financing food imports; financing was also necessary for raw material imports to permit industrial production and subsequent exports. German exports would have to take over the burden of financing the German economy, a burden the U.S. taxpayer would not and could not bear forever. The international implications of expanded German production involved the level of industry agreements, and these were tied to the agreements for reparations. The issue requiring decision was the extent to which dismantlings of German industry would be permitted. On this issue Clay at first took a pro-Allied view rather inconsistent with his usual pro-German stance. But he needed to obtain Allied agreements on German reunification, and he also had long held the belief that with so much industry idle anyway, reparations were a small price to pay.

Both the American and the Russian views of how reparations could be paid vacillated between dismantling and payment from revived German production. Dismantling was inefficient; it involved knocking the factories down into pieces, putting them on railroad cars, and shipping them off to the recipient to be reassembled, if all went well, into the same factory transplanted. In 1946 the Russians altered their previous emphasis on dismantling. Stories filtered back to the West that many factories shipped to Russia could be seen peacefully rusting into oblivion beside the railroad tracks. Reconstructing the factories was much more difficult than tearing them down. Stories were also heard of German workers forced to accompany their factories and rebuild them in Russia.

Chargé Durbrow, in Moscow, cabled Washington that Russia was willing to postpone dismantling for ten years to get reparations from production. In October Murphy reported Clay's willingness to give the Russians a small amount of reparations from production. Draper was talking with the Russians about it; if they agreed, the ban on reparations would be lifted, with provisions for necessary imports.[80] Gottlieb added:

> Draper and Clay sponsored, at least to a limited degree, the program of a reparations settlement with the Soviets involving some kind of "deal" over upward revision of the dismantling plan. Clay alluded vaguely to his desire at Moscow to "develop the issue," which Dulles took the lead in inducing the American delegation to oppose. The outcome of Clay's initiative was a curious proposal which offered the Soviets the dollar-for-dollar equivalent in current production of a fraction of the plant capacity entitled for dismantling under the March 1946 agreement but retained in Germany.[81]

It is stranger that public policy was adamant against reparations from production, the most reasonable form. Draper's assistant, Don Humphrey, worked out in November a possible program for them. He rightly predicted that if some such program were not implemented, difficulty with Russia would be much greater; reparations from production should be carefully considered.[82] Yet reparations to Russia remained unresolved.

Secretary of State Marshall left the Moscow Conference agreeing with Clay to push German recovery despite French and Russian protests. In July 1947 a crisis developed with France over this higher level of industry. Clay had come to an agreement with the British by 12 July and wished to publish it. He was forbidden to do so because the French objected that the increase in German steel would impinge on French demands for coal. Clay "desires to resume delivery to the Western Allies of reparation plants, but to continue withholding them from Russia."[83] His cable shows him willing to deliver reparations to the West, but he would have to be ordered to operate on any other basis than maintaining the industry necessary for German survival. The *Revised Plan for Level of Industry,* published 29 August 1947, increased the permissible levels to those of 1936.[84]

What followed was a tug-of-war, with Clay pushing for reparations. His opinion in early September was that it would be wise to deliver western nations some items, but none to Russia. In October, 682 plants were listed as eligible for reparations, down from the approximately 1,600 of the 1946 level of industry plan. Since Germany was to be helped by the Marshall Plan to increase industrial output, it baffled congressmen that the State and War Departments should continue to favor dismantling.[85] Congress combined with the Germans, in effect, to revise the list downward. Clarence Adcock, Clay's assistant, threatened the Germans with reprisals if they continued to protest, but the Herter Committee was also protesting. Draper wrote to Clay in December: "Both the House and the Senate Committees on Appropriations have been extremely critical of the plant dismantling programs."[86]

In January the cabinet sent a study commission, whose report was discussed at a White House conference 16 February. Marshall observed that a number of delicate relationships were involved in the reparations question— not merely with Russia, but with England and particularly with France. Truman said he did not want to default on the Potsdam agreement; he vigorously asserted that he had never supported the Morgenthau Plan, but neither did he want to see Germany rebuilt. They decided to approve Marshall's memo, which recommended a reexamination of plants in certain categories. Yet the House Foreign Affairs Committee told the executive branch in August 1948 that all plant removals needed Marshall Plan (Economic Cooperation Administration; ECA) approval.

Congressional policy meant another study, this time by ECA engineers. Clay objected; to study each plant was to find reasons for keeping it. Nonetheless, Paul Hoffman (ECA) sent the Humphrey Committee, which at the end of the year recommended keeping in Germany 167 of the 381 plants referred to it. In October, Britain and France accepted the Hoffman limits on further transfers of industrial plants.[87] Clay, although he supported reparations, wanted more ECA money for Germans. Harriman, Hoffman's representative in Paris, had great problems with Clay, who wished to deal directly with Washington. Clay was fighting France, Britain, and ECA. "Clay wanted a far greater share than anyone—including his ECA fellow Americans—was ready to give him; he opposed the Hoffman thesis that German recovery would be blended in with that of other Western economies and insisted that Germany be given distinctive treatment involving special barter and credit arrangements."[88]

As Clay shifted to demanding more recovery money, so he logically shifted by 1949 to a resistance to continued dismantlings. In describing his negotiations with the British and the French, his cable makes clear that he regarded more productive capacity as essential to the Germans, and that he felt his Allied opponents were merely trying to make greater profits by restricting German competition. For example, in remarking on the debate about the amount of electronic valve production to be retained, he said: "We consider their position to be based on purely competitive commercial grounds." Commenting on whether any synthetic rubber industry should be allowed to the Germans, he said: "Real motive is UK desire to provide additional market for crude rubber."[89] Fighting for each industry, Clay was convinced of the rightness of the German argument, but he was also convinced of the need to make concessions to the Allies to maintain their cooperation in the creation of the German state. That dismantling should reach its peak in 1949, when the conflict with ECA aid was increasingly apparent, angered Congress and the Germans.

Estimates of West German losses through dismantling vary, but they approximate 600 million dollars. Deuerlein put the value of the dismantlings from East Germany to Russia at 5 billion marks, plus a further 600 million marks taken from production.[90] He set the value of the patents taken by Allied experts at 15 to 18 billion marks. Henry Wallich placed the value of German foreign assets seized by the West at 1 billion dollars at 1951 levels. Maul thought the value of property lost to Poland was 48 billion marks, not far from Byrnes's figure of 14 billion dollars.[91] By comparison, U.S. aid to Germany, according to McCloy, was 3.3 billion dollars. Senator Jacob Javits set the figure at 3.5 billion, out of 33 billion dollars of foreign aid. Wallich saw economic aid as costing less than the various financial burdens, such as occupation costs, that the United States had placed on Germany.[92] ECA aid should be perceived in this context.

Although in 1945–46 Clay was worried about both too little and too much German recovery, in 1947–48 he was instrumental in getting western European approval for the Germans to revive economically. Although tolerant until 1949 of reparations to get British-French cooperation, he worked for as much U.S. economic aid for Germany as possible. Clay's policy, which effectively represented a German point of view internationally, was accepted in principle by his government and usually dominated that of the British.[93]

What had been Clay's exclusive domain in his zone, and nearly his domain in Bizonia, the combined British-American zones, became increasingly enmeshed in world policy. He could go no further, even toward West German unity, without some agreement with the British and French. Any unification movement increasingly required agreements at the top government level and a more active Washington support. Its passive support, simply letting him run his zone without interference, no longer sufficed. As much as he preferred to keep negotiations at his military governor level, he became increasingly frustrated with negotiations in process in three or more capitals. Frustration brought on his repeated threats to resign, partly as a tactic to get his own way, but increasingly from his real desire to be rid of a burden which had grown unbearable. Clay mentioned retirement regularly from mid-July 1947. His threats were usually protests against Washington's efforts to compromise in order to get French cooperation. He said: "Two years has convinced me we cannot have common German policy with the French. Still I am held responsible for [the] economic debacle in Germany and I can no longer accept that responsibility. Believe me, I understand full well State Department established policy and when we who are responsible for execution cannot accept it, we must go."[94]

The dismay he expressed at the resignation of Byrnes reflected his difficulty in dealing with the State Department. The appointment of William Draper, his close friend and assistant, as undersecretary of war helped, yet he was not as close to Secretary of War Kenneth Royall and Assistant Secretary Tracy Voorhees. They maintained the general departmental deference toward him, but with an increased command of the established issues, they could better deal with his knowledge and his threats. The War Department, still largely a buffer for Clay's ideas, had to convince the State Department of the desirability of moving toward the integration of West Germany, even at the expense of a permanently divided Germany. George Kennan, as planner for the State Department, was more inclined to consider some means of maintaining German unity and freedom—perhaps by an evacuation of nearly all of Germany by both the Russians and the western powers. The State Department also had the very real problem of convincing the Allies after it became convinced itself by Clay's ideas. The justice of Clay's position, that greater unity was needed quickly, was evident, but it was difficult for State to obtain the necessary agreements, even with the large amounts of ECA money it had available.

Pushing against these bulwarks against change, Clay was often frantic. As he cabled Eisenhower 28 July 1947:

> We were carrying on here under specific policy instructions when we read in the press, without warning or advice, of a complete change in policy. . . . it might be a real mistake to continue in a job when it looks as if you no longer have the confidence and support of the agencies responsible for policy.[95]

He was constantly reassured of Washington's admiration and support, but he complained repeatedly about its lack of policy, doubting that the situation could be saved from both French sabotage and American indecision. "My only feeling is one of complete futility."[96]

A favorite Clay device was to hold Congress over the heads of the bureaucrats: Congress would not like a change from his policy of German recovery or to see the amounts of European Recovery Program (ERP) money coming to revive Germany go to waste. (He carefully noted that this money was a loan, not grants like those given other countries.) For example, to put the Ruhr under international control would reduce the U.S. ability to protect its investment in German recovery. By late 1947 anticommunism also became a firm part of his attitude and arguments. "We do propose to attack communism and the police state . . . and to counteract the very obvious Soviet program of vituperation and vilification against the U.S. and democratic principles throughout Germany. . . . We are engaged in political warfare and we might as well recognize it now."[97] German support would be necessary to resist communist pressure. "The Germans can do a better job of fighting communism in Germany than we can as an occupying power and they do want this opportunity."[98] He also stressed that only a German government, not his occupation, could bring economic recovery. The date he suggested in November 1947 for a provisional German government was almost immediate: 31 January 1948.

Nonetheless, he progressed very slowly toward his goal of a West German government that would be, as it became prosperous, a bulwark against communism, until a spring thaw brought a flood of activity. On March 6 the six-power London Conference agreed to permit a West German state. Possibly as a reaction to that decision, the Communists took over in Prague what had been a multiparty government. This action brought a reaction from the West, in the Brussels five-power conference for a defense community.

On 20 March Sokolovsky left the last meeting of the ACC, fifteen days after Clay had telegraphed his feeling that something, maybe war, was imminent. It was not war but the Berlin blockade which followed the mid-June German currency reform. Clay's policy of staying succeeded sensationally. On 28 June, at a conference on whether to stay in Berlin, Truman acted with vigor: "The President interrupted to say that there was no discussion on that point, we were going to stay, period."[99] Yet the public success masked Clay's private frustration. After being buoyed up by the London agreements, he was dashed again 15 June by "the most disturbing cablegram I have received since I have been in Germany. . . . I thought we had crossed the Rubicon at London but apparently we sat down in the middle of the stream." To appease the French the United States had drifted back to no policy.[100] At the last moment the French nearly prevented the currency reform. Clay told Draper: "Robertson and I have made concession after concession only to meet further demands. We can go no further. We both fear the worst."[101] The Germans were loyally standing by, but their reform proposals had been compromised to get French agreement.

On 30 August Clay described himself as "down and nearly out." His Germany was getting too little ERP help. "German recovery is taking place and not because of ERP. If we are not proceeding satisfactorily, then you must send someone to take my place."[102] He was even angrier in mid-November over the question of whether MG would control the Ruhr.

> For three and a half years, we have insisted that sound administration required a single U.S. head in Germany to carry out U.S. policy. . . . [State message 1841] implies an inability on my part [to] represent broad interests of U.S. If such is the case, I certainly do not belong here. I know of no instance in which MG has acted contrary to orders of its Government. I have seen much of this broad interests theory which resolves itself into our refusal to place into effect certain measures desired by junior officials of State Department which were never approved by higher authority and sent to me as instructions. . . . Why we even consider such proposals is completely incomprehensible to me and I am convinced it will prove so to the Congress appropriating the funds.[103]

In January 1949 his bitterness resulted in a renewed pleading to be permitted to retire, something the blockade made even more politically undesirable. That the ECA was "sharing the authority without shouldering the responsibility" was crippling his administration. The worst problem, however, was French sabotage of bizonal government, which was "fast becoming a farce." All they had to do was to protest to kill bizonal economic legislation. "Frankly, I am beginning to wonder if we are right in supporting all three zones under the circumstances. . . . If we withdrew this support, economic necessity would force British and French policies more nearly approaching our own as they could not maintain an occupation in chaos."[104]

Forces with a less German-oriented solution to the German problem were gaining organization in Washington. The National Security Council (NSC) created a steering committee including George Kennan, Tracy Voorhees, Albert Blum of the Department of Defense (DOD), and Richard Bissell (ECA) to coordinate policy on Germany.[105] Clay lamented to Draper:

> Can you tell me frankly if there is any real importance to my continuance here? I do not have any feeling of government support and I see every day deviations

from policy and concessions made everywhere by people who know nothing of the problem. . . . I have a feeling that no one considers it important for me to stay and that it is a losing battle here on out.

Draper's only consolation was that Acheson's policies on Germany and Clay were still unknown, because Acheson had been too busy with other matters. "The irritating delays lately and failure to get decisions are largely due to changes in State Department and fact that neither Acheson nor Webb have yet become familiar with the problems nor have they set their own course so far as I can see." Clay answered, "I do not want another day and stay only because I do not now or when I go [wish to] create any possible embarrassment to anyone or above all to our policy, whatever it may be."[106]

Clay continued to lament the negotiations with Britain and France which were making the formation of the new German government nearly impossible. "Truly, we are so mixed up now that it is going to seem a travesty on government to give the Germans for trizonal government something less than the Germans in the Bizonal area now have." While French officials were deliberately delaying action, Acheson was playing into their obstructionist hands by giving highest priority to the Atlantic Pact. "Since State does not have operating responsibility for Germany as we have, and for economic recovery of Germany as ECA has, Acheson has not felt the same acute need which we and ECA feel for really satisfactory settlement of these problems on basis consistent with making Germany self-supporting."[107] Along with Clay, the steering committee's Bissell and Blum were insisting on more vigorous State Department negotiation. Clay urged that the United States play its trump card—money.

When Clay met with Foreign Minister Maurice Schuman 21 March 1949, Schuman surprisingly agreed with him that the French-created delay was disastrous. "Meeting was most friendly and cordial. Whether Mister Schuman can carry out his views remains to be seen as hitherto his subordinates in France and Germany have successfully sabotaged his effort." Four days later Clay despaired again, and on 29 March he lamented that for nine months there had been no economic or political advance.

> We have lost Germany politically and therefore it really does not matter except that history will prove why there was World War III. Not a gesture can we make to draw Germany westward so why do we spend money in Germany. Thank God I will be out of it soon, for to think that a government of 45 million people can be run on a 30-day appeal basis makes it sound like a police court.[108]

Yet by 2 April policy had somehow come together to Clay's satisfaction. The NSC steering group had a Clay-like policy statement which to Voorhees's surprise had gotten Acheson's immediate approval. Acheson had then taken it to Truman, who was "not only satisfied but pleased." Even Schuman had confirmed to Kennan his agreement with Clay eliminating various reservations on German powers.[109] With his long-requested retirement promised for mid-May, Clay received word 5 May of yet another disturbing State Department plan, one linked to Kennan. Its key feature was the withdrawal of occupation forces to enclaves, the U.S. forces to Bremen, the British to Hamburg, and the Russians to Stettin. Clay's response was that this was suicidal to U.S. objectives and would break faith completely with the Germans. "We cannot lose Germany now unless we throw it away and this withdrawal would do just that."[110] Acheson agreed with Clay. Clay's policy, West Germany as part of the Cold War defense of Europe, was frozen, not to thaw for twenty years.[111]

Clay, as both implementer and creator of policy, since 1945 had been a determining factor in German history. His willingness to act began as a result of his problems in implementing even the ill-defined U.S. policy. The German realities altered his views gradually and thus indirectly altered those of the three governments. JCS 1067 had not been as severe a crippling force as historians have often assumed because Clay changed it as necessary when he had the power of the Allies and money. What the United States might have done openly to reverse JCS 1067 it could not do because it had limited power over one or another ally or because available money was limited, not because Morgenthau's ideas dominated OMGUS. Clay would have done more if he had been less limited. He was increasingly persuaded of the better logic of the German position. In short, policy, rather than being pressured from above, was pressured from below. Clay became less and less a "master" of Germans for Washington and more and more a "first servant of the state" for Germans against Washington and the Allies. With the organization available to him he had no chance of being a master of even his own zone.

The Personnel, Structure, and Role of OMGUS

OMGUS was never able to govern. At best it could only supervise aspects of German self-government. Clay's top level staff had a variety of skills, but sufficient skill to govern foreigners was rare. Because the whole occupation was an improvisation, Clay had to rely on an improvised staff. Delbert Clark, a reporter who much admired Clay, much deplored what was done in his name, blaming the staff. "Many he did distrust, men he had no part in selecting, and who were far from equal to their assignments. Many others, whom he trusted to the limit, grossly abused that trust. . . ." Part of the fault lay in the nature of the army executive, trained to delegate authority but often unable to choose subordinates; an administrator on retiring would highly recommend an apparently competent replacement, who would then display ineptitude or imperialism. Although Clay's men never ventured to take a major step without his approval, his approval was often given without adequate consideration.[112] Quick to tongue-lash his subordinates, Clay was slow to discipline. Clark doubted that Clay was aware of "the extent to which his most trusted subordinates were discovering ways to make the established policy appear ineffective, and at the same time persuading him in the name of efficiency to approve administrative changes designed to nullify that policy."[113]

Clark's criticism reflects the split in OMGUS between liberals, more or less linked with Morgenthau, and conservatives linked with the State Department, between New Dealer bureaucrats and Republican businessmen, between the liberal hatred of Germany and the conservative hatred of Russia. This tug-of-war was fiercest from mid-1944 to the end of 1945, the major policy implementation period. State Department planning, attacked as "soft peace," had dominated OMGUS's predecessor in England, the German Country Unit. It was beaten down by wartime hatred, well expressed by one "hard peace" disciple: "The best way to kill rats is to burn down the whole house. When we go into Germany, this will be our policy: Germany will be in flames. We will be the fire department and we won't turn on the water!"[114]

The key man in the Morgenthau group at SHAEF was Colonel Bernard Bernstein, the finance director. Clay obliquely attacked him in June 1945, when he requested Washington to send an "outstanding financial expert" (Daniel Bell), who could bring with him a few key specialists in banking, governmental budgeting, and taxation. More direct criticism in September shows Clay's resentment at Bernstein's holding the Treasury Department over his head as a threat.[115] Bernstein had gone to Washington to prevent his loss of power, but Clay effected it before he could return.[116] Liberals survived mostly in the areas of finance, decartelization, information control, and denazification.

Nonideological, pragmatic lawyers like Donald McLean and Robert Bowie, who had worked in the War Department's Legal Division, were closer to Clay. They had become his assistants and followed him to Germany. Bowie, Clay's troubleshooter from August 1945 to April 1946, was first given the task of working out the administrative tangle left by Bernstein, and then led a task force on denazification. Young, bright, and experienced, with ties only to Clay, such men filled the most obvious bureaucratic holes. Later in the occupation this administrative function was performed by J. Anthony Panuch, a veteran of the Securities and Exchange Commission, the Office of War Mobilization, and the State Department. "In a remarkably frank and personal letter, Clay begged Panuch to come over and help him untangle the administrative snarl he had inherited from General McNarney."[117] Panuch became Clay's number one adviser, looking for inefficiency and trying to get done what Clay wanted done with a minimum of fuss.

During most of Clay's governorship, the two top official advisers were Robert Murphy, chief of the Political Division, and General William Draper of the Economics Division. They have been accused of ideological prejudices—that is, of having had conservative or right-wing views. Murphy was the only one in the inner circle who had had any experience in Germany or who spoke the language, but the criticism is that he lacked the political strength to make his experience effective.[118] He had a background in the diplomatic service, but was only propelled into a major role at the invasion of North Africa, when someone was needed to assist in negotiations with the Vichy French. This situation made him immediately important as liaison between the State Department and the army, and permanently suspect to the left wing; his negotiating with the Vichy regime showed them he was fascist in sympathy. There seems little in his advice to Clay to prove this belief true, although Murphy tended toward a conservative position and was less suspicious of Germans than most of Clay's advisers. A tall, handsome blond, he radiated charm, but was difficult to figure out. "As an Irishman who knew all the ways of smiling, handshaking, and saying pleasant things to people who counted at the proper moment," Murphy made an excellent front for State, but he did not push the department's ideas hard.[119] He was in a difficult position, as both State and War sent MG instructions, often incompatible. Contradictions were largely overcome at his expense, because Clay arranged to have all instructions to MG routed through the War Department; those sent to Murphy were to be regarded merely as suggestions.

Draper, on the contrary, displayed a very strong personality; he was the only one at OMGUS who compared with Clay in drive and hard work. Clay would work until seven or eight o'clock in the evening and then could relax, but Draper would head back for more work until midnight. Draper was a New York investment banker, from 1927 with Dillon Read, a firm involved in the 1920s loans to Germany. This background made him the villain to those who saw MG policy as building Germany up again so that investment firms could make more money. Yet Draper was also a combat officer in World War I and had come back from the army reserve to become a regimental commander. In 1944 he had been assigned to Washington to the Contract Termination Division, and in March 1945 to USGCC. To the liberal reporter Delbert Clark, Draper seemed to be the leader of the reactionaries who, aware that the public would not tolerate a pro-German policy; decided "to infiltrate, to advance by slow stages, to vitiate the established policy by a variety of devious devices, while loudly proclaiming that no change had been made or was contemplated." But Ratchford, also a liberal, and critical of most of Clay's organization, had nothing but praise for his boss Draper. He described him as a man of great patience and dignity, possessing an exceptionally keen and alert mind, tremendous energy and stamina, and a diplomat of the highest order; he deserved major credit for the success of the reparations negotiations, having more quickly gained a better understanding of the problems than any other officer, though it was an extra assignment for him. Ratchford could see no evidence of Wall Street influence; Draper was unusually fair and impartial.[120]

Clay's top military administrator was General Clarence Adcock, director of USFET and assistant deputy military governor; he had a good relationship with Clay and was his efficient spokesman, notably as delegate to Bizonia's Bipartite Control Board. Although Adcock seems to have had no particular preparation or policy position, Dorn praised him in 1949 for his knowledge of Bonn and Bizonal personalities, his good judgment, and his sound estimate of issues. Stubbornly anti-German, he "confessed his inability to sit down at a table with Germans in a social setting; to be under obligation to a German who invited him to his house, the very thought outraged him."[121] Clay's deputy as troop commander from late 1947 was General George P. Hays, a Medal of Honor winner in World War I, and in World War II a division commander of mountain troops in Italy, who had returned to the United States for routine administration. Clay had never met nor asked for him; Hays had not wanted the assignment, because "he doubted his own fitness and quickly proved himself correct."[122]

Clay's major policy advisers were mostly professors who took a year or so leave from their teaching. They would be invited back for inspection tours. The viewpoints of these scholars, based on a broad view of the German background, were usually in tension with those of army and civilian officials who knew little about Germany and had ill-founded prejudices based either on their remembrance of war propaganda or on their observation of the postwar Germans they met. Officials might be possessed either of unreasoning hatred for things German or of unreasoning admiration. The professors sometimes were unrealistic, but most who had had direct experience with prewar Germany neither hated nor adored Germans and their institutions.

Henry Parkman, an attorney who got a position as a political adviser because of his background in Boston politics, probably lacked this professorial knowledge, but he was the contact with a professor who did exemplify academic wisdom, Carl J. Friedrich, professor of political science at Harvard University.[123] Friedrich was told in 1945 that his help was needed because Clay's advisers "were in the dark." Clay told Friedrich he did not trust the young men in charge of his governmental affairs program, and had the uncomfortable feeling that they were trying to impose their own ideas on the Germans working out the Länder constitutions. Friedrich helped the Germans evade such interference.[124] He served several stints, in particular advising on the writing of constitutions in mid-1946, the first half of 1947, and mid-1948. German-born and German-educated, with respect for both the German and American experiences, he performed a valuable service as liaison. His main contribution was finding constitutional answers close to those of German democrats.

Another political scientist frequently consulted was James Pollock, of the University of Michigan, who was active in Michigan Republican politics. During the war he had written on the subject of German political organization and was called to Washington as an adviser in the writing of civil affairs guides.[125] His primary accomplishment was the 1945 midwifery at the birth of the zonal *Länderrat* (Council of the States). Bowie described him as a mediator and interpreter of German thought, definite on some issues, vague on others, and in general "a curious fellow."[126] Pollock encouraged Clay's efforts to restore German autonomy.

Edward Litchfield, a student of Pollock's and his successor, became education director. Bowie described him as a "can do" fellow and wondered whether his supreme self-confidence had not brought him excessive influence. Clark put it more negatively: "Litchfield, a man of great suavity, great cunning, and great resourcefulness . . . loved power and became vindictive when crossed. He was a fluent and persuasive talker, and by the beginning of 1948 there were few paths that could be travelled in Military Government without having to step over his shadow. It was not safe to get in his way."[127] His power was later limited by a control office, set up to shield Clay from persuasive department heads.

The only other professor of major consequence was Walter Dorn, professor of German history at Ohio State; his major endeavor was the much criticized denazification program. He was an important link to German leaders and their criticisms, yet Bowie doubted his effectiveness. Clark thought him sincere but myopic, his idea of collective guilt unacceptable and unworkable; therefore Dorn went home in 1947 a saddened man. Congressional investigator Meader wrote in late 1946: "I would be inclined not to share Clay's confidence in the quality of what he might do."

Meader also criticized Clay's staff: "Outstanding merit is difficult to conceal. No such unusual ability asserted itself on the level of Division Heads and top executives in Berlin, aside from that of General Clay himself."[128] Meader may have been unduly harsh, but the staff learned on the job. Most brought very little knowledge of Germany or of ideology with them. The staff's policy ideas were much more pragmatic than ideological. Reality taught them, so that they came to be a mirror of German opinion, becoming less anti-German and more anti-Russian.

The apparently unanimous judgment of contemporary critics is that the occupation suffered mightily from defects of organization, from beginning to end and from top to bottom. The most obvious defect was the abyss between MG and the army. MG was supposed to rule through German agencies; the army was merely to provide troops as enforcers. When it became apparent, to the surprise and disappointment of most, that the Germans practically welcomed Americans the troops lost their function. With the German army sent home or to prison camps, the army's real purpose for being in Germany was finished. It was in the way of both MG and German democrats. Only later did it find a new purpose: to defend Germans from Russians.

Yet the basic debate, whether the military or the civilians would be in charge, began at least a year before the occupation and never ended. The German Country Unit, predominately civilian although in uniform, saw the Morgenthau bomb shatter their policy, and in early June 1944 their organizational concept was shattered. They had assumed a political chain of command corresponding to the German political structure, but the new CAD commander announced they were to be organized like the army, military "in the true sense of the word." The German Country Unit came to an end when it was decided that even planning would be handled on a national rather than on an Allied basis. The U.S. Group, Control Council (USGCC) took its place, functioning by August and formally activated in October.[129]

The next problem was created by locating USGCC in Berlin, with the ACC, and leaving USFET in Frankfurt. Local tactical commanders argued that since the major work would be at the local level, the zonal commander should have more power than Berlin. At their best the local commanders were trying to carry out assignments. As Friedrich pointed out: "At their worst . . . they duplicated planning, hoarded and raided personnel, monopolized documents, sabotaged their rivals' efforts, and maintained veritable espionage systems against one another." In the American zone, the struggle was between Clay and W. B. Smith, in charge of G-5 of USFET. Until the USGCC became a functioning part of the ACC in Berlin, it was left under G-5. USFET maintained its supremacy into the fall of 1945, when G-5 began "to doubt whether USGCC had any authority for planning or drafting directives as far as the American zone was concerned. It went so far as to maintain that the USGCC could only deal with the few general matters which came under the Allied Control Council."[130]

Clay's policy-making USGCC in Berlin had little control over policy implementation even in the American zone. It could only send a recommendation to Frankfurt with a request that it be forwarded.[131] Since its policy-making power was to be based on agreement among the four powers on ACC, France, by preventing agreement, weakened its position. So did its isolation in Berlin: there was "a definite . . . loss of control, due to the difficulty in maintaining communications."[132] In October 1945 when Clay, concerned with the cooperation of zone officers and those in Berlin, asked which of his staff knew their counterparts, nearly none did. On 1 April 1946 USFET was relieved of MG responsibilities. Yet Clay was still not in command of the troops. Until he was made theater commander, Clay could only request McNarney to take corrective action concerning troops and officers. The local MG was usually outranked by tactical commanders and helpless except to persuade.

As Hilldring had predicted, the MG detachment commander, usually a captain, was no match for a major general, who could resort to a broad interpretation of the security of his forces to intervene. Oliver Echols, Hilldring's successor, told the Senate: "Military government had a hard time taking over. When fighting troops take an area they consider that they own it." After four months of occupation, the Seventh Army G-5 complained: "Most tactical units, troops and commanders alike, do not know what military government is or what it is supposed to do." At times the conflicts among the Americans threatened to undermine the authority of the occupation. German officials were often caught between MG, which had appointed but did not have the power to protect them, and the tactical troops, who either ignored them or treated them as if the war was still going on and they were all Nazis.[133]

MG was further handicapped in the formative months by being forced to communicate via the tortuous path of tactical command; "the relations between G-5 SHAEF and the G-5 staffs of the Twelfth and Sixth Army Groups, instead of being direct, followed a devious route through the chief of staff of SHAEF to the commanding generals of the two Army Groups and then through their chiefs of staff to the G-5 staffs of the Army Groups." As if this chain of command was not sufficiently confusing, MG operations were not in the hands of Army Groups but of the Armies. SHAEF officers desiring to visit a MG detachment had to be accompanied by Army Group officers, who decided what could be seen and when. Armies "usually displayed more feeling of independence and consequently greater unwillingess to be interfered with from above than any other unit." Visitors from Army Group often had to proceed as though they were from some foreign country if they wanted to visit the field and were prevented from visiting spots where their observations were undesired. Then came corps headquarters, which did most of the detachment assigning, and below them the divisions. These were usually the final command unit for MG administration, but regiments and even companies got involved in MG affairs.[134]

Even more organizational problems resulted from the JCS decision to model MG organization on army organization. Harold Zink says that this decision was

determined more by personal factors—the jockeying of various brass hats for power—than by the job to be done. Thus at one time public safety, public health, public welfare, education, religious affairs, local government and civil service, and communications were all jumbled together into a single division, though manpower and transportation, both of which probably had less complicated fields to plan than either education or public safety, enjoyed the status of separate divisions.[135]

The lack of coordination among army units was consistently criticized. Each level of command redrafted directives, and slight changes in wording could lead to far-reaching changes in application. "Some MG detachments conceived of themselves as perfectly free agents and a few even boasted that they had thrown away their *Handbooks* and read almost nothing which came to them from high levels. . . .Some officers expressed surprise that Washington was interested in German problems or that there was any place in field operations for policy decisions made in Washington."[136] Zink blamed the mess on the top brass, who "more or less ignored policy," in "a variety of feudal kingdoms in which they ruled supreme."[137] Friedrich also observed the lack of control. "Policy directives, often inadequate, were sometimes contradictory; moreover, staff supervision was almost completely absent." Getting policy down was not the only problem. "The path up from the working levels to the office of General Clay was a long and devious one, and the bottleneck created by the chief of staff and the control office made it difficult for many of those at the operating level to reach Clay."[138]

The top command was long determined to turn the job over to civilians as quickly as possible. On 1 October 1945 Eisenhower ordered that "MG affairs should be such that a change-over from military to civilian control could be effected on a 24 hour notice." Civilians would take over no later than 1 July 1946. Yet because no other agency was able or willing, the army remained holding the bag three years longer than it planned or wished. As a substitute policy Clay recruited civilians. When Washington complained, he dropped names: "Your cable not understood. Before I left Washington I understood from the President and the War Department that it was desired to make the organization for MG in Germany civilian in character at earliest possible date. I reported this to General Eisenhower on my arrival and found him in full agreement with this policy."[139]

Zink doubted that there was any real "civilianizing," despite the numbers of civilians. General Clay remained as military governor and later as commander of the military forces, receiving his orders from the army. He was surrounded by military officers who largely isolated him from civilians. "Relatively few civilians had immediate access to General Clay."[140] Ratchford noted that the army had no incentive to build up a strong permanent staff, only to have it replaced in a short time. "No such organization was built up and the result was inadequate personnel and confusion." The army resorted to sending special investigators or advisers, usually well-known figures, to

Germany for a few weeks. If, despite their fly-by-night appearances, their recommendations were sound, there was no organization to carry them out. Industrialists and financiers were supposed to set up an organization, to establish policies, and to train a civilian staff to take over when the army moved out. That plan failed badly; the recruiters had no clear conception of the job to be done; suitable men were scarce; some who did go could not stay long. The plan failed to provide staffs at lower levels, because of everyone's uncertainty about organization, and the rush for redeployment interfered with and took priority over the recruiting of MG personnel. Washington personnel staffs suffered from a lack of continuity; the recruiters were always having themselves sent over to join some unit they had been building up.

> Nobody in the Berlin personnel office ever quite knew what was going on because of the rapid turnover and the frequent reorganizations. Also there were employees from so many different organizations and governmental agencies connected with MG in Berlin, that no single personnel office had authority over all personnel: army, navy, War Department, State Department, OSS, FEA . . . none of them had any effective system of supervising personnel to see that men were on the job and doing what they were supposed to be doing.[141]

MG was terribly handicapped during the first year by the constant reshuffling of officials. "The Germans were bewildered by having to deal with men unfamiliar with the local situation, men who did not know what had happened under their predecessors and who would themselves be replaced as soon as they had mastered their jobs."[142] Ratchford observed confusing reorganizations at Berlin, like that of 29 June 1945 in which twelve divisions became sixteen, with six staff level offices and three assistant deputy military governors. The stated purpose was to decentralize, but Ratchford discovered that too many high-ranking industrialists had been recruited. The reorganization was to "provide positions with titles appropriate to the ideas these men had of their own importance. . . .This new arrangement was never satisfactory and had to be abandoned after a few months."

Then Clay demolished his field organization. In December 1945 he told his staff very few people would be required in the Länder MG detachments; execution of policy should be largely carried out by Germans. He would not care how well the Germans carried it out. Except in certain fields, such as food, MG should not set itself up even as watchdog of the efficiency in local government. By 1 January 1947 he had proudly reduced his manpower to 5,000 and by the spring of 1949 it was down to 2,500, much below the other zones. The French, for example, used many more for a smaller zone. Yet as Ratchford saw it, "USGCC (OMGUS) was overstaffed most of the time during the first year, although there were acute shortages in some branches and sections. In order to reduce staff, 'freezes' on the recruiting of new personnel were ordered from time to time. This happened so often that it was difficult to know at any given time, which 'freeze' was on and which was off."[143]

Even Clay accepted the criticism that the intelligence agencies were not functioning well: intelligence from both the army and the Counter Intelligence Corps (CIC) was not good, since it was built largely on German-haters and language experts, though it was more effective after it was reorganized in 1947. Meader thought poor intelligence was a serious problem. Intelligence functions were diffuse—for example, large staff were used for mere opinion polling; the principal source of information was Army G-2, which was unsatisfactory because Clay had no command over it and it was designed for military intelligence anyway. Clay's attitude was that he didn't want to spy on anyone.[144] Colonel Francis Miller of Military Intelligence made the criticism to a Senate committee that too many officers were assigned to military intelligence and too few to political intelligence. "Clay is not receiving the information that a deputy MG should receive in order to effectively and properly administer Germany." MG intelligence, he went on, was mostly from German sources. A report written by a German official of MG would come up through channels. It would have the War Department seal, but there would be no way for Americans to check the information.[145]

Faulty intelligence had continued since the much heralded OSS. "Though the OSS and Counterintelligence were supposed to have records which would guide MG officers in finding acceptable Germans ... it turned out that they were not actually able to perform this service, in large measure."[146] Conflicts led to poor intelligence: "In this general melee and struggle for information, organized intelligence work became impossible. Various groups worked at cross-purposes, information was not exchanged."[147] Ratchford reported that economic intelligence was also deficient, and the preparatory work done by the Foreign Economic Administration (FEA) nearly useless. "The men who found themselves faced with the actual task of controlling Germany discovered they must start from scratch."

Training for MG began in 1943 for some officers. They were landed in France in 1944 with the expectation of an early capitulation which did not materialize, and the repetition of training proved tedious. The great buildup of MG personnel occurred in May and June 1945. The Frankfurt staff grew quickly from some 150 officers to almost 2,000. There was a "great influx of high rank with little background in German institutions. . . . The colonels and generals fresh from the U.S. tended to ignore the many months of careful work done by the German Country Unit and the USGCC." Ernst Anspach observed many coming from field outfits at the last minute who had been "trained" for two weeks. Yet Ziemke notes that MG officials in the field often thought these tactical officers with little training had performed better than those who had suffered through training's boredom.[148]

Both trained and untrained were unfamiliar with local conditions, and they frequently camouflaged their ignorance with bluff. MG personnel had been trained mostly to get communication and transport going again behind a front line, not to govern. "With very few exceptions they knew literally nothing about Germany. They neither spoke the language, which forced them to rely upon unreliable interpreters, nor had they been given any idea of German history, politics or economics anywhere." Though sometimes possessed of technical skills, "they knew next to nothing about how to deal with the wreckage of human minds and spirits which was to constitute their major problem in Germany."[149] The Germans, who had begun by overestimating American abilities, tended to become sceptical of their intentions. Most officers who had been trained went home in the first six months of the occupation because they had sufficient "points" to be discharged. "Those who remained were disheartened by the chaotic conditions in which they had to work, by the absence of any clear idea of what they were supposed to do, and by the hopeless inadequacy of the 'teen age' replacements."[150]

An inspection of the "orientation program" of the troops in the fall of 1945 showed it scarcely existed. The message of orientation was to behave like a victor and to hate the defeated, or so General Morris Edwards described it: "There was not only an inadequate orientation program, but the program followed had a definitely erroneous and harmful slant." The 1946 orientation pamphlet began:

> You are a soldier fighting a new war. . . . we've got to watch every German 24 hours a day. . . . Making us feel sorry for them is one of the few weapons the "little" Germans have left. The children who shuffle from one foot to the other in the cold outside the mess hall . . . old men and old women pulling carts . . . the ragged German trudging along the street with a load of firewood may not look vicious, but he has a lot in common with a trapped rat.

This hate policy changed only in the fall of 1946, and thereafter "it was a slow process to turn the thinking and attitudes of the troops almost 180 degrees."[151]

Alfred Grosser, the French historian of postwar Germany, said of OMGUS: "With very few exceptions, they lacked really first-class men." Murphy saw the problem in the reluctance of most Americans to serve overseas. "Because a brief occupation was taken so much for granted, the only permanent staff originally available had to come from our regular Army and from career employees of federal departments and agencies. These are the only Americans obligated in peacetime to go wherever they are sent and to stay as long as ordered." MG was permitted to offer only one-year contracts. Many felt that they could not afford such temporary work, and had to hurry back home to get permanent civilian jobs.[152] The top salary, ten thousand dollars a year, was not very attractive. Zink emphasized the deluge of generals and colonels whose attitude was, "I always figured that MG in Germany would become the retiring center for the excess brass of the Army after V-E Day," and welcomed this chance to hold their temporary ranks. "To them, running a military government headquarters in Germany was substantially the same as operating a truck drivers' school or an airfield in the U.S." Yet having higher rank they automatically took over the chief positions. Senior officers who made careful preparations for the actual work to be done in Germany found that there was little or nothing left for them to do.[153]

The occupation elite was usually characerized by an attraction to luxury such as many had never had before and would never have again. As Kennan described them:

> Each time I had come away with a sense of sheer horror at the spectacle of this horde of my compatriots and their dependents camping in luxury amid the ruins of a shattered national community, ignorant of the past, oblivious to the abundant evidences of present tragedy all around them, inhabiting the same sequestered villas that the Gestapo and SS had just abandoned, and enjoying the same privileges, flaunting their silly supermarket luxuries in the face of a veritable ocean of deprivation, hunger, and wretchedness, setting an example of empty materialism and cultural poverty before a people desperately in need of spiritual and intellectual guidance, taking for granted—as though it were their natural due—a disparity of privilege and comfort between themselves and their German neighbors no smaller than those that had once divided lord and peasant in that feudal Germany, which it had been our declared purpose in two world wars to destroy.[154]

If power corrupts, the GI with cigarette power was corrupted. The bishop of the Protestant church stooped, as did millions of other Germans, for a cigarette butt thrown away by the GI, rich by comparison. Drinking was made easy; one pack of cigarettes would finance fifty double scotches. There was a breakdown of standards of sexual behavior: maids were expected to be mistresses or they could lose their jobs, which meant losing the food necessary for survival. Zink wrote of "the wine, women and song boys," openly flaunting their mistresses.[155] The black market flourished: the men in Berlin in one month, October 1945, sent home eighty-four million more dollars than they earned. "Officers were usually the biggest 'operators' in the markets, leaving the work on their desks to make deals in the street." The army was slow in cracking down on the market; "the practice was so prevalent and involved so many high ranking officers, it was difficult to know where and how to start a stiff program of correction."[156] The prevalence of black market activities gave many Germans the impression that "Americans are fundamentally dishonest and weak."[157]

The lower echelons could not live with the ostentatious luxury of their leaders, but what they lacked in finesse many made up for in brutality. Colonel Miller told Congress: "The German troops occupying France had a better record in their personal contact with the population than the American troops occupying Germany."[158] Activities of GIs and officers in Germany sounded like Hollywood's version of Nazi behavior: stealing valuable paintings and jewels, stabbing and bludgeoning a mother and father who refused the soldiers' demands for their daughter, black-marketing millions of dollars of goods. Molestation of women became so widespread that even women of the occupying powers were unsafe without flags showing their nationalities, and uniformed bullies swaggered down a street at night, making civilians run a gauntlet of clubs and fists.[159] Calvin Hoover observed that search operations were often misused. Looting by requisition form was common. "Substantially all automobiles belonging to German civilians were taken over by our troops."[160] A more subtle form of looting was the indirect variety, bartering cigarettes, candy, or food for valuables. This behavior was the major contact between conqueror and conquered at least until the mid-1948 currency reform.

The army took a rather tolerant view of such good spirits, particularly at first. Eisenhower observed 30 August 1945: "In many ways I feel our soldiers are very good ambassadors in teaching the German about our ways of living, for example, their lack of discipline shows another people not used to that sort of thing how we act and react. We would ask you not to quote 'lack of discipline'—I mean our attitude toward discipline as opposed to a subservient race." Such free thinking got out of hand in January 1946, when 3,000 GIs demonstrated outside McNarney's headquarters, chanting "I wanna go home." McNarney blamed the communists. Raymond Daniell, a *New York Times* correspondent, described the army as "an aggregation of homesick Americans shirking their jobs to figure out ways to make money, courting German women, counting up points." On 24 April McNarney belatedly ordered a crackdown on discipline and repeated it in September.[161]

As discipline got out of hand the army blamed the quality of men being sent from the United States to Germany. A survey in mid-1946 reported that approximately 14 percent of the white and 49 percent of the Negro enlisted men had Army General Classification Test scores of less than seventy. To eliminate the most unfit, 2,000 were shipped out "by the carloads" in November.[162] There was some merit in the army's complaint that it was sent troops not qualified by native intelligence or educational preparation for the occupation. On the other hand, the army did little to make them better able to relate to the native population. Those who did interact with Germans were usually operating contrary to army policy or for nonpolitical goals, such as black market operations or sex. Further, the army really had almost nothing for them to do of any meaning to the occupation. The peacetime army exists to train men for a possible war, and trying to use more than a few soldiers to work with civilians (in sports, for example) was nonfunctional. The troops were bored, and many turned to drinking and fighting. With so few capable Americans for responsible positions, the army increasingly gave responsible tasks to Germans.

McCloy and the High Commission for Germany

The process of letting the Germans do it was nearly complete when John J. McCloy succeeded Clay as military governor, slightly before becoming high commissioner for the new Bonn republic. His period in power was less important than Clay's, policy toward Germany and Russia already having been established. McCloy's major contribution to policy was to effect an alliance with the Germans. His status, even more than Clay's, was the persuader rather than the commander, his powers being limited by treaty. He continued Clay's job as liaison, and was more sympathetic than Clay to German arguments. He seems to have represented the German position well in Washington, but the United States also got German support against Russia. An anti-Russian stance was not something Chancellor Konrad Adenauer had to be pushed into.[163] McCloy's and Adenauer's policies generally coincided.

Like Clay, McCloy was of major help to the Germans as an intermediary with the French and British. He also helped Adenauer get German support for integration into the west. Mrs. Ellen McCloy had a better relationship with the general public. From a German family, by odd coincidence a distant cousin of Adenauer's second wife, personable and intelligent, she appeared frequently before various groups, addressing them in German and displaying concern for the country. The McCloys' function was not only to soothe Germans about American policy but also to soothe Americans about German developments. Retrospective views of McCloy in interviews were rare, because his impact was so indirect. Among the few who knew him, Reinhold Maier conceded that McCloy had by the end of his regime created a good relationship with the Germans, but Maier had found it difficult to adjust to him. "We again made the observation that the Americans could be more Prussian than the Prussians."[164]

OMGUS organization had eventually copied that of the prewar Germans, with detachments at each Kreis and Land capital. In 1945 these detachments were to command, early in 1946 to advise, and finally only to observe the parallel German units. The High Commission for Germany (HICOG) retained the same pattern of organization.[165] But its powers steadily diminished; its local powers were limited to observing and reporting. The high commissioner was legally limited to maintaining law and order if Germans were unable to do so (never the case), to ensuring protection to Allied forces (who did not need protection), to ensuring delivery of reparations (soon canceled), to looking after DPs (soon integrated into German society or emigrated), and to observing the administration of justice and the care of prisoners (who were rapidly released). The high commissioner's truly useful function was his ability to get money from Washington and to get concessions from the Allies so as to return freedom to the Germans.

The German press praised McCloy's staff, particularly the inner three, for their intelligence, deep character, and cultural convictions. James Riddleberger, after five years as legation secretary in Berlin, became a top State Department specialist on Germany in Washington, and then Clay's adviser in Berlin. Public Affairs Officer Ralph Nicholson was a publisher from New Orleans who rose from poverty and gave up a greater income, "because he respects Germans and wants to help them back on their feet." Economics adviser Norman Collison, an engineer, had moved from mining and oil into politics, becoming assistant to the secretary of the interior in 1946, then ambassador for the Marshall Plan to Germany.[166]

The work at the top, the only significant involvement in German affairs, was usually conducted informally at numerous committee meetings. The official description of the work at the bottom makes it clear that the resident officer had the vague duties of a figurehead: he was to be a jack-of-all-trades, to encourage democracy, and to emphasize youth. He was not supposed to order anything, but to win German acceptance of policy by example and personal prestige, and to act as liaison between civilians and troops.[167] Zink, who complained that many in HICOG retained the habits of victors in a conquered land, thought there was improvement on the local level. Half of these local officers were taken over from OMGUS, but they were of a new type—younger and more intelligent than their predecessors.[168] They spent much of their time trying to keep American troops in good humor and out of the Germans' way. Much energy was taken by disputes involving the army's hunting and fishing privileges and drinking water: the army insisted on quantities of chlorine, which the Germans regarded as pollution. They reported on local developments, particularly on public affairs programs. By 1951 these Kreis Resident Offices were closed, leaving only the Land Offices, which closed in early 1952.

Sent on an inspection tour by the War Department, Colonel Cheseldine made a devastating critique for McCloy and the State Department: HICOG never got close to the people; they simply got to know Adenauer and Bonn officials.

> We may have the greatest collection of technical experts obtainable from the U.S., but they are in complete ignorance of the Germany in their backyard. McCloy said to me: "I guess we here are probably too much oriented toward Bonn, but we just don't seem to have time for much else. I have to spend three

days a week up there and my people are always busy getting ready for HICOM meetings. I probably am not getting all I should out of the Land Commissioners, but I do have them up here once a week for staff meetings and I am just starting a series of meetings here with the Land Commissioners and the German Minister Presidents. . . . I guess the Land Commissioners become somewhat proconsul in attitude—a hangover from MG—and I don't believe they are exactly living up to their responsibilities. They seem to think that so long as serious trouble does not break out in these areas everything is all right."[169]

The division chiefs, Cheseldine commented, felt they were there only as specialists. Each was convinced that his particular problem of the moment was earthshaking. Many were "condescendingly there for a short period during which time they feel they can easily shape up their field so someone else can move in and mop up!" Land commissioners and staffs were dismayed; "We no longer operate, it's true, but our job now is to democratize in every field, and each one of us knows that that job is not one man's province. . . . But if we are going to be liquidated in the next six months, what's the use?" Cheseldine concluded that "the only continuity in occupation activity exists at Land Offices. There are practically no people in HICOG-Frankfurt who have any personal knowledge of the past five years of endeavor; there are more at Land levels who have lived with their Germans for almost five years." State Department people, he thought, should be those who had been in Germany before, because the Germans needed someone on the local level to explain American democracy which had been made confusing by the policies and people they had seen.[170]

Cheseldine wrote to McCloy that the most important need was to find higher quality resident officers, the kind who would make an effort to associate with the people.

> Your Office Directors have not spent any time in the Länder. Some Land Division heads claim they have never seen their HICOG 'opposite number'! Since you have practically no tie with the past at HICOG, since your top technical advisers have not lived with the development of Germany, and since many of them have, even in their short period of service there, not associated with any Germans except those at top governmental level, I submit that they cannot know that with which they are dealing.[171]

Cheseldine asked the Land commissioenrs if it were true, as McCloy had said, that as long as things were going smoothly they should not bother him. Their answer was that McCloy had given them no terms of reference. They felt they could talk to McCloy, except he was always rushing back to Bonn.

McCloy was sufficiently impressed with the denunciation to ask Pollock to verify its findings. Pollock concluded that Cheseldine was right except on the minor point that the Germans wanted more resident officers.

> I do not find that the present legal framework is favorable to the development of German initiative and I find, further, that the Allies are not securing

anything like the amount of work and cooperation from the Germans that would be possible under more favorable circumstances. . . . I would estimate that eighty percent of our desires would be carried out by the Germans, if they knew what we wanted and knew it in time. I would further estimate that no more than forty percent of our desires are effectuated, and part of this by default. . . . we need more and closer liaison at both policy and operating levels between our people and the Germans, particularly at Bonn.

Liaison was worst at Bonn.

The admirable example set by the High Commissioner, if followed by his own organization, would do the trick . . . the working relationships [between Americans and Germans] under the occupation Statute are not good or satisfactory. . . . It is today little more than a euphemism to say that the High Commission is running Germany. Both the international situation and the Germans are far ahead of its actions. It became increasingly clear to me that it is politically impossible for us to hold the present line of controls over so many aspects of German life. There is a growing disrespect among the Germans for our ability to handle the job of occupation. . . . one still finds in our zone and organization too many instances of interference by some of our functional people . . . with German operations.

Much of the HICOG organization was "out of focus, a disproportionate amount of time and attention was given to the various activities of the High Commission, while too little attention was given to the work of the Bonn government, of the Länder governments, and of Berlin. . . . it is clear that the organization is not operating smoothly, nor securing from its various units in the headquarters, and in the field, contributions commensurate with the time and money expended."[172]

A third inspector, Roger Baldwin, doubted that HICOG had even local usefulness:

From McCloy down I found what struck me as a distrust of the Germans and a naive confidence in American advice and supervision. I urged withdrawing from the bottom up, beginning with the American county agents. . . . Devotion to county agents was intense, as if they were the heart of a treasured 'reorientation,' when I knew from experience that they were, despite all good intentions, an irritating nuisance . . . the ever present evidence of a foreign occupation.[173]

It was also an expensive nuisance. HICOG was generally criticized for its vast building program to house offices near Bonn. Not only was the cost criticized, paid for as it was by the Germans, but this "little America on the Rhine" was a community self-contained and insulated from the surrounding Germans. It was a gilded ghetto.

These descriptions of OMGUS and HICOG organization and personnel should not be interpreted to mean that the occupation was composed of rascals and incompetents. It was composed of humans, for better or for worse. The lack of normal social controls highlighted rascality and the difficulties of governing unknown people in a strange country highlighted incompetence.[174] There were many well-meaning Americans, though few well-informed ones. The point is that this group's capacity to govern was limited by manifold arrogance and greed, but it was even more limited by ignorance. Not only did most participants fail to exert the power over the civilian population that has been assumed, but when they did it was often irrelevant, or even contrary to the policy ordered by Washington or Clay. Neither the United States nor its army was prepared for the responsibility of victory. But in most cases Clay had the intelligence and courage to order Americans to let the Germans solve their own problems. The one area where they needed help in 1945 was in staying alive.

Notes

1. To Field Marshal Alan Brooke, he was "just a coordinator, a good mixer, a champion of inter-Allied cooperation" (Arthur Bryant, *Triumph in the West* [Garden City, 1959], 181; Stephen Ambrose, *Eisenhower and Berlin* [New York, 1967], 22). "His heart was never in the German occupation" (Robert Murphy, *Diplomat among Warriors* [Garden City, 1964], 228–29). In mid-1944 he thought that the German general staff should be exterminated; all Nazi leaders and Gestapo also deserved liquidation (Harry Butcher, *My Three Years with Eisenhower* [New York, 1946], 609). "One of the few questions I was able to ask him was how he envisaged the political development of the country. The General looked at me in surprise. 'The Germans don't have to worry about politics. They have to make sure that they have enough to eat, for we are not going to feed them forever. . . . You have to *tell* the Germans. That's the language they understand' " (Hans Habe, *Our Love Affair with Germany* [New York, 1953], 105–106).
2. The ban on contact with Germans was easy to obey meticulously; official negotiations were delegated to his staff (Murphy, 255, 262, 283, 287). Clay explained he did this to avoid meeting anyone who was not "politically clean" (Interview Lucius Clay).
3. Harold Zink, *American Military Government in Germany* (New York, 1947), 24–25. Yet victory brought the expected promotion in the fall. He returned only in 1950 "to let bygones be bygones," and to interest Germans in serving under him in NATO. He had happily forgotten his tough words.
4. Russell Hill, *Struggle for Germany* (London, 1947), 102. McNarney lacked political flair. He would rarely talk to the press, and then only with a public relations man handy (Bud Hutton and Andy Rooney, *Conqueror's Peace* [New York, 1947], 45, 49; Murphy, 290). McNarney was praised for his belated effort to stop the misbehavior of his troops. The decision that made him noticed as a commander was his refusal to permit soldiers to marry German girls for over a year after ACC permitted it. Washington also forced him to call off the hate orientation given the troops.
5. Clay was involved in politics, pushing for more war goods over consumer goods. His having battled businessmen should prove Clay was not "the tool of Wall Street," as revisionists may assume. On his assignment to Germany an industrialist said: "Fine, they have found the right place for him, ruling over enemies. He will show them understanding but no sympathy" (*Look*, Sept. 1945). The *Washington Post* agreed: "General Clay's exceedingly high abilities are

better suited to the German situation than our own. That task calls for authoritarianism" (quoted in *Newsweek,* 26 June 1945). On 25 March FDR wrote Byrnes: "My inclinations are toward Fred [Vinson] as he is such an old friend, but if we shifted Fred at the present time, we would have to find someone to handle the loans." Marshall wanted W. B. Smith, but Stimson turned him down as temperamentally unsuitable (Jean Smith, ed., *The Papers of General Lucius D. Clay* [Bloomington, Ind., 1974], xxxi). Earl Ziemke wrote that the War Dept. already preferred Clay in November 1944 (*The U.S. Army in the Occupation of Germany* [Washington, 1975], 222).

6. W. B. Smith thought various combat generals were qualified but were still busy; he said: "General Eisenhower has always wanted Mr. McCloy as you know." Wickersham could carry on until one of the senior officers would be free. For a lesser job, Smith mentioned Clay as a possibility (W. B. Smith to McCloy, 3 Mar. 1945, CAD 014 Ger, National Archives [hereafter NA]); see also James Byrnes, *Speaking Frankly* (New York, 1947), 47; James Byrnes, *All in One Lifetime* (New York, 1958), 272. Murphy noted, "A civilian put the occupation into the hands of a professional soldier—contrary to the advice of the military chiefs" (248); see also Elliott Roosevelt, *FDR: His Personal Letters, 1928-45* (New York, 1950), 1578.

7. Lucius Clay, *Decision in Germany* (New York, 1950), 6-7; Murphy, 289.

8. Delbert Clark, *Again the Goosestep* (Indianapolis, 1949), 32. Clark was assigned as a reporter to Clay's headquarters. "Very few officers anywhere work as hard as Clay, who usually reaches his office long before the opening hour and not uncommonly remains after the closing hour far into the evening." He noted Clay's initial impetuosity; he decided after a ride through the countryside that "he didn't like the names of German streets and parks and directed that not only Nazi names but of historical figures antedating the present century be obliviated." Officials were not to carry certain titles, such as president, trustee, commissioner, and director (Zink, *American,* 27).

9. Harold Zink, *The United States in Germany, 1944-45* (New York, 1957), 69. "He depends on his advisers more for information than for advice, and it is for this characteristic that he has been chiefly criticized by subordinates" (Hill, 27). He preferred the advice of friends to that of professionals (B. U. Ratchford and W. D. Ross, *Berlin Reparations Assignment* [Chapel Hill, 1947], 58).

10. William Hale, "General Clay on His Own," *Harper's,* Dec. 1948, 88.

11. Zink, *American,* 27; Clark, 46, 50, 52. William Draper would be the outstanding exception to Clark's rule. Ernst Anspach thought Clay vain, and that obsequiousness was required of his staff (Interview Ernst Anspach).

12. "He would sit around for hours, smoking his innumerable cigarettes, and drinking whiskey and soda, regaling the company, if it was small and discreet enough, with hilarious 'inside' stories" (Clark, 39). To adviser Bowie, Clay seemed much more articulate than Eisenhower, though less "sound" (Interview Robert Bowie); Chronology of the Office of Military Government U.S. and its Predecessor Organization, Historical Section Control Office, OMGUS, Kansas City Record Center [hereafter Chronology, KCRC], 13 Oct. 145).

13. "The proper amount of centralism for Germany would be like that of the U.S. around 1910" (Clark, 36); Interview Bowie.

14. Reinhold Maier, *Ende und Wende* (Stuttgart, 1948), 365, 370, 394; Friedrich Glum, *Zwischen Wissenschaft und Politik* (Bonn, 1964), 595; Hubertus von Loewenstein, *Deutschlands Schicksal, 1945-57* (Bonn, 1957), 57. "All German politicians who met Clay in those years report that only the blockade changed his attitude toward Germany" (Hans-Peter Schwartz, *Vom Reich zur Bundesrepublik* [Berlin, 1966], 122); John Gimbel said this derived from Clay's busy life; his humanity was evident in his cables (*The American Occupation of Germany* [Stanford, 1968], 47).

15. OMGUS, "History of U.S. Military Government in Germany," 8 May 1945-30 June 1946;

U.S. Group CC Staff Meetings, KCRC, 16 May 1945; Clay press conference 16 May 1945, quoted in Hubert Schmidt, *Policy and Functioning in Industry*, USMG, Historical Division (Karlsruhe, 1950), 9.

16. He worried someone would think he was for a "soft peace" (Clay to McCloy, 29 June 1945, Chronology, KCRC).

17. Clay, 21, 45. Stimson told him in July 1945: "He would have no policy based on vindictiveness. . . . the American people would in the long run give their approval only to an occupation which was decent and humane and which was conducted under a rule of law" (Eugene Davidson, *The Death and Life of Germany* [New York, 1959], 190); also Interview Clay.

18. Michael Balfour, *Survey of International Affairs, 1939–46* (London, 1946), 27. "Only the White House could have intervened but that was immersed in domestic problems during the formative period" (Zink, *U.S.*, 31). Washington, lacking a policy, was buffeted between "modified Morgenthauism," and "Draperism" reconstruction (Basil Davidson, *Germany: What Now? Potsdam to Partition, 1945–49* [London, 1950], 180). In 1946 the Republicans took Congress. Clay associated himself strongly with Dewey, visiting him and not Truman on a trip home before the 1948 election.

19. Hale, 89–90. Yet he told Dorn in 1949 "that while there were disagreements between him and Washington, he ended up by following the decisions which Washington had made for him" (Walter Dorn, "Notes," 16, Institut für Zeitgeschichte, Munich).

20. The interpretative error has been furthered by the effort of officials to make sure they could not be accused of being soft on Nazism. Gimbel's thesis also stresses that the "Promise of Potsdam" was nullified by French, not Russian, vetoes (*American*, 2–5, 14–16).

21. "There is no friction or discord between the Departments of the Government back home on these issues" (quoted in Wickersham to Division Directors, 17 Feb. 1945, CAD 014, NA). A member of the U.S. Group assured Boettiger that 1067 was "the Bible" (Milburn to Boettiger, 20 Feb. 1945, CAD 014, NA; Smith to McCloy, 3 Mar. 1945, CAD 014, NA).

22. Clay, 8, 18. "Although reading it now will show that it deviated little from the American policy . . . proclaimed by Byrnes in his Stuttgart speech."

23. "Clay agreed and he asked Douglas to fly back to Washington at once to try to get the directive modified. But Douglas returned dejected . . . the disputes in Washington had tied American occupation plans into fatal bowknots, and before long he quietly resigned" (Murphy, 251). "The most generally expressed sentiment, met at every level of the organization from Generals Clay and McSherry down to local MG detachments, was that German economic activity must be restored" (Clay to McCloy, 26 Apr. 1945, ASW 370.8, NA; Cable from Hilldring, Clay reply, 1 May 1945, AGWAR, NA; Clay to WARCAD, Hilldring, 7 May 1945, Box 177-1/3, Washington National Record Center [hereafter WNRC]). "It is important not to minimize the capacity that local officers have for finding ways around the obstacles that high policy may set in their way," with "the understandable sympathy that administrators have for any people living in the desolate conditions in which the Germans do now" (Abramovitz to Lubin, 14 May 1945, CAD 014 Ger, NA).

24. Hilldring to Clay, 21 May 1945, OMGUS 177-3/3, WNRC; Clay to McCloy, 16 June 1945, ASW 370.8, NA; Chronology, 9 June 1945, KCRC. Privately he began to move toward "a painstaking legal analysis of the orders" (John Backer, *Priming the German Economy* [Durham, N.C., 1971], 37). He used the "disease and unrest" phrase to get around the negative phrases. On 2 July Calvin Hoover, Clay's economic adviser, gave him his anti-1067 report; Hill reported Clay as being "very well aware of the problem. . . . However, Clay had to be sensitive to trends of public opinion" (Hill, 82).

25. 4 July 1945, OSW 463.3 Ger, NA, Stimson and Bundy, 583. JCS ignored Stimson's wisdom, and simply ordered coal to be seized for export (Chronology, 25 July to 1 Aug.,

KCRC). To Clay's chagrin, JCS 1067 was classified top secret until October 1945. (A 22 May cable from Eisenhower asked that publication be withheld.) A 6 June cable withdrew objection to publication (Smith, *Papers,* 15, 20). For Clay's proposed revision of 21 July 1945, see Smith, 54. Eisenhower resisted publication because SHAEF "is now operating under policies different from those described in 1067 and its publication would therefore be embarrassing to him" (MacLeish to Charles Ross, 23 May 1945, CAD 014, NA).

26. Herbert Feis, *Between War and Peace* (Princeton, 1960), 159–60, 317; Harry S Truman, *Memoirs: Year of Decision,* I (Garden City, 1955), 411.

27. William McNeill, *America, Britain, and Russia* (New York, 1970), 612; Walter Millis, *Forrestal Diaries* (New York, 1957), 78.

28. Leahy Papers, Library of Congress, 17 July, 21 July, 22 July 1945; U.S. Dept. of State, *Foreign Relations of the U.S.: The Conference at Potsdam,* II (Washington, 1960), 59 (hereafter *FRUS*). Stalin reported incorrectly most Germans had left anyway. The conference ended with the area "under Polish administration"; Stalin would not admit he had erred in giving Poland the territory, but "the present arrangement cannot be changed."

29. Ernest Penrose, *Economic Planning for the Peace* (Princeton, 1953), 276; Truman, I, 308. The 18 May directive to Pauley noted the need for German subsistence (*FRUS: 1945,* III, 1222–27). Truman wanted someone as tough as Molotov and Pauley was a "mean-so-and-so."

30. Penrose, 281–82; see *FRUS: Potsdam,* I, 468–70, for Pauley correspondence.

31. *FRUS: Potsdam,* II, 197, 274.

32. The Russian zone was difficult to see, but the Russians had clearly stripped the factories to get the machinery out of the U.S. sector of Berlin (ibid., 873, 888–92; Pauley letters of 25 and 27 July 1945). "Mr. Pauley had learned that the Russian Army had destroyed a lot of property in Germany and what they did not destroy the American Army did" (Byrnes at the foreign ministers' meeting 27 July 1945).

33. McCloy to Byrnes, 31 July 1945, original italics; Pauley to Truman, 20 Sept. 1945, "Report on German Reparations," in *FRUS: Potsdam,* II.

34. "Truman, by then baffled and eager to get away from these trying sessions of talk, fell in with the idea. Attlee and Bevin had deeper pangs . . . but did not have the strength to prevent it" (Feis, *War,* 259). Molotov thought that a percentage of an unknown quantity meant very little, but Byrnes refused to be more specific because of the Russian dismantlings. Penrose thought this "standard of living level" was vastly worse than that adopted at Versailles in 1919: "It would be difficult to find in the recorded history of international relations a more intellectually disreputable and administratively unworkable formula for determining the economic fate of a nation" (Penrose, 284–87); see also Gar Alperovitz, *Atomic Diplomacy* (New York, 1965), 172–73; Lloyd Gardner, *Architects of Illusion* (Chicago, 1970), 94. (Revisionists accept the Russian idea of a "dangerous Germany.") Murphy described Truman's anger when Stalin brutally rejected the internationalization of the Danube (278–79). Truman said later that he had been ready at Potsdam to give the Russians a six billion dollar credit, but had received a "slap in the face" (Trygvie Lie, *In the Case of Peace* [New York, 1954], 295).

35. Although Truman later wrote that he was much impressed by the ruins of Berlin, "while there he did not ask to meet any anti-Nazi German statesman, publicly or privately, and almost everyone in the President's entourage followed his example" (Murphy, 283); see John Snell, *Wartime Origin of the East-West Dilemma Over Germany* (New Orleans, 1959), 13. Feis thought more negotiating skill might have kept Germany united and neutral (*War,* 272). George Kennan wrote: "I cannot recall any political document the reading of which filled me with a greater sense of depression than the communique . . . at the conclusion of these confused and unreal discussions" (*Memoirs, 1925–1950* [Boston, 1967], 272–81).

36. Gimbel and Backer have emphasized that the Potsdam agreement was a significant modification of 1067. Germany was to be treated as an economic unit; measures to restore transporta-

tion, agriculture, and housing would be permitted; reparations were not to deprive Germans of a minimum standard of living or to preclude imports (Backer, 26–27; Gimbel, *American*, 9–18).

37. Alperovitz, 188, 202, 235; Seyom Brown, *Faces of Power* (New York, 1968), 307.

38. In other respects, including reparations, the communiqué was a confirmation of JCS 1067 (see Chronology, 1 Aug. 1945, KCRC; Gimbel, *American*, 25).

39. *New York Times*, 8 Oct. 1945; Hilldring to Patterson, 9 Oct. 1945, CAD, WDSCA 014 Ger, NA. Republican senators blasted Morgenthauism. Morgenthau demanded that Patterson repudiate the report. Byrnes rejected Hoover's arguments: "Large scale removals are compatible with and required by other U.S. objectives in Germany and elsewhere in Europe." Clay assured Washington that Hoover's MG report was only "a basis for discussion," not policy (Clay to WD, 10 Oct. 1945, *FRUS: 1945*, III, 1339; Byrnes [Clayton] to Murphy, 12 Oct. 1945, *FRUS: 1945*, III, 1341).

40. Price's recommendations reached Clay in mid-October and Truman by 9 November (Byron Price, Memo to the President, 9 Nov. 1945, 177-3/3, WNRC; Truman to Patterson, 20 Nov. 1945, OSW 091 Ger, NA; Patterson, Memo to Truman, OSW 091 Ger, NA; Hilldring to Patterson, 3 Dec. 1945, WDSCA 091 Ger, NA).

41. Hilldring memos Nov. 1945, ASW 370.8, Ger, quoted in Gimbel, *American*, 28; Murphy, 285; McCloy to Clay, 23 Nov. 1945, 410/3, WNRC.

42. His directors could think of no further significant changes (Chronology, 2 Dec. 1945, KCRC). Supposedly none of these explanations violated the 1067 emphasis on making Germany pay damages and remain too industrially weak to endanger its neighbors (WARCAD to OMGUS, 8 Dec. 1945, 365-2/5, WNRC). This positive interpretation was not evident in the setting of the industry level; see chapter three.

43. He also recommended "the passage concerning the political and administrative structure of Germany should be revised to encourage the early promotion of a Central German Government with limited responsibility as originally directed." He suggested freeing German travel between zones, modifying denazification to permit the individual trials he was beginning, deleting nonfraternization, limiting mandatory arrests, and limiting economic controls to those necessary for industrial disarmament (Clay to WARCAD, 10 Dec. 1945, Clay Cables, NA; Chronology, 13 Dec. 1945, KCRC). Hilldring soothed Kilgore Committee fears; "General Clay and I like 1067" (Senate Hearings on Elimination of German Resources for War, 29 Dec. 1945, 1053, 1058). Clay's successful pressure on the State Dept. was evident in its bulletin of 16 December (U.S. Dept. of State Bulletin, 16 Dec. 1945, 960–65).

44. Chronology, noted under 13 Dec. 1945, KCRC. SWNCC authorized a review of JCS 1067, 10 Apr. 1946 (Byrnes to Patterson, *FRUS: 1946*, V, 539).

45. Clay's policy accepted reparations, but not such as to prevent the "minimum German economy." He proposed calling a minister-president council to create a "decentralized-central" government. Clay gave up the Oder-Neisse lands to Poland, and the Saar to France, but not the Rhineland and Ruhr. Germany should be admitted to the United Nations (Clay to Echols, 19 July 1946, CAD, Colonel Fahey's File, 1947, NA; summary in Gimbel, *American*, 76–78).

46. Clay to WARCAD, 7 Aug. 1946, CAD 014, NA; also Smith, *Papers*, 247–48. On 13 August he wrote Hilldring that the situation was completely intolerable (Smith, *Papers*, 250).

47. These aspects were: the establishment of a provisional government in Germany, admission to the UN, heavy industry, financial policy, frontiers, and the Rhineland-Ruhr (WDSCA GO to Clay, 12 Aug. 1946, NA).

48. Clay to WDSCA, 23 Aug. 1946; Echols to Patterson, 24 Aug. 1946, NA. To underline his opinion of Washington interference he also rejected CAD's suggestion of giving assistance to the anticommunist parties in Berlin. Clay's actions were based on excellent reasons; West Berlin would reject communism, no matter how much money the Russians gave their party.

Then he rejected State Dept. objections to the Länder constitutions (WDSCA GO to OMGUS 15 Aug. 1946; Clay to WDSCA GO, 23 Aug. 1946, NA). He wrote Patterson: "It was an effort on my part to summarize our policy . . . based on original directives as modified by the passage of events. I was disappointed to find out how mistaken I was and I must confess somewhat at sea to know how to proceed" (Clay to Patterson, 16 Aug, 1946, OSW 091 Ger, NA; Smith, *Papers,* 252–53).

49. Although Clay said he did not write Byrnes's speech, the letter supplied the exact phraseology in certain places. It was more general on the admission of Germany to the UN, and more vague on the internationalization of Ruhr coal and steel. Clay suggested to the War Dept. that it be the basis for a 1067 revision (Smith, *Papers,* 263; Gimbel, *American,* 85). Meader traced Clay's problems back to Washington. "In theory the State Department is responsible for policy, but what is a matter of policy and what is a matter of administration remains in considerable doubt." Confusion of responsibility was disastrous (Meader Report, confidential report to the special Senate committee investigating the national defense program, on military government in the occupied areas of Europe, 22 Nov. 1946, 37–38, based on the criticism by Colonel Miller, who had resigned in disgust as intelligence chief for OMGUS); see also Frances Pickens Miller, "Memoirs," manuscript in Miller's possession.

50. Edward Litchfield, *Governing Postwar Germany* (Ithaca, N.Y., 1948), 8. The elevation of assistant William Draper to become undersecretary of the army and the Republican 1946 victory helped push Clay toward the conservative view (Clark, 53).

51. Interview Bowie; Hill, 101.

52. Clay and Sokolovsky could trade insults at the council meetings, but afterwards stroll out, arm in arm, for a drink (Clark, 41). "American relations with Russians were undoubtedly better in Berlin than anywhere else in the world; but the time came . . ." (Hill, 101). Russians were sometimes robbing, raping, murdering, and even kidnapping from other sectors, which pushed Americans into protecting "their" Germans from Russians (Wilhelm Kaisen, *Meine Arbeit, Mein Leben* [Munich, 1967], 207). Clay long warned German officials: "Don't criticize Russians in my presence." Berlin commander Frank Howley recorded experiences which made him anti-Russian much earlier than Clay. When Sokolovsky assured Clay the Soviet army would not be used to promote communism, Howley said Sokolovsky was lying. Clay supposedly protested: "But I know Sokolovsky. He wouldn't lie to me" (*Berlin Command* [New York, 1950], 12). Kennan remembered his dismay in Berlin in the fall of 1945, when he was forced "to endure reproaches leveled at me and at us 'State Department people' generally for our anti-Soviet attitudes and our inability 'to get along with the Russians' " (207). Maj. Harold Zink of Clay's Political Division lamented that Clay not only was ignorant, when appointed, of German history, institutions, and psychology, but distrusted the British and misunderstood the French (*U.S.,* 71–72).

53. Chronology, 2 June 1945, KCRC. "However, we have not found them willing to discuss matters on a broad basis . . . which will make negotiations extremely slow" (Clay to McCloy, 29 June 1945, 410/3, WNRC); this was in response to McCloy's worried letter 21 June, suggesting tripartite or zonal arrangements in the event quadipartite action was lacking (quoted in Robert March, *U.S. Military Government in Germany: Financial Policies and Operations* [Karlsruhe, 1950], 142). Clay's problems as governor made him impatient of the long wait and he resorted eventually to the West German solution McCloy had suggested at the beginning.

54. De Gaulle reaffirmed this opposition in November (Caffrey to Byrnes, 11 Aug. 1945, *FRUS: 1945,* V, 703–704; Caffrey to Byrnes, 3 Nov. 1945, ibid., III, 890–91; Chronology, 28 Sept. 1945, KCRC). By 20 October, Clay had permission to enter into any agreement for central administrative machinery. On 1 October, Gen. Pierre Koenig had given another French reason: until France got the Ruhr-Rhineland away from Germany, he could not agree to central agencies (Cable W 77596, AGWAR, WARCAD to OMG, 21 Oct. 1945 in AG OMGUS 014.1

Ger, CAD, NA; Hilldring to Clay, 20 Oct. 1945, *FRUS: 1945*, III, 885–86). By 3 October Clay had learned another reason: France had tried to dismember Germany for centuries (Chronology, 3 Oct. 1945, KCRC).

55. Draft cable, Clay to AGWAR, 4 Oct. 1945, Clay Cables, NA. The cable actually sent said instead that the Russians had set up "a complete German administration for their zone. I have been reluctant to create any such agencies for our zone for fear it might impede the treatment of Germany as an economic entity. In view of the delay in establishing the central agencies, however, we have concluded that some German machinery is essential for coordinating the activities of the three Laender of our zone" (Clay to McCloy, 5 Oct. 1945, 410/3, WNRC).

56. Clay to Robertson, 13 Oct. 1945 in AG, OMGUS 014.1, NA. "He withdrew the proposal on October 16. His specific reason for doing so is not clear from available records, but it is clear that it was not done on instructions from Washington" (Gimbel, *American*, 24, based on OMGUS papers 99-2/5). On 19 October, OMGUS working parties on central transport and communications agencies were stopped.

57. "Clay, apparently annoyed by the suggestion that Soviet intentions might be as obstructive as French actions, emphasized that until France accepted central agencies . . . the Soviet barriers on interzonal trade and travel had a rationale" (Gimbel, *American*, résumé of meeting on 3 Nov. 1945 in Smith, *Papers*, 111–17). On 21 November Patterson reminded State to pressure France, as requested 6 November; "unless such agencies are established promptly, there is grave danger of a breakdown of the provisions of Berlin Protocol" (Patterson to Byrnes, 21 Nov. 1945, OSW 091 Ger, NA; McCloy to Clay, 23 Nov. 1945, 410/3 WNRC). Byrnes's memo of 30 November stated that only the Oder-Neisse lands should be considered outside of Germany's borders (Patterson to Byrnes, 10 Dec. 1945, *FRUS: 1945*, III, 917; Patterson to Acheson, 22 Dec. 1945, AG 091 Ger, NA; Acheson to Patterson, 12 Jan. 1946, *FRUS: 1945*, III, 923).

58. Manuel Gottlieb, *The German Peace Settlement and the Berlin Crisis* (New York, 1960), 97, 105. As late as 21 March 1946 Clay told the War Dept. there was no obstacle to reparations to USSR if they reciprocated (Smith, *Papers*, 182).

59. "This . . . appears to have more future political signficance than any other development up to this time" (Patterson to Byrnes, 23 Feb. 1946, file labeled P & P 091, OPD, NA). A Byrnes-Bidault exchange in March seemed to show that an agreement was possible on *service communs* (Byrnes to Bidault, 1 Feb. 1946; Bidault to Byrnes, 12 Mar. 1946, *FRUS: 1946*, V, 496–98, 512–13). "The French representatives will be informed . . . our attitude on economic assistance will be influenced by the French position on central agencies . . . to impress upon the French authorities the grave concern . . . in the establishment of central agencies. . . .The French request for additional grain for their zone in Germany and for more coal for France . . . were intimately linked with the problem of central German agencies" (H. Freeman Mathews to Petersen, 17 Apr. 1946, CAD 014, NA).

60. In October 1945 the War Dept. suggested "one or two plants of moderate size" to Russia, until "the resolution of outstanding issues" (Chronology, 20 Oct. 1945, KCRC).

61. James Martin, *All Honorable Men* (Boston, 1950), 181. Clay had recently suggested stopping the flow of wheat to France if she continued opposing central agencies (Clay to Anderson, secretary of agriculture, and Byrnes, 11 Apr. 1946, *FRUS: 1946*, V, 540; Murphy to Byrnes, 10 Apr. 1946, ibid., 538). Clay in an 8 April cable shows dismay at the Soviet position (Smith, *Papers*, 186).

62. Murphy to Byrnes, 2 May 1946, *FRUS: 1946*, V, 545–47; Clay Cable to AGWAR, 3 May 1946, OMGUS Chronologies, WNRC. Murphy told Byrnes a ban was possible because of the failure to agree to central agencies.

63. Gimbel, *American*, 60–61. Clay, asked about the Gimbel thesis, replied that much time had passed and that motivations had become obscure, but that the French were making things

difficult. "However, we did have access to the French Zone and thus knew what the French were doing, whereas without free access to the Soviet Zone, we did not know the extent of their dismantling except that it was on a large scale. Thus our direct motivation was the unilateral action being taken by the Soviet occupation authorities" (Clay letter to author, Jan. 1971). He wrote in 1950: "Perhaps without the French veto we could have created central administrative agencies for Germany as a whole within the first six months. . . . Six months after Potsdam the Soviet expansion program was under way. . . . agreement in Germany was no longer possible" (Clay, 42–43; Hill, 126–27).

64. Reparations could be suspended again if there was no substantial progress. This Acheson explained in detail, ignoring French obstructionism and assuming they would agree (Acheson [Hilldring] to Byrnes, 9 May 1946, 549–55). His adviser, Kennan, urged that the U.S. propose the immediate unification of Germany; the Russians would probably refuse, but this would end their claim that the U.S. was opposed to unification (Kennan to [Murphy], 10 May 1946, 555–56; Murphy to Byrnes, 25 May 1946, 559–61). He told the ACC that Soviet opposition to the investigation of war industries was blocking the way. It was important to know what was left in order to decide on reparations, but the Russians refused (24 July 1946, 581–83). Byrnes made a similar complaint to the French (Byrnes to Bonnet, 24 July 1946, *FRUS: 1946,* V).

65. Gottlieb blamed the Russian poverty on the influx of refugees, yet that was the result of another Russian decision; their Polish policy complicated their German Policy, and the poverty of their zone might easily be explained as the failure of Soviet economic policies (124–29, 135). Since U.S. economic policy had also failed, part of the Cold War resulted from the economic foolishness of both as victors.

66. Yet Clay resisted mounting pressures to take reparations out of increased production; "This ignores the real danger which Germany would still present, if restored to full industrial strength." Then Clay proved the opposite; "it will take three to five years to bring German industry to the level now agreed" (Clay to AGWAR, 26 May 1946, Cable 091, OMGUS, NA; also in Pollock Papers, Michigan Historical Society, Ann Arbor, Mich.). Clay's position quickly found its way into a Patterson letter to Byrnes: "there exists in the Ruhr-Rhineland an industrial concentration which would constitute a great threat in the hands of an enemy of the U.S.," though "any settlement of the Saar problem which you consider appropriate would be acceptable to the War Department" (Patterson to Byrnes, 11 June 1946, OPD 091, NA).

67. Yet Molotov's tougher policy recurred: programs for security against Germany were inadequate; Russia must have its ten billion dollars (OMGUS Chronologies, Jan. to Dec. 1946, 12, WNRC). Byrnes proposed treaty guarantees to appease France. "Washington's primary aim at Paris had been to use the Byrnes 25-year treaty proposal as a wedge to open serious negotiations with France on the issues that had brought a stalemate to Potsdam" (Gimbel, *American,* 73).

68. "We cannot see that these Allied bureaus would serve any purpose not already served by quadripartite committees except to extend further the tentacles of Allied Control, thus postponing any real return of self-responsibility to the Germans" (Clay to WARCAD, 18 July 1946, CAD 014 Ger, NA: Murphy to Byrnes, 11 Aug. 1946, 590–92; 29 Aug. 1946, 595–96). France's Georges Bidault admitted he was taking the Saar in order to win an election (Memo, 24 Sept. 1946, *FRUS: 1946,* V, 607–9). Forrestal and Clay disagreed on whether Russia wanted war; Clay thought not. "His theory is that we should be firm with Russia but should be very polite at the same time." He had quietly stopped the Russians from kidnapping Germans from the U.S. trains. Forrestal thought Clay was close to blowing up, and should be ordered to take a vacation (16 July 1946; Millis, 181). A report in August made it clear that OMGUS, if not Clay, had already come to regard Russia as the enemy. "Incidents, almost daily in occurrence, at first not published, later found their way around the Zone by word of mouth, usually exaggerated in the telling" (Colonel Balke to Chief CAD, 20 Aug. 1946, CAD 014

Ger, NA). Murphy agreed with the reparations ban as a way to get the Russians to live up to Potsdam; one might get them to permit more political freedoms in their zone (Murphy to Byrnes, 16 Oct. 1946, *FRUS: 1946*, V, 623).

69. Misapprehension about Soviet aggression in Greece led to a tougher U.S. policy in Germany, but "the Soviet government took no direct action with respect to the uprising in Greece." Stalin supported only revolutions which he could keep under control (Milovan Djilas, *Conversations with Stalin* [New York, 1963], 127). Kennan was critical of the Truman Doctrine (333).

70. De Conde, in Graebner, 251. Adam Ulam describes Molotov as uncharacteristically conciliatory, but lacking in concrete proposals, except on the ten billion dollar reparations and four-power control of the Ruhr. Yet possibly the hint was for a neutral united Germany. No consistent policy can be seen (*Expansion and Co-existence* [New York, 1968]; see also Ernst Deuerlein, *Die Einheit Deutschlands, 1941–49* [Frankfurt, 1957], 120–22). "The Soviet leaders felt confident that if all political power were centered in one place, preferably Berlin in the Soviet Zone, they could get control of Germany by getting control of that central power" (John Foster Dulles, *War or Peace* [New York, 1957], 103). Clay's reaction is available in Smith, *Papers*, 328–31.

71. The U.S. and U.K. agreed at Moscow to make the Saar into an autonomous area having economic and financial ties with France, and to more Ruhr coal to France. The U.S. agreed on an international control of the Ruhr (Dulles, 104). Dulles said the primary purpose of the U.S. delegation was to dispel the notion that the U.S. was committed to a program of building up a strong Germany at the expense of French recovery.

72. The Russians had done an immense amount of harm, "but have not gotten any corresponding gain because they cannot set up the plants in Soviet territory and make them work. Apparently the railroad sidings between Berlin and Moscow are filled with cars containing the scattered and rusting parts of German plants." For that reason the Soviets were not really eager to get more plants from the West (Dulles to Vandenberg, 22 Mar. 1947, 29 Mar. 1947, Council of Foreign Ministers, Dulles Papers, Princeton Library; Joseph Jones, *The Fifteen Weeks* [New York, 1955], 216).

73. Clay was opposed to Dulles's plan to set up an independent and neutral Ruhr (Interview Clay, 12 Mar. 1965, Princeton University Oral History Project; Jones, 228).

74. Clay played an active role, getting respected Republicans, Herbert Hoover, Christian Herter, industrial leaders, the *Wall Street Journal*, and columnists like the Alsops to support the policy of German recovery (Schwarz, 87, 99; Jones, 219).

75. Max Beloff traced the idea to early 1946, to W. W. Rostow, in the State Dept.'s German-Austrian Economic Division (*The United States and the Unity of Europe* [London, 1957], 10). Jones and Schwarz gave much credit to Walter Lippman (Jones, 228; Schwarz, 71, 78; Cabell Phillips, *The Truman Presidency* [New York, 1966], 177).

76. "The Marshall Plan's great contribution . . . was its focus on general European recovery rather than on Germany *per se*. It made it possible for Washington to push for German rehabilitation by arguing for Europe and without having to defend each policy change so necessary to German recovery in terms of what was being done or had been done in Germany proper" (Gimbel, *American*, 151). For an incisive analysis of the relationship between the army's need to create a viable German economy and the French demands for "silent reparations," see John Gimbel, *The Origins of the Marshall Plan* (Stanford: Stanford University Press, 1976), a profound revision of the accepted explanations.

77. Harry S Truman, *Memoirs: Years of Trial and Hope*, II (Garden City, 1956), 121; Kennan, 343; Beloff, 21; Djilas, 127.

78. Kennan wrote of "feeling like one who has inadvertently loosened a larger boulder from the top of a cliff and now helplessly witnesses its path of destruction in the valley below, shudder-

ing and wincing at each successive glimpse of disaster.'' He deplored not having made clear he was not talking about military containment of a military threat but about political containment of a political threat; he was not thinking of a worldwide system, but of selected areas, and particularly of Europe. He had never believed that Russia would invade anywhere or that there was any need of a war with Russia (375–78, 385).

79. Bevin reported three causes for failure to agree with Russia: reparations, reparations from production, and reparations by Sovietizing German businesses (Deuerlein, *Einheit,* 127–28; Djilas, 153).

80. Yet Durbrow opposed reparations from production, because this would orient German industry to the east (Durbrow to Byrnes, 6 Sept. 1946, 602; Murphy to Mathews, 14 Oct. 1946, *FRUS: 1946,* V, 622–23; Clay to Echols, 14 Oct. 1946, in Smith, *Papers,* 169).

81. Gottlieb noted it would offer reparations of less value than the Soviets would extract in six months from their zone (157).

82. Humphrey calculated that German industry, if given 2.5 billion dollars worth of raw materials, could produce 7.5 billion in reparations over a period of ten years, an idea reminiscent of Keynes's idea in 1919 and the Dawes Plan of 1924 (OMGUS, 177–313, Council of Foreign Ministers' File, 2 Nov. 1946). Clay wrote Byrnes in November 1946 that it would need an increased level of industry and unification (Smith, *Papers,* 281–82).

83. Clay, who objected to the delay, was reportedly on the verge of resigning. He got the promise (not kept) of enough food to raise the daily German calorie ration to 1,800 (Gimbel, *American,* 153–54). Marshall appreciated Clay's problem, but he had to deal with Russia and this minor matter could make major problems more difficult (Millis, 287).

84. Clay to Petersen, 6 July 1947, AD 014, NA. Steel production was one-fifth and exports were one-sixth the legal level (Backer, 82). Clay's bitter anger at letting the French sabotage recovery is evident in his cable to Petersen, 16 July 1947 (Smith, *Papers,* 383–8).

85. Gimble, *American,* 177–85. Marshall pleaded for reparations for moral reasons, and included Clay's claim that the factories were surplus anyway, because raw materials were in short supply. Clay defended this analysis to Congress and added that ''reduction of Germany's industrial output was also a security measure'' (Nicholas Balabkins, *Germany under Direct Controls* [New Brunswick, 1946], 26–27).

86. ''The real fire in the arguments comes from the large shipments to Russia so far . . . to build up Russian military potential. . . . My own thought is, and I am sure you are in agreement, that no shipments should go to either Russia or her satellite countries'' (Draper to Clay, 22 Dec. 1947, ASA Germany 300, NA). An example of Clay's argument is available in Smith, *Papers,* 464–69. On 13 January 1948 he opposed Marshall's plan to stop deliveries to the USSR (Smith, *Papers,* 542).

87. The six-week study in April and May recommended reducing the list by 300 plants. Clay and Draper objected; all were ''surplus.'' They feared the French Chamber of Deputies might reject the London Agreements (Millis, 379). Few plants had been removed until the spring of 1947. During the first half of 1948 none was removed, but in the second half 157 plants were dismantled (Balabkins, 141). Freda Utley was told that the Humphrey Committee had led to an evasive MG speed-up (*The High Cost of Vengeance* [Chicago, 1949], 59, 151). At the height of the Berlin blockade, the Ruhr minister-president asked about the workers' concern for their jobs in the dismantled plants. Clay responded: ''It's none of their business. If one wants any more help from America, one should stop talking about the dismantlings'' (Schwarz, 141; OMGUS Chronologies, 19 Oct. 1948, 54, WNRC).

88. Murphy described the nonstop debate between Clay and Harriman about how much ECA assistance Germany should get. Harriman worked out a compromise. Aid to Germany would be in two parts: that required to maintain a subsistence level would go directly to Clay; the remainder would go via the ECA (Beloff, 29). Harriman thought Clay exaggerated the useful-

ness of Bizonia. Although Murphy and Clay knew they risked being labeled pro-Nazi, they pushed for more aid, though only a fraction of what was allocated even to Italy. The other nations got aid as grants, but the Germans got it as loans (Murphy, 310; Hale, 88; Smith, *Papers*, 653–54). His dismay with ECA is evident in his 12 Jan. 1949 memo to Harriman, Smith, *Papers*, 982–88).

89. Clay to CS CAD, 6 Mar. 1949, CAD 014, NA. Balfour estimated 5 percent of capacity was dismantled, but in January 1949 Clay still saw no conflict between recovery and the dismantlings (Smith, *Papers*, 979).

90. Balabkins counted some 667 plants dismantled in the west with a value in 1938 of 708 million marks (142). Bremen Senator G. W. Harmssen estimated the 1938 value at 1.3 to 1.4 billion marks, a 1951 value of 2.5 billion marks or 625 million dollars. Mark to dollar calculations are usually close to the long-prevalent 4 marks to a dollar (*Am Abend der Demontage* [Bremen, 1951], 176). Yale professor Henry Wallich put the 1951 value at 2 billion marks (*Mainsprings of the German Revival* [New Haven, 1955], 359). Price and Schorske, of the OMGUS economics staff, doubted the value of dismantlings. "It is now recognized that, in some cases at least, the cost of transporting a plant from the German border to its new location, plus the cost of installation at the new site, would exceed its value." This estimate does not include the cost of dismantling the plant (Hoyt Price and Carl Schorske, *The Problem of Germany* [New York, 1947], 55); see also Ernst Deuerlein, *Handbuch der deutsche Geschichte* (Konstanz, 1964), 85.

91. Balabkins estimated between 12 and 30 billion marks (142). Yet Lewis Brown concluded: "Many of the patents . . . are so written . . . as to make it impossible for anyone who did not know what was intended to make use of them" (*A Report on Germany* [New York, 1947], 113).

92. House Foreign Affairs Committee, 82nd Congress, 2nd session, "Report of Special Study Mission to Germany," 8 Feb. 1952, I, 24; Wallich, 357. But Javits emphasized that ECA aid provided the vital foreign exchange so difficult for a developing economy to acquire.

93. Schwarz, 127, based on *New York Times*, 1 Aug. 1947 and 12 Aug. 1947. Francophiles like Lippmann and Welles thought he represented the interests of Germany to the detriment of France. Dulles, who was pro-French, thought "the only trouble was that he was too strong and able a person to be in charge of a limited theater like Germany; his great abilities would inevitably lead to the overemphasis of any area for which he was primarily responsible" (133).

94. Teleconference Petersen and Clay, 24 July 1947, Smith, *Papers*, 387.

95. Clay cable for Eisenhower, 28 July 1947, ibid., 390.

96. Teleconference Royall, Draper, and Clay, 8 Aug. 1947, ibid., 396.

97. Teleconference Jack Bennett and Clay, 24 Oct. 1947, ibid., 445; Clay cable for Draper, 30 Oct. 1947, ibid., 459. When urged to clear anticommunist statements, he responded that the Soviets were violently criticizing American principles in Germany.

98. Clay cable for Draper, 3 Nov. 1947, ibid., 476–77; see Clay letter for Noce, 5 Nov. 1947, ibid., 483, for his suggestions.

99. Clay was confident he could have gotten an armed convoy through. Murphy, disappointed that the U.S. did not force its way in, noted that no one had mentioned the use of the atomic bomb (Millis, 454–59). Smith gives credit to Clay for the airlift as well as the resistance (Smith, *Papers*, xxviii). Clay's blockade cables are in the *Papers*.

100. Clay to Draper, 15 June 1948, Smith, *Papers*, 678.

101. Teleconference Draper and Clay, 16 June 1948, ibid., 682, 684. Ambassador Caffrey cabled from Paris that the Gaullist Koenig was battling with his Paris government (ibid., 693).

102. Ibid., 795–96. "Visitors do not help as a rule. They simply consume the time of those doing the job."

103. Clay cable for George Lincoln, 18 Nov. 1948, ibid., 926.

104. Clay cable for Draper, 23 Jan. 1949, ibid., 990–92.

105. Teleconference Draper and Clay, 29 Jan. 1949, ibid., 994. Murphy replaced Kennan on the committee in March.

106. Teleconference 29 Jan. 1949, ibid., 996–98.

107. Teleconference 17 Mar. 1949, ibid., 1047.

108. Clay cable personal for Voorhees, 21 Mar. 1949, ibid., 1058; Clay cable personal for Voorhees, 25 Mar. 1949, ibid., 1061; Clay for Voorhees, 29 Mar. 1949, ibid., 1063.

109. Teleconference Voorhees, Draper, Litchfield, Clay, Apr. 1949, ibid., 1073–74. Clay regretted the hint of remilitarization.

110. Teleconference, Voorhees, G. Dorr, Clay, 5 May 1949, ibid., 1149.

111. In the summer of 1949, Vishinsky offered a "State Council based on the economic organizations in zones." Acheson suggested instead a political organization, an immediate end to military government, and free elections to a substantially independent German government (Deuerlein, Einheit, 130–32). Kennan's solution was for both sides to withdraw from Germany to fringe areas, leaving the Germans to find some sort of unity (445). There was a wavering in 1951–52 from the German policy emphasizing sovereignty and rearmament, with talk of a possible bargain with the Russians offering them a reunited but neutral Germany as the alternative. But the overall U.S. strategy congealed instead into NSC 68; the solution was the hydrogen bomb and balancing the Soviet potential for conventional war (Beloff, 54; S. Brown, 51–52).

112. A division chief would lay on his desk a great stack of neatly typed papers and accompany it with a brief synopsis. Clay would sign the papers. "What he had signed sometimes went far beyond what had been explained to him" (Clark, 46–47). The army officer had a special disadvantage vis-à-vis civilians; an army specialist knowledgeable outside his field was a rarity.

113. "The quirks of Clay's character caused him to keep in office men who in one way or the other were continually thwarting the policy he was supposed to be enforcing" (ibid., 56).

114. Dale Clark, "Conflicts Over Planning at Staff Headquarters," in Carl J. Friedrich, American Experiences in Military Government in World War II (New York, 1948), 212.

115. "Bernstein, while outstanding in his specialized field and of great value in investigating assets of leading firms and in decartelization, does not in my view have the broad financial background essential to the reestablishment of governmental and commercial finances in Germany" (Clay to Hilldring, 9 June 1945, Clay Cables, NA). "He claims that Treasury Department might not agree to this use of personnel. It is my understanding that all personnel sent to this theater are to be assigned where their services will be most needed. . . . Bernstein has been excellent in the investigating phases of his work. Our progress in finance and banking has been much less than in other fields and I believe that Dodge will do much to improve this situation" (Clay to WARCAD, 8 Sept. 1945, NA).

116. Bernstein resigned in November and tried to use the Kilgore Committee to reverse Clay's "softness" on Nazis; aide Russell Nixon then resigned and blasted Clay's "rightists" (Senate Hearings on Elimination of German Resources of War, June 1945 to Feb. 1946). They were later labeled communist, and Bernstein was accused of being a strong supporter of "procommunist causes." Many were German émigrés and Jewish, and were accused of warping policy implementation from personal hatreds. The men who came after 1945 were often labeled facists, anti-Semites, and Nazi dupes.

117. Clark, 76. Dorn described a visit with him as being with a "windstorm." He "had good information on how things were done . . . seems to have his hand in most things . . . clear eye for essentials . . . a hard-fisted devil, who implied that what gets by the President makes policy" (Dorn, "Notes," 19).

118. Clay and Murphy agreed in their memoirs that they had no serious disagreements. Murphy

was from Milwaukee, and of German ancestry on his mother's side. He had served in Munich in the 1920s and had met Hitler, but he had doubted Hitler's chances. Clay wrote 29 June 1945: "Bob Murphy is a cooperative person, and as long as he is here there will be no difficulty" (Smith, *Papers,* 43).

119. Clark, 75; Zink, *U.S.,* 74; Hale, 91. Since he had held only subordinate posts and had little experience in directing a sizable staff, he permitted specialists to go for months without substantial work, while others had so much to do they could not give adequate attention to their assignments (Balfour, 103; Clark, 75).

120. Interview Bowie; Clark, 57. Draper supported capitalism, and possibly for that reason he usually worked, rather unsuccessfully, to revive German industry; he would otherwise have failed as director (Ratchford and Ross. 159). Calvin Hoover, MG economist, agreed on Draper's ability; a three-minute briefing while walking toward the conference room would leave him prepared (*Memoirs of Capitalism, Communism, and Nazism* [Durham, N.C., 1965], 239). When Draper was being considered for promotion to assistant secretary of war, Clay wrote: "I have no one repeat no one approaching him in ability" (Smith, *Papers,* 385). Even the Russian negotiator Gregory Klimow was impressed by the small, dark general (*The Terror Machine* [London, 1953]).

121. Dorn, "Notes," 12, 25. Adcock was a West Point classmate of Clay (Smith, *Papers,* 40).

122. Clark, 76.

123. Parkman has been characterized as "an honest, amiable attorney, whose knowledge of politics was circumscribed by the Boston city limits" (Clark, 76).

124. Friedrich was much impressed by Clay's Saturday morning staff sessions, where he "tongue-lashed his dumb advisers" (Interview Carl Friedrich).

125. In 1944 he proposed a fairly positive program for German democratization (James Pollock, *What Shall Be Done With Germany* [Northfield,iMinn., 1944]). He was later criticized for giving too much self-government too soon (Hill, 108).

126. Interview Bowie. Clark thought him unaware "that the issuance of a directive and the execution of it were not necessarily the same thing" (74).

127. Clark, 74. He later showed a spectacular, and controversial, ability as chancellor of the University of Pittsburgh.

128. Ibid., 98; Meader Report, 18.

129. Clark, in Friedrich, 212–18. The Country Unit was set up in early 1944, with about 150 British and American officers (Zink, *American,* 42).

130. Friedrich, 213, 219, 234. The deal, formally worked out in the Treaty of Bushy Park, gave G-5 a veto power over USGCC. On 1 October 1945, USGCC was renamed Office of Military Government, U.S. (OMGUS). Friedrich also observed the extreme difficulty of transferring leadership from tactical leaders to administrators.

131. Frankfurt considered itself the source of policy (Chronology, 13 Oct. 1945, KCRC: Balfour, 103).

132. Oliver Fredrickson, *The American Military Occupation of Germany* (Darmstadt, 1953), 31. Train and motor transport and telephone service through the Russian zone was poor (Hill, 106; Balke Report to Chief CAD, 20 Aug. 1946, CAD 014 Ger, NA; Gen. Morris Edwards, *A Case Study of Military Government in Germany During and After World War II* [Ph.D. diss., Georgetown University, 1957], 84).

133. Ziemke, 313.

134. Zink, *American,* 48–52; his evaluation came partially from his experience as an inspector.

135. "Education and religious affairs... never received anything like fair recognition in the organization setup.... It was difficult to know where they might be located at any given moment." The education section, with sixty-five officers by mid-1946, represented one officer to reeducate every 270,000 Germans (ibid., 43, 55).

136. Although MG detachments had supposedly spent much time studying the places they were to occupy, confusion counteracted their efforts, leaving chaos (Zink, *U.S.*, 174; Zink *American*, 74–76, 97). "The American commandant of SHAEF at Frankfurt decided that it would be very nice if he could have a little feudal state to play with. . . . it literally paralyzed the local American MG detachments while it lasted."

137. "Our entire military system, which supposedly is so grounded in strict observance of orders from the top, is actually operated under a more or less uncoordinated arrangement that permits each Army commander in foreign theaters substantial autonomy" (Zink, *American*, 200).

138. "This difficulty arose . . . largely from the failure of top policy makers in Washington . . . putting informed, aggressive men of broad governmental experience in positions where they could have full staff supervision of, and staff responsibility for, MG" (George Benson and Mark Howe, in Friedrich, 52; Zink, *U.S.*, 50).

139. Chronology, 1 Oct. 1945, KCRC. The idea horrified State which admitted its lack of preparation (Zink, *American*, 75; Clay to WARCAD, Sept. 1945, Clay Cables, NA). Civilians were to replace demobilized officers to ease the transfer to full civilian status by 1 July.

140. Zink, *U.S.*, 124; Benson and Howe, in Friedrich, 52.

141. The army followed its usual procurement policy: get two men for each job to be sure to have one (Ratchford and Ross, 20–21, 55).

142. "The man who did volunteer to stay on . . . was generally among the least competent; he was the man who feared he could not get as good a job at home, or the man who wanted to stay because he could live cheaply and make money on the black market" (Hill, 121).

143. Chronology, 15 Dec. 1945, KCRC; Clay, 66; see also Howley, 256; Gimbel, 48; Chronology, 15 Sept. 1945, KCRC; Meader Report, 15–16; Ratchford and Ross, 23. Ratchford linked this problem to "the old army method" of pushing the least qualified into any vacancy, so that a division chief had to spend much of his time getting rid of incompetents pushed off on him by someone else. Alfred Grosser noted that the French zone was particularly overburdened with high-living officials and their families (*Germany in Our Time* [New York, 1971], 48–49).

144. Interview Clay, 30 Dec. 1968. He thought State Department and British intelligence was better (Meader Report, 18). G-2 had "pulled strings" in Washington (Col. Francis P. Miller, Senate Investigation of the National Defense Program, Chairman Mead, Meader Chief Counsel, 14 Aug. 1946, 25814). "Clay knew how much Communist influence . . . was precious little, but the CIC magnified it to justify the job" (Interview Roger Baldwin, Baldwin Project, 559, Columbia Oral History).

145. Miller testimony to Mead's Senate Investigating Committee, 25821; Clay testimony, 18 Nov. 1946, 25877. The Meader Report assumed that German reports would be designed to trick unsuspecting Americans, but in most matters German-source intelligence was the best available.

146. Zink, *American*, 91.

147. "Germany was deluged with intelligence teams and commissions of inquiry of every possible description . . . busy MG officers who had to receive some intelligence team almost every day grew less responsible to them and their innumerable, and often conflicting reports" (Robert Neumann, "Political Intelligence," in Friedrich, 82. Neumann served as an intelligence officer. "Several hundred men spent months producing reams of material of very limited usefulness" (Ratchford and Ross, 35–36).

148. "The series of pools in which military government officers were forced to stagnate for over a year was as vicious a system as can be conceived. There is hardly a man who has passed through it who has not given concrete evidence of demoralization in the most exact sense of the word. The long, sterile inactivity and the theoretical *half fish half fowl* military training killed all enthusiasm in officers and men, and many became subject to a complete moral breakdown." The trouble was most serious in the lower level detachments (Ziemke, 311).

149. James Warburg, *Germany—Bridge or Battleground* (New York, 1947), 82–83. Robert Engler's study agreed; they were competent men, but once physical problems were largely met, they were not trained for the rest; they lacked the necessary political skills ("The Individual Soldier and the Occupation," *Annals of the American Academy*, Jan. 1950, 80).

150. Zink, *American*, 45; Balke Report, 20 Aug. 1946, CAD 014 Ger, NA; Ernst Anspach, "The Nemesis of Creativity," *Social Research*, Dec. 1952, 416–17.

151. Inspector Carl Taeusch reported that his talks with the college-educated junior officers made one "wonder how effective their broader education in the U.S. had been before they entered the army." It was enough to make anyone wonder about "the best educational system in the World" ("Report on Trip through Southern Germany," 12–22 Oct. 1945, CAD Ger, Record Group 165, NA); see also Edwards, 94; USFET, *Occupation* (Frankfurt, 1946), 5–26. Correspondents Bud Hutton and Andy Rooney observed how wartime censorship added to the hate, for example by not reporting that there were occasions when Americans killed prisoners, or that frequently a German medic saved an American soldier on the battlefield (*Conqueror's Peace* [New York, 1947], 88).

152. Grosser, 76. Lewis Brown assumes that wartime agencies had closed out such men so they had flowed to MG (118–19). He thought businessmen better than New Deal bureaucrats. Clay managed to retain a few key officials only by personally promising them two years of work, a guarantee he had no authority to make (Murphy, 281).

153. "So they pulled every string known in Army circles to get assigned to Germany. . . . they concentrated on jockeying for personal power, knocking the efforts of specialist MG officers down, and making themselves generally 'difficult.' . . . The specialists on German problems . . . were so buried under the deluge of rank above them, they found it increasingly difficult . . . to get anything accomplished . . . if possible got out entirely" (Zink, *American*, 28–30).

154. Much deserved to be destroyed, but much that was precious and innocent had been destroyed with the rest. "In the presence of this tragedy even the victors had a certain duty of self-effacement and humility" (Kennan, 452); see also Alfred Grosser, *The Colossus Again* (New York, 1955).

155. "Those conditions created an atmosphere so unreal, so nightmarish, so demoralizing that efficient work was almost impossible" (Ratchford and Ross, 3); see also Zink, *U.S.*, 76.

156. Ratchford and Ross, 10, 17, 18. These men knew Germany well, having cajoled their way onto the payroll to visit relatives and to trade in the black market; "they were rarely at their desks." Ratchford accepted the *New York Times* estimate of between 250 and 400 million dollars by mid-1947. "No one could escape the completely disillusioning conditions which prevailed."

157. Zink, *U.S.*, 138–40; Meader Report, 4.

158. Senate Investigation of the National Defense Program, 25821. U.S. enlisted men's hatred of the army was related to violence toward the conquered. Brutal treatment accorded GIs surprised Germans (Robert Engler, "The Individual Soldier and the Occupation," *Annals of the American Academy*, Jan. 1950, 77–86). They were particularly puzzled by the interminable series of riots between black and white troops. For French reaction, see Hutton and Rooney, 12, 31.

159. Hutton and Rooney, 32. Looting became so serious that information officer Arthur Settel described the American troops as "the khaki-clad mob" (*This is Germany* [New York, 1950], 7, 12).

160. Zink, *U.S.*, 136. The wholesale looting was encouraged by the Morgenthau atmosphere; "at the decisive moment guidance from the top was either missing or in the wrong direction" (Friedmann, 20, 43); see also Hoover, 227.

161. Eisenhower to Berlin Press Club, 30 Aug. 1945, Pollock Papers; Hill, 112; Raymond

Daniell, *New York Times*, 16 Dec. 1945; see also Senate Investigation of the National Defense Program, 25839. "The average soldier learns only two things from his occupational experience. He learns how to drink and how to pick up a Fräulein" (Hill, 117).

162. Fredericksen, 50–52. By April 1947 the policy was to use only regular army troops, but this policy ended with the 1950 troop buildup. The 1946 creation of a "constabulary" was a device to improve discipline. They were given flashy uniforms with bright scarves "to re-instill pride;" their commander, Gen. Ernest Harmon, was colorful enough to be compared with Patton. Although credited with improving discipline, they had little effect on the black market, their raids being clumsy and rarely based on good intelligence (James Snyder, *The Establishment and Operation of the U.S. Constabulary* [Frankfurt, 1947], 70). Congressman Taber was threatening to cut off funds unless the level of personnel improved (Smith, *Papers*, 663).

163. McCloy "was not very articulate and his speaker style was not particularly impressive [nor was his physical appearance]. But he possessed sound judgment, worked effectively with his staff, and usually moved ahead only after careful preparation." His staff did not see much of him, for he devoted much of his time to the Germans. He supposedly had a strong impact because of his constructive ideas, and because "he could, with his conservative background in law, banking and business in the U.S. 'speak their language.'" Some of McCloy's staff thought Adenauer frequently outfoxed him, even using tears to break down his resistance (Zink, *U.S.*, 77–78).

164. Beloff, 59. Land Commissioner Gross, formerly with the New York subways, who "knew nothing of Württemberg," created a severe crisis with McCloy. Eisenhower happened through on a tour and saved Maier from Gross by saying to Maier, as Maier remembered his English: "You are my baby. You made a very good job" (Reinhold Maier, *Erinnerungen 1945-55* [Tübingen, 1966], 124–249).

165. Military governors became high commissioners, liaison and security officers became Kreis resident officers (Guy Lee, *Documents on Field Organization of HICOG* [Bonn, 1952], 1–14).

166. *Nürnberger Nachrichten*, 7 Sept. 1949. Dorn also had a high estimate of Murphy's successor, Riddleberger, saying he was "quick, well-informed, and on the whole one of the ablest men on German affairs I know" ("Notes," 22). McCloy's assistant high commissioner, Benjamin Buttenweiser, was severely criticized on his retirement in December 1951 for having learned so little. On the same day, the *New York Times* quoted Buttenweiser criticizing German "arrogant nationalism and anti-Semitism" (*Donau Zeitung*, 1 Dec. 1951; *New York Times*, 1 Dec. 1951).

167. In the first year there were 169 such meetings, of which only 27 were of main committees (Elmer Plischke, *Allied High Commission, Relations with the West German Government* [Bonn, 1953], 6; HICOG, *The Kreis Resident Officer* [Godesberg, 1950]).

168. The new men were young Foreign Service officers on first assignment or young men out of the universities (Zink, *U.S.*, 50, 63). Some army people resented the existence of a civil agency. HICOG made itself even less popular with the army by passing on the increasing German complaints about the officers' luxurious living, for which Germans were paying. An officer characterized the HICOG staff as "carpet baggers." An army wife who said, "We do not associate with civilians," reflected the relatively slight personal contacts between civilian and military representatives (ibid., 125–30).

169. Cheseldine, "Think Piece 13," 22 May 1950, Pollock Papers.

170. To clear up the confusion in the Bureau of German Affairs, everyone should be sent to Germany, but should avoid headquarters and "the Alice in Wonderland virus infection which constantly rages in Frankfurt" (ibid., 5).

171. McCloy's assistant, Colonel Textor, was quoted by Cheseldine: "No matter how active his people are in the Länder, he finds it almost impossible to get the HICOG Division Chiefs to take time to prepare policy guidance or directives for the Land Offices" (Cheseldine to McCloy, 1 June 1950, Pollock Papers).

172. Pollock to McCloy, 14 Aug. 1950; Pollock, Report to McCloy, 12 Sept. 1950, 11, Pollock Papers.
173. Interview Baldwin, Baldwin Project, 598.
174. As a very junior member of that force, I was certainly unqualified for the responsibility given me, but my conduct, like that of many others, was much more naive than vicious.

3 Retreat From Economic Controls

America ended the war with the hope not only of having laid down its heavy burden, but also of so altering German society that no more wars would be possible. These great expectations had to take second place to the most difficult problem, that of simply keeping the Germans alive. It was a task barely accomplished and in constant conflict with other policy objectives. The victors, with a hail of bombs, had so ruined the country that even governing it was all but impossible. The idea of keeping Germany weak by some form of partition proved a second massive barrier to policy implementation. JCS 1067 had ordered that nothing be done to revive the German economy, except as necessary to prevent "disease and unrest," but MG had to prevent mass starvation. Potsdam promised only a minimum standard of living, but even this goal proved possible only with mass shipments of U.S. food at heavy expense, and with a massive infusion of U.S. capital to stimulate the economic recovery necessary to pay for more food. Reality eventually forced the U.S. retreat in economic policy which enabled the "miracle" of German recovery.

There is no doubt that Germany's economic problems at the end of the war were enormous. The closest thing to total war Germany experienced under Hitler was the collapse in 1945. The war had destroyed one-third of German wealth, nearly one-fifth of all productive buildings and machines, two-fifths of the transportation facilities, and over one-seventh of all houses. In U.S. zone cities only 60.5 percent of the homes were usable, of which 4.5 percent were taken for the use of troops and displaced persons (DPs). Of the 870,000 houses standing in the cities, 320,000 needed vital repairs. The damage to the population base was even more lasting. Some 3,500,000 German soldiers were either dead or missing; 6,000,000 were either prisoners of war (PWs) or forced labor.[1] Some 500,000 civilians had been killed during the war; over 1,500,000 were disabled. Some 10,000,000 lost all they could not carry on their backs. All German wealth outside the country was confiscated. The impoverished country was divided into nine parts, giving each victor a zone and a piece of Berlin; the land east of the Oder-Neisse was taken by Poland; Russia took its piece of East Prussia and Königsberg; Bremen was chopped out of the English zone for an American port, and the Saar was sliced from the French zone for eventual annexation. Each zone of poverty was locked up tightly.

Despite the wartime hatred, which may be illustrated by FDR's casual suggestion that the Germans deserved soup lines, and despite the postwar fear of a revived German threat to peace, the occupation authorities very quickly accepted the responsibility of doing something about the horrible conditions they discovered. Anything approaching the genocide practiced by Hitler in eastern Europe was never considered. As evil as the Germans may have appeared to be, the occupation must keep them alive. Germans might need some punishment, but their physical needs would have to be met. Although occasional administrators might have been unaffected by the sight of suffering around them, most in authority were willing to help solve the most pressing problems insofar as regulations and circumstances permitted. What follows is a brief treatment of the policies OMGUS adopted to attempt to deal with the vast movements of people uprooted by the war, to restore food production and German industry, to reform the badly inflated currency and restore crippled foreign trade, and to provide housing for the homeless. American planners further hoped to reform the economy so that it would no longer contribute to the rise of authoritarian and aggressive governments.

Occupation Policy and the Population Upheaval

Germans made U.S. prisoners early in the war were often shipped to the United States, where they were apparently treated well. Those who surrendered to the U.S. troops in 1945 were in effect buying a lottery ticket. Some were immediately released. Many were given to some ally as forced labor. They could end up working with better rations than civilians, performing some demilitarization service, or they could end up under conditions like those of concentration camps. With millions captured very suddenly in the spring of 1945, it was understandable that the first camps would be in the open and food would be limited. Yet men were often held through the winter outside in the open or in flimsy tents, sleeping on the ground; starvation rations continued in some American camps as long as a year.[2]

At first the U.S. policy seems to have been to release PWs because they were a great burden. On 4 June SHAEF cited the urgent necessity to arrange for an early disposition of the great numbers of PWs in order to be relieved of their feeding and maintenance.[3] On 25 August a general announced that the United States had suspended discharge of PWs, as the equilibrium between "requirements," the need for their labor, and backlog had been reached.

Allied prisoners numbered nearly 5 million, of which the United States had a total of 1.6 million.

Some hundreds of thousands who had fled to the Americans to avoid being taken prisoner by the Russians were turned over in May to the Red Army in a gesture of friendship. Another grand U.S. gesture was the promise to turn over one million to the French. About one-third had been delivered when Clay in September discovered the French were not complying with the Geneva Convention.[4] General W. B. Smith showed Eisenhower photographs of emaciated PWs obviously suffering from malnutrition.[5] Clay told his staff he was quite concerned about the French PWs, who were being used as slave labor; the United States turned over none after 1 October. He cabled: "it savors quite a lot of the slave labor practices employed by Hitler."[6]

A year later, in response to prodding by the Länderrat, MG promised to release prisoners by July 1947, and asked France, Belgium, the Netherlands, and Luxembourg to release the PWs the United States had turned over to them.[7] The hottest dispute, which raged for years in Germany, was about the number of PWs and civilians seized, loaded on boxcars, and sent to Russia for forced labor. The estimated numbers range from 890,000, the Russian figure in March 1947, to 3.5 million assumed by Germans on the basis of 4 million estimated captured.[8] A MG report in 1948 stated: "Those who are returned by Russia from time to time are the most pitiable objects of starvation and suffering one could imagine."[9] The fate of these individuals, including the millions who disappeared after capture, is relevant to MG's power, not only because these men were unable to assist in feeding or rebuilding Germany, but because what happened to them proved to most Germans that slave labor and mass dying were crimes not only of the Germans, but also of the victors.

Further proof of the victors' inhumanity was the expulsion of almost all "Germans" from eastern Europe.[10] The most famous refugees were Sudeten Germans, some of whom had agitated in 1938 to be annexed to Germany with its full employment. The largest group came from territories "under Polish administration": East Prussia, Silesia, and eastern Pomerania. Clay informed his staff 1 August 1945 that ten million Germans expelled by the Poles and Czechs were expected to arrive in what remained of Germany; they were supposed to be expelled humanely. In fact, they were ordinarily permitted to take only what they could carry, and even these few possessions were often stolen along the way. The weak, the old, and the very young died by the hundreds of thousands. USFET estimated a death rate among refugees of nearly three million.[11]

Yet another population grew from the evil seed sown by Hitler when he brought people from all over Europe to work fields and factories in place of men taken into the German army. DP violence against Germans in 1945, at first half encouraged, immediately became MG's major security problem, and MG was soon anxious to be rid of them.[12] MG at first assumed that all of the

4,250,000 DPs found had been forcibly driven from their homelands. Some were not.[13] They were for years given relatively high rations, 2,000 calories daily, deleted from German food rations.[14] By 1 June 1946 there were some 368,210 DPs in the U.S. zone, who were living in various camps and in German homes cleared for them. Despite all efforts to reduce this number, it increased to nearly 500,000. Much of the increase came from Jews fleeing Poland and Russia toward Israel.

In 1945 a report told Truman: "We're treating the Jews as the Nazis did, except for the extermination."[15] Truman wrote Eisenhower 31 August: "We must intensify our efforts to get these people out of camps and into decent homes until they can be repatriated or evacuated. These houses should be requisitioned from the German civilian population." Eisenhower commanded that there "be no hesitation in requisitioning houses, grounds, or other facilities useful to DPs except as limited by essential considerations of a practical administration."[16] The DPs were not subject to the German police, although Clay thought as early as October that the DPs should obey German laws. USFET appealed to Hilldring for policy guidance about the 300 Jews coming in daily from Poland to Bavaria. The Delphic answer was: "The Army had *no* obligation to furnish safe haven to any person who was *not* the victim of Nazi persecution. But . . . the Army should not refuse to offer safe haven to persecutees simply because their persecution had been at the hands of other than Nazi oppressors." The army added them to DP camps, although Patterson and Byrnes opposed accepting Jewish refugees.[17]

Growing frustration with DPs was evident when USFET begged Truman not to announce that they would be permitted to immigrate to the United States when shipping was available, because "they would not voluntarily accept repatriation to their homeland."[18] More frustration is evident in the report that the food situation would be much better but for the DPs, who increased in numbers daily and added to the black market by selling their United Nations Relief and Rehabilitation food packages.[19] In April 1947, Clay offered them an extra food bonus if they would leave and warned that he could not feed them forever. Palestine and America eventually opened up for most to leave, and the rest were assimilated into the German population. As in most of its policies, MG had long since reversed itself to accept the German position.

Controls and Agricultural Production

Finding enough food to stay alive was the major problem faced by Germans under American rule for the first three years of the occupation.

Although MG was aware of the food shortages almost from VE Day, it was unable to remedy them until, faced with total disaster, it asked the American victors to feed the defeated. The lack of farm production was caused partly by the loss of farmland in East Germany, but also by the decline of land fertility, manpower, and farm machinery resulting from the war. It was also a consequence of OMGUS policy, which was based on the assumption that the food problem could be solved in isolation from MG's other actions, such as limiting industrial production, blocking raw materials, confiscating capital, and delaying currency reform. Warnings about impending catastrophe came to Truman in early June 1945.[20] Clay wrote McCloy that Germans should be hungry but they should not starve; he told his staff he was strongly opposed to the distribution of Allied foodstuffs to Germans until there had been complete exploitation of German agricultural resources.[21] MG would not even permit relatives to send food parcels.

In August the average German's daily ration was calculated at 1,100 calories, varying from 840 in the Ruhr to 1,300 in Hamburg. The death rate of children and old people in Berlin rose to fantastic heights; more than half the babies born in Berlin in August died. In the U. S. zone 30 percent of the children in their first year died.[22] Yet in October Clay again refused to permit a barter deal for Czech sugar, because the ACC required all sales in currency. He considered it unwise to bring up the food question until reports of German privations had convinced the American people that additional food should be given to Germans.[23] Yet Germans noted Americans threw food away and were bitter that leftovers from army kitchens were frequently forbidden to hungry children, and sometimes even burned in front of them. The rare German allowed to visit western Europe was amazed at the food available.

MG intelligence had been again faulty; it had much overestimated German agricultural capacity. The land had been tilled so long it depended heavily on fertilizers, but these had not been manufactured in quantity; OMGUS planned to reduce that production because nitrogen was basic for munitions as well as fertilizer.[24] Farmers were ordered to plow up pasture land, but were able to get legally only 1 or 2 percent of their requirements for farm machinery, spare parts, and fertilizer. To have met the needs of agriculture alone would have taken virtually all of the permitted steel output. Illegal barter was the only solution. Zink pointed out: "The amount available for German use hardly equalled the food supplied by the Nazis at such notorious concentration camps as Dachau where thousands died from starvation."[25] During the long, cold winter 1946–47, the calorie distribution went as low as 650 a day, while the average distribution in the U.S. zone was 1,040.[26]

Washington, under pressure from Clay to send food, put him under counterpressure to get more production and better distribution. Powerless to provide the normal material incentives to production, Clay resorted to threats. These were largely meaningless, because he was using Hitler's system of forced collections, but without the death penalty for sabotage. An expert accompanying Herbert Hoover on his inspection mission concluded that precisely the OMGUS attempt to solve the shortage with bureaucracy was at fault.[27] Balfour agreed: "What was becoming clear was that German recovery must be put into German hands."[28] Clay, however, defended the German collection, which he put at 90 percent of production. In mid-1947, he hoped the new "constabulary" would "have good effect on the farmers and would definitely impress upon them the determination of MG to pursue the collections." Yet he became more puzzled and bitter. "We had imported more than twice as much food as in the previous years without bettering the ration."[29] The German contribution of 975 calories per person was so low partly because six to seven million refugees had been added. Yet the 10–20 percent of the food not distributed legally was minor in comparison to the 50 percent of the industrial goods in illegal channels. Were all German production distributed equally all would still have starved.

In the fall of 1947 all hopes for rapid improvement were dashed by the worst drought in years. By January 1948 the bizonal economy had reached "dead center." Food production was less than 60 percent of that before the war.[30] Clay demanded that police power be employed to enforce the food census law, which required the entire population to report excess food. Almost no one obeyed, as to do so meant risking even more hunger.[31] Controlling Germans for the presumed security of the victors "was a luxury which the British could not and the Americans no longer wished to afford."[32] Costs were multiplying. The food cost for both victors in the first three years was 1.5 billion dollars. Yet German rations, mostly potatoes, remained at hardly one-half of the recommended diet.

Germans were both grateful for massive MG help and angry at MG mismanagement. Food Director Hans Schlange-Schöningen saw the MG bureaucracy hampering his officials. "A major portion of their time and energy had to be devoted to explaining the German situation to the Allied control officers, particularly the American, who came to Germany with completely different preconceptions about farming."[33] Understanding was excellent with the officers with whom one worked daily, "but the farther one climbed in the hierarchy of the Military Government, the farther away they were from the gray German reality, the more cool and distant they were and the more difficult to break through the ice of distrust."[34] He also felt that MG's basic mistake was to consider the food problem as separate from the rest of the economy. Had OMGUS not restricted exports, food imports could have been paid for by the beginning of 1947. Clay was intelligent, "but it was impossible either with Clay or with Robertson to get into an objective discussion about the necessary changes in the *general* economic policy as the prerequisite for the improvement of the food situation, or a recognition of the objective barriers confronting the German efforts."[35]

Controls and German Industrial Production

The pattern observable in the agricultural economy was repeated in industry. While JCS 1067 ordered nothing done to help, the Potsdam agreement permitted a "level of industry" that would permit Germany "the European average." At that time only 2 or 3 percent of the factories in the U.S. zone had been reopened.[36] Eisenhower merely ordered woodcutting projects for the winter, and the unemployed were to be forced onto farms to help with the harvest. Yet while New York papers were decrying a soft peace, some English papers were attacking the policy decided at Potsdam. The *London Times* predicted it would mean keeping Europe poor. The *Economist* attacked "the Luddite lunacies."[37] Those Americans officially involved did not agree with each other. The closer they were to the problem the more critical they were of the policies.

Calvin Hoover's September 1945 OMGUS report predicted the extreme difficulty, if not impossibility, of carrying out a severe program of industrial disarmament while still providing for a minimum German standard of living.[38] McCloy cabled: "For all practical purposes there is no industry in Germany or Austria and unless there is, it is a constantly losing game. . . . Above all we should not hesitate to encourage the re-establishment of more industry and commerce."[39] Patterson did not agree. He was visited 12 October by Morgenthau, who urged repudiating the Hoover Report, and sending Harry White to check up on MG. Patterson was noncommittal, but when he learned the State Department also disavowed the Hoover Report, he thought "the Army people in Berlin might be worrying too much about the Germans."[40]

As OMGUS historian Hubert Schmidt remarked: "Fear of German war potential was so great that only men in the field who saw the economic chaos and observed German war weariness could see that there was a greater need for rehabilitation than for restrictions." Often the little done was contrary to orders; "very few of the detachments have an understanding of the restriction on production of certain items." OMGUS was not clear either; its year-end report called for "great effort to build up," while its reorganization plan of 5 December still gave "limitations and control" as its mission.[41]

Misplaced bureaucratic energy in the fall and winter went into deciding the level of industry. How low must it be set to comply with Potsdam? Calvin Hoover, involved in setting the key steel production level, suggested 7.8 million tons, less than half the prewar figure, which Draper and Clay immediately accepted.[42] Yet on 8 October another headline storm broke, with long quotations from their secret level of industry report.

Clay took Hoover's figure of 7.8 million tons of steel to the Allied negotiations on the level of industry to be permitted. The Russians suggested

4.5 million, the French 7 million, and the British 9 million tons. Later Clay wrote: "I was convinced of the merits of the Hoover Proposal and was amazed to receive a suggestion from the State Department that 3.5 million tons would be adequate."[43] Yet he arranged a compromise at 5.8 million, despite British protests. His experts doubted this figure could be used as the basis for settling the level of industry, but Clay insisted and they had to show it could be done. Draper, accused by liberals of being an "enemy of the Morgenthau Plan," accepted the low figure of 5.8 million tons, and chemical production "restricted to a level consistent with the need for fertilizers in a country where agricultural production is to be maximized."[44]

In two months of negotiations, the U.S. plan was made more restrictive by the French and Russians.[45] German exports had been two-thirds chemicals, metals, and engineering products, precisely those things forbidden. Businessman Lewis Brown thought: "What is planned is actually a series of bottlenecks."[46] All the while the economy deteriorated even more seriously as the scanty resources available in 1945 were consumed. "In 1946 no progress was made toward solving any major problems. . . . [MG] transformed Germany into a raw material exporting country (96%), her economic status more than a hundred years before. Fantastic scarcities of raw materials and fuel resulted."[47] The German reaction: "MG has really taken hold, bringing a vicious train of events . . . channels through which permits must go are so complicated and take so long that it is virtually impossible to get anything done."[48] Brown shuddered to see "red tape and paper work barriers at a thousand points."[49]

The heart of the problem was coal. German incentive had been further depressed in June 1945, when Truman proclaimed that a large portion of the coal produced would be exported regardless of German needs. The production of Ruhr coal was 25 percent of prewar tonnage in 1945, 40 percent in 1946, 50 percent in 1947, and only 60 percent in 1948, although every possible bureaucratic incentive was used.[50] Herbert Hoover listed some of the level of industry plan's costly fallacies: (1) exports from light industry, coal, and potash could pay for imports; (2) Germany could be reduced to a pastoral state; (3) war potential could be defined and eliminated by restricting certain industries; (4) Germany could never be self-supporting under the Potsdam level of industry plan. "We can keep Germany in these economic chains, but it will also keep Europe in rags."[51]

Hoover's report came at the right time to add its weight to the Marshall Plan; results were apparent with the announcement on 26 August of the "Revised Plan for Level of Industry, US/UK Zones," into which Clay had pushed the State Department. Whereas the 1946 plan had set a level of approximately 70 to 75 percent of 1936 production, the new plan allowed production equal to that of 1936.[52] The price laws meant that what was produced were mostly items not under price control: ash trays, fancy lamps, dolls, and chandeliers, instead of the cups, pails, pots, and plates really needed. The occupation also diverted labor into nonproductive work; one-third of all people employed in public and private services were working for the occupation forces. More seriously, industrial output per man was 40–50 percent of prewar productivity; it was not unusual to have a 50 percent absentee rate, because workers were out scrounging for food.[53]

Concerning housing very little positive can be said about the occupation. Herbert Hoover noted in 1947: "The housing situation . . . is the worst that modern civilization has ever seen."[54] The policy of the German authorities was simply to distribute the poverty, apportioning so many square meters of space to each person; houseowners were required to take refugees and those bombed out into their homes. Statistical justice aimed at averaging two persons per room, but the number per room was often higher. Accomodations ranged from overcrowded peasants' rooms in the countryside to overcrowded cellars and bunkers in the cities. OMGUS had neither money nor the imagination even to consider housing construction. Its impact was negative: seizing building supplies and halting industry, at first even saw mills. Its most resented action was the seizure of housing for the troops, including luxury housing for officers. A decision in the fall of 1945 to billet families of the army brought the seizure of homes to its high point of 65,000 in 1946. The large-scale requisitioning came to an end in 1947, but houses were kept, in some cases for more than ten years.[55]

From mid-1946 the policy drift was away from industrial limitation, yet Washington hesitated to make a clean break. By mid-1947 the economy was rapidly deteriorating.[56] One result of policy was the increased need for a Marshall Plan. But this costly support was ineffective as long as it was tied to MG controls. In mid-1948, following the long-delayed currency reform, Ludwig Erhard, the bizonal economics chief, abolished this MG system of rationed scarcity. The country began to recover as soldier-bureaucrats began getting out of the way of workers and businessmen.

Currency Reform and Exports

Both cause and effect of the disaster in food and factories was the disaster in money. Even during the war, Hitler had chosen inflationary borrowing over deflationary taxing; he had diverted production from consumer goods and increased the supply of money. Even before the victors arrived, inflation was hiding behind price controls. What split the system apart was that industrial production fell off to almost nothing, making the money worth little more than the few items on a ration card. Furthermore, the victors, notably the Russians, printed billions of "occupation marks" for their soldiers to use, adding to the supply of money chasing the vanishing commodities. In December 1945, MG stated: "There is general agreement that drastic steps in the monetary and financial fields will have to be taken soon to prevent the situation from getting out of control." Yet this was not done until June 1948.[57]

The lack of currency reform is usually blamed on the Russians, yet OMGUS economist Manuel Gottlieb thought the Soviet policy in the winter 1945–46 was much more positive than the American; the Russians evidenced a readiness to agree to immediate and drastic monetary reform. In January 1946 the Russians approved a provisional central banking system, monetary liquidation, and equalization, the essential components of the reform. Until then the Russians had been concerned to retain control of currency issue to pay their troops, a billion marks a month, or a total from six to eight billion.[58] American soldiers exchanged some of these marks, acquired in the black market, for millions of dollars at U.S. Army offices. This practice, belatedly stopped by headquarters, made so strong an impression that it was Clay's stated reason for not agreeing to a joint currency reform with the Soviets. The refusal sparked the split of Germany. Russian poverty in 1945 had led to American distrust in 1946–47, which led to Germany's division in 1948.[59]

The French opposed reform, yet it was the British Gottlieb saw in 1946 leading the fight against it, mostly because their delegate held "obsolete" monetary views. "Even an aggressively oriented American policy might have been stalemated by British objection after French and Soviet support had been won."[60] A resolute monetary policy and skillful leadership would have been needed on the American side in order to win Allied approval. "These did not then exist and later only slowly and partially came into existence." Therefore no directive had been issued to maintain uniform monetary conditions throughout Germany.[61] U.S. specialists were sent early in 1946 to devise a financial rehabilitation program. Working intensively for ten weeks, they produced the the Colm-Dodge-Goldsmith Report, largely adopted two years later. It proposed a new currency, and reduction of all monetary claims at a rate of 1 to 10. It also had a 50 percent mortgage on all major property, and a progressive levy on wealth.[62]

Experts persuaded Clay, but Washington was skeptical of the far-reaching social effects of the capital levy, which smacked of socialism.[63] Clay was told 5 July of their reservations, but he preferred the plan and the deadlock persisted. Rusk blamed him.[64] After direct petition by Clay to Byrnes, his plan was approved in late August 1946. Long delayed, it was introduced to the ACC 2 September. The Soviets and French immediately agreed, and the British agreed 12 September, to the broad principle of a drastic monetary reform with some kind of capital levy.[65] Agreement was not reached, however, in the areas of currency allocations to the occupying powers and detailed provisions of the capital levy, although Gottlieb believed that agreement on the latter was very likely. A stalemate did develop over the distribution of the new currency; the other Allies feared Russian misuse.[66] The debate was carried to the Moscow Conference and left unresolved. Clay explained that the United States had had enough of Soviet promises in the printing of marks.[67]

Gottlieb described one more significant incident before the fateful currency reform: the introduction of a "last compromise proposal" on financial reform by Clay to the ACC in January 1948. The Soviets accepted the printing of currency exclusively in Berlin under quadripartite control, and arrangements for it were begun. Agreements were also reached on the capital levy and the allocation of currency. "The principal difficulty appeared to hinge about the extent of political or economic union needed to support a common monetary reform. The Soviets urged the establishment of a joint central German bank and a joint central department of finance." The Western answer to this Soviet position was apparently negative."[68] Instead, in June 1948, the Germans were given the chance to have a life-giving currency, but the price was the formalization of the division of Germany, first into a land with two currencies and soon into a land with two states. The delay, crippling to industry and trade, resulted first from MG inability to agree internally on a policy and then to agree with its allies. After the reform MG influence rapidly withered.[69]

To say something good about the MG bureaucracy assigned to control and later to increase trade, one might remark, "most Germans survived." But he would have to add that their survival might be as much despite as because of the control system, since most people evaded it.[70] The Germans were at first forbidden to export and import; domestic trade remained under the rationing system on the retail level and under raw material allocation on the production level. Clay, late in July 1945, thought he had no authority for any export program.[71] By September he had come to see that German economic survival depended on some exports, and he requested Washington permission for German export-import agencies.[72] He soon realized the greatest problem was that the victors would not treat Germany as an economic unit. OMGUS historian Schmidt admitted, "Restrictions of the four occupying powers had a strangling effect on internal trade. . . . Foreign trade came to a complete standstill . . . under MG supervision."[73]

Field reports gave glowing accounts of drives against the black market, yet the year-end report had to admit that it thrived. Illegal barter was all that was possible, given nearly worthless currency and unworkable price controls. If a manufacturer did not get some tangible value for what he produced, he could not produce anything at all. While MG bureaucrats worked all hours trying to control the economy, the natural forces found their own level and kept a trickle of trade going.[74] The Länder, encouraged by MG to be autonomous, set up border controls, to retain scarce items for their own use.

A CAD inspection reported administrative confusion in the Foreign Trade Section. In its first seven months, from June 1945, it underwent eight changes of status within the chain of command, and four changes of office location.

> In the absence of instructions from higher authority it wrote its own directives, which it endeavored to piece together from scraps of policy material and taken from miscellaneous pre-surrender military government regulations, JCS 1067, and classified reports of the Teheran, Yalta and Potsdam Conferences. . . . It was necessary to base major decisions on pure guess work. With ever-recurring changes in the chain of command and constant shifting of responsibilities and authority from one command to another, it was unlikely that the desires of one's immediate superior of today would prevail with his successor of tomorrow.

Much confusion was caused by the overlapping work of other agencies, and by the independent action of MG detachments in the field who were oblivious of directives.[75] Because of the extreme difficulty in negotiating deals with the Allies, the inadequacy of transportation and communication, the prohibition of travel into or out of Germany, and the freeze on the movement of German or foreign money across German borders, only one hundred export deals had been consumated, and these were mostly barter. Imports were largely relief supplies.

One point was very sore to Europeans, who were working for their own recovery and needed to increase their trade with their former prime partner, the Germans.[76] By OMGUS rule all exports from Germany must be paid for in dollars. The Dutch, short on dollars as were they all, were driven to the expedient in 1947 of destroying the vegetables they were long accustomed to sell to the Ruhr and Rhineland although the people there were desperate for food. Potential trading partners complained that it was easier to trade with the Russian zone than with the U.S. zone. American embassy economic advisers complained about the dollar rule; even Clay's economic adviser, Draper, questioned its advisability.[77] Under such pressure Clay had begun to moderate his export policy in January 1947, although he continued to believe that allowing the Germans to use export revenue, as they wished to buy Dutch food, would mean less money for the raw materials to revive industry, which to him had higher priority.[78] Yet the resulting shortage of food led to low production and low exports.

Exports were also crippled by MG controls that left little room for German initiative. Germans could not even travel abroad until October 1947;

trade treaties were long delayed; MG made all decisions on the use of export earnings.[79] Bizonal and German experts blamed the system. "There is absolutely no incentive for German manufacturers to export . . . the first time I saw Clay he complained bitterly that the Export-Import Program was on dead center. . . . the whole German economy is *not* on dead center but is spiraling down. . . . All decisions must come from Berlin. Seventy-five percent of everyone's time is taken up in meetings, or in preparing papers for meetings."[80] Adviser Gottlieb agreed: responsibility for foreign trade in the bizone was scattered over a host of Allied and German agencies with many of the key purchasing decisions made directly by the military governors.

The Clay system was a narrowly conceived trade policy, which reinforced a network of obstacles to private trade, and was "the policy which would destroy Germany as both exporter and importer and imposed the dollar requirement in the most critical trading area in Europe.[81] Even the Joint Export-Import Agency quoted a Swedish businessman who said, "we will under no circumstances buy in Germany . . . to be bothered by the JEIA paper war." The bizonal commerce chief in February 1948 denounced non-German control, saying: "The Export-Import Agency should be dissolved as quickly as possible."[82] Even Clay agreed: "With great reluctance I have come to conclusion German bureaucratic controls stifling expansion."[83] The oddity was that Clay, who preferred freer enterprise, was bound to a system of massive state restraint. Ludwig Erhard became the national hero by beginning in June 1948 to destroy the control system, freeing Germany and Clay himself from crippling controls. Exports and imports boomed when the JEIA was abolished in October 1949.

The Failure of Economic Reforms

Of the many postwar economic reforms envisioned by American planners, the destruction of German industrial cartels was regarded as most necessary. The planners thought of the cartels, actually trade associations, as "trusts," and saw their destruction as necessary both to achieve denazification and to punish Germany for its war crimes. Even more importantly, without these large industries Germany could not wage aggressive war. Although the other economic policies of the occupation had perforce to be directed toward sheer survival, OMGUS found the strength to attempt this one economic reform. The following sketch of the retreat from decartelization suggests the problems inherent in an army trying to effect structural changes in an economy, problems created not so much by the resistance of the Germany people, who were scarcely involved in this struggle between big business and government, as by the division among the military governors themselves about what should be done. Liberals saw "a sell-out to Wall Street." Decartelization triggered a classic fight between two ideological groups, a battle that was publicized because leaders of the anticartel group, Bernard Bernstein, Russell Nixon, and James Martin, took their case to the Congress and the public.

In his passionate account, *All Honorable Men* (1950), Martin tells how he had been recruited from college by the Justice Department to investigate German-U.S. industrial contacts. He had discovered marketing arrangements which limited U.S. production, including production of some items for war. Martin was assigned to study German "economic warfare," and by the fall of 1944 FDR wanted these economic weapons destroyed. Martin was assigned to decartelization planning in England, only to discover that Draper's Economics Division was already influenced by "reactionaries."[84]

The decartelization group under Russell Nixon was prepared to break up the trusts, but after he resigned in December 1945, he protested Draper's "laxity" with Nazis in business. On 5 June 1945 Clay had ordered the reduction of the I.G. Farben war potential, but Draper thought it should continue to produce.[85] All Farben plants were operating with a minimum of supervision. Despite the directives from Washington, OMGUS had created no decartelization law. Bernstein told Congress: "These deficiencies between action and policy developed from the fundamental fact that the officials responsible for the programs did not support the directives to destroy Germany's war industrial potential."[86] Martin had thought Clay was on the side of the angels—that is, in favor of more rapid decartelization—when Clay had called him back from Washington with great urgency in December 1945, to counter British opposition. Martin discovered that his branch had been absorbed into Draper's division, where someone was helping the British. The reformers regarded Clay's policy of giving power back to the Germans as even more dangerous.[87]

Businessmen were everywhere in MG. "In one of my first talks with General Draper, I found that the investment banker's view was uppermost," Martin wrote.[88] As a result, most of the ostensible powers of the decartelization branch were delegated to other branches; all it could do was recommend through Draper to Clay. "The written orders from Washington meant whatever the commanding general at each level said they meant."[89] A year after the occupation began, no steps had been taken to carry out the antitrust policy anywhere in the zone, except for two cases. I. G. Farben was seized and a trustee had been appointed to administer coal wholesaling firms. Martin's section had no authority over Farben; it was "a dance of the skeletons in the army's 'greatest show on earth.'" Martin found a flood of inexperienced replacements had come in with the barest briefing on official policy, and instead were condemning World War II's Trading with the Enemy Act, which limited German trade with the United States and German recovery.

Clay told Martin: "Congress was becoming economy minded; the spotlight was turning to 'recovery' and 'saving the taxpayer's money.' In his opinion we would have to move rapidly because the pressure to do nothing at all might be expected to increase."[90] Martin got Clay's approval in August for a zonal decartelization law, but in early September Draper flew to the United States, and on his return called Martin to the airport. He had talked about the decartelization law with William Clayton, assistant secretary of state. "These talks, he said, had revealed a shift of position at Washington on the subject of a 'mandatory' law." The next morning Clay asked about the delay. Martin told him of Draper's report. "Clay's face clouded up and his speech became even more controlled and precise than usual. He stated that his instructions from Washington had been that the law must be 'mandatory.' He would not alter his position unless Washington put the order in writing."[91]

On 10 October Martin asked Clay to take Decartelization Branch out of the Economics Division because of the division's briefings against an antitrust policy. Clay replied one had to expect a swing of the pendulum. "It might have to swing even further away from the original objectives of the occupation before any backswing could be hoped for." He asked Martin to stay; with a senatorial investigation in the offing he did not want a change implying criticism of the Economics Division. He dictated a memo to Draper criticizing these briefings. At the 12 October meeting, Clay changed procedures and asked for gripes. Draper said his first gripe was decartelization, because Germany would need sizable industry to compete on the world market. Clay interrupted, "his black eyes flashing, 'I don't believe that we can accomplish our purpose without striking out large corporations in Germany. The conduct of those existing in the past condemns them. I personally am fully in sympathy with decartelization based on size.'" General Draper should adhere strictly to policies which were fixed by official statements from Washington.[92] On 31 October Clay went ahead on the U.S. zone law, limiting a firm to 30 percent of any industry.[93] When the Reconstruction Finance Corporation showed interest in lending money to German industry, Clay was concerned these loans not be criticized as going to cartels, and sent an urgent telegram back to OMGUS to designate objectionable firms.[94] Resistance continued: "It was not until March 13, 1947 that our 'staff study' outlining the reorganization procedure was approved by the Economics Division.... Clay never signed the proposed order. Gradually the restrictions against allocation of raw materials to 'cartelized' firms were relaxed without a formal order, 'in the interest of promoting the export-import program' "[95]

There was also increasing pressure from American big business to get plants "put back into operation, not because they fit into any plan but simply because they belonged to Singer, International Harvester, General Motors or because an American, Belgian, or British company had had a prewar arrangement that made it desirable to get MG to reopen a particular line of German production. . . . The plants of the favored firms were all decked out with priorities and ornamented like Christmas trees. Around them clustered the little satellite industries, protected by 'hands off' and 'do not touch' signs."[96] MG surrendered its important power to allocate coal, transport, and electricity into the hands of the favored Germans. "By 1947, our files contained hundreds of complaints from independent German businessmen that although their plants were ready to operate, they had been refused the necessary license."[97]

The December Meader Report blasted Clay's administration with documents provided by Martin. Clay called him in and wondered whether "it would be possible to avoid public outbursts." Martin thought it would only if the decartelization branch were made a division again. This Clay would not do, so Martin resigned 22 May 1947.[98] Martin in his last talk with Clay saw that Clay's keen sense of history and his military habits had contributed most to MG's defeat. Since the previous occupation had been defeated by lack of congressional support, policy must be bipartisan which "meant that on many critical points the statements from 'Washington' had included contradictory points of view. It was one thing, he implied, to believe in his own mind that the objective was clear, and another thing to charge any of his subordinates with violation of orders if they adopted different interpretations." Whereas a civilian would resign, a military man would knuckle under. "General Clay, sensing a swing of the pendulum or a wave of the future, had held his fire in cases when he, as 'higher authority,' had the power to give a direct order.[99]

The decartelization staff concluded in early June 1947 that they should attack by picking five or six firms they could handle. Four teams were set up, one for each of four firms: Henschel, Siemens, Bosch, and Gutehoffnungshütte. Each team ran into trouble, though for different reasons. Most of Gutehoffnungshütte was in the British zone; Henschel caused disagreement within the section and an eventual Clay veto; Siemens had its headquarters in the Russian zone; the Bosch case was delayed[100] The decartelization program came to a precipitous stop by 9 March 1948, when Clay astounded his staff by reversing policy in the Henschel case. Richardson Bronson, chief of denazification, saw Clay again and returned to tell his staff: "General Clay has changed his policy and clarified my mind. I have a different concept of his policy." Clay's policy was "the rule of reason." As Bronson reconstructed the sequence:

> Clay stated to me that he had a responsibility for getting Germany economically on her feet and off the back of American taxpayers, that . . . the rule of reason

> would not permit the deconcentration measures at this time. . . . all hell broke
> loose. . . . I saw General Clay and he suggested that I meet with my staff again
> and tell them it wasn't a change of policy, it was a change of emphasis, a
> change of timing . . . Clay said that he realized that when this program was
> made public there would be a scream to high heaven from a strong anti-trust
> group. . . . There had been similar screams before and screams had come and
> gone.[101]

The only case continued was against Bosch, which was tried years later under
an Allied high commissioner court. Bosch agreed to sell its shares in a number
of plants and to liquidate others. I. G. Farben, for a time under direct MG
control, was broken into three large components and may have profited from a
more manageable organization. Otherwise, decartelization became merely a
pressure on licensing procedures, mostly of very small retail firms; large firms
were not bothered.[102] The Ferguson Committee held hearings December
1948-February 1949 to investigate. Among twelve strong recommendations,
it urged that Clay's top officials "be removed from any responsibility for the
conduct of the decartelization programs."[103] The army took no steps to carry
out the recommendations, but Draper resigned as undersecretary of the army
before the report was filed and Clay soon after. By 1952–53 the concentration
of economic power was regarded as greater than ever.[104]

Martin and his followers blamed administrative sabotage, but another
staffer thought zealots like Martin himself were to blame: "I think we should
have set up at the very outset . . . a very mild and reasonable program, bearing
down heavily on trade practices particularly, and that we should never have let
a single punitive overtone creep into anything emanating from this branch.[105]
MG officer Bert Schloss agreed:

> The Americans in charge of the anti-trust action in Germany seemed to
> have acted under the illusion that the Germans themselves had never recognized
> the problem or done anything about it. In fact, the Germans had a well-
> developed system of legal supervision of cartels, the administration of which
> was entrusted to the highly competent special courts. . . . The new law (which
> read like the Sherman Act) omitted any reference to established German legal
> ideas, institutions or procedures.

It was drafted by young American lawyers, who knew little of Germany.[106]
Knowledge is power.

Economic policy, given the most attention, was the least successful.
Economic reform and economic policy became a self-defeating intervention.
Although the Morgenthau Plan was not the OMGUS policy, and its aim of
crippling the economy was soon replaced by the OMGUS goal of enabling the
Germans to survive, MG's attack brought defeat. The economy and reform
stagnated. Clay was slower than most of the experts to retreat from controls,
but he was quick to recognize the need for some aid. The belated emphasis on

such aid helped to create the victory of economic recovery that restraint had delayed. Political goals, almost ignored by comparison, were the sooner successful. These political policies were less subject to dispute among Americans and were more acceptable to the Germans. The original active lecturing and threatening to denazify had an immediate countereffect, but the passive permitting of Germans to learn democracy "by doing" was victorious. With the least done, the most was achieved.

Notes

1. As partial explanation for the economic miracle after 1948, it should be noted that destruction of plant was only 10 percent for metallurgy, 10–15 percent for chemicals, 15–20 percent for engineering, and 20 percent for textiles (Alfred Grosser, *Germany in Our Time* [New York, 1971], 57; Manfred Rexin, *Die Jahre 1945–49* [Hannover, 1962], 1–3; Paul Noack, *Deutschland 1945–60* [Munich, 1960], 13). Some twenty-five million Germans were refugees, bombed out, compulsory labor, prisoners of war, or in concentration camps (Wilhelm Böge, *Ereignisse seit 1945* [Braunschweig, 1960], 9).
2. A widespread belief is that the commander at Bad Kreuznach deliberately let a large number starve to death. A Jewish lieutenant told John Dos Passos: "I find them half-starved to death in our own PW cages and being treated like you wouldn't treat a dog" (*Tour of Duty* [Boston, 1946], 251).
3. SHAEF intended in early June to disband the PW cages quickly (*Chronology*, 4 June 1945, Kansas City Record Center [hereafter KCRC]). Earl Ziemke stressed the problem of feeding PWs as a reason for rapid discharge (*The U.S. Army in the Occupation of Germany* [Washington, 1975], 293); see also Montgomery Belgion, *Victor's Justice* (Hinsdale, Ill., 1949), 56. The American Red Cross found the prisoners improperly treated. The *New York Herald Tribune* reported 12 October 1945 that the French were starving their PWs; Americans compared their emaciation to that of those liberated from Dachau (Eugene Davidson, *The Death and Life of Germany* [New York, 1959], 122). Ambassador Caffrey reported from Paris that the French had 1 million prisoners, though they admitted to only 550,000 (Caffrey to Byrnes, 12 Nov. 1945, U.S. Dept of State, *Foreign Relations of the U.S.: 1945*, III, 1382–84 [hereafter *FRUS*]; see also his report on French views, ibid., 1381).
4. When Habe asked Eisenhower about taking back German captives, Eisenhower answered: "Washington will have to decide that" (Hans Habe, *Our Love Affair with Germany* [New York, 1953], 106).
5. Chronology, 18 Oct. 1945, KCRC; Clay to WARCAD, 28 Nov. 1945, Clay Cables, National Archives (hereafter NA); Caffrey to Byrnes, 14 Nov. 1945, *FRUS:1945*, III, 1423.
6. Chronology, June 1945 to Dec. 1946, 269, Washington National Record Center (hereafter WNRC). Eugene Davidson calculated 4 million PWs in Allied hands in March 1947 (166); Belgion, 57. In Britain in mid-1946 the government was accused in Parliament of making 750,000 pounds profit a week out of nearly 400,000 PWs in Britain and 500,000 more in the Commonwealth. The French had 600,000 in France; their release was not completed until mid-1948 (Michael Balfour, *Survey of International Affairs, 1939–46, Germany* [London, 1946], 164).
7. Belgion, 52, 55. Deaths during captivity presumably accounted for 75 percent of the prisoners; out of 60,000 Italians known to be captured, only 12,500 returned. The Russians claimed over 3 million PWs captured, of which they might have returned 300,000, but for

which they had probably taken a larger number of civilians, including women; of one such group of 1,300 German women, 800 had died in two years (*Manchester Guardian*, 31 July 1947).

8. Spencer, Chief Commerce Group, Bipartite Control Board (hereafter BICO), 11 Feb. 1948, NA; Clay testimony to House Appropriations Comm., OMGUS Chronologies, 23 Jan. 1948, WNRC. Clay accepted this German view.

9. Senate Investigation of National Defense Program, 18 Nov. 1946, 26862. Clay incorrectly told Congress that many had recently moved from Germany. See the volumes published by the Bundesministerium für Vertriebene, Flüchtlinge und Kriegsgeschädigte, *Die Vertreibung der deutsche Bevölkerung aus ost-Mitteleuropa* (Bonn, 1945–60); Hajo Holborn, *American Military Government* (Washington, 1947), 128.

10. Hubertus von Loewenstein estimated 11.8 million fled, of whom 2.7 million died in flight; Deuerlein placed the figure at 13 million, of which 2 million died in flight (*Deutschlands Schicksal 1945–57* [Bonn, 1957], 31); Ernst Deuerlein, *Handbuch der deutsche Geschichte* (Konstanz, 1957), 91. In answer to Murphy's complaints that Poles robbed refugees again and again, Ambassador Lane first denied ill treatment and then conceded that sometimes people did such things, but the Poles being shipped out by the Russians were also maltreated (Murphy to Mathews, 12 Nov. 1945; Murphy to Byrnes, 23 Oct., 23 Nov. 1945; Lane to Byrnes, 4 Dec. 1945, *FRUS: 1945*, II, 1290, 1296, 1310, 1318, 1325).

11. Harold Zink noted the original MG sympathy, "but when the DPs broke out of their camps night after night and pillaged the country for miles around . . . killing the German farmers who sought to protect their property, MG officials began to worry" (*American Military Government in Germany* [New York, 1947], 106).

12. Habe, 125; see also Edward L. Homze, *Foreign Labor in Nazi Germany* (Princeton, 1967).

13. Taking care of DPs was acceptable for a time, but not indefinitely for those who refused to go home or for the hundreds of thousands, mostly Jews, who fled west after the war. America restricted its immigration, but Germans had to accept and feed anyone (Zink, *American*, 134).

14. Earl Harrison Report, Chronology, 29 Sept. 1945, KCRC.

15. "It is fantastic for anyone to say that their condition is the same as it was under Hitler except for the extermination policy. . . . Are they to receive permanently higher rations than the non-Nazis about them or preferment in business? It may well provoke a more acute anti-Semitism" (McCloy, Report to USFET, 11 Oct. 1945, Clay Cables, NA).

16. *Chronology*, 18 Oct., 23 Nov., 7 Dec. 1945, KCRC; Patterson to Acheson, 19 Dec. 1945; Byrnes to Royall, 7 Jan. 1946, *FRUS: 1945*, II, 1215, 1224.

17. "Such an announcement would also greatly accelerate the infiltration of unauthorized persons into the U.S. Zone (current rate 10,000 a month)" (Chronology, 22 Dec. 1945, KCRC).

18. Balke to CAD, 20 Aug. 1946, CAD 014 Ger, NA. The Meader Report of November 1946 complained about the 3,000 newly arrived Polish Jews who would not work (Meader Report, 42, Pollock Papers, Michigan Historical Society, Ann Arbor, Mich.); Chronology, Jan. to June 1947, 215, WNRC.

19. CAD Memo to President, 2 June 1945, CAD 014, NA, based on a Clay report. This led to a brief War Dept. effort to avoid responsibility for feeding the defeated millions.

20. Chronology, 3 July 1945, KCRC. Eisenhower said MG must feed Germany and guessed the ration would be 2,000 calories. The normal U.S. calorie intake was about 3,000; even during the war the British never had less than 2,800 (Chronology, 13 Aug. 1945, KCRC; F. S. Donison, *Civil Affairs and Military Government* [London, 1966], 270).

21. E. Davidson, 77, 135.

22. Chronology, 18 Oct. 1945, KCRC. "Everyone was sympathetic but German needs could not be given a higher priority than those of the countries allied with us in our war effort" (Lucius Clay, *Decision in Germany* [New York, 1950], 265). John Backer thought only Clay's frantic

efforts kept the rations around 1,100 calories when bread grains were practically unobtainable (*Priming the German Economy* [Durham, N.C., 1971], 52–53).

23. Zink said nitrogen production was throttled (*American*, 110). Backer wrote that OMGUS went all out to raise fertilizer production; farm equipment plants were ordered reopened (45); he reported a rapid food recovery led by Food Chief Hester, but rations remained low until 1948 (83–84).

24. For example, a sack ot twine cost 150 kilograms of wheat and a sowing machine 4,000 kilos of potatoes (Nicholas Balabkins, *Germany under Direct Controls* [New Brunswick, N.J., 1964], 87, 93; Zink, *American*, 111).

25. Victor Golancz, *In Darkest Germany* (London, 1946), 137; William Chamberlin, *The German Phoenix* (New York, 1963), 33. On 13 April 1947 Clay reported a deficit from scheduled deliveries of 335,000 tons (Jean E. Smith, ed., *The Papers of General Lucius Clay, Germany 1945-49* [Boomington, Ind., 1974], 361).

26. "The reality has long made a farce of the pretensions of MG of maintaining the appearance of stability, when under the pressure of the sheer struggle for survival, the joint effort of the whole population is directed at destroying that stability" (Gustav Stolper, *German Realities* [New York, 1948], 77, 97). The bureaucracy did prevent mass starvation; poverty was partially distributed.

27. Balfour, 151–52; Noce Memorandum to Secretary of War, 8 Sept. 1947, CAD 014, NA. Hoover was used to influence Congress (Louis Lochner, *Herbert Hoover and Germany* [Boppard, 1961], 193). In June Clay reported that the feeding level was the worst in Europe (Smith, *Papers*, 378).

28. Manuel Gottlieb, *The German Peace Settlement and the Berlin Crisis* (New York, 1960), 81, based on Bipartite Board minutes. "The Allies carried a large part of the blame since they had failed to maintain the scheduled shipment of grains to Germany" (Balabkins, 100; Spencer, Chief Commerce, BICO, 11 Feb. 1948, in CAD, CSCAD 014, Ger. 1948, NA).

29. Balabkins, 88; Food Chief Hester reported zonal production at 87 percent for 1946-47 and 95 percent for 1947-48; Backer, 85–86.

30. The law had been promulgated over the advice of Clay's experts, but he wanted to convince Congress "that the German cupboard was bare, and that continuance of further food shipments was necessary" (OMGUS Chronologies, Jan. to Mar. 1948, WNCR); Gottlieb, 81.

31. Balfour, 152; Balabkins, 100–102, 107–109.

32. "This was repeated as often as the office-holders were changed. Much depended on how much these new food officers could be made to understand and how vigorously they would advance the German arguments with their superiors" (Hans Schlange-Schöningen, *Im Schatten des Hungers* [Hamburg, 1955], 20).

33. Clay showed genuine interest. The turning point was the visit of Secretary of Agriculture Anderson, with his 5 July 1947 formal promise of 300,000 tons monthly. MG still said fats in the diet were luxuries; by January-February 1948, the ration of fats was down to 75 grams monthly (ibid., 59, 86, 135, 140).

34. "One constantly criticized German administrators for the lack of vigor against the black market, but one compelled the flight into barter, by speaking for years of the coming currency reform and constantly delaying it" (ibid., 142, 148).

35. Zink, *American*, 113; Seligman, *New York Times*, 7 Sept. 1945; Chronology, 26 July 1945, KCRC.

36. These attacks were part of the reading diet of MG officers (quoted in Hubert Schmidt, *Policy and Functioning in Industry* [Karlsruhe, 1950], 12).

37. Eisenhower told his staff on 1 October that "any assistants or officers who do not follow out the principles of their directors should be immediately removed from their positions, and cited the example of officers who feel that for one reason or another Germany must be 'built up' "

(Chronology, 10 Sept., 26 Sept., 1 Oct. 1945, KCRC).

38. McCloy to USFET, 11 Oct. 1945, Clay Cables, NA.

39. Patterson Memo, 13 Oct. 1945, ASW 370.8 Ger, Control Council, NA.

40. Schmidt, *Policy,* 43, 67, 72.

41. Calvin Hoover, *Memoirs of Capitalism, Communism, and Nazism* (Durham, N.C., 1965), 244, 246. To liberals' criticism of the "high level" permitted, Hoover responded no one associated with the report had ever any business connections in Germany. That the plan was more confusion than intrigue is evidenced by Ratchford. His predecessor Hoover had come to gain economic intelligence, only to be made chairman of the Standard of Living Board; he had been given a month to turn out a plan to reshape the entire German economy; statistics were scattered and lost; much of the plan was based on a chance copy of the *Statistical Yearbook* of 1943 (B. U. Ratchford and W. D. Ross, *Berlin Reparations Assignment* [Chapel Hill, 1947], 70–71); see also *FRUS: 1946*, V, 485–86 for meetings of Jan. 1946; see also *FRUS: 1945*, III, 1485–99.

42. Clay, 108; Ratchford and Ross, 129, 136; Schmidt, *Policy,* 91. Schmidt's criticism was that "little change in thinking had penetrated to the top levels." Backer's defense was that these MG limits had no relevance to reality because Germany could not produce that much anyway. Clay told the British the U.S. "regarded a balanced export-import program" as "definitely secondary to the destruction of war potential" and that the U.S. had "no obligation to guarantee a certain standard of living to Germany" (Gottlieb Collection, Box D, Berlin Quad. 1945/46, 15 Jan. 1946, quoted in Kuklick, 334).

43. Draper's memo even accepted the desirability of making Germany an agrarian country (Schmidt, 92, based on Draper memo 28 Jan. 1946, "Future Level of Industry").

44. "The restrictions on chemicals and machine manufacturing and engineering were severe, and the settling of levels for electric power, building materials, certain consumer goods, *etc.*, seem unjustified by any standard" (Schmidt, 96–97).

45. Textile and shoe production was set at 70–77 percent of prewar levels; the machines to equip and maintain these factories at 50 percent, steel mills to make the machines at 39 percent, and machine tools at 11.4 percent (Lewis Brown, *A Report on Germany* [New York, 1947], 35; Gottlieb, 159). Gottlieb regarded the plan as a Russian success taking advantage of the surviving Morgenthau orientation and Clay's determination to reach agreement with the Soviets at German expense.

46. Balabkins, 82, 134; Schmidt, 151.

47. "The officers assigned to production control tasks are not the most capable men that America could bring to the task, and in many cases have very little understanding. . . . There are many conflicts of authority between the branches of MG. . . . They cannot see any clear plan or direction in the American program . . . very few things can be done without prior MG approval and therefore MG over-burdens itself with a welter of details" (USFET Military Intelligence release, 11 Jan. 1946, in Schmidt, 106).

48. L. Brown, 48.

49. Gottlieb, 79. A BICO expert admitted the tragically slow recovery in coal production was because of the food shortage, which was because of "worthless money" (Barrows to Szymczak, BICO Economic Control Group, 9 May 1947, CSCAD 014 Ger).

50. OMGUS Chronology, 25 Feb. 1947, 18 Mar. 1947, WNRC. Clay's recommendation 28 June 1947 was a goal of 65–70 percent of the 1936 level the first year and 80–85 percent in the second year to assist European recovery (Smith, *Papers*, 379).

51. Schmidt, 245. Steel was up from 5.8 million to 10.7 million tons. Per capita this meant that by 1952 the standard of living could be 75 percent of the 1936 level (Backer, 81–82).

52. Balabkins, 161, 179–81. Clay wrote 16 July 1947: "I am at wit's end to do anything progressive in economic rehabilitation." He blamed Washington for assuming one could work with the French (Smith, *Papers*, 384).

53. Bombing had emphasized destroying workers' homes to destroy workers' morale. Expulsion of Germans from eastern Europe piled additional millions into the houses that survived.
54. Colonel Balke to Chief CAD, 20 Aug. 1946, CAD 014 Ger, NA. It was contrary to the Hague Convention, which excluded housing confiscation for dependents. Houses were requisitioned, stripped of furnishings and then derequisitioned (Oliver Fredericksen, *American Military Occupation of Germany 1945-53* [Darmstadt, 1953], 121).
55. Balabkins, 207-208. "Partly because of an exaggerated effort to prevent revival of Germany military power and partly as a result of Allied disunity, we had so throttled industry and trade that we were put into the position of being the first victor in history to support a vanquished enemy over an extended period" (Schmidt, *Policy*, 226); see also Hermann Behr, *Vom Chaos zum Staat* (Frankfurt, 1961), 234; Hubert Meurer, *U.S. Military Government: Trade and Commerce* (Karlsruhe, 1950), 146-47.
56. Schmidt, *Policy*, 226. Ernest F. Penrose blamed Eisenhower and Clay, who "had little understanding of monetary questions and were too preoccupied with other urgent matters to follow all that was done and all that was left undone by their staffs . . . gravely handicapped by directives" (*Economic Planning For the Peace* [Princeton, 1953], 305).
57. Gottlieb, 105-106. "Communist" White, Morgenthau's assistant, was blamed for turning over the printing plates to the Russians, who paid their soldiers for four years of war service in marks.
58. With Soviet troops being repatriated and German taxes coming in to cover their troop payroll, Gottlieb found it highly credible that the Russians stopped issuing military marks during the first winter, contrary to Clay's later fears.
59. Gottlieb thought the British could have been won over; their occupation policy did not fit with the more progressive ideas of the Labor government and the British ordinarily kept in step with Americans (109).
60. Gottlieb blamed MG's passive policy, the JCS 1067 injunction against measures designed to "maintain, strengthen or operate the German financial structure" (109-11).
61. Backer, 92-93. The levy was to reduce the disparity in sacrifice of those holding money and real assets.
62. Evident in Dean Rusk's review of the negotiation, beginning with Clay's appeal on 23 May (Dean Rusk, Memo to ASW, 4 Sept. 1946, ASW 091 OMUGS, NA; Noce, Memo to Sec War, 8 Sept. 1946, CAD 014, CAD, NA; Rusk, Memo to Petersen, 7 Oct. 1946, ASW 200.4 Eur., NA). Clay also opposed a ten cent value to the mark as unfair to the Germans (Smith, *Papers*, 274-76).
63. "General Clay declined to make any changes for reasons that are not entirely clear." Washington won in 1948; Clay removed the "socialist" feature, which brought on the major German criticism of the 1948 reform. A later Bonn law tried to equalize burdens.
64. Gottlieb, 112.
65. "When the Soviets proposed that *currency printing facilities in Leipzig be used jointly with those in Berlin* . . . a snag was struck" (Gottlieb, 116; his italics). For the Clay report see Smith, *Papers*. 302-303. Clay's report 10 May 1947 shows him alone insisting on Berlin as the only location (ibid., 350-51).
66. Gottlieb was skeptical of finance office reports: "These discrepancies and ambiguities suggest that the problem of the so-called 'Army mark overdraft' is related far more to internal U.S. procedures and fiscal delinquencies than to soviet monetary policy, although this policy was an important contributing factor" (121).
67. Gottlieb, 186. Clay's brief report of 5 February 1948 is obscure on his position, except in rejecting the property levy (Smith, *Papers*, 554). His strategy for the 11 February meeting was: "They will insist on central finance administration. . . . we will hold fast to our position that central administrations are not feasible until economic unification is agreed. This will result in disagreement which leaves our hands free. On the other hand, Soviets may concede this

point. If so, we will accept decision to print new money immediately with 60 days established as limiting date to agree supplementary details." His target date was 1 June for the western currency (Clay Teleconference with Draper, 10 Feb. 1948, in Smith, *Papers,* 559). The next day he reported them forced to accept a sixty-day negotiation period (ibid., 561). Clay's position was written but not sent to Royall in March 1948; see Smith, *Papers,* 589–96.

68. See Henry Wallich, *Mainsprings of the German Revival* (New Haven, 1955), 372.

69. Ludwig Erhard could think in 1970 of nothing to praise in the system he delightedly tore down at the first chance (Interview Ludwig Erhard).

70. Certain minor export transactions might be executed, at an army level on an exchange basis and with no currency involved (Chronology, 26 July 1945, KCRC).

71. Ibid., 15 Sept. 1945.

72 Schmidt, *Policy,* 28, 33. Backer, who worked in that bureacracy, admitted serious failures, mostly because of problems outside its power.

73. A report of 27 October said: "the hoarding of goods in towns, counties and Länder and exchange by barter is a throwback to the Middle Ages" (quoted in Schmidt, 38). Clay described channels for business as normal (Clay, 198).

74. The only success was the restoration of rail transportation "accomplished by the Germans themselves, under MG supervision, and in the face of the denazification policy which eliminated a high percentage of trained railroad operating personnel" (Col. Balke to CAD, 20 Aug. 1946, CAD 014 Ger, NA); Schmidt, 143.

75. Other European countries were unavoidably dependent on Germany for many essential raw materials, chemicals, and agricultural and manufacturing machinery. "As these countries have small if any dollar reserves, they are greatly handicapped even in the purchase of replacement parts" (E. Davidson, 212). "The British and American taxpayer was having to provide the dollars to pay for the goods which Germany was not allowed to buy by non-dollar trading" (ibid., 85).

76. Draper to Clay, 25 Mar. 1946, quoted in Backer, 148–49. Backer, defender of JEIA, admitted that the efforts of MG were "self-defeating."

77. Clay, 197.

78. Schlange-Schöningen, 149; Backer, 124. Clay protested 16 August 1947 that Washington refusal to permit a coal price increase crippled JEIA (Smith, *Papers,* 402).

79. Of Clay's search for better executives it was said: "I can't see where twelve outstanding American executives would do much more than add confusion to the present confused organizations" (Barrows to Szymczak, BICO, 9 May 1947, NA).

80. Gottlieb, 82. Germans translated JEIA as "*Jeder Export und Import Ausgeschlossen*" ("Every export and import impossible").

81. Slovner, 200, from JEIA Press Digest, 6 Aug. 1948; Spencer, Chief Commerce, BICO, 11 Feb. 1948, NA. Backer, a JEIA official, blamed "the circumstances" that 1946 exports were only 7 percent of the low permitted level; see also Wallich, 372.

82. Clay to Draper, 24 May 1948, Smith, *Papers,* 658; William Chamberlin, *The German Phoenix* (New York, 1963), 49.

83. James S. Martin, *All Honorable Men* (Boston, 1950), 14, 24.

84. I. G. Farben was founded in 1904 by Dr. Carl Duisberg, who was inspired by what he had seen of trusts while visiting the U.S. It was expanded after World War I into a quasi monopoly as a reaction to chemical industry losses to the U.S. (J. F. J. Gillen, *Deconcentration and Decartelization* [Bonn, 1953], 82).

85. Senate Hearings on Elimination of German Resources of War, Bernstein testimony 29 Dec. 1945, and R. Nixon, 25 Feb. 1946, 1107–8, 1538.

86. "Before the occupation was a year old, one could begin to observe that when . . . the top echelons of the German administrative agencies liked the advice they were given, they followed it. When they did not like the advice, there were difficulties" (Martin, 163–67).

87. The bankers' view was that "until the German economy was in a 'reasonable' state of operation, it would be unnecessary, and in fact harmful, to undertake 'drastic' reform" (ibid., 176–78).

88. Ibid., 181, 186.

89. Draper barely permitted Martin to report at divisional meetings (ibid., 193; Clark, 50).

90. Clay asked Martin to bring it up the next morning, at which time he laced into Martin for "delaying," while Draper looked on (Martin, 198–200).

91. Ferguson Commission Report, 15 Apr. 1949, 102, in Records of Army Staff, P & O 091 Ger, NA; staff meeting file in OMGUS 178-1/3; Martin, 203; John Gimbel, *The American Occupation of Germany* (Stanford, 1968), 117.

92. Gillen, *Deconcentration*, 24–25. The effective date was 11 February 1947, to be enforced by each Land.

93. This hit like a bombshell because the Trade and Commerce Branch program was built around big firms like Siemens and Bosch; they had instead put smaller independent firms on the reparations list; they argued Clay's order would bring export to a standstill (Martin, 215).

94. For export Harriman and MG used cartel arrangements (Martin, 218).

95. "MG officials were supposed to work out their economic programs without disturbing anything . . . the garden variety of Germans who were not of the industrial combines felt the full force of the controls."

96. Despite many abuses, MG did not repeal licensing laws for two years after Martin had recommended it (ibid., 219–20).

97. Martin's acting successor was Draper's son-in-law, Phillip Hawkins. Clay told Draper 16 Mar. 1948: "Phil now heads new division and once again has to get his eager-beaver trust busters in hand" (Smith, *Papers*, 578).

98. Ibid., 235.

99. A ball bearings firm was added to the list after reparations dismantled its opposition, thereby making it a monopoly, but it was Swedish, as was a match monopoly (Gillen, *Deconcentration*, 37; Schmidt, *Policy*, 313–15. 321).

100. Martin, 262; Gillen, *Deconcentration*, 57–58, 63. This was the month of Clay's sensing a war was imminent (Schmidt, *Policy*, 322–23). Wallich described ineffective efforts to break up the steel and coal industries and banks (380).

101. To Martin this was another proof of "the relative powerlessness of governments in the face of growing economic power. . . . National governments stood on the sidelines while big operators arranged the world's affairs."

102. Ferguson Report, 121. Clay responded on 24 April 1949 that he had faithfully carried out deconcentration, and that neither Draper, Wilkinson, Hawkins, nor Bronson had ever opposed it (Smith, *Papers*, 1131).

103. Harry Gross, *Dialektik der Restauration* (Freiburg, 1965), 60.

104. Interview Charles Dilley, 27 July 1949, in Schmidt, *Policy*, 333.

105. Bert Schloss, "The American Occupation of Germany 1945–52: An Appraisal" (Ph.D. diss., University of Chicago, 1955), 256.

4 Retreat from Forced Denazification

At the end of World War II, the free world took a lesson from "history" and set out to change what it perceived to be German values. Part of the program called for the total demilitarization of Germany. The Germans had cheated on the partial disarmament in the 1920s, and the accepted interpretation of the German national character was that inheritance and environment turned Germans into obedient soldiers, unquestioningly following orders to roll over innocent bystanders. Demilitarization in terms of weapons was thorough; there were no soldiers, no weapons, and even the police were disarmed. Antique hunting guns and swords from the Franco-Prussian War were collected, and destroyed or taken home by the victors.[1] Demilitarization of "the German mind" was not such a simple task, but as a beginning the externals of militarism were expunged. There could be no marching, no parades, no uniforms, no military songs or national anthems, no glorification of war in books, films, or art, no militaristic toys, no veterans' organizations or benefits. (It would be interesting to imagine attempting such a ban in the United States.)

Unlike most MG measures, these prohibitions were successful, but they were because the Germans were ready to accept them. Postwar Germany was a society where most men and some women from fifteen to sixty had been drafted, where millions of men had been killed, imprisoned as forced labor, or disabled for life. Millions of children had lost fathers. Many boys ended the war soldiering in a hopeless slaughter. City dwellers had repeatedly crouched in cellars, frightened to near hysteria by the bombing, many lived for years in ruins with their possessions destroyed. Other millions had lost their homes and lands forever. In the face of the resulting hatred of war, MG laws were inconsequential. Demilitarization was welcomed by most, resisted by none.

Ironically the Germans in time became suspicious of the American character, seeing it as one prone to violence and war. In less than three years some Americans began planning for Germans to bear arms again. That which had been dismissed as more of Goebbels's insane propaganda in 1945—an eventual American alliance with Germany against Russia—was being studied officially as early as April 1948. If the Americans failed to rearm Germany immediately it was only because they feared they might alienate their allies; they were suspicious of leftist tendencies in the German population and knew the Russians would denounce rearmament to the world. And in any case, MG realized that for the time being the West German economy could not support a military power.[2]

By 1950 the American fear of communism had swept aside most such objections, but the question was, would the Germans cooperate? James Pollock, asked by McCloy, reported no serious desire among Germans for an army. "The population has lost its military ardor and would not, without considerable difficulty, cooperate in the revival of any kind of military force." The antimilitarist attitude of *Ohne uns,* or "Count us out," very much bothered American planners. In 1951 almost everybody in the West was for German rearmament but the Germans; plans had been worked out but kept secret from the German people. The closeness of the Soviet army weakened German resistance to rearming, yet only 43 percent of the population favored it. As late as 1956, 65 percent were opposed to military service and the new army; of the first draftees in Munich only 15 percent showed up, and in Nuremberg only 25 percent. In 1959 an Augsburg veteran asked: "And where are the Americans who promised us in 1945 that none us would ever soldier again?"[3]

With weapons safely out of German hands almost as soon as the war was over, the first priority was to "denazify," a word coined to describe the process of making normal people out of Nazis. After this negative policy of denazification came the more positive assignment of making the Germans into believers in democracy. This chapter describes briefly the tortuous and tortured process of denazification, which by most accounts was a sad failure, and then the process of democratization, which, although it was at first deplored, would appear to have been a success.

Early Denazification Policy

When the war ended, there was one policy acceptable to all of the Allies—eradicating Nazism. No other occupying force was as methodical as the United States. Denazification was basic to all of MG's political policies. It absorbed a major share of OMGUS attention and staff and affected the lives of more people than any other OMGUS activity. Yet the early denazification program was based on a number of debatable assumptions. Emotional policy makers were ill-served by emotional social scientists, often émigrés, who used history to demonstrate that Nazism was so deeply rooted in German history, German culture, and "the German character" that a vast uprooting was necessary.[4] Almost everyone believed, at the least, that the structure of German society must be drastically altered. The previctory analysis was immensely fortified by the shock of discovering that what some had assumed to be exaggerated Allied propaganda was in fact true. Whatever doubts OMGUS may have had about the necessity for radical denazification were stilled by Buchenwald and Auschwitz. MG's response was to accept the idea that every German, whether man, woman, or child, was personally responsible for the crimes of the Nazi regime.[5] This theory of collective guilt remained the policy line until January 1946.

OMGUS, then, began with the official assumption that an individual's membership in the National Socialist party was a valid criterion of his support for the crimes committed by its leaders.[6] Yet those who had experienced twelve years in Hitler's Germany knew that life was more complex than theories of collective guilt would suggest. Evil could not simply be attributed to any group or even to most individuals. People had joined the party at various times and for various reasons, many because they were public employees and would otherwise lose jobs or promotions. Once in the party, most behaved much as they had before—apolitically. A few had been active. Some, but not most, party members had urged violence, particularly against Jews; some had terrorized their communities with denunciations; some had benefited from membership by getting better jobs or more profits. Yet some people not in the party were more Nazi than were party members. Some in the party hated it. Such subtleties became obscured by the notion of mass guilt for a mass crime. MG is properly blamed for basing policy on such a notion.

The denazifiers went at their job with convictions undisturbed by any doubt that Hitlerism was still very strong, and that only the sternest measures could destroy it and assure world peace. Yet one can as easily believe Nazism was for all practical purposes dead before denazification began; a common complaint by 1950 was that it had led to the rebirth of Nazism. Saul Padover, an avid liberal army propagandist, was surprised by the lack of support for Nazism among those in the Rhineland he interviewed in late 1944. He found that the youth were under the influence of their Catholic parents; only 20 percent of the population could be called Nazi in spirit. Teachers were conservative and neutral; Germans over forty were not friendly to Hitler; women resented the inferior status given them; Catholics were anti-Nazi because Nazism was anti-Catholic. Germans even showed an amazing lack of anti-Semitism. Padover concluded: "There is little evidence of racism, race pride, or race arrogance. . . . Young Germans are the paradox. . . . Many of them are sick and tired of Hitlerism and disgusted with the whole system of forced labor, forced training, forced living."[7] Hans Habe, who interrogated PWs, found the same: most youth opposed Nazism. Support for Hitler had come from the misery of the 1920s, which the young had not experienced. They had amplie experience with Hitler's miseries, however, and "had to pay a heavy toll for the wild enthusiasm of their fathers. Most of the young Germans hated the army."[8]

A War Department survey very early in the occupation found that "well over half of the German population did not accept any of the Nazi doctrines. Only a very small percentage, ranging from 4 to 5 percent among workers to 14 percent for professionals and executives and managers were 'full Nazis' on the basis of adherence to all the essential doctrines."[9] George Kennan wrote in 1945 that denazification was unnecessary and impossible. Lutz Niethammer concluded that the people who had given passive support to Hitler for personal goals, personal peace, and success, with the defeat shifted naturally to democracy when it did as well in serving their personal ends. Denazification may have thus been largely accomplished before it began. No one challenged removing the party from power, or punishing crimes, or seizing wealth gained criminally, but the majority did not support punishing those who had joined the party because they believed in something, or because they were forced to join.

Among Americans, who perhaps had seen too much pseudohistory created in Hollywood, a battle raged between those favoring tough and those favoring moderate punishment. Moderates were weakened by the assumption that it was somehow unmanly and unpatriotic not to be tough; to be moderate was to be weak which was to be pro-Nazi. Arguments on policy in 1944–45 had little to say specifically about how denazification might be implemented, but the army's experience in Italy suggested the means. MG set up "removal categories," which defined the groups of persons who were to lose their positions, and made use of detailed questionnaires which asked individuals to provide the information that would classify them into categories.[10] The category determined who would be dismissed or arrested. MG's Public Safety Division and its Special Branch were in charge of the programs, with the CIC providing them with any information it could uncover. The major issue at first was which persons should be removed, but then came the issues of what to do with the many appeal cases, what would happen to principles of justice in the cases of those sent to prison without trial, and what would happen to public services and the economy with so many people removed from their jobs.

The questionnaires were much influenced by Franz Neumann's Marxist analysis. He saw Nazism simplistically, as a coalition of militarists, industrialists, and high officials. Plans to destroy these groups were outlined in army manuals or handbooks in early 1944, but after the promulgation of the Morgenthau Plan there was a shift to a tougher line. (Morgenthau himself saw no hope for denazification; he felt the German character was incorrigible.)

The German Country Unit in May 1944 had recommended the immediate removal, pending screening, of only those officials who were most heavily incriminated. In August JCS 1067 decreed that all party members were to be forced from public offices.[11]

The first city where government could be practiced was Aachen, which had been taken in October 1944. It soon acquired about as many reporters as soldiers. Their widely publicized reports of Nazis in office frightened planners into more severity and administrators into more rigidity.[12] The local MG way of finding leaders was to ask the bishop, who suggested a conservative, who in turn chose people from the business community; 30 percent of these had belonged to the Nazi party.[13] Gen. Frank McSherry cabled SHAEF's defense against the newspaper's attack:

> The report to a very large extent is a misstatement. We do have some members of the Nazi party still in governmental positions in Aachen. These are being liquidated as rapidly as possible. . . . under our directives from the CCS, we are directed to eliminate "active Nazis" or "ardent sympathizers." If they mean party members, who in many cases joined the Nazi Party because of compulsion, it might be well for the CCS to consider a directive to that effect. . . . Initially the removal of all Nazis would make our problem very difficult, but at least we would be free from criticism.[14]

While McSherry wanted to fire more Nazis, his British counterpart thought this would be suicidal. The resulting schism meant that there was no SHAEF directive. The delay in advance meant delay in policy, until the spring offensive forced decisions by rapidly occupying more German territory.

On 11 March 1945, the deputy commander of the Twelfth Army Group, disturbed by General Omar Bradley's criticism, hastily drew up a blanket directive calling for mandatory dismissal of "Nazis, ardent Nazi sympathizers . . . members of any affiliated, attached, controlled or supervised Nazi organization" Yet this directive, which would have included most workers, was limited by the phrase, "with due regard to the basic well-being of the civilian population."[15] Policy moved to bar from public service all who had Nazi affiliations, even clerks and mechanics. It was mandatory to remove anyone who had been more than a nominal member of the party, that is, who had "held office or been otherwise active at any level." By early summer, MG was operating under four different directives; each command level sent modified orders down through its own channels. Matters seemed to stabilize with the 7 July directive, which subordinate headquarters were forbidden to modify. It created 136 categories under which removal from any kind of public service position was mandatory. Anyone with party membership before 1 May 1937 was fired.[16] The directive took the line of "guilt-by-office-holding."

Eisenhower told a MG conference in August: "We must get everybody tainted with Nazism out of every organization. If for no other reason we must remember we have to recognize the public demand in the U.S. and in the rest of the democratic world for complete denazification." In September he made it simple: "Reduced to its fundamentals, the U.S. entered the war as a foe of Nazism; victory is not complete until we have eliminated from positions of responsibility and, in appropriate cases, properly punished every active adherent of the Nazi Party." Clay added significantly: "It will require the separation of the wealthy Nazis from their property and financial resources, particularly where these have been gained through party membership."[17]

Clay took a strong denazification line from the start. By mid-June 1945 he was expressing concern that workers were being hit harder than management; an assistant was to discuss with Robert Murphy how management could be denazified. In late July Clay spoke of the "excellent" denazification of government, and the need to do something about industry; those who had become rich were presumably thoroughgoing Nazis. On 15 August, after he had visited Augsburg and been told about a butcher who allegedly saved his best meat for party members, Clay ordered the economy denazified.[18] He did not consult Public Safety, the enforcement branch, but it did not at first object. "Later however, they came to feel the directive was the first step on the road to ruin of denazification."[19] Murphy reported a denazification that had become too broad; James Pollock suggested letting the Germans do it. Yet Clay at his 22 September staff meeting put on more pressure. He felt that the transportation, communications, and industry divisions had lagged behind, and that people who came to him for approval in maintaining Nazis in their positions were "just wasting their time."[20]

Suddenly, on 26 September 1945, Clay decreed his famous Law No. 8: "It shall be unlawful for any business enterprise to employ any member of the Nazi Party or its affiliate organizations in any supervisory or managerial capacity, or otherwise than ordinary labor." Hastily conceived and badly drawn, the law affected the national union, into which nearly all workers were forced, and charity organizations such as the Red Cross, but not the more violent *Schutzstaffel* (SS) or *Sturmabteilung* (SA). It had been formulated and issued without the knowledge or advice of the USFET denazification staff, who immediately realized that the law would lead to "the confusion instead of the intensification of denazification,"[21] Enforcement was to be handled by having each firm report to municipal labor offices, and MG was to spot-check these reports, a mammoth and quite impossible task. Temporary licenses to practice were issued to physicians and other persons necessary to safeguarding public health.

Legislation designed to repair the damage done by this poorly prepared Law No. 8, Regulation 1, created three-man committees of Germans on the local level to review dismissals. Their lenience led to local MG complaints.

Appeal boards were soon swamped, yet an individual was not to be employed until his appeal was acted on. Confusion persisted as to whether a person could be employed in the same enterprise by changing job titles, a widespread means of evasion. The law did not refer to the self-employed or to those who owned a business, only to employees. There was confusion as to whether the Nazis' property should be kept from them, and which division should enforce this.[22] The worst feature of Law No. 8 was that it included so-called little Nazis, by forcing them into manual labor when their skills could have been more productive elsewhere.

That the program was too inclusive became the universally accepted criticism of denazification. The law was not seriously crippling only because it was not seriously implemented. All through the fall of 1945, reports on the degree of enforcement completely contradicted each other. Some reported denazification 99 percent completed; others reported it scarcely begun. Russell Nixon told Congress that "the contrast between what is claimed and what has been accomplished for Law No. 8 is very great," and the reason for the failure was that "we do not have a staff in Germany which from top to bottom possess the will and the understanding to carry out denazification."[23] Donald Robinson, MG historian, agreed: "Even months after the Patton affair, USFET had to send telegrams to the Third and Seventh Armies threatening court martial for officers of more than one hundred MG detachments unless the purge was speeded up."[24] William Griffith, who was to administer the law, blamed Clay that it was not implemented:

> Law No. 8 threw the denazification program into a state of confusion, uncertainty and flooding with work from which it never really recovered. . . . Uniformity was never established, even within districts; interpretations were often left to untrained members of local detachments; German authorities were in a state of complete confusion and uncertainty and German public opinion was now finally alienated from any support of the MG denazification program. No statistical reporting system was ever really set up and higher supervising MG levels had only the vaguest idea of what was actually happening in the field. Responsibility within MG for control and enforcement of the law was never made clear.[25]

Griffith's bitter criticism is largely supported by Clay's top two implementers. Chief denazifier M. K. Wilson said later that the review boards would not have been swamped but for Law No. 8. He thought it would have been better if removals had been left to MG commanders, if party members had been excluded only from policy-making positions, and if the property of those removed by Law No. 8 had not been blocked. Extending the law to include minor shopkeepers and all persons employed at more than ordinary labor diverted his office from the important job. Robert Bowie, who took over the denazification planning in December, agreed that it had been all fouled up by

Clay's arbitrary order that no one could be employed until cleared.[26] Banning people from jobs until they were proven innocent was an unhappy presumption of guilt. Although Special Branch reported to Clay on 9 January 1944 that "it is not working satisfactorily in the field," he told the press on 14 January that Law No. 8 had done a "pretty good job."[27] Yet the fact that it was already being replaced was an admission of failure. Law No. 8 set denazification down the road to ruin, and limited MG's power to persuade in matters where it acted more wisely.

SHAEF had prepared an arrest categories handbook in April 1945, and arrests were made by the tens of thousands, as quickly as titles could be checked with the list. A small-scale reign of terror was led by CIC detachments, while pressure from various U.S. groups forced headquarters to add ever more names to the arrest list.[28] Arresting people without a hearing, simply because they held some office, was one of the least defensible aspects of denazification. Sometimes simply having the title "councillor" (*Rat*), as in *Studienrat*, a pompus name for a teacher, sufficed for arrest. Anyone could be denounced and lie in a camp for months, ignorant even of the reason for his arrest. The army had arrested 70,000 by July 1945; at the end of the year, Clay announced that 100,000 "dangerous Nazis" were in jail. Alfred Grosser puts the numbers at the end of 1946 into perspective: the British had interned 64,000, the Soviets 67,000, and the French 19,000.[29]

Those arrested were put in what the Americans called internment camps, but which to Germans were concentration camps under another name. Murphy described one such camp for "little Nazis": "I was startled to see that our prisoners were almost as weak and emaciated as those I had observed in Nazi camps. The youthful commandant calmly told me that he deliberately kept the inmates on starvation diet, explaining, 'These Nazis are getting a taste of their own medicine.' " Murphy told Clay, who had the officer transferred. Murphy added: "On another occasion we were informed that a Nazi torture camp, equipped with devices to extort confessions, was still operating under American auspices."[30]

Clay at first took a hard line on internment. As late as 15 September 1945, he opposed changing the mandatory arrest categories as proposed in his staff meeting; he preferred to wait for a directive from Washington. But by 18 October, observing that 94,000 in mandatory arrest had been held incommunicado without trial, he was recommending that they be allowed to exchange letters with their families, and that their cases be investigated by German courts. A few days later, USFET ordered that new prisoners, even those taken by CIC, be notified of the reason for their arrest within twenty-four hours. On 15 November USFET gave instructions for setting up review boards for some categories, with MG boards to review German boards. But the boards did little to correct injustices. CIC retained wide discretion in arresting "security suspects," and the arrest level was in fact raised. The matter of the mandatory arrest of anyone who had held "high position" came to a head in the case of Dr. Hans Ehard, for over a postwar decade Bavarian minister of justice and minister-president. He was clear of guilt, yet subject to automatic arrest because he had been a judge from 1933 to 1945. "The absurdity of the situation became obvious, and USFET issued a directive in November 1945 allowing denazification boards to make exceptions to these categories."[31]

By 2 December Clay was worried by the increasing numbers of prisoners and the very slow review of their cases; lack of coordination resulted in some Germans being released by the British and rearrested by Americans.[32] On 6 December his Legal Division responded to Washington inquiries that of about 100,000 arrestees, 80 percent were members of organizations under indictment at the International Military Tribunal, and that quadripartite agreement on criminal organizations was unlikely until that trial was over. Any release of prisoners would take at least four months more.[33] On 8 December Clay recommended limiting mandatory arrests to active members of the indicted organizations, dangerous security suspects, and individuals against whom specific evidence was available on participation in war crimes. His reasons were crowded facilities, winter conditions, and the slow screening by German tribunals.[34] A February 1946 rule permitted the release from prison of general staff officers and high officials of any Land, but only after a review, which occurred in few cases.

The number interned had been reduced to 49,000 by January 1947, when the camps were turned over to German authorities. Yet when Clay ordered that sentences to camps should not wait for the appeal decision, thousands more were arrested, most of whom after appeal would not have been arrested. According to Niethammer, very few of the elite were arrested; those arrested came largely from the middle class, and were mostly persons holding public office. Of party "leaders" arrested, 80 percent were peasants from small villages, which was "not only an injustice but a mistake." In November 1948 Freda Utley visited a camp: "The prisoners included people who were not even party members and three former inmates of Nazi concentration camps. . . . many were old and sick . . . a pitiful collection of forgotten men who had no money and no influence"[35] Although Utley was prejudiced, M. K. Wilson Clay's assistant, agreed in principle to her account. He criticized the internment policy, arguing that it differed in important respects from the categories of JCS 1067; that no plan existed for the disposition of the interned; that few internees were made eligible for release, that the vast majority held for security or intelligence reasons should have been released; and that it was undemocratic to hold them indefinitely awaiting trial.[36]

In fact, the camps probably hindered denazification. Putting Nazi leaders together revived their badly shaken esprit de corps; judgments in camp trials were relatively mild. Moreover, if defendants were important figures, trials in their home communities would have reassured the public that the big ones were not getting away free.[37] There was slow improvement in both physical and psychological conditions, but even after the Germans took over management of the camps in 1947, prisoners were still not being given reasons for their arrests. When the tribunals started in 1947, five-sixths of the prisoners were put in the least serious "follower" category, and one-half of the prisoners would not have interned at all had there been any hearing before their arrests.[38]

Prisoners released in 1948 came under the wheels of the local tribunals, which were by then passing out lighter sentences; rarely did a sentence imposed equal the length of time already served.

Creating and Destroying the Law for Liberation

The OMGUS effort to denazify had become so great a mess, including such features as automatic arrest and automatic loss of employment, that as early as September 1945, Clay's key legal advisers, Charles Fahy and Robert Bowie, concluded that a comprehensive law was needed to replace the sporadic directives. It was clear that such meat-cleaver tactics by outsiders would not provide justice and maintain a functioning society. Therefore on 6 October 1945, Fahy suggested to Clay that a study group be authorized, and Clay set it up in November as the Denazification Policy Board. With Fahy as its chairman, and with its working committee headed by Bowie, it pushed for moderation in denazification policies.[39]

When the Americans looked about for ideas, they could utilize the plans already begun by party leaders in Bavaria, Anton Pfeiffer of the Catholic party, and Heinrich Schmitt of the Communist party. Their formulation criticized the OMGUS severity on ordinary party members, its failure to publicize directives, and the lack of German participation in implementing the policy. Their plan proposed German tribunals with judges as chairmen. These should have no prosecutor and make no clear presumption of guilt.[40] On 22 December 1945, the justice ministers of the Länder presented their proposal, which was essentially the Bavarian plan with some modifications coming from the state of Hesse. Their problem was to convince the American authorities that they had a better idea.

In early January negotiations began between Germans and Americans. The responsible branch of OMGUS, Public Safety, thought that the German proposal was too soft. American experts correctly foresaw that the tribunals, "in the climate of misery," would be frustrated by social pressures on the lay judges of the tribunals, by political pressures exerted by various groups, and by public opinion in general. Yet the decisive comment was also the shortest. Clay told Fahy, "I like it."[41] The Denazification Policy Board therefore accepted the German plan as a basis for negotiation on 7 February 1946.

While this negotiation was proceeding on the zonal level toward moderation, Clay was pushing through the ACC statement on denazification, Law No. 24. Bowie and Fahy were strongly urging him not to try to reconcile the zonal legislation with the ACC Law No. 24, but in early February, Clay decided otherwise.[42] His decision meant that anyone who had joined the Nazi party before 1937 could perform only ordinary labor until his trial, and then must be classified as a "lesser offender,"—that is, guilty. Bowie could not change Clay's mind, and was forced to tell the German planners that they must work both ACC Law No. 24 and zonal Law No. 8 into the new law. They were thunderstruck. Two of the three Land delegates were instructed by their home governments to refuse, but Pollock was able to work out a compromise. The Germans were led to believe that the apparently rigid categories of guilt could in operation be modified by the German courts, in which Americans would rarely interfere.

Only the most severe OMGUS pressure, and the fear of even worse practices by ill-informed MG officials, persuaded the Germans to sign. A draft of the new version was worked out in the second week of February 1946, and even this, under Public Safety Branch pressures, was made more severe before being published as the Law for Liberation from National Socialism 5 March. The provision with the greatest impact was the ranking of all party members who joined before 1 May 1937, and all officials of all other organizations, as "offenders."[43] This inclusion in the new law of Law No. 8 meant that the accused could not practice their occupations until they had been cleared by the tribunals. To permit large numbers of people to continue in their occupations was so urgent a task that the cases of nominal party members had to be handled before those presumed guilty of more serious offenders. This necessity led to the result that those convicted early, when the law was more strictly enforced, often received harsher treatment than those convicted later, when the law was being abandoned.

German doubts were temporarily outweighed by the satisfaction of ending direct MG operations, but the system was not ready to try its first case until late summer. Some twelve million questionnaires had to be distributed to all Germans in the U.S. zone over the age of eighteen. They asked not only for party affiliation, but also for any titles of nobility back to grandparents and for income during various years. The answers made possible a mechanical sorting of the twelve million into four classes subject to penalties: Class I, major offenders; Class II, offenders; Class III, lesser offenders; and Class IV, followers. Some three million persons, it was discovered, would have to be brought to trial. Tribunals of politically clean amateurs had to be created to try one-fourth of the adult population.

MG exerted pressure to get the new ministries for denazification going quickly, but their haste created the next problem. Their supervision was inadequate, which led to "the startling leniency and often sheer ignorance of the law," which many tribunals displayed, and to continual controversy when MG attempted to fill the gap left by inadequate German supervision.[44] From the German standpoint, MG intervention prevented the adjustments which had to come. The law made no mention of MG supervision and the Germans had assumed they had a free hand.[45] But on 17 May OMGUS Public Safety issued an implementation order which specified that local Special Branches could not permit follower status to anyone who had "held office or otherwise been active at any level . . . in the party and its subordinate organizations." OMGUS also decided, contrary to the 18 April directive, that MG would have to clear all tribunal members.

At this juncture, Clay's personal adviser, Fritz Oppenheimer, an émigré German attorney who had too bitterly criticized this Special Branch corruption of the directive, was replaced. His successor, Walter Dorn, at first stood between the factions, agreeing with the 1945 dismissal policy, but accepting, as Special Branch did not, Clay's "turn it over to the Germans" policy. His solution, which Clay backed, was to form a coordinating committee which was organized on 10 June. The committee's decision to separate policy and operations led immediately to serious policy differences. M. K. Wilson criticized Dorn as simply flitting about finding fault. Within a year Dorn was bitterly at war with Special Branch.

By August Special Branch, which never really supported turning its job over to the Germans, had found one great legal loophole: a Land denazification office could force the Land minister of denazification to correct "erroneous" decisions. Although MG denazification personnel approved of this arrangement, Dorn opposed it and prevented an OMGUS directive making it mandatory. On their own, however, Länder Special Branch offices set up a Delinquency and Error Report System. Officially begun in November 1946, this system was largely operated by the German employees of the Kreis level Special Branches, as the American officers nominally in charge changed too rapidly to exercise control.[46]

In early October, while Dorn was in the United States, a report from Dorn's assistant greatly perturbed Clay. It estimated that 67 percent of the verdicts in Bavaria were susceptible of error, which meant that presumably these cases would have to be tried again. But the Special Branch struggle to discredit the law and to regain full control was set back at the 22 October staff meeting when Clay dismissed these statistics and stated that the law's purpose was to return most party members to work. On the other hand, their 1 November study of German sabotage convinced and angered him. Clay lowered the boom on 5 November, in his bitterest speech to the Länderrat. He had "personally examined" 575 cases put by the law into Class I, major offenders. Of these, 355 were put by the court all the way down into Class IV, followers, and 49 were exonerated. He could not understand how people in high offices could be classed as followers.

> I have never spoken to you in terms of threat and I do not approve to do so now. However, I must say to you that MG cannot in full conscience restore self-responsibility of government to a German people who have shown they are unwilling to denazify their public life. . . . Regardless of its effect on the German economy, regardless of the additional time which it may take, if this will does not develop, MG will necessarily have to take measures to see that denazification is carried out.[47]

Clay's pressure on the Germans possibly was actually intended to show the American public that denazification would not work.[48] He resisted worse Washington suggestions, opposing mass trials or mass extradition of accused war criminals. He would have no single officer trying fifty cases a day.[49]

Clay's anger seemed to be the great chance for Special Branch, which decreed that no one could be reinstated in his job unless his local Special Branch concurred. It worked out a plan to take over denazification again. But Clay's anger was more in the tone of his speech than in the content, for he still believed his system could work. Antagonism grew rapidly. German denazification officials said intervention made the Rechtsstaat (rule of law) impossible, to which MG replied that Clay could issue any orders he wanted to. For a while there were more classifications of persons as I, II, and III. In two months, however, matters reverted to where they had been, as it became clear that Clay could not carry out his threat to resume direct MG operations. Classification became consistently more lenient.[50]

With tribunals swamped with more cases than they could handle, amnesty was used to reduce the numbers to be tried. On 8 July 1946, the minister-presidents obtained amnesty for those born after 1 January 1919, unless they were in the top two categories.[51] At its December 1946 meeting the Länderrat suggested an amnesty for those in low income groups, that is, those having a yearly income of less than 3,600 marks. This action reduced the numbers to be tried by 800,000, leaving 1,000,000 still to go. "All his advisers strongly urged him to make basic changes in the law itself, but Clay decided otherwise."[52]

Although amnesties were intended to clear the deck for major cases, processing them diverted the organization machinery. Negotiations on how broad the amnesty should be lasted for months, and the tribunals took three more months to process what was a much larger group than expected. All the while Clay was pressuring for statistical progress. One such statistic of progress was that 28 percent of the population over eighteen years old had been dismissed from their professional jobs. On 4 February Clay told the Länderrat it should pass laws to draft people to serve on the tribunals. Two days later he instructed field offices to see that this was done. "This law proved to be 'a blow into water,' as most of those who were supposed to be drafted knew how to get out of the duty."[53] Special Branch stressed that Clay's law was "administratively impossible and politically unacceptable to the German people." Although the ministries had practically sabotaged it, they could not be criticized, because real implementation would be political suicide. Wilson's solution, to punish criminals and fire others from leading positions, entailed in effect a return to pre-Clay policy, with Special Branch in "complete control."[54]

Dorn opposed this plan. He hoped, by reporting on his inspection in early April, to influence changes in the law in accordance with German wishes. It was asking the impossible of German democracy, he said, for a minority to purge the majority, and this was what was being asked. While only 10 percent of the total population were party members, this amounted to 29 percent of the adult population. Furthermore, 60 percent of the population were affected indirectly as families, and 70 percent of the middle class. The monthly meeting with denazification ministers was a "tug-of-war," because they were responsible to parliaments who reflected the widespread German opinion that too many people were being tried. The quality of tribunal personnel was deplorable; some judges were not only untrained but uneducated. Witnesses were on strike against the prosecution, but increasingly ready to help the defense. The law required an automatic indictment of large numbers into the top two guilt categories, even though the investigators found charges unjustified, and verdicts supported the investigators. The practice of automatically putting an official into Class III was also unfair. Many such officials were poor people who had been forced into trifling jobs, for the rich and powerful rarely held offices. The party had gloried in giving everyone some high-sounding office; one local group of nineteen members held among themselves sixty-one offices.[55] Niethammer thought Dorn was trying to take advantage of Clay's vanity, but Clay regarded his report as "the most damning criticism of what we have been trying to do here that has yet come to my attention." After ten minutes he put the report into his drawer, where it remained for ten weeks, and he followed nearly none of his adviser's recommendations.[56] Dorn left. Congress would force a change.

The masses of congressmen who came to Germany in the summer of 1947 to see what was happening concluded that something had to be changed. American public opinion was being pushed by American critics of OMGUS denazification activities.[57] This outcry paralleled rising German criticism made louder by party leaders needing votes. The Case Committee, led by MG adviser Carl Friedrich, recommended in the fall that denazification be ended by 8 May 1948. Clay cabled in September that denazification might take a year or so longer, but should not be abandoned. His Public Safety Branch reported that it was having only a very minor effect on industrial revival, a favorite congressional concern, stating: "Of all the factors at present having a deterrent effect upon the general economy of the country, denazification is a poor last."[58]

But in any case the system was also cracking from the top. On 16 August 1947 the Soviets made a bid for the support of the party small fry, by letting them out of the net. The United States saw this action as the end of any Allied denazification program. Negotiations with Britain for a bizonal de-nazification law had also failed. Army Secretary Kenneth Royall requested Clay to close up denazification as soon as possible in order to relieve congressional pressure. In late August Clay personally drafted a memo for reform, including a point not asked for by the Germans—permission for the return of Class III persons to technical and managerial posts.[59] For the first time some Americans were more interested in relaxing denazification than were Germans. Clay directed Special Branch to use error reports only in cases of seriously incriminated Nazis, whose clearance might make them eligible for influential positions. But his order had little practical effect. "The MG de-nazification staffs, who by then practically alone fully understood the complicated denazification structure, were able effectively to delay the effects of policy relaxations."[60] On 9 September Clay gave the presidents of the Länderrat an oral summary of concessions which his own denazification personnel learned of only at the 23 September meeting. German efforts, as in Augsburg, to speed up the cases were discontinued by MG despite optimistic publicity, because denazifiers labeled them a "whitewashing machine."

Then Congress got involved in the person of John Taber, chairman of the House Appropriations Committee.[61] Washington opinion, simplistic before on the subject of denazification, remained simplistic but was now on the other side. Cox of Georgia, for instance, said the Nazis were being persecuted for being patriotic. At a January 1948 hearing, Taber and Congressman Clifford Case put further pressure on Clay. In a deficiency appropriation debate, the committee apparently demanded that denazification be ended before more funds were voted. The War Department cabled Clay, urging him to declare an immediate amnesty and to bring the program to a conclusion. Clay replied that the "big Nazis" were still to be tried; not to try them would be a major blow to U.S. prestige. He played his usual trump card; he "would only do so if he were given a direct order to that effect." Since this threat was weakened by the fact that his retirement was scheduled for 30 June, he proposed a speedup, so that by 1 May only a few cases would be left. His offer was accepted by

Royall and Taber. Clay ordered cases to be tried limited to 30,000, of which 5,000 could be those of persons currently interned.

Clay sent Theo E. Hall with oral orders to Länder ministers to have all those in the offender category, unless they had been in criminal organizations or personally active in the party, moved down to the follower category. The ministers resisted this equalizing of leaders with members. At the end of April there were still 450,000 cases, not including appeals, and 17,000 prisoners in internment camps. Clay ordered Hall "to negotiate" with the German ministers, that is, put them under intense pressure. Roles were reversed; the Germans were resisting OMGUS efforts to break down MG's system, while Hall practically dictated changes like the almost total end to occupational restrictions and to automatic classifications. When Gottlob Binder, minister from Hesse, raised some practical objections, Hall offered a deal; he would remove the entire supervision system if the Germans would accept his proposal for changing the law. What would have taken the Germans months of waiting was done in four hours, but the changes came too late.[62]

Hall, with full powers, instructed the state denazification ministers, who instructed local agencies. The quota of 30,000 was subdivided down to the Kreis level and those in internment camps were subjected to the same procedure to reach the 5,000 figure. The whole operation was done largely under verbal orders, for this quota procedure was supposed to be kept a complete secret from the German denazification authorities. By 1 May, OMGUS claimed only 28,065 remained to be tried. In May MG denazification staffs were cut back by as much as 80 percent; in August all units below the Land level were abolished.[63] In October Hall told the ministers that all that was left of his entire organization was one adviser to Clay. The tribunals, however, moved more slowly than had been predicted. Although people had been reluctant to serve, once involved they did not want to quit, since they had become outcasts and jobs were scarce for them. The MG goal of dismantling the German denazification system was defeated by the denazification ministers, who had been told for years that denazification was the number one goal. They had appeals to hear, and new cases from refugees and returning PWs. And indeed, although the German ministries closed in 1949–50, appeals dragged on for a decade.

German public opinion meanwhile became steadily more critical. Some 57 percent of those polled in 1946 were satisfied with denazification procedures, but only 32 percent in 1948 and 17 percent by 1949. In 1953 only 17 percent thought denazification had generally fulfilled its purposes, 23 percent considered it wrongly executed, and 40 percent thought it harmful.[64] Niethammer, in his definitive analysis of denazification, found that little survived of the great MG effort. Party members, except for obvious criminals, had been reabsorbed without discrimination. The opportunity for real social change had been forfeited by MG. It had chosen instead to have a power base against Russia. Partly for that reason MG had no partner for its policy of political housecleaning. At first it had rejected partnership with the Germans, choosing instead to attempt reform by authoritarian repressive action. But to succeed this course required a strong German administrative organization, and MG had destroyed it. MG was then forced into recreating the political parties, but their existence prevented its administrative solution. While the parties of the left might have assisted the kind of denazification MG desired, they would also have pushed for basic social change which MG feared. Therefore MG allied itself with conservatives, although their ideas of *Rechtsstaat* were contrary to its own.[65]

The Army and Reeducation

All OMGUS political actions were, at least in theory, supposed to reeducate the German people toward acceptance of democratic values. Americans assumed that their personal example and their reforms of German school and German communications media according to American models would lead the Germans to become as democratic as they thought themselves to be. In actual fact, the program of democratization got off to a very slow start, taking three steps backwards before taking any step forward. The denazification and internment program followed procedures ordered by U.S. generals over the protests of the German people and their elected leaders. The early OMGUS prohibition of American and German fraternization was a second backward step. Finally, an American attitude of self-righteous superiority characterized the occupation from beginning to end.[66]

The policy of nonfraternization was adopted on a governmental level before the 1944 Quebec Conference, but it has been impossible to identify the individual or group responsible for the decision.[67] Some of the reasons for it, however, are clear enough. The complete failure of the nonfraternization rule following World War I was attributed to the practice of billeting troops in German homes; officials agreed that billeting should be prohibited. Nonfraternization was partly an answer to a security question based on the assumption that there would be a long resistance. It was also designed to protect the GI from German propaganda and to convince Germans of their defeat.

It was a tyranny redeemed only by mass disobedience. No sooner were GIs in Germany than pictures appeared of them giving children chewing gum, which prompted Eisenhower to say: "This must be nipped in the bud immediately." Tight censorship was imposed to prevent news of such behavior from reaching the home front, yet charges increased that MG was coddling the

Germans. The ban created insoluble problems. For example, what was to be done about GIs with German relatives? This question led to the March 1945 directive that all troops with blood relatives were to be transferred from the theater, but implementing the directive would have meant the loss of most interpreters.[68]

The army in effect invited contact when it employed large numbers of Germans to do the menial work in offices and camps, a practice which had the further effect of leaving the troops with little to do but search for souvenirs, wine, and women. Most of the mass violations of the nonfraternization edict went unnoticed by headquarters, but they learned officially of a large number of rape cases between March and the end of June.[69] Joseph Starr listed 402 in March, 501 in April, and 241 in May. The high venereal disease rate was also proof of disobedience to the more suspicious—perhaps even proof of female sabotage. Hans Habe noted a very tangible result: in the western zones there were 94,000 illegitimate occupation babies.[70]

MG officers puzzled whether it was legal to have contact with Germans for the purpose of obtaining information required for official duties. It was clear, though, that they were forbidden to shake hands with any Germans. There could be no eating together, even with leaders of the anti-Nazi underground. Even after the ban ended in the fall, it remained policy to stay officially aloof. GIs could then consort with *Fräulein* without breaking regulations, but MG officers were instructed to keep their social relations with German officials to the minimum.[71] Other zones had a similar policy but it was more rigidly enforced in the American zone. The French, for example, were regarded as more harsh but also more human. Although conditions were physically better in the U.S. zone, Germans resented the ''We come as conquerors'' attitude, and the superiority complex of a people whose superiority they had never admitted.[72]

Unfortunately the policy was withdrawn so gradually that many Germans assume it existed until the end of the occupation. On 8 June 1945, Eisenhower permitted contact with ''very small children.'' Not speaking was ended on 1 October, but there was still to be no billeting with Germans and no marriage. In January 1946, soldiers were told they could associate with Germans as ''ambassadors of democracy.'' A bulletin of 29 September 1946, following the famous Byrnes speech in Stuttgart, emphasized the change which commanders were to explain: ''Re-education and the general salvaging of the German population is now the order of the day. . . . Every element of the occupation forces is involved in this program and those running the show consider it the most important single job we have to do.'' In November troops were no longer told to reject any friendship; instead they were urged to behave well and respect respectable elements.[73] By May 1947 Americans could take German guests to snack bars; by June 1948 they could take them to military messes twice a week. Yet in spite of the changed policy, contact declined, largely because new troops were concentrated in military posts and communities. They usually saw Germans only as servants at home or clerks at the office.

Housing requisitions were a form of contact that had an effect opposite to creating admiration for Americans and democracy. Correspondent Russell Hill compared the American rapaciousness for houses with Russian rapaciousness for machines. "It was a scandal that an American officer and wife could live in a house of from 8 to 15 rooms in a city where the average residents were living three to four in one room. There was no differentiation. They were all Germans and could be booted out."[74] CAD conceded the great bitterness created by the military communities, entire suburbs put behind barbed wire for U.S. families. The practice was rationalized as "presenting to the peoples of the occupied countries good examples of democratic American family and home life."[75] Through the barbed wire, perhaps?

Furthermore, Americans sent to Germany maintained wartime attitudes even after the official hate program was discontinued.[76] There was no doubt that Americans were encouraged in their feelings of superiority by the practice of bringing their families to Germany and supporting them out of occupation costs in a luxury rare for Germans for years. "If the average soldier knew little about re-education, his wife or mother knew even less. The American women . . . entered Germany as the real conquerors." These women, usually lower middle class, were supplied with servants and sometimes deigned to do social work among the conquered. Much of the isolation of American troops and their families grew from the policy of creating "little Americas" that made everything as much like home as possible. No one had to have contact with natives.[77] Although the Berlin blockade of 1948–49 and the common front against communism altered the official line from regarding Germans as a conquered people to regarding them as allies, the psychological nonfraternization barriers remained. In May 1952, Acheson, Eden, and Schuman arrived to sign the treaty giving West Germany a considerable measure of independence, but members of the occupation were still officially forbidden to spend the night under a German roof, and American autos still could not be stopped by a German policeman. "On the Petersberg, near Bonn, where the High Commissioners resided, there was a carpet on which no German was allowed to step."[78]

A further serious impediment to the democratization program was the bureaucratic restraint on individual liberties, which was not unlike that imposed by Hitler. Americans had a stereotyped view of Hitler's Germany as a place where everything was forbidden—*Alles verboten*—yet it also often seemed true of the Germany created by OMGUS in 1945. The Germans had to be taught a lesson, and therefore, as Eisenhower made clear, they had no rights. His 14 July proclamation told them they were to obey orders "immediately and without question." Americans, fearful of nonexistent guerilla "werewolves," ordered extreme curfews as soon as they arrive, allowing Germans as little as one hour daily outside their homes. Germans were not to travel more than a few kilometers, although millions were left far from home by the war. Meetings of more than five people were prohibited; all mail service was stopped; no telephones were to be used. Germans were sealed off from the world. They were forbidden to receive books, newspapers, and magazines from outside, and in fact to possess one was a crime. "Instructions posted at the German-Swiss border told the Germans it was forbidden to attempt to communicate with the people on the other side of the frontier whether by words or by making signs." Movies and theaters were not permitted for several months after VE Day, although the Soviets authorized such entertainment almost immediately.[79] The Psychological Warfare Division, which rebaptized itself the Information Control Division, undertook rigorous control over all media. The army's right to carry on search and seize operations handicapped MG efforts to reestablish a humane judicial system, as Clay admitted. "In January 1947, however, I was able to persuade the Army Command not to undertake searches without previous notice to MG. . . . Later the detention of security risks for more than a few hours required the appearance of our Army Intelligence personnel, making the arrest, before a MG court, to show justification for the detention."[80]

The hermetic seal was only gradually loosened. In November 1947 the first businessmen were given permission to leave for business in the United States and the first correspondents were allowed to leave the zone. In October, censorship of civilian communication came to an end.[81] Yet in November 1948, Roger Baldwin of the American Civil Liberties Union reported many limitations, such as MG control over all communications through licenses. He noted: "Books critical of the Occupying Powers may not be published nor imported." Organizations were also controlled by the device of licensing. All officials were subject to summary removal; many were removed without hearing or appeal. No German might leave without an exit permit which took an unreasonably long time, entailing, for example, a six-month wait to visit sick relatives in Holland. No German might move his residence without permission from the housing authorities.[82] Baldwin's report in April 1949 noted several other limitations on German liberties: the censorship of printed matter and motion pictures from abroad; the CIC practice of hiring undercover informers and paying for each bit of information; the trials of Germans in occupation courts for offenses not involving occupation personnel or property; the irregularities in requisitioning properties and in their return; and the discrimination against Germans in Allied establishments.

The negative impact of troop behavior and army regulations was in some part balanced by more positive efforts to reeducate the German population toward democracy. Most of these efforts were indirect, for example, stemming from the reeducation policy makers at OMGUS or from the Information Control Division, which influenced the newspapers. The exception that proved the rule was the announced program to work with German youth, the group presumably least corrupted by the German past. The German Youth Activities program (GYA) evolved relatively quickly. Although no youth organizations were supposed to be permitted, MG soon discovered there were many young people who required society's attention. In August MG created a juvenile delinquency section and then a youth office. By mid-September officers were being encouraged to organize youth activities, but this ran counter to nonfraternization orders and to the policy of making Germans responsible for youth. In October a theater directive authorized the formation of youth committees on the Kreis level, and later directives ordered committees on the Land level.

In 1946 there was little progress because of fear of coddling the Germans, but the formation of a youth activities section in April 1946 signaled positive participation by a few troops.[83] The principal activity was athletics, but food, gum, and Cokes were an attraction. Generally the idea was to give youth something to do, with the notion that democratic principles might be passed along in the process. There were obstacles from all sides. It was difficult to get equipment after the practice of requisitioning it from Germans was stopped. A 1947 inspection in Munich showed that GYA there had nearly come to a standstill for lack of gasoline and funds. There were no trained personnel to run the activities. Almost all of the direction was in the hands of young soldiers who had little idea of what they were supposed to be doing and therefore did the one thing they knew how to do—teach American games. By 1948 whatever activity existed was operated by Germans, with military personnel mostly in supervisory positions.

While statistics of growth were impressive, in fact the program expanded very slowly. An opinion survey in major cities showed most youth had never heard of GYA. Most of those who participated said they came for food and assumed providing it was GYA's major function; about 10 percent thought they had learned something about democracy.[84] Outside the larger communities, the program simply did not exist. It was attacked from the left by socialists and from the right by Catholics, who preferred their own organizations; peasants preferred their children to work in the fields. Everyone resented the requisitioning of buildings for GYA. Large Christmas parties—a total of 1,689,046 persons attended in 1948—brought much publicity but little real personal contact. Perhaps the prize anecdote about GYA is the story of the soldiers in charge of an outing in Nuremberg. They turned over bats, balls, and gloves to the boys and told them to bring them back at 1600 hours; the soldiers then disappeared for the afternoon with their German girl friends, the more interesting German youth activity.

A more specific reeducation program was that which attempted to reform the German educational system. It dealt primarily with elementary and secondary schools, although reformers occasionally hoped to reform the universities. It could have effected organizational changes, and involved new textbooks, the introduction of adult education, and teacher and student exchanges between German and American schools. By 1948 reeducation was labeled the most important goal, but there were constant disputes about its feasibility and bitter criticism of its personnel and procedures.

Although OMGUS had an education section from the beginning, it was given very little support for at least two years. Clay was at first sceptical about a reeducation program. In March 1946, in response to Hilldring's offer to send over a "big-name educator," he wrote that OMGUS had tried in 1945, and finding no such person had developed its own staff. Clay felt that reeducation of the German people was a part and parcel of MG as a whole. The restoration of the secret ballot, the reestablishment of self-responsibility for local government, the revival of local initiative and pride, and many other factors had to combine to reestablish a liberal Germany. It must be done by Germans.[85]

Yet school reform was investigated by OMGUS. In September 1946 an educational mission headed by George Zook, president of the American Council on Education, made three recommendations. It called for a comprehensive school system, rather than one divided by intellectual aptitude, for a common six-year elementary school, rather than a four-year, and for increased emphasis on social studies. In January 1947, while its education section was led by Dr. Roger Wells, OMGUS put these recommendations into directives. A CAD inspector, however, remained sceptical of reeducation, noting the lack of sufficient qualified personnel, of status in the organization, of supplies, and of comprehension of what the program was trying to accomplish.[86]

In early 1947 more disagreement developed regarding its future. CAD argued that the new Land constitutions precluded MG intervention at that level; only OMGUS could advise and suggest. The Education and Religious Branch resisted this interpretation, using as evidence the draft of the directive which emerged in July as JCS 1779: "You will require the German Länder authorities to adopt and execute education programs designed to develop a healthy, democratic educational system." In February Clay said: "Education or Re-education is the one constructive field in which we have a positive mission . . . I side with education."[87] In February 1948 CAD gave education "top priority," and on 1 March OMGUS advanced the branch to division status. By the fall of 1948, Edward Litchfield convinced Clay and

Washington that OMGUS should get the authority to recruit officers to work in a "program which goes variously under the name of democratization, reorientation, or cultural affairs."[88]

When adviser Wells left the OMGUS education section, he reported that the problems of reorganizing German education along American lines had been surmounted. Zink commented: "Actually most of the plans, probably fortunately for both Germans and Americans, remained on paper and were never executed." Wells's successor, Dr. Alonzo Grace, dismissed Wells's work with the statement that the previous years had been "more or less devoid of an educational and cultural relations effort," but according to Zink his own reign was marked by waste of money and "a great deal of fuzziness of reasoning and too much rather pompous talk."[89] Carl Friedrich wrote in the 1948 Herter Committee report: "After two years the urgent request of German institutions of higher learning for visiting American professors had not been heeded."(Dozens of French and British scholars had visited their zones.) Instead OMGUS had tried to force upon the Germans certain purely organizational features of American education, some of which were highly controversial even among Americans. Friedrich thought MG should do as the Germans asked, and send teachers, books, and exchange students. "Unfortunately, until very recently... every kind of bureaucratic obstruction was thrown in the way of those who wished to help."[90] He observed that Information Control Division (ICD) officials often lacked an educated background and spent their time imposing their personal views rather than helping reeducate.

Zink thought that despite the great increase in personnel and funds, "too many of the new education staff were 'empire builders,' who knew very little about German problems and cared less, but saw in the Education Division an opportunity to gain recognition, build up personal power. ... People were selected who sought the jobs because they were offered more salary than they could command in the U.S.; or surplus military personnel needing jobs or friends of officials were picked out."[91] As Roger Baldwin described the absurdity: "Few Americans spoke German—few knew German history or institutions. ... Instead of knowledge they had titles. 'Director of Reorientation,' 'Director of Re-Education,' 'Director of Democratization,' and finally, supreme above all, the 'Coordinator of Democracy'."[92]

General Morris Edwards counted thirty-five different devices for reeducating the Germans, but praised only one, the public forums, even though they had failed in the cities. A May 1948 MG report noted a need to change "the predominantly negative relationship" between Germans and MG.[93] An OMGUS conference "universally agreed that democratization should henceforth be regarded as a major function and mission of the CAD, but that to date OMGUS had taken little action to make it such." There was criticism on all sides of the "failure to submit a well-planned and coordinated program to the Länder."[94] There was no training program for new teachers until four years after the war was over. New schoolbook publication was slowest in the U.S. zone, where in mid-1947 there were still only two million books, and these did not include a single elementary book about modern history or government. At the end of 1947, for every 1,000 children in school the French had published 800 textbooks, the Russians 700, British 400, and the U.S. only 150.[95] Under HICOG education had a low priority. Arthur Settel noted: "The Resident Officers had 103 functions, of which education was but one and concluded that their influence on German education is minute." The French sent four times as many educators for one-third the number of students. Education was allotted but 1 percent of the occupation budget.

The general failure of American attempts to reeducate the Germans was partly caused by the assumption which underlay them. Reeducation was necessary because the German character was assumed to be antidemocratic, although William Thayer, OMGUS liason officer to the Bundestag, wrote that this belief was largely based on a myth.[96] Bavarian Commissioner George Shuster believed the German bureaucracy had been willing to reform until it realized that Americans planned to reshape the supposed German character. The unwarranted generalizations forced them into angry opposition. Shuster criticized OMGUS for its unwillingness to learn about the true character and culture of the people they were to reform. Those responsible for handling cultural problems showed great reluctance to meet with Germans socially, see a German play, or look at a German book. "They sat in their offices and issued orders, frequently reflecting appalling unawareness of the German educational pattern." A few first-rate men with greater freedom could have collaborated with good results. As it was, the Germans gave in only as long as they had to, and then "went back to their dear old days with badly concealed jubilation."[97]

Toward the end of MG, and during the HICOG period, a few more effective programs were created. They were effective because they offered some Germans something they wanted: exchange programs and information centers. Exchange programs began in 1947 with four categories of candidates: political leaders, trainees, students, and teenagers. The peak years were 1950–52, when the total number of persons sent to the United States exceeded 2,000 annually. The number was then cut drastically, though the Fulbright program took up some slack. By the end of 1956 more than 12,000 Germans had been sent to the United States, and more than 1,800 Americans had gone to Germany.[98] Some younger Germans did in time come to see some advantages in U.S. colleges, in subjects such as political science, for example, or in modifying the "professor is king" pattern.

Information centers (*Amerika Häuser*) with reading rooms and bookmobiles did not cost much, but they attracted the attention of serious-minded

Germans at a time when books were hard to get. For the first two years after the war it was difficult to get books, and indeed the Americans carried out a purge of libraries. In one small Bavarian town the library was reduced from 10,000 to 3,000 books, on the basis of a 1945 list later labeled as communist, which banned even the *Nibelungenlied* as nationalist propaganda. The books of large numbers of authors were banned; some authors were arrested by mistake.[99] There were also frustrations from the top. In Washington the program faced indifference and even hostility, both in the State Department and in Congress, so that much time and effort had to be spent merely to keep it alive. When OMGUS was replaced by HICOG the question arose of whether information centers were still a legitimate activity of the occupation. Further waste was occasioned by congressional delay in passing authorizing legislation and in working out the transfer of funds from the army to the State Department.[100]

There were eventually 26 Amerika Häuser and 137 smaller reading rooms. The average center had some 16,000 books, one-fourth in German. Attendance rose from 3.7 million in 1948 to 13 million in 1951. Unfortunately, very few Americans showed any interest and most American officials were less proud of the centers than were Germans. As in other areas, the program was handicapped by a lack of qualified personnel. "Since much of this program is financed through marks, the actual operations have been to a large extent carried out by Germans. . . . effective policy execution requires a background which many of the German staff members simply do not possess."[101] Habe, however, observing that some junior officers did a remarkable job with Amerika Häuser and community meetings, remarked: "They were simply powerless against an incapable policy . . . our positive attainments in Germany have nothing to do with our policy and are not the results of deliberate planning." Edward Litchfield, the director of education, told Baldwin he recognized "the futility of propaganda to promote democracy, but he was caught by directives."[102]

OMGUS policy could have encouraged reeducation with lecturers, films, books, and buildings. It spent money on other things. It could have facilitated, not hindered, travel of people and information. It could have stimulated, not censored, controversial ideas. Germans might have appreciated advice, had the U.S. experts shown more understanding and less ignorant arrogance. Yet the negative effect was moderated by the fact that reeducation consisted chiefly of talk, and few Germans heard MG talk, fewer paid attention, and even fewer changed.

The most effective instrument of reeducation was the press. Most publishing was done by Germans on their own initiative for their own power or profit, and they succeeded the more when MG left them alone. Yet as former officers of the ICD have written, what success they achieved was also beset with policy frustrations. From the first there was conflict. On 10 May 1945, the Office of War Information announced that Germans would get only the information U.S. officers thought they should have. The public outcry that followed brought a quick reversal from Truman, who announced 15 May that Eisenhower intended there to be a free press as soon as conditions would permit.[103] Another area of conflict was apparent 22 May, when General Robert McClure, founder of the Psychological Warfare Division of SHAEF, directed that news policy be to make the Germans feel guilty about the concentration camps. The wartime appeals to the sympathy and confidence of the Germans were at an end.[104] The "collective guilt" line meant a severe restriction on editors, as did the ICD ban on criticizing any of the Allies.

But simply getting the newspapers going suffered long delays. The ICD blamed the lack of suitable personnel. Its staff man Harold Hurwitz, thought the problem was the ICD lack of urgency; the "Russians had moved much faster."[105] Rather than trying to use older publishers with non-Nazi views, ICD closed all of the old papers and created only a few totally new ones, the licensed press. Finding even a few new people qualified by training and political persuasion took valuable months, and the examiners and their procedures were open to criticism. They were accused of being far to the left; the leading ICD figure, Cedric Belfrage, is usually cited because he later fled to communist Czechoslovakia. Belfrage created a board of seven men for the Frankfurt paper, four of whom were communist, and the other three socialists. Communists, however, were soon forced out or moved to the political center.[106]

Hurwitz thought the psychological testing and the psychiatric interviews of applicants were absurd, but whoever passed the tests and was given a newspaper became the protégé of the ICD officers who sponsored him.[107] For the first weeks of publication each paper had a press control officer as adviser, but he was instructed not to exercise any prepublication censorship. ICD was involved in the battle between the German political parties and the licensed press, partly because the press was not as respectful as expected, and partly because MG prevented the parties from owning their own newspapers, as had been the practice formerly.[108] Newspapers feared political pressure because of "a bitter experience of licensed newspapers with antagonistic civil authorities and critical, often jealous, party officials."[109]

Habe, the long-time editor of the OMGUS-operated newspaper, *Die Neue Zeitung*, thought that the close relationship of "the licensing teams with their selected German editors was a partial explanation for the opposition to his newspaper." (In addition there was a "monstrous lack of understanding" in higher quarters.) His idea of one German-language newspaper for zonal distribution somehow got verbal approval from Eisenhower, eliminating a staff study. Its circulation quickly rose to one and one-half million and could have increased another one-half million. Although it was highly respected, having attracted some of the best German talent, its closing by the spring of 1946 was prevented only by Eisenhower's intervention. Habe's problems with headquarters continued over what he could and could not print. For instance, he did not try to print Churchill's "Iron Curtain" speech. He did, however, disregard orders to stress the Morgenthau line. While he got McClure's support for this evasion, he thought if McClure had been able to read German he would probably have disowned him.[110]

Division Chief McClure was able to retain a significant degree of autonomy from MG until late in 1945 when Clay forced him to relinquish some authority to the Germans. Clay's idea was that MG control should be limited to the protection of the public against "fraudulent enterprises" and "malicious information" through granting or withholding licenses.[111] McClure, favoring a slow and cautious policy, wanted MG to teach Germans what they must do; Clay wanted only to list those things which Germans must not do, leaving the remainder of the field free. In line with Clay's policy, German newspapers were granted permission to carry factual accounts of world events as legitimate news stories, although "Nazi and militarist and malicious" material was still banned.

Increasingly ICD was also operated by German employees, who at first were émigrés. "Native-born Americans, because of their lack of knowledge of Germany, its people and institutions, were inclined to depend on the refugee groups rather than to interfere." The émigrés tended to put returning friends into publishing enterprises and return things to the Weimar pattern. More importantly, there were the "indigenous personnel" on the ICD staff, who had menial positions but were making decisions because of the turnover among Americans. "The new American chief was frequently dependent on his German staff to tell him what duties he must perform."[112]

The licensees retained a monopoly longer than expected. The paper shortage, a result of poor planning elsewhere in MG, meant even licensed papers had to be reduced from fourteen pages to two.[113] From December 1946, for a year and a half licensing came to a near stop. Only with the currency reform in June 1948, when industrial goods began reappearing, was liberal change possible. Another delay was brought on by the conflict over a "press law," first suggested to the Länderrat by Clay in 1946 but not enacted until 1949.[114] German officials opposed the suggested law because it gave fuller protection to the press and required public officials to disclose information. In 1949, in eight months of disappointing debate, the MG defenders of a free press retreated from one position to another. They tried for a radical revision toward U.S. precedent, only to discover that "they were insufficiently prepared, out-classed, and well-advised to rely on the German press tradition which protected the freedom of the press in some fashion." At the end of the debate the German press was legally better protected than in 1945, but in many ways it lacked the security it had had under Bismarck.[115]

In 1948 information policy changed from control to positive orientation and the Information Control Division was renamed Information Services. One major effort was to make sure the licensed press would be guaranteed long-term use of plant facilities, originally requisitioned by ICD for the new publishers, and protected by law from encroachments from officials and interest groups. As with much of the MG apparatus, the efforts of one department were largely exerted in battling another department on behalf of the Germans. For example, journalists had enormous difficulties getting permission to leave the country from the Combined Travel Board.[116]

When licensing was finally abolished in 1949 and anyone could start a newspaper, some feared that Nazis or other reactionaries would reassert their old position. From May to October, 650 new papers were started as competition with the 66 licensed papers. By the end of October, to the relief of MG and German liberals, the licensed press had lost but 15 percent of its circulation. Most of the new papers that survived were small town provincial papers catering to regional demand. These were poorly financed and no threat to the metropolitan papers with a four-year headstart. One major oversight, on the other hand, was MG's disregard of the Germans' love for weeklies. This field was taken over by a series of illustrated and nationalistic papers which initially aroused readers' interest by featuring Nazi memoirs. (They later discovered that sex sold better.)

Hurwitz thought the change effected in German journalism by U.S. influence rather minor, being limited to some use of letters-to-the-editor columns and interviews with citizens. The impact was minor because of the "lack of a systematic and well thought-out program. . . . The belief that the best thing for the German press would be for it to become an American press survived throughout the MG period. And when officials realized that this was impossible, they were unable to imagine how broad changes could be implemented in German terms. At this point American officials were inclined to consider the Germans—who are a relatively 'educatable' people—beyond hope, a lost cause." Effects of training were hit-and-miss, and the austerity program nullified most positive plans.[117] Yet the arbitrary transfer of the major newspapers from relatively conservative owners to those relatively liberal was as close to a revolution as MG effected. In terms of democratization the newspapers had limited immediate impact, but over the years their influence grew. It was one of the few cases where MG allied itself in 1945 with "good Germans" for mutual goals.

In attempting to change German attitudes, U.S. personnel were most successful when they tried, and interfered, the least. The vast effort expended to denazify was thwarted by bad planning, poor assumptions, internal struggles, and massive public resistance. Germans resented and resisted any reeducation; little was accomplished directly by any change in the school system, or by any of the dozens of gimmicks used, because the system was unwilling to change. Yet new newspapers, which were created with MG permission and assistance, achieved, by constant repetition of fact and opinion, a gradual change of values, although they were of course aided mightily by the unmistakable implications of the 1945 disaster. The eventual establishment of a functioning German democracy by 1949 under Clay's aegis constituted a practical education in democracy, a case of learning by doing.

Notes

1. Any German who violated the weapon ban was to be given at least eight years in jail (OMGUS, Chronology, 26 July 1945, Kansas City Record Center [hereafter KCRC]).
2. P & O, Military Survey, to Col. Fahey, 12 Apr. 1948, CAD Pol. & Govt. Br., CAD, "Limited Armament for Germany," National Archives (hereafter NA).
3. Pollock Report to McCloy, 12 Sept. 1950, 4, Pollock Papers, Michigan Historical Society, Ann Arbor, Mich.; *Müncher Allgemeine*, 7 Jan. 1951, Wilhelm von Schramm; Drew Middleton, *New York Times*, 26 June 1951, 1 July 1951; John Dornberg, *Schizophrenic Germany* (New York, 1961), 66-72.
4. They often assumed an evil German race. This was later modified to the assumption that Germans, as far back as Luther at least, had had "authoritarian personalities" (Theodore W. Adorno, *The Authoritarian Personality* [New York, 1950]).
5. "This policy had the reverse effect upon the Germans from the one contemplated by the U.S." It ignored the 800,000 Germans who suffered in concentration camps and the 5,000 leaders killed after the 20 July 1944 *Putsch* (Albert Norman, *Our German Policy* [New York, 1951], 14-15). Norman was in the ICD Historical Section.
6. The most thorough work on denazification is that of Lutz Niethammer, *Entnazifizierung in Bayern* (Frankfurt, 1972). He blames the Cold War for the failure to change German social structure.
7. Americans were hostile and suspicious, but "many Germans will greet the Allies, either openly or deep in their hearts, as liberators" (Saul Padover, *Experiment in Germany* [New York, 1946], 17-18, 112-13, 116).
8. "The majority revolted against the coercion . . . none of the young people had any free time left; the desire for leisure thus resulted in a practical and perfectly healthy love for freedom" (Hans Habe, *Our Love Affair With Germany* [New York, 1953], 134). Most young Germans had a romantic image of America.
9. Gabriel Almond, *The Struggle for Democracy in Germany* (Chapel Hill, 1949), 62. Liberal editor W. L. White saw Germany in 1946 and remembered from 1939 "the frightened anti-Nazi majority," of which 80 percent had opposed the war, 70 percent disapproved the known anti-Semitism, and over 90 percent would have opposed the gas chambers (*Report on the Germans* [New York, 1947], 14, 16, 39); George Kennan, *Memoirs. 1925-1950* (Boston, 1967), 185-88; Niethammer, 319.
10. William Griffith, "The Denazification Program in the U.S. Zone of Germany" (Ph.D., diss., Harvard University, 1950), 6. Griffith was Bavarian chief of denazification. The ques-

tionnaires were first intended to be evaluated by MG officers, but the job was immediately too much for Americans to handle and Germans were increasingly given the task of deciding who fit into which category. By early 1946 Germans were openly and legally making the decisions, with MG employees, usually Germans, evaluating the original German decision.

11. Ibid., 7. The army manual of September still limited this to party officials and pre-1933 party members, officers of the SA or SS, very high government officials, and high military officials; see Franz Neumann, *Behemoth: The Structure and Practice of National Socialism* (New York, 1944).

12. The MG setup in Aachen was typical—officers "who knew little about Germany" and a SHAEF G-5 staff "where confusion reigned" (Griffith, 34, 37, 39).

13. There were almost no representatives of the SPD or KPD, although these had received 25 percent of the votes in the 1933 elections.

14. McSherry to Hilldring, 8 Feb. 1945, CAD 014, NA; Donald Robinson, "Why Denazification is Lagging," *American Mercury*, May 1946, 566.

15. "The directive was impossible of accomplishment, and the great majority of MG officers, recognizing this, simply ignored it, and many, reacting to its unreasonableness and impracticability, became disgusted with denazification in general, and neglected it completely" (Griffith, 45–46, 51–54); Harold Zink, *American Military Government in Germany* (New York, 1957), 135; John Kormann, *U.S. Denazification 1944–50,* HICOG (Bad Godesberg, 1952), 25.

16. More severe than JCS 1067, the 7 July directive was less severe than the Twelfth Army Group's directive, which specified no date of entry (Senate Hearings on the Elimination of German Resources for War, 1546–47). Russell Nixon claimed credit for getting the 1937 date. Murphy wanted mandatory removals only for party officials. The assumption was that the earlier a man had joined, the more guilty he was. See Niethammer, 61, for commentary.

17. *Weekly Information Bulletin* No. 9, 22 Sept. 1945, OMGUS; MG *Weekly Information Bulletin*, First Military Gov. Conf., 27–29 Aug. 1945, 5–6; Griffith, 81. Clay's move to expand denazification to the economy is further evidence of his lack of business orientation.

18. *History of Military Government,* Staff Meetings, 16 June 1945, 17 July 1945, OMGUS. After eating meat in Augsburg he asked where it came from and learned of the "Nazi butcher" (Niethammer, 63).

19. Griffith, 82–83, based on letters from M. K. Wilson, chief of Special Branch. His 15 August directive meant "that the anti-Nazi Germans were alienated" and "such a serious interference with German economic recovery that a reaction in American public opinion was inevitable." See chapter seven on Augsburg for background.

20. Murphy to Sec. State, 8 Sept. 1945, U.S. Dept. of State, *Foreign Relations of the U.S.: 1945*, III, 960–61 (hereafter *FRUS*); Niethammer, 96; Chronology, 22 Sept. 1945, KCRC.

21. Griffith, 90, 96. Law No. 8 came after a few hours of preparation by his assistant Charles Fahy, and was the immediate result of the public pressure and Patton crisis. War hero George Patton was fired for allegedly not cleaning Nazis out of Bavaria; see chapter six. Only Clay and Fahy knew of the law. Fahy confessed blame: "I should have avoided the poor draftsmanship. . . . I expected to be able to have another shot at the draft . . . but Clay . . . put the law in effect before I saw him again" (Interview Charles Fahy, Patterson Project, 260, Columbia Oral History).

22. Griffith, 96; Niethammer, 103; "Failure of Law 8," 29 Dec. 1945, OMGUS 124-3/15, Washington National Record Center (hereafter WNRC).

23. Nixon sensed the constant hostility of MG officials to anyone who came down from headquarters to enforce directives; they implied that denazification was a Jewish matter. These and the following statements of denazification are from Senate Hearings on the Elimination of German Resources for War, 1547–49.

24. "The response was to flood headquarters with requests to exempt" (Robinson, 566).

25. Griffith, 105.
26. Col. M. K. Wilson, in Morris Edwards, "A Case Study of Military Government in Germany" (Ph.D. Diss., Georgetown University, 1957), 366–67; Interview Robert Bowie.
27. Griffith, 107–108. Griffith held Clay almost completely responsible for the Law No. 8 fiasco. Niethammer agrees and notes that the economic elite remained unchanged (108).
28. Zink, *American*, 140.
29. Alfred Grosser, *Germany in Our Time* (New York, 1971), 43; Eugene Davidson, *The Death and Life of Germany* (New York, 1959), 87. At the same time all of the victors were recruiting rocket experts, scientists who had done more to help Hitler. An OMGUS report said internees numbered 117,512 (Denazification Policy Board Report, 15 Jan. 1946, 9–11. OMGUS 124-3/15, WNRC).
30. Robert Murphy, *Diplomat Among Warriors* (Garden City, 1964), 293. Russell Hill saw a Nazi-like secret police in the CIC and the Criminal Investigation Division (CID). They were "inexcusable from any point of view. . . . These agents repeatedly embarrassed MG by making stupid arrests" (*Struggle for Germany* [New York, 1947], 145).
31. OMGUS Legal Division to WARCAD 6 Dec. 1945, Clay Cables, NA.
32. Yet Clay thought it inadvisable to change current policy until completion of the international trials, and he urged that German boards review cases as quickly as possible (Chronology, 15 Sept., 18 Oct., 26 Oct., 2 Dec. 1945, KCRC). Niethammer reported MG's fear by September that too many were being arrested, and a reversal of the order to arrest all *Ortsgruppenleiter* (10). These were the lowest officials in rural areas.
33. Clay to Hilldring, 8 Dec. 1945, Clay Cables, NA. The State Dept. approved Clay's request by 5 January, published 31 January. Yet the MG newspaper reported some 280,000 to 300,000 interned in the U.S. zone (Petersen to Asst. Sec. of State, 3 Jan. 1946, OPD 091, OPD, NA; OMGUS Chronology, 31 Jan. 1946, WNRC; *Die Neue Zeitung*, 28 Feb. 1946).
34. He listed some 90,000 plus 25,000 members of military or paramilitary organizations (Griffith, 119, 122–23).
35. Niethammer, 111; Freda Utley, *The High Cost of Vengeance* (Chicago, 1949), 215.
36. M. K. Wilson, in Edwards, 375–77. Griffith thought the program was based on a false premise—that there was a large-scale underground resistance to the occupation. "Above all, the G-2 and CIC personnel assigned to it were—in numbers, in preparation and in quality— inadequate for their tasks" (125–26).
37. Justus Fürstenau, *Entnazifizierung* (Neuwied, 1969), 92.
38. Niethammer, 270–72.
39. Special Branch was able to keep the concepts of mandatory sanctions and the burden of proof on the accused (Interview Fahy, Patterson Project, 258; Griffith, 150–54). Niethammer noted two bankers, two generals, and one diplomat on the committee, but no Special Branch officer (116a, n. 48).
40. The plan also included no labor camps, property confiscation, or permanent dismissal from offices (Griffith, 160–62). The best account is in Niethammer, 112–19.
41. Griffith, 173–74; Niethammer, 120–36. Public Safety criticism was directed mostly at OMGUS Legal Branch. It was in principle opposing Berlin policy replacing JCS 1067. Special Branch made the mistake of criticizing Law No. 8, which was tantamount to a criticism of Clay.
42. Griffith wondered why MG was the prime mover for this law while it was conducting negotiations with the Germans based upon almost diametrically opposed propositions (177, 179–80). Niethammer assumed OMGUS simply overlooked the conflict. He explained that Clay's rejection was based on the facts that he wanted the ACC to work for German unity, he identified with Law No. 8, and he feared public opinion aroused by the Kilgore hearings (130–36).

43. "This extension, made at MG insistence, was . . . responsible for the slowness of case processing in the first year and a half of operations" (Griffith, 205, 303). Niethammer thought MG's threat an empty one, because MG had no alternative (103); see also Fürstenau, 66.

44. Griffith, 305.

45. Griffith agreed: "The whole directive clearly established a policy of minimum MG interference" (310–12). Niethammer noted delays MG caused, including their failure to release documents (149–53).

46. Niethammer, 154–155, 183; Griffith, 324.

47. Kormann, 107; Niethammer, 185–86; see chapter six.

48. In 1970 Clay wrote: "the American people had to be convinced that [denazification] was being undertaken vigorously before it could respond to a more liberal policy which would prevent Germany from becoming a political and economic vacuum which would endanger the recovery of all Western Europe" (Clay letter to author, Jan. 1971).

49. "Even the drumhead courts of our friends to the east, which mete out punishment rather than dispense justice, could reach no such figure" (Clay to Echols, 28 June 1946, OMGUS, 177–3/3).

50. Griffith, 331, 334, 377. Niethammer concluded that Clay had only the power of his rhetoric (188).

51. Yet "as quickly as cases were completed, the backlog increased just as rapidly and the tribunals struggled constantly to keep their heads above water" (Kormann, 100–101).

52. Griffith assumed he was unwilling publicly to reverse his position because it would expose him to the charge of weakness (384, 388); see also Edwards, 349.

53. Fürstenau, 87; John Gimbel, *The American Occupation of Germany* (Stanford, 1968), 159. On 1 April Wilson reported that only 7 percent of the serious cases had reached the tribunals, and only 4 percent had been acted on. Even in an optimistic view, he said, it would take five more years to finish processing them, because the law was too broad, much broader that JCS 1067. Niethammer linked this amnesty to a Clay meeting with Byrnes in November (199–200).

54. Staff Study OMGUS, I. A. & C. Div., "Desirable Changes in the Law of Liberation," OMGUS 148–1/15, 29–1/11; "Notes on Denazification," 3 Mar. 1947, Pollock Papers.

55. Walter Dorn also criticized a point on which Clay had overruled everyone, to limit any fine to 2,000 marks, a laughable sum in the inflation and particularly to the rich ("The Failure of the Law for Liberation," sent 15 May 1947, OMGUS, 125–1/15, 148–1/5, WNRC); Fürstenau, 79.

56. Niethammer, 222–23. Dorn later wrote: "He was too stubborn and obstinate an absolute monarch to change when the denazification process was becoming ridiculous and falling apart in large measure because of the system set up by this law."

57. Herbert Hoover, Freda Utley, Gustav Stopler, Lewis Brown, and Louis Lochner were probably exaggerating the economic impact of denazification. See L. P. Lochner, "The Idiocy of Our Denazification Policy," *Reader's Digest*, Jan. 1948, 130–32; Niethammer, 227–32; see also House Select Committee on Foreign Aid, 80th Cong., 2nd sess., *Final Report on Foreign Aid*, 127–29.

58. In eighty-four firms studied, employment had risen from 88,000 to 103,000; 3,900 persons had been removed from their positions, 2,800 by Law No. 8; of these 1,200 had been reinstated, after an average absence of 14 months. "Employees awaiting action or requiring replacement represent only 6 percent of all personnel engaged." Griffith observed that few such employment reports were ever filed; the MG effort to enforce the sanctions had soon collapsed from lack of personnel. Noce to Sec. War, 8 Sep. 1947, CAD 014, NA; Theo Hall, Public Safety Branch, Internal Affairs and Communications Div., to Deputy Mil. Gov., "Report on Effect of Denazification on Industry," 9 Oct. 1947, OMGUS, NA.

59. Griffith, 437–38, 454, 483–85; Niethammer, 238; see also E. W. Wendt, "Report to Murphy on Clay's Rewrite," OMGUS, 18–1/15, WNRC.

60. "There existed a sort of unwritten agreement among them—arising from their sincere conviction that such relaxation would mean the failure of the program—to 'interpret' orders and directives so as to lessen, if not completely to nullify, their effect" (Griffith, 428-29). Niethammer described Clay's anger at the Länderrat's taking extra advantage of his concessions, though he was responsible for the misunderstanding (238); also based on OMGUS 92-1/13 and 29-1/11.

61. With at least two deficiency appropriations bills per year, Taber had numerous occasions to enforce his will on the War Dept. and even on Clay (Griffith, 472, 502-504; Niethammer, 239-40, 244).

62. "The Americans still had developed no sense for a kind of policy which took into account, even psychologically, the complex situation in Germany" (Fürstenau, 92, 96); Griffith, 504-6; Niethammer, 239.

63. Griffith wrote that statistics had become completely unreliable, being regularly adjusted to present as favorable a picture as possible (502, 506, 508, 515), Fürstenau, 98.

64. John Montgomery, *Forced to be Free* (Chicago, 1957), 34; Griffith, 520, 583-84. Grosser puts the results in some perspective. The proportion of charges dismissed was 52 percent in the French zone, 33 percent in the American, and 29 percent in the British. In the British zone, 58 percent of the cases fell into Class V (not guilty) and only 10.9 percent into Class IV, whereas in the American and French zones, Class IV accounted for 51 percent and 45 percent respectively, and Class V for only 1.9 percent and 0.5 percent. Classes I to III represented 14 percent in the U.S. zone, 1.3 percent in the British zone, and 2.6 percent in the French zone (Grosser, 44-45).

65. Niethammer, 310-12. The trials before the International Military Tribunal of the major war criminals were partly to denazify. The effect was limited, except in that the most obviously guilty were punished. The trials were criticized as a victor's justice; the victors' leaders could also have been found guilty; the British and American bombing of cities indiscriminately killed civilians. Kennan thought that the trials held under Soviet judges were a mockery after Stalin's mass murders (Kennan, 274); Lucius Clay, *Decision in Germany* (New York, 1950), 253. The U.S. on its own then conducted a series of trials against a few officials and businessmen, but sentences were relatively moderate and quick reprieves were granted when the Germans regained their sovereignty. MG's sensational trial was held at Dachau to find those guilty of the "Malmedy massacres" of about 100 American prisoners during the Battle of the Bulge. Its irregularities created a large-scale protest, an appeal by a U.S. colonel to the Supreme Court and a War Dept. commission to investigate in 1948. Clay conceded that improper methods had been used to obtain evidence. The reputation of MG war crimes trials was such that further prosecution by Germans was delayed for a decade (253). Utley quoted a judge: "All but two of the Germans in the 139 cases we investigated had been kicked in the testicles beyond repair." She also mentioned the use of matchsticks under fingernails (186); see also Montgomery Belgion, *Victors' Justice* (Hinsdale, Ill., 1949).

66. German armies, allegedly told to behave like a "master race," had no rule against fraternization (Joseph R. Starr, *Fraternization with the Germans in World War II*, Office of Chief Historian, European Command [Frankfurt, 1947], 29 [hereafter OCH]).

67. Starr, 2-4, 13. Eisenhower was given the policy 28 April 1944; the SHAEF directive was dated 18 September 1944. It cannot be blamed on Morgenthau, who thought U.S. troops unqualified for occupation and recommended their immediate withdrawal.

68. Starr, 52. The order was modified to exclude those with German grandmothers, uncles, and aunts, but even this was never really enforced, although the chief of staff was told it was being scrupulously followed (Oliver Fredericksen, *American Military Occupation of Germany 1945-53* [Darmstadt, 1953], 130).

69. "There was a suspicion on the part of some commanders that the many rape charges were

merely another manifestation of resistance against the conqueror; yet a high proportion of these charges were proved in court" (Fredericksen, 81). The cases usually involved a soldier's entering a private home on the pretext of searching for forbidden goods. To divert GIs from female temptation, the War Dept. suggested "letters from home and special movie trailers."

70. Habe, 10.

71. Zink. *American*, 238–40.

72. A German official told Habe: "A French officer invites me for a dinner made of food he has taken from me. The Americans don't take my food and don't invite me—but man cannot live by bread alone." He was told by a Hamburg newspaperman: "The American fraternize with everybody except us; the British don't even fraternize among themselves." The anti-Nazi Dr. Hans von Eckhardt wrote: "We were starved and humiliated. But we were more humiliated than starved" (Habe, 10, 12–14).

73. Margaret Geis, *The Relations of Occupational Personnel with the Civilian Population, 1946–48*, HICOG (Karlsruhe, 1951), 1–5. Troops were to avoid "emotional entanglements" with German women by self-control and active participation in army athletic and educational programs (Fredericksen, 130–32).

74. "It was not necessary to throw the owners out in a brutal manner with one-half hour's notice, letting them take only what they could gather together in the short time to whatever cellar they could find. It was not necessary to forbid them to come back to collect the potatoes stored in their cellars or the vegetables in their gardens.... Moreover no time limit was set on the requisitioning of houses" (Hill, 143).

75. Edwards, 182–83.

76. "Throughout the whole occupation . . . members of the occupation forces and their families continued to regard the Germans through the eyes of 1945" (Habe, 22).

77. Ibid. Some escaped the pressures; real friendships were achieved by the more sensitive and determined.

78. Ibid., 12. This should remind anyone who saw the occupation of the signs on toilets: Not For The Indigenous Population.

79. Eugene Davidson called the U.S. zone "an immense concentration camp" (89). ICD's seven departments "neatly replaced the Reich Chamber of Culture, with its seven chambers of press, literature, radio, film, theater, music, and art" (Zink, *American*, 162); Joseph Dunner, in Edwards, 274. "The ICD in its practical effect can be considered to have replaced the Propaganda Ministry to the following extent: . . . ICD officers achieved an independence of action which permitted them to act in a manner quite as arbitrary as their Nazi predecessors . . . character assassination . . . was practiced covertly by persons protected by the Division" (Edward Breitenkamp, *The U.S. ICD, 1945–49* [Grand Forks, 1953], 35).

80. On 7 January 1948 the right of habeas corpus was extended to persons other than "security risks," and in a few months it included these (Clay, 249). There was never any security risk to the occupation.

81. OMGUS Chronology, 15 Oct., 8 Nov. 1947, WNRC.

82. Americans who married Germans were banned from Germany (Roger Baldwin, "Report on Civil Liberties in Germany." Nov. 1948; Roger Baldwin, "Memorandum on Civil Rights in Germany," 12 Apr. 1949; Interview Roger Baldwin, Baldwin Project, 542–44, 554, Columbia University Oral History.

83. Charles Campbell, *German Youth Activities of the U.S. Army 1945–46*, OCH (Frankfurt, 1947), 3–6, 14–15, 22.

84. The Munich survey in 1947 showed people thought GYA's chief value was keeping children off the streets; some suspected it was a new Hitler Youth organization (Joseph Starr in Campbell, 66); see also Edward James, *The U.S. Armed Forces German Youth Activities Program, 1945–55*, Historical Div., ASUUSA, Europe, 1956, 7, 27, 38; Litchfield Memo, 18

July 1947, from "Theater Inspector General Report on GYA," OMGUS Internal Affairs and Communications Division, Education and Religious Affairs Branch, 22 Sept. 1947, WNRC; Delbert Clark, *Again the Goosestep* (Indianapolis, 1949), 79–80; Fredericksen, 135, 138.

85. Clay to Hilldring, 6 Mar. 1946, OMGUS 177-3/3, WNRC.

86. Report Lt. Col. R. B. McRae to Clay, 20 Jan. 1947, CAD Plan and Govt. Branch, NA.

87. Then came more money from Washington, three times the previous budget (Clark, 86; discussed in Gimbel, *American*, 249–50, from OMGUS 256-3/17).

88. Gimbel, *American*, 250–51.

89. Harold Zink, *The United States in Germany 1945–55* (New York, 1957), 202–4.

90. "Unwise decisions in highest quarters were made . . . [there were] many cases where the spirit of Germans . . . was destroyed, because instead of support they received unrealistic orders, and instead of encouragement ill-considered criticism" (Friedrich Report for Herter Committee, 1 May 1948, 136–38). Junior officials prevented writers from publishing because they did not like some paragraph they had written.

91. Ibid., 210–12, 222.

92. Interview Baldwin, Patterson Project, 542–44, 554.

93. Edwards, 250–58; OMGUS Governmental Structure, Frederick Dirks Memo, "Status of CAD Program for Developing Local Interest in Government," to Litchfield, 3 May 1948, NA.

94. "Memo on Conference on Democratic Progress," Stuttgart, 8 July 1948, OMGUS, NA.

95. The U.S. was still last in 1949, with 700 compared to the French 1,300. "The large amounts expended on the textbook program do not seem to have produced the results anticipated. In some of the projects were some outright scandals, but more important was the indifferent work submitted" (Arthur Settel, *This is Germany* [New York, 1950], 101–3).

96. The "authoritarian" German family existed only among those with enough wealth for the father to dominate through his power of disinheriting. The German woman was not just the *Hausfrau* "experts" described; the Bundestag had a higher percentage of women than the American Congress (Charles Thayer, *The Unquiet Germans* [New York, 1957], 38–39).

97. American experts who looked into the German system had growing doubts about their own; "having compared the intellectual menu available there with what was served to German youngsters, they were tempted to believe that their children were the ones who were faring badly" (George Shuster, "American Occupation and German Education," *Proceedings of American Philosophical Society*, 1953, 160).

98. The semiofficial evaluation organized by Litchfield and Pollock praised the programs but even it found an "increase in democratic values" only among those in the teenager program (Richard Hiscocks, *Democracy in West Germany* [London, 1957], 247; International Public Opinion Research, *German Exchanges: A Study in Attitude Change* [New York, 1953]; International Educational Exchange Service, *A Follow-up Study of German Teenage Exchanges* [Washington, 1954]). "Too much emphasis was place on bringing the German teachers to the U.S. and too little on sending them to nearby European democratic countries. . . . This would have cost much less and permitted larger numbers to travel" (Zink, *U.S.*, 222).

99. Breitenkamp, 5, 11.

100. "While some of the administrative and budgetary uncertainties were ended by the beginning of 1950, it was not yet clear what the new policies would be" (Henry Pilgert, *The History of Information Services Through Information Centers and Documentary Films*, HICOG [Bonn, 1951], 5–6).

101. Ibid., 12, 31.

102. Habe, 25, 55. When Baldwin asked Clay, "Where do the really effective forces lie?," Clay said without hesitation: "They lie in the trade unions, the liberal middle class, and the tendencies toward socialism." Baldwin was dumbfounded: "Why do not our policies conform to that prescription?" The general was frank; "Because it would be quite impossible in view of public

opinion in the U.S. The whole tendency of the 'Right' in American is to be fearful of a strong socialist Germany. The whole 'Left,' meaning the liberals and labor, is fearful of a strong capitalist Germany. Between the two I have to choose the strong—the Right on whom our Congressional appropriations depend.'' It seemed to Baldwin Clay's answer revealed the whole tragedy of the occupation (Interview Baldwin, Baldwin Project, 542-44, 554).

103. Franz Gross, "Freedom of the Press under Military Government in Western Germany, 1945-49" (Ph.D. diss., Harvard University, 1952), 6.

104. Harold Hurwitz in Harry Pross, *Deutsche Presse seit 1945* (Bern, 1965), 31, quoting PWD/SHAEF Directive 22 May and 28 May 1945.

105. Harold Hurwitz, *U.S. Military Government in Germany: Press Reorientation*, HICOG (Karlsruhe, 1950), 38, 51-53.

106. Ibid., 156-66, 248. Their influence in that early period is still regarded by Germans as having created a leftist climate of opinion (Hurwitz, in Pross, *Presse*, 32, 29).

107. Sponsors protected the licensees to the point of telling generals and congressmen their aim was to create American-style papers when this in fact was not their intention at all (Hurwitz, in Pross, *Presse*, 42). Hurwitz wrote the advisers were soon much more concerned with keeping the papers going under difficult conditions than with controlling editorial policy. Only one Munich newspaper was mildly penalized for violating policy—in June 1946 for an article criticizing the manner of expulsion of Sudeten Germans.

108. This was a Clay decision. The State Dept. recommended a party press as early as October 1945, to which MG acceded in January 1946, but nothing was done.

109. "From the beginning . . . MG was forced to intervene to protect press freedom from encroachment by Land governments" (Hurwitz, *U.S.*, 135).

110. In one typical encounter with headquarters in the fall of 1945, Habe quoted Eisenhower as saying: "Germany must become a country of pioneers, capable of exercising individual initiative, or it will have no future." Eisenhower was furious at the word "pioneer." "Pioneers were our forefathers. You will omit any comparison between our ancestors and the Germans" (107-9).

111. "By the continued selection of German personnel, a healthy press cannot be established. . . . the actions of MG at the earliest possible date should be restricted to disapproval of personnel rather than to their selection" (Norman, 27).

112. Hiring practices were casual, but the calibre of Germans was high; they were attracted by the noon meal (Breitenkamp, 42-44).

113. German critics have assumed this restriction was more policy than paper shortage. The *New York Times* consumed 1,200 tons of newsprint for one Sunday edition, while the entire zonal press got 1,050 tons for June 1947.

114. Clay told the Länderrat in March 1947 he had changed his mind; this was a matter for each Land. Since it took the states two years to produce press laws, the delay had the effect of extending U.S. licensing for as long (Hurwitz, *U.S.*, 144, 228).

115. Hurwitz, in Pross, *Presse*, 49. Gross saw this new law as based on one of 1848 which prohibited newspaper chains. Some in MG wanted laws against former NS owners, yet the final decision was to restore full freedom (206).

116. "Press control officers were forced to devote enormous time and energy to facilitating the processing of visas by this stubborn organization" (Hurwitz, *U.S.*, 272, 308).

117. Ibid., 316, 324.

5 Restoring Self-government: Successful Noninterference

The victorious American army entered Germany intending to make its victory meaningful by reconstructing faulty German political institutions. The present flourishing condition of the Federal Republic of Germany might be said to evidence that its goal was achieved. In a sense, it is true that the Bonn government is the result of OMGUS and British operations; OMGUS contributed to the various stages of its creation. But OMGUS could contribute by obstructing or permitting. In retrospect, it is clear that obstruction failed and permission succeeded in the establishment of a viable West German state.

Unlike the Russians, who had a cadre of German communists trained to take over as Russian troops moved into German territory, the United States rarely went beyond finding the least objectionable person on the spot and asking him to form a new government.[1] Not only did MG not bring an exile government or cadre in its baggage, but it ended what might have been considered resistance governments by its treatment of the various local *Antifa* (antifascist) groups, who had occupied party offices in some towns, erased Nazi slogans, changed street names, seized houses, food, and clothing from Nazis, and nominated persons for local administrations. These resisters were downgraded to little more than informers.[2] The policy probably reflected the ideas behind "unconditional surrender," that Germans could not be trusted and that any initiative must be American. JCS 1067 made it official. All political activity by Germans was forbidden.

MG did not give permission for political parties until after the Potsdam meeting, when they were authorized only on the local level, and grudgingly. In the fall of 1945 they were permitted to organize at the state and zonal level, as a result of pressure exerted by the earlier Russian permission to parties and by the Potsdam agreement. The new parties were largely those that had existed in 1933, with the obvious omission of the Nazi party. Old leaders and old ideas of the Socialist party (SPD) and the Communist party (KPD) returned from prison and exile. Instead of the narrow Catholic Center party, Christian politicians who had learned the necessity of unity created the Christian Democratic Union. Bavarian Christians remained autonomous when they expanded the Catholic Bavarian Peoples' Party into the Christian Social Union.[3]

Although MG boasted of aid to the revival of parties, it was mostly in the way. Its regulations made the movement of party leaders more difficult. Central party organizations were held back in their coordination of local parties because MG assumed that the traditional parties had been too centralized. MG also put a serious limitation on the parties by forbidding them their traditional publication of party newspapers. With the exception of a few individuals, mostly German émigrés with a native's command of the German language and political practice, MG personnel showed little understanding of the importance of party leaders. Few officers, certainly not Clay, developed any relationship with them. OMGUS probably had the least contact with the new parties of any of the occupying powers.[4] Any significant advice to them was on how to deal with MG, not with politicians' constituents or colleagues.

The German leaders were usually clever enough to avoid the MG regulations limiting their activity, but they could not avoid zonal poverty, which hampered their contact with the people. They did the job of recreating political activity, often by violating MG policy.[5] The parties also overcame the MG effort to keep them out of the new administrations—in fact it would have been difficult to find a German administrator who was not either a member of a party, or closely connected with one. J. F. J. Gillen, historian for OMGUS, concluded that "the parties were distinctively German and there is no indication of any attempt on the part of the U.S. MG to foster the growth of any party which would represent American rather than German political traditions and ideals."[6] OMGUS critics thought that the German parties, like most of those in Europe, were too centralized, too bureaucratized, and too dominated by a central committee; but they remained organizationally what they had been, for better and for worse. Perhaps thinking of U.S. practices, MG stressed elections and constitutions instead. By the fall of 1945 Clay was pushing a rapid return to local and state self-government, rapid compared to the leisurely pace in the other zones. Harold Zink, OMGUS political adviser, speculated: "Perhaps the frustrations in the economic field led to a concentration on constitution-drafting and elections so that some progress could be reported by the Military Governor at an early date."[7] Although most analysts regard this as one of Clay's wisest moves, Zink thought it had made little difference one way or another to the recreation of German democracy.

Zink also commented on the limited capacity of his fellow MG political experts. The early CAD in England consisted of but three officers, none of whom had specialized training on German government and politics or had spent any considerable time in Germany. When an Air Force brigadier general had arrived in England, fresh from the United States, planning divisions were rapidly set up to deal with regional and local government, civil service, elections, administrative courts, and the reorganization of the German government, together with an elaborate system of administrative, research, secretarial, supply, coordination, and records sections. The staff ballooned in a short time to fifty officers, few of whom had substantial knowledge of German government or problems or any military government training at all. "The result was that a very elaborate administrative organization was set up to support, or perhaps it would be more accurate to say be supported by, the ten or a dozen officers who had sufficient knowledge to draft plans."[8] Whatever the powers of MG organization, it was weakened in the fall of 1945 by demobilization, which meant that people with the longest training had the right to go home. Even worse, Clay's order of 5 October 1945 limited the power of his field organization at the city, county, and state level. According to this very important decision, local detachments were no longer to command German authorities, but merely to observe and to report delinquencies to higher headquarters.[9]

Even his remaining large central staff was often limited by Clay's opposition to its advice. He ordered elections although everyone else agreed the Germans were not ready. Smaller towns and rural districts were not producing any political activity. Clay said: "The German masses are entirely unready for self-government and ignorant of democratic responsible German government." Yet as he had explained to McCloy, "with so many officers returning to the U.S. during the coming months, we will certainly not be able to staff a large number of the local detachments with qualified men even by a vigorous recruiting program. Yet, we can hardly withdraw the local detachments until the officials appointed by us have been replaced by others selected by the Germans."[10] He set the election dates for villages in January, for rural counties in March, and for cities in May 1946. The elections, described as progress, represent a tactical retreat by MG personnel.

The success of these elections, success in the sense that high percentages voted and did not vote for extremist parties, encouraged Clay to push for state constitutions. Successfully resisting State and War Department pressures, he limited his role to keeping American hands off the Germans, and letting them do it their way.[11] As a result the new state constitutions were very much like those of Weimar, altered only to allay German fears of another 1933. Restoring local, state, or even zonal government required a real effort on Clay's part, mostly to keep the British and French from delaying German sovereignty. Even the power of the zonal Länderrat was crippled by his need to appease the British.

The Länderrat: Zonal Government

The Länderrat, the beginning of the reforming of central government, was organized October 1945, following Clay's failure to reverse the decentralization order of JCS 1067.[12] JCS 1067 worked out the policy of zonalization so thoroughly that the zonal commander was given supreme legislative, executive, and judicial authority over travel, courts, schools, social insurance, trade, banks, and other institutions. Independent commanders in 1945 had carried decentralization down to the Land level and the local level. With responsibility for the zone, Clay was immediately concerned to regain centralized power for the zone. Although his June letters to McCloy hinted that the U.S. zone might have to go it alone, Clay knew by midsummer that such decentralization to the zonal level made no economic sense. By 26 July, his staff had lists of five hundred suitable German ministerial personnel ready to organize the national agencies accepted at Potsdam.[13] When centralization at the national level was vetoed by the French, Clay moved quickly to centralize on the zonal level, creating the Länderrat. Perhaps the most praised institution Clay created, this meeting of minister-presidents was organized rather precipitously on a suggestion made by James Pollock in late September. It followed the Russian creation of zonal administration, but preceded centralizing efforts by the British and French.

The principle of the Länderrat was simple: the minister-presidents of the three Länder (Hesse, Bavaria, and Württemberg) would come together and decide matters which were "zonal." (The mayor of Bremen was later added; the United States wished to control the port, and carved the enclave from the British zone.) The Länderrat was given certain specific assignments—those burdens MG chose not to assume. Significantly, its first task was to take care of refugees; in November it was given responsibility for the railroads and postal service.[14] By December Clay, beginning to see some of the problems of denazification, permitted the Länderrat to become involved in the program. Then came another problem which neither the states nor MG could solve: food shortages.

The device of having the Land chief executives come together monthly to coordinate answers to zonal questions seemed properly federalist, but it was quickly proved inadequate by economic problems. A permanent organization was necessary and as early as December 1945, a Länderrat *Sekretariat* was created to prepare for such decisions. Its general secretary was the former Reichstag member Erich Rossmann. The Länderrat was not supposed to issue orders to the Länder, but when the food situation got very bad in April 1946, its food director was given plenipotentiary powers. By 4 June 1946, the secretariat was ordered expanded into a *Direktorium*, composed of nine men, two from each state, and the secretary. At its peak the Länderrat secretariat had nine departments.[15] Most of the work was done in a large number of specialized committees.

As his liaison with the Länderrat, Clay created the Regional Government Coordinating Office (RGCO). It was directed successfully by Pollock, and then by the highly praised William Dawson until his accidental death, and finally by Charles Winning. Offices were housed in the Villa Reitzenstein on the outskirts of Stuttgart, where despite the continued suspicion of fraternization, Americans and Germans worked under the same roof. Correspondence was supposed to go through the secretary, "yet there developed as a result of this common housing in the same building, an ever closer cooperation, and it was usual that the corresponding directors and specialists visited each other for an exchange of ideas. Difficulties worth mentioning did not arise, because the Americans when they had direct contact with the German population and knew the conditions from their own observation showed much understanding of the German problems." That Clay appeared monthly to speak to the Länderrat was helpful, although he showed a "remarkable mixture of command-force and democratization pedagogy."[16]

RGCO officers came to see their major function as protecting the German authorities from the OMGUS bureaucracy.[17] RGCO was able to be protective because its director had direct access to Clay. This special position aroused the envy of OMGUS officials and contributed to the Länderrat's fall from grace. Heinz Guradze, an RGCO officer, thought that anti-OMGUS efforts, such as discouraging OMGUS attendance at meetings by holding them in German, were fully justified. It seemed to him that the fundamental error of OMGUS was its glorification of the states and their legislatures, with "little regard for, and less knowledge of, the historical development of German law and social conditions." Although they should have known that "if Bavaria . . . agreed with the other three states, there must be a strong case for uniform legislation, OMGUS officials were fascinated by the imaginary importance of the little state legislatures for the democratization of Germany."[18] This led to OMGUS's "sabotaging" Länderrat activity by 1948. Clay, in 1946, was sympathetic to giving freedoms: "No matter how much MG organization or personalities would try to cling to their authority, he would say, 'That is not our function. It goes to the Germans . . . we may be wrong but this is it.'"[19]

Although easy to build, the Länderrat represented little more than a United Nations of three neighboring states. In theory, when the minister-presidents agreed on something they could simply order their state bureaucracies to comply. In fact they could not compel obedience, as, for instance, on matters of food, although food was their basic problem. The other states bitterly accused Bavaria of not living up to the agreement to share food supplies and Bavaria as bitterly rejected the charge. When MG criticized his organization for being weak, Rossmann answered that when he had taken over the organization was practically nonexistent. It was crippled by MG censorship and the resulting poor telephone and teletype contact with the various states. Rossmann tried to expand the organization's power but any such expansion was based on concessions of the Länder and could easily be withdrawn by them. "If I were to carry out MG orders as quickly and properly as necessary, I would in many cases have to overstep my powers." He pointed out that he was subject to four masters, the three minister-presidents and OMGUS.[20]

Pollock realized that the Länderrat organization must have more power, because problems were not being solved. The result was a reorganization on 4 June 1946, supposedly strengthening it.[21] Clay was "extremely angry" about the difficulties in getting national economic unity and had therefore decided to push zonal activity and to give more responsibility to the Länderrat. If the Länderrat had a heyday, it was in this gap between the failure of Clay's national economic unity effort in the spring of 1946 and the bizonal effort with the *Wirtschaftsrat* (Economic Council) in the early spring of 1947. But as early as August 1946, the Länderrat noted the shifting of Clay's attention toward a bizonal solution and they needed reassuring. On 12–13 August, RGCO officers appeared to reassure Rossmann that despite the bizonal talks the Länderrat was not to be abandoned.[22]

This reassurance was also meant to counter fears that cooperation with Britain would mean adopting British practices, which allowed less German involvement. The Länderrat supported the bizonal negotiations as a step to economic unity, but thought the British should adjust to the more progressive American practices.[23] Wilhelm Hoegner noted with concern that "in the area of economy and transportation there has been a development whereby the centralizing and bureaucratizing of governmental organization must seriously diminish the democratic institutions already created."[24] RGCO shared his fear of the centralism pushed by the British, their German officials, and Americans like General Draper who saw advantages in central direction of the economy. They were not sure about Clay, who ran a tightly centralized OMGUS and was working for central ACC powers at Berlin, although Clay told OMGUS to keep hands off the Länderrat. He ordered that "every effort be made to conform to recommendations of the Länderrat; their requests should not be denied unless they clearly violated MG policy or Quadripartite agreements and in each case the policy or agreement violations must be clearly stated in recommending disapproval."[25] Both the Länderrat and RGCO doubted that OMGUS really would be so liberal, as indeed it was not when Clay's attention was elsewhere.

Länderrat fears of impotence were partly allayed at Clay's October 1946 visit. He convinced people like Reinhold Maier of his brilliant command of the details of the various state constitutions under discussion. Yet at the November meeting he blasted the minister-presidents for their lack of energy in denazification.[26]

After November Clay came to the Länderrat less often because the Stuttgart zonal council was being steadily replaced by bizonal institutions. In January 1947 Clay's brilliance was necessary to explain to them the relationships among the Land, zonal, and bizonal institutions which he had created. He had first blessed the new Land parliaments (*Landtage*), but because of the delays occasioned by referring zonal or bizonal matters back to them, he said the minister-presidents should be allowed to issue laws ignoring the Land legislatures. (The bizonal directors should also be allowed to issue directives without consulting the minister-presidents.) Clay's pragmatic reaction to an impossible situation brought more confusion. Survival became the major matter for debate at subsequent meetings of the Länderrat. The minister-presidents thought the only way out of the mess was for MG simply to issue laws itself, as acting for the Reich.[27]

On 16 February, they requested MG permission for a meeting with the bizonal directors to straighten out lines of authority, possibly by creating a legislative council or an ad hoc arrangement for political control of the bizonal economic administrations. This Clay vetoed. At their 23 February meeting, when Maier reported a degree of confusion which could halt the entire legislative process, Clay explained that in view of the coming Moscow Conference the economic agencies would have to be made to work without a political apparatus and state parliaments should be ignored. The United States was spending millions in Germany; to placate Congress OMGUS had to show that industrial capacity was increasing, and this required effective economic union. OMGUS could not

> after having determined something is essential to the economic revival of Germany... submit the question to a state parliament.... We cannot permit a proposal to be defeated by one parliament which is absolutely essential to the success of our economic program, and I certainly don't want to be in the position to have to disapprove a parliamentary act. I am sure it is more democratic never to submit that act to parliament.[28]

To the proposal to establish a bizonal coordinating committee, Clay answered: "It would be considered, in effect, a provisional government of the two zones. I have enough charges against which to defend myself without adding that one too.''[29] On 1 March Clay proclaimed the right of minister-presidents to declare Länderrat resolutions law without consulting their Landtage. Then, as an effort to involve these legislatures in the process, he created on 11 March, a zonal *Parlamentarischer Rat* (Parliamentary Council), composed of seven members from each Landtag and three from Bremen, to approve the laws and presumably to get their colleagues' support for implementation.[30]

With the failure of the Moscow Conference, bizonal authorities were given more powers and the Länderrat was increasingly ignored. Rossmann told the RGCO on 4 June that certain Germans were being kind to the Länderrat because "one should not speak evil of the dead." Clay admitted that "we have been too tough and . . . it is destroying our Länderrat . . . which I don't want to do just yet."[31] He reassured the minister-presidents, acknowledging that OMGUS had been too restrictive in rejecting laws they had proposed. But their position worsened despite his assurance, and even Clay was criticized on the grounds that his sessions were deficient in the free speech guaranteed by the Atlantic Charter, and promised under the new JCS July 1947 directive. Alex Möller, a socialist delegate, observed:

> The situation as it has developed in the last months is not in keeping with the dignity of a legislative body . . . to be called to a meeting to receive a declaration of *Herr* General Clay, which is often delivered like some schoolmaster, without the opportunity to say a word. *Herr* General then disappears to a reception with the press, which has the right to discuss things with him, and to ask him questions. . . . We delegates sit then in these meetings with *Herr* General Clay with fewer rights than school boys, who at least can clear their throats and say something.

Several members of the Länderrat noted that the British had come to permit more give and take than did Clay; MG had sharply increased the vetoing of Länderrat proposals, negating large amounts of work. At the 9 September meeting Clay permitted questions for the first time.[32]

Yet criticism increased after the 23 September meeting on denazification. The legislators were confused by Clay's rapid change of position, though willing to exploit any concessions to the limit. Hans Ehard (Bavaria) thought the most important goal was to end the Law No. 8 prohibition on employment of party members. He feared that as had happened before, the concessions that Clay had granted would be withdrawn by his administrators.[33] Binder (Hesse) observed that the *Herren* of OMGUS were upset because they too came to this meeting ignorant of Clay's proposals; they seemed to agree with the minister-presidents that Clay was the barrier, and that the insoluble problem was how to move him.

Although the Länderrat continued to meet, it was pretty well reduced to debating the question of whether Clay would prefer it dead. Clay was quoted as having said that "although he hated to say it, the Länderrat should fold up; the zonal concept should disappear." Delegates warily observed that Clay had expected to get the British to give their Länder the same powers as those in the American zone, but that in fact the British had no such idea. They felt Clay was very impulsive, and that they should not be taken by surprise; and that the Länderrat was democratic but the Wirtschaftsrat was a creature of MG. Rossman conveyed some of these opinions to Winning, who reported that

Clay had not yet made any decision on the Länderrat; both the British and American officers wanted a bizonal organization like it, but zonal organization must disappear. The Germans, however, should take the initiative, because MG did not want to be responsible for any split in Germany.[34] The Länderrat reaction was that the British zone's bureaucracy dominated the Wirtschaftsrat and would dominate any bizonal Länderrat—it would be another case of the north running over the south.

In March 1948 Clay found the same reason for continuing existence of the Länderrat as he had in 1945–46—denazification. This time, however, the task was to end it quickly. The minister-presidents had learned in the newspapers that a speedup was desired, and they now heard from Binder, who had had better contacts, of the great pressures for change. Perceiving the growing shambles, they lashed back at the earlier foolishness forced on them.[35] Denazification machinery was dismantled, but more importantly for the Länderrat, so was RGCO. That Clay removed this liaison could only mean that he did not think their work worth noting. By 10 June Winning reported that his staff had been disbanded, but that he could stay. The Länderrat knew that Clay was counting on the formation of a new federal government by 1 January 1949, and that this expectation accounted for his nearly total neglect of the Länderrat.[36]

The long lists of laws awaiting approval during 1948 show that the Länderrat continued passing laws, but no one knew what to do with them once they were passed. With RGCO disbanded, OMGUS was ignorant of zonal administration and legal affairs.[37] In the fall of 1948 the Länderrat was moribund. When by January the hope for an early federal government proved a delusion, Clay broke his long deliberate absence; he reported his surprise that ninety Länderrat requests had been simply ignored by OMGUS.[38] Frustration is evident in the bitter remarks of Emil von Wedel, Länderrat liaison to OMGUS;

> If one has repeated dealings with OMGUS it becomes clear OMGUS does not operate like ministries, but rather just like a military government. For decisions only the orders of *Herr* General Clay are important. Therefore, one does not consider the legal aspects, rather simply the question, "How would General Clay judge the matter?" . . . OMGUS organization is exceptionally complicated, so that every decision involves many offices. The process is therefore very tedious and . . . decisions take weeks. Even the leading officers do not have the right to make decisions. They emphasize again and again that they are only small wheels in the big machine. They are therefore never willing to express an opinion about a definite question, even if one assures them that one will make no use of that expression.[39]

At the last meeting of the long-dying Länderrat, Wedel gave a bitterly critical overview of OMGUS. The Länderrat, he said, had been kept in a "half-dark" position because of Clay's unsuccessful efforts with the British. The result had been that from June to October 1948 there had been no official link to OM-GUS. He had been told the Bonn Parliamentary Council must approve the continued existence of the Länderrat. OMGUS had agreed to consider the Länderrat laws when that was done, but only on matters already in its area of jurisdiction. "The processing of the requests moved very slowly and would probably have come to a total halt, if the minister-presidents had not re-fight the question through with OMGUS of the necessity of zonal uni-formity." Wedel had repeatedly asked OMGUS for guidelines or even oral indications about the principles on which OMGUS made its decision. An expression of opinion on the questions had always been refused. There had been no clear line evident in OMGUS decisions and it had been impervious to rational arguments. Enormous efforts, he thought, had gone for naught.[40] On this bitter note the first stage in the restoration of self-government came to an end.

Yet at its short-lived best, the Länderrat was a forum working with MG on something approaching reasonable cooperation. It was certainly prefer-able to a remote OMGUS issuing orders and vetoes to divided, confused, and resentful German leaders. This working together lasted from early 1946 to early 1947, the period when Clay needed cooperation from the Länderrat badly enough to give it his important blessing. Thereafter he needed a wider economic unity for which the Länderrat was obsolete. Although the mun-daneness of the operation is indicated by the fact that a major topic was the German need for tires, the Länderrat can be regarded a significant step back toward German self-government.[41] Its abandonment represented another re-treat from the 1945 policy of decentralization. Another step toward recen-tralization was the withering away of the minister-presidents' conferences, which had also helped to facilitate the interchange of opinion and to overcome the localisms of 1945. The minister-presidents were replaced by the national party leaders, who seized the power in the Bonn government.[42]

The Wirtschaftsrat: Experiment in Bizonal Administration

Clay clearly saw the need for German reunification, which was the fervent desire of most of the Germans he was trying to govern. Yet he was so crippled by the necessity of maintaining the agreement made with the British to unite the two zones, and he was so limited in his policies in their zones by the need to reach future agreements with the French and Russians, that it seemed he had no choice but to hamstring the *Wirtschaftsrat* (Economic Council). Even its name was meant to obscure the fact that it was trying to function as a government, at least for the economic sector. To avoid the unavoidable criticism from the USSR that the United States was responsible for splitting up Germany by creating a West German government, Clay had to go through repeated convolutions to affirm, as he consistently did, that he was creating only an economic organization.

Clay was forced into this most difficult position of frustrating the German leaders, and yet not convincing the French and Russians by the fact that his mounting economic disaster could be ameliorated permanently only by economic unity, which the French openly opposed in 1945. When stopping reparations did not change French opinion in mid-1946, Clay fused his zone with Great Britain's, the only willing ally. He had discussed this fusion with Byrnes in Paris in the spring of 1946, but his cable had "somehow been lost" in the maze of bureaucracy.[43] The British accepted on 30 July, and plans were laid in August and September.

Clay insisted that the coordinating agencies for food, economics, finance, transportation, and communication be scattered about the country further to avoid the appearance of a government.[44] The result resembled a combination of American federalism and British centralism. The eight members of each of the five central agencies were each responsible to a different Land government; there was little provision for coordinating the work of the agencies, and they were not responsible to any legislative body.[45] The contract for each agency was negotiated separately, the first on 11 September for the *Verwaltungsrat für Wirtschaft* (Economics Administration). Located in Minden, it was empowered to issue directives to all Länder and agencies, and to control the execution of its decisions and regulations through its own administrative agency. This power to make law conflicted immediately with the constitutional right of the newly created Landtage, a conflict never resolved. Clay was caught between his commitment to democracy and his commitment to centralized economic unity.

Each failure to reach agreement with the Russians and the French forced the British and Americans to take another sidestep toward more logical solutions. The failure in Moscow in April 1947 led to Secretary of State Marshall's instructing Clay to strengthen the bizonal authority. On the same day Robertson, the British commander, wrote Clay that he had no authority to create political institutions and his government would take a long time to agree to a political parliament, but that an "economic council" would help. Clay agreed two days later, adding that German parties would not be satisfied without some legislative authority, which would bring the protests of "other powers."[46]

The German leaders did not participate in this planning. By 29 May, Litchfield and his British counterpart had drawn up the plan for the Economic Council: there were to be fifty-two delegates, to be chosen by the Landtage;

the council would have legislative authority, but only in the field of economics and subject to MG veto. The institution of directors of the five agencies survived in a *Direktorium*, but they were to be coordinated by an *Exekutivrat* (Executive Council) which would consist of one representative from each Land appointed by the Land government; the Executive Council would nominate the directors, who would be elected by the Economic Council. All was now brought together in Frankfurt, too involved in its own survival to offer the new institution much help. This joining together was certainly an improvement on the scattered agencies, but "no really effective government had been formed, and some of the difficulties which had hampered the separate agencies remained."[47] The Wirtschaftsrat organization was baffling because Clay assumed that anything good enough to govern the zones would anger the Russians and French.

To supervise this nongovernment the British-American Bipartite Control Office (BICO) was created, with some nine hundred officers.[48] Its director, Hermann Pünder, noted that the two allies were at first reserved in dealing with their German counterparts, but unlike the case of the Executive Council, "there was no question of simply receiving orders, rather an exchange of views around a table. Informal discussions continued after the meetings with coffee and cakes." Direct contact between corresponding officers worked more quickly than the supposed routing of everything through the top executives.[49] Of the 171 Economic Council laws, MG disapproved 8, a further 18 were returned as premature, and 18 held for approval of an eventual parliament.

There is general agreement that these unwieldly institutions were confronted with such problems as to make them very nearly powerless. Tilman Pünder concluded that the administrative confusion among the Economic Council, Executive Council, and the Directors condemned the experiment to failure. In addition, MG wanted politics to be kept out, but the Economic Council was immediately political; the parties were, from the beginning, the real power.[50] The parties took over because the delegates were elected by political Landtage. The bourgeois parties had a narrow majority in the Economic Council and the SPD in the Executive Council; any action needed bipartisan support, which was difficult to achieve. The big problems they faced, the only ones supposedly permitted them, were economic, and their ideologies differed most sharply in this area.

T. Pünder attributed this administrative monstrosity to another compromise between American federalists and British centralists, and to their ignorance of German organizational practices. "Most obvious were the violations of the principle of division of powers. . . . The small membership proved a serious handicap. . . . The ever increasing work, particularly in the committees, was very quickly beyond its powers." The Executive Council was to coordinate departments, but it did not stand directly under the Economic Council as would a government under a parliament; a vote of no confidence was not possible. The Executive Council was in fact superfluous. The coordination of the various administrations could have been more quickly achieved through regular meetings of the directors. "Implementation, though assigned to the Executive Council, was much more easily accomplished within each agency." The Executive Council had the further weakness that it was supposed to represent Länder while at the same time it was supposed to compel them.[51]

The surface activity of this complex of organizations is seen in Economic Council debates which were conducted in the tradition of German parliaments. MG was infrequently mentioned and usually with bitter criticism. At the first session the Christian Democratic Union (CDU) spokesman blamed "our monstrous catastrophe" on their negative measures, "negative in taking parts of the territory away, negative in demolishing factories, negative in putting limits on production, negative in taking patents from the German people and giving them to all the world, negative in taking away German technicians and scientists, negative in keeping our best and most vigorous workers as prisoners of war."[52] The SPD added: "These difficulties would be overcome only when the occupation would not limit itself to speaking about giving us the responsibility, but when they actually do it." There would be no recovery of exports until they could end the flood of MG regulations.[53]

After more angry remarks, the Economic Council reverted to meaningful activity: organizing on the basis of political philosophy and power. The crucial decision, lasting in principle until 1966, was for the bourgeois parties to overlook their differences and to ally against the socialists. On 23 July 1947, the alliance of CDU and the Christian Social Union (CSU) with the Free Democratic Party (FDP) brought a vote of twenty-seven to twenty-two which gave them control of the vital economics directorate and the rest. The *Rhein Echo* blamed the relatively unknown Konrad Adenauer for preventing compromise.[54] What Adenauer was accused of seeking was party control over the key Economics Administration, the crucial point of dispute with the socialist party and their murky Marxist goals. Adenauer's effort to control economic policy and the fortuitous choice of the then obscure Professor Ludwig Erhard would prove highly significant to the future of his conservative party and to the history of West Germany until the mid-1960s. Erhard would give Adenauer the issue, economic freedom, and the results, the economic miracle of the 1950s, which would keep the old Adenauer and Erhard, his successor, in power for twenty years. While only a delegate to the Economic Council, Erhard on 7 October was already denouncing the lack of economic freedom. In his view the problem of the Economic Council was "too many laws." Laws depended on implementation and the Council was full of confusion, with laws popping out of drawers; no one even knew whose laws they were.[55] Erhard might well not have achieved a position of power, had it not been for "the Semler affair," wherein Economic Director Johannes Semler lost his directorate because of those fatal words, "chicken feed." A sketch of the dispute will illustrate the problems which remained in the relationship between the Wirtschaftsrat and OMGUS.

The Semler case was a throwback to 1945 when MG put men into top positions and took them out again with barely an explanation. From northern Bavaria like Erhard, Johannes Semler was the CSU man put into the economic directorate in July 1947 by the Adenauer coalition. Leftists could wonder about his activities in Hamburg before the war or in Paris during the war, but there was little to suggest that he would become a cause célèbre. He seemed to be on good terms with Americans. In October he spoke of the consumer goods the Americans had agreed to give without asking for immediate payment. His gratitude elicited shouts of "bravo" from the Council.[56] Semler's worried report of 12 December listed few problems that Clay had not reported to Marshall six months before. But Semler emphasized MG's blame: "We are at the moment surrounded by an MG system of trade treaties which are actually killing export."[57] On 4 January at a CSU meeting, Semler, perhaps to rouse the party faithful, said the Americans had sent corn, which Germans, who had not eaten it before, thought of not as human feed but as "chicken feed." This had to be paid for, yet Germans were supposed to be grateful. "The time has come that German politicians should stop thanking the Americans for these food subsidies." Allied representatives were in the audience and the word was out.[58]

In what Pünder described as a "historic case," Semler was fired 27 January in a "deliberately demonstrative way." The Bavarian Landtag, just as demonstratively, elected him immediately to the Economic Council. Clay canceled that election two hours later and ordered the Bavarian leaders, Ehard and Müller, immediately to Berlin to tell them that Semler was disqualified for any bizonal job and that he would refuse the entire Bavarian delegation if Semler were in it. MG handled the Semler case badly, giving no refutation of the charge for three weeks except to call him a "damned, unmitigated liar."[59] Yet Semler was out, and Erhard was in. Owing his earlier career in Bavaria to Americans, he would be much more careful in his attempts to undermine the occupation. He would succeed because MG and controls were ready to retreat.

While Semler's discharge was proving to many that the Economic Council really was a puppet, Clay was about to give it more powers. With the failure of the London Foreign Ministers' Conference in November 1947, Clay and Robertson had been ordered to move at their discretion toward a real government for the two zones.[60] Something had to be done. The Economic

Council's powerlessness had become evident in the winter's "potato wars" or "meat wars," during which various Land ministers and Landtage defied the Frankfurt agencies and ignored their directives. When the Economic Council's food office organized a hundred field inspectors to make spot checks, the Bavarian food minister ordered that no bizonal inspectors be allowed in without his written authorization and supposedly said farmers could chase any unauthorized snooper out of the country.

With the system clearly not working where it most mattered, and a hostile lineup forming on both right and left, Clay took the initiative. He had suggested as early as September that OMGUS proceed to establish a government for the two zones—three, should France join—if the London Conference failed. On 4 November he hinted to the minister-presidents that a government might have to be created for only western Germany.[61] On 7 January 1948, he assured the Germans that the meeting was for real discussion, not for the usual presentation of an MG plan for acceptance. Yet he had such a plan in his pocket, worked out with the BICO board on 2 January.[62]

The new Clay plan for the Wirtschaftsrat was another effort to solve problems by another retreat from the original decentralization, another expression of OMGUS disillusionment with federalism or states' rights. The plan was in principle that of a typical government, but was camouflaged to obscure its essential features. It had in effect a prime minister, who was elected by a parliament. He would appoint heads of departments with political functions, although in theory the parliament remained only an economic council. The membership of delegates sent by the various states to make parliamentary decisions was doubled to make it more representative of the people. A second house replaced the Executive Council; it was formed like the U.S. Senate with two delegates from each Land. Clay properly sensed that what he was creating could well be the form of the future German government. Clay modified his plan, in response to German suggestions, only in the title of the second house, which was called the Länderrat.[63] (This name had the unfortunate effect of bringing confusion between this bizonal council of states and the U.S. zone's Länderrat.) It was implemented as Clay, with Robertson's support, ordered.

To this reasonable conception of the future government, Clay added "the pantry law," which was as ridiculous as anything since nonfraternization. It assumed that because the United States was meeting its import schedule, blame for food shortages must lie with the Germans. Therefore, a law was necessary to require every individual and firm to report available food. If the Germans would not enact such a law, MG would, since it must be done quickly. BICO ordered an immediate Economic Council session to work out a law "which will prescribe that within a certain brief period every holder of food submit a sworn statement as to his holdings in flour, grain and potatoes. . . . Within a week after passage of the law. . . . all holdings in excess of authorized quantities [are to] be turned in as surplus."[64] The pantry law was designed to influence opinion in the United States, for Clay was appealing to Congress for more food to offset communist attempts to lead German workers into "serious disturbances." He told reporters that the authorities were collecting a higher percentage than the Nazis had collected. This statement might have had some effect in Washington. It had no effect in Germany. Of the millions of persons required to make a report, thousands did, and dozens admitted to having enough food for a good party.[65]

After the absurdity of the pantry law, open criticism increased rapidly. Schlange-Schöningen deplored the farce that Germans had any authority. Knowing that theirs was only pseudopower, officials did not carry out orders. "When a mayor gets this or that order pressed into his hand and passes it on to his community, what should he do when the orders are not followed? What happens? Absolutely nothing happens!"[66] MG told them there were no fats available. "My answer is, 'Let us look for ourselves, we'll find some.' " Clay was sincerely seeking their good in Washington, but MG did not understand the German problems. Eugen Kogon doubted that the MG juggling of institutions would help. "When *Herr* General Clay delivered his threat against German peasants, 'I still have an army,' nothing came of that either . . . no army can do anything if not enough is being produced." The Economic Council had been totally superfluous; it should have had a defined authority, but MG kept a large number of rights to itself. "The result was a fiasco." Kogon thought what was needed was a German authority. Instead came the sudden order for bizonal centralism, and thus the general resentment and bitterness.[67] Hartrich, a reporter for the *New York Herald Tribune*, perceived a crisis in March because the United States could not decide whether to support a West German state.[68]

Everyone seemed frustrated. On 4 March Generals Clarence Adcock and Gordon Macready severely criticized the Germans for having achieved so little; MG might lose interest in the Economic Council unless it got to work.[69] BICO blamed the delay on party conflict; Robertson suggested that there be a party truce of six months and that officials be selected for ability not party allegiance; the blame was all the Germans', he said, because "everything was under German control." The Economic Council made the opposite judgment: "All significant questions rest in the hands of the occupation, with no satisfactory provision for consultation, to say nothing of a provision for cooperation in making decisions."[70]

Yet change occurred in mid-March, more probably the result of Clay's panic about the Russians than attention to German complaints. On 15 March Clay met with the German leaders and announced that he wanted to meet them monthly. Schlange-Schöningen told the council: "That was a completely different atmosphere. For the first time one could really begin to hope again.'' Yet the council became more bitter. Otto Seeling, a director, condemned the plunder of German patents. He resigned a few days later because of ''the insuperable disparity which exists between the capabilities of the Economic Council on the one hand and its responsibility towards the German people on the other hand,'' which made it ''the target of bitter sarcasm owing to the unproductive and unsuccessful results of its work.''[71] Haffner, a spokesman for the CDU, was angry at MG for using food as blackmail: ''MG explained that Germany would receive no more food from America if we protested the dismantlings. . . . we were assured . . . that we should be quiet because of the London Conference, and the dismantlings would be significantly moderated. In this whisper-propaganda was no truth.'' The Marshall Plan proved America was not dominated by the desire to prevent competition, yet the German party leaders had observed how ''again and again the good intentions of the American people were turned into the opposite by a tough occupation bureaucracy. (Cheers of 'very true.') Nothing had more poisoned public opinion about the Allies than the experience that in many MG offices there are people with power who still are possessed of the Morgenthau spirit.''[72]

Another source of discontent during the frustrating period before the currency reform was a deal made for army surplus. Desperate at the lack of consumer goods, the council agreed to buy army goods sight unseen. The agreement in December 1947 estimated a cost of some 875 million dollars. In March, Robert Pferdemenges, an industrialist and confidant of Adenauer, urged the acceptance of more surplus at an estimated 21 percent of its original value. (A KPD report revealed its true value: of 4,000 army shoes only 90 were usable.) By the summer the cat was getting out of the bag, when an Economic Council committee issued a report on a vehicle park: ''With the inspection of the dump one feels the enormity of the losses in the bulk-deal contract.'' An estimate put the value at 3 to 3.5 percent instead of the 21 percent charged; the U.S. army had simply left the goods untended and in the open for three years, and nearly everything was ruined.[73] Pferdemenges limply explained later that it had been a sincere mistake and offered his hope that MG would reduce the charges by at least 50 percent. BICO rejected the complaints, saying that the price had been fair and denying that the United States had already sold off the better items.

Erhard had the better idea of using the coming currency reform, and the slim CDU majority, to strike at MG controls. On 22 April he delivered *the* Erhard speech, repeated with variations for the next twenty years. The gist of it was that a planned and controlled economy cannot work because of human nature. Economic incentives are needed; controls bring shortages; freedom would bring prosperity. Erhard suggested loosening controls but just before the currency reform Clay firmly refused: ''We can unfortunately not negotiate with you before we have negotiated with a third power.'' To Erhard's appeal to loosen the MG requirement that all German trade must be conducted in dollars, Clay answered: "I cannot on the one hand request dollar credits from my government and at the same time permit the export of German goods to the dollar-weak countries. The Marshall Plan will end these difficulties. If you think that the dollar clause damages you, then conduct your own foreign trade without dollar help."[74]

There is little in these exchanges to have presaged Erhard's joyous disobedience, which became the cornerstone of his reputation, when he presented Clay with the fait accompli of a major dismantling of OMGUS controls while at the same time he announced the currency reform.[75] As Erhard recalled his happy "rebellion," he gave a radio speech on Sunday and announced the end of price controls on industrial products without having warned anyone. On Monday, everything broke loose. He was called to MG very early to face the denunciation of all of the MG economic advisers. He asked where the law said that he could not do it. They read him the law that he could not change MG regulations. His answer was that he had not "changed" them, but had ended them. He asked to see Clay. "I was in good with him." Clay said, "Don't tell me you didn't know." Erhard answered: "Naturally, but if I had told your officials, they would have stopped me. You have to help me, the entire horde is against me." They had a long talk, after which Clay supposedly said: "I have the impression that you are right and I will help." This episode began their friendship. Erhard went back to the astonished advisers and told them that Clay backed him.[76] By 25 June most prices were freed from control.

A September conference shows the more typical Erhard flabbiness. During a debate on JEIA limitations, Clay firmly beat him down with statistics and argument. In October Bavarian delegate Gebhard Seelos listed eleven MG actions which proved the increased MG toughness. He thought that the MG personnel were reacting to the expected loss of powers under the new Occupation Statute. A December conference provides another good example of the usual situation. Erhard presented very polite requests which were met with repeated refusals until the generals finally remarked: "It does not seem fruitful to discuss the question any farther." The issue was Erhard's appeal to permit craft associations to examine prospective members. Clay also refused to give the Economic Council responsibility for decartelization.[77] The minutes show how the generals operated. Robertson was kind; Clay was sarcastic and sharp. The Germans were respectful before the new authority, with its toughness, hard work, and accessibility.[78]

Clay's toughness and knowledgeability and Erhard's hesitation to challenge authority are still evident in the debates in 1949. In February Erhard complained that the price for German coal was two or three dollars a ton lower than the world price. Clay said confidentially that he would make up the difference from Marshall Plan funds if the price were not raised. Yet in April Clay took a contradictory position in complaining that the Germans always relied on Marshall Plan money for projects when they should be gathering German capital.[79] (A less courteous Erhard might have asked whether Germans could gather such capital by raising the price of coal.) In July, when Erhard complained that the price paid for U.S. wheat was higher than the world market price, McCloy answered toughly that the Germans were free to join the Wheat Organization, but only if they were prepared to accept a lower subsidy from the United States.[80]

In addition to thus fighting a rearguard action with the weapon of economic assistance, OMGUS tried to push through reforms at a time when any strong German receptivity to reforms had ended. MG's autocratic manner of trying to make the civil service more democratic caused major bitterness among German leaders. In August 1948, BICO ordered that a new *Beamten* (civil servants) law be prepared by the Germans by 1 October.[81] On 8 November, BICO told the Economic Council leaders the law should make it through the required three readings no later than 19 November, ignoring objections that it was a complicated bill of twenty-four pages. The council brought in a draft law by 9 November which was discussed in committee. It was due to be made law 18 February. All of this was well known to MG, yet on 16 February, without warning, MG announced it had the day before taken the matter out of German hands and issued its own law.[82]

Walter Dorn, back in Germany for an inspection, was puzzled as to why the Economic Council was not working properly. "Why is it that two such important laws as Civil Service and Free Trade must be issued by MG, and the liaison with Bonn is apparently so ineffective? . . . clearly the Economic Council is not doing its job. . . . The same pattern seems to be repeated now at Bonn. . . . too weak to take a strong position . . . this whole thing was a failure."[83] Whether the failure was, as the Economic Council believed, the fault of MG or, as MG believed, the fault of Germans who behaved "politically," it appears another period had passed with another MG failure of government. There had been a currency reform, but whatever advance there was had been achieved by reducing government—that is, MG—controls. Even the currency reform, so long delayed, prolonged the economic suffering of most Germans.

Clay and the Bonn Constitution

If anything has survived the occupation, it would be the Bonn constitution, written under the supervision of *Herr* General Clay. Clay's role was highly significant, not because of what he put into the constitution but because he kept himself and his organization out of the way and worked very hard to keep everyone else, notably the French, out of the way too. He had decided in the spring of 1946 that new constitutions would have to be developed in Germany and fashioned by elected representatives, beginning in the American zone.[84] After the failure of the Moscow Conference, March-April 1947, Clay rejected the joint Kennan-Nitze-Lippman concept which envisioned a West German state incorporated into European reconstruction as a neutral buffer zone.[85] If the Western zones were to be attractive, they must not only become economically viable, but also attain political unity. Throughout 1947, the notion of a West German government drifted ever closer to the policy mainstream, finally reaching it at the London Conference in the spring of 1948. Clay led the struggle against the French, who preferred to push the idea into some more slowly moving channel.

Compared to Clay's problems with the French, and occasionally with a hesitant Washington, opposition from Germans was nearly nonexistent, which shows that Clay had become the German spokesman. Most Germans were willing to risk a split with the Soviet zone in exchange for the freedom he promised them, if that choice had to be made. The behavior of the Soviet troops, the experience of the refugees, and the experience of millions of German soldiers in Russia convinced 95 percent of the electorate that Russia had too little to offer to make unity on Russian terms acceptable. But slamming the door on unity as long as any hope existed was politically all but impossible, so everyone seemed to mumble.

There was not then nor later any articulate opposition to the idea of a democratic state. As Peter Merkl pointed out: "Even the ex-Nazis and members of the old ruling class by and large failed to object to the revival of democratic principles and reserved their venom for the Allies and the persons in power." Fascism had failed totally. Whereas many observers emphasized the political apathy among the disillusioned masses, who were devoting every thought to finding food, Merkl perceived a dynamic faith in democracy in the dominant minority.

> The spirit of founding a new society upon ideals of justice, brotherhood and democracy pervaded everything written during the first two years after the war . . . democracy and federalism were a natural choice long before the Western Allies chose to include them in the London Agreements. . . . There was a traditional democratic strain in Germany. . . . The most important single influence on German public opinion during these years was that of the traditions and tried institutions of the past.[86]

There was also a wide area of agreement on the second Allied principle, federalism. "The antipathy of the Germans to the excessive centralism of the Third Reich was so large, that without any allied doing federalism installed itself immediately after the collapse."[87] Merkl stressed the strength of federalism, the many intellectuals who supported it, and the entrenched defense of it in the various states: Bavaria, Lower Saxony, Bremen, and Hamburg. The major counterpressure came from the national SPD organization, which saw socialism as possible only with a strong central government. It assumed the cities would give it national majorities impossible to achieve in each of the states. There were some who blamed postwar hunger on federalism, citing the reluctance of farm states like Bavaria to share enough food with the industrial states. (Federalists blamed the central institutions and OMGUS for unproductive interference.) A new doubting of federalism was also noticeable at OMGUS: Clay confided to Dorn in April 1949 that he was not sure the federalist policy was right, but it was too late for him to change.[88]

The real problem was the French insistence that German government be kept weak. After the Allies in their early 1948 talks failed to agree on the structure of the German government, "subsequent conversations in Berlin also produced little until Clay negotiated a compromise with a French Foreign Office representative which paved the way for the later agreement in London."[89] This was the turning point in the plans for the West German government. At the London Conference, February-March 1948, the six powers agreed on little more than "democratic federalism." Refining this concept required another classic push by Clay. He negotiated with Zonal Commander Pierre Koenig and Foreign Ministry official Couve de Murville to get permission for a central government with some power. He was also holding back General Robertson, who wished to put the limits on this government into writing; to avoid the image of a puppet government, Clay thought the less said the better. German reaction to the London agreement, the terms of which were made known in June 1948, varied from lukewarm to unfavorable. The Allied "reserved powers," particularly the continued control over foreign trade, were generally criticized as worse than the status quo. The Germans were bitter about the international control over the Ruhr.[90]

At their 30 June meeting, Clay, Robertson, and Koenig could not agree on how specific to make the limitations on the new German government. Koenig, preferring to keep the Germans under control, wanted the terms to be precise. Clay and Robertson argued instead that it would be better for the Germans to come up with their own recommendations. Clay assumed that these German-stated limitations would be largely acceptable, and the German reaction would be less critical than if MG spelled out the terms in advance.[91] After this difference of opinion, each general read a part of their specifications to the assembled minister-presidents. Clay told them that they should call a constituent assembly by 1 September; the government created there should be federalist and should guarantee individual rights. Appropriately, Koenig specified the reserved areas, those to be kept under the military government: foreign trade, domestic trade affected by occupation commitments, the Ruhr authority, reparations, demilitarization, and some scientific research. The Allies reserved the right to resume full powers in an emergency. The effect was near disaster as the minister-presidents more clearly perceived Koenig's severity than the willingness of Clay and Robertson to negotiate. "The meeting came to an end in an atmosphere of mutual suspicion."[92]

The shocked minister-presidents agreed to delay a response and met for the purpose, 8–10 July, in Koblenz. At preparatory party caucuses, Carlo Schmid (SPD) and Josef Müller (CSU) agreed it would be a mockery to draft such a constitution. Misled by Koenig into thinking the 1 July statement was tentative, the German leaders suggested changes. Then, at the Koblenz Conference, they resolved to postpone a constitutional convention "until a solution for all of Germany is possible and until German sovereignty has been sufficiently restored." They wanted a parliamentary council to draw up a "basic law," and a further definition and limiting of the occupation powers. Clay, who had dismissed Allied fears of a German nonacceptance as "looking at ghosts walking," then "moved with determination to turn the precarious German compromise of Koblenz to his own purposes." He expressed to them on 14 July his fear that their rejection would simply put their fate in General Koenig's hands; the position they took at Koblenz would require discussion by the foreign ministers and home governments, and delay change for many, many months. They would be charged with splitting Germany no matter what they did. When the generals met the following day, Clay and Robertson insisted the Germans could and should be persuaded to accept the London decisions. The international situation made it imperative that the western Allies put their plans into effect as rapidly as possible. The mayor of Berlin, Ernst Reuter, at the follow-up meeting at Rüdesheim, 21–22 July, persuaded the minister-presidents that the split with Russia had already occurred.[93]

The minister-presidents accepted with only minor changes the offer to let them create a government. But they still objected to the word "constitution," choosing instead to call it *Grundgesetz* (Basic Law) and, fearing a national referendum and the communist charge that they were splitting Germany, they asked again for ratification by the various Landtage. These relatively minor issues came close to postponing a decision at a conference of the two parties on 26 July, but all muddled through to agree that a parliamentary council could start to work.[94] Even before the Parliamentary Council formally began in September, a committee was at work at the Chiemsee Conference, 10–23 August, shaping a document which presaged the eventual Basic Law. In forty-six sittings it produced not only guiding principles but a complete draft of the constitution. This thorough preparation was one reason for the peaceful constitutional convention; but in addition "the mood of the Parliamentary Council was most conciliatory and pervaded by a fundamental willingness to make compromises among the parties." The politicians had learned from the debacle of their Weimar predecessors.[95] CAD's Hans Simon had a different explanation, saying that "everybody agreed except on technical tax matters."[96] When the Allies did not intervene, things moved steadily ahead. The parties were well disciplined; with the exception of the CSU on the matter of federalism, voting blocs held steady.

Clay was able to realize his objective of a less centralized state because of the CSU states' rights position and the party's brief cooperation with the SPD. When Hans Ehard saw he was getting nowhere with his ally Adenauer, he had his famous breakfast agreement with Walter Menzel of the Rhineland SPD. "Sensing a widening rift between the CSU and the CDU, the national SPD hastened to take advantage of the situation. Ehard was more concerned about a pure *Bundesrat* (representation of the Länder in a second house) than about its equality with the lower house, and on this basis Menzel and he struck a compromise." To the CDU's surprise, the SPD came out in early November 1948 in favor of a Bundesrat with a suspensive veto on legislation. Yet on the second issue of financial federalism—taxing powers—it was the CSU that was outmaneuvered. To iron out a compromise, the convention appointed a committee of five which did not find room for any CSU members. With the formation of this committee the initiative passed to the alliance of the SPD and FDP with the British zone CDU.[97]

The major debate centered on the relative strength of the new central government and the states. MG was involved scarcely at all, mostly because the Allies were having difficulty coming to an agreement. The German draft document was finished before the Allies could agree on how to advise them. The Occupation Statute, setting out the powers the Allies would reserve to themselves, was not completed until many weeks after the Parliamentary Council had completed its third reading of the Basic Law.[98] Thus the Parliamentary Council got no specific guidance from the Allies. They were involved only at the end and only negatively.

There were, however, two major crises, both caused by MG interference. The first was the Allied *aide-memoire* of 22 November, after the Ehard-Menzel breakfast brought agreement on the Bundesrat. The *aide-memoire* demanded that the states be represented on the Bundesrat and have the power to safeguard their interests. The majority decided to ignore the Allied recommendations and to keep merely the Bundesrat's suspensive veto. The second crisis was the rejection of the Basic Law in Clay's memorandum of 2 March which demanded a weaker federal government. His objections concerned the appointment system of the civil service, the distribution of specific finance powers between the states and the federal government, the ambiguity on judicial independence, the nature of the federal administrative agencies, and the place of Berlin in the federal structure. The memo reflected Clay's inability to persuade the French to permit a stronger government.[99]

The impasse of 2 March took about six weeks to resolve, with Germans and Allies arguing among themselves. On the German level, it meant that the CDU, which had moved toward the SPD's centralism, had by 30 March slipped a notch back to the federalist CSU position, as demanded by Clay and the French. The "great compromise" was abandoned under the pressure of the governors, with the SPD going into the opposition, accompanied at first by the liberal FDP and the German Peoples' Party (DVP). Later the FDP and the DVP abandoned the SPD for fear of endangering the work of the Parliamentary Council by refusing to accept the Allied proposals. By the end of March it was a fight between the SPD's Kurt Schumacher and the three military governors.[100]

Clay still had to counter those in the State Department and Defense Department, like Kennan and Nitze, who preferred the neutralization of Germany in hopes of an agreement with Russia.[101] His greater struggle continued with the French, but he was aided by the quiet shift in French policy from the hard line of Koenig and the Gaullists to the moderate line of Foreign Minister Maurice Schuman. In March, Schuman asked for a secret talk with Clay, during which Schuman agreed to reducing the occupation controls.[102] By 8 April, the foreign ministers had agreed on the short, less restrictive U.S. version of the Occupation Statute.

This agreement left Clay alone in his duel with Schumacher. Washington instructed him to release the agreement on 20 April, but Clay delayed telling the Germans of the change in policy until 23 April. Clay who had been the compromiser, was now the resister. Perhaps he was concerned to save face. He cabled Washington he did not mind being defeated, but thought Schumacher merely spoke for himself and top party bureaucrats; he should not let this small group dictate to the SPD majority, particularly to gain votes.[103] Paul Weymar, Adenauer's authorized biographer, thought Schumacher had scored a major victory in convincing the SPD on 20 April not to accept the first Allied offer, for it put Clay in the position of seeming to make the concessions the party demanded.[104]

Two days after Clay's delayed release of the agreement, the Germans were ready with compromise proposals. These provided for the administration of major taxes by the Länder, as the Allies wished, and a reduction of the powers of the Bundesrat as the SPD wished, but retained for the federation power to legislate "to maintain economic and legal unity," as well as provision for financial equalization among the Länder.[105] After the Germans had accepted certain changes of phrasing, Clay gave way. The impasse was broken. All the pieces fell into place: on 25 April the German-Allied agreement was reached; on 27 April the Russians agreed to lift the blockade; on 8 May the Basic Law was adopted; on 10 May Bonn was selected as the capital; on 12 May the blockade ended.

To summarize the Allied impact on the new government's creation, one could begin with the immediate psychological effect. Merkl thought Allied intervention had been more display than reality, having only a negative psychological impact. He said, "the emergency powers retained by the occupation . . . the military style of the instructions, and the condescension of the military governors dampened the exalted spirits normally associated with constitution making. . . . The adverse effect of the Allied approach on the very aims they intended to foster was striking."[106] MG had little positive influence, even on the wording of the Basic Law. Even Clay observed much of the document was taken from the Weimar constitution and its various Land constitutions.[107] Friedrich put it positively: the basic cooperation between Germans and Americans came about because the United States proposed what the Germans wanted.

Merkl had the highest praise for the Germans' skill and discipline, their courage, self-restraint, and moderation. Under the March-April pressure, one might have expected them to pass on the responsibility to the occupiers, or to have been cowed. But in fact the majority of the Parliamentary Council seemed to be rather anxious to take on the full responsibility. "Far from being cowed, they defied the Allied governments repeatedly and were quite ready for a final walk-out during March and April 1949." John Golay discounted occupation influence on the constitution, noting only its mention of the Occupation Statute and its omission of provision for defense. "In all other respects, the Basic Law reads as though the occupation powers had never existed. . . . It follows the German tradition, with adaptations to take account of contemporary conditions and to accommodate varying interests and political views in West Germany today." The change that MG had imposed gave the Länder control over the assessment and collection of major taxes, thus buttressing states' rights.[108] "A more significant effect of Allied intervention was the quite unintended one of weakening the powers of the Bundesrat." The effect was "to raise doubts in German minds as to the sincerity of Allied professions of neutrality in issues of internal German politics, to discredit . . . the Parliamentary Council and its work, and to embitter relations between the German parties at the start of parliamentary life under the Basic Law." But MG's constant retreat from intervention, evident by 1950 under HICOG, gradually convinced the German public that the victors did not control Bonn.

The HICOG Epilogue: 1949–52

With the constitution approved, and occupation powers much reduced by agreement, occupation involvement in German politics ended except at the top level. The major debates with Bonn concerned not what the occupiers did—nearly nothing—but how much they charged for doing it. Occupation costs were therefore an issue, and so was the question of how quickly HICOG could reverse the key OMGUS policy of German demilitarization.

As the rules of the game changed, so did the players. The three high commissioners, McCloy, Ivone Kirkpatrick, and André François-Poncet, were diplomats and generally sympathetic to Germany. Their single opponent was Adenauer, and he is generally credited with having outfoxed them repeatedly. Yet when he was elected chancellor by one vote (his own), he was known to perhaps as little as 8 percent of the German people. The traditional party-style democracy, unchanged by MG, left decisions to party leaders, which HICOG privately lamented. "The German people have no real representation in government through the political parties and generally cannot effect governmental policy or action on any given issue."[109] Although Republican Washington was later devoted to Adenauer, "his election was received by the western powers with a marked lack of enthusiasm, even by the Americans who backed the CDU. His uncompromising personality and dour criticism had scarcely endeared him to the American officials with whom he had had contact."[110]

The already old Adenauer, born in 1876, had had a distinguished but regional political career as mayor of Cologne 1919–33, and as chairman of the Prussian state council. Forced from office by the Nazis, he had suffered economic hardship, during which he was helped financially by an American Jew.[111] Arrested in 1944, he escaped death by remarkable cleverness and good luck, although his first wife acquired a fatal blood disease in prison. After the Allies arrived, he resumed office as mayor of Cologne at the request of one British officer, but was abruptly fired for alleged lack of vigor by another and banned from the city. This left him free for party politics. He had the effrontery to take over the founding meeting of the Rhineland-Ruhr CDU with the excuse of being the oldest man there, and thus began his leadership of that party. With the most populous and industrially strongest Land as his power base, he added an organizational command post, the CDU British Zonal Council. This organization started as nothing more than a meeting of the CDU Land leaders, but it quickly became the most effective policy organ in the zone. In the formative years of the party Adenauer patiently travelled his zone creating it. "The hard work spent in explaining, compromising, cajoling and exhorting began to pay off in steady political support and a respectful following of secondary leaders."[112]

Competition with Adenauer for national leadership could possibly have come from Catholic Bavaria, then under Josef Müller, but Müller had his own problems and in any case, Bavarians were suspect to northern Germans as separatist. Another possible competitor was Jakob Kaiser, leader of the CDU in Berlin and the Russian zone, but he had a base of operations with obvious disadvantages and had held no important position before 1945. In contrast to Adenauer, he was at his best on a podium before a cheering audience, but he lacked Adenauer's administrative ability and the analytical capacity, flexibility, and tactical finesse necessary for the political bargaining table.

Thus at the crucial early stages, Adenauer was able to dominate the leading bourgeois party. All he needed was the support of the lesser bourgeois parties, notably the FDP, and he was fairly certain to get a majority over the SPD. As leader of the antisocialist bloc he came to interest the Americans. He had meant little or nothing to General Clay, and still less to Washington. "He merely happened to be an elderly German Conservative who, by one way or another, had become the head of the chief anti-Socialist party in West Germany."[113] Adenauer's chairmanship of the Parliamentary Council could have been a dead end, as it was for Pünder of the Economic Council. The socialists, who accepted him as chairman, assumed they were putting him on ice, and also assumed he was so old he could not be a serious problem. He chaired the meetings efficiently (though he was criticized for political absences), but his power came mainly from his clever use of his position to become the representative of the German people to the Allies.

Adenauer's victory over Schumacher was achieved partly because although he was often sour and irascible, he seemed charming and rational compared to Schumacher. Schumacher was the leader of the common man, the period's outstanding speaker, and vastly better known at first. Crippled and dying from an illness acquired in a concentration camp, where he spent most of the Third Reich, Schumacher appeared to many, particularly MG, as autocratic, arrogant and inflexible. He had no high opinion of the victors, thinking they carried a far greater share of "collective guilt" than did the SPD, who had fought Hitler from the beginning. He was outraged at the victors' assumption that Germans deserved their misery for having submitted to Hitler; "their meddling efforts to pacify, re-educate and democratize the German people were certain to backfire unless someone compelled them to do the 'right thing.' "[114] Schumacher began to recreate the SPD, even before the end of the war, although party activity was prohibited under both the Nazis and the Allies. By his brilliance and intensity, Schumacher controlled the central committee which controlled the party congresses; his autocracy was less often challenged than Adenauer's. The executive council of the CDU was elected from the party faithful, and able younger men, mayors like Ernst Reuter, were kept from power in the national organization. Schumacher refused to join any coalition with bourgeois parties, a great mistake. By choosing foreign policy as its major emphasis, the SPD, formerly accused of being unpatriotic, came to seem more overtly nationalistic than Adenauer, whose responsible position forced him to become more pragmatic.

Actually Adenauer's real interest was also foreign policy, that is, restoring German sovereignty. At the beginning of his effort to change the Occupation Statute, he told confidants: "We must have patience. I think that patience is the sharpest weapon of the defeated. I have a great deal of patience."[115] He needed it. Some Allied officials frankly resented the appearance of a German government and continued to show little regard for it. Their attitude much annoyed Adenauer, who often in public was unable to restrain his acid tongue. Some reports suggest he blundered in timing and tact, yet he was the most prominent German politician who consistently came out for total cooperation with the West. The Cold War was his standard weapon.[116] Playing each side against the other, he used his position with the Allies for domestic victories. "Through his CDU newspapers he launched a campaign demanding, often in offensive terms, precisely those concessions which, he was tolerably certain from the hints of his American friends, were to be granted within the next few weeks."[117]

Adenauer's actions in connection with the Ruhr dismantlings in the summer of 1949 demonstrate his typical astuteness. The workers were resisting with clubs and rocks. Adenauer's prestige depended on stopping the dismantling. His only chance was to accept the Allied offer of three seats out of fifteen on the International Ruhr Authority, which meant accepting Germany's being outvoted twelve to three in its own coal and steel industry. Adenauer gambled with his patriotic constituency and won. Bonn promised only to join the international authority, to maintain demilitarization (soon reversed), to cooperate on the Military Security Board, and to eradicate Nazism. In return the Allies agreed to curtail the dismantling of German industry, stop dismantling entirely in Berlin, relax restrictions on shipbuilding, and allow gradual reestablishment of consular and commercial relations with other countries.[118] This so-called Petersberg Agreement led to the prompt revision of the Occupation Statute, and was a major victory over the victors.

Schumacher pointed out that many evils still existed in the statute. In reply, Adenauer noted that because of the greater evil done by the Nazis, the rest of the world did not trust Germany, and its confidence had to be regained. Revision of the statute, he said, was a matter of psychological timing; it had to be done slowly, piece by piece. Joining the Ruhr Authority was a matter in which they had no choice; the decision for Germany to be involved had already been made by the military governors. As the debate grew hotter, Schumacher called out the famous insult, "Chancellor of the Allies," starting a demonstration which stopped barely short of a brawl.[119] Later events showed that Adenauer bet on the Allies and won West Germany prosperity and sovereignty, but not the German unity which was supposed to follow.

In July 1950, an intergovernmental study group, including Lewis Douglas, brother-in-law to McCloy, was already at work on the question of German sovereignty. By September they were ready to recommend relinquishing more authority to impress German public opinion. The Foreign Ministers' Conference of September 1950 approved most of the group's recommendations, which entailed a "major extension of the authority of the Federal Government," including a ministry of foreign affairs. The major documents were ready by early December, but were delayed until 7 March 1951, following six months of intensive negotiations.[120] Adenauer was gambling again by accepting Germany's foreign debts of 14.3 billion marks. A few weeks later the Allies gave up the economic limitations they had been imposing. At the end of April the dismantling ended, and negotiations got underway to replace the Occupation Statute with a security pact, and to integrate Germany into the European Defense Community.

By the summer of 1951 the Americans had accepted the French Pleven Plan for an integrated European army. "With General Eisenhower's consent, Mr. McCloy 'sold' the European army plan to the Pentagon and the State Department in Washington. Late in June he returned to Germany with orders 'to get on with it—and get Adenauer's agreement.'" Within a few hours of his return, at a garden party, he sounded out the key German generals Hans Speidel and Adolf Heusinger. "Adenauer, well-informed as always on Allied thinking, realized just how desperate the Americans were . . . to get a German army in the field at any cost. The crafty old man in the Chancellery raised his price."[121] He told the Americans he would have to get greater concessions to win over a German public, heavily influenced by *Ohne mich* neutralism.

The State Department was concerned about supposed Nazis in the foreign ministry and neo-Nazi parties, yet Adenauer knew he held the cards. His private contacts with the Pentagon, probably through the massive American-financed Gehlen Service (for spying on Russia) assured him the American generals were behind him, no matter what the State Department might say. The concessions he won for Germany became apparent at the September 1951 foreign ministers' meetings: the ending of the occupation as such, and the ending of interference in domestic affairs by the western powers were to come into effect in exchange for the agreement to place German troops in the European army. "Adenauer never played poker, but he certainly completely outbluffed the Americans."

During the winter of 1951–52 there was strong U.S. pressure to seal the West Germans into the western European community. The threat was that otherwise the Americans might reconsider their whole German policy, and the flow of dollars might stop. Adenauer and McCloy took turns working on the German public for the same goal. The SPD was making the tough charge that Adenauer was more for integration into the West than for German unity, which the Russians seemed to be offering as the alternative.[122] Integration into the West was accomplished by the European Defense Community Treaty of

26 May 1952, which promised German independence. Since implementation was related to ratification of the treaty, which was delayed by the French, the occupation did not come to an official end until 1955. German sovereignty was promised, and in effect achieved. The high commissioners for the last three years were little more than ambassadors. They never finally and completely disapproved any federal law or annulled any federal regulation, although they provisionally disapproved a very few federal legislative enactments. Their positive influence was also limited because they did not maintain close contacts with the political leadership, or legislators, or parliamentary committees, or with various interest groups, such as business, trade, labor, and management.[123]

The major failure of HICOG concerned one of the very few projects surviving from liberal days, civil service reform. In February 1950, A Bundestag bill in effect restored the civil service law of 1936. It reinstated the distinction between *Beamten* (officials) and *Angestellten* (employees) which MG Law No. 15 had eliminated. The bill eliminated the central personnel office, MG's major effort to break down the caste system. HICOG negotiations with Adenauer dragged through April and May, but HICOG historian Elmer Plischke wrote that Adenauer failed to implement his promises of reform. The provisional law was continued and tolerated by HICOG for its own political reasons. After a HICOG lecture December 21, Adenauer made more promises, also not kept.[124] According to critics, the civil service legislation that emerged in May 1951, achieved the "renazification" of the German civil service. Based on the popular conviction that public officials had borne unfairly the brunt of the denazification, nearly all of them having been forced out of office for years, after most had been forced into the Nazi party, the law provided for the restoration of pension rights or the reinstatement in office of all but those few who owed their original appointment to a close connection to the party, or whose only appointment had been to the Gestapo.[125] Americans, who usually oversimplified and in 1951 still equated party membership with party conviction, were horrified, though the expert on the civil service wrote that only a negligible number of civil servants had approved of Nazi inhumanities.[126]

From a public relations standpoint, HICOG could not be faulted for interfering seriously because it did not. It could not be faulted for lack of concern with German development; McCloy and his wife showed public concern. Yet like any other fading nobility whose service to society was no longer commensurate with the privileges it enjoyed, HICOG could be faulted for its luxury, still obvious in a society just beginning to rise out of the ruins. The costs of troops stationed in Germany as part of the common western defense have remained a burden on the German economy and a constant and irritating reminder of the occupation. It was left entirely to the occupation powers to determine what goods and services must be supplied to them. They had not recognized the provisions of the Hague Convention. However, over the years the percentage of German tax funds going to pay these costs declined markedly from that early in the occupation. In the three western zones from 1946 to 1950, the annual total taxation reserved to meet occupation costs was, in the successive years, 42, 38, 33 26, and 28 percent. The 1950 figure represented 210 marks per worker, or about the monthly salary of a clerical worker. Too often the money was used to buy luxury goods for occupation personnel and their families.[127] The official total of occupation costs to 31 March 1950 was 21 billion marks, but a German investigation found it to be at least 25 billion. Gottlieb thought such expenses drained off more wealth than did the Russians with their reparations.[128]

In 1945 perhaps one-third of the working force was used by the occupation. In 1951, of a working population of 20 million, 1,250,000 were working for the occupation. It was a luxury that West Germany could not afford, because one-third of its population was already on public assistance, in particular its eight million refugees. It took two German employees to support each Allied soldier. A directive said households should be limited to two inside housemaids and one outside worker, "to avoid unnecessary burdens" on the German economy. As a specious justification for this luxury, army wives were quoted as saying that "having a servant for the first time in their lives freed their energies for the good works they were doing among the Germans." Another argument was that "American officers must live in a style to impress the Germans and this involved household maids." The troops and their families were also extravagant in their demands on German resources; they used almost as much electricity as all of German agriculture or as much as 8 million Germans; they absorbed 54 percent of all automobile exports. Since hotels and services were supplied by Germans, soldiers and their families could vacation at requisitioned deluxe hotels at only $1.50 a day for first class accommodations, with train service at a fraction of the regular fare. HICOG was helpless against the military.[129]

In spite of such abuses, West Germans were increasingly free and satisfied. Clay's policy of restoring self-government was no doubt his wisest and most successful, although not until MG had surrendered its power was its general policy implemented. Clay was not consistently willing to let the Germans do it, but he was more often than were most advisers and Allies. His policy was certainly superior to that of his counterparts in the other zones, where self-government was delayed for months. Had his power not been limited, by France and England more than by Washington, he would probably have come to an earlier and more reasonable surrender of occupation prerogatives.

It is less clear that he tried to save German unity; for the first half of his regime he was unduly worried about what a stronger German government might do. At least until 1946 he seemed willing to work with the Russians to get that unity. Thereafter he worked so efficiently with the British and French that the original U.S. policy mistake of partitioning Germany was partially redeemed. In permitting the Germans to reconstruct their government, he took the admirable Jeffersonian line that military government which governs least governs best. The Germans as a result reconstituted their system as it had been before.

Notes

1. The only policy remotely like the preparation of a cadre was the reorientation of a few prisoners in the U.S. When they returned to Germany, long after area governments had begun, their involvement at a low level was strictly coincidental. Clay rejected the idea of pressuring Germans to hire them (Clay to War Dept., 7 Oct. 1945, in Jean Smith, ed., *The Papers of General Lucius Clay* [Bloomington, 1974], 98).

2. Revisionists can argue that suppressing Antifa was not only undemocratic but justification for Russian suppression of noncommunist groups. MG's argument was that these were very small groups, badly organized, unimportant, and unrepresentative. MG soon pressured the new governments to include communists; the KPD was not hindered; the SPD was encouraged (Gabriel Almond, *The Struggle for Democracy in Germany* [Chapel Hill, 1949], 67; Lutz Niethammer, *Entnazifizierung in Bayern* [Frankfurt, 1972], 47–52).

3. Only marginal parties were banned. Clay turned down a party for the refugees with the argument that they should work within the established parties. Pressured by Murphy to prohibit the Bavarian Monarchist party, Clay in May 1946 correctly judged that that would be unnecessary and undemocratic.

4. Washington forbade party youth groups until 1947 (*Monthly Report of the Military Governor*, Feb. 1947, 23; Vera Eliasberg, "Political Party Developments," in Almond, *Struggle*, 232).

5. "From the very beginning, in fact, they nearly always operated beyond the limits of MG authorization, engaging in activities ostensibly prohibited, but which were usually, later, informally authorized, all the way from building local party cells to re-establishing international contacts. . . . Most of the activities were initially unknown to the occupying authorities (Solomon Lebovitz, "Military Government and the Revival of German Political Activity" [Ph.D. diss., Harvard University, 1949], 165, 230).

6. J. F. J. Gillen, *American Influence on the Development of Political Institutions* (Karlsruhe, 1950), 68–69, based on AG OMGUS 000.1 Political Parties; see Murphy to Clay 5 Feb. 1946; Murphy cable 19 Apr. 1946; CAD cable to Clay 5 May 1946; Clay cable to CAD 8 May 1946.

7. Harold Zink, *The United States in Germany, 1945–55* (New York, 1957), 179, 181.

8. Harold Zink, *American Military Government in Germany* (New York, 1947), 169.

9. Letter USFET 5 Oct. 1945, AG 014.1. This order, like many others, was not necessarily obeyed; a local military governor could exert extralegal influence, but with the exception of denazification, this was not supported openly from above.

10. Clay to Sec. of War, Cable CC 17554, 14 Oct. 1945; Clay to McCloy, 16 Sept. 1945, in Gillen, *American*, 14, and Smith, *Papers*, 74–82.

11. Gillen, *American*, 39–44; Clay to AGWAR, Cable CC 2418, 23 Aug. 1946, Smith, *Papers*,

252–53. On 14 August 1946 Clay protested in the strongest possible terms against making any of the changes suggested by the State Dept. and was willing to have his protest referred to the president (Smith, *Papers*, 272; OMGUS Chronology, Oct. 1946, 142, 146, 149, 151, Washington National Record Center [hereafter WNRC]).

12. "This almost amounted to American sponsorship of the policy of dividing Germany into four different countries." It represented the commander's autonomy on which the army thrived (Carl Friedrich, *American Experience in Military Government in World War II* [New York, 1948], 230, 234; Manuel Gottlieb, *The German Peace Settlement and the Berlin Crisis* [New York, 1960], 18–23). Reinhold Maier thought the talk of decentralization amusing in view of all the burdens MG dumped on Bonn (*Erinnerungen, 1948–55* [Tübingen, 1966], 263).

13. OMGUS Chronology, 26 July 1945, Kansas City Record Center (hereafter KCRC).

14. Lia Härtel, *Der Länderrat des amerikanischen Besatzungsgebietes* (Stuttgart, 1951), 23, 31; Gillen, *American*, 105.

15. The secretariat's departments were: Coordination, Legal, Finance, Economics, Transportation, Food, Social Policy, Cultural, and Administrative.

16. Hans Schlange-Schöningen, *Im Schatten des Hungers* (Hamburg, 1955), 59–60, quoting a food specialist.

17. An RGCO January 1946 memo to OMGUS said: "The prestige of German authorities should not be lowered nor their enthusiasm impaired by MG interference" (quoted in Robert W. Miller, "The South German Länderrat" [Ph.D. diss., University of Michigan, 1960], 85).

18. Heinz Guradze, "The Länderrat—Landmark of German Reconstruction," *Western Political Quarterly* (1950), 205. Like so many officers, Guradze and Miller came to see things the way their German counterparts did, which was usually anti-OMGUS.

19. Winning to Dorn, 10 June 1949, quoted in Gillen, *American*, 95. He is also quoted as saying: "I am sick of doing all the work for the Germans" (Geiler Papers, Staatsarchiv, Wiesbaden, quoted in John Gimbel, *The American Occupation of Germany* [Stanford, 1962], 43, 73).

20. Rossman to Pollock, 20 May 1946, Länderrat File 70, Z-1, Bundesarchiv (hereafter BA); Länderrat File 1213, Gesetz zur Befreiung, BA. MG censorship meant that it took four to twelve hours for a telegram and two to four hours for a telephone call (Seelos to Pollock, 2 May 1946, File 70, Z-1, BA). The problem was evident when Wilhelm Hoegner (Bavaria) marched out, complaining of "unfriendliness" toward Bavaria; it was willing to cooperate on the food question, but regarded the powers granted to the food plenipotentiary as a greater threat than the hated centralization of Weimar (Minutes of meeting, 2 Apr. 1946, File 18, Z1, BA).

21. Minutes of meeting, 27 May 1946. Maier feared Pollock's seriousness meant Clay would soon come to scold them (Rossmann Report, 4 June 1946, File 18, Z1, BA).

22. On 18 August, Dawson soothed Rossmann with the promise that there would be no interfering with the functioning of Land government or the Länderrat (File 15, File 72, Z1, BA).

23. Any central offices should not be under MG but under the minister-presidents and their Landtage. The opposite occurred (Grundsätzlicher Entscheidung der Minister Präsidenten der amer. Zone, 21 Aug. 1946, File 15, Z1, BA).

24. Hoegner letter, 22 Aug. 1946, File 15.

25. Confidential remarks of Lt. Pabst, File 20, Z1, BA.

26. They assumed his anger was for Washington's benefit and were slightly mollified by Dawson's immediate effort to smoth it over (Interview Reinhold Maier). Maier had much respect for Clay, but thought it took two years to convince him of the correctness of the German position. See also Hoegner/Dawson memo, 5 Nov. 1946, Bav. Sk., 360/1.

27. Gimbel, *American*, 94–95, based on WNRC 34 1/1 and Länderrat meeting 8 Jan. 1947; Rossmann Report, 11 Feb. 1947 conference, File 18, Z1, BA.

28. Gimbel, *American*, 98–99, taken from WNRC 99-1/15, Conference of Clay with Minister-Presidents, 23 Feb. 1497.

29. "Both General Robertson and myself fully recognize the desirability of a coordinating

committee or some political body having responsibility for all these agencies'' (Transcript of discussion, 23 Feb. 1947, in Pollock Papers, Michigan Historical Society, Ann Arbor, Mich.).

30. Härtel, xiv; it should not be confused with the bizonal council of the same name.

31. "Interne Besprechung mit Winning," Hessen Staatskanzlei, 1a08/01; Clay to Parkman, Memo 28 July 1947, OMGUS 166-3/3, quoted in Gimbel, *American*, 129; OMGUS Chronology, 5 Aug. 1947, WNRC.

32. Remarks of Alex Möller, SPD, 4 Aug. 1947, Parl. Rat Stenog Protokolle, U.S. Zone Länderrat, 89, Wissenschaftliche Dokumentarstelle des Bundestages (hereafter WDS); ibid., remarks of Keil, Seelos, Rossmann, 12–14, 31–32; OMGUS Chronology 9 Sept. 1947, 412, WNRC.

33. Clay had said the "less incriminated" could work except in "key" offices and when asked to define that, he said: "It would have to be worked out." The result had been that party members could not have a responsible position in public service, or be employed as teachers, preachers, editors, writers, or radio commentators. This had a disastrous effect on education (Interne Sitzung, 23 Sept. 1947, Z1-19, BA; WDS, 23–43); see chapter six.

34. Sitzung, 2 Feb., 12 Feb., 19 Feb. 1948, Z1-20, BA.

35. Parl. Rat., 28 Mar. 1948, WDS.

36. Sitzung, 10 June 1948, Z1-21, BA. Rossman assumed there was no other job for him.

37. Miller, "Länderrat," 86. Guradze thought OMGUS was taking advantage of weaker RGCO chiefs, that is, those less close to Clay (Guradze, 194, 211).

38. One law, which merely implemented ACC action on labor conciliation, was turned down without explanation. Ehard's explanation of the confusion: Clay was trying to reduce the Länderrat to put pressure on the British to agree to a bizonal arrangement. This did not work either (Miller, "Länderrat," 104–105; Sitzung, 15 Feb. 1949, Z1-19, BA).

39. Report Graf Emil von Wedel, 5–9 Apr. 1949, Z1-16, BA.

40. Report Wedel, 22 Oct. 1949, Z1-16, BA.

41. Länderrat correspondence with RGCO responses show neither argument nor depth of analysis, only general principles. The futility of their efforts is dramatized in a letter from a cabinetmaker who answered he could not supply workers to an RGCO project because two were ill, two others were seeking relatives expelled from the east, and no one worked Saturday because of the reduced food ration (Files 69–79, Z1, BA; letter, 17 June 1946, File 70, BA).

42. The most famous minister-president conference was the one held by Ehard in Munich in June 1947. The relevant question is whether Clay prevented cooperation with the minister-presidents from the Russian zone by forbidding talk of political matters. German authorities seem to agree that Ehard's supposed clearing of the meeting with OMGUS 6 May led to "the fatal limitation" of the agenda to economic matters (Gerhart Binder, *Deutschland seit 1945* [Stuttgart, 1969], 183; Elmer Krautkrämer, *Deutsche Geschichte nach dem II Weltkrieg, 1945-49* [Hildesheim, 1962], 121; Ernst Deuerlein, *Die Einheit Deutschlands, 1941-49* [Frankfurt, 1957], 191; Hans-Peter Schwarz, *Vom Reich zur Bundesrepublik* [Berlin, 1966], 633). Gimbel offers an impressive rebuttal—that there is no record of "the May 6 conversation" or of MG objection to the inclusion of political matters in Ehard's early publicity. The objection came instead from Schumacher's SPD (*American*, 131–39). Then the French stepped in and forbade talk of political unity (*Die Berliner Zeitung*, 10 June 1947; *Main Post*, 3 June 1947). Ehard continued to insist that the motivation for the conferences was economic. He put the blame for the failure of the conference on the Russians (Interviews Dr. Hans Ehard, 1970). OMGUS was little involved, and maybe even pleased, as Ehard thought, that somebody else was doing something to achieve what MG had failed to accomplish at Moscow. With all of the other saboteurs of the conference, not excluding the Russians and Ulbricht, it is exaggerating U.S. powers and clarity of policy to say it was responsible for the failure, and it would be exaggerating the importance of this effort to assume that because of it German unity was lost.

43. Lucius Clay, *Decision in Germany* (New York, 1950), 78. In his book Clay emphasizes the

need to nullify the communist appeal to nationalism, and this was the argument he used to convince Byrnes to make the offer on 11 July to join with any other power.

44. Most Germans were opposed, not only because of the scattering, but because any coordination would have to come from MG, a step backward from the Länderrat. Litchfield told the army historian in 1949 that everyone knew at the time that this concept was doomed, but Clay stuck to it. Washington was not involved at all (Gillen, *American*, 138; Col. Dawson to Gen. Adcock, 14 Aug. 1946, in AG OMGUS 014.1, Länderrat, quoted in Gillen, *American*, 142).

45. A Hessian plan of August 1946 for parliamentary control was turned down by the military governors as they feared the accusation of "political unity" (Tilman Pünder, *Das Bizonale Interregnum* [Spichltroisdorf, 1966], 86).

46. Robertson to Clay, 25 Apr. 1947; Clay to Robertson, 27 Apr. 1947, in AG OMGUS 091.3 as quoted in Gillen, *American*, 148, 150.

47. Gillen, *American*, 161. On 13 April 1947, Clay admitted: "Certainly the Bizonal organization is weak and equally certainly as a result of my compromises." He assumed he was to decentralize (Smith, *Papers*, 359).

48. BICO was authorized to make most decisions, referring only basic political questions to Berlin (Wörtlicher Bericht über die Vollversammlungen, 4, Wirtschaftsrat Protokolle, WDS; T. Pünder, 119).

49. Hermann Pünder, *Von Preussen nach Europa* (Stuttgart, 1968), 344; T. Pünder, 12. Yet Schlange-Schöningen thought getting approval from BICO bureaucracy went terribly slowly; BICO memos were curt and had a gruff military tone (156).

50. T. Pünder, 105, 108, 226–27; Robert Slover, "The Bizonal Economic Administration of West Germany" (Ph.D. diss., Harvard University, 1950), 75, quoting W. Hallstein.

51. T. Pünder, 119–21. This possibly reflects his CDU leanings. Patient, hard-working liaison officer Kenneth Dayton from OMGUS said the Länder needed a defense, the various administrations needed Executive Council coordination (6 Aug. 1947, Akten des Vereinigten Wirtschaftsgebietes, Z4/183, BA).

52. Wirtschaftsrat, Protokolle, 24 June 1947, WDS, remarks of Dr. Friedrich Holzapfel.

53. Ibid., 9, remarks of Erwin Schöttle.

54. *Die Neue Zeitung*, speaking for OMGUS, regretted that the directors were not experts but politicians, not bipartisan but all from one party (ibid., 26–36; *Die Neue Zeitung*, 28 July 1947; *Rhein Echo*, 30 July 1947).

55. The Wirtschaftsrat was not democratic and the blame was not German but Allied (Akten des Vereinigten Wirtschaftsgebietes, Z4/183, BA).

56. Wirtschaftsrat, Protokolle, 29 Oct. 1947, 154. His speeches seemed less inflammatory than those of Food Director Schlange-Schöningen, who described Germany as "the poor house of the world" about to become "the sick house of the world," or as "the concentration camp, Germany" (Wirtschaftsrat, Protokolle, 4 Sept. 1947, 80, 94, WDS).

57. Gimbel, *American*, 193; Protokolle des Exekutivrates, Bericht von Dr. Semler, 12 Dec. 1947, Akten des Vereinigten Wirtschaftsgebietes, Z4/182- , BA.

58. Semler promptly apologized to Clay, but added he would not have said such things if he had known "strangers" were there (T. Pünder, 152–54). At the same time Clay was writing Washington that food distribution problems arose mostly "from lack of authority of Bizonal administration," and that German sovereignty was necessary (Smith, *Papers*, 545–46).

59. Slover, 196. Semler wrote a lengthy defense: Germany could have paid for the food if her foreign assets had not been taken away, if use of German boats were not forbidden, if farm lands had not been taken away, if coal prices were not kept well under the world price level (Semler Folder, in OMGUS, 103–215, WNRC).

60. The U.S. agreement 2 December to assume a much larger share of the costs of German imports increased Clay's influence (Gimbel, *American*, 189). Gimbel described the latter half of 1947 as the period of least initiative and experimentation and the most indecision.

61. OMGUS to AGWAR 24 Sept. 1947, OMGUS 9-25/16; "Interne Besprechung mit General Clay am 4 Nov. 1947," Z1/26, BA, quoted in Gimbel, *American*, 195.

62. The *Verwaltungsrat* (Administrative Council) should be reformed to consist of a chairman selected by the Economic Council and confirmed by the second house for a fixed term of office. The chairman was to choose his own heads of departments and they were not to be subject to confirmation except by MG (Gillen, *American*, 166).

63. Ibid., 167. German reaction is well shown in "Nachlass Pfeiffers," Bayerische Staatskanzlei, 010b (hereafter BSK).

64. OMGUS Chronology, 8 Jan. 1948, 23, WNRC; Bipartite Control Office, 12 Jan. 1948, WDS.

65. OMGUS admitted failure: Wiesbaden handed in 824 positive declarations out of 72,000 households. In Frankfurt there were 10 out of 197,000, declaring only 72 pounds of flour and 1,714 pounds of potatoes (OMGUS Chronology, 22 Jan. 1948, 41, 44; Feb. 1948, 148, WNRC).

66. Wirtschaftsrat, Protokolle, 21 Jan. 1948, 271. "MG often tells us: 'We are giving you all the authority you want! Up to now this has meant only a paper-authority. When does authority collapse? Always when orders from above have to be put into effect."

67. *Rheinischer Merkur*, 14 Feb. 1948.

68. The U.S. appeared to be the wavering "democracy," which was "a very much depreciated idea" (*New York Herald Tribune*, 22 Mar. 1948).

69. The council had passed but five laws in three months; the election of Dr. Hermann Pünder as chairman had been a sorry affair, for he got but forty of ninety-six votes. The problem was that the CDU-CSU coalition was looking for a weak man, but one who could still get as much as possible out of MG (H. Pünder, 322; Peter Eckhardt, *Wiesbadener Kurier*, 5 Mar. 1948). Adenauer turned down the post because he was "too old."

70. BICO, "Lack of Progress in Bizonal Legislation," 5 Mar. 1948, WDS; Wirtschaftsrat, Protokolle, 2 Mar. 1948, 350, WDS.

71. Ibid., 16 Mar. 1948, 406; 25 May 1948, 562; T. Pünder, 263. A common German judgment is that Clay's distrust and hostility altered only with the Berlin blockade (Otto Seeling to Erich Köhler, 11 June 1948, BICO, WDS).

72. Another CDU spokesman said the entire council must consider resigning, as Seeling had done. The long economic stagnation was the fault of the occupation (Wirtschaftsrat, Protokolle, 25 May 1948, 595–96; Ketels (CDU) and Dahrendorf (SPD), 14 June 1948, 607–609).

73. The committee report was an exhaustive treatment in five volumes. "Ausschuss Amerika Geschäft," 7 Sept., 15 Oct. 1948, 4 Feb. 1949, WDS; Wirtschaftsrat Protokolle, 16 Mar. 1948, 398; 8 Aug. 1949; BICO Correspondence, 24 Nov. 1948, WDS.

74. Conference of 14 June 1948, Akten des Vereinigten Wirtschaftsgebietes, Z/4, BA. When asked about supplying Berlin in any blockade, Clay answered that if the Germans did not subsidize Berlin they could write the city off. Clay was a very heavy smoker, but defended the limits set on foreign trade, saying that otherwise the Germans would import luxuries like cigarettes.

75. BICO had ordered a decentralization of German economic controls 9 June. Erhard had obtained a fifty to thirty-seven Economic Council vote 17–18 June to limit controls to those items "capable of control" (BICO, "Decentralized German Economic Controls," 9 June 1948, WDS; T. Pünder, 301).

76. Interview Dr. Ludwig Erhard. The BICO file indicates a tough Clay and a critical MG, but both were increasingly on the outside looking in, and their efforts were primarily directed toward ending German restraints on domestic trade. BICO complained that the law for decentralization of economic controls did not protect the public from industrial groups. It threatened that if there was not a new law by 3 September MG would step in (BICO to Sec. Gen., 3 Aug. 1948, BICO Correspondence, WDS).

77. Conference 15 Sept. 1948, Akten des Vereinigten Wirtschaftsgebietes, 211; Seelos to BSK, 8 Oct. 1948, Ehard Papers, Akten der Abteilung II, BSK; Besatzungstatut, BSK; Conference 15 Dec. 1948, Z/4, BA; Direktorial Kanzlei des Verwaltungsrates, Dept. 1b6 for Pünder, 27 Dec. 1948, Z/4, BA.

78. Clay complained that lumber was available for housing, although there was not enough for coal mining; none would be imported. He could not approve German whale fishing or sailing the seas, or minor local exports to East Germany in exchange for necessary local electric power (Conference of 14 Jan. 1949, 212, Z/4, BA).

79. Ibid., 15 Feb., 13 Apr. 1949.

80. In August, Erhard was held responsible for an article in a journal of which he was the publisher, which stated that Germany was not so much the receiver as the giver of economic help (ibid., 15 July, 16 Aug. 1949).

81. BICO Correspondence, 13 Aug. 1948, WDS.

82. BICO, 8 Nov. 1948, in Erhard Papers, Akten Abt, II, BSK; T. Pünder, 231. OMGUS specialist Wolfsburger was elated at having gotten his law in. Adcock opposed reconsidering it, although Walter Dorn thought that best; he also thought MG action necessary because of the "stall" to preserve party nepotism, which was "even worse than it was at any time during the Weimar Republic" ("Notes," Institut für Zeitgeschichte, Munich).

83. Ibid., 80, 88.

84. One could more simply have amended the 1919–33 constitutions, but to Americans and some Germans these were discredited by the events of 1933.

85. The hope was that Russia, after exploiting its zone, would drop it like a squeezed-out lemon (Schwarz, 121–23). Until the 1961 Berlin wall, the "economic magnet" theory worked to make the East German state untenable.

86. Peter Merkl, *The Origins of the West German Republic* (New York, 1963), 21–33, 44. Merkl also praised CDU politicians as evangelists.

87. Theodor Eschenburg, "Der Neue Start," in Hans Netzer, *Adenauer und die Folgen* (Munich, 1965), 29–30, 35. Eschenburg says the powers of the Weimar president were necessary to pay reparation demands.

88. Adcock's assistant Dayton said that bizonal agencies failed because the Länder sabotaged them, and that Americans had lost some love for federalism (Glum Memo, 25 Jan. 1948; Staatskanzlei, Wiesbaden, 1d02; Gimbel, *American*, 197; Dorn, "Notes," 114).

89. E. H. Litchfield, *Governing Postwar Germany* (Ithaca, N.Y., 1948), 39–42. Litchfield emphasized Murphy's unauthorized push for a pooling of European coal and steel, see also Gillen, *American*, 184–86, 192. He cabled of the lack of French cooperation (Clay to Draper 1 Apr. 1948, Smith, *Papers*, 608–11). Gillen thought French obstructionism was upset when the Soviets walked out of the ACC. No council, no French veto (196, 219). Clay praised the diplomacy of Douglas and described himself as "the tough so and so injecting the needle" (Smith, *Papers*, 664).

90. Lebovitz, 141; Merkl, 52. The currency reform angered German authorities because German experts had been rounded up, kept isolated, and ignored (Carl Friedrich, "Memorandum concerning Governmental Developments," 11 Oct. 1948, CSCAD 014, NA). Friedrich thought this high level of dissatisfaction encouraged the Soviets to try the blockade; see also T. Pünder, 233. Clay said the secrecy was necessary to avoid repercussions in France (Smith, *Papers*, 672).

91. Gimbel, *American*, 209, based on draft verbatim minutes, "Meeting of Military Governors," 30 June 1948, OMGUS, 110–2/11, WNRC.

92. Friedrich Memo, 11 Oct. 1948, CSCAD 014, NA. Friedrich blamed Allied clumsiness for the crisis; there had been a basic agreement all along.

93. Gimbel, *American*, 216, 218, based on Robert Lochner, "Summary of General Clay's

Meeting, 14 July 1948," dated 23 July 1948, 177–2/3, WNRC; see also John Golay, *The Founding of the Federal Republic of Germany* (Chicago, 1958), 15; Krautkrämer, 180.

94. Friedrich Memo, 18 October 1948, CSCAD 014, NA. Friedrich gave Max Brauer and Hans Ehard, not MG, credit for saving the conference from a disastrous failure (Gimbel, *American*, 225). For Clay's optimistic report see Smith, *Papers*, 746.

95. Golay, 18. MG was not represented at the conference, but Friedrich was on the shore. Some leaders came at night by boat to get his advice (Merkl, 61). Clay's 19 Aug. 1948 report is in Smith, *Papers*, 773–76.

96. The exception was Reiman (KPD) but he was so inept that he was voted down 65–2 (Hans Simon to Baldwin, 22 Oct. 1948, OMGUS: Merkl, 88). For Clay's 29 Sept. 1948 report, see Smith, *Papers*, 882–86; for the 16 Oct. report, ibid., 901–6.

97. Merkl, 93–95.

98. Golay, 22. Clay's report on the 5 November meeting doubted that Koenig was speaking for his government (Smith, *Papers*, 915).

99. Merkl, 97. Robertson scolded Adenauer for council slowness; MG might take the initiative (Abschrift des Berichtes der Aussenstelle, Bad Godesberg, 22 Nov. 1948, WDS; Gillen, *American*, 229, quoting Clay cable to DA for CSAD, 28 Feb. 1949; Litchfield, 42). Clay later regretted the 2 March veto (Clay Cable to DA for CSCAD, 10 Mar. 1949, in Gillen, *American*, 229; Clay, 421–22).

100. The "friendly message" by the governors may have facilitated the compromise; "It was little more than an attempt by the military authorities to gain credit for the final solution of the crisis of the Council which they had obstructed for so long" (Merkl, 94, 101). Clay defended his action to Voorhees as a defense of decentralization (Smith, *Papers*, 1067).

101. Schwarz, 142–44. Schwarz thought the USSR was also unwilling to risk a different policy. "They united quietly on the preservation of the status quo."

102. Golay, 96–97; Gillen, *American*, 221–22; Elmer Plischke, *History of the Allied High Commission for Germany*, HICOG (Bonn, 1951), 23.

103. On 2 April, Clay emphasized the folly of giving Schumacher a victory for his minority position. The SPD was "close to a totalitarian party in operation and lacks the democracy which comes from local pride" (Smith, *Papers*, 1077, 1090, 1095, 1102). On 14 April Riddleberger reported a masterful Clay conference with German leaders (ibid., 1107–10, 1114). To the pressure to announce Clay responded on 19 April: "If you want to judge German political situation there, please simply give me instructions and take away my discretionary power. My real suggestion is you let me come home tomorrow" (ibid., 1117). On 21 April Clay told Voorhees he would come home if the remarks were an order, but Voorhees said: "No order has been issued you." The next day Bradley said that Schumann wanted the message forwarded and that soldiers are used to accepting orders. Clay answered that the Nuremberg judges had found no excuse for a soldier carrying out political orders (ibid., 1123–25). He wanted to be relieved as soon as the message was delivered. Golay thought the holdout was a mistake (108).

104. Paul Weymar, *Konrad Adenauer: His Authorized Biography* (New York, 1957), 247, 259. To counter this Schumacher "victory," Adenauer claimed in a 22 July speech that the SPD had known all along from Allied friends that "no" would win. Hans Simon, Clay's liaison to the Germans, emphasized Allied confusion and errors, particularly the disagreement between State and War, which made the unnecessary concessions "the historic blunder" that convinced the Germans to procrastinate, to evade, and to get what they wanted ("The Bonn Constitution and Government," in Hans Morgenthau, ed., *Germany and the Future of Europe* [Chicago, 1951], 117–18).

105. Golay, 106.

106. Merkl, 116. Dorn reported "much misunderstanding, and communication something less than adequate. Feeling that there has been a reversion to intervention of 1946" ("Notes," 25).

107. Clay, 89. Interventions were "far less significant than public opinion in Germany and abroad has been made to assume." Allied contact was uncoordinated. "Each liaison office tried to sell the view of its particular government, and the Germans quickly became wise to it and tried to exploit it" (Hans Simon, in Morgenthau, 117; Interview Carl J. Friedrich).

108. Merkl, 102. But since this arrangement suited a substantial minority of the Germans and was in keeping with earlier German practice, "it cannot be described . . . as having altered the fundamentally German character of the Basic Law" (Golay, 23, 108–10).

109. Richard Hiscocks, *Germany Revived* (London, 1968), 12. Others estimate as many as 50 percent of the people had heard of him (Lewis Edinger, *Kurt Schumacher* [Stanford, 1965], 243; U.S. Office of High Commissioner for Germany, *A Program to Foster Citizen Participation in Government and Politics in Germany* [Frankfurt, 1951], 18).

110. Without significance until later was the fact that his second wife was half American; her father, Professor Zinsser, was an American-born German. Frau Adenauer had three American cousins, one of whom was a member of the Morgan financial empire. His two sisters had married two promising young men from the same circle: Lewis Douglas, an early Clay adviser and later U.S. Ambassador in London, and John J. McCloy (Charles Wighton, *Adenauer* [New York, 1963], 109, 40).

111. This man was the first person Adenauer visited on his first official trip to the U.S. (ibid., 61). The reason given for his dismissal was the slow progress made in revival of the city. Adenauer's memoirs gave as reasons the SPD links with the Labor party and his effort to save the trees of the green belt around Cologne from becoming firewood (*Erinnerungen: 1945–53* [Stuttgart, 1965], 33–37).

112. Arnold Heidenheimer, *Adenauer and the CDU* (Hague, 1960), 61, 71.

113. Wighton, 89.

114. From the beginning he saw foreign leaders as cynical realists engaged in a game of power politics in and over Germany (Edinger, 144).

115. Wighton, 111, 120. "Too often, Adenauer and his ministers were treated as reformed criminals on probation. The High Commission as a whole was often gauche and exhibited a complete disregard for that inevitable German super-sensitivity."

116. Rudolf Morsey, "Die Rolle Konrad Adenauers im Parlamentarischen Rat," *Vierteljahreshefte für Zeitgeschichte*, Jan. 1970, 83. "The Americans were willing to pay an unlimited price for Germany's support in the Cold War" (Wighton, 116).

117. During the fall of 1949 Adenauer used that technique over and over; he could not be asked to push through unpopular Allied demands. On 24 November he announced he had extorted major concessions, which American friends had assured him all along he would get (Wighton, 114).

118. Paul Noack, *Deutschlands Nachkriegzeit* (Munich, 1966), 99; Hiscocks, *Germany Revived*, 35.

119. Schumacher would not apologize, and was banned from twenty days of meetings (*Verhandlungen des Bundestages*, 24 Nov. 1949, 472–525).

120. Plischke, *History*, 29. De facto changes in the practices had frequently been made on the initiative of high commissioners or foreign ministers (Gunter Moltmann, *Die Entwicklung Deutschlands, 1949–55* [Hannover, 1963], 17). Britain and France ended the state of war on 9 July, and the U.S. on 18 October 1951.

121. Wighton, 144, 145, 152.

122. The Adenauer decision for the West was linked by his critics to his long-standing opposition to "Prussia," to "separatist" leanings toward France, and his "Catholic fear" of Protestant eastern Germany (*Die Neue Zürcher Zeitung*, 17 Dec. 1951).

123. Elmer Plischke, *Allied High Commission, Relations with the West German Government*, HICOG (Bonn, 1952), 158, 168.

124. Ibid., 19–29. The Bundestag was not committed; "we as legislators are in no way bound by these conferences." The draft legislation was so faulty it had little hope of being passed (*Verhandlungen des Bundestages*, 6 Oct. 1950, 3335; Plischke, *Relations*, 41).

125. Arnold Brecht, "Personnel Management," in Litchfield, 268–69; Richard Hiscocks, *Democracy in West Germany* (London, 1956), 202–203. All but the smallest public authorities were obliged to fill 20 percent of their posts with officials still unemployed. "If the original denazification of civil servants had been unwise, this sweeping enactment went too far in the other direction. It was the product of a national reaction against Allied measures." This kindness to the conforming majority Hiscocks contrasts to the neglect of the resisting minority.

126. Brecht, in Litchfield, 271.

127. Alfred Grosser, *Germany in Our Time* (New York, 1971), 59.

128. Eugene Davidson, *The Death and Life of Germany* (New York, 1959), 261–63. The French zone occupation costs exceeded the value of the entire production of the zone (Institut für Besatzungsfragen, *Occupation Costs: Are They a Defense Contribution?* [Tübingen, 1951], 1, 5–6, 29, 51).

129. E. Davidson, 262, 321; Zink, *U.S.*, 128.

6 Letting Bavarians Do It Their Way

Clay's power over the central level of government was limited, but OMGUS's power to implement its policies proved to be even more restricted at the lower levels of the state, city, and village. Its experience in Bavaria clearly reveals its inability actually to control the population and institutions over which it had authority. Bavaria composed over half of the American zone's area and population and seemed to generate over three-fourths of the problems faced by policy enforcers.

OMGUS frustrations were basically caused by the geography of the state. Bavaria was made up largely of villages, scattered from the flat lands of the Danube valley to the Alps on the south and highlands on the north. For centuries relatively isolated from the rest of Germany, Bavaria had developed its own political characteristics. It was marked by a stubborn peasant conservatism which found its focus in the Roman Catholic church, dominant everywhere except in Franconia, which did not become part of Bavaria until 1806. United with the scorned northern Prussians only in 1871, Bavaria had maintained a separatism in its monarchy until 1918 and in its Bavarian Peoples' Party (BVP) until 1933. Disliking socialist Berlin, it had at first preferred the Munich-spawned Nazi party to what it assumed to be the Marxist alternative, and then retreated after 1933 more deeply into loyalty to the authority of the church.

The Bavarian state government had remained after 1933, although it was much crippled by Nazi centralization. It had been formed by the election of party leaders to the Landtag, which then chose from the majority party the minister-president and his cabinet ministers. This state government traditionally had more powers over local governments and schools than would be true in the United States. For example, it appointed the *Landräte* (county executives), controlled teacher preparation and assignment, and, in the European fashion, set a standardized curriculum for local schools. Bavarian conservatism was a tough nut for the Nazis to crack and would offer even more effective resistance to the Americans who came with goals of reform. Bavarians were proud of their ways and increasingly determined to maintain them. Americans first used the Third Army to recreate and control the Land government. The army was replaced in the fall of 1945 with the Office of Military Government–Bavaria (OMGB), which was organized to parallel the various ministries, such as justice, economics, labor, and education. The Land military governor was a link in the chain of command from USFET and OMGUS to the local MG units. This link could occur either through the Land commander to the county commander or through the Land departments to the corresponding local officers. The same system supposedly linked Land MG to the civilian Land government, with the military governor issuing orders to the minister-president, or his department heads issuing orders to civilian ministries.

In order to arrive at a broad understanding of OMGB's limited power in Bavaria, one must understand the personalities and policies involved in its daily operations. For the purposes of clarifying the evolution of policy implementation, I have somewhat arbitrarily divided my analysis into periods which correspond roughly with the tenures of the OMGB commanders or commissioners. These were General George Patton (April–October 1945), General Walter Muller (October 1945–November 1947), former Michigan governor Murray van Wagoner (December 1947–October 1949), and two professors, George Shuster and Oron Hale (July 1950–February 1952). Nonetheless, the periods are arbitrary because while these men were important figures in the context of MG itself, they were in a sense irrelevant to Bavarian affairs. None so seriously influenced events as to be comparable to minister-presidents in importance.

The Patton Period: Mistaken Intervention

Although General George Patton's period of command is the best known, mostly because of his precipitous fall from Eisenhower's grace, it is doubtful that he was sufficiently involved in Bavarian affairs to be more than a symbol. Like Eisenhower, he preferred the role of combat commander and left decisions about peacetime matters to his civil affairs staff. When he was finally confronted with significant decisions for the occupation of Bavaria, his method of operation and personality led him to defend his variation or interpretation of central policy. He had relied heavily on his staff in combat operations and continued to rely on them to produce occupation decisions. He did not so much act differently—his local commanders did the acting—as think for himself and sometimes talk without thinking sufficiently about how others would interpret his casual remarks. On receiving criticism from above, he would usually try to comply with the orders along the command structure, but at the same time that he would publicly defend his past policy in a way which brought down more criticism from above. He was privately contrite and publicly an apparent rebel.

Although Patton had a most complex personality, his political values apparently included the military preference for authority and scorn of civilian politicians, not excepting American ones. He seems to have been an anti-communist earlier than most, and was therefore willing to work with German conservatives. Suspicious of Russians, he had urged in April 1945 that he be permitted to take Prague, and apparently proposed to Eisenhower that his troops continue moving east. "We shall need these Germans, and I don't think we ought to mistreat people whom we shall need so badly."[1] This was not an idea whose time had come. Clearly his feelings toward Germans were ambivalent, yet it is difficult to prove that his attitudes made much difference. He had delegated responsibility to the local commanders. Some were tough and some were lax. Patton himself exerted little influence locally.

MG's basic practical decision was to give grudging permission to a few Germans to begin self-government again, although some Bavarians in a resistance who tried to organize a government were frustrated. When Munich was taken early in the morning of 1 May, the only political organization the American army encountered was the *Freiheitsaktion Bayern* (Liberation Bavaria). Its activity had commenced about seventy-two hours before, and MG reported "no single instance in which this organization aided any agent of the Allied Powers, communicated any message to any office outside Germany or engaged in active resistance against Nazism." MG felt this inactivity justified suppressing the organization, although it had seized the radio station and kidnapped the nominal head of the government, Ritter von Epp.[2]

The first Munich military governor, a Swiss-American named Colonel Eugene Keller, installed conservatives—pre-Nazi mayor Karl Scharnagl from the Catholic party and an aged police chief of the 1920s. Both remained in May when Colonel Charles Keegan of Patton's Third Army took over Bavaria. Keegan had been a member of the New York City Council, "a creature of Boss Flynn," or, some critics said, a creature of Cardinal Spellman.[3] Keegan's qualities as a political leader are illustrated in his answer to the Germans who raised the question of rights. "Rights? You got no rights. You're conquered, ya hear? You started the war and you lost. . . . You got no rights." In a conversation with a captured general, Keegan ordered his translator: "Tell that thick-headed kraut that there'll be no changes, and that I'll throw that damn bum into the can if he yells again. Tell that lousy monster I'll put him on ice. . . . I'll throw you in the can too if you don't translate the exact words I said and in the same tone."[4]

Keegan wanted action, the quick installation of a government. His adviser, a Captain Landeen, wrote: "We had not been ordered from SHAEF to do this. But Colonel Keegan was extremely anxious that the Germans take over as early as possible."[5] For advice as to who might head up a government, Landeen and Lieutenant Colonel Arthur Bromage simply asked the opinion of Cardinal Michael Faulhaber and the Protestant bishop, Meiser. At the top of Faulhaber's list was Fritz Schäffer. A wiry lawyer and politician, a leader of the BVP before 1933, he had been fired and imprisoned by the Nazis and seemed the logical choice to men in a hurry. (He probably would have been the majority choice with any election.) Bromage and Landeen recommended him on 25 May; he was immediately made minister-president. Schäffer, who had been working with the "sympathetic" Bromage in recreating a court system, was "totally surprised" when he answered a request for a meeting and found the room full of reporters. He was given his certification of office without being asked whether he wanted the job or even having the matter discussed with him. His certification threatened arrest for violation of any MG order, but his supervisors reassured him this should not be taken seriously. The meeting was "cold, no handshake or standing close together."[6]

Schäffer quickly created a cabinet acceptable to Keegan. The men he chose were mostly old and conservative, but there was someone from each party except the Communist. Three (Otto Hipp, Karl Lange, and Karl Fischer) were soon thrown out by MG as "Nazi sympathizers." Three others (Wilhelm Hoegner, Hans Ehard, and Anton Pfeiffer) remained leading figures for decades, the first two as minister-presidents. With but two rooms for his government, Schäffer called on the civil service to group itself into the former ministries wherever rooms could be found. He tried to make contact with district presidents and county executives. Things seemed to be moving more rapidly in Bavaria than elsewhere, as Clay cabled Washington: "Consensus of opinion here is that Keegan is doing exceptionally fine job in reorganizing the German administrative machinery. Rather than being strutting type, he is highly regarded by religious leaders in Bavaria. . . . He is tough on those deserving to be treated toughly."[7]

Yet a bomb was ticking away under Schäffer and Patton. It could be heard in a report to Clay in July that "political faiths were not equitably represented in the administration, that the main liberal elements in the Land had not been given proportional representation and that there has been considerable delay in the exclusion of Nazi influences from the administration . . . no steps or measures had been taken to give qualified elements of alleged anti-

Nazi parties any representation in the administration of the Land."[8] This was the report of an SPD émigré at USFET, Lt. Ernst Anspach, who "had some vague feeling . . . that it might be useful to have a fresh look at the unexpectedly fast formation of a German government in Bavaria." He found that Munich Special Branch believed that the Land government was deceiving MG about denazification; they began in June to gather material against Schäffer's government. Special Branch could not get through to Frankfurt, but Anspach went directly to Clarence Adcock, aroused his suspicions, and was sent back to convince Keegan.[9] The move to democratize was about to be reversed by the greater urge to denazify.

The official MG story is that Schäffer was sabotaging denazification, because of "Nazi leanings," and that in this he was tolerated by Patton, who had proved himself to be politically unsophisticated by his known ability to say the wrong thing at the wrong time. The reality is not so simple. To be sure, Patton played a relatively simple role; he was probably only vaguely aware of what was happening. He had been gone for a victorious month in the United States, returning only on 5 July. He was trapped by the bureaucracy and by his reputation. He had no contact with the German leaders; he had never met Schäffer.

He was suspicious of MG, which he thought leftist. This was one reason why he had refused the services of the Psychological War Division (PWD), which was fighting for a place in the occupation sun. He said he had enough intelligence services. To show him he was wrong, a Colonel Powell of the PWD sent two investigators to Munich with orders to "dig up as much dirt as you can." They reported the Bavarian regime to be a clerical, monarchist, military clique, filled with senile, stubborn reactionaries.[10] Eisenhower and Clay told Patton to clean out the Bavarian administration. Changes in the cabinet toward broader representation were announced on 31 August; Schäffer offered to resign but MG declined. When Patton said the discharge of all party members would lead to a breakdown, Eisenhower warned him on 12 September that it was policy and must be complied with. The discussion stage was over, and "any expressed opposition to the faithful execution of the order cannot be regarded tolerantly by me."[11] Third Army headquarters issued secret orders 15 September for every Bavarian MG office to check all questionnaires, and report in ten days, and also to report in one month what percentage of officials had been politically cleared and when the rest would be cleared.

Adcock of USGCC also asked two OSS men, Walter Dorn and Howard Becker, to investigate; they came to agree with the previous Third Army studies. Meanwhile Anspach, having failed to convince MG-Munich to make a change, had taken the matter to the press, specifically to *PM*'s Victor Bernstein. Under the headline, "American MG Can't Stand Bavarian Government, Schäffer's Cabinet Clique of Fascists," *PM* published the essence of the Anspach report, naming names.[12] With reporters sniffing a sensational story came the famous Patton interview, unluckily for him just after USFET had lifted the ban on direct quotation of general officers. From the unplanned 22 September interview Patton emerged as having apparently compared the Nazi party with the Democratic and Republican parties, and having said that entirely too much fuss was made about denazification. The interview created an even bigger press storm and Eisenhower ordered a retraction. Patton in a second interview said he had been ordered to regret the comparison, but added one could not fire people if it meant hunger to them; many had joined the party just to keep their jobs and one could not blame them for that.[13] To the *Stars and Stripes,* Patton admitted that his choice of analogies was "unfortunate," but added:

> the point that I was trying to bring out was that in Germany practically all, or at least a very large percentage of tradespeople, small businessmen and even professional men... were beholden to the party in power for the patronage which permitted them to carry on their business or profession, and that there-fore, many of them gave lip service only.... when they paid party dues, it was still in the form of blackmail. These are the type of people who eventually will be removed, but we must put up with them until we have restored sufficient organization to Bavaria to insure ourselves that women, children and old men will not perish from hunger and cold this winter.... there are no outstanding Nazis whose removal has not already been carried out.[14]

Patton was closer to the truth than Eisenhower. Carl Friedrich wrote: "Actually denazification had progressed so far that all but a very few Nazi Party members had been removed from public employment." The incident showed how little the correspondents understood. "It also revealed how limited was General Patton's own knowledge of what had been going on under his command."[15]

On 28 September Patton was summoned again to Frankfurt and "read the riot act" by Eisenhower. (Orders were issued that all "mandatory re-movals" in Bavaria still in office were to be removed within twenty-four hours.) The Dorn report had reached Eisenhower, so Dorn was asked to attend. Eisenhower asked him whether the Bavarian agricultural ministry could operate without the sixteen key people accused. Dorn said it could. "Suddenly Eisenhower was righteously indignant: 'What in the devil the American army was doing in Germany, if not to denazify the German gov-ernment and administration.' The Russians killed their Nazis; the Americans put them in office." He spoke at length about the soldiers he had sent to their deaths. Schäffer had to go; he belonged in prison, as did those ministers who had helped against denazification. Eisenhower asked Dorn who could replace Schäffer, and Dorn suggested Hoegner, but added he belonged to SPD, only a minority party in Bavaria. Eisenhower answered: "I don't care what kind of a political majority Bavaria has, as long as our MG orders are carried out obediently." Dorn was to dictate the cabinet to Patton, who was eager to be given the name of every minister, but Adcock told Dorn to let Hoegner choose.[16] Patton called his officers, who that evening threw Schäffer out and installed Hoegner, to the astonishment of both. In three days Patton was transferred to a pseudocommand; he died in December in an auto accident.

If one moves from the reality as perceived by Eisenhower to the reality as perceived by most Bavarians, it seems that two faulty charges were later directed against Schäffer. The first concerned what he had said between 1919 and 1933, and the second what he had done in the summer of 1945. Although a few sentences spoken by a politician twenty years in the past may not be a fair criterion for dismissal, it was a criterion common to the times. The indictment included a 1922 speech in which Schäffer was "more critical of the Treaty of Versailles than of the Nazis." The next event mentioned was a conversation Schäffer had with Hitler in 1932, in which MG assumed, but Schäffer denied, that he had suggested his BVP join Hitler in a coalition government. He had written 8 April 1933 that "the collapse of the national government would be a disaster and a danger to all of the German nation." He had also written Himmler 26 April 1933, making reference to "our common goal of rebuilding a nationalistic Germany." MG admitted that his party was dissolved and Schäffer immediately dismissed from public office despite these words, but noted that he had kept his pension—the common practice—and was permitted to practice as a lawyer. The report dismissed the persecution he suffered as having amounted only to his being "briefly" arrested in 1933, for which von Epp had apologized. After the 1944 attempt to assassinate Hitler, he had spent "several weeks" at Dachau (actually from 23 August to 9 October).

His appointments of Fischer to the interior ministry and Lange to the economics ministry were also criticized, though neither had been party members. Fischer, a devout Catholic, had stayed in a Bavarian ministry to defend Catholic rights until forced out in 1939, but his having held high office until 1939 made him a "mandatory arrest." Lange was in the brewery business, and MG charged that "he had increased his business through close association with notorious Nazis." Schäffer's personal staff appointments of a former member of the German general staff and of Otto Gessler, thought by some to be responsible for the illegal rearmament in the 1920s when he was defense minister, were also at issue. MG accused Schäffer of having lied about these two appointments. To the MG mind of 1945, these "nationalistic" conservatives were guilty of Nazism.[17]

Whatever the guilty thoughts or associations conservatives might have had, or still harbored, the action that brought Schäffer's rapid dismissal was his so-called sabotaging of denazification. He had criticized denazification;

his associates' questionnaires were slow in coming in; he had been concerned to find other jobs for those fired. Schäffer certainly said the mass dismissals endangered administration of a government beset with great problems and were ill-advised. The German argument then and later was that associates of the officials knew best which were really Nazi, and that Americans were using guilt by association. Basing guilt on the mere fact of party membership not only was unjust but would transform the public's antagonism toward Nazis to sympathy. The German point of view finally became the MG position in 1947, when it permitted officials to return after having been cleared by a denazification tribunal and classified as "followers."[18]

From the records, statistics, and correspondence, one can scarcely support the case of significant sabotage. Schäffer had made no secret of his position from the time of his appointment. He was consistent; it was MG policy that changed. Twice in the first week, he had stated his agreement with the dismissal of active party members, and had ordered all ministries to be clean by 12 June in terms of MG policy.[19] By 22 June Schäffer had a sophisticated argument, supported by statistics, for this removal of active Nazis and ardent sympathizers. Simple membership, he said, was very high among officials because their careers had been dependent on Hitler's state. The state was involved in many more activities than in the United States, including railroads, all public transportation, and all public communication, so that often "non-denazification of officials" referred to streetcar conductors. Schäffer gave a detailed breakdown of Nazis in each layer of the administration of all ministries; it was so thorough that he devoted a full page to foresters.[20]

Schäffer wrote MG for general instructions how to proceed in order not to paralyze the whole administration. He asked that previous instructions be retained, that is, that any party member be taken out of a leading position at once. "As far as these officials who have not been active Nazis, they may be employed in lower positions at least as employees, that means subject to revocation and dismissal." This was punishment enough to people accustomed to lifetime tenure in office. All active Nazis were to be removed at once. If the number of them in any one branch should exceed 25 percent, its head could spread out the dismissals for a few months until replacements were trained. Nominal party members would be kept in lower positions, but "not on an equal footing with officials who have from conviction resisted the pressure from the party." All promotions and hirings since 1933 would be reexamined to be sure they were warranted. "The decision whether an official has to be enumerated amongst the active Nazis rests, of course, entirely with MG." USFET moved in the opposite direction: all members must go. This order was conveyed orally by Keegan 5 July, and in writing by the USFET order of 7 July, forwarded by the Bavarian military authorities 19 July. "He

[Keegan] wished to push the clean-out, so that he could at a certain period, perhaps in August, report that the government in Bavaria was completely free of Nazis, and therefore be in a position to be granted fuller plenipotentiary powers, so that the American MG could pull back, leaving only a few supervisory and directive organs."[21]

The files show Schäffer besieged by complaints from all over Bavaria that the governmental machinery, just beginning to operate again, would collapse if the new rules were carried out. Actually mass firings had preceded the 19 July order. The president of Upper Bavaria reported he had to fire ninety-two officials; he could scarcely continue to govern because the records of pre-1945 governmental actions had been destroyed by bombings and only the memories of those just released from their positions were available to maintain continuity. Munich's mayor complained that all sorts of officers were hiring and firing members of his city administration without consulting him. The finance director for Northern Bavaria wrote: "A full breakdown of the administration must be expected. The government's main cash office is no longer in a position to do any business at all . . . ; tax payments cannot be accepted; tax collection, supervision of tax payment, examination of tax-payers are completely impossible."[22]

While MG was rushing about blasting chunks out of the dam against disorder, Schäffer was trying to hold them back with finespun distinctions too subtle to be persuasive. He wrote his SPD labor minister, Albert Rosshaupter, concerning the latter's order of 16 July that labor offices give "active Nazis" only inferior work, and that army officers be considered "active Nazis":

> Our primary task is to fight the spirit of Nazism. That can only happen if we do not use methods which contain the same spirit. . . . We would be doing that if we used the social welfare institution of the labor offices to discriminate permanently and to defame certain groups of the population, thus creating in them the feelings of a lack of rights and an enslavement. . . . Second, such a discrimination is contrary to the guidelines, personally given me by MG. Col. Keegan and Col. Bromage emphasized over and over again to me that a permanent discrimination against the former National Socialists was fundamentally rejected.[23]

One must avoid popular nihilism, and therefore be very careful that all actions could be defended morally.

Such objections, and not noncompliance, made up the resistance which brought his fall. Schäffer wrote MG that the members of his government were anti-Nazi and that they

> understand the situation in Germany for the last 12 years better than outsiders. . . . now as before I am possessed by the most ardent desire to thoroughly extinguish from my people the spirit of Nazism and militarism. The government has executed all the orders for the removal of officials and employees, even if in individual cases it was convinced these orders originated from erroneous sup-

positions. . . . the present methods lead and have led to the following consequences: (a) instead of denazification there has grown in many cases a silent and
dangerous renazification; (b) many innocent people have been affected and
among the population the impression of a complete lack of justice and protection has spread, whereby a serious obstacle for the coming democratization has
been created; (c) the administration has been hit hard—it will lead to a breakdown.

He estimated that of those released, 30 percent were clearly not Nazi; of 30
percent one could not be sure; only 40 percent could be considered Nazi in
fact. What was phrased as a courteous request ended with the appeal to be
allowed to present his views in person in Frankfurt.[24] Instead, the answer was
the 15 September order to push the questionnaires and the cleanout. This order
Schäffer loyally forwarded with his own order to implement it "with all
powers." Evidence in the communities I researched shows Schäffer complying, but with little influence on local affairs. Niethammer concluded that
Bavaria actually had a higher percentage of releases than the other Lands by
September; the impression of slowness came from the fact that it had rebuilt
its government faster.

Clay sent Murphy "to broaden" the government, not with the intention
of excluding Schäffer, but merely to change the lineup to divert attention from
Patton's remarks. Murphy remembered Pfeiffer, whom he had known from
before the war, and whom he knew from captured documents, to have been
consistently anti-Nazi. Pfeiffer introduced him to Schäffer.

> The three of us had an agreeable conversation and I was favorably impressed
> with Schäffer. But early the next morning, Pfeiffer telephoned in great agitation
> to tell me that a message had arrived from Frankfurt ordering the dismissal. . . .
> I was able to find out that Schäffer's dismissal had been ordered in Frankfurt
> without consulting Clay or the State Department. A subordinate Civil Affairs
> officer, who had been recruited from the history department of an American
> college [Dorn], was convinced that Bavaria should be governed by the Social
> Democrats, notwithstanding that this socialist party had always been a small
> minority in this predominantly Catholic state. Schäffer, as a leader of the
> People's Party, opposed the Social Democrats, so the American professor con-
> sidered him pro-Nazi.

Murphy's report at the time differs from his memoir, according to which he
had gone to investigate the denazification "failure."[25] Murphy wrote in his
report that press accounts were misleading. Schäffer had personally reviewed
about 5,000 questionnaires and only one of these German judgments had been
reversed by MG; 49,887 officials had been removed from office; Schäffer's
failure was one of public relations. The OMGB report of 18 October implied
his removal was a mistake: "The removal of Schäffer is causing much discussion; public opinion is definitely 'pro-Schäffer.' " Hoegner was welcomed by

the Social Democrats and Communists. The Nazi element display decided fear of Schäffer, but not of Hoegner."

The scene of Schäffer's dismissal and Hoegner's installation, as described by Hoegner, is a minor classic of 1945 MG. He had just returned on 28 September from a trip as minister of justice, when Schäffer phoned to say that he should be at MG headquarters at eight o'clock in the evening. Neither knew why. At seven, Captain (later Senator) John Sherman Cooper, who had been extremely helpful from the first, appeared to escort Hoegner. At headquarters Col. Roy Dalferes told Hoegner he had just received telephone instructions to make him minister-president. As Hoegner put it: "I fell from the clouds." There was a sudden clamor around him.

> What then transpired was comparable to a scene from Shakespeare. I was led into the room of Col. Dalferes. He stood behind his desk in front of a number of officers complete with steel helmets. Minister-president Schäffer and his group were called into the room. Then we Germans had to stand around Col. Dalferes in a semicircle. A particularly bad electric light spread a dismal brown-yellowish glow. Col. Dalferes picked up a letter and began: "You, Herr Fritz Schäffer, minister-president of Bavaria, are herewith dismissed. Here is your letter." Schäffer took the letter with an impassive face. Col. Dalferes continued, "You, Herr Lange, economics minister of Bavaria, are herewith dismissed. Here is your letter." Then, "You, Herr Rattenhuber, agricultural minister of Bavaria, are herewith dismissed. Here is your letter." Then he turned to me, "You, Dr. Wilhelm Hoegner, are herewith named minister-president of Bavaria. Here is your letter.... Have the gentlemen anything further to say?" asked Col. Dalferes. We said no. Then they were all told not to enter their offices the next day and to say nothing for the time being about the events of the evening.[26]

Another dimension to the story of democracy defeated by denazification was known to Robert Neumann, an officer in G-2, Third Army. He thought Schäffer had been intransigent and should be removed, but "the selection of Hoegner was undoubtedly a mistake, which would not have been committed had MG possessed an adequate intelligence organization." He said an alliance had been formed between the left-wing Catholics under Josef Müller, the SPD, and the KPD, which would have gotten the right-wing Schäffer out. "The advisers to Eisenhower had no idea of the policy agreement reached between the three groups in Munich.... in Berlin and Frankfurt, Hoegner was the only Bavarian liberal known. And the political record of the MG in Bavaria did not make it desirable to consult Munich." OMGB might not have known anyway. Yet the coalition headed by the leader of the Catholic party was a natural one.[27] CSU leader Müller had already drawn up his cabinet and program; the Murphy mission was sadly uncoordinated with the Dorn visit. Although MG was moving toward democratic government, Hoegner arbitrarily became minister-president through the historical accident that Dorn had read his OSS file.

MG's failure is evident in Third Army intelligence reports of November.

> In Southern Bavaria the general attitude of civilians is gradually changing from obviously genuine friendliness and devotion, which they cherished for Americans at the beginning of the occupation, to a definitely reserved and cold attitude.... One German intellectual [thought] America was repeating... "Germany's crucial mistake," namely, failing to contact the right people and failing to promote mutual understanding and goodwill.... unpopular and bitterly resented police measures overshadow all honest intentions and constructive measures to such an extent that agitators successfully promote their slogan of "an American policy of extermination."... Local military government officers are said to have dictatorial ambitions, trying to run their places like little kingdoms.... opposition to Law No. 8 is universal.... people were being arrested in the night and disappearing as under the Nazis.... Every community had teachers who joined the NS under pressure, who warned students against the NS and now are fired.... Clergy and laymen alike regard the occupation policy as unfriendly to the churches.... It was the universal German expectation that, as American radio propaganda told them, there would be freedom of religion.... In six months of occupation that expectation has turned into deep disappointment.... Catholic clergymen protest that not even under the Nazis did they have to submit to censorship.... Hours of instruction have been limited, refresher courses cancelled, seminaries for priests in Bavaria forbidden.... Germans contend that MG is indifferent, even callous—an oppressive burden of red tape, restrictions, and complications.... The people were first wildly hopeful, and are now completely discouraged. Desperation is more and more turning into bitter resentment.... "You will ruin us and yourselves if you do not give us hope."... the arrival of American troops was equivalent to the end of air-raids, tension and privation. Most Germans also thought that the arrival of American troops spelled the end of Nazism and the beginnings of a new and democratic era with freedom from tyranny, personal security, and economic reconstruction.... That is probably the *reason* why everybody is disappointed now.[28]

A summary with hindsight of policy implementation in Patton's period would be that it had permitted a revival of self-government by trusting the traditional leaders. These leaders were much more concerned with solving the problems of eco omic survival than with reforms, but were willing to denazify as they understood it, that is, to remove active Nazis from important office. This sometime MG policy was implemented, on orders from Eisenhower, at the expense of progress toward democratization. Yet the predictions of the denazifiers that a Nazi revival was under way and the predictions of officials that denazification would lead to an administrative collapse were exaggerated. The years of denazification were also the years of poverty, but the two conditions were not in a cause and effect relationship. The state had power to do little more than register the disasters and distribute some of the poverty. The democratization interrupted by MG was not to be denied. Bavarians got their way within a year, forcing the socialists out and the Catholics back in.

The Muller Period: Mutual Frustration

While Bavarians were increasingly frustrated that the Americans were blocking their efforts at self-government, the Americans increasingly perceived the Bavarians as unrepentant reactionaries, frustrating the American plans for liberal reforms. No matter whom the Americans put into power, the Bavarian government resisted. The names of the protagonists changed, but the struggle between Bavarian officials and OMGB officials continued. Methods altered, as rough commands, which the Bavarians compared to the Nazi style, were gradually replaced by polite conferences and by written correspondence which was somewhat less polite. Newspaper headlines prolonged for a time the image of tough Americans. For example, when General Lucien Truscott replaced his commander Patton, he was introduced to the American public with the reassuring story, *"Will Make Nazis Stop.* Truscott hated Germans in battle and he'll govern Bavaria with the same strong policy.... 'If I were a Nazi I'd be more afraid of Truscott than of any other American leader.' "[29] Truscott in fact promised Hoegner "complete independence" except for "necessary controls and checks;" he even told Hoegner to report to him "if any of the agencies under his control bothered him."[30] Although the short Truscott was described in the press as the most fear-inspiring man in the army, he cast a very small shadow over Bavaria. Partly because of the lack of coordination in the Patton-Schäffer affair, the army was being pushed out by OMGB. The firing of Schäffer was the Third Army's last major action.

Walter Muller, another Patton general, took command of OMGB 9 October 1945.[31] His first contact with MG was as a Third Army supply officer, when he was assigned to organize the production control branch to survey what German production the army might use. The reaction of those few Germans who had contact with him after he became commander varied. Hoegner praised his helpfulness; although he "often appeared to be a rough professional soldier he was actually good-hearted; he had given Bavaria important service. He repeatedly and strongly presented the special desires of Bavaria to General Clay. In difficult situations he always stood by me." Hoegner's successor, Hans Ehard, echoed these kind thoughts, adding that when Muller got an order from Clay he did not agree with, he would simply begin the conference by asking Ehard, "What do we do now?" At their first meeting in December 1946 Ehard told Muller: "If we are going to play democracy, and play it right, I cannot have just anyone in MG telling just anyone in my government what to do." He suggested all orders go through him. Muller agreed and "the system worked well." Assistants to the minister-presidents were less kind. Fritz Baer described Muller as "touchy" (*Rauhpelz*). The atmosphere was tense at the beginning of his command because one did not know whom Muller would arrest next; not even Ehard was sure. All the top people were ordered to appear at the CIC, with its unrestrained powers of arrest.[32]

General Muller's partners in governing Bavaria may in retrospect have found him very helpful personally, but they remember the period of his command as very frustrating. Not only were they frustrated in governing by the horrible economic conditions, but they found the bureaucracy of MG as frustrating as Americans found the Bavarian bureaucracy. Dr. Wilhelm Hoegner, Eisenhower's sudden choice for minister-president, was caught between a population which had not elected him and military authorities who demanded that he compel their obedience to very unpopular policies.

Although not the people's choice for minister-president, Dr. Hoegner was professionally qualified for the position.[33] From a small town railroader's family and solidly Bavarian, he had come as a student to Munich and there saw the pre-1914 bloody attack of cavalry with sabres against the suffering working class. The 1919 slaughter of innocent workers decided him for the SPD. Otherwise an academic type, a lawyer and a judge, he had achieved sufficient prominence before 1933 in speeches denouncing Hitler that flight to Switzerland became a judicious act. His twelve-year exile made him "clean" for MG, but an outsider for some voters, as he had not experienced their suffering under Nazis and war. He was much impressed with Switzerland, and returned with a draft of his constitution for Bavaria.

Hoegner's relations with OMGB were amicable, although his subordinates, Gebhard Seelos and Friedrich Glum, were later critical and said that the amicability had come from his obsequiousness. They spoke of his humbly taking notes on the wishes of any American captain.[34] Hoegner later complained that his first real difficulty was complying with the MG request that he include a communist in his cabinet. Goldhammer, the Bavarian communist leader, told him that General Muller had promised him the interior ministry and the press secretariat, two vital posts. Hoegner regarded Goldhammer as "a stubborn Stalinist," and instead offered him the denazification ministry and two harmless state secretariats. After first refusing, the KPD accepted.[35]

OMGB also selected Hoegner's economics minister. Although he wished to have a man from industry, a Colonel Jackson presented him with the unknown Dr. Ludwig Erhard. This Bavarian who became the German chancellor was a "professor" with MG friends. He was "the creature of the Americans;" his major function seems to have been as liaison with MG. Americans liked him. Baer remarked Erhard was: "Flesh of their flesh, spirit of their spirit. He had their informality, their happy self-confidence and said, quite openly, 'I like the American style.' "[36] Erhard himself remembered his association with Americans as beginning near Nuremberg in May, when an officer with a jeep appeared and said, "Come on." Erhard had been quickly installed as regional chief of distribution, "simply administering the poverty," and was rarely bothered by MG supervisors. As to his career in Munich, Erhard observed that he was "an American discovery." Hoegner never tried to influence him, knowing he was persona grata.[37] He approved Erhard's good relations with MG. "The always good humor of Dr. Erhard made the Americans feel at home, as they were from nature mostly good humored and approached difficult tasks with happy self-confidence. Dr. Erhard avoided presenting German complaints because this got on the American nerves, as they could not understand why we could not solve our difficulties." Erhard arranged for theater presentations, an export show, and a very popular weekend house for officers.

In December 1946, Hans Ehard left Erhard out of his cabinet, partly because OMGB had less influence. Erhard's ministry was chaotic and particularly violated MG denazification policy, but other MG officers had protected him. A story in September had Erhard "vacationed" on MG orders, and by month's end many of his ministry had been released.[38] In January the new SPD minister announced a cleanup, and released thirteen officials for falsifying their questionnaires. The newspapers reported: "It was an open secret that in the ministry a reactionary spirit was dominant and furthered by various people in leading positions. If complaints grew too loud, one hid behind the MG work permits or blamed the former minister." These defiant officials had MG permission to govern but could not qualify for their positions under Hoegner's rules.[39] A parliamentary commission to study the economics ministry took four thousand pages to describe enormous corruption and administrative confusion. The CSU spokesman said Erhard was not involved; he simply did not have the ability to head an economics ministry.

What Hoegner and Muller thought became more and more irrelevant, however. Political power in Bavaria rested with the Catholic party, the CSU. Its influence depended in the first months on MG tolerance, but soon afterwards on how effectively it maintained its unity. What happened in government during the occupation period, except for the ineffectual administration of Hoegner and General Muller, was primarily a result of CSU decisions. When MG got something accomplished, it was because it was something the CSU wanted accomplished.

The CSU was in operation from 21 August 1945, but officially the founding date was a few weeks later, when MG gave permission.[40] The two most significant founders were Adam Stegerwald, who died suddenly in December, and Dr. Josef Müller, around whom CSU battles were fought during the entire occupation. Stegerwald, the spiritual father of "the Union idea," in 1920 had conceived of a party which would replace the Catholic BVP with a Christian party having a definite democratic and social philosophy. This party was to combine the numbers of Catholic peasants—in Northern Bavaria, Protestant peasants—with the urban middle class against working-class socialism. The common Catholic and Protestant suffering from 1933 to 1945, particularly in concentration camps, sealed this unity for many leaders.

The driving force behind the new CSU was Müller, who somehow— presumably with MG help—traveled all over Bavaria and with countless talks and meetings started local parties and brought them all under the CSU title. For this service, he was elected chairman 17 December, beating out Schäffer, who had tried first to recreate his BVP. Müller, a lawyer by profession, had been a relatively unknown politician before 1933, although he was a friend of BVP Minister-President Heinrich Held. He became important as a member of the resistance, being its liaison to the Pope and the Allies.[41] His cooperation with the wartime enemy did not help Müller with many Bavarians, and only helped at first with MG. A series of scandals, involving wartime links to German and Allied spies and postwar finances kept Müller in his own twilight war as a man of shadows.

Americans were less perturbed than Germans by his apparent lack of firm principle. Robert Neumann called him "a very clever, down-to-earth politician, of an almost American type." To William Griffith he seemed a natural politician, representing generally the northern, centralist, anti-separatist elements of the party. Both agreed that "his claims to represent the 'liberal' wing were largely for the benefit of gullible MG officials and correspondents."[42] Americans were not sure why Müller visited Russian headquarters in Berlin, but heard rumors that the Russians had a file on Müller which they could use to influence him. Müller professed good relations not only with the Russians, which he said would help to gain their cooperation for German unity, but also with the Americans.

When Dorn visited his creation in January-February 1946, his horrified description put Bavaria on the verge of restoring the king, with Hoegner hoping to split the CSU and become the king's first minister. He reported that the monarchists, including Müller and Schäffer, were planning the creation of a Bavarian president as the first step.

> Hoegner has many enemies among the Bavarians, who want to throw him out. He wants to do something for Bavarians, but is watched closely by Americans and his power is limited. He is only MG's administrative organ. . . . This can't last. Americans from convenience want to keep them till autumn. Hoegner's conviction, gradually obtained, is that they have no real interest in Germany, especially not in the economic field. . . . France has greater interest in German problems and thinks more European than the Americans. . . . Hoegner is fed up with playing messenger boy for the Americans and ruining the rest of his prestige. . . . Schäffer is now firmly convinced that he will become Minister-President again because the Union has no one with the ability.

MG was frustrated in its efforts to halt the centralization which its Land government was pushing, although OMGB assumed decentralization was a step toward democracy. "Decentralization painstakingly set up and nurtured by early MG is rapidly deteriorating into a strong central Land government due to the installation of independent ministerial agencies which parallel constituted channels of authority and administration. . . . The Landrat's authority and prestige, and the District President's too, are being rapidly usurped by armies of local officials all claiming special independence and authority, direct from the ministry." Hoegner told Dorn he agreed with decentralization but blamed centralization on OMGB, which had given special powers to the labor and economics ministry.[43] By odd coincidence, OMGB preferred the same solution as had, in theory, the National Socialists: power ought to be in the hands of the Landrat and mayor. Neither succeeded in the face of the Munich government's arguments that policy must be coordinated. The result was a powerful central bureaucracy in Munich, despite the efforts of both.

Into this Bavarian beehive of intrigue, Clay introduced the great American hope, elections, to begin at the village grassroots in late January. That General Muller thought Clay was taking a risk is evident in the concern he communicated to Hoegner 29 December: "The submission of candidate lists for the villages is causing everywhere great difficulties, because the local and county parties have not been built yet. Therefore, someone should make sure that the Land level parties take form as quickly as possible, and that they can submit the necessary lists." MG blamed Bavarians for public apathy and party weakness, but MG delayed normal post and telephone service; where there had been two hundred newspapers, there were only four as late as October 1945 because of MG. Yet the first election brought a large turnout, which seemed to show that Clay's policy was a success. Another evidence of success was that 76 percent of the rural mayors appointed by MG were reelected to office.[44] Privately MG doubted Germans could handle their own affairs, believing that campaign talk was gibberish, merely hearty endorsements of the Ten Commandments and the Beatitudes, that the election should have been delayed, and that the clergy and old men were too much involved.

MG's involvement in the spring elections was to ban Schäffer from politics as a "Nazi sympathizer . . . an exponent of ultra-nationalistic and militaristic ideologies."[45] An ICD officer said it was done precisely to avoid his inevitable victory over Müller. Although OMGB reported that press reaction generally favored the ban, privately OMGB officials admitted that Schäffer was the real party leader.[46] OMGB later reported the CSU did not follow Müller, but rather Schäffer, who was willing to appear as the one who most resisted Americans. MG also suspended the CSU parties in various counties because they were admitting "Nazis" to party membership. But however incompetent or dishonest Bavarian politicians seemed to be, Clay's policy was to reduce MG intervention. Therefore General Muller told Hoegner that proposed governmental action no longer had to be submitted for prior OMGB approval, except for a list of matters dealing with government structure. General Muller told the ministers all correspondence with a political content should go only from him to the minister-president; any MG letter without his signature was to be returned.[47]

Part of the rationale for MG's hands-off policy in Bavaria was the creation in early 1946 of a new Bavarian constitution. The Bavarians' right to rule themselves was buttressed by this documentary foundation that- Americans revere. The Bavarian constitution was the first state constitution to be completed, partly because Bavaria was the only state left largely intact. Hoegner forwarded his draft to Clay by 27 October 1945. OMGUS rejected it as "an extreme form of Bavarian particularism," having "dictatorial features," and giving the Bavarian republic "unrestricted autonomy" in all fields. OMGUS Legal Division wrote: "It is the embodiment of the dream of Bavarian independence nursed for two generations by Bavarian extremists of whom Dr. Hoegner permitted himself to become the tool. . . . a thinly veiled declaration of the secession from Germany. . . . It makes . . . the Minister President . . . a dictator." MG could take credit for halting this first Hoegner constitution, but MG had also just made its author minister-president.

Thereafter the MG involvement was small, although it did set a timetable for completion and specify there should be a bill of rights. "The Americans kept almost totally out of the negotiations. They were primarily concerned that the Bavarian constitution would not prejudice the future German constitution, because they wanted Germans to decide on its form."[48] Clay's major involvement was to keep Americans, and Washington in particular, out of it. He found effective arguments to let even Bavarians have wide freedom in their constitution. In particular MG stayed out of the hottest controversy, about the kinglike state-president. Of 188 articles, MG took a firm position on only a few. These included concern for the emergency powers of the head of state, Bavaria's position in the new *Bundestaat,* its treaty-making powers, and denazification. The document was more conservative than that of the other states, having a senate based on Catholic corporative ideas. This senate was to be a group of experts serving as a counterweight to the Landtag formed by popular votes. It also contained provisions for "confessional schools." Clay thought stopping this latter provision would have caused the rejection of the proposed constitution in pious Bavaria.

In September OMGUS ordered OMGB to recognize the changed relationship under the new approved constitution. MG functions were limited to observation, examination, reports and advice, the disapproval of measures which were clear violations of principles, dismissal of officials in violation, the creation of full controls where goals were in danger, military courts, and direct administration of matters the Germans could not take over (such as denazification). Yet Clay threatened to reimpose direct MG rule because of denazification, and getting MG out of Bavarian affairs was more easily ordered than done.[49] Years later, Hoegner complained that OMGB frustrated democracy.

> Throughout 1946 my life was made sour by blunders of local MG officers. . . . an American fanatic combined two communities against their wishes. . . . Alien *Landräte* who were guilty of irregularities were protected by American officers. . . . the American commander in Kulmbach threw into prison on a false denunciation the SPD mayor . . . I told Major Schweizer, if rights and justice had become worthless, I had no reason to stay in the American zone of occupation.

Jean Stock, SPD district president, was thrown out of office by MG because a criminal had falsely denounced him; MG regretted its mistake but someone else was district president. In July State Secretary Ficker was arrested, confined without food for seventeen hours, and asked about his connections with the Red Army; CIC agents had broken into his house and forced him from bed at pistol point. Three more KPD leaders were arrested for black marketing; four others had been arrested for traveling to Berlin without permission; a KPD paper had been banned for criticizing MG. But the intervention most bitterly resented was the confiscation of homes:

> an entire residential sector was surrounded by MPs, then sealed off with barbed wire. The residents, forced to move, were forbidden to take any of their possessions. In some sectors, DPs had already plundered the houses they had been allocated, burned the furniture, screwed-off door knobs and water faucets, and stolen everything not nailed down.[50]

Yet while Americans at one level were tyrannically driving people from their homes without their possessions and placing entire neighborhoods behind barbed wire, those at a higher and more public level were permitting the return of self-government. Elections were held, with the result that the minister-president imposed in the fall of 1945 was voted out of office a little more than a year later.

Hoegner's year of tribulation with Americans and the Catholic majority was ended by the 1 December election results. The CSU received 52.2 percent and the SPD 28.2 percent of the vote. The only question was who was to lead the CSU. Schäffer was still banned by OMGB and Josef Müller was explaining away one of his many scandals. MG intelligence saw no other qualified candidate.

> Pfeiffer is regarded as academic, reactionary and lacking in political acumen and personal force. Dr. Ehard, however capable as an administrator and however honest and personally above suspicion, may have the format of a minister but scarcely that of a Minister-President. Dr. Hundhammer, self-styled agriculturalist but in reality a vain, self-centered, suave poser, who prides himself on his monarchist leanings, has not the necessary administrative experience or personal influence to be seriously considered.[51]

Dorn told Hoegner that MG had planned to fire Müller as party chairman while Clay was in Washington, but Clay had cabled that nothing was to be done against him. OMGB officers were at war among themselves. Some, notably Anspach, were leading a left-wing drive against Müller and the CSU, using Gestapo files.[52] Müller was accused of having profited from an "Aryanization" case, the transfer-theft of Jewish property to Aryans. There was also the murky point that as member of the resistance working with *Abwehr* (Counterintelligence), he could be considered a Nazi if he had helped Nazis, or a traitor if he had helped the Allies. Suddenly somebody in OMGB decided that as he neared Bavarian leadership he had to be "denazified."

Murphy conferred with party leaders who came to Berlin at Clay's invitation. He cabled the decision that Müller, just reelected CSU chairman, would be allowed to keep that position.

> As it appears obvious that Müller may be the choice of his party for position of Minister-President, an agreement was reached by General Clay and myself with Müller that he will refrain from taking office, if elected . . . until he is either cleared of charges recently made against him by the public prosecutor at Munich or until he is found guilty. . . . If cleared, he will assume office. We feel it of considerable importance in formation of first freely elected State Government in Germany since 1933 that proceedings be free from our intervention if at all possible. It is expected that Müller will appear before the denazification tribunal shortly. His defense will be that he used his position in the *Abwehr* to promote German withdrawal from the war, incident to the July 20 abortive Putsch. (Secret, what he will be unable to testify, is that he supplied intelligence material to Allied contacts as this would be a source of embarrassment.)[53]

The Müller case had at least one virtue: "For the first time since the surrender of Germany, the Bavarians have taken a serious interest in politics." Some who also had "egg on their vests" from compromises with the Nazis sympathized; others feared Müller as a danger to separatism. "In between the two are some who insist that if MG meant business in stressing free elections, Müller would become the head of the new cabinet since as the leader of the largest party he has to be regarded as the choice of the people, and since the charges against him are known to be trumped up."[54]

Although members of OMGB had successfully torpedoed Müller as successor to Hoegner, they could not control the CSU even if they had perceived a suitable alternative to Müller. They were saved from an embarassing public veto of Müller by the CSU party convention's surprising decision for the Hans Ehard scorned by OMGB experts. The decision developed out of the deep split in the CSU over the issue of creating the constitutional office of Bavarian state president. It had been pushed by the particularist, and allegedly monarchist, wing of the party led by Hundhammer, which bitterly accused the Müller faction of being "centralist," that is, of preferring to sacrifice Bavarian autonomy to a central government. Müller's party minority had combined with the majority of the SPD on the state president issue to defeat the CSU majority and Hoegner. At the party convention, therefore, the Hundhammer faction was determined to defeat Müller, using as a further weapon his allegedly ambiguous position on communism.

With Müller blocked by OMGB and Hundhammer, the American observers assumed that Pfeiffer, not Ehard, would be elected. "Ehard's showing (2 votes) was poor because he is unknown to most of the faction members; he has no following in the party and he made a poor showing in Eichstätt at the party convention."[55] Pfeiffer, with a long conservative career, had most recently had the responsibility for denazification, which cost him some support. He reputedly had good relations with MG, partly because of his excellent English—by profession he was director of a language institute—but like Müller he was torpedoed by a story from the past. At this precise juncture he was accused in a newspaper article of having favored in 1932 a coalition government with the Nazis. Pfeiffer denied the charge; a copy of the alleged letter could not be produced or remembered with certainty. The SPD, however, decided they would not join with him. Müller again seemed destined for victory, but at the last moment Hundhammer roused support for Ehard, who was acceptable to the SPD.[56]

CSU conservatives' dislike for Müller was so intense that they preferred cooperation with Hoegner's SPD. Ehard accepted a coalition government, which Müller had opposed. His combining CSU conservatives with the SPD was barely thinkable, but including the demagogue Alfred Loritz in order to secure his few Landtag seats was an even stranger decision and one which he would soon regret.[57] The next Third Army intelligence report, which finally began spelling Ehard's name correctly, regarded him as the "dummy" for the Hundhammer-Pfeiffer group, "the proto-type of a bureaucrat who with his exaggerated pedantry can be content only in a state where the power of the police is unlimited."[58] This kind of faulty political intelligence is reflected in subsequent OMGUS skepticism of their reports: "Much confusion is created by high sounding, but meaningless commonplaces."

Actually Ehard, although short, slight, and reserved, had a distinguished career as jurist; his most recent post was minister of justice. (He had also been state's attorney against Hitler in the sensational 1924 trial.) Ehard had been unwilling to join the party, as most in the ministry did after 1933. He was not thrown out, but shunted to backwater cases so unpolitical that after the war no significant "Nazi" decisions could be found to destroy him. However, that he had remained in high office should by MG law have meant his automatic arrest. He was temperamentally an administrator, not a politician, the opposite of a Müller. He left political work to Pfeiffer and his assistant, Karl Schwend. He socialized little, rarely inviting CSU leaders for the beer evenings typical of Bavarian politics.[59] His strengths in his twenty-year career of CSU prominence were his moderate and tactful manner, his vital ability to keep disagreeing groups from ruining the organization, his exercising power without appearing to need it, and his evident integrity and reasonableness. Although he was Catholic, a necessary condition for leadership in Bavarian politics, he had a Protestant wife.

Ehard recalled his election in the temporary quarters of the university auditorium, still showing the effects of the bombing. "The floor was burned in many places, the windows still blocked up with boards, the lighting extremely limited, and the heating just sufficient so that one did not freeze to death." He left the room with heavy heart considering his problems, the first of which was dealing with Americans. "Until my entry into office, it was customary that every German officeholder could be summoned to account by any number of captains, majors, or colonels of the most varying departments. Every officer gave assignments for his domain without concerning himself with the domain of someone else. This administrative chaos could not be allowed to continue." He worked out the arrangement, in a long conference with Muller, that orders would go only to him.[60]

Frustration persisted on both sides. MG observers watched the elected Landtag with dismay. It had done nothing; the free spirit was missing; the speaker was authoritarian; members merely obeyed party leaders. They had agreed to a nineteen-day wait until the Landtag's next meeting, presumably because the cabinet was too busy to bother with legislators. Hoegner partly agreed with this evaluation in a letter which MG censorship neatly intercepted:

> Our situation is approximately the same as in 1920–21, and the old game of the Bavarian reaction can start all over again. The occupation powers sit back, watching this, and leave the politically incorrigible Germans free to do what they like. There is no trace of guilty feelings among the broad masses. . . . My family is longing to get out of this chaos of hate, libel, and lewdness back into the purer atmosphere of Switzerland.[61]

Whatever criticism OMGB had of Ehard's regime, OMGUS was reported as very pleased; Ehard was much trusted and OMGUS was happy that the Müller wing was coming to support him. It criticized only the taking of Loritz into the government, but OMGUS was determined even there not to interfere.

Yet OMGB rejected Ehard's protest against the military police arresting a member of the Landtag: "It must be recognized that Article 28 of the Bavarian Constitution is not applicable to action by the occupying forces. Members of legislative bodies have no more inherent privileges *vis à vis* the Occupation than any private citizen."[62] OMGB orders were still being given, for example, to implement decartelization and to report how it was done within fifteen days. Under heavy OMGUS pressure, the OMGB Education and Religious Branch investigated the universities and found many faculty working without MG approval and contrary to the Law of Liberation. "The work of a department had to be stopped and in one or two cases the program of an entire faculty was all but brought to a standstill."[63] The attempt to restrain the *Süddeutsche Zeitung* from printing stories about refugees by punishment backfired; the paper merely increased in popularity.

OMGB was still planning decentralization, but reported strong opposition from "power greedy" ministers and bureaucrats. The special agencies were out of control, with ministers quarreling over who should get them. The interior ministry "appears to be falling over backward rather than take action that would offend the majority party." It opposed the popular election of the Landräte, leaving the old system of their being chosen by Land party officials, who often chose people not even known to the local electors, or by powerful cliques in the communities.

> The department concerned with local administration is operating perhaps better than it was, but is a long way from showing any degree of efficiency. Its channels to local governments are still slow and unwieldy. It has indicated little leadership or encouragement to the many local officials new at their jobs who are insecure in their duties and basic responsibilities, nor has it shown enough strength or purpose to gain any particular respect from these officials.[64]

OMGB continued to intervene with dubious results.

OMGUS democratization chief Litchfield's criticism of OMGB was that it had continued to be heavily involved in Bavarian affairs despite OMGUS orders to curtail its activities. Events in 1945 had attracted attention to OMGB, and this explained why "OMGB divisions have taken MG regulations and OMGUS directives and instructions more literally than have the other OMGs, and hence have been more active in enforcement." These activities were not well designed to solve the problems, including those of democratization, and Clay should make sure intervention was indeed limited. "MG intervention, especially at Land levels, needs to be reoriented toward more high level supervision and away from dealing with individual cases . . . the bulk of MG personnel is now assigned to activities involving operations . . . such as information control and denazification with a concomitant weakness in those fields which ought to be promoting the foundation of a sound economy and democracy." The complaint in Munich was that

> Land MG was allowed little voice in policy-making, and was serving more and more as a mere message channel between OMGUS and the German ministries. It would seem that this particular type of faithful literal-minded leadership may have proved very useful in the past but the time is at hand when considerably more must be expected from the Land MG leaders. They should be more intimately acquainted with local conditions and problems than the OMGUS divisions and, even if not invited to share in policy formation, Land leaders must be capable of giving mature judgments and adapting OMGUS instructions to local circumstance.

After this blast at General Muller, Litchfield noted that 30 to 50 percent of OMGB and local MG officials' energy went to solve problems actually created by the miltary. He cited personnel practices, and the army's insistence that "military procurement needs be covered 100 percent before allocations are permitted to the civilian sector," which deprived Germans of both basic necessities and their civil liberties.[65]

Other inspectors also found much wrong with OMGB operations, such as its duplication of reports by simply copying the statistics from German reports. The industry section was guilty of poor administration, including its orders to the minister-president directing allocation of scarce materials. "MG tends to intervene with specific instructions and personnel, in effect taking the problem impatiently out of German hands." German firms or authorities used MG to forward special requests to the minister-president, urging that scarce materials and supplies be immediately allocated to them. OMGUS thought such decisions should be high level policy advice and not local intervention.

> Regardless of MG attitudes, however, the political relationship of MG authorities toward German groups will continue to be precarious. . . . Many German officials . . . await MG inquiry, before taking action, and they tend to find excuses for not accepting MG advice. . . . various German factions frequently attempt to elicit MG support for their proposals or candidates against those of opposing factions, and that such support is often claimed when, in fact, it has not been extended. Conversely, there is evidence that many German officials are ready to attribute an unpopular action by their office to MG orders, regardless of whether such orders have been issued. . . . Unfortunately since untrue allegations of these sorts have been passed around orally . . . there seems little hope that effective measures can be taken by MG to suppress them. Since corrective action was taken with respect to MG activities in the Josef M ller case, OMGB officials have tended to favor a hands-off policy in internal political party disputes.

Therefore OMGB had not intervened in the Loritz case; one OMGUS official who gave too many press comments about Loritz was withdrawn. The report concluded that incompetent Kreis MG should be weeded out and detachments reduced.[66]

OMGUS intervention in OMGB affairs was primarily in the form of critical reports about how OMGB intervention in Bavarian affairs was counterproductive. The exceptional activity was denazification, for which Special Branch could not follow OMGUS's general orders against intervention because OMGUS was specifically ordering it to make German denazification activity more effective. "The Ministry of Political Liberation is directly responsible to the Land Special Branch Officer. . . . Orders currently being received from Berlin are adding to this operative load." Even so detachment reports were a waste.[67] Yet another OMGUS study not only found more problems but raised the question whether someone should inspect the inspectors to be sure they were functional. The Economics Division was supposedly advising German authorities, but these seemed less able to handle their own problems than the year before. Their intervention probably impeded the orderly allocation of scarce materials. Forty percent of the Economics Division staff was assigned to reparations, which seemed out of proportion to the need, as did the heavy investment of personnel in denazification, amounting to some 50 percent of German employees. MG attention should go to internment camps where presumably the major offenders were. As for the Manpower Division, most of its efforts went into two tasks. One was "straightening out difficulties of Army personnel with indigenous labor; these arise largely because many Army Personnel Officers are not trained in civilian personnel management, and even disregard employee rights as specified in EUCOM [European Command] regulations;" the other was putting pressure on German labor offices at the request of Economics Division to recruit labor for programs with high priority. The inspector thought this was further unproductive intervention. In conclusion he noted that the Legal Division continued to operate and inspect to a degree exceeding that of most other fields and thought it could be cut back 30 to 50 percent.[68]

The Legal Division, criticized for inspecting too much, criticized MG courts. Qualified men had gone home in 1945–46; replacements were inferior, often combat officers with no training in law. There were no outstanding lawyers at any level; of fifty-six judges studied, only four were lawyers; only twenty-one had any college; and one had only an elementary education. "Most of the more able officer judges with whom I talked stated frankly that they felt themselves incompetent to preside as judges and do not want to continue." Many cases showed poor preparation. "The judges are under the direction of the Chief Prosecutor and are thus not in a proper position to criticize the preparation or presentation of cases tried in their courts." A review board of six men handled a thousand cases a month. "Until February of 1947 the review procedure was dominated by the policy of the then Chief Legal Officer and was extremely harsh." There was no real provision for interpreters and that job was usually done unsatisfactorily. "An examination of the 'death cases' now under review at this headquarters reveals an extremely low standard of performance on the part of the courts in the field." The summary courts, 282 officers in 140 counties, were too far away for control or advice. Many were former local commanders with almost autocratic power. Control of the Bavarian summary courts was not practicable. "Personnel changes are rapid and, as a result, many officers are never contacted during their tours of duty."[69]

At the top Muller was using praise and criticism to gain Ehard's compliance. The points he raised show Muller's frustration and the general triviality of OMGB intervention. For example, he passed on Clay's concern about hoarding and black marketing; telling Ehard, "your government has not to date effectively attacked this problem. . . . give this matter your personal attention."[70] A rather typical amicable conference followed, at which MG raised trivial points. Muller wished that "the population" be given driving instruction, and wondered whether Bavaria would accept the offer of army jeeps (Muller seemed pleased that it would). He would help businessmen get to an export fair. The Bavarian government should close down a few "luxury night clubs." He would invite Landtag members to meet with his staff to discuss common problems.[71] But after this mild personal confrontation came another harsh letter: "It is desired to call your attention to the unsatisfactory performance of the Reparation and Restitution Section, Ministry of Economics. . . . [which] has increased rather than diminished since last brought to your attention and has culminated in a complete failure to carry out orders." The letter noted that reparations deliveries for April were still undelivered: "It is requested that you present any available evidence why the person responsible should not be prosecuted under MG."[72]

Through September Muller wrote a variety of criticisms and warnings. "You are hereby advised that the entire hop crop was frozen by order of OMGUS, and that it has been sold to foreign buyers. Any losses due to lack of pickers and black market operations will not only reflect upon your ministry but will cause a serious monetary loss to the German people." To the Bavarian request for an extension of the deadline on land reform, Muller said he would ask Clay, "but for the time being I would follow that interpretation closest to Clay's order." By 17 September he had three objections to the budget: occupation costs must be a first claim on the budget; Bavaria could not pay pensions to released officials; the deficit should be liquidated. Arthur Schweizer complained to the interior ministry that its bureaucrats were sabotaging MG efforts to create more autonomous local government; the minister fully agreed and promised to cooperate in every way.[73]

When Muller left he tried to make his departure as sad for the Bavarians as it was for him, but he still fired two more barrages. The first accused Ehard's government of passive resistance by unreasonable delays in compliance, and told Ehard he must answer the charge in eight days. "Excessive delays in compliance with requests suggest an existent passive resistance to the American occupation in some quarters." The same minister who "fully agreed" with MG denied any such resistance, pointing out that his staff was overburdened with work, lack of rooms, moving of offices, and reorganization.[74] Muller next complained that a Landrat had criticized a member of a local MG. This was improper. Ehard properly informed his ministries: "An individual case prompted MG to order that local German authorities are not authorized to criticize actions of local MG offices." This must have been remembered when the same day Muller made an impassioned appeal as his last word: "Before my departure from Bavaria, I should like to impress on you the value of a strong independent press." He quoted Voltaire: "I disagree with what you say . . . "[75]

The major struggle between the Bavarians and Americans during the Muller-Hoegner regime was denazification, which might occasion some surprise because Hoegner had been brought in so dramatically to replace Schäffer for that purpose. The man who had fled Hitler to save his life was clearly anti-Nazi, and one of his first acts was to issue what was later called "Hoegner's law," a strict standard which exceeded MG requirements. The law stated: "In no ministry may a civil servant or contractual employee be employed who at any time was a member of the NSDAP, SA, SS, or the SD [*Sicherheitsdienst*], or held any office in any other of the NSDAP-connected organizations or was known as a follower or exponent of National Socialism."[76] His assistant, Anton Pfeiffer, responded to the thousands who lost their jobs and who had written to Hoegner for help by placing the blame entirely on the Americans. "I must unfortunately tell you that all of these affairs were arranged without the Bavarian Government being able to exert any influence." Appeals should go to OMGB.

Hoegner began eager to denazify, yet in his first month he found reasons to modify policy. The mass arrest of officials was without apparent reason; their families were not informed and no contact was permitted; they were not interrogated for months; they had inadequate quarters and food, and had had no chance to take sufficient clothing. The denazification law then worked out for Bavaria by Pfeiffer and Ehard on how to deal with party members was largely taken over by OMGUS and issued on MG orders for the zone.[77] Hoegner's choice of Heinrich Schmitt (KPD) as his denazification minister could not be faulted in terms of Schmitt's intent. Yet Schmitt had many problems: his inexperience, a shortage of employees, and for weeks no building and few supplies. He used "special delegates," one for each district, of which four of the five could be considered communist. Schmitt and his assistant spent their time traveling and giving speeches. He complained about lack of help, but when Hoegner sent some capable officials, they were not put to use.[78]

In May MG had its own denazification program, Operation Zebra. Hoegner described it only as troublemaking, noting that it "suddenly cancelled all work permits." He was able with great difficulty to get some postponements and to retrieve his finance state secretary, unjustly dismissed. MG orders were to have work camps ready for another 50,000 prisoners. Pressure was on party leaders to give full support to denazification. Hoegner wrote: "In my presence, Müller was so worked over by Col. Reese and Major Vacca that beads of perspiration could be seen on his forehead. Finally they squeezed out of him the promise to recognize the law and to cooperate in its implementation."[79] Reese and Muller warned Hoegner that "Clay was angry at the situation in Bavaria and would use the army if necessary. Then there could be no elections in Bavaria and the right to self-government could not be honored. On June 14 the party leaders had to sign the proclamation to the people and to promise to implement the law."[80]

As late as April the responsible OMGB officers thought Schmitt "useful and dependable, but a bad organizer." Then Clay's assistant, Fritz Oppenheimer, reported that Schmitt was "honest and energetic," but that his "ministry was packed with incompetent and inexperienced Communists."[81] The ministry was reorganized and Hoegner was made personally responsible for its proper functioning. In June Dorn reported it on the verge of chaos; he suggested that Pfeiffer replace Schmitt. Schmitt resigned 5 July, claiming that Hoegner was giving the ministry to the CSU to make it easier for the party to sabotage denazification.[82] Pfeiffer set out to regularize the denazification process, getting little CSU support and much criticism from the left. He quickly sent MG a long report on how he would clean up the mess. He would select people on the basis of ability, not politics, straighten out administrative confusion, inform tribunals of the texts of the laws, and better public relations. Hoegner told Ehard, then justice minister, to supply trained judges; this was MG's highest priority. On 3 August he put more pressure on Pfeiffer to stop so many exonerations.[83]

Although Colonel Reese had said 10 June that "It cannot be overemphasized that higher headquarters has indicated that it will tolerate absolutely no interference by MG with German officials charged with carrying out the Law for Liberation," on 12 August he ordered all tribunals suspended because of the many decisions "contrary to the law."[84] MG itself was delinquent. Muller found a former Gestapo man in his own headquarters and ordered a new program of investigations, with new questionnaires distributed to everyone. On 17 August, he found people in the "mandatory removals" category still in his employ.

The cabinet meeting 7 August saw Hoegner holding a tougher line, although the ministry's State Secretary Kraus thought the law's purpose was to make possible the reinstatement of officials in their old careers. Hoegner called this "a fundamental mistake, which one must oppose with all severity. Being an official was an honor. The Americans were watching with extreme sharpness."[85] With Clay watching Dorn and Dorn watching Hoegner and Hoegner watching Pfeiffer, things were as orderly as they would ever be, yet the verdicts brought Clay's greatest anger. His spot check of 575 firms in Bavaria revealed "a widespread failure to comply" with the law; Hoegner was to report in a week on what he had done to get all firms to submit the required reports, to conduct spot checks, to select the most flagrant cases for prosecution, and to publish the prosecutions as a deterrent.[86] Two shrill voices criticized Pfeiffer. One was that of a radio commentator, Herbert Gessner, whom OMGB ordered Pfeiffer to answer on the radio. (Gessner soon fled to the East.) The other major critic was Loritz, making political hay by denouncing denazification.

OMGB misjudgment and Bavarian politics created another period of chaos in the ministry when Ehard put the demagogic Loritz in as the minister in charge. His speeches showed a brilliance in oratory which brought comparison to Hitler's. No one attracted as many thrilled listeners. There was little question that Loritz was anti-Nazi. From a respectable family, his father a former district president of Upper Bavaria, he had been active in the resistance. He claimed (falsely) to have placed the bomb in November 1939 that almost killed Hitler, and had cooperated with various Allied intelligence agencies in Switzerland. Because Loritz was mysteriously back in Germany so quickly in May 1945, Niethammer assumed that MG got him there; Loritz began his career on the general assumption that he was an American agent. Certainly he was an important MG informer in 1945; he was favored by OMGB, particularly in its intervention in the summer of 1947 and spring of 1949. OMGB intelligence officers doubted the charges made against him of lying and corruption; they admitted he was fanatic but thought him useful to MG. He had some corrupt men thrown out, but other corrupt men taken in. Loritz had attacked camp corruption as "champagne to the rich and hunger to the poor," but lacking authorization for more police, he recruited his private police force, the *Kontrolldienst* (KD), which introduced more corruption. As early as February MG was criticizing this KD, but Dorn supported Loritz almost to the end, ignorant until mid-June 1947 of the conditions which Griffith observed: "His ministry disintegrated into a state of complete administrative disorganization. The promised detailed report-newsletter was never published; letters went unanswered; favoritism and corruption ran rampant, and denazification in Bavaria was hurtling down the road toward complete collapse." OMGB found in March that denazification had nearly stopped, though Loritz had processed some name cases and sent some 5.7 million Bavarians a signed card that they had nothing to fear. Niethammer thought only MG intervention kept the tribunals from collapsing.[87]

What brought Loritz down as minister was MG's reversal from support to criticism. Muller wrote Ehard on 20 May that the KD had the characteristics of a secret police; its members were either from the Loritz party or KPD; and many were not screened by MG. Furthermore, it was set up without MG permission and should be dissolved immediately. Two top Loritz aides were to be fired, because "they have proved themselves unwilling and incapable of carrying out the denazification program in consonance with the policy of MG." The Landtag should be informed that Loritz lied when he said he had MG approval. OMGB concluded that he had accomplished little other than providing patronage jobs for his followers. He had promised a large increase in appeal courts, but there were fewer than when he had started. He had fired sixty-seven chairmen and prosecutors on charges of corruption, falsification, and insanity. Many others had quit in disgust. "Among other failures of Loritz as minister was the complete lack of cooperation between the ministerial level and the various tribunals. Loritz repeatedly stated that circulars, clarification of the law and new instructions had been issued throughout Bavaria. In every instance, investigations disclosed these statements to be false."[88] He had spent so much money for party purposes that it was rumored he had sold denazifications. A better-supported explanation was that he was very deeply involved in the black market.

He was not alone to blame, however, that the spring of 1947 brought mounting protests about the internment camps. Tens of thousands of people arrested two years before were still awaiting trial. In February 1947, Clay, despite protests, ordered that those sentenced to labor camps be locked up, even though their cases were under appeal. Even OMGB had come to agree that many had been sentenced unjustly and that conditions were bad. Although Ehard could justly have answered that the fault was MG's, Muller told him on 3 April to solve the mess: "The internment of large numbers of civilians who have been held under unsatisfactory physical conditions and without trial for nearly two years is repugnant to American concepts of justice and humanity and presents a problem which requires your personal attention. In spite of the efforts made by MG during the past eight months to effect the speedy trials of internees, only 289 of approximately 225,000 inmates have been disposed of."[89] Protestant Bishop Meiser was more specific in his protest, particularly of abuses when the United States was in full control. He charged that the arrests had been made without evidence of guilt; people arrested had homes and property confiscated; family members lost pensions and right to work. Those arrested, even in February 1947, had not been permitted to take necessary articles; the sick and aged had been arrested; some persons were forced to sleep on the ground in bitter cold without blankets or coats; many died in the camps; the piling of ever more people into the camps had made it impossible to improve conditions.[90] Camille Sachs conceded for the ministry that conditions for women were terrible, the worse because the women did not know how long they would be imprisoned.

Even while Muller was telling Ehard to get people out of the camps, he passed on the OMGUS order for Ehard to arrest "the following classes of persons": members of the leadership corps, anyone of any leadership position in the Nazi party, and members of the Gestapo, SD, and SS, including the Waffen-SS. This new automatic arrest of those in "criminal organizations" was left to the Germans and largely ignored, partly because Americans had already arrested any they could find. Ludwig Hagenauer, Loritz's replacement, denounced the arrests for membership in organizations as violating "every principle of civilized justice," but Griffith defended him as honest and dependable. Hagenauer's deputy, Camille Sachs, who was part Jewish, played the more active role in denazification. Politics were largely removed from the ministry; the organization began to function, and relations with MG improved.[91]

But the OMGUS tide was ebbing. In March 1948 Muller's replacement, Murray von Wagoner, wrote Ehard that MG would no longer veto tribunal decisions or veto the reemployment of anyone. Internment camps could release without MG approval, and the MG order compelling internment during appeal was canceled, as was the order arresting members of criminal organizations. By 2 June, Wagoner wrote that MG would interfere no more; Law No. 8 was canceled. The Bavarian machine limped along; appeals lasted for two more decades. What had been accomplished? The statistical result: 6.7 million questionnaires; of those replying 72.5 percent were judged not incriminated; 23 percent were amnestied; 4 percent were tried in 33,000 hearings; those tried comprised 0.5 percent of the population. As Niethammer concluded, denazification had become purely a matter of paper shuffling. By July 1948, out of 12,000 teachers dismissed, 11,000 had been reinstated.[92]

Thus Muller's two years were marked by a degree of American intervention in Bavarian affairs mutually frustrating to both sides. The intervention led to a weakening of democratic impulses in those whom OMGB could not control (except on occasion to ban them from office). American intervention in denazification had the effect of preventing a reasonable solution. The result was regarded at the time as disastrous, but in retrospect it would appear little more than an irrelevant waste of time and effort. The solid steps forward were taken by party politicians working to recreate parties and a government with the power derived from public support. Yet the government and parties remained weak, partly from MG intervention, but mostly from the economic problems which MG also could not control.

The Wagoner Period: Retreat with Anger

The general left and OMGB was placed under a new civilian "commander," Murray van Wagoner, in December 1947. Formerly Michigan highway commissioner, his one previous trip to Germany had been to inspect the Autobahn in 1937 for the American Road Builders' Association. Briefly governor of Michigan (1940–42), he was referred to as a "lame-duck politician." He had recently come to Clay as an engineering consultant. His lack of precise qualifications for his new position was partly obviated by the fact that Ehard increasingly went over his head to Clay by simply making a telephone call.[93]

When Wagoner arrived Bavaria was resisting where it could. His first major action was in the "Great Potato War," the struggle over who would get Bavarian potatoes. Externally it was a fight against Economic Council demands; internally it concerned potato deliveries to the DPs. MG demanded that DPs get their potatoes first; then Wagoner compromised, ordering that Bavarians could be given potatoes when the 12,000 tons for the DPs were safely stored in a warehouse.[94] In May MG protested that only 2,500 tons had been delivered, but Wagoner had lost the potato war.

There were other discontents in addition to food shortages. Bavarians were incensed at Clay's dismissing Semler as bizonal minister and forcing Bavaria to ban him from office. The Bavarian Dr. Josef Baumgartner had already sensationally resigned as bizonal agriculture minister.[95] His experience with OMGUS centralization led him to join the newly formed separatist Bavarian Party (BP), by June becoming its chairman and making it the most serious threat to the CSU. Another Bavarian delegate to Frankfurt, Otto Seeling, resigned with a bitterness which Ehard wrote that he shared.

> I regard it as humiliating to belong to a parliament, whose laws are under the criminal law of an alien military power.... democracy is led *ad absurdem.* After the victors in nearly three years have proved themselves to be incapable of recreating a peace and a legally organized condition, all German parliaments and governments should demand the immediate end to MG rule.... The triple administration; MG with offices down to the Kreis level, the bizonal administration, and the Länder administrations have created an administrative hypertrophy, which must lead to the financial and economic ruin of Germany and to an intolerable bureaucratization. If the German people is supposed to be trained for democracy... this military command is the worst teacher.

The draft of the bizonal economic charter was denounced by another delegate to Frankfurt, Seelos, as more centralist than Weimar. Hundhammer went one historical precedent farther: it could be compared only to Hitler's Reich.[96] Seelos also left the CSU for the BP and Hundhammer was rumored to follow.

MG found more and more noncompliance. The most sensational was resistance to its "pantry law," but there was also noncompliance in housing. MG felt Nazis were not required to give up extra rooms, and people with contacts had extra rooms. "To continue to keep refugees in barracks and camps when they can be assigned to private homes is contrary to MG policy." Wagoner complained that dismantling was not proceeding because of "a complete lack of cooperation among the various departments and ministries, so that this headquarters is constantly being asked to save some object or services from some other department." And rather oddly, after so much effort to get the Nazis out of office, Wagoner canceled the Land government's right to intervene when former party members were elected to public office.[97] With this charitable line, MG let Schäffer engage in politics in mid-February 1948; he was immediately elected head of the Upper Bavarian CSU. The same agreeableness was shown at the new German-American Cultural Relations Group, where all agreed "that the German people in 1945 were more ready than at present for re-orientation, but that the Americans did not at that time understand the German mind, [and] that the Americans have not adequately explained their policies and the reasons for their actions to the Germans."[98]

The winter of discontents passed and the June currency reform began the release of the economic stranglehold, but not in time to save the CSU from the BP challenge. It lost heavily in city elections to Baumgartner's demagoguery, which promised an end to misery by keeping Bavaria for the Bavarians. Yet Ehard's increased confidence demonstrates that MG was more and more leaving Bavarians on their own. "We have never been told by the Americans what position we are to take, and I must say I have always had the freedom to tell the Americans what I think. They have not taken offense. One has to remain objective and not to violate the procedures, because with courtesy, good humor and kindness, one can solve many problems." Ehard needed his humor to deal with Wagoner's August order setting another deadline for catching up on reparation deliveries.[99]

In general, however, MG activity came to center on civil service reform, education, and on vetoing a variety of minor laws.[100] Hoegner told the Landtag that this latter activity sometimes came after a law had been operating for months and thus created legal problems. He was interrupted frequently by Landtag members shouting other criticisms of MG action. OMGB reported: "Certain Bavarian parliamentary and governmental officials of ministerial rank have lately evidenced an antagonistic attitude toward MG, the legislators objecting to occasional suspension of Bavarian legislation and governmental officials resenting almost any manifestation of MG's supreme authority."[101] Dorn described the situation in March 1949 as one of nearly unrelieved frustration and failure:

> Saw Shell and Wood [OMGB officials], who tried to explain failure of denazification in Bavaria to me and were generally expressive of the ignorance and fatuousness of OMGB. The Governor a breezy, well-meaning politician who wants to be helpful; they thought that Intelligence was particularly inefficient. Then saw Governor, who had a mere toe-hold on situation, who said that land reform was not executed in Bavaria,... who said that *denazification failed if you believe in it;* believed of course in reorientation which like everyone he thought was a great success... Winning chairman of Reorientation... admitted that every meeting was not necessarily a blow for democratic idea. (Some people say no definite direction outside of discussion and talking. And every Bavarian likes to do that.) Parties protest, ostensibly because, once having refused to take a hand in re-education they would be compelled to introduce party democracy; success measured in terms of an occasional mayor ousted or a *Beamter* who was taught responsibility to the public.... Only ten laws dis-

allowed in a long time; yet Hoegner was mad recently. Are they talking past one another? Friedman [editor, *Süddeutsche Zeitung*] seemed to think so—and I can say ditto as far as the impression van Wagoner made on me . . . knows what Clay does not want him to do. What is he in terms of moral influence on Germans—nil or thereabouts. . . . I should say again that MG is absorbed by the Bavarian atmosphere. . . . Denazification people *tired and almost hopeless and speak of failure . . . so many marginal people are admitted to high public offices.*

Dorn reported at length Ehard's reactions, stressing that he was incensed with MG's contradictory policy of trying to build up a responsible democracy and at the same time continuing interventionism. "He was really outraged by lack of encouragement, lack of acknowledgment of what had been accomplished; continuous criticism of the regime which undermined his authority which was also being attacked from below. But he kept coming back to the spirit of interventionism. The spirit of 1946." Ehard also resented the public education program which was stirring up the people against his government. Dorn concluded:

Perhaps man for man our present Bavarian staff is better than it was under General Muller—it is, with the exception of a few, still not good enough to do its job at the peak of efficiency which this job requires. . . . There has been indeed an unmistakeable transformation of MG in the past 18 months: we have abandoned the early doctrine of hands off in the matter of German internal affairs, and MG has gone far beyond its original objective in the matter of democratization; there is not merely the reorientation program, but the civil service law (both good and bad features), free enterprise in trades, civil rights, local government authority. . . . Much of this will vanish with the disappearance of U.S. authority.[102]

Despite Dorn's pessimism, the CSU demonstrated great political skill in early 1949. The issue was the Basic Law. Ehard privately was quite prepared to accept the constitution, but the CSU's small town and rural conservative wing opposed it. In a public opinion poll in Rosenheim, 71 percent of the males and 91 percent of the females were opposed; even in cosmopolitan Munich 45 percent of respondents wanted either an independent or an autonomous Bavaria. CSU politicians contrived a baffling piece of Bavarian politics to defeat the BP. "The spectacle they presented to the public induced even the Bavarian SPD, the FDP, and members of their own party to believe momentarily that they were toying with separatism and the restoration of the Wittelsbach dynasty." Hundhammer thus maneuvered the BP into an extreme position. Baumgartner apparently felt he had to go all out for monarchy in order to maintain his radical appeal. He demanded a referendum, not on the Basic Law but on the restoration of the Bavarian monarchy. Then Hundhammer denied having mentioned the restoration of the monarchy. While the BP thus appeared too extreme, Ehard then formulated the manner in which

Bavaria could show its dissatisfaction with the Basic Law and still remain a part of the new federation. The Landtag rejected the Basic Law, but accepted it as binding upon Bavaria when ratified by two-thirds of the other Länder.[103]

MG's last summer showed diminished but still annoying intervention. After years of telling the Germans to keep their hands off DPs, MG ordered a crackdown on DP blackmarket operators, without mentioning most were Jewish. A greater matter for anger concerned the arrest of Loritz by Müller, minister of justice, just prior to the August election. Clarence Bolds, acting for Wagoner, brought the German leaders in to tell them it was undemocratic to start a court case against an opposition leader in the middle of a campaign. "He could only describe the action of Müller as political chicanery . . . every school child knew that Müller was trying to stop opposition . . . it stinks." Müller said MG's asking for Loritz's trial documents just before the trial was "equal to the methods applied during the Third Reich. . . . Under such conditions the building up of an independent democratic rule of law is not guaranteed. I feel after ample consideration that I must in good conscience resign my office as minister of justice and request a release from my duties."[104] The case got messier when the state's attorney informed Müller that Paul Farr, aide to Wagoner, had called the previous winter to inquire about a case then being considered against Müller. When he was informed no indictment would be asked for, Farr had told the attorney he "should be careful because of the public interest and that of Auerbach." (Philip Auerbach was a Bavarian official who represented Jewish interests.) Farr was told MG intervention could not influence the decision, but the state's attorney resented Farr's effort to interfere. Müller then wrote Wagoner of another dubious legal issue, that Farr had told a member of the Bavarian *Staatskanzlei* (State Chancellory): " 'Whatever action the minister of justice will take, MG will be advised since we have tapped his telephone circuit.' I made known this fact to the president who told me Mr. Bolds recently assured him that no telephone conversations were overheard. . . . Dear Sir, you will certainly understand my wish to get released from nondemocratic measures since during the Nazi regime my conversations per telephone were always being overheard."[105]

A more positive OMGB aspiration was a reform of the *Beamtentum* (Civil Service) in Bavaria, for the German bureaucracy had not only a positive reputation for efficiency, but also a negative reputation for reactionary views. MG assumed that for democracy to take effect the civil service should also be democratized. Much as the Nazis had, MG tried to do something about the "excessive power" of the *Beamten* (civil servants), and with much the same result. Just as the Nazis were convinced that Beamten were anti-Nazi and would sabotage Nazism, so Americans were convinced that they were Nazi and would sabotage democracy. They were actually conservative and could oppose either. The 1945 firing of most officials because of Nazi party membership caused an earthquake. The action was meant to solve the problem of Beamten Nazism, but it was based on the false premises that party membership meant real support to Nazism and that persons who had not joined were less reactionary than those who had. Actually, those most bitterly resisting OMGB were usually devout Catholics who had also resisted Hitler, and MG could more legitimately have complained of a Catholic resistance than of a Nazi one. MG policy also assumed that the people and elected leaders would support the American reforms, whereas the Beamten were given much more support from both than was OMGB.

When Hoegner informed OMGB 27 June 1946 that MG requests for civil service reform had been carried through, he evidenced his fundamental misunderstanding of what was intended by the Americans.[106] Diverted by more pressing problems, OMGB did not seem to be aware that the more things had changed in 1946 the more they had remained the same. The parties were still dependent on Beamten for expertise. Of the first Landtag members, elected in December 1946, nearly 35 percent were Beamten.[107] OMGB reaction seems to have been delayed until February 1949, when Wagoner wrote:

> the democratic objectives of the law itself and MG policy are not being realized. Actions indispensable to the democratic implementation of the Civil Service Law have not been taken. . . . The Civil Service Commission should establish a position classification system; it should revamp its examination system to eliminate undemocratic caste features; it should discontinue its secret meetings; it should provide for adequate publicity on open positions; it should be able and willing to provide important statistics on government employment in Bavaria. Discrimination on account of formal education, age, sex, race, and origin, and discrimination against persons with good democratic records in favor of persons having a dubious political past, should be eradicated.[108]

Wagoner protested again in June that public servants were being fired to make room for those who had been "denazified," adding that it "cannot be allowed to continue."[109] He then deplored his failure to McCloy:

> All attempt to induce the Bavarian government or legislature to democratize the public personnel system have come to naught, due to the unwillingness of the bureaucracy to give up such class privileges as almost absolute security in office, lucrative pension rights, military-like rank and titles, traditions of secrecy that keep the public in ignorance of what the civil servants are doing, and the "insult" law that is so interpreted by the courts as to make it extremely dangerous for a citizen to criticize an official, and undemocratic restrictions on admission to the civil service. The concentration of privileges and power in the *Beamte* caste in public affairs is the more dangerous because the high positions in the executive branch of the government are in the hands of the privileged official class and because the Bavarian legislature is largely controlled by them. Moreover, their influence is heavily felt in all the political parties.[110]

Commissioner George Shuster was hopeful for reform in 1951, assuming a wide agreement, but HICOG analyst J.F.J. Gillen in 1953 despaired.

American efforts to democratize the Bavarian civil service, during HICOG, have not been productive. A draft which was prepared in 1949 was less democratic than the original code, and the 1950 amendment represented another step backward. It is doubtful that anything more can be done in Bavaria. The old civil servant caste is particularly strong in the Bavarian Landtag where approximately one-fourth of the deputies are civil servants on the active list. On the whole, they are the most active and competent members, and farmer and labor representatives in the Landtag tend to defer to them.[111]

The changes desired in the structure and spirit of local government, properly advanced, could have tapped long-standing support for more *Selbstverwaltung* (local autonomy). (This had been a stated National Socialist goal as well.) It represented a common hostility of MG, the National Socialists, and organized city and county leaders toward the Munich ministerial encroachment, which seemed like coordination to Munich but like tyranny from below. The struggle had begun 2 October 1945 when Major Peter Vacca ordered Hoegner to submit a new local government code, based on fifteen listed democratic principles, by 10 October. There were two noteworthy provisions. First, the code was to guarantee "the right of a governmental unit governed by an elective body or elected official to exercise definite powers and functions of local importance without supervision from any body or official of any other governmental unit, and to provide adequate revenues for the support of these functions." Second, the code should not permit "any chief executive to veto decisions of the legislative body of his unit."[112]

Matters did not move quickly. By February 1948 MG and the Bavarian government had agreed only that the terms for Landrat and mayor be set at four years. Thereafter the election of the previously ministerially appointed Landrat was a significant change and MG played an encouraging role. These candidates need not be Beamte. The voter could vote for individuals instead of merely party lists. In January 1949 Wagoner praised this "Democratization of Local Government in Bavaria," as it was described by the interior ministry, as a job well done.[113] He had apparently not noted the dismay of his own Political Affairs Division five days before when it lamented that discussions had dragged on for two years; the old Beamte had been busy making reactionary changes; Interior Minister Ankermüller had spoken for progress, but his actions did not back up his words. There was further delay.[114] The code ordered in 1945 was completed 25 January 1952, and called "the most modern and progressive in Germany." Gillen thought it less so than the version originally proposed, although Americans got more ideas into the Bavarian code than into the Hessian code of the same year. But the core was German and went back to nineteenth-century precedents.[115]

The matter of school reform was even more thorny than that of civil service reform, because it involved the position of the family and the church. Wagoner discovered that the problem had been conveniently passed over before, but during his time it became the cause célèbre of OMGB versus the government of Bavaria. School reform was made more difficult because the leader of the opposition was Alois Hundhammer, who was referred to respectfully as *Doktor Doktor,* having earned two doctorates. His incorruptibility was illustrated in the popular story that he could be left together with a sack of gold and a beautiful maiden, and neither would be touched. Son of a large peasant family, he had fought the Nazis and been sent to Dachau in 1933, where he was singled out for humiliation. On his release he had refused to compromise. Instead he changed professions, leaving the vulnerable academic life for shoe repairing, and throughout the dictatorship he remained self-sufficient and defiant. Called into military service and taken prisoner, he returned in late 1945 from prison in France.

Before Hundhammer took over the school reform struggle it had been waged by Dr. Josef Mayer, an equally determined Catholic, who had left the education ministry in 1939 after six years of protecting Catholic school rights against the Nazi Gauleiter. He had refused to join the Nazi party, which made him the obvious person to be the top official of the reconstructed ministry. By July 1945, Mayer was fighting the ignorant Americans with something of the same determination he had shown against the Nazis. The first problem had been denazification. As he later proudly noted in his memoirs, he had protected the party members in the ministry who were ordered to be fired. He regarded those ordered dismissed as harmless followers, men who had not had his strong convictions for the church; he illegally kept their positions open for them.[116]

On 23 July 1945 the ministry had reestablished "confessional" schools, that is, schools for either Catholics or Protestants but not for both, as contrasted to the *Gemeinschaft* (communal) schools preferred by liberals. Hoegner, anticlerical at least by Bavarian standards, had his SPD education minister reverse the 23 July order and restore the communal schools, on the grounds that Bavaria had not had a legal government in July. Mayer's battle continued, the true faith against the Marxists and MG. His antagonist Hoegner worked out a law which left the decision up to the parents—a community with a mixed population should have a communal school. But MG prevented publication of the law.[117] After long, bitter debate and more MG intervention, it was finally signed 8 August 1950, in theory providing for both kinds of schools.

The question of communal versus confessional schools was an old German debate and only a side issue for the real battle, which began as Hundhammer took over the ministry, and which concerned the U.S. objective of reeducation. Mayer wrote: "It remains the indisputable and permanent achievement of Minister Hundhammer that these [American reform] attempts were defeated . . . despite the massive pressure." Hundhammer's support came "to him from almost every side, from the universities, from the Bavarian Academy of Science, from associations, from both churches."[118] As Hundhammer wrote later: "America was indeed a world power but that was no reason why Germany should give up her cultural tradition which stretched all the way back to the Greeks and Romans." Although some American officers, like Dorn, did not think Hundhammer well educated, and although most of his colleagues thought him a better agriculture than education minister, Hundhammer was very proud that he could speak both Greek and Latin, which was true of almost none of the Americans he met. He had proudly saved the *Gymnasia* (preparatory schools) where they were taught.

Friedrich Glum, who had worked for Professor Alexander in the OMGUS education section before joining the Bavarian government, traced the bitter debate back to Americans who had "very primitive ideas about the conditions in Germany in the Nazi period." Glum noted with regret the

> many reports on how the undemocratic and militaristic German people could be re-educated. Each MG unit had officials who were to achieve this education. Constantly, commissions from America came for the same purpose. Unfortunately, most of these efforts had the opposite effect.... Germans therefore went back to the old ways, which they might not have done had the Germans had the education for democracy in their own hands.[119]

Glum also blamed the unyielding leadership in Bavaria, in particular Faulhaber's assistant in school policy, Father Zinkl. Glum heard Zinkl scold a teacher like a recruit and understood why Bavarian teachers disliked clerics and had flocked to the Nazi party. Glum thought even Hundhammer would have been more reasonable, but he fell under the influence of the old bureaucrats of his ministry.

The battle of the Bavarian schools began in January 1947, when General Clay demanded that good American principles of education be implemented quickly. Some of his demands had to do with a more democratic school organization; the others had to do with designing a curriculum which would better prepare young people to be citizens. The problem as perceived by the American reformers was that German like other European schools were in effect divided along class lines. Peasant and working-class children attended a grade school until they were fourteen, and then went to work or into vocational training or an apprenticeship. Middle-class and upper-class children (and the occasional very bright lower-class child) at the age of ten or eleven went to gymnasia where they were given intensive training in preparation for the university and a profession. Clay therefore ordered that compulsory education for all be extended to age fifteen, after which all should attend at least half-day school until eighteen. The grades seven to twelve should be in a common high school, which presumably would have the advantage of creating a greater feeling of equality among citizens. These later grades should remain general education, and not be limited to class-bound vocational education. Private school should conform to these public school goals. Teacher training should be upgraded for elementary school teachers by requiring them to attend a university rather than the less academic teacher-training institutions. There should be community participation in education, presumably through something like the parent-teacher associations in bloom in the United States.[120] Pfeiffer quickly wrote to Hundhammer that MG demands were for nothing less than a change to the American system. His eight years of experience with an American school in Munich made him much opposed to such a change. He advised taking it to the Landtag—that is, to stop it.

OMGB then rejected the liberalizing curriculum changes that had been proposed by the former SPD minister in the fall of 1946. The minister was told that these must be revised by 1 April to conform to the Clay principles, and that long-term programs were due by 1 July; the work should not be turned over to the ministry but to a specially created Land curriculum committee. On 5 March the ministry presented its analysis of Clay's plan. Putting everyone into the same school was based on the assumption that all children were equally talented; since they were not, society must have different educational programs, because otherwise it would produce only half-educated persons, such as those who supported the Nazis. Moreover, having children start their college preparation at ten or eleven was wise because they were ready then for intellectual development. Germans could not add to the length of schooling because with the war losses they needed the extra workers. Since 70 percent of Bavarian schools were village schools, it would be inappropriate to have teachers university trained. In summary, they argued that the American style of school was neither necessary to democracy nor conducive to the intellectual development of the academically talented.[121]

At a meeting 21 May Hundhammer, Alexander, Glum, and others tried to work out a settlement. Alexander did not object to beginning Latin at an early age, but he felt that both rich and poor should have the same chance. They should be in the same school and in some classes together until relatively late, and then could be divided into humanistic and vocational students. It should also be possible for a child to shift later from the vocational to the humanistic curriculum.[122] The Bavarian negotiator reported that the initial harmony of this meeting was nearly destroyed because Hundhammer's ministry bluntly rejected some of the American demands, and "several clumsy expressions, which were interpreted as a criticism of General Clay, had brought a strong bad temper at OMGUS, which together with other misunderstandings had almost led to a serious crisis." He thought he had worked out a compromise calling for six years of common school and a delay of teacher-training changes until a study outside Germany was completed. Unfortunately the Landtag's CSU had gone much farther in conciliation, offering eight years of common schooling with special classes for bright students. Even Hundhammer accepted the Landtag compromise, but later changed his position. The Americans preferred this CSU plan, which unfortunately, he thought, followed the American suggestions point by point.[123] The politicians were more flexible than the officials.

Five months later Clay complained to Hans Ehard about the unsatisfactory Bavarian proposals of April. Clay had conferred in Munich with Hundhammer, who had promised to have a revised program by 1 October. But on 18 November Clay wrote to Ehard:

> I must regret to inform you that this second program shows no substantive improvement over the first. . . . It ignores the basic principle of equal educational opportunities. It does not end the overlapping of schools (*Grundschule* and *Höherer*) after the fourth year, but proposes a two-track system and even proposes a third track, a *Mittelschule*. . . . It proposes a complete separation of the training of grade school from high school teachers. Hundhammer said publicly that he would make no substantive changes in the school system. Give this your personal attention.

Ehard, to mediate, suggested a committee to work with the Americans, and volunteered for the committee.[124] Rising MG impatience with Hundhammer and his bureaucrats was evident in the 1 December notice that teacher-training institutions were forbidden and must be closed no later than 1 February 1948. The ministry drew up a plan for increasing the curriculum to six semesters at these institutions by 16 January, but MG turned it down and ordered that no more new students be accepted in such institutions.

The Germans, mounting a counterattack, gathered criticism of American schools. Hundhammer was sent an article from *Vogue* which described American public school students as having a dulled curiosity, being politically illiterate, and lacking in moral values. German scholars at the University of Chicago noted that MG was actually criticizing the European, not just the German, system of education. Thus the school systems of clearly democratic countries were included in the attack. The American high school system had much expanded because of the depression, but it still relied on college to continue the education; the high school might prepare citizens, but it was much weakened as a preparation for an academic training and in general education.[125]

Faulhaber appealed to Bishop Muench from North Dakota, an adviser to Clay on Catholic affairs, pointing out:

> The MG controlled press and radio have given a false picture and kept the public uninformed on the real issues. All agree change is necessary, but the parents must keep the first duty to educate. . . . Every dimunition of this parental right is a step toward statism and collectivism, even if in the name of democracy. We accept the MG goals of protecting the world from a revival of Hitlerism, but the school reform program contains provisions which have nothing

to do with those goals. This intervention is contrary to the principles of federalism and of natural rights of the individual. It would be contrary to the establishment of a true democracy.[126]

The first of April brought more deadlines. Wagoner told Ehard that beginning in September school would be free for all children, as would all materials and books. Furthermore:

> The Munich Pedagogical Institute will be elevated to university level by October 1, 1948. A commission to plan the fifth year of the new six years basic school will be created by May 1; it has until January 1, 1949, to present a detailed plan for starting the new fifth year in 1949. A commission to plan the raising of pedagogical institutes to university level will be appointed May 1, 1948, and will have its detailed plan by January 1, 1949, for the opening of such an institute in 1949.

Wagoner exerted as subtle a pressure on Hundhammer, on 6 May canceling his scheduled trip to the Hague. He wondered a few days later why Hundhammer was reneging on his 5 April promise to have the Munich institute raised to a university as scheduled.[127] A 15 May Clay-Ehard conference about "the Hundhammer problem" ended with Clay accepting Hundhammer's statement that he had never said he could wait out the Americans and that he would still be in office when they had long since left Bavaria. Yet on 27 July, OMGB was informed that "Bishop Muench has further excited the Cardinal [Faulhaber] on the question of the moral right of an occupation power to interfere with the educational system of a conquered people . . . Dr. Hundhammer, presumably in collusion with Bishop Muench, has regained the Cardinal's support of his opposition to school reform." The advice was to issue the order in a few days and tell Faulhaber later.

Wagoner followed the advice. His 4 August order began with the statement that the Landtag had recessed without making a decision. The time had come when MG could no longer watch such delaying tactics. Therefore he issued the following order: (1) from 1 September 1948, no student would have to buy books or other materials; (2) all books and materials were to be given free to students; (3) no school fees would be asked or paid; and (4) no school books would be sold to anyone. All school books and materials were confiscated by MG. According to an observer's report to OMGB the order had an effect.

> On August 4, at 11 a.m., Dr. Ehard called me into his office. I never saw him so furious. He had just received the order. . . . "Are the Americans crazy," he cried, "to send me such a rude order? Are they trying to wreck democracy completely? That is my reward for my attitude at Koblenz and Frankfurt! How can they expect us to work on a constitution for West Germany when such an action is just as bad as the Russian methods; it slaps a constitution and any democratic-minded man in the face. They could not give a better pretext to the Bavarian Party and the Nationalists and the Communists! . . . . I refuse to coop-

erate and have social intercourse with such people in the future. They treat us just like a backward colonial nation. This order will have most serious political consequences and you can be sure that I will speak before the Landtag and will not hide my indignation. I have received many rude letters but this is the worst!"[128]

Life is real and compromises are necessary. Wagoner revised the 4 August order: (1) not less than 50 percent was to be paid by the Land for the first school year; (2) not less than 75 percent was to be paid for the coming school year; (3) for the school year 1950–51, 100 percent would be paid by Land Bavaria. It seemed settled, yet OMGB complained on 15 October that the draft law was not living up to the agreement, and again on 9 December that the draft law provided only for 1948–49, with no mention of the agreement for subsequent years. He would not approve the budget if the deal were not honored. The law was finally passed 5 March 1949. Wagoner expressed his approval. "The accomplishments of the past year, which have been made possible largely through the friendly spirit between the Minister of Education and the Education Branch of MG, are the best proof that democratic cooperation is the most effective way to work."[129]

Nonetheless, Wagoner soon had further reason to be unhappy. He was disappointed that no action had been taken in establishing new pedagogical institutes. He rejected the ministerial argument against increasing the training of elementary teachers. He again had to be concerned with school finances. Writing to Ehard, he restated the terms of the agreement, and then pointed out: "Written and verbal complaints to MG from all parts of Bavaria indicate that during the past year these laws have not been put into effect as many citizens rightly expected them to be. . . . Innumerable complaints report that parents of children attending all kinds of schools have been under duress to purchase textbooks for their children." He was aware of the financial problems from the war, yet tuition was only a fraction of 1 percent of the budget. "It is the considered opinion of MG that the Bavarian Government should fulfill its agreement."[130] Nearly a year later MG was still trying to get compliance with the January 1948 ministerial plan for reform of teacher training. It was also trying to prevent an amendment to the free tuition and textbook deal.

Bavaria came to accept part of these reforms and to delay others, remaining in the rear guard of change in Germany. MG did not leave the scene without another flurry linking reform to confessional schools. Faulhaber felt called upon to complain to McCloy in February 1950 that even Hitler had recognized the Bavarian Concordat with the pope. "Therefore the statements of the deputy U.S. Land commissioner on 4 February to the Landtag represented the sharpest attack ever made on the Concordat and the legal position of the confessional schools." McCloy answered he had not the least intent to make Bavarian schools like American ones or to attack the concordat. Shuster put the matter back to sleep: "The confessional school was a Bavarian matter in which no American wanted to intervene. He could criticize aspects of the Bavarian school system, but ossification was too universal a problem to be regarded as a Bavarian problem."[131] A similar perspective is evident in the judgment of Hildegard Hamm-Brücher (FDP), a liberal expert on Bavarian education and the state secretary for education in the first Willy Brandt cabinet:

> Already in 1945 we had these problems, only then it was a demand of the "victor." I believe that the Allies wanted to help Germany, as they tried to bring a new structure to our educational system—at first they were dictatorial and unfortunately without the least sensitivity; later they were almost touchingly concerned and helpful. What did the "victors" demand then? Scarcely more than had already been demanded in school reform discussions of the 1920s: free education and the same chance for education for all citizens, an extension of compulsory schooling, academic teacher training, democratization of school administration . . . the reaction then was that "the German way was much better." Therefore Germans did everything simply to gain time. Later, with increased sovereignty, people spoke unblushingly of the superiority of the traditional German educational system and refused any further intervention. And the "victors" retreated, at first protesting, at last resigned. . . . One victory in the American zone was the regulation establishing free tuition and supplies. . . . After this era, which was perhaps too critically named an era of "reeducation," no politician dared for years to propose anything which could be construed as approaching the American conception of education. . . . Under the motto "Our schools need peace and quiet," nothing was done for ten years.[132]

Wagoner's period marked at one level the end of one issue. Denazification had pretty well been demolished. It marked the high point of another frustration. It was impossible to effect any school reform as a part of democratization. The more solid democratization had proceeded apace with the continuation of the power of the parties, yet the occupation frustrations experienced by Germans pushed them toward the more reactionary solutions of the BP and briefly away from the conservatism of the CSU. OMGB intervention may have been rarer than before but was perhaps more irritating to confident Bavarians.

The Shuster and Hale Period: A Graceful Bowing Out

On 23 September 1949, Wagoner politely informed Ehard that the Occupation Statute was in effect, something Ehard might have overlooked because he continued to get letters of instruction (take care of the Czech refugees), letters of correction (maintain free trade in the milk industry), or letters of criticism (not enough attention has been shown to Dachau graves). Finally came a friendly farewell from Wagoner. "It has been a pleasure indeed to work with you and your ministers, and I am going away with the feeling that there has been some progress made since I have been Land Director of Bavaria—maybe not as much as we hoped for but being Americans we are never satisfied. . . . Look me up if you ever get to Detroit."[133]

Clarence Bolds, who became acting Land commissioner, had worked his way up through the ranks of MG from labor officer. He began his tenure by explaining to the press that things would be different. His was a new kind of position, a mixture of ambassador and adviser; he was not a commander. Yet a few days later he wrote Ehard that the many American letters which had gone unanswered should finally receive his attention and listed those matters where he expected reform. One of Bolds's innovations was to issue courtesy cards to all Bavarian leaders that said: "The bearer. . . . is by virtue of [his] high position entitled to the utmost courtesy from all American officials."[134] Some Bavarians thought Bolds's style was not courteous enough.

Bolds was replaced 15 July 1950 by Dr. George Shuster, an able president of Hunter College, who has since been praised by all as the ideal representative, an American the Bavarian leaders could regard as their equal and possibly their superior. Ehard described him as extraordinarily well educated: "He knew more about Germany than we did." He was a Catholic of German descent, spoke fluent German, and had already learned through contacts with the Vatican of the Catholic resistance and had met Adenauer in 1938. Because of the war Shuster had dissolved his organization, Loyal Americans of German Descent, despite an FDR request.[135] Soon after Yalta Shuster spoke to the Foreign Policy Association, stressing that such an agreement might have been inevitable, but "would result in the division of Europe into two parts, the reunification of which we should in all probability not see in our time; and second, that the only hope of keeping West Germany lay in proceeding as soon as possible to work with reputable groups in the German population for the rehabilitation of their country." Very few applauded the speech; one listener told him; "That speech of yours was nothing less than an act of high treason."[136] Suspicions of his loyalty closed doors to him, including some opportunities to publish. In the summer of 1945 Patterson asked him to head an historical commission to Germany. On the day when passports were to arrive, he was told he would get none: "A high official said that I could not because of my pro-Nazi past." Patterson intervened and he had permission.[137]

By 1950 Shuster was a man whose time had come. He knew Hoegner, having met him in Zurich during his exile; he described Hoegner as "anticlerical but with a special nuance, a socialist but also a lover of the Wittelsbachs.'' He had met Hundhammer in 1948, and realized that MG difficulties with him had come from "a failure of communication.'' He observed that Bavaria had been regarded as the most Nazi part of Germany because Americans assumed conservatives were the next thing to Nazis. Consequently most American leaders had never bothered to make the acquaintance of Germans except in the most perfunctory way. "Both sides talked to each other across a sort of wall and the resulting misunderstandings were as natural as anything could well be.'' He learned from his first visit that Faulhaber had become troubled because the English *suggest* had been translated into German as *demand*. Shuster also noted: "The U.S. was often represented by good men, but alas also by lechers, traffickers in women, manipulators of the black market, petty protagonists of illiteracy, and fools.''[138]

During his time as Land commissioner Shuster improved relations, making use of kindly suggestions in the hope they would work when brusque orders had not. When he left, McCloy asked him why the cooperation with Bavaria had become so excellent. He replied:

> When I came to Munich the reason for my presence was that relations between ourselves and the Bavarians had reached a kind of sub-zero latitude. . . . I had really done very little except talk to people in their own language, talk to them whenever they wanted me to do so, in the spirit that the new world upon us which we were entering would require of us on both sides the largest measure of friendly cooperation for freedom and justice that we could manage.[139]

One could regret that America sent so few administrators with Shuster's qualifications and that five years of the occupation passed before he could be used. Certainly the increased goodwill during his eighteen months in Bavaria was also due to the less painful policies he was asked to implement. One could also regret that with so much American scrutiny, important abuses, such as the delay in payment to Jewish invalids, continued to be overlooked.[140]

Shuster's successor, Oron J. Hale, later a professor of history at the University of Virginia, continued in the Shuster tradition. He was knowledgeable and physically and intellectually impressive. His wife is often mentioned along with Mrs. McCloy as an ideal ambassadress. During his short term, his major function was to close out the land commissioner's office, transferring its diplomatic functions to the Munich consul, Charles Thayer.

Unfortunately, while relations were excellent at the diplomatic level, American-Bavarian problems persisted. The many troops stayed, and from them came repeated violence against Germans. The month Hale was closing out his office, Ehard had to protest some fifty-six incidents of assault by American troops in Bamberg alone.[141] Ehard's files contain hundreds of cases, usually involving drunken soldiers beating up old and helpless civilians. The bitterness rarely appeared in print, but the Bamberg editor wrote Ehard's office:

this time it can not be pushed away by a few nice words, a cup of coffee and a glass of whiskey. . . . How impossibly we are treated you can see from the following which I can not print. The Press Officer of the 26th Infantry Regiment complained that our paper made too much out of a brutal murder of a taxi driver. His sergeant told us, "You have no right to get excited. Remember what happened in your concentration camps." I never told Americans that because of what they prepared in Yalta, they were responsible for the treatment of the Sudeten Germans by the Czechs and of the Silesians by the Poles. . . . All press officers are now forbidden to give us information. They want to force us to deal with them. Never.[142]

Another matter that caused deep bitterness was housing. As Helmut Penzel reported for the Bavarian government:

> The feelings of these people who have been driven from their houses for seven years has reached a low point and must be taken seriously. One cannot argue with their assertion that the confiscation of their houses seven years after the end of hostilities is against constitutional, international and humane law. . . . it is high time that the federal government gets from HICOG some action as a solution . . . the immediate release of houses standing empty . . . the building of new housing. . . . almost nothing has been built in Bavaria.[143]

Although economic distress was a contributing factor, the period of OMGB's supervision was also the period when there was the most political confusion, corruption, and radicalism. The numerically dominant Catholic peasants and middle class, from whom the CSU in normal times obtained its majorities, were restless. The danger to the CSU came from the BP, who attracted voters angered by MG policies and by the millions of refugees whose expulsion without property meant painful sacrifices to already impoverished Bavarians. The hopes aroused in 1945 by MG's moves toward decentralization were frustrated as Bavarians were again joined to the more numerous "Prussians." Schäffer, kept out of power by MG, returned in 1948 eager either to resume what he considered to be his just place or to carry his massive support to the BP, which he nearly did, leaving the CSU in October 1948.

The party was further shaken in June 1949 by the fall of Josef Müller, brought down by the constant scandals surrounding him and by Hundhammer's unwillingness to compromise with someone so suspect. A group associated with Müller and with August Hausleitner had long held the top positions in the party but had little influence on Ehard's government. Hausleitner was critical of the old men the victors had put in power, and although a deputy party leader himself, broke from the CSU in September 1949 to found another splinter group. A Protestant, he denounced the CSU and Ehard as creatures of the "reactionary" Catholic Hundhammer. Schäffer then rejoined the more purely conservative party. Yet the problem of his competition was resolved when he was immediately elevated to Bonn to be Adenauer's finance minister. (He got a measure of revenge there by resisting occupation costs.)

He and Hundhammer joined the party executive committee in December 1949, and stabilized the right flank defense against the BP. Although the CSU lost enough votes to be forced into a February 1951 coalition with the SPD, it was sufficiently conservative that it could wait for the BP to dissipate itself in what became a corner of extremism and outdated parochialism. Ehard provided the stability and compromise, in coalition with Hoegner, who returned to the justice ministry.

While Ehard was acting the statesman of coalition, a representative of the younger generation of the party, Franz Josef Strauss, was acting the persuader in the back country with the voters.[144] Born in Munich, son of a butcher, Strauss had a brilliant academic record, as good as any in Bavarian history. He served in the war and could speak for the so-called front generation. He returned from war in 1945 with several advantages for a politician. He was very intelligent, he had not been a party member, and he spoke English well, becoming an interpreter for MG and then Landrat in Schongau. He joined the power party and became a passionate missionary for Müller's concept of the CSU as the party of choice for everyone but the socialists. In March 1946 he had shown his oratorical ability in party debate, assisting Müller to victory over Hundhammer, and after brief service in Munich ministries, Müller gave him the job of reorganizing the party. In this task he rarely granted himself even a weekend's rest. "Tirelessly he travelled through the countryside to fight for his party. Provincial functionaries invited him into the most isolated villages. He spared himself nothing." He spoke to peasants in broad dialect, and to intellectuals with foreign phrases. His dynamic, often abrasive, drive was diverted at the proper time for CSU harmony, when he also went to Bonn, there to fight for Adenauer as he had for Müller and the CSU. This left Ehard to mend the party's wounds with gentler phrases.

Quiet descended on the long turbulent party. Hundhammer was eased out as education minister and replaced with a CSU man who could at least talk about reform. By 1952 Müller was all but totally discredited by his involvement in the Auerbach affair. Philip Auerbach, as head of the Jewish community and with apparent MG support, had been so helpful to the Jews, most of whom he furthered toward Palestine, that he had not been overly careful with funds to help them. An enormous scandal brought his trial and suicide.[145] To defeat him, Müller so far exceeded the traditional practices of a justice minister that Ehard had little choice but to release him.

The giants were gone. The big issues pushed by MG were gone, perhaps underground to surface more quietly years later. The biggest issue, whether Bavaria would get its freedom from MG by cooperation or resistance, had been solved by those who cooperated as they resisted. Yet Bavaria in its search for things Bavarian did not retreat to Nazism, contrary to the pessimism of non-Bavarians. It remained perhaps more authoritarian than other sections of Germany, but with a Bavarian touch, and certainly with the support of the majority, who seemed to prefer it that way. Shuster had been essentially America's first ambassador and he performed his role very successfully. His function was not to change Bavaria by any intervention, but rather gently to influence Bavarian leaders toward a consideration of the policies the United States desired. That he attempted to do so very little made for better feelings on both sides. His predecessors had accomplished little but to make the Bavarians angry. Perhaps the Shuster approach changed even less, but it began the reconstruction of goodwill.

Notes

1. Lutz Niethammer emphasized Patton as anticommunist (*Entnazifierung in Bayern* [Frankfurt, 1972], 96). He reported that the Third Army had modified the 20 July 1945 order denazifying industry. Patton described his intent in August as "to occupy myself with the denazification of Bavaria, and the recruiting of the industries of the German people so that they can be more self-supporting" (Constantine Fitzgibbon, *Denazification* [London, 1959], 93).

2. Office of Military Government, *Yearly Report of Political Activities in Bavaria*, 1 July 1946, 1 (hereafter OMGB). Their radio broadcast had led to the surrender of the German army in Norway (Hermann Behr, *Vom Chaos zum Staat* [Frankfurt, 1961], 56). The *Freiheitsaktion* was no alternative to the government, yet it made the U.S. entry easier, as did uncoordinated local groups (Lutz Niethammer, "Amerikanische Besatzung und bayerische Politik, 1945," *Vierteljahreshefte für Zeitgeschichte*, 1967, 177, 194; see also Niethammer, *Entnazifizierung*, 47–48).

3. Some reporters regarded Bavarian affairs in the next few months as an extension of the Flynn-LaGuardia struggle for control of New York City.

4. *PM*, 25 June 1945. Niethammer compared the rule of Keegan's MG to that of the previous Gauleiters; it was an effort to control the bureaucracy from outside by threats (*Entnazifierung*, 64).

5. Quoted by Niethammer, "1945," 179. Critics assumed Keegan was more concerned about the next election in New York. Landeen was a history professor from Washington State College, and Arthur Bromage was a political science professor from Michigan.

6. Karl Hnilicka, ed., *Die Bayerischen Ministerpräsidenten der Nachkriegszeit, 1945–63: Schäffer* (Munich, 1963), 5. Keegan also appointed a farmer, Rattenhuber, as food director because he liked how he had organized milk deliveries to Munich; he was also threatened with arrest should he fail (Behr, 58).

7. Clay Cable to Hilldring, July 1945, National Archives (hereafter NA). Keegan left on "emergency leave" in July.

8. J. F. J. Gillen, *American Influence on the Development of Political Institutions* (Karlsruhe, 1950), 13. The proportion of socialists to Catholics was perhaps not conducive to many of the changes MG desired, but it was representative in terms of subsequent elections.

9. Interview Ernst Anspach; see also Niethammer, "1945," 195; Third U.S. Army of Occupation, *Mission Accomplished* (Frankfurt, 1947), 17.

10. Arthur Kahn, *Betrayal: Our Occupation of Germany* (Warsaw, 1950), 80. Kahn achieved notoriety by fleeing to Warsaw and there writing the book denouncing "the right-wing occupation." Patton had reported other problems, such as internment camps, recommending that

civilian internees arrested by the CIC be released; many were aged or pregnant (Chronology, 27 Aug. 1945, Kansas City Record Center [hereafter KCRC]). Niethammer reports that Patton had some men with unimportant offices released from camps, but that CIC reversed the releases (*Entnazifierung*, 96).

11. Headquarters Third Army, 15 Sept. 1945; "Fragebogen," 3600 B2, *Bayerischestaatskanzlei* (hereafter BSK).

12. *PM,* 31 Aug., 2 Sept. 1945. Howard Becker was a sociologist at the University of Wisconsin.

13. Niethammer, "1945," 201. The *New York Times,* 23 Sept. 1945, quoted him: "This Nazi thing is just like a Democrat-Republican election fight." The other quotation begins with the reporter's question: "After all, general, didn't most ordinary Nazis join their party in about the same way that Americans become Republicans or Democrats?" Patton's answer was: "Something like that" (Ladislas Farago, *Ordeal and Triumph* [New York, 1972], 776).

14. Quoted by Julian Bach, *America's Germany* (New York, 1946), 179.

15. Carl Friedrich, *American Experiences in Military Government in World War II* (New York, 1948), 248.

16. Niethammer, "1945," 205–206.

17. Sims to Ehard, 8 July 1947, *Korrespondenz Militär-regierung* (hereafter *Korrespondenz*), BSK. These arguments were worked out by July 1947 to keep him permanently out of politics. Dorothy Thompson, writing for the liberal *New York Post,* took the same position as that taken by Bavarian leaders: conservatives were also anti-Nazi, and a democratic Bavaria in 1945 would be conservative (*New York Post,* 8 Oct. 1945). Certainly Bavaria voted conservative.

18. Most people forced out before and after Schäffer's dismissal were later cleared and reinstated. Their politically clean colleagues, such as Baer and Riedl, agreed with Schäffer that the real Nazis were already out of office (Interview Dr. Fritz Baer and Dr. Riedl). Baer emphasized that Schäffer's action was out of Christian charity for people he knew were innocent of wrongdoing. MG forbade paying pensions, whereas nearly all persons released in 1933 had been treated less harshly.

19. BSK Files 360, 3600, 3602, 3603, 3615, 1537. One could doubt that Schäffer had sufficient control to have sabotaged even if he wanted to (see Niethammer, *Entnazifierung,* 74–76). "This order is in concord with my own inner attitude and I shall, therefore, be happy to comply with it" (File 3602-1, 30 May, 6 June 1945, BSK; see also "Kleindienst Nachlass," 12 June 1945, Augsburg Stadt Archiv).

20. The Ministry of Education and Religion, in which Nazis had fought to reduce the power of the Catholic church, was also an objective of Schäffer's liberal critics. The ministry had many nominal Nazis. At the top level, of twenty-nine officials, twenty-eight were members, of which nine were active; at the second level, of three officials, three were members, of which two were active; at the third level, of fourteen officials, twelve were members, of which eight were active; at the bottom level, of fifty officials, forty-five were members, of which ten were active (Schäffer to MG-Bavaria, 3602-1, BSK). This policy agreed with the instructions then given him: dismiss members before April 1933 and party officers. Dr. Josef Mayer, who had battled the Nazi foes of the church as he would the American "foes" of the church, was in this ministry, and he objected bitterly to MG's firing of nominal party members as sabotaging the ministry (*Der Wiederaufbau des Bayerischen Volksschulwesens* [Passau, 1965], 40).

21. Miner B. Phillips, Headquarters MG-Bavaria to Minister-president, 3602-1, BSK; handwritten note, presumably Schäffer's, "Aus dem Gedächtnis," 5 July 1945; "Vatican's Hand in Bavaria," *New Masses,* 18 Sept. 1945. A July *Stars and Stripes* quoted Keegan as saying that MG might leave Bavaria by the fall and let the Germans rule it.

22. Regierung President Oberbayern to Schäffer, 11 June 1945, 1537, I; Scharnagl to Schäffer, 8 June 1945, 1537, I; Schäffer to Regional MG, Financial Div., 14 Sept. 1945, 1536, I, BSK.

23. Not all officers were active Nazis. "There were thousands who became officers to avoid the pressures of the party" (Schäffer to Rosshaupter, 20 Aug. 1945, 360, Dmla, BSK).

24. Schäffer Memo to MG, 1 Sept. 1945, OMGUS; "Fragebogen," 3600 B2, BSK; Niethammer, *Entnazifierung,* 107.

25. Robert Murphy, *Diplomat Among Warriors* (Garden City, 1964), 295; Niethammer, *Entnazifierung,* 95. Murphy assumed Patton and some of his officers were not in sympathy with policy, and Bavarian MG had kept Berlin and Frankfurt badly informed. He recommended that Schäffer be replaced, and intended to recommend Rosshaupter (SPD), but Eisenhower had named Hoegner (Murphy Report to Secretary of State, 5 Oct. 1945, CAD 014, NA; OMGB Weekly Report, 18 Oct. 1945, 3).

26. Wilhelm Hoegner, *Der schwierige Aussenseiter* (Munich, 1959), 199–200. The next day Murphy got the public statement changed to "a voluntary resignation."

27. Robert Newmann, "The Political Parties of Germany," *American Political Science Review,* Aug. 1946, 756; Niethammer, "1945," 202–209.

28. Unit 11021, Box 79, 11071, Box 79, passim, KCRC.

29. From a small Texas town, he taught school in Oklahoma until 1917 when he enlisted; after the war he traveled as a polo player; at war he had formed a Ranger unit, and then commanded the Third Division from Sicily (*Overseas News, 7* Oct. 1945, NA).

30. *Süddeutsche Zeitung,* 26 Oct. 1945.

31. Muller was a West Point graduate of November 1918 and served with the occupation near Koblenz. In 1956 he recited a long poem about Koblenz he had written in 1919, "The Flag on Ehrenbreitstein," conveying the sentiment that Germany deserved to be crushed and the proud American flag would return if it tried to rise again. The poem is now in the General Walter Muller Papers in the Hoover Library; the papers are primarily published MG material. In the interwar period he had served as a mathematics teacher, rejoining the army at the end of the depression. As a colonel in an armored division, he entered Morocco and France with Patton and became a highly regarded supply officer.

32. Hoegner, 205; Interviews Dr. Hans Ehard, Baer, and Ernst Deuerlein; Ministerpräsident to Ministries, 7 Nov. 1945, 9731-Bd 2, BSK. Deuerlein remembered that Muller's tantrums had given the minister-presidents many headaches.

33. Baer, CSU head of the chancellory, conceded him to be "a very good administrator . . . a man who could think" (Interview Baer).

34. Friedrich Glum, *Zwischen Wissenschaft und Politik* (Bonn, 1964), 586, 593; Interview Dr. Gebhard Seelos. Glum noted Hoegner's joyous defiance when exceeding the MG speed limit whenever MPs were not to be seen.

35. Third U.S. Army on Hoegner Appointment, 18 Oct. 1945, Muller Papers, CAD, vol. 1. Kroth was rejected as a Nazi; he said he had joined on Communist orders, but MG called him a KPD spy. Scheringer was rejected because he had "resisted" the Rhineland occupation. Herinrich Schmitt was something of an outsider in the KPD because he was too moderate; he moved to the SPD in 1947.

36. Behr, 128.

37. Interview Dr. Ludwig Erhard. He thought there had never been more fraternization than when it was banned (Hoegner, 264).

38. Erhard's reaction at a press conference was: "If it is true, as the saying goes, that subordination is trying to be dumber than your boss we must admit that we belong to those who tend to insubordination" (*Südost Kurier, 7* Sept. 1946; *Tagespiegel,* 28 Sept. 1946).

39. *Die Neue Zeitung,* 6 Jan. 1947; *Wiesbadener Kurier,* 11 Nov. 1947; *Münchener Mittag, 7* Oct. 1947.

40. Not only had MG prevented the party from being "public," but by forbidding travel and not permitting enough paper even to write letters, MG severely handicapped it (Walter Berberich,

10 Jahre CSU in Bayern [Würzburg, 1955], 4). Niethammer criticized MG delay in approving parties. One exception was the speedy approval of the extremist Loritz party, approved on the Land level when it had but one weak county organization. He assumed "connections" (*Entnazifierung*, 84, 95).

41. Berberich, 7; Harold Deutsch, *The Twilight War* (Minneapolis, 1968). Deuerlein quoted Father Leiber of the Vatican as saying that Müller did much less than he claimed, and that when Ehard learned this he lost respect for Müller (Interview Deuerlein).

42. Neumann, 758; William Griffith, "The Denazification Program in the U.S. Zone of Germany" (Ph.D. diss., Harvard University, 1950), 731. Anspach spoke of him as a colorful figure and a brilliant man; he was not fascist nor reactionary, merely a very bad opportunist (Interview Anspach). He also thought Müller guilty of profiting from Nazi pressures on the Jews, as political enemies later charged. Harold Hurwitz describes his anger at not getting a newspaper (*U.S. Military Government in Germany: Press Reorientation* [Karlsruhe, 1950], 136).

43. Walter Dorn, "Notes," 254–72, Institut für Zeitgeschichte, Munich. His fear of monarchism was unwarranted (Paul Burns, Local Government Section, to Director, 14 May 1946, OMGB). Although Burns denied that MG was at fault, Schweizer admitted that it was divided on centralization, and that some MG offices were behind the centralist push (Government Structures Branch, 3 Oct. 1946, Arthur Schweizer, CAD, OMGB, Washington National Record Center [hereafter WNRC]).

44. Third Army G-5 Report, 29 Jan. 1946, 30 Jan. 1946, KCRC; OMGB, Cumulative Historical Report, 30 June 1946, WNRC.

45. Muller to Ehard, 14 Apr. 1946, with copy of MG to Schäffer, 24 Apr. 1946, *Korrespondenz*. *Time,* and most German analysts, thought MG had foreseen his victory and so banned him on election eve (*Time,* 6 May 1946; *Passauer Neue Presse,* 6 May 1946).

46. "Schäffer enjoyed a popularity in the party because of his definite programs, whereas Müller is greatly criticized because of his lack of a decided platform" (OMGB Weekly Report No. 53, May 1946).

47. Muller to Hoegner, 9 July 1946; Muller to Bavarian Ministers, 20 July 1946, 9731-Bd. 2, BSK.

48. Gillen, *American,* 24, based on AG OMGUS 010.0 Const. Bavaria. Hoegner's views explain why he was often on good terms with conservatives like his close friend, Hundhammer (Glum, 586; OMGUS Chronologies, June 1946 to Dec. 1946, 24 Oct. 1946, OMGUS; J. F. J. Gillen, *State and Local Government in West Germany, 1945–53* (Mehlem, 1953), 50.

49. Col. Garde, Adj. Gen., to MG Directors, 30 Sept. 1946, 9731-Bd. 2, BSK; see also Dorn, "Notes," 357; Dorothy Thompson, *New York Post,* 8 Oct. 1945.

50. *New York Herald Tribune,* 18 July 1946, 23 July 1946; Hoegner, 261–63. A macabre local MG tyranny was reported in October 1946. Bodies were found, presumably killed two years before by some SS unit. All villagers over six years old living near the spot were ordered to dig out the bodies, to clean them, removing eyes and brains, and to brush the teeth. Then they were ordered to run a gauntlet; fifty-two were beaten (Report in Box 102-3/15, OMGUS, WNRC).

51. The analyst found the SPD equally lacking in talent except for Hoegner, "the only urbane, cultivated, adroit, and political personality in the present political life in Bavaria" (Third Army Intelligence Reports, No. 80, 4 Dec. 1946, KCRC).

52. Hoegner, 281. Müller had more support at OMGUS than at OMGB (Niethammer, 196).

53. Murphy, 16 Dec. 1946, Cable, OPD 091 014, NA.

54. Third Army Intelligence Report, No. 82, 18 Dec. 1946, KCRC; Dr. Hundhammer, "Dokumente zur Bayerischen Politik, Die Bildung des Kabinets Ehard," Vertraulich, Ms, n.d.

55. Burns Memo, 13 Dec. 1946, OMGB.

56. Hundhammer, 9; Hoegner, 284; Glum, 596. Hoegner wrote privately that he had stopped

Müller despite the latter's MG friends, and that Pfeiffer's past had taken him out (Hoegner letter intercept, 102-2/15, OMGUS, WNRC).

57. One can believe Ehard wanted Loritz to ruin himself by denazifying. Niethammer thought Ehard assumed MG would make him behave. Ehard said again in 1970 he did it for votes, since he could not be sure of his CSU support.

58. Third Army Intelligence Report, No. 83, 25 Dec. 1946, KCRC. "Few units have sufficient personnel to conduct intelligent polls of public opinion and only too often the conclusions of local detachments are based on flattery of people who want favors or on denunciations of persons whose attitude is not objective" (OMGUS letter 14 Jan. 1947, OMGB Legal Division, OMGUS). The anti-Müller people at OMGB were transferred: Anspach, Reese, and McMahon to Hesse, and Jackson and Vacca to Württemberg-Baden. Special Branch Officer Johnson left for the U.S. and was replaced by Griffith (Niethammer, 198).

59. Deuerlein blamed his social reticence for the cool relations with the rising young man of the party, Franz Josef Strauss (Interview Deuerlein).

60. Hnilicka, *Ministerpräsidents: Dr. Hans Ehard* (Munich, 1963), 9–10.

61. OMGB, CAD, Bradford to Schweizer, 22 Jan. 1947, OMGUS 98-1/5; Third Army Intelligence Report 87, 22 Jan. 1947, KCRC.

62. Glum report 4 Mar. 1947 on Berlin conferences 24 and 28 Feb. 1947, Ehard *Nachlass*, BSK; Schweizer, CAD to Min. Pres., 11 Apr. 1947, *Korrespondenz*, BSK.

63. OMGB, Education and Religious Branch, Annual Report, 14 July 1947. This interference particularly affected medical facilities. OMGB reported that OMGUS had handled the case badly (OMGB, ICD, Annual Report, 15 July 1947).

64. OMGB, CAD Memorandum to Deputy Director OMGB, 15 May 1947.

65. Litchfield, OMGUS, CAD Division to Clay, "Operations of MG in Bavaria," 6 Sept. 1947, 147-3/15, OMGUS, WNRC.

66. OMGUS, CAD, Policy Enforcement Branch, "Review of MG Relationships with Civil Authorities in Bavaria," to Director, CAD, 14–22 July 1947, OMGUS, WNRC.

67. "It is doubtful that the statistics on this form are used in OMGUS; they are definitely not used in OMGB" (OMGUS, Government Structures Branch, "Report on Internal Affairs Division and Staff Branches of OMGB," Comstock Glaser, 21 July 1947, OMGUS, WNRC).

68. OMGUS, "Review of Functional Divisions," August 1947, 2, OMGUS, WNRC.

69. OMGB, Legal Div. to Director, 20 Aug. 1947, OMGUS, NA. A woman was given a fourteen-day sentence because the judge thought someone else should run her movie theater and a jail sentence would take her license. A woman was given six months because she charged an officer with having "goosed" her; he had denied it. A mother was given one month because she had said that a soldier during a house search had fondled the "pelvic area" of her thirteen-year-old daughter; no attempt was made to prove it had not happened. A man was given eighteen months for writing General Muller that Special Branch had used violence to get a statement; he was charged with a false statement, although no evidence was presented.

70. Muller to Ehard, 12 Aug. 1947, *Korrespondenz*, BSK.

71. The meeting would end on a sad note: Clay had decided that Muller would return to the states on 15 November ("Gespräch mit General Muller," 20 Aug. 1947, Ehard *Nachlass*, IV, BSK).

72. Muller to Ehard, 22 Aug. 1947, Reparation, 977, BSK.

73. Muller to Ehard, 2, 3, 4, 17 Sept. 1947, *Korrespondenz*, III, BSK; Schweizer, "Vermerke über die Besprechung der CAD mit Ankermüller," 24 Sept. 1947, *Korrespondenz*, IV, BSK.

74. Muller to Ehard, 11 Nov. 1947, *Korrespondenz*, Innenminister to Ministerpräsident, 19 Nov. 1947, 9731-Bd. 3, BSK.

75. Muller to Ehard, 15 Nov. 1947, *Korrespondenz;* Ehard to Ministries, 26 Nov. 1947, 9731 Bd. 3, BSK; Muller to Ehard, 26 Nov. 1947, *Korrespondenz*, BSK.

76. Hoegner, 9 Nov. 1945, 3600-B2, BSK. He later expressed concern for the fate of the "little

man'' entangled in this law, but many who lived under Nazism doubted he understood that little man's problem (Pfeiffer, 14 Nov. 1945, 3600-B2, BSK). This file includes more varieties of life than MG had dreamed of in its philosophy. Niethammer thought implementation had been erratic. The "Morgenthau Boys" had cleaned the finance ministry though it was unpolitical. Businessman Lange, less sympathetic to officials, had been tough. Rattenhuber, food director, threatened a slowdown in deliveries and got a deal with MG to slow down denazification (Niethammer, 74–76).

77. Minister-president notes for discussion with Truscott, October 1945, *Massnahmen*, 360 Dmla., *Protokoll, Ministerialrat*, 24 Nov. 1945, 360 Bd. 3, BSK.

78. Niethammer, 158–60.

79. Hoegner, 233–34; John Kormann, *U.S. Denazification, 1944–50* (Bad Godesberg, 1952), 25, 28; Niethammer, 164. Hoegner told his cabinet 11 June of Clay's threat to suspend the government. Müller later said he hadn't signed. Dorn wrote Clay: "If Dr. Müller is unable to commit the CSU Policy Committee to an unreserved support for the law, some reorganization of . . . that committee is called for" (Kormann, 84; Parkman to Clay, 11 June 1946).

80. Hoegner's defense was that compared to the former MG enforcement, this law was an improvement.

81. *Vormerkung für Reden mit Reese and Johnson*, 23 Apr. 1946, *Staatsministerium für Sonderaufgaben*, 1537, BSK; Kormann, 75. Keeping Schmitt in office countered objections that Bavaria was dominated by reactionaries.

82. Kormann, 92–93. Griffith speculated that Hoegner saw the job as a way of crippling Pfeiffer (726–27); Niethammer, 166.

83. Pfeiffer to Reese, 15 July 1946, 360-1, BSK; Hoegner to Ehard, 18 July 1946; Hoegner to Pfeiffer, 24 July 1946, 360-1, BSK. He told Pfeiffer that claims of "resistance to the party" must mean "active" resistance, and not just a vague "noncompliance" with party orders.

84. Reese, "Elaboration of 17 May Denazification," 10 June 1946; Reese OMGB order, 12 Aug. 1946, General Walter Muller Papers, Hoover War Library; Muller to all Detachments, 29 July 1946, 17 Aug. 1946, Muller Papers.

85. Niethammer provides the Bavarian cabinet reaction and that of the Bavarian constitutional convention reaction (191–95).

86. Al Sims to Erhard, 19 Nov. 1946, with copy of Clay to Director OMGB, CC8318, 360-1, BSK. Hoegner got helpful advice from Col. Dawson: "When Clay drags out his statistics of poor denazification, the only way to counter is have more statistics about good denazification." Dawson said confidentially: "Clay was under heavy attack when he permitted these tribunals, and many people are trying now to prove that he was wrong" (Hoegner memo of conference, 5 Nov. 1946, 360-1, BSK.

87. Niethammer, 202–15; John Wickham, 11 Oct. 1945, 1537 Bd., 2, BSK; *Newsweek*, 7 July 1947; Griffith, 736, 739; Special Branch, OMGB report 10 March 1947, OMGUS 92-3/13, WNRC.

88. Muller to Ehard, 20 May 1947, 3621, BS1p, BSK. Ehard passed the letter on to Loritz and again asked him to reply to his earlier requests for information (OMGB Denazification Branch, Quarterly Report, July–September 1947, 6).

89. Sims to Ehard, 11 Feb. 1947, including TWX Office of MG Germany, 7 Feb. 1947. Appeals courts later would cancel most sentences. "Clay has ordered that the ratio of one tribunal per 500 internees be established by 15 April 1947" (Muller to Ehard, 3 Apr. 1947, *Korrespondenz*, I, BSK). This is a very large number for inmates, and possibly mistaken.

90. Meiser to Loritz, 16 Apr. 1947, 3621 BS10, BSK. A Landtag member protested the Augsburg camp for women: with the women were 24 children between six weeks and two years old; 55 women were under twenty years of age; 69 had children under sixteen; there were nine cold water faucets for 400 persons, and no warm water even for infants; wash rooms were

open, with no light; latrines were open and distant; rooms had only beds, and no privacy (Maria Deku to Sachs, 7 July 1947, 3621 BS10, BSK; Sachs to Deku, 5 Sept. 1947; 3621 BS10, BSK).

91. Muller to Ehard, 19 July 1947, 360 Bd. 2, BSK; *Main Echo*, 2 Sept. 1947; Griffith, 740.

92. Wagoner to Ehard, 30 Mar. 1948, *Korrespondenz*, VII, BSK; Niethammer, 253–54. He analyzed in depth 300 cases picked at random.

93. OMGUS, Public Information Release, 8 Oct. 1947; Interview Deuerlein.

94. Wagoner to Ehard, 12 Dec. 1947, *Korrespondenz*, V, BSK; Fuller description in BSK, Pfeiffer *Nachlass*, No. 8, "Ernährung-Landwirtschaft." An MG spot-check potato dig found 45 percent more than the German estimate (Ingwalson to Ehard, 13 May 1948, *Korrespondenz*, VII, BSK). Most Bavarians resented the higher DP ration which they thought destined for the black market; they believed that many DPs were not in Germany as a result of Hitler, but had fled after the war away from communism or toward Palestine.

95. Baumgartner to Ehard, 6 Nov. 1947, 1101 Bizonal, BSK. He complained to Ehard that the Frankfurt organization was a dictatorship, recreating the hated Reich Food Office with all of its Prussian bureaucrats, led by Schlange-Schöningen's socialist deputy.

96. Otto Seeling to Ehard, 1 Jan. 1948; Ehard answer 4 Feb. 1948; 1101 Bizonal, BSK; OMGUS Chronology, 1 Feb. 1948, WNRC.

97. Loriaux to Ehard, 16 Jan. 1948; Sims, 20 Jan. 1948; Wagoner to Ehard, 16 Jan. 1948; Wagoner to Ehard 27 Jan. 1948, *Korrespondenz*, BSK.

98. OMGB memo, "First Meeting of German-American Cultural Relations Group," at Haus der Kunst, 3 Feb. 1948.

99. Ehard to CSU, 17–18 July 1948, 150-3/13, OMGUS, WNRC; Wagoner to Ehard, 4 Aug. 1948, *Korrespondenz*, BSK.

100. Wagoner to Ehard, Order No. 11, 10 Jan. 1949 and Order No. 12, 21 Jan. 1949, *Korrespondenz*, BSK. For example, MG vetoed the "Bavarian Law on the Auditing of State Accounts," and the "Law for Market Regulations for the Food Economy."

101. OMGB, CAD to Director, Intelligence Division OMGUS, 9 Mar. 1949.

102. Dorn, "Notes," 27–29, 37–41, 44–64. Emphasis in original.

103. Peter H. Merkl, *The Origins of the West German Republic* (New York, 1963), 154–59. Merkl gave Hundhammer credit for more sophistication than Ehard did, if MG understood his position; MG reported Ehard saw Hundhammer as his greatest problem in joining Bonn. Ehard was pressured by the Franken CSU, which threatened to join Adenauer's CDU if Ehard cooperated with the BP (Penzel Report to Bradford, Chief, Government and Politics Branch, CAD, OMGB, 31 May 1949; OMGUS Intelligence Report, signed Sear, 17 June 1949; Report to CAD on Annual CSU Assembly, 3 June 1949, 150-3/13, OMGUS, WNRC).

104. Wagoner to Ehard, 20 June 1949, and 5 July 1949, *Korrespondenz;* Section on WAV, 25 July 1949; J. Müller to Ehard, 25 July, 26 July 1949; *Parteien*, Bd. 12, 112, BSK.

105. *Oberstaatsanwalt München* I to Müller, 27 July 1949, *Parteien*, Bd., 12. Auerbach was in a long feud with Müller which would destroy them both (J. Müller to Wagoner, 2 Aug. 1949, *Parteien*, Bd., 12, 112, BSK). Ehard doubted that OMGUS was happy with Bolds's intervention, because the impression was created that MG was protecting a demagogue. "Loritz goes all over the country insulting everyone, but also saying over and over again that he wants the trial before the election. Then he runs to MG and says, 'You have to protect me, I don't want the trial right now.' I would not like to assert that MG wants to protect him, but in many things they are so formalistic that you can only wonder" (*Akten der Abteilung* II, BSK; Interview Ehard).

106. Gillen, *State*, 76. Hoegner in October showed his lack of support for the MG order for the personnel office. He was not sure whether he could find a room for it; the office had no authority (Bavarian Ministerrat, 19 Oct. 1946; Niethammer, 181).

107. The conflict was between two democratic conceptions. The Germans wanted to continue the political rights of the officials, but Americans saw a conflict of interest (Eckhard Heintz, "Der Beamtenabgeordnete im bayerischen Landtag" [Ph.D. diss., Berlin University, 1966], 113). Perhaps because of MG criticism, the level dropped to about 28 percent until the 1960s, when it returned to the 34 percent level.

108. Wagoner to Ehard, 7 Feb. 1949, *Korrespondenz*, XIII, BSK.

109. Wagoner to Ehard, 18 June 1949, *Korrespondenz*, XIII, BSK.

110. Wagoner, quoted in Gillen, *State*, 75.

111. Shuster to Minister-president, 17 May 1951, *Korrespondenz*, BSK; Gillen, *State*, 91. In 1970 Dr. Riedl, ministerial director of the interior ministry, saw considerable change. The personnel office had worked well, relieving him of a worrisome chore; his deputy had worked his way up from the ranks and did not possess the legal degree formerly required (Interview Riedl).

112. Vacca to Hoegner, 2 Oct. 1947, "Gemeindeordnung," 2400, I, BSK.

113. OMGUS Chronology, Feb. 1948, 154, WNRC. The system has since evolved into a more sophisticated system for voter choice than the U.S. has. See Wagoner, 17 Jan. 1949, *Korrespondenz*, XII, BSK.

114. Ritter von Lex had gone along with MG suggestions, but Lex had been pushed upstairs to Bonn (Clark to Dayton, 12 Jan. 1949, Political Affairs Div., OMGB).

115. A democratic device, pushed hard for in 1948–51, was the *Bürgerversammlung* (Citizens' Assembly). Gillen gave the occupation credit that the idea was retained even in a watered-down form. Munich Consul Thayer observed that it was little used, considering the effort made. Other than in villages, where the idea was old, it caught on mostly as a device which skillful mayors used to make contacts and win votes (Gillen, *State*, 23–25; Charles Thayer, *The Unquiet Germans* [New York, 1957], 35).

116. J. Mayer, 40. OMGB ordered no offices held open for party members and Hoegner assured them none was (Hoegner to CAD-OMGB, 4 Sept. 1946; Niethammer, 181).

117. J. Mayer, in Hans Seidel, *Festschrift zum 70. Geburtstag von Dr. Hans Ehard* (Munich, 1957), 165.

118. Mayer, 70; Karl Hnilicka, *Bayerische Profile: Hundhammer* (Munich, 1965), 10.

119. Alexander was personally sympathetic but very impractical and undiplomatic, a pure theoretician who never understood the opposition. Glum assumed the American concepts derived from Deweyism and the teachers' colleges (Glum, 599, 604–8).

120. OMGUS to OMGB, 10 Jan. 1947, in *Akten des Bayerischen Staatministeriums für Unterricht und Kultus* (hereafter BSUK); Pfeiffer to Hundhammer, 3 Feb. 1947, Ehard *Nachlass*, BSK.

121. Al Sims to Minister-president, 27 Feb. 1947, *Korrespondenz*, BSK; *Ministerial Denkschrift*, 5 Mar. 1947, BSUK; Hundhammer to MG, 31 Mar. 1947, BSUK.

122. Gumppenberg Report, 23 May 1947, Ehard *Nachlass*, IV, BSK. That a child must remain in one or the other educational track has long been a bitter German complaint about the system.

123. Gumppenberg Report, 19 June 1947, Ehard *Nachlass*, IV, BSK. The reform had been proposed by Prelate Meixner without consulting the ministry. It suggests that bureaucrats, not CSU politicians, prevented change.

124. Clay to Ehard, 18 Nov. 1947, *Korrespondenz*, BSK; Ehard to Hundhammer, 18 Nov. 1947, BSUK; Mayer, 115.

125. Critics quoted Lydia Sherwood, "Lost in the World," *Vogue*, 1 Feb. 1947, *Spezialia*, 1947, BSUK; *Arbeitsgemeinschaft für deutsche Fragen*, University of Chicago, and "Memo re Report of U.S. Educational Mission to Germany," 11 Feb. 1948, all in 1948 file, BSUK.

126. Faulhaber to Muench, 7 Jan. 1948, *Schulreform*, Pfeiffer *Nachlass*, BSK; Martin Mayes Office Memo, Jan. 1948, OMGB. The OMGB education office thought Faulhaber was much

more reasonable than those about him, including Muench; the latter's secretary called the reform "communistic;" Hundhammer had misinformed the cardinal on the number of new teacher-training institutions and on the feared closing of the *Caritas* kindergartens; neither Faulhaber nor Meiser was against school reform, and both wanted the matter settled quietly.

127. Wagoner to Ehard, 1 Apr. 1948; Wagoner to Ehard, 6 May 1948; Wagoner to Ehard 10 June 1948, *Korrespondenz*, VII, BSK; also Clay remarks 6 May, 14 May 1947, Pfeiffer *Nachlass*, BSK; Edward F. Kennedy to Land Director, OMGB, "Muench and Faulhaber," 27 July 1948, OMGB.

128. Wagoner Order, 4 Aug. 1948, *Korrespondenz*, BSK; Penzel to Sims, 4 Aug. 1948, CAD Information Office, OMGB. Hundhammer and Finance Secretary Krauss were quoted as saying that Bavaria could not raise the education money because it was paying so much in occupation costs.

129. *Hochlandbote*, 10 Aug. 1948; Wagoner to Ehard, 22 Sept. 1948, *Korrespondenz*, BSK. This deal he based on a Clay letter to Ehard of 21 September. See also Winning to Hundhammer, 15 Oct. 1948; Wagoner to Ehard, 9 Dec. 1948, 15 Apr. 1949, *Korrespondenz*, BSK.

130. Wagoner to Ehard, 8 Sept., 22 Sept. 1949; Winning to Hundhammer, 11 Aug., 18 Aug. 1950, *Korrespondenz*, BSK.

131. Quoted in Mayer, 87; Shuster press conference, 17 May 1951, 9731, BSK.

132. Hildegard Hamm-Brücher, "Das Schulwunder fand nicht statt," in Helmut Hammerschmidt, ed., *Zwanzig Jahre Danach* (Munich, 1965), 439–40.

133. Wagoner to Ehard, 23 Sept., 14 Oct., 10 Oct., 21 Oct., 24 Oct. 1949, *Korrespondenz*, BSK.

134. Clarence Bolds, press conference, 4 Nov. 1949; Bolds to Ehard, 9 Nov. 1949; Bolds, 1 May 1950, 9731, BSK.

135. "On this occasion he assured me of his interest in and respect for the German people, despite the necessary hostility to Hitler. But we felt that we could not put ourselves so blatantly into the political arena" (George Shuster, *The Ground I Walked On* [New York, 1961], 70–71).

136. Ibid., 72.

137. Ibid., 75.

138. Ibid., 191–94, 195.

139. Ibid., 208.

140. Society of Jewish Invalids to McCloy, 2 Apr. 1951. "Not a single pension payment has been fixed for Jewish widows, orphans and invalids to date."

141. Hale to Ehard, 2 Jan. 1952, "Besatzung," Ehard *Nachlass*, BSK; Ehard to Hale, 11 Jan. 1952, BSK.

142. Editor, *Fränkischer Tag*, Bamberg, to Deuerlein, 9 Jan. 1952; 974, BSK.

143. Helmut Penzel, *Betr. Besatzung beschlagnahmter Wohnraum*, 12 May 1952, Ehard *Nachlass*, BSK; Albrecht Montgelas and Carl Nützel, *Wilhelm Hoegner* (Munich, 1957), 80.

144. Erich Kuby, *Franz Josef Strauss* (Munich, 1963), 94–97.

145. See File under "Auerbachprozess," 5703, BSK.

7 Local Variations: Augsburg, Friedberg, Eichstätt, Nuremberg

Among the many fine analyses of the American occupation of Germany, there is only one which discusses the occupation in depth at the local level, John Gimbel's study of Marburg in *A German Community under American Occupation* (1962).[1] This pioneering work describes a German liberal elite whose efforts to reconstruct a democratic order were frustrated by an ill-advised local MG. Marburg, as a relatively small town with a relatively large university, was possibly atypical. One must examine many more communities in order to discover the many variations in local implementation of central policy. Neglecting to tell how government actually touched the lives of the people leaves the story of the occupation only half told. Too much historical writing looks only at the top, leaving to the imagination what happens elsewhere. But in fact, if one looks at the grass roots, it becomes evident that the policies bitterly argued, and the decisions proudly if sometimes hesitantly made, would appear to have had few results and rarely to have reached the average person.

The four communities studied in the following pages are by no coincidence the same four I studied for the Hitler period.[2] My investigation of persons and documents in Augsburg, Eichstätt, Friedberg, and Nuremberg not only incited further curiosity about the history of these interesting towns, but also served as a necessary introduction to the leading personalities of each and, to a lesser extent, to the available documentary sources. To evaluate the occupation one should have some knowledge of what occurred before it, or one can be amazed, as, for example, by the fact that the mayor of Augsburg from 1933 to 1945 was treated gently by the denazification trial after the war. The documentation of MG activity in the four communities, however, was disappointingly scanty. From that scarcity of footprints on the sands of MG time came the conclusion that the sound and fury in Washington and Berlin meant very little at the local level. Interviews of participants and the evidence of local documents, whether of German or American origin, were noteworthy for their triviality. People remembered very little of consequence and they recorded very little of consequence. It may be embarrassing to Americans that the occupation all came down to so little, but so says the record.

What should also be evident in this community-by-community analysis is that there were certain important variables in each town. These included the personalities of American officers and of German officials, at first selected by Americans but later elected; the nature of the communities themselves, large and small; the presence or absence of occupation troops; and the strength of other institutions, such as political parties, unions, and churches. Some communities were peaceful; some were turbulent. In some the personalities of the military governors were noticeable; in others the personalities were lost behind the bureaucracies necessary to govern more than a few thousand people. Yet throughout, one's impression is that there was great German continuity and very little American change.

The Augsburg Experience: From Disruption to Petty Annoyance

Augsburgers have long prided themselves on being atypical. They are, on the one hand, more conservative than other Germans, which is evidenced by a CSU strength unusual for an industrial center of 180,000. On the other hand, the city could properly also consider itself unusually liberal in its commitment to freedom, which it traces to its medieval and Renaissance glory, an urban autonomy that persisted in part even under Hitler. It strove also for freedom from the occupation in resisting the advice and intrusion of outsiders, who were welcomed as long as they enabled the Augsburgers to live their own lives as before.

The events of April–May 1945 in Augsburg were like those in many communities, except perhaps in the degree of disobedience by its mayor. Almost half the city had already been destroyed by Allied bombing.[3] To prevent further destruction, Mayor Josef Mayr and Gauleiter Karl Wahl defied the Berlin order to fight to the last man. So did a Resistance group, which became active only to assist the surrender. On 27 April, its leader got a call from the U.S. Third Division threatening an attack of 2,000 bombers in a half-hour unless the city surrendered. The resistance and Mayor Mayr cooperated in taking prisoner the commanding general, who believed that orders were orders.[4] The city was taken with little further damage and little loss of life, but oddly all those who arranged the surrender were later ignored or arrested.[5]

The Augsburgers were relieved that no one need fear the war or the Nazis any longer. Fritz Aumann's mother's "Thank God," on seeing Americans was a sentiment echoed by most. Aumann remembered the immediate GI friendliness to him and other children.[6] Some women also had privileges. "The Americans had everything that was so bitterly lacking: candy, stockings, soap, liquor, cigarettes—and an untroubled joy of life."[7] But while some soldiers were giving children and some women food, other soldiers were robbing other adults. Ironically, the members of the resistance, the first to see the Americans, were the first of many to lose cars, watches, and wedding rings.

The next group systematically plundered were the police; those at headquarters were taken from their bunker to the street where the thefts were supervised by American tankmen. All police cars were stolen.[8] Those police not arrested were told the next day they could continue as police, but in civilian clothes with an armband and without weapons. Not only were the police helpless against the plunderers, particularly the DPs, but these were often protected by sympathetic Americans. Several police were killed. "It was strictly forbidden for the German police to try to stop American soldiers with weapons from any crime or even to defend themselves from attacks by drunken GIs. And violence from the Americans was even more frequent during 'The wild year' than later."[9] Weeks later MG relented. Each station got one rifle and five bullets.

The hardship caused by plunder and senseless destruction was made worse by the long-time lack of industrial production. Augsburgers later blamed the occupation for not having supported law and order until nearly everything was stolen. Even MG reports registered complaints when plundering by one American unit caused problems for another: "Very shortly after the capture of Augsburg, 7th Army HQ was established in the city. When the 7th Army HQ moved to Heidelberg, a very large amount of furniture and a large number of automobiles (German) were removed from the city and the Landkreis causing considerable difficulties on the part of this detachment in reestablishing the adequate transportation facilities."[10]

Amid the ruins and chaos faint glimmerings of order emerged. As the city was taken, Dr. Wilhelm Ott, who had been retained as city treasurer 1933–45 by Mayor Mayr, though he had never joined the Nazi party, was told by Mayr he should take over the city. At 3:30 the first afternoon, Ott was ordered to MG headquarters in the railroad offices. Mayr and his two assistants were there; they were soon called out and arrested without warning.[11] Ott recalled the scene: "Then I was asked to come into the office. At the desk sat two officers . . . Colonel Joublanc spoke no German, or very little, and I no English . . . the interpreter was a fluent German-born soldier. . . . Without much introduction Joublanc observed that the former mayor was no longer there and they had heard that I could work hard; they wanted to make me mayor!" Ott, whose stubbornness had kept him politically clean, answered he thought that was illegal because Mayr was the elected mayor. According to the law he could be acting mayor if the two men above him could not act. Joublanc agreed. "I could hire staff where and how I liked. The only limitation was that men who had been active politically for the NSDAP should not be given a leading position. The officer made this limitation quite clear by stating, 'A member of the NSDAP who was not particularly active politically could be given a leading position in the city administration, and a member who had been active could, for example, be employed as streetcar conductor.'" Ott should merely tell them the next day who would be employed.

Ott worked out the lists "to keep the level of efficiency at least equal to that during the Third Reich." He knew only he and Dr. Josef Kleindienst as department heads had avoided joining the party, but most of the others had joined only after 1933 and had not been active. MG had no objection. "Dealing with MG was not only without friction but almost without exception took place in a pleasant fashion, even courteously." He could discuss matters freely with his counterpart, a Major Towe, a former professor of administrative law at the University of Toledo.[12]

Much of the German-American communication was oral, particularly at first. (A German official who had observed the German occupation in France noted that what was not in writing would be hard to prove later.) The written record, however, gives the best available insight into MG activity, though like most of the interaction that can be documented, this activity was strangely trivial. The city file for the first month contains several items. Taken together, they suggest that MG was concerned first with its own comfort, second with keeping Germans out of the way, and third with merely passing on orders. For example, the first written MG communication was an order to take the piles of rubble away from the luxury hotel where the officers were staying, while the second announced that *die Herren der Militärregierung* wanted a barbershop set up at their headquarters. MG also made clear it was not only permissible but expressly desired that businesses reopen; Hitler's rationing system and price controls should continue.[13]

Other MG orders were more disruptive of German life. A mimeographed sheet listed MG's ten commandments: (1) everyone must obey MG; (2) curfew was from 1830 hours to 0700; (3) no one could leave the city; (4) DPs had the first claim on all necessities; (5) weapons, munitions, carrier pigeons, and radios must be turned in; (6) no Germans were allowed in MG buildings; (7) any streets used by military convoys were closed to civilian traffic; (8) everyone was to read and obey the orders; (9) if the city needed more police, it should get them; and (10) it should not expect MG to provide food, clothing, or medicine.[14] On 16 May MG ordered that no German could be outside his home except to purchase food between 11:00 a.m. and 1:00 p.m.; guards were to shoot violators. No one was allowed to go more than six kilometers from his home.[15] Other orders included the requirement that Ott set up a special city account to pay all army bills and that "stores" could be open but approval was necessary for "factories."[16] On 24 May Major William Wiles asked for a list of all city employees, and reminded the city to circulate "the questionnaires."

Other early occupation documents reveal a strange mixture of compassion and brutality. One letter makes clear that MG did not want to be bothered with civilians: anyone wanting something from MG must go to the city administration.[17] By 30 May Joublanc and Towe agreed the animals in the zoo must be saved; early the same day a man riding a bicycle to work was shot by an American sentry.[18] Yet Ott was impressed to see the town major show concern for the long lines of people waiting to get permits to travel; he might notice PWs trying to get home and order a truck to take them as far as Ulm. The reasonable Schwaben MG officers were "less impressed with the extent of their power than with the extent of their responsibility," but Ott noticed "the cold wind which was to end the spring blossoms of recovery." He was ordered by the CIC to fire his department heads.[19] MG had appealed to a general "with wide-reaching authority," but to no avail.[20] Ott's spring came abruptly to an end with the arrival on 8 June of Major Everett S. Cofran as commander for a new city MG. Unfortunately Cofran is the only MG commander whose name and image have survived clearly in Augsburg, although he was there for a single summer.

Major Cofran had a sign hanging behind his desk: "I hate all Germans." Why did he hate them? "Were it not for them, I would be America's most famous architect."[21] On his desk he had a large card with the number of American dead, and he told Ott: "If I ever weaken in the fight against National Socialism, a look at the number of the dead always gives me new strength."[22] Cofran took a large apartment house for himself and his officers and an imposing building near the police headquarters for his offices.[23] He demanded the city hall's Rathskeller as his restaurant, but he came to Ott's office only once—to collect furniture, including a gold lamp. He also demanded two cameras, including the customary Leica. On the other hand, Cofran was satisfied with the flowers delivered to his office each morning, while other officers were not.[24]

Cofran's treatment of Ott was usually dictatorial. He was ordered to be at Cofran's office punctually every morning. He sometimes had a long wait, but received no explanation or apology, and there was sometimes no reason for a meeting. Ott kept making up the required reports twice a week, but since they took so much time, he had half of his department heads to report on the first one, and the other half on the second. The half-report was apparently not noticed; it was always praised. He had to get approval for every trip outside the city. His phone was tapped and once Cofran demanded that Ott defend an admittedly wiretapped statement. Ott observed that Cofran reacted in a "human fashion" only on one occasion. He had threatened to send Ott to prison, to which Ott answered, "Any time." Cofran became thoughtful, saying: "You are older than I." Then he sent the interpreter out of the room, got up and handed Ott a pack of cigarettes over the desk. A pathetic effort at conversation followed; Cofran spoke no German.

Much of the MG activity during Cofran's summer concerned denazification. At his first meeting with Ott, Cofran had said: "The previous policy is at an end. You should know that today a new policy begins." He ordered Ott to implement a new questionnaire. Schwaben MG had not been particularly interested in the old ones, even those of the leading office holders. Yet Cofran had given otherwise no new definition of policy; on the contrary, Ott was told by officers assigned to technical jobs that more consideration would be given to the needs of city administration.

Part of Cofran's difficulties with Ott and the turmoil they created can be inferred from an inspector's report of a visit on 30 June. It gave Cofran short praise: "Ambitious, alert, interested in MG assignment, 42," but it credited Lieutenant Edgar Milton with doing an outstanding job on denazification. This is strange because the report notes that he had not yet removed many Nazis from office when the officer called the first time. Three days later Milton had ordered 154 Nazis from office, which was "indicative of excellent progress."[25] This pressure explains why Cofran, without any warning, called Ott and Kleindienst into his office on 4 July and began to harangue them, charging that the city had worked against his policy of firing every party member. All of them, without exception, should be out by 31 August at the latest.[26] Ott noted that he would have fire forty-three of the forty-eight doctors at the city hospitals, fifty-eight of the sixty firemen, the entire forestry staff, and nearly all of the policemen; he proposed instead releasing only those who could be considered active, that is, those who joined the party before 1933 or had been members of the SS. Cofran refused, saying: "America had not fought the war to maintain German administration but to destroy Nazism." It did not matter that other cities had a different policy. Headquarters agreed to his radical measures; "they" thought a successful local radical policy would lead to a zonal radical policy.[27]

Cofran released Kleindienst as head of personnel, but refused Ott's resignation: "MG would do the firing; it was his job to find new people." Yet MG appointed its own personnel director, Xaver Sennefelder; Ott was largely ignored.[28] In December 1945 the detachment reported it had released 2,035 of 3,192 city officials and employees between July and September.[29] In July it had quoted an inspector, Mitchell Wolfson, who "put his finger on certain public opinion in Augsburg which thought that the Americans were missing 'the worst Nazis, such as shopkeepers, who were Gestapo informers.' . . . As a matter of fact, denazification of commerce and industry seems to have gone faster in Augsburg than it did anywhere else."[30] Cofran notified all firms that everyone down to department heads must fill out the denazification question-naires or the firm would be forced out of business. On 13 July the leading industrialists of the city had been arrested and their property seized.[31]

Ott, whose position had never been pleasant, did not remain in office much longer. He had been bothered that under the Nazis the mayor had to get the advice of a council, but under MG the mayor was a dictator. On 12 June he proposed an advisory council, a suggestion accepted two months later. Cofran, however, asked for "Ten Good Men" to act as MG advisers instead of a revived city council.[32] Then Ott heard in early August that Cofran was planning to change mayors. After being ordered to give a full report on his activities 1933–45 and on any "Nazi friends," Ott was informed 23 August, during a routine talk, of his release from his position for trying "to sabotage the denazification" of the administration. Dr. Dreifuss, the Jew selected to replace him, told the city council a year later: "Dr. Ott was unjustly dis-charged by MG. He was in no way politically compromised. In truth he was fired because he did not suit them and therefore they gave the false reason that he had sabotaged their orders."[33]

As it happened, Cofran was fired at almost the same time. The reasons are obscure; the only official hint came in a later report: "The present com-mander is cooperating well with the *Regierung-Bezirk* Schwaben [Joublanc], which was not the case with Cofran transferred in September."[34] Somehow his moderate superiors got rid of him. A more tragic oddity of the Cofran story is that he was murdered in January 1946 in Passau by a fellow MG officer who mistakenly killed two other men before he axed the sleeping Cofran.[35]

The real kingmaker in Cofran's summer was not Cofran, who under-stood no German, but Alfred Kiss, an émigré from Dresden. As a young member of the SPD he had fled to Czechoslovakia in 1933 and with luck escaped to London in 1938. Briefly interned as an enemy alien in 1940, he volunteered in 1944 to return to assist the British. They were not interested; they had enough colonial civil servants. Yet the OSS employed him to find out how Germans reacted to the occupation. Kiss chose to go to Augsburg, partly because Cofran had a good reputation for cooperation with the OSS.[36]

Kiss arrived in mid-June and, after an afternoon's study of the SPD directory, began to make contacts. He was soon convinced he knew what was going on, but he knew only of the pre-1933 SPD men from the book. Al-though the OSS had ordered him to stay away from MG, an SPD contact told Lieutenant Milton, who told Kiss, that Cofran wanted a new personnel chief; Kiss was the one who selected Sennefelder, whom he praised for "throw-ing 300 Nazis out a week." When Cofran then wanted a new mayor, Kiss learned through a Jewish contact of the Jewish lawyer, Dr. Dreifuss, who had survived the war because he had an "Aryan" wife. He was still hospitalized, recovering from the concentration camp, but his legal training and "race" would seem to make him someone Cofran could use. Kiss was also the source of the ICD report about the struggle of the radical city MG versus the moderate district MG. "Three top officials who had been appointed by MG for Augsburg could not start denazification procedures for a considerable length of time since District MG told these officials they could not exercise the functions of their office. This intervention on the part of MG-Schwaben amounted to an outright slighting of MG-Augsburg." The Kiss report praised Cofran, Milton, and Glass. "These three officers had to overcome strong resistance to their denazification policies on the part of officers as well as German civilians. . . . As far as denazification of authorities under the supervision of MG Schwaben is concerned, progress was much slower or hardly existing. . . . Neither the District-president Kreisselmeyer nor his subordinates nor MG-Schwaben have attempted to denazify thoroughly."[37]

Kiss remained in Augsburg, as did Milton, when Cofran left. He could no longer name city officials but there was much he could do, mostly correcting MG abuses. For example, the town major had his mistress as his secretary. She interfered with the city labor office, and when she was opposed she demanded the firing of its chief. Kiss used Milton to counter her influence. The town major also ordered vegetable dealers to stop selling to Germans, presumably so that DPs would get what they wanted. Kiss got Milton's support and the order was ignored.[38]

With the precipitous changing of the guard, Cofran was out and briefly a Colonel Charles Mathews, civil engineer from Milwaukee, was in. Mathews was quickly replaced, after barely becoming known even to the mayor, by Colonel Richard A. Norton, who arrived with the Clay law for getting MG out of local business. Commanders were rapidly losing importance. A Jewish mayor could scarcely be dismissed as a Nazi sympathizer and Dreifuss proved himself a more agile buffer between MG and the city than Ott could have been.[39] Evidence of MG contact in the city records is varied and spasmodic. One episode involved the deputy mayor's car, stolen by men in U.S. uniforms.[40] Dreifuss tried to find out what men in uniform were doing: "Complaints are increasing that civilians with papers from some office or with American soldiers appear in our offices and try under pressure to get something." He ordered that he should be informed and any decision left to him, except in obvious cases. Each official reported his American contacts, which were "occasional" and usually requests for information.[41]

On his side, Norton was frustrated trying to implement Law No. 8:

The month of October started badly for MG with the slipshod promulgation of Law No. 8. In some cases, civilian officials received word of the law through their radio and newspapers, before MG officers knew such a decree was in effect. Even after distribution of the edict through military channels, its sweeping undefined provisions made it unenforceable, unless complete paralysis of the civilian economy was to be effected. The MGO of this detachment wisely ordered all sub-commanders to defer action until clarification had been received.

But a version was implemented. "Large factories and firms of active Nazis have already been taken under control, and detachment property control officers are now working down to small businesses."[42] The November report termed implementation of the law MG's biggest problem, although only 600 appeals had been received instead of the thousands expected.[43]

The property control officer reported at first a happy division of the spoils, taking property from the bad and giving it to the good, yet he was irritated that his office was "literally pestered" with party members trying to find out what would happen with their property. By January 1946 the problem created was overwhelming. About 1200 pieces of property, factories, and businesses, had been seized in the district. "Proper administration of the controlled properties is a never-ending task beyond the scope of the present military personnel available for property control . . . complaints are now piling up in the chamber of commerce by the hundreds of abuses of prerogatives by the custodians . . . for mismanagement of the business due to professional incompetency or for personal gain." There had also been delays in getting people screened.[44] Confusion persisted into the spring. "To set up a checking system to determine and prosecute violations of Law. No. 8—something that Trade and Industry had failed to do since Law No. 8 was hatched in October 1945—Special Branch organized a 'Trade and Industry Section' in March 1946."[45] The March Law for Liberation gave the Germans the mess to clean up as best they could.

A greater problem faced by the detachment was Clay's October directive which ordered the withdrawal of MG functional control at the local level by 15 November. Actually the date by which MG was to stop issuing orders was 1 January, but that day passed without even observant Germans aware of any change. MG continued issuing orders, but the documents show them to have become more trivial, like the order keeping people off "military streets." In November the big issue was that all returning German soldiers must be demilitarized, that is, out of any uniform. Since they often had nothing else to wear, MG forced them to have the uniforms dyed.[46] In February MG urged everyone to see the documentary film on concentration camps, *Mills of Death*.[47] A one-day raid on book stores netted 2,150 objectionable books.[48]

Responsible German self-government formally began with the 26 May 1946 revival of the elected city council, but a predecessor, the Advisory Council, was appointed by Captain Glass in October on the basis of pre-1933 party strength, excluding the NSDAP. The party leaders, predominately SPD and CSU, began meeting on 18 October 1945. They could not legally compel Dreifuss, but it is evident they were powerful advisers from the beginning because they were closer to the people than Dreifuss was. Advisory Council discussions also document MG's collapsing importance. The number and seriousness of references to MG declines steadily, and each shows MG's frustration in any effort to influence the council. Yet the city, hoping at first for some assistance from MG, was also frustrated because local MG had neither economic resources nor any influence on policy decided in Munich, Frankfurt, or Berlin.

The first council meeting was almost entirely devoted to matters in which MG or the occupation troops were directly involved. It dealt with thirteen points, including housing, labor, fuel, and food shortages, but the minutes of the meeting show that the council was unified in attempting to find solutions to the problems MG had created. Council members were also willing to use MG when it served their purposes, but MG compulsion rarely worked. Point thirteen, for example, concerned the confusion about Law No. 8. Dreifuss calmed their fears of being overrun with petitioners: "When people come you can say we don't have the last word, MG has. . . . You could also keep them down by saying, 'We have to follow the MG rule,' to avoid any influencing of our decision."[49]

The next meeting showed markedly less MG involvement, although the problems dealt with, chiefly shortages, were occasioned by American policies. MG was most involved in the denazification of the administration. The mayor noted many departments had to be rebuilt, but "the denazification to my own surprise could be much better implemented than one thought at first." Other comments were not as positive. Dreifuss lamented that food rations were worse than in Theresienstadt, the concentration camp he and his wife had been in.[50] He was very angry with MG.

> Orders come back and forth from every possible side. If one would not always leave us in the dark, it would help. Usually we hear, "Think what you did to the other peoples." First we did not do it; secondly it was then the Nazi war of the worst kind; and thirdly, one cannot make one war right with another war. Someone should tell that to people at the highest level. Our present [local] Governor does what he can; he is understanding, but his power is very limited. We keep hearing the MG complaint, "We can't do anything about that. That is the army."[51]

On 26 March, Captain Glass made MG's first and only personal appearance, speaking for Colonel Norton. He explained briefly how he had pushed denazification and had advised the creation and expansion of this council, and then left immediately with his interpreter. His advice sufficed only to excite old SPD member Wernthaler into a rebuttal. "We know much

better how things should be done, and the suggestions are by no means new."
To have answered Glass "would not have been flattering for the Americans. . . . This is a democratic administration. If only one commands, then it is
no democracy. We Germans have the best democracy." Germans had not
become scoundrels after 1933, but retained the good institutions they had
created in 1914 and improved in 1919. Augsburg had developed an improved
democracy by having both the majority and minority party members learn
about each department by working within it. New members should know how
their tested system operated, so he proposed creating such party caucuses to
prepare for council discussions and votes. The leaders would advise the
mayor. "We secured our rights from the beginning. We therefore gave the
Americans no information. We do not plan in the future to approach the
Americans, because we find it more useful to settle our affairs ourselves."
This proud statement expresses the real local attitude toward a superfluous
MG, and it certainly reflected what happened in city government. Officials
did things the old way without asking MG advice.[52]

MG, however, retained a power base through its influence on the city's
hiring. At the May council meeting, Sennefelder said the city could not hire
anyone because Special Branch was two months behind in clearing applications. No one was working on them and no one answered his requests for
information. Things had gone well until the last two months only because MG
had not interfered. "They issue orders for things to be done at once, then
prevent us from hiring anyone to do it." By the time MG approved, applicants
had usually found a different job. The city had approximately 5,000 employees; MG had 4,600, who were better paid, better fed, worked less, and
were less helpful. "Wherever I go I find the greatest cooperation from the
American officers; our work is sabotaged by their German employees."[53]
Dreifuss, the other major American appointment, agreed totally with Sennefelder, but said that apparently Norton could do nothing about it: "It appears that here, as with every military organization, certain countercurrents
exist, so that the commander cannot get through."

The 26 May election of a true city council in place of the Advisory
Council isolated MG even farther and restricted MG's power more than
Clay's orders, since the council could speak with the authority of the people.[54]
Wernthaler and Josef Miller (CSU) organized the council, agreeing that the
bourgeois majority would choose the mayor. The CSU chose Otto Weinkamm
and the SPD proposed Dreifuss for second mayor. All would have gone
perfectly but Weinkamm suddenly resigned on 12 July, explaining that "his
friends had originally talked him into the job." The CSU looked about for
someone else and came up with a non-Augsburg civil servant, Dr. Heinz
Hohner.[55]

The council was emboldened by its popularity. It first protested against the army's venereal disease raids, during which any women caught on the streets could be hauled in for examination.[56] It also rejected the American proposal for unsubsidized theater; it unanimously agreed that American-style boxoffice competition could lead to bad taste.[57] Hohner blamed the city's slow recovery on MG's mass dismissals in 1945, saying that Bavaria had a much more radical denazification than Württemberg, and that Augsburg's was the worst in Bavaria. But since he was speaking confidentially, Hohner admitted things were not really as bad as all that, but one should not let the other cities find out.[58]

For twenty months MG virtually disappeared from council deliberations. An interesting reminder of its existence came on 28 July 1948, from the brash journalist and eventual SPD mayor, Wolfgang Pepper. He had used a subtle antioccupation line in his articles to gain voter appeal and an eventual council seat. He asked the identities of two uninvited men at the closed meeting. When he was told they were Germans sent by MG, Pepper said he knew of no rule that MG employees could attend secret meetings. His colleagues answered that MG was the sovereign power and could do what it liked, but Pepper denied such a law. "If it has been this way, then the time has come to stop the practice."[59] He pushed the issue to a vote, but the two Germans left, after explaining they had been sent because Americans could not understand German. Thereafter the council recognized the existence of MG only when it vented its rage that Americans would not give Germans their houses back.

Skepticism or hostility toward MG was evident not only in the city council, but in the ICD opinion polls. Weinkamm protested MG's constant interference in the economy and administration.[60] The president of the chamber of commerce reported that America had lost a great opportunity to earn friendship: "It is regrettable that practically no occasion has been missed to prevent it. Americans apparently were not interested; not enough contact had been established with qualified Germans."[61] Criticism reached its hungry high point in January 1948; no one believed any MG assurance that the food crisis would improve.[62] "The feeling of the population toward the Americans and their offices is still very unfriendly." Those interviewed lamented: "Three years after the end of the war, the occupation has still not developed contact with the leading political parties and other leading men."[63]

Actually the local MG commanders probably were increasingly inclined to want contact, but they were coming and going. As the German press noted in polite brief news items on back pages, Colonel Norton left in February 1947. For about seven weeks a Major John Rhea was in command; the only thing he left behind was a picture in the paper which made him look like a Hollywood villain. Colonel John Hector took his place in April 1947, and expressed his desire to help Augsburg rebuild.[64]

Whether MG was able to assist the rebuilding could be disputed, but not that contacts with the civilian authorities became more congenial. Most of the credit belongs to the new mayor, Dr. Klaus Müller, who from 1948 to his retirement in 1964 was very popular with Augsburg voters and with American commanders. Until 1945 Müller had worked as an administrator in a textile factory. The son of a Catholic sexton, his loyalty had been too Catholic for him to have joined the NSDAP.[65] His experience and purity made him eligible to be a trustee of three firms seized by MG, including a large textile factory owned by a school friend. He had never been active politically, but one brother was on the city council and another brother was a monsignor. His brother told him over a Sunday coffee that he was to be the new mayor, and Müller was duly elected on 12 November 1947.

At first nearly unknown and kept in office by only narrow majorities on the city council, Müller eventually became unbeatable as a fatherly politician. He embodied the Augsburg mentality: conservative, respectable, moderating. Not even the Americans could be long angry with this white-haired father figure, who learned enough English in time to be gracious and flattering. For his services in improving German-American relations he received more medals from the American army than he had gained from the German army in both world wars. Müller's major interest was the city's cultural life, which is fortunate from an historian's point of view because he supported the city archives and kept notes of each meeting with the *Herren der Militär-Regierung*.[66] These notes add substance to the idea that however friendly Müller and his American counterpart, local MG could do little to change the city and the city could little to change MG or army policy in those few areas which had any local meaning.

Hector expressed interest in a wide variety of matters, including juveniles on the street, crowded schools, getting the schools heated, rubble on the streets, the use of the city archives as MP headquarters, the control of city swimming pools by the army, and, of course, the chlorine in the water. In each case he promised to see what he could do. In each case he could do nothing. He politely asked for assistance in finding out where the occupation had made its mistakes. He also politely asked the mayor to see what he could do to extend Hector's assignment to Augsburg.[67] In the spring of 1948 Hector's major effort was to gain the return of confiscated buildings. Some were controlled by the International Relief Organization (IRO) to house DPs, and others were controlled by the army. In both cases he admitted failure. Just talking about it had made the IRO angry. The army was equally unmovable in regard to beer halls, houses, or swimming pools.[68] Hector was also helpless to reduce the large number of Germans working for the occupation troops and worsening the labor shortage.[69]

By May 1948 Colonel Hector was transferred to Heidelberg. William

Rhyne, who became the most important American in Augsburg for the next four years of the occupation, was made director of Schwaben. Lieutenant Donald Root was director for North Schwaben, and a Mr. Neil was director for the city.[70] The issues remained much the same as they had been under Hector. Discussions, friendly but nearly fruitless, were ever more devoted to German requests for Americans to give something back. General Pierce said that the army needed the little-used longer swimming pool "for certain tests;" Americans needed their own pool because Germans had "too little soap" and because of the hunger they had "certain illnesses."[71] The requests for the return of the West Hospital have continued for thirty years.[72] When Müller asked for the return of a certain empty house, the answer was: "The officers were very interested in that, because they were looking for better quarters for themselves." In the summer of 1948 began the tedious negotiations for a suitable building for the Amerika Haus, as part of a trade to get the archives building back from the MPs. Müller got lucky and obtained the Gestapo headquarters, which became the Amerika Haus. (It had been purified by the Special Branch's using it to ferret out Nazis.)[73]

Although most MG-city relationships seemed inevitably to involve buildings in some way, MG also concerned itself with Augsburg's cultural and political life. On the one hand, it pushed for some citizen meetings to discuss such matters as school reform. On the other hand, it protested Pepper's discussions in the newspaper of current affairs, as he seemed to be using his position on the city council to get information that was supposedly secret.[74] Donald Root, who by February 1949 had replaced Petitfils, made repeated proposals for public forums, though what the city wanted was the return of housing. (Root was able to get the Riegele beer hall back, a cause of rejoicing to some.) He suggested a column in the newspaper for citizens' questions and complaints. This became a permanent feature. In a good American tradition, he suggested the "Youth Mayor for a Day" idea.[75] He was upset, however, at the cold reception given an American unit's desire to sponsor a sports group and to open a football game by throwing the football from an airplane.[76] By the time that the negotiations over the only auditorium had reached the point of Germans and Americans sharing the building, Müller had to regret that the city, wanting to use it for plays and operas, found the Americans using it for boxing matches. "Captain Stone did not see the point. For him boxing exhibitions are more important than theater." Müller added sadly: "Here the points of view of the two peoples differ."[77]

Discussions with the new MG officers, Mr. Hart and Mr. May, continued along the same frustrations, except that there were apparently funds available, such as "the McCloy funds," which were marks collected in payment for Marshall Plan aid that could be used for projects in Germany. The German hope to get some McCloy fund money to rebuild schools was dashed by the observation that Americans did not agree with the German system of education.[78] There was hope that new housing might be built for Americans from such funds, which would free the confiscated homes. The Germans were wary because housing suitable for Americans would be too luxurious for Germans to afford if the Americans ever left.[79] The Germans sadly noted that the Korean War brought a buildup of troops; three times as many troops were coming. Not only would housing remain confiscated but there would be more disturbing tanks and artillery moving through the neighborhoods.[80]

In September 1951, May explained further his convictions about "a moral rearmament, namely in the awakening of a civil spirit and the training of the people to cooperate on community affairs."[81] Müller by chance began his next report: "The Americans are very hard to bring to the point of living in the same building with German families."[82] May had also returned to one of Cofran's ideas in 1945, that of compiling a list of the most influential men from every part of the community. Müller noted: "He wants to have these gentlemen given lectures for democracy." At the same meeting May expressed his concern about an obscure city official because the official's son was allegedly active in the Communist party. When May attempted "open conferences" with the press, the questions concerned housing.[83]

At their last meeting, May came to Müller and expressed his disappointment that the Germans had learned so little about becoming involved in community affairs. His last hope was for a group of five Augsburgers to visit the United States for a three-month stay.[84] The irony was that hundreds of thousands of Americans living in Germany had kept their distance. When their leaders had come together, as in the MG-mayor conferences, the result had been triviality and frustration.

While Mayor Müller was recording his gently ironical views of the occupation, others, both German and American, were expressing either bitterness or frustration. For example, a newspaper account reflected candidly on the progress of the occupation:

> In 1946 it was possible for an education officer of the local MG to declare categorically that "Silent Night" had become a song of the Hitler Youth and therefore was now forbidden. And long, long thereafter the leading officers, despite honest efforts, had still not come to understand the German mentality, so that their efforts for public forums and youth activity did not fit the situation, and so that there was nothing else for us to do but to practice passive resistance. Sipping cocktails, we listened time and time again to what they wanted to force on us (usually poorly translated). We looked at each other silently, went home and did—nothing. Alright, that is finished. They had a limited time with the nice task of playing Santa Claus with money from the profits of *Die Neue Zeitung*, the McCloy funds, and other praiseworthy institutions. Now that has come to an end and guns are more important than culture-butter. Now the entire apparatus, with its camp-followers, albeit reduced, exists simply for its own sake, with its job reduced to a minimum so that its clothes flap in the wind.

From the time of the Romans and earlier, that was the natural destiny of an occupation; after a number of years they fastened themselves to their positions and began to take nothings as somethings. One could, as generous as we will have to be, ignore that, if it were not for the painful question of occupation costs.[85]

The sincere Donald Root, who served the occupation from the beginning in Sicily and training in Shrivenham, would have been hurt by this judgment of his work. He had served in Bavaria at Wasserburg and "ran everything." He had served in lovely Sonthofen as "supreme boss," with an "awfully good life" for him and his wife. Throughout that time there had been no problems with the Germans, who were grateful, he thought. Problems had come from the army and the DPs. Yet reading through his diary, one notes his frustration as a decent man counfounded first by Americans who could not or would not do their jobs properly, and later by some German leaders who could not or would not learn how to govern themselves.[86] His diary covers 1945–49; in his previous assignments he was horrified at the folly of his leaders and the antics of his peers and then, as commander at Sonthofen, he could concentrate on good works and the good life. His time in Augsburg was less filled with scandalized notations of aberrant officer behavior and more filled with frustration and wasted time. He was no longer in charge. When he came 27 May 1948, he observed that Augsburg's MG was "a first class mess." Rhyne's conferences were tiresome, "not sticking to Regierungs-Bezirk business." On 6 June he noted that with all the enlisted men transferred, each of the eight officers had more than he could do merely writing the required reports. If the mayor wanted to defy MG, all they could do was report the fact to Berlin. The only possible result would be some criticism coming down through German channels. "By the time that is done the chances are good that personnel changes will make it nothing more than a gesture." On 15 June he wrote: "All quite confused as normal." Root's frustration with HICOG climaxed when he was released 10 May 1952 with but a few more months to serve. He regarded J. J. McCloy as one of the coldest fishes on earth and as one of the world's worst windbags, without a sincere bone in his body. "I shall never be able to forget McCloy's going to sleep in my office at a conference with the Landrat and the Oberbürgermeister, and chiseling on the price of one ticket to last year's Bayreuth festival."

Mayor Müller, twenty years later, remembered the occupation with neither the bitterness of the newspaper nor the frustrations of Donald Root. He even seemed to have forgotten the irony of his notes. Always the diplomat, he expressed high admiration for the professional officers who shared his values. The reserve officers were less commendable, to be sure, and the American soldiers were like grown-up children. But he had seen so many fine officers come and go.

Among the very few Germans who came to know these officers was Harald Modrow, an interpreter-assistant to the later Augsburg MG. Like Kiss he had come from the Russian zone, having flown out of Berlin in 1948 to escape the Communists. He praised all the officers, except one later caught in Turkey trying to smuggle silver disguised as car bumpers, as fine men. William Rhyne had been the best, "the good American, agile, vital, jovial, just, open-minded, and understanding." He had often invited Germans to his home; he spoke perfect Bavarian and sent his children to German schools. Herbert Hart was the professor type, very quiet, thoughtful, and humorous. Germans took him seriously, but he had not stayed long enough. Francis Lambert and John J. May were outstanding in their piety. Mrs. Sophie Bernard, the Jewish German-American who ran the Amerika Haus, was well liked except by her German staff. Her Amerika Haus attracted many people when books were in low supply, but by the time it had started there was already a reaction against things American.[87]

Modrow, looking back on his former bosses, saw their accomplishments as very limited in spite of their goodwill. Some had emphasized trying to Americanize the Germans and had failed. He thought that most soon saw that they could not get much done, so they had limited themselves to maintaining "good contacts" in order "to influence" the politicians. Actually only Rhyne had achieved much contact. When he came he got introductions to the leading people and got them to come to his parties.[88] A German-American club and a women's club had been created, but when HICOG left these had been allowed to slumber.

In addition to noting these general evaluations of the impact of Augsburg MG, it is illuminating to look more closely at those areas where it was most active and where it had the greatest impact, for better or for worse. One important area was denazification, where the influence of the local MG was even less fortunate than elsewhere. One can also point to its activity in police reform, which had a largely negative result in those cases when OMGUS policy or local MG decisions made any difference. Newspaper reform was belated but successful in the sense of creating a liberal and critical press. Finally, Augsburg MG's most negative impact was the requisitioning of German homes and businesses; it was in this area that the occupation forces remained in the way for the longest time.

Denazification perhaps left an even more negative reaction in Augsburg than elsewhere because Augsburgers had not experienced a very harsh local Nazi regime and were more inclined to forgive and forget. Hundreds would testify for the arrested Mayor Mayr and Gauleiter Wahl. A further difference between Augsburg and some other places would be the image Cofran created in 1945 of an extremely rigorous denazification policy. In November, for example, Augsburg MG proudly announced the success of firing some 2,000

Nazis.[89] With the city administration cleaned out, MG began the implementation of Law No. 8 to clean out industry. Colonel Norton made it clear that any active Nazi must be reduced to manual labor or the entire business which employed him would be closed.

Dreifuss, the new Jewish mayor, tried to convince Bavarian Minister Heinrich Schmitt that Augsburg denazification was so far advanced that Munich need not interfere. Schmitt assured him that all would be done in an orderly fashion with tribunals. With some hope Dreifuss in December selected a fine group to serve as lay judges, including the leading people in his administration and the local parties.[90] Unfortunately, when the system began to function in March, Schmitt sent his fellow Communist, Helmut Menzel, to be the local director. Menzel set up his own tribunals, giving the small KPD extra positions. The lack of formal training of those he selected and their assumed prejudices gave the tribunals a bad image.

The tribunes became involved in accusation and counteraccusation. The CSU blamed Menzel for delaying the tribunals' activity. The mayor in turn was blamed for not helping, but Dreifuss said that he simply could not find qualified people. The trade unions, though clearly anti-Nazi, could not suggest anyone. Menzel blamed MG for refusing to accept two-thirds of the people he had nominated. MG blamed the CSU for nominating people who required long investigations to clear. Some thought MG was sabotaging the process to show that only Americans could handle denazification.[91]

Public opinion, led by Dreifuss, turned against denazification. Dreifuss thought that MG had acted on false denunciations in dismissing many city employees.[92] The head of the chamber of commerce answered an ICD inquiry: "In May 1945 National Socialism and militarism were dead. Today they have been brought to life again by wrong measures."[93] Menzel brought further public disdain by occasioning repeated stories of his constant drunkenness and of lavish parties financed by black-market profiteering. In December 1946 he was arrested for having falsified his own questionnaire. He had neglected to mention eight prison sentences.[94]

By 1947 the Augsburg denazification was being dragged along in the general struggle to get the job done one way or the other. A technique worked out to facilitate the processing of thousands of cases, "the Augsburg system," or "B procedures," got much publicity as a solution. The prosecutor simply classified former party members into Class IV, who were subject to a fine. If no one objected to this judgment, the individual, instead of going to trial, would receive notification of his "denazification" in the mail.

Although this procedure was frequently criticized as farcical, in 1948 Clay concluded, under the Congressional pressure described earlier, that faster procedures were necessary. The Augsburg MG, unaware of Clay's reasons, had nothing but contempt for the results: "In many cases the

Chamber [court] appeared more interested in defending the respondent than in arriving at the truth . . . the people who had previously been considered the big Nazis were coming out better than the block-leaders tried earlier. To increase the difficulties the public lost what little interest it had left in denazification, because they felt that the American MG at high level had no further interest in it and was only trying to finish it off as fast as possible, without regards to results. . . . As a result of this feeling no person would give testimony against the respondents.'' The tribunals had practically ceased to operate.[95] As a later news story put it: "One waited in vain for the cooperation of the population."[96] It is now agreed that denazification failed in Augsburg as a process. It is also generally agreed in Augsburg that Nazism died despite denazification.

Another major reform attempted by the Augsburg MG was that of the police, because Nazism in the minds of Americans was almost synonymous with the hated concept of the police state. Police support was assumed to have led to Nazism and the police force was assumed to be full of Nazis. Naturally all policemen who had joined the party were discharged by MG. At first they were not allowed to carry weapons. Uniformed police were also suspect because the German love of uniforms had supposedly contributed to the rise of Nazism. The centralization of the police, carried through by Heinrich Himmler, chief of the Reich SS, had to be reversed; local control was assumed to be necessary to democracy.

Major Joseph Zapitz, a lawyer from New Jersey, was assigned the task of police reform in June 1945. He had had no police experience, but was taken from a combat command and given an eight-day training he regarded as useless. His policy was the commonsensical one of getting only the worst Nazis out and training some replacements before firing the remaining police. His jails were filled to overflowing with curfew violators, crowded together for the night with no facilities and released the next morning. Zapitz later recalled: "Crime was horrible. The DPs would attack Germans on any pretext."[97] Radio and newspaper announcements of openings in the police department brought a stream of applicants whose credentials could not be checked; it took years to separate the wheat from the chaff.[98] George Knapp, a former police lieutenant from Darmstadt, was considered to be qualified for police chief because he had been in a concentration camp. MG fired him under mysterious circumstances in January 1947. In a later court case, Frau Knapp said that he had been released because he had violated the rationing laws and had made much extra money; he had encouraged an employee to falsify a questionnaire; he had tried to get an abortion for a girlfriend. The city administration had given him the choice of resigning or being arrested.[99]

Other attempts to find suitable replacements for ousted policemen were little more successful. One Trillich, a former Augsburg police lieutenant, seemed to be the perfect solution; he had not joined the party although remaining with the police until 1938. As deputy chief he became a subject of local argument; the Communists said he had been too tough, but Mayor Dreifuss noted that he had suffered much by not having joined the Nazi party. Yet MG fired him as the Nazis had done, because he was insufficiently pliable. His replacement was an electrician, Eugen Wolff, named deputy police chief in April 1947.[100] He left quickly in November 1947, with the parting statement: "I had to leave Germany in 1933 because of my political and religious position. After the capitulation I thought it my duty to help rebuild my Fatherland. Unfortunately I discovered that not all Germans have learned what democracy is. Anti-Semitism is growing again."[101] It was not as simple as that. In January 1947 he had already been called on the carpet by MG's public safety officer. He and Knapp had been given twenty-four hours to resign or perhaps be arrested for black-marketing, bribery, incompetence, and pressuring the housing office. MG worked out a deal: he would be given a two-month probation if he would get back his letter demanding a hearing. In November Wolff said he was going to the United States to study police law and return to help his country again. His return to Augsburg would be difficult because the newspaper gave the real reason for his leaving: he had embezzled 10,000 marks from confiscated occupation money; in addition there were "women problems."[102]

The replacement for Knapp, January 1947, was a Herr Drzimala, who had begun as a policeman in Wuppertal in 1906. He had been briefly with the Augsburg police 1941–43, but had not joined the party. He remained as chief until his death in 1953, although he had been strictly a police administrator, with little knowledge of police work as such. The actual police leader was naturally Trillich. When Wernthaler of the city council objected, the city answered that Trillich had kept most of his officials out of the party and had arrested two SS men for the 1938 pogrom against the Jews, which had cost him his police job. MG had fired him without consulting the city and by virtue of "a confusion." To rehire him would be the proper restitution.[103] The police history praised his devotion; he was a man of integrity, a simple man who had suffered very much.[104]

Of the variety of reforms, the much-heralded change to an American-style uniform came to nothing. By 1954 the uniform was as it had been in the 1920s, but without the pointed helmets.[105] In 1948 MG tried to weaken the police by separating its administrative functions from its law enforcement functions, but the order made little practical difference; both elements were in the same building but entered through different doors. The decentralization of police, which meant going back to the pre-1929 system, had considerable conservative support. It survived in Augsburg, but the problem of financing the police has meant that most small towns lacking a tax base have given police control back to the Bavarian state. By November 1950 the banned political police was recreated in the centralized Office for Protection of the Constitution. U.S. concern for civil liberties was outweighed by its post-Korea fear of Communist infiltration. Whether the previous officiousness, or authoritarianism, of the German police had been altered could be debated. Public awe probably declined. The police complained in 1948: "the public because of the systematic propaganda from all sides against the state's authority has taken a basic position against the police and made its work more difficult." The police president in 1970, August Schepp, said the police were not given "proper respect." Another change was the creation of a somewhat less military atmosphere, although the MG ban against saluting had been reversed.[106]

Chief Drzmila and his successors had little interference from MG and matters became routinized in amicable relations with their MP counterparts. Police dealings with Americans were more often with drunken or violent GIs, who at first could not be arrested by German police. In the fall of 1949, when GI violence reached one of its peaks, Drzmila presented a short history of affairs to the city council which expressed the public concern about being beaten up. He passed off the attacks until then as normal for an occupation, but added: "The picture changed seriously when the rule keeping German taverns off limits was lifted. Although most Americans behaved themselves, there were fights, because of girls and drunkenness, in which the German usually was helpless and was thoroughly beaten up." Robberies had increased, presumably because soldiers had less money, as the black market had declined after the currency reform. A high point had been reached at the end of October with fourteen beatings and six robberies. "In all of these outbreaks of American soldiers, the German police have their hands completely tied. They cannot even hold the Americans until the MP comes. Even if they try to help the wounded, they can be charged with an attack on an American soldier."[107] There was some satisfaction perhaps, as well as amazement, at the harsh manner the American MPs used with their drunken compatriots. It was like the German policeman's use of the billy club before the reforms.

After pointing out so many rather fruitless MG efforts, it is a pleasure to note that the reform of the Augsburg newspapers was a relative success. It installed a new newspaper, at first called *Die Schwäbische Landeszeitung,* later *Die Augsburger Allgemeine,* which became so powerful in the entire district that it invited criticism as a monopoly.[108] The newspaper has been regarded by some conservatives as Communist, but it never was, although one of the two original editors selected by MG, Curt Frenzel, began at least as far left as the SPD and had good relations with the Soviets. He was neatly balanced by a pious Catholic, Johann Naumann, who had worked for the major preoccupation newspaper, *Die Neue Augsburger Zeitung,* which had a Catholic tinge until 1933. He had been released in 1935 for political unreliability and had survived the Nazi period by working for the church. His editorial contribution to the new MG paper was limited to two feature stories, one written for Christmas and the other for Easter. He left *Die Schwäbische Landeszeitung* in 1948 to attempt to start a Catholic paper; informed opinion is that he was outmaneuvered by Frenzel, who treated him shabbily.

Although Frenzel came to the newspaper as a critic of capitalism, no one has since disputed his business acumen: he came penniless to Augsburg and died a presumed millionaire in 1970. He gained the approval of the ICD by his solid socialist and anti-Nazi background. As an assistant editor of the SPD newspaper in Chemnitz, he had been arrested; after beatings in a concentration camp he had suffered unemployment and ended the war in hiding. He could have been employed in the Soviet zone, but with some reluctance he accepted the ICD offer of the Augsburg paper.[109]

Frenzel's opening statement for the new paper was that it "appeared without any control or censorship, headed by Germans who alone were responsible for its content."[110] Yet observers report that he was kept under strict controls during the first years; he received the guidelines every week in Munich and carried them out loyally.[111] Frenzel's editorials in the first years show a clear evolution. His blazing hatred for the Nazis meant a boundless gratitude toward the Allies, and he hoped for some revolutionary change in the Germans who deserved the Allied distrust. If anything was wrong (bombed cities, hunger, refugees), only the Nazis were to blame; punishing the Nazis was the best solution. The Russians were the allies of the Americans and all were the blessed liberators.[112] But by 1946 Frenzel's editorial line was perceptibly more sceptical of the Russians. "Frenzel regrets very much the rift between the Social Democrats and Communists and believes in unity on the left, but resents the strong-armed methods of the KPD and the SMA [Soviet Military Administration]."[113]

Frenzel moved to the center; he came more often to the defense of his fellow Germans and by 1948 he came to open criticism of the occupation. He gained the undying dislike of Valentin Baur and Kiss, the socialists who had first recommended him, because he dropped his party membership when he moved to the suburbs. His paper would not further the SPD, and he was later proud of his friendship with Adenauer. The sharp Frenzel pen was first aimed at his benefactors just before the currency reform and reflected the despair of a hungry people; the electorate was radicalized by its hunger. "The dissatisfaction is growing among the people. The unhappy solution of denazification, the constant promises of more food have unmistakably led to a growth of radicalism and to an inner resistance to the occupation."[114] Frenzel felt that MG had increased nationalism and communism.

In December 1948, Frenzel rejected the American criticism of the Germans as arrogant and nationalistic; instead he criticized the Allies for the high costs of occupation, the dismantlings, their lack of unity, and their failure to permit German democracy. He also described the Russian zone as a dictatorship.[115] His real biting of the hand which had fed him came with the denunciation in July 1949: "For the first time since 1945 it has come to a crisis of faith between the state leaders and the occupation power, or better said, the longstanding tension has exploded. Because back of every minister's chair stands unseen the representatives of MG, which always has the right, by virtue of its power, to intervene, as long as the Occupation Statute has not been put into effect." In response to the MG defense that it was always easy to get the Germans united against MG, he replied:

> If that is the case, then the question should be investigated, why it has come to this, and why during the passage of the years, the relationship between the responsible German authorities and the representatives of MG has not improved.... It has not been possible to convince the outside world and the occupation that we want nothing else but the reconstruction of a government on a democratic basis. One cannot handle a people forever like a schoolmaster.

He was grateful for MG help, "but when gradually there awakens in Germans a national consciousness, then this indestructible love of homeland and fatherland dare not be immediately suspected as a revived nationalism, which truthfully does not exist."[116] This eloquent statement of loyalty to the new Germany represents a reversal of Frenzel's 1945 suspicions. Yet his paper remained pan-European in tone and in its increasing skepticism of things American. Even though this MG creation declared its independence and went its own way, it is likely that it had done what MG planners should have wished. Its editorial policy represented a new Germany—liberal, skeptical, and critical, even of Americans.

Frenzel's three best-known writers could be taken as examples of the newer German state and as symbols of the real changes that have occurred. The first, Wolfgang Pepper, began literate attacks on MG policy, as when he wrote in November 1948 that the crisis was whether Germany would become sovereign or whether an unpopular pseudosovereignty would rest entirely on Allied bayonets.[117] A Prussian from Kiel, Pepper had come to Augsburg, his wife's home, after the war. (His career in journalism had been destroyed in 1933 because of his membership in the SPD.) With little tolerance for fools, whether Nazi, American, or socialist, he used his position as local editor to gain leadership of the local SPD, and election as Augsburg's second mayor. He quickly learned city administration, while Müller represented the city with courtly speeches. Although lacking the Augsburg softness of manner, he won the mayorship in 1964; a factor contributing to his success was his assumed toughness with rowdy Americans.

Alois Schertl is a good example of an older man who successfully made the transition from a career as a professional officer to that of an incisive liberal journalist. In 1946, on his release from a Russian PW camp, he could not enter on a university-based career, but when he entered a short story contest of Frenzel's he won the prize of 60 marks and an offer of a job.[118] He viewed the occupation bitterly, recalling the waste and even burning of food in front of starving Germans, the violence of the troops, and the scandals of officers and their women.[119] On the other hand, when Schertl's baby was born and the family had nearly no food, his wife and child had been saved by the large amounts of food given to the sanitorium.

Despite his reputation with Mayor Müller as an American-hater, Karl Pflugmacher, long assigned to "the American beat," had probably developed the closest relationship with Americans. The American impact was evident from the many photographs on his office wall, mostly American jazz musicians, from his anachronistic Rockefeller for President sign, and from the sign in English, No One Is Perfect. He had been drafted out of high school and taken prisoner in 1945, his first contact with Americans. They were searching for SS men, and he observed primitive techniques, including beatings. Released, neither harmed nor embittered, his next contact in a small city near Augsburg was with a so-called sport officer, who delighted in teaching the schoolboys how to play baseball. The ball games always got them a bean lunch; the officer had scrounged up extra food. This instructor took particular pleasure when home runs were hit, and for each home run passed out Hershey bars. To afford him more pleasure, the boys arranged for more home runs; fielders misjudged fly balls or threw wildly. These officers were "harmless big children."[120]

After joining the newspaper in 1948, he had for many years a wonderful contact with American athletes, some of whom, particularly the black basketball players, he regarded with awe. For some reason during the 1960s the quality of men and officers had declined; was it Viet Nam? Commanders forbade troops to join German teams. The climax of disillusion was General Walker; Pflugmacher took pride in having disclosed him as a purveyor of John Birch Society ideas to his troops. His story led to the general's dismissal. In 1969–70 Pflugmacher wrote about General George Young coming from Viet Nam and "behaving like a conqueror." At the height of the agitation, Young was suddenly recalled by Washington for alleged involvement in the My Lai massacre.

Whatever the favorable impact of individual soldiers and officers, the primary army impact at the local level was the seizure of German homes and businesses, to be used mostly as officer housing. Getting houses free was the major German activity involving the local MG; defending houses from the army or holding back the angry Germans was MG's major activity until the last. The process began with officers touring the city, picking out the best-looking house, and then ordering its owners to evacuate within a few hours and to take only clothing and personal effects with them. Some of the remaining unbombed commercial establishments were seized for the use of the troops as bars or post exchanges. What was most bitterly resented was the seizure of an entire section of town to house DPs who would not or could not return to their homes.

Many of the early confiscations occurred without entering into the city's records. Its file on confiscations, the bulkiest one dealing with the occupation, begins with the notice of the seizure of ninety-one houses in Bärenkeller to hold captured German officers and top Nazis.[121] The next notice is a list of furniture which Cofran had seen in various homes and which he took for his own. The file continues with pitiful letters asking Ott to help.[122] All requests were brusquely rejected by MG. Ott tried to find out whether international law would help. He was told MG had issued no statement on legality, although the Hague Convention said that private property should not be seized.[123]

In August the Hochfeld workers' apartments were seized for DPs; all buildings bounded by certain streets had to be evacuated by 0800, 13 August, another group by 21 August, and a third group by 28 August. The residents might take their personal effects, but all furniture and fuel had to be left.[124] Although the Americans considered the Lithuanians, Esthonians, and Poles forced labor as well as allies, Fraunholz protested that most had been Nazi party members and some were SS.[125] In October the city reported "another exciting incident between the American troops, their Polish guards, and German civilians." The residents of confiscated houses "saw their furniture, household goods, clothing, shoes, *etc.*, thrown from windows on all floors into the street, and quickly carted off to a dump. Although men and women begged the soldiers and foreigners to let them take their last little property away, they were held back by rifles and driven away." When the 140 apartments had been taken on 2 May, the residents were told that everything would be kept in good order and they could soon return, but the troops occupying the buildings had changed repeatedly.[126] To the city's inquiry about what had been thrown away, the officer who answered said that it was only rubbish.

In January 1946 panic broke out all over the city when UNRRA officials were seen measuring houses; the city was first told not to worry and then told that 4,000 Jewish refugees were being shipped in. MG deplored the new burden on housing but had its orders.[127] In February 1946 the Ninety-first Division moved into Augsburg and made what MG described as "unusual and excessive demands for housing," including more downtown businesses for its own stores.[128] The city council was told that between 12,000 and 14,000 soldiers, 1,800 officers and 500 dependents were coming, as well as 3,000 to 4,000 administrative personnel. Some 10,000 more refugees were also expected.[129] When an anti-Nazi complained to Dreifuss that his house had been inspected, Dreifuss answered that the army had recently confiscated the home of a city councilman, which showed how little they considered the circumstances.[130] Dreifuss also received a letter from a half-Jew, who remembered how happy he had been when the Americans came in May, but since then his house had been taken by the troops. He had just seen the interior again and found it in shambles; everything was gone or ruined.[131]

American families came to Augsburg in the fall of 1946, and with them came more confiscations. In September the mayor noted that sixty-five houses in Spickel, a new section of town, were already surrounded by Polish guards. "The population of the city who live in those sections desirable to American families live in constant fear whether their house will be confiscated. For unknown reasons confiscations occur here or there, then are suspended, then confiscated again . . . they absolutely do not know what is going to happen. After reassurances suddenly guards appear around a large number of houses and the confiscation is announced."[132] Norton expressed his sorrow. On 26 December more houses in the Pfersee section were taken.

A new problem emerged beyond the ability of the city to deal with. Without consulting any Germans, MG wrote to house owners that their furniture had been appraised and they should collect the appraised price. The residents instead organized to protest this forced expropriation of their property.[133] The owners told the city administration that the action was simply theft. What complicated the problem was that the Americans, who had come and gone, often traded furniture from one house to another; one could not be sure, with the German owner barred from his house, whose furniture was where. The issue was presented to two colonels and two captains, who after two and a half hours of listening rejected the suggestion of later compensating the German owners for any damage.[134] By July OMGB agreed to no more forced sales, and 95 percent of the Germans declined to sell their furniture.

The newspaper escalated the protest by printing a series called "The Injustice in Augsburg," pathetic stories of those people who were waiting to get back into their homes. Its most sensational story reported that the DPs had been raising livestock for sale on the black market in the Hochfeld apartment buildings.[135] A public outcry led to the organization of a group called Augsburgers Injured by the Occupation. Pressure mounted on Mayor Müller, who was accused of being apathetic because he still had his own house. A report was finally compiled of the properties still kept from their German owners. The IRO had 736 apartments with 2,690 rooms. The army had 128 houses, 316 residences, 1,616 rooms, 3 hotels, 4 restaurants, 2 cafes, 1 casino, 1 theater, 2 movie houses, 6 department stores, 1 reading room, 3 factories, 5 gas stations and garages, 1 laundry, 1 cleaning plant, 2 swimming pools, 1 school, 1 bakery, 1 printing plant, 7 office buildings, 1 athletic field, 2 tennis courts, and 7 barracks.[136] All of these were in a city with few buildings being rebuilt after the wartime bombings, and with people legally allowed one-half room per person.

MG officers Rhyne and Root began freeing the business district in November 1949. The newspaper hailed their action with the headline, *The Occupation frees furniture.* The results were again disappointing. The liberated furniture was mostly junk and badly damaged. Some owners had received nothing for their losses; others had received compensation, but since the currency had been devalued to 10 percent of its previous value, their compensation was calculated at 10 percent of the original value or of any replacement cost.[137] Relief came only as the number of DPs declined through emigration in 1950–51. Hochfeld was turned back to the Germans 8 December 1951; the return was, a colonel suggested, "a Christmas present." There were 680 homes freed, as well as another 100 destroyed homes. All had to be rehabilitated from top to bottom. Most of the electric installations had to be replaced, and stoves and furniture were nearly all gone.

Army housing remained, then, the major MG problem. The only hope was for new housing to be built. The project, discussed first in 1949, became a reality in Centerville, begun in October 1951 and completed by April 1955; it was built from German tax monies. But in 1956 there was still bitterness because 171 German dwellings were still occupied. The American authorities showed "no concern for hardship cases" and used "delaying tactics." Finally, in January 1957, the last 22 houses were returned.[138]

Despite the intense bitterness created by the housing policy and by the continuing violence of drunken GIs, knowledgeable participants neither damned the evil done by the occupation nor praised any good it had accomplished. Instead, I had to conclude that very little for good or evil had survived. It is almost as though MG had not happened. It had thrown many people out of their jobs; most were soon reemployed and some that MG had put in jail even became community leaders. Troops threw people out of their houses, but these were eventually recovered. (Centerville twenty years later looked shabby by comparison with recent German housing.) Although Americans have been in Augsburg in large numbers since 1945, anything outside their housing areas more significant than a bar with an American name is hard to find. Some of the local officers were idealists who tried to help the Germans up, and others were arrogant fools who tried to keep them down. Both sorts briefly succeeded, but mostly the occupiers were only in the way. At no time did they show locally the capacity to govern, as though military government by a conqueror was never a real possibility. The Augsburg experience leads to the conclusion that Augsburg MG was mostly irrelevant. This lesson would seem to be repeated in the following shorter studies of the small towns of Friedberg and Eichstätt, and of the large city of Nuremberg.

The Friedberg Experience: MG's Servant Becomes the County Master

The city of Friedberg was the historic county seat for rural Friedberg County, on the highland rising out of the Lech River valley just east of Augsburg. Friedberg was pulled economically by the industrial center of Augsburg on the west, and by the many conservative villages, such as Dasing and Laimering, on the east, villages which it had governed quietly for hundreds of years. Under Hitler's rule its staunch Catholics had been shocked by the bitter struggle among the new Nazi local leaders. Perhaps because of its quiet traditions, it had passively watched influential Nazis fight over issues irrelevant to Hitler's central policy. Another bitter personality struggle occurred during the occupation, involving new but similar petty scandals and petty tyrants. Again the events were irrelevant to the governing power's central policy. What is surprising is how passively MG authorities merely observed the struggle, perhaps unaware that their unused power had been usurped by a man they had employed as an interpreter.

The occupation began with the support of Friedbergers, who wanted the war to end without ending their thousand-year-old city. The women scolded the few local SS men, who disappeared, and they destroyed the barrier of felled trees erected to keep out the advancing army. The unpopular Nazi mayor, Franz Schambeck, was driven by the Americans about town on a jeep as a trophy, and then disappeared into an internment camp. The first American commander, Captain Paul Webb, reinstated the pre-1933 mayor, a publisher and editor, Karl Lindner.[139] In the county government, Landrat Siegfried Fürst, a nominal party member, was left in office for another month. Then he suddenly became, on 31 May, an "automatic arrest."[140] MG mysteriously ordered a merchant, Dr. Sigbert Sohn, to take over, and Sohn explained to the surprised staff: "The MG made me your Landrat today. It was done without my doing anything. I could not refuse. . . . I will keep asking MG to take the job away."[141] His prayer was answered 17 June, and the Kreis had its third Landrat in as many weeks. This was Dr. Anton Schropp, an attorney from Augsburg who had avoided joining the party. Two young Americans appeared and said that the people wanted him.[142]

Mayor Lindner was the natural leader of the city or county. Yet he was no more likely to work well with MG than with the Nazis, because he was stiffly old-fashioned, patriarchal, dignified, and authoritarian.[143] The few possible competitors for leadership were at first too compromised by part activity. Lindner had under pressure joined the party from 1939–45, but the fact was ignored during the entire occupation. The town knew he was not really a Nazi. Rarely guided by MG, Lindner moved at his own pace. By July he had a city council in operation, and began the session by stating that the council must vote on everything. They voted that officials would be released only if they had been active in the party. Georg Kerle, who later ran city hall, was kept throughout. As far as he was concerned, "Nothing changed." Lindner had merely said he needed him.[144] Four other party members were retained throughout the occupation contrary to orders. The only mention of the occupation by the city council was a reference to the quartering of troops.[145]

With local government operating almost independently, Friedberg MG seems to have done little more than cause problems. It issued a few of its very infrequent orders to the council in early November; they were chiefly concerned with regulating the use and appearance of the streets.[146] In November Lindner tried to resign, purportedly "for reason of poor health," but apparently actually because of difficulties made by soldiers.[147] By January the MG problem was denazification; even the non-Nazis opposed it.[148] Mayor Lindner was permitted to resign by the council, and thanked "for all he had gone through." Mathias Sepp, an elderly member of the SPD, was given the job, but he repeatedly tried to resign because of army demands for housing.[149] Captain David Moran's 1946 command was reported to be ineffective: "Lag in information from Munich, Germans know sooner. . . . Officers do not have answers, refer you to another, different answers from different offices." Friedberg MG was heavily dependent on its German employees. "Enlisted personnel now supervising work of Germans who are more clear than they. . . . Special Branch turned over too much to Germans."[150] With MG isolated, leaving a power vacuum, a battle began among local politicians for control of city and county.

The CSU won the May 1946 county election, but the local party was badly split, largely because of the feud between two newcomers to politics, CSU chairman Dr. Hugo Kellner and Landrat Schropp. Kellner was the flashy meteor of Friedberg politics by virtue of his close ties with MG in 1945. When in July 1946 he proposed scrapping Clay's law and tribunals, MG became skeptical. "He is known in Friedberg to be a little dictator and to have created a CSU machine, which is railroading his propositions into effect."[151] In September Kellner was challenged by a rebel group.[152] In October, Kellner proposed an official complaint against Schropp, listing fourteen Landrat delinquencies.[153] In January, Kellner asked the district president to discipline Schropp for misuse of ration cards and clothing; Schropp said MG had given him the authority.[154] Mayor Sepp had been trying to resign and also blaming Schropp; the city council was backing their mayor in all things.[155]

MG watched the political dog fight with lofty detachment. It merely reported from some anti-Schropp German source: "The Landrat dominates the meetings and does not delegate responsibilities, but rather likes to govern himself. . . . He is by profession a bookkeeper and is a typical Mr. Milktoast.

However, he gets the cooperation of all parties."[156] The less cooperative Kellner called a CSU meeting on 10 March 1947, and after a seven-hour marathon thought he had CSU support for his list of loaded questions Schropp must answer. But the CSU men deserted him and he resigned. The MG analysis was written by a German interpreter, Viktor Kolesnikow, who sympathized with Kellner's goals:

> There is no doubt that Dr. Kellner is impulsive and drives the democratic supervision of public institutions to extremes; however, his objectives in economic problems would surely be of benefit. . . . His party friends . . . do not care to express an opinion in his presence and therefore call him "dictatorial." . . . Both opponents have practically organized a system for supervising each other.

Kolesnikow observed that there was no one else in the Kreis who could lead the party but Kellner's friend, Georg Köninger, the mayor of Mering. "Furthermore, Kellner sees that it is impossible to get on politically with democratic means with the dead masses which hate intelligence and flexibility."[157] Kolesnikow himself later became a more successful dictator.

Matters were complicated by denazification, which dragged the parties from apathy into antagonism. Alfred Loritz's party, the Union for Economic Reconstruction (WAV), was getting applause saying "a large part of the party members were decent people, whereas there were proper scoundrels among the non-party members."[158] The local head of denazification, Georg Blümle (SPD), blamed the intensity of feeling on the order that all of those classified I and II had to be sent to work camps before their appeals had been acted on.[159] Adding to the turmoil was the influx of refugees. In a county with a 1945 population of 23,000, 10,000 refugees had been resettled in private homes by the spring of 1947.

The surprising thing is that with so much conflict among the German leaders, no one seemed particularly annoyed with Captain Moran, in command from March 1946 to October 1947. "An official going-away party was held with statements . . . of the affection held for Captain Moran, who was extremely *Korrekt,* thereby a conciliator, understanding the popular wishes in every way. He was the quiet spot in these turbulent times."[160] Officials who worked with MG remember it with amused tolerance. When talking among themselves, they smile about the little aberrations of this or that "nice boy," mostly incidents concerning women and minor black market activities.[161] The exception to the goodwill toward MG was the attitude toward the CIC man, a Belgian Jew.[162] His secretary-mistress ended up in prison. One of his German investigators had been hired in the belief he had been a "political prisoner in Dachau," but as it turned out he was a criminal who had stolen gold teeth from corpses; he was rather soon back in prison for illegal confiscation of shoes.

An exception amid the black-marketing and other dubious enterprises was Captain R. C. Talcott, whom Kolesnikow described as a puritan. Talcott, who replaced Moran for a period of six months, owed the position to a friend in the Pentagon.[163] He later wrote:

> I had no experience that would qualify me for the job he enticed me with: occupation duty in MG, one of those soft, "reward" jobs for tired ex-combat officers. . . . After about six months as Number Two in the Landsberg Detachment, I was given the Friedberg assignment. . . . In one of the more idealistic decisions of my life, I decided to get out before I was completely demoralized by the rich life, the castles, the women, the drink and black market. . . . The only duties I can recall were counting potatoes before harvesting for an economic report . . . acting as judge in minor MG offenses, writing a weekly summary for Munich and visiting some innocuous regional MG field office in Augsburg, intermittently. Once in a while someone would report a Nazi and there would be some excitement with the *Landpolizei*. . . . The things that occupied most of my life were personal: going to PXs, worrying about food and help at my quarters, visiting other MG officers in more exciting places . . . and entertaining visiting officers and friends. . . . the whole operation seemed a holding action, to maintain a semblance of order. . . . Munich MG seemed to be indecisive, and I had no decisions to make—by order—on my own. To keep things quiet was the aim.

One of Talcott's rare contacts with Friedberg's political reality came when Schropp complained that "MG methods were like those of the Gestapo." He meant Kolesnikow's methods. Schropp had been accused of violating the law by having accepted some meat from a farmer, which was the long-standing courtesy occasionally shown the Landrat.[164]

Mayor Sepp resigned again in December, apparently because he did not want to force people to surrender parts of their houses to refugees. The council was under bitter attack. Critics charged that the city had terrorized the community and the bureaucracy had ballooned in size, and they organized themselves into the Emergency Association.[165] Kellner was involved in it, and, strangely, so was MG. ICD investigator Kiss and the city wondered in February why MG was helping this radical group.[166] The answer was the political ambition of Kolesnikow, MG's strong man. Schropp observed that working with Moran had been easy because of his tolerance and understanding, but: "Now under the new leadership of MG everything has changed. Above all I am bothered that MG has so little contact with the leaders of the parties and authorities and thereby does not support the democratic and progressive men of the county."[167] A former ICD investigator agreed sadly: "Local MG has supported in recent times circles which, seen politically, do not further progress. In Friedberg a group has been formed, The Emergency Association, whose purpose and goal it is to sabotage and undermine the work of the authorities in every way possible. I cannot understand why this group is supported so completely by MG."[168]

The answer to many of the mysteries in Friedberg from mid-1946 lies in the first obscure and later dominating personality of the interpreter, Viktor Kolesnikow. By working within MG he established a power base in 1946–47 that made him the most powerful man in the county. He is an example of the outsider with skills, primarily the skill to speak the language of the conqueror and of the defeated, who took advantage of the immediate postwar turmoil to rise to a temporary power. Kolesnikow, a large, imposing man, described even by his enemies as brilliant, was a German expelled from Czechoslovakia.[169] He had lost everything, and when he was enticed by the Americans into a PW camp, presumably to be discharged, he was nearly forced to volunteer to work in French coal mines. Released instead, he had come to Friedberg, where he was alloted a small room, presumably to find work as manual labor. When he filled out his questionnaire at the county labor office he indicated his English language capacity. Two days later he was called to MG, where a Lieutenant Barker had signed him up immediately as an interpreter-investigator. The next day he was sorting MG papers in his own office.[170] Soon he was doing much of the field work for the detachment. As "Mr. Kay," he became a familiar figure riding about the county in his own jeep. He learned much—for example, who was violating what MG rule—and he reported only what he wished. He gained credit with the Germans for being a friend in dealing with MG. He promised to help if he could; if things went well, he could take the credit; if things went badly, he had done the best he could. Knowing what was going on, he became the de facto MG for the county. He could also take advantage of grievances of the younger element against the conservatives in office; he promised to bring in industry. He became leader of the refugee organization. He also was able to exploit anticity sentiment against Friedberg, particularly in Mering, the second largest town.

In the chaotic year of 1948, Kolesnikow put together a coalition of disparate elements and, on 1 June, got nineteen votes in the *Kreistag* (county legislature) to Schropp's fourteen. The CSU was divided; many were bitter about Schropp's housing actions. Kolesnikow, backed by The Emergency Association, went to the overawed members of the Kreistag and convinced them.[171] As Landrat he frightened the majority by his "quick responses filled with cynical sarcasm." So began the four years of the Kolesnikow "dictatorship." Yet he made enemies; the most important was editor Lindner, who in 1948 was elected mayor of Friedberg again.[172] Although Kolesnikow helped get some industry, mostly to Mering, critical letters appeared regularly in area papers. For example, anyone getting public assistance was forbidden to visit movies, theaters, or inns, or to eat white bread. At the same time his office had bought two new cars, one of which was quickly destroyed by an assistant while drunk. His regime was compared to that of the tsars.[173] He was accused of using the official county newspaper for personal attacks on his critics and on the CSU, which started falling apart when Kellner emigrated to the United States.

Then began the biggest fight, the affair of the stamps. This complex matter involved a chest filled with valuable stamps which had been left in the city savings office for safekeeping toward the end of the war. When the owners asked for the chest after the war, they were misinformed that it had been accidentally destroyed. In 1947 Kolesnikow heard of its existence; he tried to get possession, and kept the chest briefly in his room.[174] When the stamps were finally turned back to the owners, they discovered that the most valuable, worth about 49,000 marks, had been stolen. When the Kreistag mustered the courage to vote eighteen to seventeen that he be suspended pending an investigation, he coolly answered that a two-thirds vote was necessary. Those who voted for him allegedly feared him; there was still "U.S. wind in his sails."[175]

The district president took note of the press campaign against Kolesnikow and began an investigation of the charges, including one that his election was illegal because he was not a citizen.[176] An eighty-page analysis, completed when Kolesnikow was out of office, reported that the Kreistag had been totally subject to him. The public, even the Kreistag, did not know what he was doing.[177] The organization he created to further industry had helped some, but at high cost, and was partly conceived to provide a job for him later. The official paper had been used for his personal gain, with county contracts going to those who supported it with advertising. There had been subsidies granted without Kreistag knowledge, including some to his Sudeten refugee organization. While spending lavishly on his own expenditures, he had been very frugal with aid to the poor.[178] Nevertheless, no Bavarian or MG action had been taken by 1952, when Kolesnikow was up for reelection. A citizens' committee chose an attorney, Dr. Josef Hohenbleicher, to run against him. At nearly the last minute Kolesnikow had ruled as Landrat that Hohenbleicher, as former member of the party, was ineligible; therefore, he himself was the only candidate. Lindner, already running for reelection for mayor, ran as a write-in candidate for Landrat. He won both elections, with 60 percent of the total to Kolesnikow's 39 percent. He relinquished the mayor's job, and became the new Landrat.[179]

In 1948 the local MG had lost its main strength, Kolesnikow, to the Landrat's office; it had also lost its autonomy. Freidberg's MG was absorbed into Augsburg's. A German, Walter Herrmann, the brother-in-law of Harald Modrow, assistant to Augsburg MG, was put in charge of the branch office. He was visited once or twice a month by someone from Augsburg MG. His work was largely issuing passes to travel to another zone and permissions to have weapons. He was supposed to organize the town meetings desired by

MG; he got to each area's meetings once or twice. He remembers the peasants as reserved, and he is remembered by the peasants as having been very quiet during these visits. Root recorded his impression of his own visits in early 1949: "In the afternoon to Friedberg where the reorientation committee, which was to meet with me, petered out into one man. . . . So I talked with the young man and asked him to call another meeting. . . . February 20: First of forums at Friedberg, a first class flop."[180]

With Lindner at the Landrat office and Hohenbleicher at city hall, things were pretty much back to normal by 1952. Although Lindner was logically a CSU type, local personality conflicts had put him on the BP ticket. The CSU regained its normal leadership in 1956, when he retired and administrator Fabian Kastl was elected.[181] The city hall also stabilized with Hohenbleicher, despite his having been, in the 1930s as a struggling young lawyer, aide to the Nazi mayor Schambeck and naturally a party member. He was automatically arrested in 1945, interned, and his house occupied, but he maintained, as mayor from 1952, excellent relations with Americans in the Augsburg area. A competent, popular mayor, he looked every inch a dignified representative of his city when in full regalia. There could be no question of his having brought any Nazism back to the city hall. Except for the pensions claimed by the former NS mayors, the NSDAP was irrelevant, and both claims were rejected. Hohenbleicher was thought just a bit harsh on them, particularly on his former boss, who died in poverty.

As one might expect, MG's impact on the villages of Bavaria was minimal, even less than that noted in the Nazi period, when the impact was much less than in small towns and cities. To illustrate how little contact there was, I include very brief accounts of two villages in Friedberg County. The first is Dasing, only ten miles from the center of district government at Augsburg, whose experience was described by Mayor Cajetan Schlech. The second example is Laimering, a mile or so farther off the beaten track, whose experience was recounted by Georg Haas.

The occupation had less effect on Dasing than the NS. There was no party member there until 1938, and then only in the person of the school teacher, forced in as the party official. (The nominally Nazi teacher was kept out of the school for three years after the war, but the village council then got his job back for him, knowing that he was in reality a good Catholic.) In 1945 the villagers, ordered to fight with pitchforks against tanks, had avoided contact, just as the American tank going through had politely avoided hitting Schlech's ox cart. Americans, with bottles of wine on each hip, had moved through, doing no more than tearing up his fireman's cap as "Nazi" and taking his camera. Perhaps twenty soldiers had stayed until the end of the year; they bothered no one.

The mayor continued in office as did the five-man village council. When the man who had been mayor since 1925 resigned in January 1946 for reasons of age, Schlech was overwhelmingly elected. MG forced him out for a time, because he had collected for the Nazi equivalent of the Red Cross. He was reelected in 1947, and this time MG threatened to lock him up if he refused the job. All contact with MG was through the Landrat. Schlech never met an MG officer. When asked what MG had commanded for Dasing, he could think only of the refugees which MG had ordered the village to accept. He had been ordered later to have the citizens' meetings once a year and had no objection. Some mayors opposed them, because they were not capable of discussing things. He was proud of his village's good record of expanding its schools.[182] Schlech had been chosen democratically, as mayors before, and had served his village well. MG had simply stayed out of the way.

Georg Haas had been mayor of Laimering through the NS years. With the urging of the priest, he had joined the party to keep a real Nazi from the job. When the Americans invaded, they bothered only to take a radio, some eggs, and a little meat. The only threat to his village had been when troops came with orders to evacuate the entire village for troop housing. He had convinced them that his village was solidly Catholic and not at all Nazi, so the army evacuated the next village down the road, remaining there until September 1945.

As a nominal party member he had been released 27 March 1946; Moran had refused his reinstatement in May 1946. As Haas remembers it, his village council had met as usual from 8:00 to 10:00 p.m., and then came to him, when he was already asleep, and begged him to come. "We need you. We'll ask the Landrat and MG." The village had appealed that their beloved Haas be permitted to be their mayor.[183] As soon as the law was changed in 1946, he was officially back into office, elected with 92 percent of the votes. His village had been democratic as long as he could remember. He kept the citizens' assembly once a year, listened to their opinions, and "took a middle path." He had had no other contact with MG. Nothing had changed, neither his relationship to the Landrat nor with his village.

Villages were barely aware of American commanders. Although the town of Friedberg came to know MG personnel as individuals, even it possessed few political memories of an occupation which was notable for not having gotten in the way. The personnel were remembered as romantic young men, almost none of whom had done anything disagreeable or significant. By their not doing anything political, they permitted a much more capable interpreter on whom they were dependent to take control of the county, at first as their agent and then as elected Landrat. Political sins were mostly those of omission. Eichstätt would have been envious.

The Eichstätt Experience: Tyranny and Corruption

Located in the heart of rural Bavaria, roughly halfway between Augsburg and Nuremburg, the county seat of Eichstätt was a small, isolated, pious, conservative Catholic town. Surrounded by villages even more agrarian than itself, it had the fine baroque structures of a bishopric and the intellectual stimulus of a Catholic seminary to add to its local pride. In Nazi times it had fallen into the clutches of an irrational tyrant, Kreisleiter Dr. Krauss, who had flaunted his power only to be defeated locally by the stubborn loyalty to the church. Eichstätt under the U.S. occupation remained nearly as isolated, pious, and conservative, and again it fell into the clutches of an irrational tyrant, albeit one friendly to the church. Like Kreisleiter Krauss, Captain Raymond Jordan Towle became a legend in his time. Those who spoke of him later approached the legend with awe, some hatred, and considerable humor.

Eichstätt's first contact with Americans was fairly typical of the experience of other German towns occupied as the war came to an end. Bombs fell in February 1945 on the train station, and again on 12 April.[184] As the Americans came closer, the Abtess persuaded the mayor not to offer resistance, but an SS unit insisted on blowing the bridges. After hanging two men who had tried to prevent them, the SS withdrew to the hills east of the city. By 6:25 a.m. on 25 April, artillery shells began falling, and at 9:15 Americans filed in from the west. The acting mayor sent a city worker with a white flag to arrange a surrender.[185] After he worked his way back, white flags appeared on the city hall tower at 10:20. By 10:45 the first tank was parked in front. The first commander, Captain Ben Reed, was decent; the first troops were well behaved.[186] A crisis came with the order from headquarters for the Catholic seminary, long a Nazi target, to be evacuated for a hospital. Bishop Michael Rackl fought again to save his seminary, and decided to stay in order to force the liberators to carry a bishop and priests out bodily. At the last moment someone got the order changed, and the United States was spared an embarrassment.[187]

Fräulein Anni Spiegl, a Catholic resister well acquainted with the Gestapo, made an early acquaintance with the CIC. Three officers appeared in her store and said abruptly, "*Mit.*" She preferred not, but they insisted that it was only for information. Their commander wanted to ask her how her Catholic group had gotten away with so much anti-Nazi activity. At city hall a Captain Reuter, German-born, was impressed enough to permit her to denounce CIC injustices, much as she had told the Gestapo of its foolishness.[188] Reuter stayed for two years and she thought helped save several from unnecessary arrest.

Although Captain Towle was at first second in command to a Major William Staats, he appears to have been the intellectual force in Eichstätt's local MG from the time in June that the unit of seven officers and fifteen enlisted men first entered the city. Some regard Staats as the more harsh. For example, he arrested the gardener who had failed to deliver flowers and closed the milk stores, rejecting the protest that this was equivalent to the murder of children. Towle was his executive officer and took over the command in the fall of 1945. Towle remained the dominant figure until he left in January 1947.

Of his command we have two versions, the first in the many lucid reports he filed with his superiors. These reports made it clear that he was a modern Sisyphus, pushing up the hill the great stone of Eichstätt Nazism, stupidity, and sloth.[189]

> Upon arrival in Eichstätt, a very tight and definite control was exercised over all departments of the civilian administration. Conditions were so chaotic as to necessitate the Detachment personnel doing the work rather than supervising. The Kreis government was heavily staffed with men who were politically unacceptable. An intensive denazification program resulted in the dismissal during the first ten days of 60 out of 77 Bürgermeister with proportionate dismissals throughout the civilian administration. This resulted in a lowered efficiency.[190]

An example of the kind of control he asserted was his 29 June order: "Every building in which German civilians or refugees are living will have posted on the front door a complete list of the occupants. Occupants who have any reason for sleeping away from their homes at any time may do so only by permission of MG or the local Bürgermeister."[191] There is no evidence that this order was honored except in the breach.

By Towle's account matters had stabilized under his supervision to the point that on 1 November the new Landrat and the mayors took over completely. He attested to their being politically clean and assured his superiors that by frequent spot checks and visits he maintained "a close control." He assumed that his charges preferred to have MG run their lives rather than to build up a government for which they would be responsible. He opposed the early elections ordered by Clay. In fifty-eight of the seventy-seven communities there were no candidates and no party organization. "This is due to the conservative and, as to the more remote villages, to the medieval standard of living within this Bavarian peasant area." Democracy to them meant only material comforts, food, autos, radios, and good housing. Towle concluded that these people preferred "to obey the orders given by somebody else."[192]

In August 1945 an advisory council for denazification had been formed but Towle felt the new appointees lacked aggressiveness and feared responsibility. Many were inept, and "there is no pool of politically acceptable, trained men to fill this gap. . . . almost all the able, intelligent younger men

whose training fits them for these professions are politically undesirable. . . .
It has often been said that 'the only men who did not join the Party were those
who were too stupid to be acceptable to the party.' "[193] Denazification of
officials had been completed by 4 August, but those dismissed expected to get
their jobs back when MG left and their replacements "fear the responsibility
and apparently do not wish or cannot command authority." During the first
week of September the denazifying of trade and industry began. "Throughout
the Kreis all shops, stores and business enterprises were closed completely. . . . In order to break down completely the Nazi system, ownership of
farms was carefully investigated and individuals were appointed for all property owned by ardent Nazis." Twenty-six food shops were ordered closed, the
rest were allowed to open forty-eight hours after Law No. 8 was received.[194]
In the next week the detachment screened everyone with a driver's license;
Nazis were forbidden to drive a vehicle. All questionnaires had been screened
by 3 November, but Towle said: "Vigilance can not relax." Unfortunately,
the Bavarian minister-president interpreted the law to mean that only active
Nazis should be dismissed. "The above mentioned detriment has been offset
by the aggressiveness of the advisory council. . . . They are reporting non-
party members who were active sympathizers or workers and are cooperating
whole-heartedly in the properly controlled removal from houses of those who
gained materially from party association."[195]

Despite his November joy in this revival of free speech and German
assistance, Towle was dubious by May 1946 about the denazification tribunals. "Personal experience has shown that the average German committee,
when faced with the denazification of an old acquaintance will fall down
miserably. They allow their judgment to be vitiated by the strong ties of blood
and association." German parties were making a political football out of the
denazification.[196] The schools had been denazified, but it was impossible "to
judge the extent to which these teachers are actually teaching in compliance
with democratic ideals and principles."[197] The school superintendent had to
be fired because of nationalist books he had written earlier, and because he
had rejected the idea of parent-teacher organizations and student committees.
The PTAs were set up and the parents showed themselves "very interested."
Efforts to set up a youth committee, however, had problems.[198] Since nothing
else worked, Towle had ordered the Landrat to appoint a committee and to
force it to meet. "From this conference one fact emerged: that all past efforts
to organize a youth group have failed because the young men and boys don't
want to be organized. They assert that they were sufficiently regimented
through the Nazi regime and that now they want to keep their freedom."
Towle reported he had organized seven groups, all to make music. They
apparently had no more political interests.

Although unhappy with the people, Towle was most happy with the

Roman Catholic church, elsewhere usually regarded as keeping the masses from democracy and change.[199] "The bishop of Eichstätt has always been extremely cooperative. He appears to be imbued with the praiseworthy desire to comply with the spirit as well as the letter of the denazification program." The church was pleased with Towle. He had accompanied the casket of the papal nuncio from Eichstätt to Rome, where he was received by Monsignor Montini (later Pope Paul) and the pope. He modestly added: "Captain Towle was awarded a papal decoration."

Despite the church's assistance, he reported danger of a Nazi revival. "A MG detachment of one man and one officer with a CIC agent who visits the Kreis once daily is in no way able to check. . . . We are asking for trouble. . . . The Germans can be ruled only by might and force."[200] An August 1946 inspection by the district MG commander reported: "Relations with the civilian officials are good. The detachment commander seems to feel that this is due to close supervision rather than to a willingness on the part of the officials to do their job."[201] Yet in September 1946 Towle admitted an insufficient supervision and his last report indicated a scandal.[202] An October inspection had found two Landrat assistants who should have been fired long ago. Towle answered that they *had* been fired long ago, in August 1945, but they had appealed. Landrat Otto Betz and Chief of Special Branch Richard Keil, "an extremely trustworthy man, one of the very few real anti-Nazis in this Kreis," had testified that both men, despite their bad records, were in fact non-Nazis. The two had been rehired until August 1946 when the Landrat was told that MG approval had been withdrawn and they left the office again. Another German Special Branch agent, also since fired, told the Landrat they could work in a subordinate capacity without MG approval. The inspection in October had led to their third dismissal. Towle asked that Betz not be brought to trial; he had done his best as an honest man; it was a question of how one defined "ordinary labor." Inspector Jan Chadwick agreed; Betz would not be tried, but the men were dismissed for the fourth time.[203]

Previous inspections had found other denazification irregularities. An inspection in December 1945 had shown that despite MG claims of 100 percent dismissals, the figure had meant only those who joined the party before 1 May 1937. As a result the chief of police, the head of the finance office, the school superintendent, and the health officer were illegally in office.[204] Towle left Eichstätt in January 1947. He may have gone because the Betz case disturbed someone, or it may have been that his superiors found out about the other world of Towle, the one that did not get into his eloquent reports. But the latter is unlikely—there was no hint of such a discovery in the many inspection reports which emphasized neat jeeps and clean quarters.

The Towle that is remembered in Eichstätt, usually with smiles, is quite different from the conscientious and democratic leader that could be inferred from his reports. With the exception of former Mayor Romauld Blei's memories, stories about him are not recounted with anger, and all tend to convey the same picture, which lends credence to the side of Towle seen by the people. (It is perhaps a matter of interest that the German pronunciation of Towle is "Toll," which can be translated as either "sensational" or "insane.") The least critical German description of Towle is provided by one of his assistants, an outsider, Dr. Theodor Krause.[205] In July 1945 MG had ordered Krause to the city hall and suddenly made him chief interpreter, office clerk, and then private secretary to Towle. Years later, he wrote:

> To my knowledge, he was about thirty-two, born in Massachusetts, Bostonian type, Catholic, unmarried, very sophisticated, graduated from a Jesuit college; his parents were owners of a silver mine business and wealthy. Towle was a type of brilliant American playboy. . . . Very casual and extremely independent. His general look, his appearance and habits were, so to say, "seigneural." . . . He impressed the population immensely by all of his actions, and his gestures like a sovereign, and the manner in which he presented the victorious USA made of him sort of a god of might, brilliancy, and power, like Pizarro or Cortes. . . . He became a mythical personage. . . . He still lives in the memory of the populace as the tremendous *Hauptmann Toll,* who once introduced himself to the *Beamten* by his unforgettable words, in his also unforgettable German (all substantives always *feminin generis*): "Ick am eine einfache amerikanische Boy, welke khat eine grosse Wagen und so vill Gäld zu gehen an every Punkt der Wällt. And this is nikt serr vill in USA."

This simple American boy with his big car and so much money managed in Eichstätt to achieve the award of *Cameriere Segret di Sua Santita,* and therewith became a member of the papal family. "The people of Eichstätt were amazed to see in the newspapers that he was on duty (in 1947 or 1948) at Saint Peter's. After his return from Rome almost all of the artisans of Eichstätt were put to work to create his papal court costume . . . including sword, chain, etc., etc., and this provoked also a lot of admiration and awe."[206] Krause could not come to a final judgment on this unforgettable character, but he was convinced "that Towle considered his presence in Eichstätt as a very colorful page of his very colorful life. A hedonistic life. I had the impression that the whole was for him sort of a new fascinating adventure."

Krause remembered Towle as an "American playboy," but Mayor Blei bluntly called him an "American gangster."[207] Blei said he had not wanted to be mayor as MG ordered; he understood nothing of communal government, having been chairman of a farm cooperative for forty years. The interpreter had said the commander didn't ask what one knew, but only what he could accomplish, and furthermore: "You might as well be quiet. The Americans are such stubborn men, once they decide on something, nothing can be done about it." At his first meeting with Towle, Blei had been scolded because he had not given up his business. In the course of the argument Towle had jumped to his feet, taken his riding whip, and beaten it on the table. (By odd coincidence former Gauleiter Julius Streicher had been notorious for the same practice.) Towle said: "You will obey all orders completely. Otherwise I will have you locked up." Blei told him that as a World War I veteran he would not be talked to that way. He wanted to be discharged and taken to jail. Towle calmed down and instead issued orders for enough plates and sterling silverware to serve two dozen, with wine glasses, crystal glassware, and damask tablecloths, to be delivered by the next noon to the officers' casino. Blei had answered: "No sir. I do not have it and do not know where I would get it." Towle said he should requisition it from Nazis. Blei answered: "I am not a thief or a plunderer." Towle, enraged, ordered all officials to evacuate the city hall in four hours, but then relented.

Towle often raged but could be faced down, as when he had ordered the police chief that a Frau Hofer, who talked too much about the Americans, should be stripped naked and paraded to the city hall. Blei appealed to Krause who straightened it out, but Blei insisted on seeing Towle, who said: "I know why you came. I did not mean it." Blei's answer: "You did mean it. When I read Eisenhower's declaration, I was happy that the dictatorship of the National Socialists was broken, but since, I have become convinced that the Americans are worse than the Nazis because they behave not as victors but as sadistic oppressors." Towle "terrorized" the town with his riding whip, screaming at people to get out of his way. "People ran at the sight of him." He had party members arrested without any discrimination, right off the streets; they were crowded into the city jail, and there robbed and beaten. On one occasion Towle had called the city veterinarian to come immediately, but he had been delayed on a call. Towle said in enraged broken German: "Why you not come at once? My dog sick." When told that the veterinarian had just gotten home, Towle screamed: "When I command, right away, or I arrest you." To make his point he hit his riding whip on the table top, only to break the glass, which enraged him so much he kicked the desk door with his boot, only to splinter it.

Towle behaved better toward the end; Blei thought that the more evil Staats had pushed him at first. The Abtess Baronin Spiegel von Bechtelsheim could restrain him. (She had frightened the Nazi Kreisleiter the same way.) When the mayor needed help, she would say: "Don't worry about it. . . . I will have Towle come over." Then with all of her great authority, she would say in fluent English: "My dear captain. I'm telling you. This is really the last time." He would get very small and answer: "Excellent Mother. I will do it." Spiegl described Towle as pious but foolish and not to be taken seriously; he often seemed merely a badly behaved boy.[208] Blei, however, regarded the group about Towle, Germans or Americans, as scoundrels and whores. Towle's agents plundered where they could. Towle even had works of art forged; he had a statute of the Virgin Mary made, then had holes drilled in it and put it in a smoking room to make it seem old. Blei could only snort at the suggestion that MG had "governed." They terrorized! He could think of nothing positive MG had accomplished.

Blei's bitter memories no doubt emphasized the negative, but others add corroborating details from their own experience. Xaver Hartmann was the artisan who made baroque items which Towle sold as antiques. Karl Gabler made furniture on command, copying antique chairs and a Louis XIV desk. He also made boxes which Towle used to send vast amounts of goods gained by requisitioning or from his many black-market agents. Gabler had records of over four hundred large boxes made for Towle, and he knew of others who were making such boxes for Towle's plunder. Towle used different airports to avoid suspicion. Hartmann knew of three different craftsmen making nativity scenes or baroque miniatures. (The sword Towle used for his papal uniform had been stolen from the city museum.) Edouard Liepold also made boxes for the requisitioned silverware, works of art, carpets, furniture, and pictures. As head of the housing office, he knew that Towle had seized about twenty-five houses for various people, including criminals. Everyone I interviewed emphasized the numbers of houses seized in 1945 and the large amounts of furniture which disappeared. Some documentary corroboration exists. It begins with a Towle letter of authorization for two Germans to seize anything for MG. In the file were many pages of house furnishings seized in 1945, but nothing about their return: long lists of items seized for the officers' casino include the place settings Blei refused to find, but which Towle had found for himself.[209]

The people working for Towle were generally regarded as Nazi-implicated. One had been a Hitler Youth leader in Berlin. Another had been a party member and had a prison record. A third, his right-hand man, allegedly found boys for Towle, usually from the Hitler Youth. (Several interviewed were certain Towle was homosexual.) The natives even thought the "Prussian" Krause had been a party member, but no one had the courage to tell Towle. Worst, in August Hammerl's eyes, was the fashion in which the new government had been organized. The meeting at which Betz had been made Landrat was filled with Nazis. Hans Schellkopf explained that the invitation went out to nonparty members; the non-Nazis invited were to bring along a friend and there had not been enough non-Nazis to go around. Hammerl was angry that so many Nazis remained in the Betz Landrat office.[210]

School Superintendent Hans Seifferth, who was not fired as Towle reported, remembered the education officer, a Major C. L., a so-called professor from Texas. His first order had been for absolutely no instruction. Seifferth had tried to give some private instruction, but had been threatened with arrest. Then suddenly in September the major ordered the schools to open 1 October. Seifferth answered that with 112 of the 128 county teachers released because of party membership, it was impossible. The major said to go out and get housewives, to which Seifferth answered they were not prepared and the law would keep them from being paid. The major, like Towle, used his riding whip, hitting the table and shouting: "I'm in charge. The schools will open." When Seifferth said he had no way of getting to all the villages, the major gave the only help to the schools in MG's entire time—a car with gas, and 2,000 marks for supplies. When the schools opened, the major was as happy as a child. Yet he demanded all the teachers be brought together in the city theater. As Seifferth recalled his short speech: "You Nazis. I cannot help you. I don't want to help you. I wouldn't help you, even if the law let me." With this concise message, he left the room, but stayed in the area for four years as education officer. The major would give no instructions in writing, which caused difficulties; he was seen but three times a year. Seifferth did not know of any efforts made in Eichstätt to democratize, either in the schools or out. As a pious Catholic the major had wanted a vestment; but the church had told him that he would not get one unless he behaved himself.[211]

Clear memories of the occupation in Eichstätt seem to end with Towle's departure in early 1947. Later impressions are only of nice men who appeared from time to time, for example to admire the American-inspired soap box derby. Yet MG reports continue, and continue to describe frustration. This mostly concerned the reemployment of party members, who were reemployed by the city council by a unanimous vote as soon as they were cleared by the denazification tribunals.[212] One of Towle's successors, a Captain Richard Julian, was critical not only of Eichstätters but, unlike Towle, also of the church. "The city has been for several hundred years the seat of high church dignitaries who have up until recent years more or less ruled the population of the Kreis, and even in recent years to a great extent influenced the officials.... The progress in the development of the Eichstätt Kreistag as a democratic assembly has been negligible."[213] Reports through 1947 complain that nothing was being done. The June 1948 report complained of MG inadequacy; the officers were much handicapped because they could not speak German. The policy of automatic transfer after one year meant that the new officer "has to rely far too much on indigenous personnel in the first weeks of his tenure. He is frequently confronted with unsubstantiated statements concerning verbal agreements, promises or orders, and is required to make decisions which can be based only on the trustworthiness of officials and employees with whom he is not familiar." Seventy percent of MG time was devoted to writing reports. As an MG detachment report wryly observed: "The people consider their present government both democratic and incompetent, and assume that the two characteristics are inseparable."[214] The correspondence file ends in 1949, with a Josif Marcu as MG officer. He got a large number of pitiful letters from people who had problems, such as cars or pianos taken by Americans in 1945, and he coldly answered that they should take their problems elsewhere. So ended MG in Eichstätt, as least in the local records.

The man who brought progress and presumably democracy to Eichstätt received his training not from American MG, but in a Russian slave labor camp. Dr. Hans Hutter appeared as MG was leaving in despair, and took the Eichstätters out of the wilderness and into the promised land. His Catholic humanism had made him an opponent of the Nazis; he had been moving toward a university position until he was called up in 1941 by special order of the commanding general and sent to the Russian front, where he remained until the end of the war. Taken prisoner by the Russians 10 May 1945, Hutter was sent to Magnitogorsk, where he stayed until 20 December 1949. After two-and-a-half years of heavy labor under the special observation of the NKVD, he was sent on a punitive expedition lasting to 16 March 1949. In December 1949 he was suddenly and inexplicably released.[215] A non-Nazi and a veteran, Hutter had tried to take up his old university career, but he was told by the Munich bureaucracy that his position had been filled. He took the job at Eichstätt as legal adviser in January 1950, and in October 1951 was elected mayor. He was repeatedly elected overwhelmingly.[216] While he was mayor his intellectual capacity simply dominated the town, although he was a firm believer in democracy.

Like Friedberg, Eichstätt began good government as MG left. The citizens remain pleased that the United States freed them from Hitler, but none could think of any positive aid they derived from the local MG.[217]

The Nuremberg Experience: Benevolence to Disruption to Irrelevance

This second largest city in Bavaria is an industrial center located in the northern and Protestant section of Bavaria. As a medieval walled city it had resisted the incursions of Catholic Munich to the south. It had become, earlier than most cities, oriented toward nationalism (that is, toward Berlin), and toward National Socialism, partly as an anti-Catholic movement. Its medieval Germanic charm was another reason why Hitler had made it the convention city of the party, and he made it more famous for the anti-Semitic Nuremberg laws he declared there at the 1935 party convention. This distinction had added to its attractiveness as a bombing target during the war, and afterwards it was chosen as a special Nazi city for the famous war crimes trials.

Not only was wartime Nuremberg helpless against the Allied bombers, but it had been helpless against acting Gauleiter Holz. (Gauleiter Julius Streicher had been banned from the city for his excesses.) Gauleiter Holz ordered everyone to fight to the last, with the result that when the Americans reached the edge of the city 16 April 1945, many more houses were destroyed by artillery. Although Holz and the SS killed police trying to give up, the 5,000 hopeless defenders were able to surrender on 20 April. Nuremberg statistics showed it to be the most badly destroyed city in the U.S. zone, and the first act of the conqueror was to requisition many of the houses still standing.[218]

From the beginning, MG relied on Germans to govern the large city, needing its large bureaucracy. Resistance groups were dispersed.[219] On 21 April, every member of the city council was called for a CIC interrogation. MG ordered the city to recreate the police force, yet there was practically no enforcement of law and order during the first days.[220] The city was also ordered to get everyone out to clean away the mountains of rubble.[221] The MG unit commanded by a Lieutenant Colonel Delbert Fuller had ostensibly been precisely prepared for the occupation of Nuremberg, but the two whose work is most evident were a Second Lieutenant Arthur Forbes and Captain Richard Mershon. Mershon, interviewed in 1969, could not understand how he ever got in the position of trying to run the city as civil affairs officer. He knew no German and knew absolutely nothing about Nuremberg. He regarded himself in retrospect not only as incredibly naive but uninterested in government. He regarded his selection of mayors and his daily meetings with the city council as misguided. "As a naive young man, sick of the war, I was absolutely inadequate." Meeting with the council was also frustrating, because his orders were "not to rock the boat."[222] Mershon's frustration is evident in letters to his wife. On 6 July 1945 he noted he missed the cooperation which had won the war. A week later, he said: "This new C.O. of ours is really something. He's all spit and polish and I don't believe he knows his fanny from a hole in the ground about MG." On 24 July: "They have again put me in civilian supply, because the major has left. I'm glad because I'm sick of politics and local government."[223]

The chief German interpreter during the early days, Dr. Hans Raab, put in charge of the schools because he spoke English and was politically clean, agreed that the unit was not prepared. From long talks, usually answering naive questions of a Colonel James Barnett, he noticed how little MG knew. None of the officers spoke German. Raab had listened to the forbidden BBC radio broadcasts before the occupation, and had heard that many were trained to take over the administration of each area. But when they came, they knew almost nothing.[224]

Nuremberg did not produce an MG dictator like Towle in Eichstätt, nor an MG-backed German tyrant like Kolesnikow in Friedberg. It had no MG officer with the negative image of Cofran in Augsburg. Not able to govern the city itself, it needed someone to govern for it. The pre-1933 anti-Nazi Mayor Luppe had unfortunately been killed 3 April 1945 in Kiel, during a late air raid. Mershon, looking for someone to take over in Nuremberg, logically picked the aged Martin Treu, who had the most experience in city affairs.[225] He was also the senior statesman of the majority SPD. He had been released from office in 1933 and had not joined any NSDAP organizations. The lesser-known Hans Ziegler, put in as second mayor, was slightly younger.[226] To balance out the age and inflexibility of these SPD leaders, MG by chance discovered a remarkable young man, Dr. Heinz Levié, and permitted him to try to solve the city's problems until 1948.

Levié was certainly the most spectacular figure in Nuremberg in the MG years, and thereafter one of its wealthiest men, with a worldwide fur business headquartered in neighboring Fürth. He was practically given control on the June day in 1945 when he first saw the city. From a family of Leipzig lawyers, his "racially" Jewish father a judge, he had finished his legal training in 1930 at the very early age of twenty-one. Presumably he would have continued in a civil service career, but he was forced out in 1933; although a lifelong Lutheran, he was half-Jewish.[227] In 1941 he was arrested as implicated in a resistance group and transferred to the infamous concentration camp at Mauthausen. He avoided nearly certain death there thanks to a series of lucky breaks, including help from some good people and the cleverness of his wife.[228] On 13 April 1945, he was saved by Americans, beginning immediately a life of close empathy with Americans. He was taken from the camp to the Leipzig MG commander, who decided that Levié would be his chief adviser. Levié could have been made mayor of Leipzig, but decided in June to move to the U.S. zone before the Russians took Leipzig. A doctor recommended Bavaria as a healthy climate, so with furs from his father-in-law's business, he set off for Nuremberg. The morning after his arrival he went to the helpful Americans to get gasoline, but was suspected by the first officer he contacted of being an SS officer. After describing his past difficulties, he was taken to Lieutenant Colonel Carlyle Klise, second in command, who informed him he had already checked up on him in Leipzig, and on the spot Klise offered him the job of *Amtsdirektor* (office director). In effect, Klise was asking him to solve Nuremberg's real problem, economic survival. Levié took the job, but only for three years, and with the stipulation that he could also begin his fur business.

Levié had what the formal heads of the city did not have. He possessed vast amounts of energy and imagination, and, what was then most important, the ability to get along with Americans. He owed his easy relationship with Americans partly to his history, which made him someone they could trust; nearly every non-Jew and nonconcentration camp veteran was suspected of being a Nazi. He also had the personality, relatively rare among Germans, to charm American officers into agreement, and every Saturday night there was a party bringing Germans and Americans together.[229] He remembered MG officers as extremely kind, trusting him completely. He remembered the procedure: every morning at nine o'clock he went to the officers' mess, where he would start things off pleasantly by a bit of piano playing. After jazz and some whiskey, the officer in charge would then ask kindly: "Well, what's your problem today?"[230] Levié felt more at home with the easygoing Americans than with the German politicians; the regime of party hacks he thought worse than under Hitler.

The Americans gave him a free hand for his unorthodox wheeling and dealing to get supplies. MG accepted his "compensation deals." For example, a large factory had asked him whether he would permit them to trade a few trucks they produced for some bricks they needed to rebuild their bombed buildings. Strictly contrary to law and MG policy, he gave them permission for this necessary black-marketing, with the understanding that they would also get some bricks for schools. MG knew about it and thought it great, saying: "*Du, du bist unser Mann.* Do what you want." They accepted his liberal interpretation of Law No. 8. Party leaders should be treated roughly, but other party members used to help rebuild. Levié treated denazification with the same generosity, but MG never interfered.[231] He also distributed justice quickly. For example, a Polish Jew was sent to him from Auerbach in Munich and asked that the confiscated luxury Hotel Carleton be given him. Levié did not like his character, but soon thereafter a Herr Rubsamen, who was a nicer man, asked for the hotel. Levié arranged for its transfer from MG Property Control and for some building materials when they were needed.[232] The system of trustees for confiscated businesses he commonly modified by having the owner take the office next door to the MG trustee while business proceeded as before.

It is impossible to retrace the quick and confident steps of Levié in the written records. In those chaotic years, nearly all of his actions may have violated some rule. The only action in the records was his decision in 1946 to provide clothing for the prisoners from concentration camps, or PWs or refugees, by simply taking excess clothing from leading Nazis. MG approved. In one case he came across an American major who was taking dozens of the best pieces for himself; he told Klise, who had the major transferred.[233] Although Levié was tempted by his popularity to stay on in 1948—he described nostaligically his final speech in May 1948, when he was carried from the open meeting on shoulders of admirers—he did not find the political parties easy to adjust to, and certainly not German bureaucratic procedures; both were reestablishing themselves.[234] The currency reform and the gradual withdrawal of MG made his services less uniquely necessary. He returned to a business career and the city returned to normal. The nominal authorities had been marking time in either MG or mayor's offices, coming and going with an empty public flair.

The MG unit, which received unwanted international publicity as the site of the war crimes trial had three commanders before the year was out. The first was Delbert Fuller, soon described by inspectors as ready for retirement: "Lt. Col. Fuller, DMGO, has outlived his usefulness."[235] The report continued with praise for Colonel Charles Andrews, age forty-seven, "by his own declaration, one whose adult life has been devoted to nothing other than the Army and politics." He had gone directly from Wentworth Military Academy into World War I, afterwards serving in the Reserve and in the Arkansas National Guard. Back into wartime service, he had spent three years filling one administrative job after another until ordered to MG in 1943. He came to Nuremberg in July 1945. The inspector reported: "In civil life Andrews operated a country store with his father. The depression took all he and his family had. In the early thirties, Andrews caught on in politics, regained a modest substance, found a deep interest in the troubles of others, and served, for several years prior to the war as State Welfare Commissioner. He will return to this, or some similar political post when discharged. Andrews is small, possessed of a high pitched voice and would draw no attention in a crowd."[236]

Andrews's successor, Lieutenant Colonel Carlyle Klise, a younger graduate of Wentworth Military Academy, regarded Andrews as a political appointment and a disgrace, as he admitted openly he had been a barker in front of an Army-Navy store back home.[237] Klise thought most older officers were in the way of abler younger officers, and too many officers were doing nothing, interested only in furthering their own nests filled with German girls and later their children.[238] Klise observed that even he could not keep track of so many officers and know whether they were doing their jobs.

Yet Klise was better prepared than most for his assignment. Impressive in person, tall and elegant, he had a master's degree in history. After infantry school he had been assigned to the Caribbean; in the fall of 1943 his training brought him to the MG school at Charlottesville.[239] He was elevated very quickly, sent in a rush to England, and given the assignment of organizing COSSAC's Political and Economic Intelligence Section. Then he was sent to the CAD Shrivenham collecting center, where masses of officers were gathering. The inexperience of these nonprofessionals was made worse by faulty intelligence. At COSSAC information had been based on bombing reports and radioed reports from agents, but at Shrivenham they were using 1890 travel guides to plan the occupation. He found the unrealistic thinking and jealous guarding of status frustrating, "a ludicrous play game."[240]

After a brief MG assignment in Würzburg, by virtue of an officer friend who just took him along, Klise was assigned as deputy commander in Nuremberg. An early memory there was a summer 1945 visit from J. J. McCloy, who inquired about the detachment activities. When Klise began describing how the city was being put back into operation, McCloy had become enraged. He pounded the desk and shouted he did not give a damn about such things. What were they doing about demilitarization and denazification?

Actually, nearly all the detachment did was interrupt the reconstruction of the city and its government by interventions dictated from Frankfurt or Berlin. The administrative history of the city in the city archives records that everything of importance had to have MG approval. At any time any case could be picked up by MG, which would tell the city how to handle it. Because this frequently happened, according to the official history there began an "extraordinary instability of the civil service in the most difficult time."[241] At their 31 July meeting MG presented Treu with a list of acceptable people and those to be released from city service. The next day he was told that although the firings would proceed as planned, no one could resign without MG permission.[242]

A conference of the aged Mayor Treu with the young Lieutenant Arthur Forbes on 3 August showed what MG was really concerned about: signs with a swastika must go; three questionnaires of officials were returned with no objections to employment but the head of the police department would be released. Treu responded: "If all officials who were ever members of the NSDAP were released, we might as well lock up city hall."[243] The city was told the name of its new police chief, a Dr. Speicher, who lasted a few months, and the name of the new head of a city clinic. New lists of department heads and others to be released were given to the mayor. Two department heads, including the head of the police department, were arrested by the CIC for not having disclosed the hiding place of some antique imperial jewels, and sentenced to five years in prison. On 8 August, MG told Treu more of his top people would be fired.[244]

Colonel Andrews was not as tough as the orders and in one of his rare meetings with the mayor, he showed the concern of the welfare commissioner he had been before, asking whether people could really survive a winter in the air raid bunkers many had to use in the bombed city. Treu thought they could, but that the wooden barracks used by many others would be worse. Andrews emphasized that any of his comments should not be taken as a reflection on the good work being done by Treu, saying: "The mayors can use their best judgment at all times and for all purposes. The department heads could do the same." When Andrews asked how the police were functioning, Treu said: "They are not functioning at all. Crime is increasing.... We'll give Dr. Speicher a chance to see whether he has the qualifications to be chief of police." Treu said he had only three department heads left; disorganization was taking over the administration. Andrews merely noted he had no complaints about either Treu or Ziegler; as far as he could see, they were doing a fine job.[245]

MG showed more concern about fuel. On 13 August Klise told Treu he had a plan for getting wood; he would use troops. Mershon was given the order a month later to get some 300,000 cords of wood. He had not the foggiest idea how and he got no directions.[246] He solved the problem by getting the use of 1,500 SS troops, 500 guards, and two truck battalions and stealing the necessary axes and saws. In an unforgettable scene, his SS men, stripped to the waist, marched by in perfect formation singing "Lili Marlene." All ready to cut, but what? Mershon simply picked a forest at random, asking no questions, and in three weeks his SS crew had leveled it. Through this combination of American ingenuity and German resources, Nuremberg had wood for the winter.

The most celebrated achievement of the Nuremberg MG was the firing of Treu. This episode provides an interesting example of an American reporter forcing a detachment into a decision it regretted then and later. As Klise described the affair, he was called on 4 December to Andrews's office, where he found the special Branch Officers, the reporter for *PM*, Victor Bernstein, and the Treu file from the city records. The file had been stolen by one of the German employees in Special Branch and given to Bernstein, who told Andrews and Klise: "This is what I am going to tell the American public and they'll believe me. You have kept a Nazi in office." Andrews, shaking with panic at the thought of a political career ruined, left the mess with Klise and was out of town by the next morning. The evidence in question consisted of two letters from Treu to the former Nazi mayor, Willy Liebel; both of them were brief and formal. The first thanked Liebel for helping Treu to keep his pension on his release from city service in 1933. The second was a birthday congratulation, but Treu had used the common salutation at the end, "Heil Hitler." The fateful two words might not have sufficed to bring him down, but Treu was blamed by Bernstein for having sabotaged denazification of the Nuremberg city administration, as Fritz Schaeffer had earlier been blamed in the Bavarian government. The evidence was that a few days earlier, while talking with Minister-president Hoegner and District President Hans Schregele, who was particularly eager for a total denazification, Treu had allegedly shown an unwillingness to fire all party members permanently. He had also argued the point with second mayor Ziegler, who opposed passionately Treu's idea that "decent" party members be taken back.

The available correspondence, however, shows that in a November conference with Hoegner, Treu was given clearly to understand that Hoegner did not think it necessary to fire nominal party members unless they held prominent positions. Schregele had demanded Treu do precisely that, but

Hoegner told Treu that Schregele had no right to demand it; it was a policy which he was not following as minister-president.[247] On 26 November, Schregele wrote Treu he had heard Treu had complained that Bavaria was less tough on Nazis than Schregele was.[248] Treu answered he had noted the difference between the Schregele policy and that of Hoegner and Schmitt in Munich. He had not told MG about the discrepancy in the interest of the state's authority, yet he had been called to the district MG in Ansbach and asked there to report on his visit in Munich, which he had done in a factual manner. Ansbach MG said the matter was closed.[249] Treu was convinced his policy was that of Bavaria and the district MG.

Whatever Treu's intent, Klise reluctantly bowed to Bernstein's threat. He suspected that Ziegler's ambition was behind it all, called him in, and "read the riot act"; if he could prove Ziegler had the document stolen, he would ruin his career.[250] His colleague Hans Raab thought Ziegler was a poor mayor and totally uneducated; his every speech was an embarrassment. So far as the city's denazification was concerned, Ziegler had done exactly what Treu planned to do, because it was the only possible course of action. Even the KPD's Frau Anni Finger dismissed Ziegler as a mere opportunist, although much of the rest of the town came to consider him a near-Communist. He was not reelected at the first chance to change in 1948, and was even dismissed from the SPD in 1949 for his Russian-leaning policy, after he became internationally known as a critic of MG "hunger politics."

By January 1946 there is a rapid decline in the record of city contacts with MG.[251] MG influence declined with the election of a city council on May 26, 1946; the SPD began its unbroken domination, getting by far the largest number of votes.[252] The most important issues involving MG, however, still were those affecting the health and economic welfare of the city. MG, for example, continued to search vigorously for housing for its own dependents. By the end of the year it had confiscated 1,286 residences, as well as 500 more for the International Military Tribunal. Ziegler's weekly report 31 January 1947 put housing as the greatest concern. The town major had promised no more confiscations, which brought great joy, but the next day more housing had been taken for dependents.[253] And the hungrier Nuremberg got, the more bitter its leaders.[254] As Ziegler put it: "This condition of unconditional surrender is a mixture of tyranny, humiliation, insecurity, uncertainty, and derived from distress and fear." The situation was worse than the year before.

Ziegler's famous attack on MG came in the miserable winter 1947–48. He began it by saying that there would be no meat for two weeks. "No longer can one say that Hitler and the war are to blame. It was the mismanagement in the central bureaucracy. The strike called by the workers should at least have the effect of calling attention to the near starvation."[255] The anger continued in February, the immediate issue being Swedish fish: the Swedes were either destroying the fish they caught or working only two days a week, because MG forbade the only kind of deals possible, the barter of coal or bottles for fish. "Maybe the Germans were supposed to starve a certain period. Nuremberg should tell MG that the city government is no longer prepared to continue unless something is done."[256] At this emotional crisis, Ziegler made his famous statement: "Everyone should strike, from the minister-president on down to the street sweeper." Shades of a general strike![257] In March the hungry city council believed the world food shortage was not nearly so bad as it had been pictured; the people were losing their faith in the goodwill of the occupation.[258] In May came another protest, that MG had decided that Bavaria would get less imported food. The city council said it was at the end of its strength and would quit if things did not improve. The Bizonal Economic Council should reverse its policies; if it could not, then it should quit.[259] Only the currency reform ended this dangerous discontent born of hunger.

As was the case in other communities, the questions of confiscated housing and law and order in the streets continued in correspondence between the city and MG and in public debate until the end of the occupation. A Communist city councilman thought the people only wanted the Americans to go home, but a socialist member answered that Russia's aggressive policies forced them to stay. As in Augsburg, GI violence came to a peak in the fall of 1949, when they were allowed in German taverns.[260] A member suggested that the occupation could last thirty years, so Nuremberg had better get used to it. Yet in the nearly thirty years of American residence in Nuremberg, the random GI violence seems to have been more readily accepted than in Augsburg, presumably because there were fewer troops in a larger city.

The size of the community may also explain the fact that among the few Germans who came to know them, MG officers are generally favorably remembered. Most Nurembergers do not remember them at all, although the Amerika Haus became so popular that the city took over the responsibility for keeping it open as an information center about the United States. It would seem to be the only survivor of the occupation. MG remnants otherwise seem nearly washed away. With a party as strong as the SPD overwhelming every election since 1945, MG intervened only when the two SPD leaders they had given power were divided by Ziegler's envy of Treu. Other than the mistaken dismissal of Treu, brought on by the intervention of U.S. newspaper reporters, it is difficult to find a local MG political impact. The local commanders usually had the common sense to mind their own business.

Thus among the four communities the available evidence suggests that the original commanders took the practical course of finding the most qualified and politically clean person and transferring the responsibility of governing to him. In the small towns the first choices stuck, although purists could later observe that nominal party members, presumably those qualified by experience, remained in office. In the two larger towns, there was more outside interest, which compelled—in the summer in Augsburg, in the fall in Nuremberg—the dismissal of the original mayor on the specious grounds that he was insufficiently anti-Nazi. The replacements were in turn replaced as the party system began its own winnowing process, and by early 1946, with the communal elections ordered by Clay, the search for politically popular and professionally competent mayors found acceptable replacements for the men MG appointed. In the small towns, either the MG commander could terrorize, as in Eichstätt, or the German interpreter could terrorize, as in Friedberg, but these were also temporary phenomena. Clay's ordered withdrawal from intervention in local politics was gradually achieved even there. The small towns were, in effect, abandoned as the machinery of military government clustered in the more comfortable cities. These clusters provided the real German-American contact, first through black-marketing amid economic scarcity, and later through extra pressure on the housing shortage. Germans came to admire American athletes and gadgets. Americans came to admire German scenery and occasionally German culture. In the cities the defeated and conquered evolved into allies, living together yet segregated.

Notes

1. John Gimbel, *A German Community under American Occupation: Marburg, 1945–52* (Stanford, 1962).
2. Edward N. Peterson, *The Limits of Hitler's Power* (Princeton, 1969).
3. The statistics of Augsburg's worst night were: 1,499 dead, 2,325 severely injured; 43 percent of the buildings destroyed, including 12,423 homes, with 32,000 damaged; of the 70 industries, only 11 were undamaged (Fritz Aumann, *Schwäbische Neue Presse* [hereafter *SNP*], "Augsburgs Wilde Jahre," 7 Mar. 1969). Some 8,400 men were killed at the front or died in captivity. Farmers, school classes, and trains filled with civilians were also bombed and strafed (ibid., 18 Apr. 1969; also evidenced by many eyewitnesses interviewed).
4. Letter Maj. John O'Connell, Fifteenth Infantry, 30 Apr. 1945, in Augsburg Stadtarchiv; see also OMGUS, 76-2/10, Washington National Research Center (hereafter WNRC). Franz Hesse, given all the credit by the Americans for helping take the city, was arrested two years later for a minor crime. Another member of the resistance, Achatz, was charged in his denazification trial as a major criminal until he proved he had used his party office to help others (*Schwäbische Landeszeitung* [hereafter *SLZ*], 5 Dec. 1947). When the city archivist in 1950 tried to get statements from ten resistance leaders, only two answered and both declined to help; they did not want to be called "the traitors of 1945."
5. An exceptional incident occurred near the train station when someone fired a carbine at an American tank. Civilians, watching with curiosity and relief, saw a tank slowly turn its turret and fire back. The shell missed the house the shot came from, but hit a neighboring house, killing eight civilians who were standing in the front yard.

6. Despite the fraternization ban, each GI had his German child as "helper." At the arranged whistle, a horde of children appeared to share lunch.

7. "In a destroyed greenhouse on Stettenstrasse, immediately after the invasion an ingenious GI had a busy brothel in operation" (Aumann, *SNZ*, 2 May 1969). Such stories cannot be proved, but any GI, vintage 1945, knows soldiers could accomplish such miracles. See Augsburg Stadtarchiv file on "Einmarch."

8. The soldiers marched the police off, presumably for imprisonment, but an officer appeared to take them back to the police presidium, where they were given a certificate that they were not to be arrested (letter from Police Inspector Joachim Schlichterle, 17 Feb. 1970). Police in precinct stations were taken prisoner and gotten out of jail only with difficulty.

9. Aumann, *SNP*, 6 June 1969. The MPs arrested a policeman trying to help a drunken GI who had fallen through a bakery window; he got two days' arrest, and lost his suspenders, shoe-strings, watch, and rings (*SNP*, 13 June 1969).

10. "In addition to furniture and automobiles that were removed, many other commodities from stores and business houses, such as leather goods, clothing materials, wine, liquor, *etc.* were taken by the troops" (Report, Augsburg MG Detachment, 30 June 1946, OMGUS 83-2/10, WNRC).

11. Mayr had been told by the first American officers they knew he was a good mayor, and that he should stay on for a while (Wilhelm Ott, *Memoir*, Augsburg Stadtarchiv, 10–12).

12. Ott was impressed that Towe neither smoked nor drank and was always friendly and happy. They met as necessary in Towe's office. Ott had other American visitors who would sometimes march in, throw their machine pistols on his desk and sit on it, smoking or chewing gum (ibid., 16).

13. *Hauptamt der Stadt Augsburg* (hereafter HA), *Besetzung der Stadt,* 30 Apr. 1945; ibid., MG Communications, 30 Apr., 3 May, 4 May 1945.

14. Ibid., 5 May 1945. Augsburgers were often amazed when a soldier would seize their bicycles and throw them on a fire; they had ventured on a "military street" without knowing it.

15. The city was ordered to have someone who could speak English on duty at any hour at the utility plant to remedy any breakdown (ibid., 16 May 1945).

16. Ott thought the local MG wanted to help Augsburg's recovery but was hindered by orders (Ott, 30–32, 38).

17. Civilians somehow kept getting a paper which got them into the MG building. Usually the matter was a complaint about American behavior or a request for goods that only Americans could provide (HA, "Verkehr mit den Besatzungsmächten 1945–51," William Wiles, 24 May 1945).

18. The army said he had refused to stop when challenged; two witnesses said no such command had been given. The army then said it was accidental; the sentry had been shooting at pigeons. The sentry was not punished; the widow and children were not compensated (HA, Besetzung, 30 May 1945; Ott, 30).

19. The order came as a surprise even to MG, who recognized in these peremptory dismissals a disavowal of their policy (*Die Mitteilung,* Sixth Army Group, 19 May 1945, Augsburg Stadt-archiv). Dr. Max Utz, in charge of coal distribution, was arrested and spent two years in an internment camp; he returned to a distinguished career as police chief and CSU candidate for mayor in 1964.

20. As Major Towe reported his failure, he said, "CIC," and made "an unmistakable gesture of thumbs down" (Ott, 35).

21. During a quiet conversation about fuel he threw a member of the resistance out of his office when he learned he had been a party member. His closest colleague, Lt. Edgar Milton, said that Cofran also treated his underlings in an insulting fashion (Interview Alfred Kiss).

22. It may be significant that he had a French mistress instead of the usual German (Ott, 51). He had enlisted in World War I when he was only fifteen and possibly served in the Rhineland

occupation. A native of New York City, he had gone from a prep school to MIT to become an architectural engineer. He had designed the Bermuda Yacht Club and prepared a city plan for Pontiac, Michigan. A lieutenant in 1942, he had served in the Air Transport Command (*Washington Post*, 15 Jan. 1946).

23. Ott praised the Schwaben detachment for living simply in a hotel.

24. When Ott objected that the city greenhouses had been badly damaged, Cofran ordered him to buy the flowers elsewhere, but Ott said Americans had bought the other flowers too (Ott, 47–50). Cofran tried to bill the city for 500 bottles of wine. Ott refused (HA, Besetzung, 13 July, 30 July, and 31 July 1945). The file does not show who paid the bill; Ott was soon fired.

25. Lt. Col. Mitchell Wolfson, "Report on Detachment G1H2, F214 to G-5 SHAEF," 30 June 1945, OMGUS 418-2/3, WNRC. Milton's civilian occupation was "news analyst."

26. "Why he had not mentioned that at the daily conference an hour before, I cannot say for sure." Ott suspected orders had just arrived. Assuming Ott would get Joublanc to intervene, Cofran emphasized he had the support of Frankfurt (Ott, 54).

27. Cofran said that officials could change careers; he had been an architect and as a soldier was earning only 2 percent of his former income (ibid., 57).

28. Although Sennefelder was the OSS choice to clean out "Nazis," he agreed with Ott that the entire city administration could collapse. When President Schäffer asked whether much injustice occurred, Sennefelder answered, "great injustice." Schäffer asked: "Do you think that you could keep the city going until September or October when they could be hired again?" Sennefelder thought so, but MG put the time period variously at three months, six months, or three years. Schäffer noted: "The American MG wants as quickly as possible to have the most favorable report to give their superiors. Thereafter one can hope something can be saved" (Bayerische Staatskanzlei 2401, *Schriftverkehr, Besprechung*, 14 July 1945).

29. Detachment Report, Dec. 1945, OMGUS 83-2/10, WNRC. The city administration stagnated for two years until the officials were rehired. A man hired as city doctor performed all medical duties, including surgery, until it was discovered that his only training had been as an army medic (Interview Alois Schertl).

30. G1H2 Detachment Report, July 1945, OMGUS 83-2/10, WNRC. This occurred in advance of OMGUS policy. The "certain public opinion" was probably OSS man Alfred Kiss telling Milton who told Cofran who told Wolfson. The report suggests the "butcher of Augsburg" incident which prompted Clay to issue Law No. 8.

31. Report on the Augsburg Detachment, 31 July 1946, USFET. The proud report expressed surprise that "anti-fascists" were not cooperating.

32. Detachment Report, Dec. 1945, OMGUS 83-2/10, WNRC. As Ott was bringing his list he learned the industrialist he had placed at the top, Otto Mayer, who had had difficulty with the Nazis because of a Jewish wife, had already been arrested.

33. That Ott was discharged instead of being permitted to resign cost him his pension rights, but both he and Kleindienst were quickly employed by the Schwaben government with its tolerant MG. Ott returned in 1946 as city treasurer; Kleindienst was repeatedly elected to the Bundestag.

34. Report on the Augsburg Detachment, 31 July 1946, USFET.

35. Cofran had refused to approve a loan to the father of the officer's German mistress (HA, Besetzung, 22 May 1954).

36. Alfred Kiss, *Memoir*, 5, Augsburg Stadtarchiv, borne out by interviews with Valentin Baur, long-time SPD Bundestag member. (Kiss learned from Belgians that German troops had behaved better than he had supposed. From PWs he learned that Germans were not as persuaded of Nazism as he had assumed.)

37. ICD Report, 3 Apr. 1946, "Denazification in Augsburg," OMGUS 76-2/10, WNRC. "Thoroughly" was written in afterwards.

38. Kiss concluded nearly every officer had a mistress-secretary (Kiss, 9). The town major was a

liaison for goods and services. Kiss spoke well of Milton, a fine man who brought his secretary from Bonn and later married her. Another officer with whom Kiss worked closely was a "Communist;" his secretary was feared because she had been pro-Nazi; she later had come to marry him in the U.S., but married someone else. An ICD officer was also "Communist" and a major black market operator (Interviews Kiss and Valentin Baur). The two Communist officers, according to Kiss, tried and failed to convince the local SPD to work more closely with the KPD.

39. Kiss, who put Dreifuss in office, was disappointed; he was not energetic enough against Nazis. Baur thought him too forgiving, resisting pressures to throw Nazis out of their homes (Interviews Kiss, Baur, and Schertl).

40. The assumption was that they were DPs. By September MG agreed with the Germans that the DPs should be sent home (HA, *Besetzung,* 3 Sept. 1945).

41. These contacts were not problems, except that time was consumed. Sometimes the contact was helpful; the big MG service was providing twenty-six saws and four power saws to cut wood for the winter. Yet when the health office requested penicillin to combat the rampant venereal disease, the MG health officer said he could not give the Germans any; "if one American should die for lack of penicillin, there would be great unrest in public opinion" (ibid., 4 Sept., 21 Sept., 18 Oct. 1945). Banning party members meant that of seventy-nine doctors in the city, only fifteen to twenty would be left in their practices.

42. "The Trade and Industry section reports that production has been definitely curtailed by the operation of Law 8" (Augsburg Detachment Report, Oct. 1945, OMGUS 83-2/10).

43. The city had acted on 120 appeals, and approved 62, of which MG disapproved 16 (Report on Augsburg Detachment, Nov. 1945, USFET).

44. Augsburg Annual Regierungsbezirk Report, Jan. 1946, OMGUS 83-2/10.

45. Augsburg Detachment Annual Report, 30 June 1946, OMGUS 83-2/10.

46. When the city reported a lack of dye, MG's answer was it was not required to furnish dye, merely to arrest violators (HA, *Besetzung,* 29 Nov. 1945).

47. ICD reported the film "has completely failed in its objective in reaching German youth," who thought "the occupation brings more misery to Germans than the concentration camps brought to a few" (Augsburg ICD Report, 12 Feb. 1946, OMGUS 65-1/10).

48. These were turned over to the Library of Congress and the U.S. Information Service (Third Army Monthly Reports, Mar. 1946, 40, Kansas City Record Center [hereafter KCRC]). By 7 July MG opened its own book room, precursor to Amerika Haus.

49. Complaints concerned soldiers stealing streetcars, troops taking the coke used for heating, and the Americans putting chlorine in the water. Breweries had to remove the chlorine (HA, *Niederschift über die Beiratsitzungen,* 18 Oct. 1945).

50. Cofran had promised more food for overburdened city administrators, but Norton said it was none of MG's affair (ibid., 26 Jan. 1946).

51. *Niederschrift,* 29 Jan. 1946. The next mention of MG was when Fraunholz reported pressure by Captain Wilson to have the city buy a factory. Americans had taken all the tar and roofing and would not give any back. The council accepted the MG suggestion that it increase its size to thirty-six members in order to give more persons political experience (ibid., 5 Mar. 1946). Coincidentally, Sennefelder had been knocked down by soldiers strolling with their girlfriends (HA, *Besetzung,* 19 Mar. 1946).

52. HA, *Besetzung,* 26 Mar. 1946. The next item of business concerned more army requisitioning.

53. When MG employees came looking for work with the city they were all refused, "because we have no need to employ people who have forgotten that they are Germans. If one goes into the MG offices, one hears these people speaking only English" (ibid., 21 May 1946).

54. The CSU victory was probably irrelevant to MG, although local MG would have regarded CSU as the less cooperative party.

55. Ibid., 4 June 1946. Baur said the real reason for Weinkamm's resignation was that although he was politically clean, Frau Weinkamm had enjoyed riding horses and unfortunately had joined an SS riding club. Weinkamm moved successfully into Land level CSU politics. Hohner was a noncombatative person who left the city's political wars in late 1947 for a quieter civil servant job at the Land level.

56. The city had suggested regular medical examinations of likely suspects instead of mass arrests; local MG agreed, but Frankfurt had ruled this would be the equivalent of legalized prostitution (ibid., 17 July 1946). MG was able to veto the city's choice of librarians, who simply took jobs in Munich (ibid., 7 Aug. 1946).

57. Ibid., 20 Aug. 1946.

58. Hohner therefore would play down city achievements (ibid., 19 Nov. 1946).

59. Ibid., 28 July 1948.

60. "This is particularly the case with American MG because every office appears to act on its own hook and according to its own policies" (Augsburg Detachment ICD to OMGB-ICD, 7 Feb. 1947, Otto Weinkamm, OMGUS 65-1/10). Most ICD reports were written by Kiss, though others might sign.

61. Ibid., Kiss interview of Vogel.

62. A worker's wife said: "One simply does not want to hear any more from the Americans. They have been giving big speeches for two-and-a-half years, giving many statements, promises of improvement, etc., and in reality it gets worse from week to week" (Augsburg ICD, Kiss Report, "Öffentliche Stimmung," 15 Jan. 1948, OMGUS 65-1/10). Kiss was told by an official: "The Americans deserted the democratic Germans and swing to Reaction. One observes this in their every movement."

63. Ibid., report 11 Feb. 1948.

64. Hector participated in the invasion of France; he returned to Germany in 1946 to a series of assignments in Bavaria (*SLZ*, 18 Feb., 28 Feb., 12 Apr. 1947).

65. Müller was therefore politically clean in 1945, although a picture of him with Gauleiter Wahl and hints of cooperation with the party-dominated union could have been given greater publicity.

66. HA, Oberbürgermeister Dr. Klaus Müller, "Besprechungen mit der Militärregierung," 1 Jan. 1948 to 27 Nov. 1951 (hereafter "Müller").

67. HA, "Verkehr," 4 Dec., 9 Dec. 1947. Müller observed: "The Americans are not happy about their achievements as occupiers. If they are aware of mistakes, this should facilitate improvements" (ibid., 12 Dec., 19 Dec. 1947). Hector was very concerned about suspected communist influences in a strike (HA, "Müller," 8 Jan., 22 Jan. 1948).

68. "They [IRO] do not work as desired with the Americans. . . . For local conditions it has no understanding" (HA, "Müller," 31 Jan., 5 Feb., 12 Feb., 26 Feb. 1948). The IRO explained that the DPs did not want to stay but that no one would take them. Only the UN could free the housing; one could expect more DPs to come to Germany, so the empty homes had to be kept (ibid., 4 Mar. 1948).

69. Ibid., 8 Apr. 1948. Müller suggested using DPs; Hector noted very few of them were interested in work, and anyway DPs were not worth much (ibid., 22 Apr. 1948).

70. Ibid., 29 Apr. 1948.

71. Ibid., 20 May 1948.

72. Ibid., 3 June 1948. Extra houses were needed "as a reserve." Müller was told that the army did not like to agree to the civilians' desires and had certain privileges which it wanted to retain (ibid., 19 June 1948). A parallel debate was whether the city could get back its only auditorium; if the army allowed them to use any part of it, it was only "a courtesy" (ibid., 15 July, 31 July, 20 Aug. 1948). Müller noted that the American Women's Club wanted a list of children to whom to give Christmas presents. Despite this Christmas spirit, the army would not trade swimming pools (ibid., 14 Oct. 1948).

73. Müller was to try to keep van Wagoner from taking some lovely local MG furniture. The city should request that it stay with the Augsburg MG (ibid., 28 May 1948).

74. Americans were also pushing for a beauty contest (ibid., 28 Oct. 1948).

75. Ibid., 16 Dec., 30 Dec. 1948.

76. Ibid., 6 May 1949. "The Germans had answered that you could as easily bring the football to the field under your arm."

77. Ibid., 11 Oct. 1949. The fall of 1949 was a high point of soldiers beating up civilians (ibid., 15 Nov. 1949).

78. Ibid., 26 June 1950.

79. Ibid., 28 Dec. 1949, 3 Jan. 1950.

80. Ibid., 4 Apr., 5 Apr. 1951.

81. Ibid., 22 Sept. 1951.

82. He was not sure it would be a good idea because the American way of life was so much different from the European (ibid., 9 Oct. 1951).

83. Two of the five items discussed were not to be published for fear of arousing the public (ibid., 1 Aug. 1951).

84. Ibid., 6 Nov. 1951.

85. Schwäbische Donauzeitung, 9 Sept. 1951.

86. Donald S. Root, "Diary of a Retread," in Root's possession, Utica, New York; Interview Donald S. Root, Nov. 1969. I discovered no other comparable document.

87. Interview Harald Modrow.

88. Augsburg's real elite went perhaps once to American-sponsored affairs, but otherwise had as little contact with Americans as possible (Interview Schertl).

89. OMGB, Weekly Report, week ending 22 Nov. 1945. The report failed to mention that this discovery was made in a scrapbook kept by the Augsburg police. Special Branch later discovered one of their staff had been a party member since 1934, was hated because he had behaved like the Gestapo, and had black-marketed heavily (Augsburg, Special Branch, Memo to Ehlers, 11 June 1946).

90. HA 100/1704 Gesetz zur Befreiung von Nationalsozialismus, 10 Oct., 17 Oct., 29 Oct. 1945; ibid., Dreifuss, 22 Nov. 1945; Schmitt, 10 Dec. 1945; Dreifuss, 13 Dec. 1945. Special Branch Officer Glass ordered that he be told how each member of the committee voted. The city refused; such interference violated not only every democratic principle but also those of civilization. Glass answered: "The Military Government is not a democracy, but military men who have the right to command" (ibid., memo 13 Dec. 1945).

91. Special Branch was reportedly putting arbitrary questions to the prospective members (ICD, Augsburg Detachment Report, 19 June 1946).

92. The new law lacked the necessary higher court to equalize penalties (HA, 105/0500 Privatkorrespondenz).

93. Interviews by ICD, Augsburg Detachment, 27 June 1946, OMGUS, 65-1/10, WNRC.

94. OMGB, Cumulative Historical Report, Sept. 1946, 21. His trial defense was that he had not wanted his wife in Dresden to find him. His three-year prison sentence made him easier to find (SLZ, 20 Dec. 1946, 3 Jan. 1947).

95. "A review of the past year's activities shows . . . a complete rout for MG and a victory for the Germans." The case which attracted international attention was that of Mayor Mayr, who on his release from three years in an internment camp was put into Class IV. After MG protest he was elevated to Class III and fined 200 marks (Augsburg Detachment, Annual Historical Report to 30 June 1948, OMGUS 83-2/10; SLZ, 19 May 1948, 17 Nov. 1948. Mayr presented an impressive defense, "Spruchkammer Akten," in Gerichthof, Augsburg.

96. Aumann, SNP, 14 Aug. 1969.

97. Cofran, "who saw things in black and white," complained that Zapitz was releasing too many prisoners (Interview Joseph Zapitz).

98. The city's memory corresponds to the headline, "Americans Fill High Positions with Criminal Elements; Gangsters in Augsburg Offices." A case in point is that of Christian U., an army sergeant who came home from the war and found his wife living with an American. He joined the police in Ansbach and was quickly fired. He joined the police in Würzburg and was again fired. With falsified papers, he was employed in Augsburg as a precinct commander, but "curvy women interested him more than his duties." He stole money from a widow, became active in the black market, and was finally arrested (Aumann, *SNP*, 13 June 1969).

99. *Verwaltungsbericht der Polizei*, Stadt Augsburg.

100. HA, *Niederschrift*, 27 Nov. 1945. Wolff came from Special Branch; "Since all special knowledge was lacking to him (except for blowing up railroads for the *Maquis*), the entire organization was on the shoulders of Inspector Hieber" (*Schutzpolizei Verwaltungsbericht*, 2).

101. Quoted in Aumann, *SNP*, 13 June 1969.

102. Eugen Wolff, events of 23–24 Jan. 1946, in OMGUS, 76-1/10; *SLZ*, 28 Nov. 1947.

103. HA, *Niederschrift*, Uhde Report, 21 Jan. 1948. Wernthaler responded that Trillich before 1933 had been vicious with his billy club; MG had released him because he "looked like a militarist" (Interview Waltherr Feldbaur, *Polizeibeamter*).

104. *Schutzpolizei Verwaltungsbericht*, 1 Feb. 1948. Trillich was very well liked by the police; he literally lived in his office, sleeping on a cot in the corner.

105. "They were back to Bavarian blue after 20 years of Prussian green" (ibid.).

106. Ibid.

107. HA, *Besetzung*, Drzmila, 29 Nov. 1949. An increasing contribution to GI violence, noted by March 1952, were racial battles among American soldiers.

108. ICD could have purged the Catholic-oriented newspaper, *Die Neue Augsburger Zeitung*, which had outcirculated the party paper by conforming to the party line yet displaying nuances of interpretation. The ICD policy was to start fresh, which meant the owners lost everything and the city lost a paper until October 1945.

109. He had gone to France in the 1920s, and "dedicated himself to German-French problems as a journalist" (Curt Frenzel, *SLZ*, 3 Nov. 1945).

110. *SLZ*, 30 Oct. 1945.

111. Interviews Kiss and Schertl. Schertl observed once or twice a week his loud argument with ICD officers. Frenzel spoke no word of English and these ICD men no German, so that often the problem was the translation, which took hours to straighten out.

112. His visits to his former home in the Russian zone made him suspect to some Germans and Americans. He explained the delay in starting the paper because he could not make up his mind. "I did not hide my conviction from the Americans. They asked me not to go to another occupation zone."

113. Augsburg ICD, "Brief Concerning Character of Licensed Press," 27 Sept. 1946, OMGUS, 76-2/10. "Hoegner has tried repeatedly to interfere with the editorial policy of the *SLZ*, but with Frenzel, Hoegner will not have much success."

114. *SLZ*, 1 June 1948.

115. Ibid., 17 Dec. 1948.

116. The issue was Commissioner Bolds's intervention in the Loritz trial, which raised the question of judicial autonomy (ibid., 29 July 1949).

117. Ibid., 15 Nov. 1948.

118. Interview Schertl. Frenzel feared that the Americans would not let a former German officer work for the paper. He arranged that when the Americans were there, every morning from nine to eleven o'clock, Schertl would simply walk around, unidentifiable. He remained thus "in hiding" until the denazification tribunals cleared him in 1948.

119. Such women were the basis of the black market. Only priests spoke up against them, which they could do since it was taboo for the Americans to be in a German church.

120. Interview Karl Pflugmacher.

121. Joublanc said that American officers would not want to live in barracks; therefore he could not ask German officers to do so (HA, 100/1801 *Beschlagnahme von Häusern, Wohnungen für die DPs;* 100/1701 *Beschlagnahme von Betrieben, Häusern usw. für die Besatzungsmacht;* 5 May, 7 May 1945).

122. Ibid., 1 June 1945. A school custodian saw instructional materials destroyed; people had been forced out so quickly, with two-hour notice or less, that they had to leave food in their basements and had nothing to eat; leaving beds, they had to sleep on a floor; requests came for years from people who would like only to enter their gardens.

123. The Hague Convention, they later learned, was not recognized by the Americans because the Germans had surrendered unconditionally (ibid., Ott to Hohenner, 11 June 1946).

124. HA, 100/1801, Vaughn to Bürgermeister, 6 Aug. 1945. The mayor on the same day got a letter from a citizen whose house had been taken for DPs; when the Russians left, nine doors, all the door frames, eighteen windows, and all pipes, electric fixtures, and faucets were missing.

125. Ibid., Fraunholz Memo, 4 Sept. 1945. The SPD called them fascists. Local MG came to believe they had not been "forced labor," but followed the pro-DP policy.

126. "The certificate of the Town Major, which was given to us for the purpose of getting our winter clothes and other needed articles, was not respected by the troops" (HA, *Besetzung,* 23 Oct. 1945, Singer; 26 Oct. 1945, Statement; 14 Nov. 1945, Lt. Ponder). I witnessed furniture thrown from confiscated apartments and trucked away to some unknown dumping area.

127. HA 100/1801, Uhde Report, 5 Jan. 1946. The city council was told the Americans were trying to keep Jews out, or if possible trade Baltic DPs for them; there were difficulties among the Americans about the Jews for which the American head of the local UNRRA had been fired (HA, *Niederschrift,* 29 Jan. 1946).

128. Augsburg Detachment Report, 30 Jan. 1946, OMGUS 83-2/10, WNRC.

129. Fraunholz reported that when Frankfurt had seen the costs of MG confiscations, they had clamped down on MG, but no one could stop the troops (HA, *Niederschrift,* 5 Mar. 1946, 26–27).

130. HA, 105/0500, 26 Mar. 1946.

131. With the help of Jews he had gotten more furniture, but heard his substitute rooms would also be confiscated (ibid., letter of H. Mühlheim).

132. "The fine words of Byrnes in Stuttgart must be doubted when Germans saw the difference between theory and practice" (HA, 100/1701, Hohner to Norton, 26 Sept. 1946).

133. Ibid., Lethmaier Memo, 3 Feb. 1947. MG had not considered that furniture could not be bought and money was so inflated that the appraised price would not begin to replace the loss.

134. "This suggestion was rejected because it did not agree with their orders. . . . To the question whether the individual could refuse to accept the money, it was stated this was a command of the Occupation and had to be obeyed" (ibid., Conference, 10 Feb. 1947).

135. Some 300 hogs and a few cows were discovered in the houses, mostly in the cellars (*SLZ,* 30 Jan., 17 Aug. 1948).

136. HA 100/1701, Report, 26 Apr. 1948.

137. *SLZ,* 11 Nov. 1949. Hart responded angrily to Müller's appeals (HA, Müller file, 26 July 1950).

138. *Augsburger Allgemeine,* 8 Dec. 1951, 14 Apr. 1955, 28 Apr. 1956, 25 Jan. 1957.

139. Hans Selder, *Friedberger Volksbote,* 28 Apr. 1965. Resisters to the SS included a Dr. Lohmüller, later a resister to MG.

140. Sixty-three years of age, partially crippled by a stroke after his son was killed in the war, he soon died in the camp.

141. Résumé written by Caroline Hefele, 24 Apr. 1970.

142. Schropp did not complain of treatment by Americans until the rise of MG interpreter Viktor Kolesnikow, yet his assistant, Caroline Hefele, remembered Schropp mocked by drunken CIC

men, forced to stand at attention, to do push-ups, and so on. A soft personality, he was worn down by Kolesnikow's attacks and by MG demands, notably to find housing for troops and refugees (ibid., 2; Interviews Lindner, Anton Schropp).

143. According to Hans Selder, he had come to Friedberg with little academic training. From a poor family, he had "the psychology of the typesetter," and was a fairly good speaker, but not the political sort.

144. Lindner had known Kerle and his family well (Interviews Georg Kerle). Of six officials later released, all but one was taken back by 1950; the exception was the man who had been most unpleasantly active.

145. Twenty houses were taken; ten were kept for more than a year. In the fall some 1,400 men were brought in, but stayed only a month or two, and no major damage was reported. The real pressure came with the thousands of refugees.

146. Sitzungsniederschriften des Stadtrates, Friedberg, 6 Nov. 1945.

147. Mayors of several communities resigned because ill-treated by troops. The Ninety-fourth Division, returning from Czechoslovakia, caused many cases of assault and threats with firearms (Friedberg, Historical Report, Nov. 1945, OMGUS 6-3/5). The December MG report was critical of the Russian DPs who could not be forced to relocation camps and simply stole.

148. The chairman of the Law No. 8 committee wanted to resign because he was treated like an outcast (OMGB Reports of Operations, Jan. 1946, KCRC).

149. "Because of the MG curfew the meeting had to be quickly ended at 10:15" (Sitzung, 15 Jan. 1946).

150. "No property control work . . . not effective buffer between troops and civilian population. . . . Calls in Landrat once a week, Bürgermeister three times, CSU leaders once. Gets written report from Landrat once a week, discusses matters" (Dorn, "Notes," 458–59, Institut für Zeitgeschichte, Munich [Spring 1946, presumably May]).

151. A manufacturer of camera filters, he had been made chairman of the denazification board; out of fifty cases handled, ten resulted in sentences. "Because of this fact Dr. K. made himself disliked in Friedberg." He also made himself disliked in CSU circles (Friedberg, ICD Report, 9 July 1946 on Kellner, signed Ehlers, OMGUS 76-1/10).

152. It tried to call a special meeting, but the Land CSU forbade it (Friedberg, Political Activity Report, 1 Oct. 1946).

153. He had misused his official car, said Captain Moran was unfriendly to Germans, and sabotaged democracy by his actions against Kellner at meetings; he had tried to get rid of Mayor Sepp, who had looked at Schropp's house for refugees; he had retained an NS police chief as his secretary; 12,000 items of clothing had been confiscated and lost; two employees had been arrested and gave incriminating information on a ration card scandal; he refused to answer to the Kreistag, saying he was responsible only to MG (BSK 2401 Landraete, Kellner gegen Schropp, 14 Oct. 1946). The Kreistag developed into an argument over whether Schropp could stop the CSU leader, Köninger, from talking (ibid., 18 Dec. 1946).

154. Kellner wrote again that the recent arrest for major theft from the Landratsamt had indirectly involved Schropp (ibid., 2, 7 Jan. 1947).

155. "The Landrat had attacked him as mayor 'in an inn in front of the other mayors in a most unprecedented fashion,' to convince them that he [Sepp] was incompetent" (Sitzung, 30 Aug., 20 Sept. 1946).

156. He had the support of CSU mayors and the farmers. "However, the town people in Friedberg and Mering have no use for him." The young people said he had no interest in their problems (Friedberg Detachment to CAD, OMGB, 17 Jan. 1947, OMGUS 153-1/9).

157. Ibid., 29 Apr. 1947, signed by Moran, written by Kolesnikow. Although the CSU had gotten 71 percent of the vote in March 1946, and still had 58 percent in December 1946, the party had only 215 nominal members and top speakers drew at most 45 listeners.

158. Political Activity Report, 1 Apr. 1947. A village mayor declared denazification a fiasco; it

merely picked on peasants who had been picked on before by having a party office forced on them.

159. This included the popular Lohmüllers, father and son (ICD Report, Alfred Kiss, Apr. 1947, OMGUS 76-1/10).

160. Moran was quiet and better remembered because he married a German doctor (Hefele résumé, 4).

161. Kolesnikow dramatized things more: most had their mistresses, but they did not run things. The Hungarian girl friend was remembered for sunning herself flamboyantly on an MG villa balcony. A major abandoned his German mistress, but when she wrote to his mother, she forced her son to marry the girl. Another officer married after the child's birth (Interview Viktor Kolesnikow). A major who had married a local girl wrote to complain that a baker was spreading vicious rumors about him and his wife; MG should punish him. The three Germans involved agreed to contribute twenty marks to the orphanage for false statements made about the bride (Friedberg, Correspondence File, May 1948, OMGUS 152-1/9).

162. He was interested in valuable stamps and got two party members back into their offices in return for such stamps.

163. Letter R. C. Talcott, 21 Oct. 1969. "I did avoid getting involved in the black market. The results on other officers, of middle-class background were too obvious for me to ignore."

164. Schropp to Talcott, 25 Nov. 1947, OMGUS 152-1/9. The NS mayor had gotten into similar trouble with the Gestapo. Talcott answered that Schropp could not discharge the mayor who made the charge.

165. "MG should not believe that these men of low character represented the true wishes of the community" (Sitzung, 23 Jan. 1948).

166. Kiss Report, ICD, 6 Feb. 1948, OMGUS 76-1/10.

167. "With our MG it has become so that with the help of a German employee [Kolesnikow] dirty denouncers and libelers go in and out.... On the basis of such lying reports, the authorities are combed through and inspected for a month . . . and the entire population brought into an uproar" ("Attitudes Toward MG," 11 Feb. 1948, OMGUS 65-1/10).

168. "At a recent public meeting, at which the MG was officially represented, they used auto horns to drown out anyone who tried to defend the committees and the authorities. The meeting which was well attended had the character of a meeting before 1933, sponsored by the NSDAP.... MG gives its trust to certain circles, which stand close to the Emergency Association. They let Lohmüller denounce the housing office in public meetings and let someone give thousands of confiscated cigarettes to employees of MG" (ibid., J. Thiele).

169. That he spoke Russian convinced several Friedberg leaders that he was Russian or that he was a Russian spy. His account of his life before he came to Friedberg in June 1946 was that he had a large textile business in Prague, but had been forced to slave labor by the Czechs in 1945.

170. There he had come to know and respect Kellner, an MG confidant (Interview Kolesnikow).

171. Enemies said he bribed them (Bayerische Landeszeitung, 26 Nov. 1949).

172. Kolesnikow later said his greatest mistake had been taking the county's publishing contract away from Lindner's paper and starting his own official paper. The Augsburg newspaper described it as a newspaper war (NAZ, 23 Feb. 1952).

173. SLZ, 2 Dec., 7 Dec., 9 Dec. 1949. He had threatened to give officials intelligence tests and fire those who did not pass.

174. Kolesnikow allegedly told the savings office custodian MG should not be told. "The Americans have enough" (Friedberger Volksbote, 21 Mar. 1952).

175. Freie Deutsche Presse, 18 Dec. 1949. The Augsburg paper headlined, "Dictator Methods of Kolesnikow Intolerable." He threw Schropp off the Kreistag, an action soon reversed as illegal (NAZ, 10 Jan. 1950).

176. *BSK*, 1 Feb. 1950. The interior minister and Minister-president Ehard had written, concerned because the BP used the scandal (ibid., Ankermuller, 27 Dec. 1949; Ehard, 15 Dec. 1949).

177. He had presented them repeatedly with fait accompli, spent much more for projects than authorized, and used the official car for personal purposes. To such charges his answer had been: "The Kreistag had known about it and said nothing" (Bayerische Prüfungsverbank, Geschäftsführung Kolesnikow, 1953, in Akten des Landratsamt, Friedberg, 015).

178. Ibid., Report 22 Jan. 1953.

179. Kolesnikow remained a member of the Kreistag, but moved to Augsburg, where he was active in one party and then another, allegedly working for U.S. intelligence.

180. "A long talk with Landrat of Friedberg this afternoon about discussion groups. I am sure that I do not like this character. He seems to be a most insincere man . . . a feeling which everyone else in MG shares" (Root, "Diary of a Retread"). Root tried again, observing that information from MG was simply not getting to the mayors, so he wanted a committee to plan the meetings. The answers were either that the villages were too small or that similar practices had been in effect for centuries, and his proposed meetings were superfluous (Akten des Landratsamt, Friedberg, 070, May 1949).

181. From a devout peasant family, his brother a long-time village mayor, Kastl was a perfect expression of the majority. Although conservative by urban standards, a supporter of Strauss, he considered his administration very progressive, with new industry, schools, and hospitals. Easygoing, he was repeatedly reelected without serious challenge.

182. Interview Cajeten Schlech.

183. Landratamt Friedberg, Laimering file, Georg Haas. Haas knew of two mayors, nominal party members, who served without interruption. Two villagers were subject to denazification. Haas paid his 1,950 marks fine; the other was a PW.

184. On 14 April the PW camp was being evacuated when dive bombers appeared, killing twelve English prisoners and wounding forty-two (*Eichstätt Kurier,* "Vor 25 Jahren," 25 Apr. 1970).

185. Fritz Halbich encountered Americans who at first ignored him, except one who threw his white flag away (ibid., 15 Apr. 1965). Some troops, invited to breakfast, enjoyed fresh eggs and lettuce; their hosts enjoyed the luxury of candy and cigarettes.

186. The real problem was 10,000 DPs in search of food. Reed did what he could; food was found and the danger receded.

187. Interview School Director Bauch.

188. A teacher who had been forced into the party to avoid arrest had been arrested by the CIC although he was anti-Nazi (Interview Anni Spiegl). At her apartment one evening the doorbell rang. An American soldier pushed his way into her room, mumbling *"Suchen"* ("House search"), and locked the door. She backed away and said, *"Nix."* He persisted, ignoring her statement in German, "You American, worse than Nazi." As this lacked effect, she pointed to the cross on her wall and said, "You a Christian. Shame yourself." His answer, *"Ich nix tun. Freiwillig?"* ("I do nothing. Voluntary?") She said, *"Nix."* Grudgingly he unlocked the door and left. The next day when she passed him, he stood up and gave her a salute.

189. Towle's reports are a brilliant exposition of his goals and frustrations (OMGUS 120/9, 124/9, 139/9, 418/3).

190. By mid-1946 there was but one officer and one enlisted man (ibid., 120/9, July 1946; 139-2/9).

191. Ibid., 120/9.

192. Ibid., 5–6.

193. Towle thought there was truth in that (ibid., 11–12).

194. The next week 162 more shops were investigated and 136 approved for reopening; a

committee took over essential shops (ibid., 14–15). No one interviewed could remember stores being closed for any length of time. Spiegl said a few owners were out for a few days. She knew of no case where MG put in a trustee.

195. Towle noted that in contrast to the Nazi time, when "no one dared to think or to speak because he knew not the attitude of his neighbor or his supposed friend, the people can now have a voice in dispossessing their oppressors" (ibid., 17).

196. Ibid., 19.

197. Ibid., 32–33.

198. "As has been invariably true, the local authorities were spiritually and mentally incapable of undertaking even so simple an organization" (ibid., 37).

199. MG found no clergy needed be dismissed, but the bishop insisted that two who had not been active enough fighting Nazism should be removed. "He himself has a long record of anti-Nazi activity and is well known as an active opponent of Nazism. Partly because of his opposition, Nazism never succeeded in establishing itself as firmly in this Kreis as in the majority of Germany" (ibid., 42).

200. Ibid., 54–55.

201. The only criticism was that three people did not need four houses (ibid., Inspection Report, Tillinghast, 16 Aug. 1946).

202. Headquarters said tribunals would receive intensive training; they were addressed by the Franken denazification chief, who said he had read the law only twice, and knew no more than what was contained in the published version (ibid., Detachment Report, Aug. 1946).

203. Ibid., 124/9, Report Towle to Chadwick, 2 Dec. 1946.

204. Ibid., 139-1/19; Inspection, Dec. 1946. A June 1947 inspection found "Special Branch directives not being carried out . . . no 'Observation and Reporting Machinery' had been set up. Furthermore no provisions had been made to check on enforcement of sanctions imposed by the Trial Tribunal" (ibid., 26 June 1947).

205. Krause was born of German parents in Saint Petersburg, leaving Russia after the revolution. He had worked in Riga and Reval as a banker and journalist until he became an interpreter for the German Supreme Army Command. Taken ill in February 1945, he had moved to peaceful Eichstätt. He said of himself: "During the absence of MG officers . . . I 'ruled' the Kreis and the town" (Letter Theodor Krause, 12 Sept. 1970).

206. "One of the famous painters from Munich was called to Eichstätt to paint him and he performed an excellent work, painting him as a papal chamberlain and as a captain of the U.S. Army" (ibid.).

207. Interview Romauld Blei.

208. Towle had come to cathedral services only once, but in his own memorable style. The cathedral pastor had to escort him to a special chair set in front and roped off from the rest of the worshippers. There he had sat in splendid isolation, wearing riding boots and spurs.

209. One document bills Towle for a full Bavarian costume (File on Towle's unpaid bills in OMGUS, 139-3/9).

210. MG later discovered that "*Bürgermeister* Blei has proved that he does not dispose of the qualities required of officials in key positions. . . . His appointment resulted from a provisional election at which many Nazis took part and, presumably through the ignorance of the situation, was approved by MG." The SPD men believed Blei was against Nazism, but thought that because he had remained mayor until 1934 he had made too many compromises. The Betz-MG administration was known as the "Land of Smiles," because Betz smiled when he should have said no; Hammerl thought this was because Betz needed a few years more to get his pension.

211. Interview Hans Seifferth.

212. OMGUS, 124/9, Report Mar. 1947; *Sitzungsprotokolle des Stadtrates,* Eichstätt, 17 Mar. 1947; Letter Arbeitsgemeinschaft Political Parties, 1 Aug. 1947; Detachment Report, 30 June 1947; OMGUS 139-2/9, WNRC.

213. MG had disagreed with less than one percent of denazification verdicts, yet many witnesses were "afraid that in a few year Nazis and Nazism will be forgotten and that people will remember that they testified, not against a Nazi, but against a neighbor" (OMGUS, 124/9, Report 30 Dec. 1947). A Major Householder noted bitterly: "They are not interested in German politics let alone world politics. . . . As far as setting up a democracy, they all claim to know and understand democracy and not one out of one million has the faintest conception of it as we do."

214. Ibid., 139-2/9, Detachment Report, 30 June, 9 Sept. 1948, Lyle Edgar.

215. From Rebdorf, a neighboring village, his father the long-time workhouse director, Hutter studied at the local Catholic gymnasium from 1924–33. Not permitted to start university study, he continued at the seminary in church law. He finished university having avoided joining even the compulsory NS student organization. After he fought in Russia for four years his battalion was destroyed in January 1945; only one other returned. In transport German PWs died by the dozens; in one camp, 2,500 of 5,000 died in six months from cholera and diptheria. He was saved when a Russian doctor noticed a picture of Frau Hutter and their five-year-old son and took an interest in him. The labor was heavy construction work, such as building a new section to a city (Interview Dr. Hans Hutter).

216. Hutter had the courage to lead a revolt against Franz Josef Strauss and was resoundingly defeated, ending any chance of a bigger political career.

217. He thought political attitudes may have been healthier in 1950, with memories of dictatorship and war fresh enough that people were concerned.

218. In 1945 the center of the city, with no targets, was almost leveled; killed were 2,292 men, 2,512 women, 456 children, and 30 of unknown sex, a total of 5,290, including 820 foreigners (*Chronik der Stadt Nürnberg*). Dr. Luppe, probably mayor again as Streicher's foe, was killed by bombs in Kiel, 3 April 1945. The city lost 682 more, including 371 civilians. Of the city's houses, 91 percent were damaged and 36 percent totally destroyed. Of 123 schools, only two were undamaged; none of forty-two Protestant churches was intact (ibid.).

219. "Immediately after the fall of the city, a number of anti-Nazi and anti-fascist groups were formed. Since their activities were difficult to control, their leaders were ordered to cease functioning on 10 July 1945. It is assumed that the members of these groups joined the Communist Party" (Nürnberg Detachment, Annual History, 28 June 1946, 2 OMGUS, 81-3/10).

220. Many cases of rape and robbery by Americans were reported (ibid., 11).

221. MG did what it could; it offered 10,000 PWs to help (*Akten des Stadtrats Nürnberg, M.R. in Nürnberg*, Lt. Forbes, 18 May 1945).

222. Only twenty-six when he was suddenly ordered to MG, he had been commanding a field artillery unit since the Battle of the Bulge. The only reason he could imagine for his new position was that he had spent two years at Yale, majoring in government and international relations. The men in his MG unit who were able were technicians, rarely in command. The occupation was "the most poorly managed, poorly handled thing . . . with nothing of a positive nature done" (Interview Richard Mershon).

223. "We have small time politicians and businessmen who are riding the gravy train and fouling up the whole postwar administration and government. . . . The good Senator Dahlquist of Minnesota came through . . . all he is doing is sight-seeing here and wasting a lot of gas and taxpayer's money. . . . They used to call me the *Oberbürgermeister* of Nuremberg. In other words I told the mayor and city council just what to do and what they could or could not do. If the mayor tried to get frisky, I sat on him. Imagine me the mayor of a city twice as large as Duluth" (Letter Mershon to wife).

224. Yet early MG decisions, based on common sense, were better than those later made on the basis of principles enforced from a Frankfurt reacting to newspaper reporters (Interview *Schulrat* Dr. Hans Raab).

225. He had been in the city administration from 1909, as second mayor 1919–33, and served in high positions with the Kreistag and the state legislature (*Akten des Oberbürgermeisters Nürnberg, Schriftverkehr mit der M.R.*).

226. In the 1920s he had been active in SPD politics and unions in various parts of the country, though born and raised near Nuremberg. In 1933 dismissed and jailed, he had lived there 1939–45 as a bookkeeper.

227. He thus began a fascinating odyssey. He worked briefly as laborer, but because he could not join the NS union he moved to a schoolbook firm, and then became private secretary to a rich family. In 1935 an automobile accident altered his face, giving him more "the look of a boxer than a Jew." At this juncture he "stumbled" into the fur business, and then married the daughter of a Greek fur merchant in Leipzig (Interview Dr. Heinz Levié).

228. She had a doctor friend declare him "dying from a hopeless case of tuberculosis." Since he was "dying," no one killed him.

229. That the lieutenant who had to approve economic decisions was enamored of the solo dancer at the opera helped make things "less bureaucratic."

230. One morning Levié brought along a box of apples and bananas, which implied black-marketing; he was taken to Colonel Klise. When Klise learned this was for the animals in the city zoo, both left immediately to feed them.

231. He described vividly, acting out the scene, the little official who came into his office, flung himself at his feet, and begged not to be fired as a party member. Told to get off the floor, he worked hard in Levié's own office.

232. When asked by the city council why, with so many people living in hovels, he had started a luxury hotel, Levié answered every city had to have a luxury hotel; this would bring guests, which would bring work, and the people could work their way out of their hovels. He sponsored a motorcycle race in 1946 when almost no German could get gasoline for any purpose.

233. "Aktion Dr. Levié" later got involved in the bureaucracy; people whose clothing had been taken demanded payment from the city. The bill totaled 130,000 marks (*Akten des Stadtrats Nürnberg*, Evakuation and Vertriebenenamt, 2 Jan. 1959, 1 Dec. 1959).

234. His fur business, left with his partner Märkle, a fellow political prisoner, had grown. They had fed enough rabbits to become prosperous.

235. "He is now 50, tired, disillusioned, and anxious to return to Mrs. Fuller, who has been invalid for years" (USFET, Field Inspection Report on MG Detachment, 6 Aug. 1945).

236. "But he knows the Army, is a firm but reasonable disciplinarian, is a better than average administrator, follows directives literally, respects the intelligence of his staff, and is considered by that staff, a commanding officer of understanding and one worth serving under. Andrews has no driving urge to go home. The army remains a good living and one of his two hobbies" (ibid., 8).

237. At the first staff meeting Andrews announced that if any officers wanted a promotion or a medal, "tell me and I'll get it for you. That's what my exec. and I did for each other before the Corps was dismantled" (Interview Col. Carlyle Klise).

238. Confronted with Justice Robert Jackson's demand for two grand pianos, the property control officer found some, but did not even keep records about where.

239. This school had tried to be practical, but Klise thought common sense had been much more important than this training.

240. COSSAC included "some dregs of the Regular Army," building large empires and keeping officers from meaningful activity, so that the general could call it a division and get himself a second star.

241. *Verwaltungsberichte der Stadt Nürnberg*, 1945–49. Klise doubted Patton knew what was going on; certainly there was no "Patton policy" in Nuremberg.

242. He should also pay the bill for the ten 15,000 army employees in the city. The substance of the meeting 2 August was Treu's request that MG protect the forests; people were panicky with no fuel for winter (*Schriftverkehr mit M.R.*, 2 Aug. 1945).

243. Ibid., 3 Aug., 7 Aug. 1945. The first item at the next meeting concerned the employees of the city orchestra and opera. Theater and opera had been forbidden 14 June; two days later the same people were giving variety shows, but only for Americans; they were forbidden again 8 July and again permitted. The city received the bill of 55,000 marks as "war costs" (*Stadtchronik*, 14 June 1946).

244. No one released would be paid a pension. (Treu had been given his by the Nazis when he was fired.) The police force, but a fraction of its normal size, was to be completely reorganized on the English model. Forbes saw no help in getting fuel for winter (ibid., 8 Aug. 1945).

245. "Would you object if we took these [hungry] people to the countryside where they could eat?" Treu thought some would object. Andrews criticized city officials because they used too much gas and used it on pleasure trips, because lists posted outside the houses would name people who could not be found, and because many eighteen to twenty-year-olds were not working (ibid., 9 Aug. 1945). Andrews asked what the city had done to get winter fuel; the city lacked labor and transport. By 1 September, Treu had lost the last of his department heads, Rühm, MG's first acting mayor. A total of 1,951 persons, mostly at the Beamten level, had been released, including 441 policemen.

246. He asked G-4 for tools, transportation, and men. The answer was, "I won't give you a damn thing," but when Mershon saw the officer had a flyrod and began talking fishing, he got some useful advice. He should beg, borrow, or steal what he needed.

247. Hoegner said the Bavarian cabinet had agreed 21 November to make the distinction between active and nominal members. "The Bavarian state could not permit a fourth or even a third of its residents to be made into enemies. . . . The Minister-president expressed the opinion that for the time being no further dismissals should be made, until the ministries could come to a decision" (*Schriftverkehr Reg. Mittelfranken*, Nov. 1945).

248. Treu had "created this insecurity in Nuremberg," which made Schregele's job more difficult (ibid., Schregele, 26 Nov. 1945).

249. Ibid., Treu, 29 Nov. 1945.

250. He wished later he had made Levié mayor because Levié was the only one who worked for the people, but he did the work of lord mayor anyway (Interview Klise). Raab knew what Klise suspected: Ziegler knew the girl who controlled the Special Branch personnel records and told her to find something incriminating in Treu's file. Raab was sympathetic, as was nearly everyone, with Treu. He had no hearing and no one in the city administration or his SPD was consulted (Interview Raab).

251. In the summer of 1946, while Klise was on leave, his deputy and successor, Colonel Callicott, demanded that Ziegler justify the city's having withheld questionnaires on all city employees who were employed after October 1945 in violation of MG's directive (*Schriftverkehr*, 18 June 1946).

252. MG had predicted the CSU would win (OMGUS, Weekly Report, 29 Nov. 1945). In May OMGB issued an interesting order: "The housing office is to put any member of the NSDAP or militarist out of any room which looks more comfortable than a room occupied by a non-member of the NSDAP." OMGB warned: "The above is not left to the judgment of the housing official, rather he is forced to the action" (*Verwaltungsberichte*, 340).

253. Ibid., 342. Providing for VIPs assigned to the trials diverted MG. "Nothing would improve the image of the American nation more than the stopping of these house seizures" (*Schriftverkehr, Wochenbericht*, 31 Jan. 1947).

254. Ziegler defended the city: it had never been a Nazi town but had always been democratic, free, and progressive (*Niederschrift*, 29 Apr. 1947).

255. Ibid., 16 Jan. 1948. Bitter speeches by the council demanded MG recognize it must have free trade. "They [MG] do not want the German economy to recover. They do not want us to have the advantages of 1919" (ibid.).

256. Another said the city should force MG to accept the fish and chances to obtain olive oil and sugar (ibid., 11 Feb. 1948).

257. Ziegler said the Economic Council was a dictatorship. Delay in Marshall Plan aid was because American capital wanted to get control first. "When an American puts a dollar into a business, he wants to get another dollar out of it" (ibid., Ziegler).

258. Ibid., 24 Mar. 1948.

259. Linnert (FDP) declared: "they still believe they can leave us barely alive" (ibid., 5 May 1948).

260. Anger concerned the 450 houses still requisitioned, mostly from people on pensions who had put their savings into them. MG answered it had no money to build any houses, or even to repair houses (ibid., 9 Sept. 1949). The Nuremberg Opera House had to be shared with the "Stork Club" run for the troops. McCloy got so sick of complaints that he built new facilities (ibid., 14 June 1950).

261. The police chief tried to minimize the danger. The council scorned this defense; attacks "decreased" because people near Americans did not dare to leave their houses after dark.

8 The Occupation in Perspective

A favorite theme of recent German historiography has been the interplay between the forces of continuity and change—that is, the extent to which things have remained the same while changing. The clear import of my research is that the occupation per se changed very little. One could conclude that Bonn represented the continuity from Weimar. One might even argue that the authoritarian aspects of the occupation represented a continuation of the authoritarian elements in Germany's past, albeit ineffectively. Much of West Germany did remain the same from the 1920s into the 1950s, as the person of Adenauer evidences in Bonn. Old men, with ideas from the past, were long dominant. There was much continuity and not only negatively, for there were also positive elements in the German heritage.

On the other hand, there was much that had changed between 1933 and 1939, and much more was altered by the war. Much was destroyed, including hopes and illusions. The end of the war was the beginning of something new. Superficially the new Germany could be seen in further industrialization and its continued modernization. Beneath the surface there was also a political maturation. Monarchism, dying before 1933, was long dead politically. Dictatorship had not worked. War had not worked. Many of the core practices of the adult Germans would continue, but the political turning away from dictatorship represented a great change effected before the occupation began, and the change solidified rapidly once the occupation ended.

If one assesses the accomplishments of the occupation from the perspective of almost thirty years, one can consider it victorious in that Germans have fought in no more wars. But the war and the defeat itself convinced the vast majority of Germans that war is hell, the worst of all calamities, a conviction many shared already in 1939. MG's tinkering with textbooks and uniforms was a molehill compared to the mountain of war-created hatred of war, and oddly in the meantime the United States moved toward its own kind of idealistic militarism. It was the United States which pushed Germany toward a limited remilitarization, a policy reversal which was lamented by alarmists who saw it as a prelude to more goose-stepping storm troopers. Yet West Germany is still basically unmilitaristic. The German army is no danger to the world. The West German attitude remains much more skeptical of military solutions than does the American.

U.S. policy shifted from a restraint on the German economy to an effort to revive it. The folly of the Morgenthau Plan should be sufficiently evident that no one could take it for more than a madness born of the other madness of war. Yet the image of a Morgenthau Plan having been implemented survived because MG, with little money, had to be primarily passive. Unfortunately passive controls made it difficult for raw materials to enter the country, goods to be processed, and exports to leave. Policy also involved dismantling factories, but this action gave less aid to the victors than if the factories had remained standing. Even the dismantlings, however, were not as crippling as Germans then claimed. German hard work built new factories, with the temporary aid of American food and materials. Much the same noneffect resulted from decartelization. One firm was divided into three parts. German industry has grown in size since, mostly to compete with the much larger U.S. industry.

Although little can happily be said about deindustrializing, Americans do make happy assumptions about the U.S. impact on the reindustrializing. Certainly a victory, the Marshall Plan is one of the few jewels, or semiprecious stones, in the now criticized policies of the Cold War. One might debate whether the costly occupation, which absorbed a large capital and labor potential, or the burden of MG economic bureaucracy, did the German economy more harm than the Marshall Plan did it good. One could also debate whether it stopped the spread of communism, which remained weak in West Germany. The voting percentage to Communists throughout western Europe has remained remarkably stable despite a quarter-century of Marshall Plan prosperity. This economic victory, linked to the nonexpansion by Russia, seemed to prove that American economic power could work similar miracles elsewhere. It led Americans to an overestimation of the power of economic aid, even as American victories in both world wars led to illusions of military power. Both assumptions ignored the importance of the other elements of the Marshall Plan miracle; the recipients contributed a population willing and able to do what it had done before, which was to operate a modern economy with a base in roads, railroads, and factories. These factors made recovery relatively simple.

Denazification initially seemed simple, but became very complicated. The war brought Hitler's death and the end of Nazi power, but the occupation worked to eradicate the remnants. Every political policy was related to denazification, and the formal OMGUS process meant that millions of people had to be sorted through the giant sieve of ritualized questionnaires and amateur courts. This logical solution to an illogical dilemma was probably the only area where Clay's government was much more than passive, but after the quick failure of direct MG action in firing and arresting people, it had to depend on Germans to finish the job. German leaders soon recognized the folly of trying to determine the guilt and punishment of millions, but OMGUS could not admit to seeing the obvious, possibly for fear of a misguided public opinion and a confused Congress. Yet it was Congress, or more precisely its pursestring committee, which decided in 1948 the machinery must stop, probably for the wrong reasons. It ordered MG to reverse itself immediately, which added to the chaos. The least guilty seemed to be the worst punished. The image of denazification was bad, probably worse than its reality, and that image has persisted.

Yet the dangerous renazification, proclaimed by American journalists, did not happen either. Conservatives were permitted back into power by a weakened MG, but contrary to the opinion of some Americans, these were not Nazis in 1945. They considered themselves anti-Nazi and feared a Nazi revival which could cost them life and liberty as well as power. Unless one is forced to look through red eyes, West Germany did not turn brown; it combined large patches of rural black conservative with urban patches of liberal pink, for reasons irrelevant to MG policy.

That West Germany has not given power to another Hitler, as experts predicted in 1945, is probably as much despite as because of occupation policy. Germany was in large part denazified by Hitler, because Nazism was based on success and Hitler failed. In losing a war he committed crimes which put Germans into such a bad moral position that crimes committed against them, during and after the war, have yet to attract much sympathy. The occupation diminished the horrors of Nazism by creating some horrors of its own, because the elements of life impressive to most people, food and housing, got steadily worse. If anything could have justified Hitler's fanatic war, it might have been what happened when Germany was at the mercy of his enemies, particularly those from the east. At least the majority of the population under Hitler had their homes, land, jobs, and food. Until the occupation ended, many Germans could be sure of none of these. After West Germany got its essential independence and began to solve its essential problems, German regard for Hitler steadily withered away. (Only 2 percent of West Germans in 1970 thought him a great German leader.) The dismal failure of an overt right wing to be more than a lunatic fringe, despite the loss of so much land by so many millions and the nearly permanent presence of alien occupation troops, bears evidence to the anti-Nazi impact of World War II.

Democratization is more difficult to assess because both East and West Germans claim to have democracy. One could argue, variously, that the stability of open elections proves the West Germans have created a democracy; that their party system, tight by American standards, created only a party oligarchy; or that the bureaucracy has reigned supreme no matter who won elections. All things are relative, yet by the standards of other countries, many of which have maintained neither parties nor elections, Bonn has been as consistently and openly supported by the majority as any country in the world. Schools, scarcely changed by OMGUS, are about as democratic as those of other western European countries; they are somewhat more authoritarian and less egalitarian than the American. Society is probably less democratic than the American, but it is comparable to other western European societies, and possibly more open than the British. The weakening of class lines was a result of the war, the loss of lands, and the gains of industry, not of any MG policy.

This increased democracy may be causally related to the occupation, whose commanders reported, as did many historians, a determined German lack of understanding or concern for self-government. Historiography has tended to regard the Weimar democracy as merely an antechamber to an inevitable Nazism, the nuances of interpretation being whether the politicians as fools opened the door to Hitler or as weaklings lay down as stepping stones. Yet one could consider the Germans in 1945 to have been not nearly as antidemocratic as MG assumed, but rather to have provided a real potential for building free institutions. This potential was then affirmed by German leaders, who returned to power astonished at how unsuccessful Goebbels had been. In 1945 MG seemed to cancel out the alternatives of monarchism, fascism, and communism, but the early 1946 election showed that none of the three had popular support. From the first the Germans voted for parties affirming democratic values.

Perhaps they were more dissuaded from fascism and communism than persuaded to democracy, but the silent majorities elected leaders for Bonn who had been leaders for Weimar. These operated much as before, although they were better united for fear of Nazis and the occupation. They took up, for better or for worse, the practices of 1919. Local institutions, with the exception of the elected Landrat, remained as before. State and federal constitutions show slight modification, but these modifications were made to remedy what the Germans observed as weaknesses in the Weimar period. Allied influence on the constitutions was remarkably minor; the victors tended to nullify each other's influence. Bonn is assuredly not Weimar, but the major change was not constitutional, but rather psychological and indigenous. That democratic America was rich and powerful seemed a self-evident proof that democracy was potentially good, but few if any specific features of American democracy were added to the German practices.

MG had little influence in assisting German democracy, but not necessarily because of the insincerity or incapacity of its idealists. Some tried hard, but their problems began with the fundamental fact that the occupation was a military dictatorship. Germans therefore saw firsthand the least democratic facet of U.S. society. Generals can scarcely command a society to be more democratic. As soon as a government of soldiers, or tyrants, makes a concession of freedom—as was made by Clay very early—it loses the capacity to force other changes. For example, MG gave German political parties the freedom to organize. In so doing, it could not dictate party organizational policies, even to change those it considered relatively undemocratic. MG permitted elections. It then had to accept the decisions of the people, though MG also diagnosed some of those as undemocratic. Democracy requires faith in the people. This is precisely what the occupation experts usually lacked, because most were convinced that Germans could never understand anything but brute force. Clay guessed better. He felt he had to trust them, and when he did, it worked.

The soldiers, or later the civilian bureaucrats, could not begin to compete with German politicians for persuasive popularity. Germans in 1945 said apologetically, "I am not a politician"—that is, "I am not to be blamed." The same could be said for the emissaries of democracy: very few American officers were politicians or even students of politics. Those few politicians who got into MG were absorbed quickly into MG's internal politics instead of contributing to German politics. MG did not operate politically with Germans, even behind the scenes. It rarely sought out pressure groups as allies to effect MG goals, either among the people or the politicians, who were long distrusted as reactionaries, socialists, or simply as Germans. Clay kept his distance to avoid the implication that Germans close to him were collaborators. A public MG blessing to any party would have been a curse.

It was rare for Germans to look for advice on how to run a democracy; the advice they did seek was usually on what tactic would satisfy OMGUS. Most Americans were poorly trained ideologically. They knew democracy was the best system, that it had something to do with freedom, with being tolerant and peace-loving, but that was about as far as ideological discussion usually could go. The few émigrés could at least speak German, but they were handicapped by being fully trusted by neither side. Furthermore, their skill came from a knowledge of German, not American, institutions. The governmental forms which worked were those copied from pre-1933 Germany. Those which did not work effectively were the MG organizations created ad hoc at the level between the old Länder of 1945 and the new Bonn Republic of 1949. They were artificial entities made nearly unworkable because Clay could not let them follow precedents for fear of giving the Russians more reason to be obstructionist.

Debureaucratization, although not an MG goal in the same overt way as denazification and democratization, was involved in most MG policies. Distrusting "Prussian" bureaucracy, MG fired most bureaucrats for having been in the party, but then rehired them in a year or so, because the anti-Nazi Germans, whom MG needed, said they needed the dismissed "Nazis." The "renazification" of 1948-52 can be better described as a "rebureaucratization." Strange as it may seem, the MG experience with bureaucrats was much the same as Hitler's, even including the lament that officials were impolite. Discourtesies lose or gain in translation, but Germans discovered that some American officials could give lessons to German bureaucrats in discourtesy. If one thinks bureaucrats should be limited by their conscience in their obedience, the MG bureaucrat was probably more inclined to follow orders than the Nazi. Significant and deliberate policy diversion was uncommon. Disobedience was rarely on matters of principle; as aliens MG officials had little personal reason to resist unjust orders. For everyone who resigned for reasons of principle, many more left or stayed for reasons of personal advantage. More importantly, a commander who wanted to help the local population usually was powerless to do so. The occupation bureaucracy well demonstrates the frequent modern perception of powerlessness. Everyone was in everyone else's way.

Certainly the occupation period of German history was that in which the bureaucrat was condemned to decide matters of food and home for millions, and he made cruel decisions by necessity. In response there arose as massive a campaign of civil disobedience as Germany has ever known. The entire nation, or at least the 99 percent who could not live on the ration card allotments, engaged professionally or amateurishly in black-marketing, all generals' threats notwithstanding. One may in the abstract say that ration laws probably should have been obeyed, but the statement is most easily made by those with full stomachs. It may be that Germans could not stage a revolution because that would be against the law, but Germans by the millions violated MG law constantly to stay alive. Most then delighted in Erhard's reduction of the MG-sponsored bureaucracy.

By 1945 policy had moved from the dismemberment favored in 1943 to decentralization. The American commitment to that goal contributed to the division of Germany into four, and later two, compartments, because the behavior of the Prussian "monster" had made it seem that power must be taken from Berlin and given to the people. (Decentralization was also the sometime desire of the Nazi party, which found the Berlin bureaucratic centralism hard to control.) As part of the process the victors adopted the fiction that the central government had ceased to exist. Hitler was dead; Admiral Karl Dönitz was scarcely competent to gain support, and some ministries had moved out of the Berlin bomb target. Nevertheless, all that would have been necessary to recreate a central government, as was in fact done easily and quickly in each part of the country, would have been to appoint some German chancellor, give him authority to govern in the name of military government, and encourage local German leaders to respect him. He could have appointed ministers, who would in turn have paid the bureaucrats to come back to rooms called offices. The government would then have functioned if military government could agree to support it. Clay, as early as the fall of 1945, urged such central agencies to handle centralized problems. There was no central government in 1945 and later because one or more of the victors preferred it that way; certainly the French, and maybe the Russians, did. By 1948 the United States feared German political unification, but not because a Hitler but because a Stalin might control Germany, and this fear played some role in the OMGUS acceptance of a divided Germany.

Moreover, OMGUS was at first pleased to have its own zone to govern as it wished, although the toy proved expensive. Going to the grass roots caused problems because it weakened the cooperation necessary to survival. Because MG was permitting autonomous local government, it also had to permit state governments, the natural enemies of local autonomy. When these states, in order to survive, looked out for themselves, MG was quickly forced to try for zonal cooperation. Humpty Dumpty, which MG had pushed off the wall, had to be put together again. Clay's zonal Länderrat was a beginning of recentralization, but it could not compel MG's Länder in important matters like food distribution.

Nor was the zone big enough for survival. Clay was forced in the first months of occupation to try to unite the zones, but this brought conflict among the Allies, the Länderrat, Länder, and the local governments. Clay proposed centralization in September 1945, but he got cooperation only with the British and not until late in 1946. Throughout the occupation, bizonal institutions had insufficient power to master the economic crisis. Faced with the responsibility and the bills, MG reversed itself, tried desperately to centralize, and failed until it let the Germans do it. Localism was compelled in 1949 only by the centralized political parties with the popular majorities which meant power.

Parties organized centrally, in spite of MG desires, to win elections. With party organizations recreated as centralized machines, Schumacher and Adenauer had the power. The parties probably could not have been decentralized. Any MG pressure would merely increase the counterpressure and public support to the resisters. The Bonn constitution, as it emerged in 1949, was almost as centralized as Weimar's. It might have been slightly stronger without MG pressures, although Bavaria deserves more credit for the limitation on federal power. Yet with economic revival after 1948, neither party nor state needed so much power. People responded instead to economic pressure. The economic problems MG could not solve between 1945 and 1948 were then solved largely outside the realm of government policy by German workers or businessmen.

OMGUS was throughout a model of centralization, and was probably more centralized than Hitler's Reich. Policy was laid out in great detail by Clay's office, which was more dominated by his energy and intelligence than the Berlin administration was ever dominated by Hitler, although much happened, even at headquarters, which Clay could not control. Apparently distrusting local and regional subordinates, Clay took away their authority with dazzling speed. In less than seven months local commanders legally could no longer command. Their extralegal influence was handicapped by their lack of permanent assignment, funds, information, and language. All the Germans had come to hope for from local MG was aid in getting Americans out of the way, out of the confiscated homes, stores, pools, fields, and factories.

This catalogue of policy failures resulted in large part from the fact that the United States simply did not have the kind of power necessary to achieve its rather intangible goals. Power of one group over another is a complex and temporary relationship, although wars are based on the premise that those who can keep their guns pointing at others get what they want. (Keeping a gun pointed is hard work, as is having enough guns pointed in the right direction.) Three kinds of power clearly were involved: military power, economic power, and political power. In 1945, the United States had one further possible power: moral force. The victors profited morally from Hitler's fanaticism, the horror of Auschwitz. It seemed to Americans, and at first to many Germans, that MG had a moral right to change Germany. Yet to many other Germans, the Allied attack on cities, the killing of women and children by the hundreds of thousands, and the bombing of Hiroshima tarnished the generally bright image of the New World. The postwar behavior of some victors was also disillusioning.

The power of moral force quickly eroded, and MG's ability to exercise any of the other forms of power was more limited than a superficial evaluation might suggest. In 1941, an industrially strong United States created its wartime military power by producing weapons, particularly airplanes and bombs. American military power has since been largely bombing power, a force that is almost useless to an occupation. Moreover, from the time it entered the war, the United States has been much more dependent on allies than it has admitted. Allied support meant that the United States was forced to accept their presence, most significantly that of the Russian army in central Europe, whose power brought the most obvious defeat for U.S. hopes. Given the power balance, there was little Americans could have done in April 1945 except to push forward toward Berlin and occupy a slightly larger chunk of Germany. Thereafter staying in place was all the United States could accomplish without a hot war.

The decision to share western Germany with France as well as with Britain seemed reasonable in 1945. FDR assumed that he lacked the power to keep troops in Europe and only France could help maintain a balance of power. There is no reason to doubt the United States tried and failed to get French cooperation in Germany in 1945–46. It took nearly four years of political and economic pressure to get French agreement to a common policy of West German unity. The Marshall Plan was one price, but there was also the persuasive power of German realities transferred to Washington and Paris by the able Clay.

Another potential ally, prodemocratic forces in Germany, was rejected during the war and only gradually accepted thereafter. During the war the United States refused to support the resistance movement in any serious way, even publicly welcoming the slaughter of resistance officers for having tried to kill Hitler. With victory Americans were forced into a cold alliance with some Germans, as the victor had to have natives to implement policy. The army was immediately powerless to govern on its own; it never directly ran the country, but from the beginning tried to influence the Germans who did. Direct governing of the population was formally relinquished to the defeated in early 1946, less than one year after victory. This was the wisdom of Clay, but also a weakness. MG simply did not have the people with skills to run the country. MG had officers who could presume to observe through interpreters' eyes small parts of the activities of millions of aliens. The army's large numbers of officers and enlisted men were only in rare cases qualified to know what was going on, much less to take any active role.

Nor did the United States have the surplus industrial goods to solve the German economic problem. Only German industry could. The United States could provide some materials and machines for a time at the expense of the U.S. taxpayer, but only if the occupation policy were such that the demand was temporary. The Marshall Plan could provide some amounts of public capital briefly, but most of this aid went to the rest of western Europe, and Clay controlled only a small part. For a time Clay used one hand to restrain the economy while helping it up with the other, but the major American economic power was not Clay's to use. The private holder of capital or skills could be attracted to Germany only by the chance of profit. MG made that very difficult, at first deliberately, because the policy of investors was often contrary to government policy. Only after businessmen could make their own arrangements, when MG got out of the way, was it possible for a part of U.S. economic power to effect its changes in Germany.

The power more consciously applied by MG was political power. This power, as Truman said, is the ability to persuade. In the case of the occupation, it would have meant the ability to persuade all people concerned of the desirability of supporting American policy. The United States would need to persuade its allies, the American public, and the entire administrative organization from Washington down through channels to the local commanders and staffs. They would also have to persuade the German leaders and the German public. Such persuasion was limited even at home, partly because the policy was long kept a secret. It was long kept hidden because it was vigorously resisted by somebody as soon as it was leaked. By the time policy had become known to the public it had usually been made obsolete by events. What the American public first understood as policy was that peace was wonderful and Nazis meant war; therefore the Nazis would be crushed. The Germans were fortunate that the American public understood by 1948 that Communists meant war; therefore the Germans were needed to help defeat Communists.

American institutions were scarcely adapted to a more precise occupational policy than this simple emphasis which defined the primary objective. In theory the American public was enlightened by a free press and made rational decisions, in turn influencing Congress and the executive branch (including the War Department), each of which was also enlightened by the free press. This process broke down at every level. The U.S. press was not well represented in Germany; only a handful of eastern newspapers had men there. The reports, now available in the National Archives collection, were so wildly contradictory that Solomon could scarcely have made a decision based on the information available. Probably to generate headlines, reporters picked up sensational "facts": "Nazis everywhere and Patton must go," or later, "Communists everywhere and Morgenthau must go." Looking first at the record and then reading the newspapers could destroy one's belief that the free press informs as much as it confuses the public.

The public was uninterested. Its attitude was that the war was won, so get rid of the Nazis and forget it. Isolationism continued under a veneer of internationalism sold as national defense. The country's business was business and everyone was really concerned about his own business, avoiding unemployment and another depression. Those few interested in Germany had some emotional drive. Jews were concerned about fellow Jews, a few veterans were passionate about national glory, some German-Americans were concerned about relatives, and occasional church groups were concerned about fellow Christians. Such minority pressure could be significant, but it rarely did more than delay a decision or keep it private. Anti-Nazis acted as a vague veto group for the first year or so, as did the anticommunists thereafter, but they had little direct effect on Clay or McCloy.

The apathy and ignorance about conditions in Germany displayed by leaders in Congress and the administration seems more disturbing. Before 1947 only a few public officials went to observe German conditions, and they saw only the obvious. They were seldom motivated by anything more specific than anti-Nazi or anticommunist feelings and the desire to keep taxes down. The attention of Congress and of the executive branch was naturally directed toward domestic issues. These were so all-engrossing that it took real and simple issues of national defense to divert them, such as the fear of communism which led to the Truman and Marshall Plans. Individual leaders took an occasional look and possibly became less susceptible to propaganda, but Washington acted mostly as a semiinformed buffer between the vocal minorities and Clay. Rarely was any president, cabinet member, or major assistant in Washington really involved in occupation policy. That was soon Clay's business.

In his role as zonal commander, Clay had become first the buffer, and increasingly the conductor, between German vocal minorities and Washington. At first he leaned far toward the Washington prejudice, but under the weight of information flowing through his office, he was gradually tipped toward the German point of view. Although a general and able to coerce with a glare, he was also a human being with American values of democracy and freedom. On many issues, he held back his military machine and granted the conquered more freedoms—for example, early elections and local autonomy—and he was sometimes concerned for civil liberties. As an individual, he experienced a conflict between his belief in America's righteousness, its right to exercise power, and his equally American belief in freedom, the Germans' right to exercise power over themselves. These liberal values certainly limit American power as an imperial state, but they preserve America as a national state. They also make real and permanent alliances possible, because it was clear to most Germans that Americans would get out of their way.

Clay lacked some of the will for domination, but also he lacked an organization capable of domination. Despite all of its educational pretensions, America did not have people prepared by language and historical knowledge, much less by political skills, to do much more than pass on reports fed them by German employees who had these skills. Their lack of understanding prevented Americans from adding their weight to German reform ideas and forces. By contrast, the Russians brought in a trained cadre which they could impose and largely control with their own type of political skills and a wall.

Whatever capacity Americans of goodwill had for explaining democracy person-to-person was largely nullified by their disappearance into their ghettoes, and thus isolated, they usually made a new world just like home. The official policy all during the occupation was that Americans could not live in the same building with Germans. Those who did venture out were usually looking for wine, women, or black-market profit, and those whom Germans noticed on the streets and read about in the papers were often poor arguments for the virtues of democracy. The capable few, like Shuster, Friedrich, Pollock, and Dorn, were known to few Germans and had only occasional power in the policy struggle.

With only superficial involvement in German affairs, the occupation was dependent on Germans as information gatherers. This dependence could have badly warped occupational policy and might be considered to have forced the retreat from the objectives of 1945. It could also be considered to have furnished a belated education in reality for the victor. If political power is persuasion, the Germans were the more persuasive. American attitudes changed more than German ones, and reflected what their once despised German servants told them. This included anti-Russianism. Justifiably or not, victor and defeated had agreed by 1947 that something must be done to keep the Communists out. Most Germans were so inclined in 1945 in reaction to visible Russian poverty, the misbehavior of Russian troops, or the fact that Russian power had driven Germans from their homes in the east in a most cruel fashion. It was Russian treatment of Germans and East Europeans to which MG reacted by 1947.

One might thus argue that the United States was cajoled into protecting West Germany because their anti-Russian sickness had spread. What was obviously in the German interest was less obviously in America's, but MG was persuaded of it. Clay, who came to Germany prepared to let the Germans suffer, had by 1946 or 1947 decided he had no choice but to limit their suffering or lose them to communism. Although often angering his subjects, Clay became the most influential advocate with the West that the Germans could have wished. He was able, politically clean, energetic, and persuasive. His reaction to the reality he gradually perceived altered American policy. Germans can properly criticize much in his policy, but what he did for them on the international front and in Washington by 1949 should have made him the patron saint of the Bonn republic. Yet he had little choice: either he got German support, or America would lose Europe as ally. If the German interest became paramount by 1948, it was partly because the German interest had been clear since 1945 and the American interest was clarified only with the Cold War. The United States lacked purpose in Germany after VE Day. Nazism was defeated, and making sure it would not rise again was neither a clear task nor, as it turned out, a necessary one. By 1948, MG had clearly recognized that its purpose was to save the peace by building German democracy, by rebuilding the German economy, and by keeping the Russians out. These goals coincided with the inclination of most people on the scene and could be sold as in the interest of national security in Washington.

Earlier indecision in Washington and Berlin had limited policy. The conflict was between those out to punish Germany, at first the great majority, and those out to rehabilitate Germany, with the apathetic pulled first one way, then the other. This limitation by indecision came precisely when Germans were so dismayed by defeat that resistance would have been less organized. In these early years, the public MG policy was its most unrealistic. By the time public policy caught up with the situation of 1945, it was 1947 and Germany had changed. American folly and bluff had been made evident. Back talk might be glared down by Clay, but by then no one would really get hurt for resisting. With this MG policy indecision and delay, one could debate whether Germany was pushed more to the left or to the right. Surely the intent until 1947 was largely liberal, that is, to change things, but the intent thereafter largely conservative. As a result MG left the Germans with a liberal press but with most of the rest of the power structure conservative. Even unions were largely unaffected; they were liberal in principle, conservative in procedures. Yet reaction meant going back not to Nazi, but to pre-Nazi practices, and the reaction was democratic in that the people voted for it.

My research has led me to the conviction that the occupation, soon after it had begun, became largely irrelevant to its goals. It could prevent some things from happening, but it could by itself make very little happen. The victor could permit the defeated to do what they wanted to do, but it could make them do very little. Successes came when its policy corresponded to German wishes. The failures occurred when the Germans either could not or would not do as MG wished. Thus MG quickly became irrelevant, except that it was in the way. It delayed solutions to problems until, strategically retreating, it permitted the Germans to solve them, if they could, and as they saw fit. West Germans could not solve the problem of the Soviet zone and Berlin. Berlin was at once a symbol of American resourcefulness and of its powerlessness to solve a problem. The United States simply stayed in the Russians' way, but Clay took himself and his Allies out of the Germans' way.

That MG was mostly irrelevant is an unusual conclusion, but during the height of MG power, almost everyone but the writers of official progress reports concluded that it had failed miserably. Liberals saw failure already in 1945 because of the beginning of the anticommunism which put conservative businessmen back into power; they perceived it wrongly as the revival of Nazism. Conservatives saw failure, at least until 1948, because the liberals, the naive New Deal reformers, were serving Germany on a platter to the Communists. The Cold War meant that the conservative fear of communism gradually replaced the liberal fear of fascism. If foreign policy must be based on fear, it is evident that the fear of Nazism, anachronistic by 1945, so crippled MG policy that it had no chance of success. Fear of communism had as a by-product the freeing of West Germany from this first irrational policy.

Yet the MG policy retreat had already occurred before the Cold War. Instead of the Cold War defeating liberal reforms, it simply provided the psychological framework for the public 1947 retreat by discovering the new enemy, Russia. The retreat away from the front against Germans became the moving into position against the Russians, containment.

In simpler terms the reasonable but submerged goals of 1945 were partially achieved, after 1948 in West Germany, because circumstances forced Washington to a new policy, a change from a largely negative passivity to a largely positive passivity, which permitted problems to be solved by means other than MG activity. Whatever was accomplished was because enough Germans desired it; MG desires at best tipped the wavering scales of German indecision, as, for example, toward federalism. MG became rapidly irrelevant; it was locally unimportant by the beginning of 1946, and succeeded to the extent that it accepted its irrelevancy. The more it tried to influence, the worse the results; the one important exception was to bring in food to remedy German hunger worsened by the earlier policies of bombing, dismemberment, and control.

The American presence in Germany—just being there—was in its increasing passivity useful in the sense that one knew things would not change radically. Whatever slight chance there may have been of a radical German change, a revolution from within, was thereby nullified. Whatever chance there may have been of an invasion from without was also nullified. This hope of stability offered a modest but necessary encouragement to a German people desperate to climb out of the misery created by the war and occupation. By 1948 they were relatively unimpeded by the western occupiers.

Thereafter West Germany became a permanent ally, integrated into the Atlantic community as quickly as France would permit. What happened after 1949, when the artificial walls MG had created were dropped and Germany was open again to the world, was that Germans became more and more internationalized or Americanized, as MG hoped. The young in particular were open to the West in thousands of unofficial ways; the official exchange of persons was minor by comparison to the private contacts with the culture of the Atlantic community. Young Germans were as knowledgeable about rock and roll music as young Americans. With the exception of the army's radio station music, much of this cultural exchange bypassed the isolated troops. The values of the young are formed by the mass media, and there the impact of American or Western or industrial values has become overwhelming. Germans became much less isolated than Americans. America at home or abroad remained in significant ways a golden ghetto, prisoner of its own inability to absorb from the outside.

The occupation succeeded when it stopped trying. It advanced by retreating. That it trusted the defeated with freedom instead of keeping its wall about them was its basic strength. The war against the Nazis perhaps diverted Americans from their traditional value of trusting people with freedom. The "Nazified" German people supposedly did not deserve freedom. Wisdom or necessity forced a retreat from the goals of an imperial America with the right to dominate inferiors. By accepting Germans as members of the human race, by thus being true to its basic principles, the United States won the real victory and gained an ally. The continuity of the increasing German integration into an Atlantic civilization based on common values, brutally interrupted by Hitler, was resumed to the advantage of us all.

Bibliography

Books and Articles

Abosch, Heinz. *Menace of the Miracle*. New York: Monthly Review Press, 1963.

Acheson, Dean. *Present at the Creation*. New York: W. W. Norton, 1969.

Adenauer, Konrad. *Memoirs: 1945–53*. Chicago: Henry Regnery, 1966.

Almond, Gabriel. *The Politics of German Business*. Santa Monica: Rand Corp., 1955.

———. *The Struggle for Democracy in Germany*. Chapel Hill: University of North Carolina Press, 1949.

Alperovitz, Gar. *Atomic Diplomacy: Hiroshima and Potsdam*. New York: Simon & Schuster, 1965.

Ambrose, Stephen. *Eisenhower and Berlin, 1945*. New York: W. W. Norton, 1967.

Anderson, Patrick. *The Presidents' Men*. New York: Doubleday, 1968.

Anspach, Ernst. "The Nemesis of Creativity." *Social Research* 19 (December 1952): 403–29.

Armstrong, Anne. *Unconditional Surrender*. New Brunswick: Rutgers University Press, 1961.

Ayer, Fred, Jr. *Before the Colors Fade: George S. Patton, Jr.* Boston: Houghton Mifflin, 1964.

Bach, Julian. *America's Germany*. New York: Random House, 1946.

Backer, John. *Priming the German Economy*. Durham: Duke University Press, 1971.

Bader, William B. *Austria between East and West*. Stanford: Stanford University Press, 1966.

Baer, Fritz. *Die Ministerpräsident in Bayern: 1945–52*. Munich, 1971.

Balabkins, Nicholas. *Germany under Direct Controls*. New Brunswick: Rutgers University Press, 1964.

Balfour, Michael. *Survey of International Affairs, 1939–46: Germany*. London, 1946.

Baruch, Bernard. *Baruch: My Own Story*. New York: Holt, Rinehart & Winston, 1957.

Bayerische Staatskanzlei. *Dokumente zum Aufbau des Bayerischen Staates*. Munich: Staatskanzlei, 1948.

Becker, Rolf. *Niederschlesien, 1945*. Bad Nauheim: Podzum-Verlag, 1965.

Behr, Hermann. *Vom Chaos zum Staat*. Frankfurt: Verlag Frankfurter Bücher, 1961.

Belgion, Montgomery. *Victors' Justice*. Hinsdale, Ill.: Henry Regnery, 1949.

Bell, Coral. *Negotiations from Strength*. New York: Knopf, 1963.

Berberich, Walter. *10 Jahre CSU in Bayern*. Würzburg, 1955.

Bernstein, Barton, ed. *Politics and Policies of the Truman Administration*. Chicago: Quadrangle Books, 1970.

Bernstein, Barton, and Matusow, Allen. *The Truman Administration*. New York: Harper & Row, 1966.

Beyersdorff, Peter. "Militarregierung und Selbstverwaltung: Studie zur Besatzungspolitik... Beispiel Coburg." Ph.D. dissertation, Erlangen University, 1967.

Bialer, Seweryn, ed. *Stalin and His Generals*. New York: Pegasus, 1969.

Binder, Gerhart. *Deutschland seit 1945*. Stuttgart: Seewald, 1969.

Blum, John M. *From the Morgenthau Diaries: 1941-45*. Boston: Houghton Mifflin, 1967.

Böge, Wilhelm. *Ereignisse seit 1945*. Braunschweig: Westermann, 1960.

Bolton, Seymour. "Military Government and the German Political Parties." *Annals of the American Academy* 267 (January 1950): 55-67.

Boberi, Margaret. *Tage des Überlebens, Berlin 1945*. Munich: Piper, 1968.

Breitenkamp, Edward. *The U.S. Information Control Division 1945-49*. Grand Forks, N.D.: 1953.

Brockway, Fenner. *German Diary*. London: Gollancz, 1946.

Brown, Lewis. *A Report on Germany*. New York: Farrar, Straus, 1947.

Brown, MacAlester. "The Diplomacy of Bitterness, Genesis of Potsdam Decision to Expel Germans from Czechoslovakia." *Western Political Quarterly* 11 (1958): 607-26.

Brown, Seyom. *Faces of Power*. New York: Columbia University Press, 1968.

Bryant, Arthur. *Triumph in the West*. London: Doubleday, 1965.

Burns, James MacGregor. *Roosevelt, the Soldier of Freedom*. New York: Harcourt, 1970.

Butcher, Harry. *My Three Years with Eisenhower*. New York: Simon & Schuster, 1946.

Byrnes, James. *All in One Lifetime*. New York: Harper & Row, 1958.

———. *Speaking Frankly*. New York: Harper & Row, 1947.

Campbell, Charles. *German Youth Activities of the U.S. Army 1945-46*. Frankfurt: Office of the Chief Historian, 1947.

Cash, Webster C. "A Comparison of the Effects of Governmental Policies n Industrial Recovery in West and East Germany, 1945-53." Ph.D. dissertation, University of Chicago, 1957.

Chamberlin, William. *The German Phoenix*. New York: Duell, Sloan & Pearce, 1963.

Childs, David. *East Germany*. New York: Benn, 1969.

Christen, Peter. *From Military Government to State Department*. Munich: OMG Bavaria, 1950.

Churchill, Winston. *The Second World War*, V, VI Boston: Houghton Mifflin, 1952, 1954.

Clay, Lucius. *Decision in Germany*. New York: Doubleday, 1950.

Clark, Delbert. *Again the Goosestep*. Indianapolis: Bobbs, Merrill, 1949.

Coles, Harry and Weinberg, Albert. *Civil Affairs: Soldiers Become Governors*. Washington: Office of the Chief of Military History, 1964.

Cottrell, Leonard S. "The Aftermath of Hostilities." *The American Soldier: Combat and Its Aftermath*. Edited by Samuel Stouffer. Princeton: Princeton University Press, 1949.

Cube, Walter V. *Ich bitte un Wiederspruch*. Frankfurt: Verlag der Frankfurter Hefte, 1952.

Curry, George. *James F. Byrnes*. New York: Cooper Square, 1965.

Czempeil, Ernst-Otto. *Das Amerikanische Sicherheitssystem, 1945-1949*. Berlin: De Gruyter, 1966.

Dahrendorf, Ralf. *Society and Democracy in Germany*. New York: Doubleday, 1967.

Daniels, Jonathan. *Frontier on the Potomac*. New York: Macmillan, 1946.

———. *Man of Independence*. London: Lippincott, 1951.

Davidson, Basil. *Germany: What Now? Potsdam to Partition, 1945-49*. London: Muller, 1950.

Davidson, David A. *The Steeper Cliff*. New York: Random House, 1947.

Davidson, Eugene. *The Death and Life of Germany*. New York: Knopf, 1959.

Davis, Franklin. *Come as a Conqueror*. New York: Macmillan, 1967.

Day, Donald. *Franklin D. Roosevelt's Own Story*. Boston: Little, Brown, 1951.

Deuerlein, Ernst. *Die Einheit Deutschlands, 1941-49*. Frankfurt: Metzner, 1957.

———. *Handbuch der deutsche Geschichte: Deutsche Geschichte der neuersten Zeit*. Konstanz: Athenion, 1964.

———. *CDU/CSU, 1945-57*. Cologne: Bachem, 1957.

Deutsch, Karl and Edinger, Lewis. *Germany Rejoins the Powers.* Stanford: Stanford University Press, 1959.

Deutsch, Harold. *The Twilight War.* Minneapolis: University of Minnesota Press, 1968.

Dillard, Hardy. "Power and Persuasion." *Yale Review,* 42 (1953): 212–25.

Djilas, Miloyan. *Conversations with Stalin.* New York: Harcourt, 1963.

Dokumente der Deutsche Politik und Geschichte, vi–viii. Berlin, 1946–55.

Dollinger, Hans. *Deutschland unter den Besatzungsmächten.* Munich: Desch, 1967.

Donnison, F.S. *Civil Affairs and Military Government: N.W. Europe 1944–46.* London: Her Majesty's Stationery Office, 1966.

Dorn, Walter. "The Debate Over American Occupation Policy in Germany, 1944–45." *Political Science Quarterly* 72 (December 1957): 481–501.

———. "Notes," April 1949, Institut für Zeitgeschichte, Munich, published as *Inspektionsreise in der U.S. Zone.* Stuttgart: DVA, 1973.

Dornberg, John. *Schizophrenic Germany.* New York: Macmillan, 1961.

Dos Passos, John. *Tour of Duty.* Boston: Houghton Mifflin, 1946.

Dulles, Allen. *The Secret Surrender.* New York: Weidenfeld & Nicolson, 1969.

Dulles, John Foster. *War or Peace.* New York: Macmillan, 1957.

Ebsworth, Raymond. *Restoring Democracy in Germany—The British Contribution.* New York: Praeger, 1961.

Eckmeier, Otto. *Die Flüchtlinge in Bayern.* Munich, 1949.

Eden, Anthony. *The Memoirs of Anthony Eden: The Reckoning.* Boston: Houghton Mifflin, 1965.

Edinger, Lewis. *Kurt Schumacher.* Stanford: Stanford University Press, 1965.

———. "Post-Totalitarian Leadership." *American Political Science Review* 59 (March 1960): 58–82.

Edwards, General Morris. "A Case Study of Military Government in Germany during and after World War II." Ph.D. dissertation, Georgetown University, 1957.

Ehard, Hans. *Bayerische Politik—Reden.* Munich: Pflaum, 1952.

Eisenhower, Dwight. *Crusade in Europe.* Garden City: Doubleday, 1948.

Engler, Robert. "The Individual Soldier and the Occupation." *Annals of the American Academy* 267 (January 1950): 77–86.

Feis, Herbert. *Between War and Peace: Potsdam.* Princeton: Princeton University Press, 1960.

———. *Churchill, Roosevelt, Stalin: A Diplomatic History of World War II.* Princeton: Princeton University Press, 1967.

———. *From Trust to Terror.* New York: A. Blund, 1970.

Ferrell, Robert. *The American Secretaries of State and Their Diplomacy: Marshall,* XV. New York: Cooper Square, 1966.

Fitzgibbon, Constantine. *Denazification.* London: Joseph, 1969.

Frankel, Heinrich. *Farewell to Germany.* London, 1952.

Franklin, William. "Zonal Boundaries and Access to Berlin." *World Politics* 16 (October 1963): 1–31.

Fredericksen, Oliver. *American Military Occupation of Germany, 1945–53.* Darmstadt: HICOG, 1953.

Freidel, Frank. *Franklin D. Roosevelt: The Triumph.* Boston: Little, Brown, 1956.

Freeman, Dexter. *Hesse: A New German State.* Frankfurt: OMGUS, 1948.

Friedrich, Carl J. *American Experiences in Military Government in World War II.* New York: Rinehart, 1948.

———. "Military Government and Dictatorship." *Annals of the American Academy* 267 (1950): 1–30.

Fromme, Friedrich Karl. "Zur inneren Ordnung in den westlichen Besatzungs-Zonen 1945-49." *Vierteljahreshefte für Zeitgeschichte* 10 (1962): 206-23.

Furstenau, Justus. *Entnazifizierung.* Neuwied and Berlin: Luchterhand, 1969.

Gaddis, John L. *The U.S. and the Origins of the Cold War, 1941-47.* New York: Columbia University Press, 1972.

Gannon, Robert. *The Cardinal Spellman Story.* New York: Doubleday, 1962.

Gardner, Lloyd C. *Architects of Illusion: Men and Ideas in American Foreign Policy, 1941-49.* Chicago, Quadrangle Books, 1970.

Geis, Margeret. *The Relations of Occupational Personnel with the Civilian Population, 1946-48.* Karlsruhe: HICOG, 1951.

Gillen, J. F. J. *American Influence on the Development of Political Institutions.* Karlsruhe: HICOG, 1950.

———. *Deconcentration and Decartelization.* Bonn: HICOG, 1953.

———. *The Special Projects Program.* Bonn: HICOG, 1952.

———. *State and Local Government in West Germany, 1945-53.* Mehlem: HICOG, 1953.

Gimbel, John. *The American Occupation of Germany.* Stanford: Stanford University Press, 1968.

———. *A German Community under American Occupation: Marburg, 1945-52.* Stanford: Stanford University Press, 1962.

———. *The Origins of the Marshall Plan.* Stanford: Stanford University Press, 1976.

———. "Die Byrnes Stuttgart Rede." *Vierteljahreshefte für Zeitgeschichte* 20 (January 1972).

Glum, Friedrich. *Zwischen Wissenschaft und Politik.* Bonn: H. Bouvier, 1964.

Golay, John. *The Founding of the Federal Republic of Germany.* Chicago: University of Chicago Press, 1958.

Goldman, Eric. *The Crucial Decade.* New York: Vintage Books, 1959.

Gollancz, Victor. *In Darkest Germany.* London: Gollancz, 1946.

Gottlieb, Manuel. *The German Peace Settlement and the Berlin Crisis.* New York: Paine-Whitman, 1960.

Graebner, Norman, ed. *The Cold War: Ideological Conflict or Power Struggle?* Boston: Heath, 1963.

Graebner, Norman. *An Uncertain Tradition: American Secretaries of State.* New York: McGraw-Hill, 1961.

Griffith, William. "Denazification Program." *Annals of the American Academy* 267 (January 1950): 68-76.

———. "The Denazification Program in the U.S. Zone of Germany." Ph.D. dissertation, Harvard University, 1950.

Gross, Franz. "Freedom of the Press Under Military Government in Western Germany, 1945-49." Ph.D. dissertation, Harvard University, 1952.

Grosser, Alfred. *Germany in Our Time.* New York: Praeger, 1971.

———. *The Colossus Again: West Germany From Defeat to Rearmament.* New York: Praeger, 1955.

Guradze, Heinz. "The Länderrat—Landmark of German Reconstruction." *Western Political Quarterly* 3 (1950): 190-213.

Habe, Hans. *Our Love Affair with Germany.* New York: G.P. Putnam's Sons, 1953.

Hale, William H. "General Clay On His Own." *Harper's,* December 1948, 86-94.

Halle, Louis. *Cold War as History.* New York: Harper & Row, 1967.

Hammerschmidt, Helmut. *Zwanzig Jahre Danach.* Munich: Desch, 1965.

Hammond, Paul. "Directives for the Occupation of Germany." *American Civil Military Decisions.* Edited by Harold Stein. Birmingham: University of Alabama Press, 1963.

Harmssen, G. W. *Am Abend der Demontagne.* Bremen: Trüjen, 1951.

Härtel, Lia. *Der Länderrat des amerikanischen Besatzungsgebietes.* Stuttgart: Kohlhammer, 1951.

Hassett, William. *Off the Record with FDR.* New Brunswick: Rutgers University Press, 1958.

Hauser, Heinrich. *The German Talks Back.* New York: Holt & Co., 1945.

Hayward, Edwin. "Coordination of Military and Civilian Civil Affairs Planning." *Annals of the American Academy,* January 1950.

Heidenheimer, Arnold. *Adenauer and the CDU.* The Hague: M. Nÿhoff, 1960.

Heimerich, H. *Die Kommunale Entwicklung seit 1945.* Frankfurt: W. Metzner, 1950.

Heintz, Eckhard. "Der Beamtenabgeordnete im Bayrischen Landtag." Ph.D. dissertation, University of Berlin, 1966.

Hemken, R. *Sammlung der vom Allied Kontrollrat und der Amerikanischen Militarischen Regierungerlassenen, Proklamationen, Gesetzen, Verordnungen, Befehlen.* Stuttgart, 1946.

Herdeg, Walter. *Grundzüge der deutsche Besatzungsverwaltung in den westlichen und nördlichen Ländern.* Tübingen: Institut fur Besatzungsfragen in Tübingen, 1953.

Herz, John. "The Fiasco of Denazification." *Political Science Quarterly* 63 (1948): 569–94.

———. "German Officialdom Revisited: Political Views and Attitudes of the West German Civil Service." *World Politics* 7 (October 1954): 63–83.

Herz, Martin. *Beginnings of the Cold War.* Bloomington: Indiana University Press, 1966.

Herzog, Robert. *Grundzüge der deutsche Besatzungsverwaltung in den östlichen und sudöstlichen Ländern.* Tübingen, 1955.

Hill, J. W. F. "Local Government in Western Germany." *Political Science Quarterly* 20 (1949): 256–64.

Hill, Russell. *Struggle For Germany.* New York: Harper & Row, 1947.

Hiscocks, Richard. *The Adenauer Era.* Philadhia: Lippincott, 1966.

———. *Democracy in West Germany.* London: Oxford University Press, 1957.

———. *Germany Revived: An Appraisal of the Adenauer Era.* London: Gollancz, 1968.

———. *The Rebirth of Austria.* London: Oxford University Press, 1953.

Hnilicka, Karl. *Bayerische Profile.* Munich: BSK, 1965.

Hnilicka, Karl, ed. *Die Bayerischen Ministerpräsidenten der Nachkriegszeit, 1945-63.* Munich: BSK, 1963.

Hoegner, Wilhelm. *Der schwierge Aussenseiter.* Munich: Isar, 1959.

Hofstadter, Richard. *The American Political Tradition and the Men Who Made It.* New York: Knopf, 1948.

Holborn, Hajo. *American Military Government.* Washington: Infantry Journal Press, 1947.

Hoover, Calvin. *Memoirs of Capitalism, Communism, and Nazism.* Durham: University of North Carolina Press, 1965.

Horowitz, David. *The Free World Colossus.* New York: Hill & Wang, 1965.

Howley, Frank. *Berlin Command.* New York: Putnam, 1950.

Hull, Cordell. *Memoirs,* II. New York: Macmillan, 1948.

Huntington, Samuel. *The Soldier and the State.* Cambridge, Mass.: Random House, 1964.

Hurwitz, Harold. "Die Presse Politik der Allierten." *Deutsche Presse seit 1945.* Edited by Harry Pross. Bern: Scherz, 1965.

———. *U.S. Military Government in Germany: Press Reorientation.* Karlsruhe: HICOG, 1950.

Hutton, Bud and Rooney Andy. *Conquerors' Peace.* New York: Doubleday, 1947.

Institut für Besatzungsfragen. *Einwirkungen der Besatzungsmächte auf die westdeutsche Wirtschaft.* Tübingen, May 1949.

———. *Occupation Costs, Are They a Defense Contribution?* Tübingen, 1951.

International Education Exchange Service. *A Follow-up Study of German Teenage Exchanges.* Washington: Department of State and HICOG, 1954.

International Public Opinion Research. *Cooperative Action Teams*. New York: Department of State, 1954.

———. *German Exchanges: A Study in Attitude Change*. New York: Department of State, 1953.

Irving, David. *The Destruction of Dresden*. New York: Kimber, 1963.

James, Edward. *The U.S. Armed Forces German Youth Activities Program, 1945–55*. Historical Division, ASUUSA, 1956.

Janeway, Eliot. *Economics of Crisis: War, Politics, and the Dollar*. New York: Weybright & Talley, 1968.

Joesten, Joachim. *Germany, What Now?* Chicago: Ziff-Davis, 1948.

Johnson, Donald. *The Dynamics of the American Presidency*. New York: Wiley, 1964.

Jones, Joseph. *The Fifteen Weeks*. New York: Viking Press, 1955.

Jünger, Ernst. *Jahre der Okkupation*. Stuttgart: Europäischer Buchklub, 1958.

Junker, Heinrich. *Aus Bayerns Innenpolitik, 1945–65*. Munich, 1965.

Kahn, Arthur. *Betrayal: Our Occupation of Germany*. Warsaw, 1950.

Kästner, Erich. *Notabene 45*. Frankfurt: Fischer, 1965.

Kennan, George. *Memoirs, 1925–1950*. Boston: Little, Brown, 1967.

Kern, Erich. *Weder Frieden noch Freiheit*. Göttingen: Schütz, 1965.

Knappen, Marshall. *And Call It Peace*. Chicago: University of Chicago Press, 1947.

Kogon, Eugen. "Das Recht auf den politischen Irrtum." *Frankfurte Hefte* 2 (1947): 641–55.

———. *Die unvollendete Erneurung, 1945–64*. Frankfurt: Europaische, 1964.

Köhler, Erich. *Ohne Illusionen: Politik der Realitäten*. Frankfurt: Der Grief, 1949.

Kolko, Gabriel. *The Politics of War*. New York: Random House, 1968.

———. *The Roots of American Foreign Policy*. Boston: Beacon Press, 1969.

Kormann, John. *U.S. Denazification 1944–50*. Bad Godesberg: HICOG, 1952.

Kowalski, Häns Gunter. "Die European Advisory Commission als Instrument Allierter Deutschlandplanung 1943–45." *Vierteljahreshefte für Zeitgeschichte* 19 (July 1971): 261–93.

Krautkrämer, Elmar. *Deutsche Geschichte nach dem II Weltkrieg 1945–49*. Hildeheim: A. Lax, 1962.

Kubek, Anthony. *Morgenthau Diary*, Subcommittee to Investigate the Administration of Internal Security Act, Committee on the Judiciary, U.S. Senate, 89th Congress, 1st Session, 1965.

Kuby, Erich. *Franz Josef Strauss*. Munich: K. Desch, 1963.

Kuklick, Bruce R. "American Foreign Economic Policy and Germany, 1939–46." Ph.D. dissertation, University of Pennsylvania, 1968.

———. "The Division of Germany and American Policy of Reparations." *Western Political Quarterly* 23 (1970): 276–93.

———. "The Genesis of European Advisory Commission." *Journal of Contemporary History* 4 (October 1969): 189–209.

LaFeber, Walter. *America, Russia, and the Cold War 1945–66*. New York: Wiley, 1967.

Landmann, Robert. *Gewerbeordnung*. Munich: Beck, 1956.

Langer, William and Gleason, S. Everett. *Challenge To Isolation*. New York: Harper, 1952.

Leahy, William. *I Was There*. London: Whittlesey, 1950.

Lebovitz, Solomon. "Military Government and the Revival of German Political Activity." Ph.D. dissertation, Harvard University, 1949.

Lee, Guy. *Documents on Field Organization of HICOG*. Bonn: HICOG, 1952.

———. *Guide to Studies of the Historical Division Office of the U.S. High Commissioner for Germany*. Bonn: HICOG, 1953.

Leonhardt, Rudolf. *This Germany*. New York: N.Y. Graphic, 1964.

Leuchtenberg, William. *Franklin D. Roosevelt*. New York: Hill & Wang, 1967.

Litchfield, E. H. *Governing Postwar Germany*. Ithaca: Cornell University Press, 1948.

Lochner, Louis. *Herbert Hoover and Germany*. Boppard: Macmillan, 1961.

Loehr, Rodney. *The West German Banking System.* Bonn: HICOG, 1952.

Loewenstein, Hubertus Prinz von. *Deutschlands Schicksal, 1945-57.* Bonn: Athenäum, 1957.

Loewenstein, Philipp. "The Bavarian Scandal." *New Republic,* 18 June 1945, 841-42.

Lorei, Madlen and Kirn, Richard. *Frankfurt und die drei wilde Jahren.* Frankfurt, 1962.

Lubell, Samuel. *The Future of American Politics.* New York: Harper & Row, 1951.

McClaskey, Beryl. *The History of U.S. Policy and Program in the Field of Religious Affairs under the Office of the U.S. HICOG.* Bonn: HICOG, 1951.

McCloy, John J. *Bericht über Deutschland.* Bonn: HICOG, 1952.

—————. *The Challenge to American Foreign Policy.* Cambridge: Harvard University Press, 1953.

McNeill, William. *America, Britain and Russia, Their Cooperation and Conflict, 1941-46.* New York: Johnson Reprint, 1970.

McSweeney, Edward. *American Voluntary Aid for Germany, 1945-50.* Freiburg: HICOG, 1950.

Maier, Reinhold. *Ein Grundstein wird gelegt.* Tübingen: Wunderlich, 1964.

—————. *Ende und Wende.* Stuttgart: Wunderlich, 1948.

—————. *Erinnerungen, 1948-55.* Tübingen: Wunderlich, 1966.

March, Robert P. *U.S. Military Government in Germany: Financial Policies and Operations.* Karlsruhe: HICOG, 1950.

Martin, James Stewart. *All Honorable Men.* Boston: Little, Brown, 1950.

Maul, Michael. *Sieger und Besiegte.* Seebrück: Herring, 1948.

Mayer, Dr. Josef. *Der Wiederaufbau des Bayerischen Volkschulwesens.* Passau, 1965.

Merkl, Peter H. *The Origins of the West German Republic.* New York: Oxford University Press, 1963.

Merritt, Anna J., and Merritt, Richard L. *Public Opinion in Occupied Germany.* Urbana: University of Illinois Press, 1970.

Meurer, Hubert. *U.S. Military Government in Germany: Policy and Functioning in Trade and Commerce.* Karlsruhe: HICOG, 1950.

Middleton, Drew. *The Struggle for Germany.* Indianapolis: Bobbs-Merrill, 1949.

Miller, Robert W. *Die amerikanische Deutschland Politik, 1945-55.* Frankfurt: Forschungsinst. der Deutschen Gesellschaft für Ausw. Politik, 1956.

—————. "The South German Länderrat," Ph.D. dissertation, University of Michigan, 1960.

Millis, Walter, ed. *The Forrestal Diaries.* New York: Viking, 1951.

Moltmann, Gunter. *Amerikas Deutschland Politik.* Heidelberg: C. Winter, 1958.

—————. *Die Entwicklung Deutschlands, 1949-55.* Hanover: Verlag für Literatur und Zeitgeschehen, 1963.

—————. "Die Fruhe amerikanische Deutschland Planung im zweiten Weltkrieg." *Vierteljahreshefte für Zeitgeschichte* 5 (1957): 241-64.

Montgelas, Albrecht, and Nützel, Carl. *Wilhelm Hoegner.* Munich, 1957.

Montgomery, John. *Forced to be Free.* Chicago: University of Chicago Press, 1957.

Morgenthau, Hans. *Germany and the Future of Europe.* Chicago: University of Chicago Press, 1951.

Morison, Elting E. *Turmoil and Tradition.* Boston: Houghton Mifflin, 1960.

Morsey, Rudolf. "Die Rolle Konrad Adenauers im Parlamentarischen Rat." *Vierteljahreshefte für Zeitgeschichte* 18 (1970), 62-94.

Mosely, Philip. "The Occupation of Germany." *Foreign Affairs,* July 1950, 580-604.

Mowrer, Edgar Ansel. *The Nightmare of American Foreign Policy.* New York: Knopf, 1948.

Muhlen, Norbert. *The Return of Germany.* Chicago: Regnery, 1953.

Muller-Marein, Josef. *Deutschland im Jahre 1.* Hamburg: Nannen, 1960.

Murphy, Robert. *Diplomat among Warriors.* Garden City: Doubleday, 1964.

Niethammer, Lutz. "Amerikanische Besatzung und bayerische Politik, 1945." *Vierteljahreshefte für Zeitgeschichte* 15 (1967): 155–210.

——. *Entnazifizierung in Bayern.* Frankfurt: Fischer, 1972.

Nettl, J.P. *The Eastern Zone and Soviet Policy in Germany.* London: Oxford University Press, 1951.

Netzer, Hans Jochim. *Adenauer und die Folgen.* Munich: Beck, 1965.

Neustadt, Richard. *Presidential Power.* New York: Mentor, 1967.

Newmann, Robert G. "The New Political Parties of Germany." *American Political Science Review* 25 (August 1946): 749–59.

Noack, Paul. *Deutschland 1945–60.* Munich: G. Olzog, 1960.

——. *Deutschland's Nachkriegszeit.* Munich: G. Olzog, 1966.

Nobleman, Eli. "American Military Government Courts in Germany." *Annals of the American Academy* 267 (1950): 87–97.

Norman, Albert. *Our German Policy.* New York: Vantage Press, 1951.

Notter, Harley A., ed. *Postwar Foreign Policy Preparation, 1939–45.* Washington: Department of State, 1949.

Nye, W.S. *Military Government in Munich, 1945–47.* Frankfurt: OMGUS Historical Division, European Command, 1951.

OMGUS. *History of U.S. Military Government in Germany, May 8, 1945 to June 30, 1946.* Frankfurt, 1946.

——. *Land and Local Government in U.S. Zone Germany.* Frankfurt, 1947.

——. *Property Control in the U.S. Occupied Area of Germany, 1945–49.* Frankfurt, 1949.

——. *Reparations, September 1945 to June 1949.* Frankfurt, 1949.

Operations Research Office, Johns Hopkins University. "A Survey of the Experience and Opinions of U.S. Military Government Officers in World War II." Chevy Chase, Maryland, 1956.

Oppen, Beate Ruhm von. *Documents of Germany under Occupation, 1945–54.* London: Oxford University Press, 1955.

Padover, Saul. *Experiment in Germany.* New York: Duell, Sloan & Pearce, 1946.

Penrose, Ernest F. *Economic Planning for the Peace.* Princeton: Princeton University Press, 1953.

Peterson, E. N. *The Limits of Hitler's Power.* Princeton: Princeton University Press, 1969.

Pfeil, Elis. *Fünf Jahre Später, Die Eingliederung der Heimatvertriebenen in Bayern.* Frankfurt: W. Metzner, 1951.

Phillips, Cabell. *The Truman Presidency.* New York: Macmillan, 1966.

Pilgert, Henry. *The History of Information Services through Information Centers and Documentary Films.* Bonn: HICOG, 1951.

——. *The West German Educational System.* Bonn: HICOG, 1953.

Plischke, Elmer. *Allied High Commission.* Bonn: HICOG, 1953.

——. *Allied High Commission: Relations With the West German Government.* Bonn: HICOG, 1952.

——. *History of the Allied High Commission for Germany.* Bonn: HICOG, 1951.

Pogue, Forrest. *George Marshall.* New York: Viking, 1963.

Pollock, James. "The Role of the Public in the New Germany." *American Political Science Review* 39 (1945): 464–73.

——. *What Shall Be Done With Germany.* Northfield, Minnesota: Carleton College, 1944.

Pollock, James, ed. *German Democracy.* Ann Arbor: University of Michigan Press, 1955.

——. *Germany Under Occupation.* Ann Arbor: Wahr, 1947.

Pribilla, Max. "Umerziehung des deutschen Volkes?" *Stimmen der Zeit* 140 (1946): 16–36.

Price, Byron. *Memorandum to the President.* Washington, 1945.

Price, Hoyt, and Schorske, Carl. *The Problem of Germany.* New York, 1947.

Pross, Harry. *Deutsche Presse seit 1945.* Bern: Scherz, 1965.

————. *Dialektik der Restauration*. Olten: Walter, 1965.

Price, Harry. *The Marshall Plan and its Meaning*. Ithaca: Cornell University Press, 1955.

Pünder, Hermann. *Von Preussen nach Europa*. Stuttgart: Deutsche Verlagsanstalt, 1968.

Punder, Tilman. *Das Bizonale Interregnum*. Cologne: Grote, 1966.

Ratchford, B. U., and Ross, W. D. *Berlin Reparations Assignment*. Chapel Hill: University of North Carolina Press, 1947.

Reichenberger, Father Emmanuel. *Europa in Trümmern, Das Ergebnis des Kreuzzuges der Allierten*. Graz: A. Purstet, 1950.

Rexin, Manfred. *Die Jahre 1945–49*. Hannover: Verlag für Literatur und Zeitgeschehen, 1965.

Ries, John C. *The Management of Defense*. Baltimore: Johns Hopkins Press, 1964.

Robinson, Donald. "Why Denazification is Lagging." *American Mercury*, May 1946, 563–70.

Rogow, Arnold. *James Forrestal*. New York: Macmillan, 1963.

Roosevelt, Eleanor. *This I Remember*. New York: Harper & Row, 1949.

Roosevelt, Elliott. *F.D.R.: His Personal Letters, 1928–45*. New York: Duell, Sloan & Pearce, 1950.

Ropke, Wilhelm. "The German Dust Bowl." *Review of Politics* 8 (October 1946), 511–27.

Rossiter, Clinton. *The American Presidency*. New York: Harcourt, Brace, 1956.

Rudzio, Wolfgang. *Die Neuordnung des Kommunalwesens in der Britischen Zone*. Stuttgart: Deutsche Verlags-Anstalt, 1968.

Russel, William. "Reeducation in Germany." *Foreign Affairs*, October 1948, 68–77.

Rümelin, Hans. *So lebten wir . . .* Willsbach: Scherer, 1947.

Rumpf, Hans. *The Bombing of Germany*. New York: Holt, Rinehart & Winston, 1962.

Salomon, Ernst von. *Fragebogen*. New York: Doubleday, 1955.

Schäfer, Emil. *Von Potsdam bis Bonn-Dokumentation, 1945–50*. Lahr: M. Schauenberg, 1950.

Scharf, Adolf. *Osterreichs Erneurung*. Vienna: Wiener Volks, 1955.

Schieder, Theodor. *Die Vertreibung der deutschen Bevolkerung aus Ost-Mitteleuropa*. Bonn: Bundesministerium für Vertriebene, Fluchlinge und Kreigsgeschadigte, 1956–60.

Schilling, Warner, Hammond, P., and Snyder, Glenn. *Strategy, Politics, and Defense Budgets*. New York: Columbia University Press, 1962.

Schlange-Schöningen, Hans. *Im Schatten des Hungers*. Hamburg: P. Parey, 1955.

Schlesinger, Arthur, Jr. *The Age of Roosevelt*, II. Boston: Houghton Mifflin, 1959.

Schloss, Bert Peter. "The American Occupation of Germany 1945–52: An Appraisal." Ph.D. dissertation, Chicago University, 1955.

Schmidt, Eberhard. *Die Verhinderte Neuordnung 1945–52*. Frankfurt: Europäische Verlagsanst, 1970.

Schmidt, Hubert G. *The Liberalization of West German Trade, 1949–51*. Bonn: HICOG, 1952.

————. *Policy and Functioning in Industry*. Karlsruhe: USMG Historical Division, 1950.

Schmidt, Paul. *Der Statist auf der Galerie, 1945–50*. Bonn: Athenäum, 1951.

Schnitzer, E. W. *Soviet Policy on the Reunification of Germany, 1945–52*. Santa Monica: Rand Corp., 1953.

Schorr, Helmut. *Adam Stegerwald*. Recklinghausen: Kommunal-Verdag, 1966.

Schrenck-Notzing, Caspar. *Charaktwewäsche, Die americkanische Besatsung in Deutschland und Ihre Folgen*. Stuttgart: Seewald, 1965.

Schwarz, Hans-Peter. *Vom Reich zur Bundesrepublik*. Berlin: Luchterhand, 1966.

Seidel, Dr. Hans. *Festschrift zum 70. Geburtstag von Dr. Hans Ehard*. Munich: BSK, 1957.

Sendtner, Kurt. *Ruprecht von Wittelsbach, Kronprinz von Bayern*. Munich: R. Pflaum, 1954.

Settel, Arthur. *This is Germany*. New York: Sloane, 1950.

Sherwood, R. E. *Roosevelt and Hopkins*. New York: Harper, 1948.

Shuster, George. "American Occupation and German Education." *Proceedings of the American Philosophical Society* 97 (1953): 159–62.

————. *The Ground I Walked On.* New York: Farrar, Straus, & Cudahy, 1961.

Slover, Robert. "The Bizonal Economic Administration of West Germany." Ph.D. dissertation, Harvard University, 1950.

Smith, Jean E. *The Papers of General Lucius Clay, Germany 1945-49.* Bloomington: Indiana University Press, 1974.

Snell, John. *Wartime Origins of the East-West Dilemma Over Germany.* New Orleans: Hauser Press, 1959.

Snow, Edgar. *Journey to the Beginning.* New York: Random House, 1958.

Snyder, Major James. *The Establishment and Operation of the U.S. Constabulary.* Frankfurt: OMGUS, 1947.

Spiethoff, Bodo. *Untersuchungen zum Bayerischen Flüchtlingsproblem.* Berlin: Duncker & Humblat, 1955.

Starr, Joseph R. *Fraternization With the Germans in World War II.* Frankfurt: Office of Chief Historian, European Command, 1947.

Stearman, William L. *The Soviet Union in the Occupation of Austria.* Bonn: Siegler, 1961.

Steinberg, Alfred. *The Man from Missouri.* New York: Putnam, 1962.

Steinmetz, Heinz. "Problems of the Landrate." *Journal of Politics* 11 (1949): 310-34.

Stimson, Henry, and Bundy, McGeorge. *On Active Service in Peace and War.* New York: Harper & Row, 1948.

Stolper, Gustav. *German Realities.* New York: Reynal & Hitchcock, 1948.

Stouffer, Samuel. *American Soldier: Combat and Its Aftermath,* II. Princeton: Princeton University Press, 1949.

Straeter, Arthur. "Denazification in Postwar Reconstruction in Western Germany." *Annals of the American Academy* 260 (November 1948): 43-52.

Swarm, Lt. Col. William. *The History of Military Government Detachment F1B2.* Frankfurt: OMGUS, 1947.

Thayer, Charles. *The Unquiet Germans.* New York: Harper & Row, 1957.

Third U.S. Army of Occupation. *Mission Accomplished, May 9, 1945 to February 15, 1947.* Frankfurt, 1947.

Totten, Christine. *Deutschland Soll und Haben.* Munich: Rütten & Loening, 1964.

Truman, Harry. *Year of Decisions.* Garden City: Doubleday, 1955.

————. *Years of Trial and Hope.* Garden City: Doubleday, 1956.

Tüngel, Richard, and Berndorf, Hans. *Auf dem Bauche sollst du Kriechen.* Hamburg: Wegner, 1958.

U.S. Department of State. *Occupation of Germany, 1945-46.* Washington, 1947.

————. *Foreign Relations of the U.S.: The Conference at Malta and Yalta.* Washington, D.C., 1955.

————. *Foreign Relations of the United States: Conferences of Cairo and Teheran: 1943.* Washington, D.C., 1961.

————. *Foreign Relations of the United States: 1946,* II. Washington, D.C., 1970.

————. *Foreign Relations of the United States: 1946,* V. Washington, D.C., 1969.

————. *Foreign Relations of the United States: 1945,* III. Washington, D.C., 1966.

————. *Foreign Relations of the United States: The Conference of Berlin.* Washington, D.C., 1960.

————. *Foreign Relations of the United States: 1947, Council of Foreign Ministers: Germany and Austria.* Washington, D.C., 1973.

U.S. Forces European Theater. *Occupation.* Frankfurt: USFET, 1946.

U.S. Office of the High Commissioner for Germany. *A Program to Foster Citizen Participation in Government and Politics in Germany.* Frankfurt: HICOG, 1951.

————. *Quarterly Reports on Germany.* Bad Godesberg: HICOG, 1949-52.

———. *Resident Officers Handbook*. Bad Godesberg: HICOG, 1950.

———. *The Kreis Resident Officer, HICOG's Ambassador in the Field*. Bad Godesberg: HICOG, 1951.

U.S. Strategic Bombing Survey. *The Effects of Strategic Bombing on the German War Economy*. Washington: U.S. Government Printing Office, 1945.

Utley, Freda. *The High Cost of Vengeance*. Chicago: H. Regnery, 1949.

Vogel, Walter. *Amerikanische Sicherheitspolitik und das Deutschlandproblem 1945–49*. Koblenz: Bundesarchiv, January 1971.

———. *West Deutschland 1945–50*, 2 vols. Koblenz: Bundesarchiv, 1956–63.

Vogelsang, Thilo. "Die Bemühungen um eine deutsche Zeutralverwaltung 1945–46, Vf2G." *Vierteljahreshefte für Zeitgeschichte* 18 (1970), 516–28.

Walker, Richard. *Edward R. Stettinius, Jr*. New York: Cooper Square, 1956.

Wallich, Henry. *Mainsprings of the German Revival*. New Haven; Yale University Press, 1955.

Warburg, James. *Germany—Bridge or Battleground?* New York: Harcourt Brace, 1947.

Wann, A. J. *The President as Chief Administrator*. Washington: Public Affairs Press, 1968.

White, W. L. *Report on the Germans*. New York: Harcourt Brace, 1947.

Wighton, Charles. *Adenauer*. London: Muller, 1963.

Williams, William A. *The Tragedy of American Diplomacy*. New York: Cleveland World Publishing, 1962.

Willis, F. Roy. *The French in Germany, 1945–49*. Stanford: Stanford University Press, 1960.

Wolfe, Thomas. *Soviet Power and Europe*. Baltimore: Rand Corp., 1970.

Wolff, Klaus. *Blick zurück ohne Zorn*. Munich: Kreisselmeier Verlag, 1960.

Zentner, Kurt. *Aufsteig aus dem Nichts*. Cologne: Kiepenheur, 1953.

Ziemke, Earl. *The U.S. Army in the Occupation of Germany*. Washington: Office of Military History, 1975.

Zink, Harold. "The American Denazification Program." *Journal of Central European Affairs* 6 (October 1946): 227–40.

———. *American Military Government in Germany*. New York: Macmillan, 1947.

———. *The U.S. in Germany, 1944–51*. New York: Van Nostrand, 1957.

Documents

U.S. DOCUMENTS

National Archives. U.S. Army Chief of Information, Public Information Division, *News Summaries, 1944–48*, CA in Occupied Territory

National Archives Collections
 War Department (Modern Military Record Section)
 OMGUS (WNRC–Suitland)

Hoover War Library. Muller, General Walter. *Papers*

Office of Military Government–Bavaria
 Weekly Report
 Monthly Report
 Cumulative Historical Report, 30 June 1946

Kansas City Record Center. Third Army
 Chronologies, 1945

Monthly Intelligence Reports, 9 May 1945 to 22 January 1947
Congressional Record
Columbia University Oral History Project
   Baldwin, Roger
   Eberstadt, Ferdinand
   Fahey, Charles
   Gross, Ernest
   Patterson, Robert
Library of Congress manuscripts
   Patterson, Robert B. *General Correspondence*
   Leahy, William. *Papers*
Michigan Historical Society
   Pollock, James. *Papers*
Princeton University
   Baruch, Bernard. *Papers*
   Clay, Lucius. Oral History
   Dulles, John Foster. *Papers*
   Forrestal, James S. *Papers*

GERMAN DOCUMENTS

Bundesarchiv, Koblenz
   Z1 Länderrat
   Z2 Zonenbeirat
   Z4 Länderrat Bizonal, 1947–49
   Z5 Parlamentarischer Rat
   Z13 Direktorial Kanzlei des Verwaltungrates der Büro der Min. Pres., 1947–49
   B-120 Institut für Besatzungsfragen, 1947–60
Verhandlungen des deutschen Bundestages, Stenographische Berichte, Bonn, 7 September 1949–
Wissenschaftliche Dokumentarstelle des Bundestages, Bonn. Documents on Länderrate, Wirtschaftsrat, Parlamentarischer Rat, Bipartite Control Office
Wirtschaftsrat. Protokolle der Stizungen des Wirtschaftsrats, June 1947 to August 1949 *Wörtlicher Bericht über die Vollversammlungen.*

Bavaria

Bayerische Staatskanzlei
   Aus Nachlass Pfeiffers
   Ehard Nachlass
   Korrespondenz Militärregierung Bayerischen Staatskanzlei, 26 vols., 1947–652.
   Parlamentarischer Rat Akten
   Presse Archiv
Akten des Bayerischen Staatsministerium des Innern
Akten des Bayerischen Staatsministerium für Unterricht und Kultus
Stenographischer Bericht über die Verhandlung des Bayerischen Landtags

Hundhammer, Dr. Dr. Alois
Dokumente zur Bayerischen Politik
"Die Bildung des Kabinetts Ehard"

Augsburg

Stadt Augsburg. Hauptamt Akten Verwaltung. Müller correspondence, meetings with Military
Government
100/1801 Beschlagnahme von Häusern
100/1701 Beschlagnahme von Häusern
100/1704 Gesetz zur Befreiung von Nationalsozialismus Niederschrift über die Beiratsit-
zungen, 18 October 1945–
100/17   Besetzung der Stadt Augsburg durch Am. Truppen
100/1602 Verkehr mit den Besatzungsmächten
105/0500 Privat Korrespondenz des Oberburgermeisters Dr. Dreifuss
Augsburg Police Reports at Polizei Presidium
Chronik der Polizei
Dienstanweisungen
Schutzpolizei Verwaltungsbericht, 1945–54
Tagebuch der Aussendienstpolizei
Verwaltungsbericht 1954
Regierung von Schwaben
Ernährungsamt
Landesgelegenheiten
Militär-Regierung Sachen
Monatsbericht
Wirtschaftsamt
Augsburg newspapers
Augsburger Anzeiger, Amtliches Nachrichtenblatt von der 12 Amer. Heeresgruppe, 1945
Neue Augsburger Allgemeine, NAG Presse Archiv, 1949–70
Schwäbische Landeszeitung, 30 October 1945–
Schwäbische Neue Presse, 1968–70
Schwaben-Monographs, Augsburg Stadtarchiv
Krause, Dr. Johannes. *Gersthofen.* Gersthofen, 1969
Landkreis Donauwörth. Munich, 1966
Landkreis Gunzenhausen. Munich, 1966
Augsburg-Manuscripts, Augsburg Stadtarchiv
Kiss, Albert. *Der Neubeginn in Augsburg, Mai, 1945.* Stuttgart, 1970
Ott, Dr. Wilhelm. *Erinnerungen 1945–46.* Augsburg, 1960
Kleindienst, Josef Ferdinand. *Nachlass.* Augsburg Stadtarchiv
Root, Donald S. "The Diary of A Retread." In Root's possession

Friedberg

Die Kreisfreien Städte und Landkreise Bayerns, Landkreis Friedberg. Munich, 1966
Friedberg, Altbaiern in Schwaben

Hefele collection, newspaper file on Kolesnikow. In Hefele's possession
Friedberg Stadt. *Dokumenten. Sitzungsniederschriften des Stadtrates.* Friedberg, 1945–52
Landratsamt
150 Gesetz zur Befreiung
015 Besondere Angelegenheiten der Landräte
025 Wahl Bürgermeister
030 Verhandlungen *re* Schambeck
070 Anordnungen der Militärregierung

Eichstätt

Sitzungsprotokoll des Stadtrates. Eichstätt, 1947—Stadtarchiv.
Nürnberg Staatsarchiv
Regierungsbezirk, Ansbach—Franken, Schregele Akten.

Nürnberg Stadtarchiv

Akten des Oberbürgermeisters. Schriftverkehr: Militärregierung-Spruchkammer
Chronik der Stadt Nürnberg
Niederschriften über die Sitzungen des Stadtrats
Verwaltungsberichte der Stadt Nürnberg
Wilhelm, Dr. Kurt. *Chronik des Amtsgerichtes.* Nürnberg, 1945–52
Nürnberg Polizei. *Wochenberichte an die Mil. Reg.*, 1946–
Manuscripts
    Barnett, James Calvin, *Totalitäre und Demokratische Besatzung.* Erlangen dissertation, 1948
    Erdmenger, Elizabeth, *Kommunalpolitische Entwicklungen und Entscheidungen in Nürnberg, 1945–49.* Erlangen University, Magisterarbeit, 1967

Interviews, 1969–70

OMGUS

Bowie, Robert
Clay, General L. D.
Friedrich, C. J.
Griffith, William
Gross, Ernest
Riddleberger, James

GERMANY, FEDERAL LEVEL

Erhard, Dr. Ludwig
Globke, Dr. Hans
Krautwig, Dr. Carl
Maier, Reinhold
Seelos, Dr. Gebbard

BAVARIA

Baer, Dr. Fritz. Staatskanzlei
Bleier, Dr. Josef. Just. Ministry
Brandt, Philip Freiherr von. Staatskanzlei
Deuerlein, Professor Ernst. Staatskanzlei
Ehard, Dr. Hans. Ministerpräsident
Godfrey, George. OMGB
Hoegner, Dr. Wilhelm. Ministerpräsident
Horvay, Frank. OMGB
Hundhammer, Dr. Alois. Staatsminister
Knöringen, Waldemar von. SPD
Mayes, Martin. OMGB
Painter, Dr. Ministerialrat, Interior Ministry
Riedl, Dr. Ministerialdirektor, Interior Ministry
Wiebel, Dr. Ministerialrat, Interior Ministry

AUGSBURG

Aumann, Fritz. Author, official
Baur, Valentin. SPD leader
Bezen, Bernhard. Director
Feldbaur, Waltherr. Stadtamtmann
Hector, Col. J.R. Commander
Hoffman, Dr. Friedrich. Schuldirektor
Kammerer, Josef. PW
Kiss, Alfred. Investigator
Kreibich, Fritz and Marie. Refugees
Modrow, Harald. Investigator and interpreter
Müller, Klaus. Oberbürgermeister
Pflugmacher, Karl. Journalist
Root, Capt. Donald. Commander
Schlepp, August. Polizei Direktor
Schertl, Alfons. Journalist
Schlichterle, Joachim. Polizei
Schub, Josef. Regierungsdirektor
Wahl, Karl. Gauleiter
Zapitz, Major Joseph. MG, Public Safety

FRIEDBERG

Grossman, Hans. Stadtrat
Haas, Georg. Bürgermeister, Laimering
Hefele, Caroline. Landratsamt
Herrman, Walter. MG interpreter
Kastl, Fabian. Landrat
Kerle, Georg. Stadtoberamtmann
Kolesnikow, Victor. MG interpreter, Landrat
Menzel, Roderick. MG interpreter
Schlech, Cajetan. Bürgermeister, Dasing
Schropp, Anton. Landrat
Selder, Emanuel. Denazification official
Letter
 Talcott, Captain R. C. MG

EICHSTÄTT

Bauch, Professor. Seminardirektor
Blei, Romauld. Bürgermeister
Gabler, Karl. Schreinermeister
Hammerl, August. SPD, Stadtrat
Hartmann, Xaver. Kunstschlossermeister
Hutter, Dr. Hans. Oberbürgermeister
Liepold, Eduard. Wohnungsamt
Niklaus, Magnus
Reiter, Father. Priest
Schellkopf, Hans. Stadtrat
Schorer, Dr. Denazification chairman
Seifferth, Hans. Oberschulrat
Spiegl, Anni
Letters
 Hammerl, August. SPD, Stadtrat
 Household, Capt. R. Commander
 Julien, Capt. R. Commander
 Krause, Theodor. Interpreter, secretary
 Seifferth, Hans. Oberschulrat

NUREMBURG

Berggold, Friedrich. FDP, Stadtrat
Drexler, Hans. Publisher
Finger, Anni. KDP, Stadtrat
Klise, Col. Carlyle
Levié, Dr. Heinz. Bürgermeister
Mershon, Capt. Richard

Moosberger, Georg. Journalist
Pfeiffer, Gerhard. Professor, Erlangen
Raab, Dr. Hans. Schulrat
Schirmer, Hermann. KDP, Stadtrat
Letters
    Haight, Col. Edward M.
    Wilson, Col. Frank S.

Index

Edward N. Peterson is professor and chairman, Department of History, University of Wisconsin-River Falls. He attended junior college in Missouri, and received his B.A., M.A., and Ph.D. from the University of Wisconsin-Madison. The author of several articles and two previous books, he is a recognized authority on World War II and recent German history.

The manuscript was edited by Sherwyn T. Carr. The book was designed by Richard Kinney. The display type is American Typewriter, and the text face is Mergenthaler VIP Times Roman, designed by Stanley Morison in 1931.

The book is printed on EB Natural antique paper and bound in Holliston Mills Novelex cloth. Manufactured in the United States.